# Here's Looking at You

This book is part of the Peter Lang Media and Communication list.
Every volume is peer reviewed and meets
the highest quality standards for content and production.

PETER LANG
New York • Washington, D.C./Baltimore • Bern
Frankfurt • Berlin • Brussels • Vienna • Oxford

ERNEST GIGLIO

# Here's Looking at You

## HOLLYWOOD, FILM & POLITICS

FOURTH EDITION

PETER LANG
New York • Washington, D.C./Baltimore • Bern
Frankfurt • Berlin • Brussels • Vienna • Oxford

**Library of Congress Cataloging-in-Publication Data**
Giglio, Ernest D.
Here's looking at you: Hollywood, film & politics /
Ernest Giglio. — Fourth edition.
pages cm
Includes bibliographical references and index.
Includes filmography.
1. Motion pictures—Political aspects. 2. Politics in motion pictures.
I. Title. II. Title: Here is looking at you.
PN1995.9.P6G56 2014   791.43'6581—dc23   2013043404
ISBN 978-1-4331-5126-2 (paperback)
ISBN 978-1-4539-1255-3 (ebook pdf)
ISBN 978-1-4541-9079-0 (epub)
ISBN 978-1-4541-9078-3 (mobi)
DOI 10.3726/978-1-4539-1255-3

Bibliographic information published by **Die Deutsche Nationalbibliothek**.
**Die Deutsche Nationalbibliothek** lists this publication in the "Deutsche
Nationalbibliografie"; detailed bibliographic data are available
on the Internet at http://dnb.d-nb.de/.

Cover design concept by Marc Luedtke,
Graphic Designer, Prescott, Arizona
Author photo by CKG Photography

The paper in this book meets the guidelines for permanence and durability
of the Committee on Production Guidelines for Book Longevity
of the Council of Library Resources.

© 2014, 2017 Peter Lang Publishing, Inc., New York
29 Broadway, 18th floor, New York, NY 10006
www.peterlang.com

All rights reserved.
Reprint or reproduction, even partially, in all forms such as microfilm,
xerography, microfiche, microcard, and offset strictly prohibited.

Printed in the United States of America

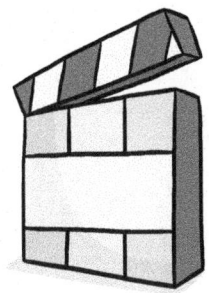

In Memory of Thomas F. Powell
*Scholar, Mentor, Friend & Noble Mon*

# Contents

| | |
|---|---|
| List of Illustrations | ix |
| List of Tables | xi |
| Preface | xiii |
| Acknowledgments | xv |
| Prologue. President Obama Returns to the White House | xvii |
| Chapter 1. Film and Politics: The Hollywood-Washington Connection | 1 |
| Chapter 2. In Search of the Political Film | 23 |
| Chapter 3. Nonfiction Film: Picturing Reality? | 39 |
| Chapter 4. Kiss, Kiss, Bang, Bang: Hollywood, Sex and Violence | 67 |
| Chapter 5. HUAC and the Blacklist: The Red Scare Comes To Hollywood | 89 |
| Chapter 6. Real to Reel Politicians: Idealists, Saviors and Scoundrels | 111 |
| Chapter 7. Picturing Justice: The Law and Lawyers in Hollywood Films | 141 |
| Chapter 8. Hollywood Goes To War: From the Great War to the Good War to the Forgotten War | 177 |
| Chapter 9. Remembering Vietnam on Film: Lessons Learned and Forgotten | 203 |
| Chapter 10. Mission Accomplished? Hollywood and the Afghanistan-Iraq War Films | 225 |
| Chapter 11. Hollywood Confronts Nuclear War and Global Terrorism | 245 |
| Chapter 12. Hollywood, Race and Obama: Feel-Good Racism | 267 |
| Chapter 13. Hollywood and Women: Cracks in the Celluloid Ceiling | 291 |
| Chapter 14. Epilogue: Is There a Future for Political Films in Hollywood? | 309 |
| Notes | 321 |
| Selected Bibliography | 361 |
| Selected Filmography | 371 |
| Index | 395 |

# Illustrations

*Permission to include movie stills and to reprint cartoons is acknowledged.*

0.1. Obama's Election Victory: The White, Black, Brown, Yellow
and Red House, election cartoon, 2012. Reprinted with permission,
Clay Bennett Editorial Cartoon, the *Washington Post* Writers Group
and the Cartoonist Group .......... xx

2.1. The Roosevelt Clan at Hyde Park, *Hyde Park on Hudson*, 2012.
Reprinted with permission, Focus Features/Photofest .......... 34

4.1. *BULLY* Poster: 2011.
Reprinted with permission, The Weinstein Company/Photofest .......... 76

6.1. A Pensive Lincoln in Steven Spielberg's Film, *Lincoln*, 2012.
Reprinted with permission, Walt Disney Studios Motion Pictures/Photofest .......... 125

8.1. Korean War Memorial, Olympia, Washington, 2009.
Reprinted with permission, David Giglio .......... 195

9.1. Vietnam Wall Memorial, Washington, D.C., 1985.
Reprinted with permission, Michael Roskin .......... 204

10.1. The Hunt for Osama bin Laden in *Zero Dark Thirty*, 2012.
Reprinted with permission, Columbia Pictures/Photofest .......... 238

11.1. *Unthinkable*, 2010.
Reprinted with permission, Sidney Kimmel Entertainment/Photofest .......... 258

12.1. *The Help*, 2011. Maid Octavia Spencer Delivering Her Special Pie
to Her Ex-Employer.
Reprinted with permission, Walt Disney Studios Motion Pictures/Photofest .......... 282

13.1. Recreating the Judith Miller-Valerie Plame Affair
in *Nothing But the Truth*, 2008.
Reprinted with permission, Yari Film Group/Photofest .......... 303

# Tables

| | | |
|---|---|---|
| 0.1. | 2012 Presidential Election Profile | xix |
| 4.1. | CARA's Ratings Assigned to Films, 2000–11 | 82 |
| 4.2. | CARA Ratings and Catholic Church Classifications | 88 |
| 7.1. | Women in the Judiciary | 169 |
| 7.2. | Law School Enrollment | 172 |
| 13.1. | Suggestions and Action Plans | 307 |
| 14.1. | Major Studio Market Share | 311 |
| 14.2. | Comparison Box Office for Pirates of the Caribbean Franchise | 314 |

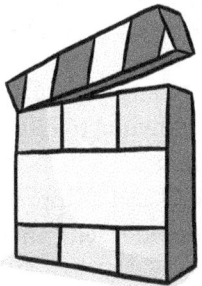

# Preface to the Fourth Edition

The idea for this book began a long time ago in the imagination of a young boy whose childhood became entwined with the movies. Little did this kid know that one day he would be writing on a subject that he loved. The first edition was printed in 2000 and was a nostalgic journey back in time, covering Hollywood movies from the silent era up to the millennium. But the second and third editions were much more critical of the film industry and the films it produced. The author has continued to find film "the most creative and interesting" of the arts while his disenchantment with Hollywood grows. While he applauded the end of censorship and the creation of a self-regulating classification system as its replacement, he soon became disenchanted with its application. The movies, it seems, had abandoned the good stories of the past in favor of gimmicks and special effects. Hollywood, for whatever reasons, became fascinated with the technology of the medium, replacing the spoken word with loud noises, digital filming, and violence that is mind-numbing. True, mainstream Hollywood has always produced entertainment, but it also told stories that dealt with social and political issues. Today, those movies are usually left to the independents. By the third edition, the author was in a state of despair over the future direction of the industry.

When Peter Lang presented me with another opportunity to revisit the state of Hollywood, I was hesitant. Could the fourth edition be more optimistic, offer more hope for those of us who still love the movies? In all honesty, I had a "book party" after the third edition because I felt, at age 80, that there might not be another opportunity. But with the re-election of President Obama in 2012 and with the support of Peter Lang's editor, Mary Savigar, I decided that a re-examination of the relationship between Hollywood, film, and politics was justified. Honestly, I wished that the results would be less acerbic and more optimistic about the future of the industry. But while there are some favorable developments, the overall tone remains somewhat pessimistic.

Still, a new edition provides the author with the opportunity to right a couple of factual mistakes, update new developments, and expand the breadth of the text. In that regard, the fourth edition divides the subject of Hollywood's treatment of minorities and women into two chapters so as to expand their content and fully develop both topics. The evolution of the wars in Afghanistan and Iraq since 2010 required substantial changes in that chapter. The opening and closing chapters are completely new, while the remaining chapters and the statistical data have been updated.

A new feature of the fourth edition is the eight case studies of films that warrant special consideration due to their subject matter and content. These are intended to raise substantial issues and questions that my colleagues hopefully will use as "talking points" for class discussion. The author accepts that not every reader will agree with the perspectives and views expressed in these in-depth film studies, but I sincerely hope that they will stimulate interest and possibly serve as class writing projects. Readers also are invited to visit my blog (ernestgiglio@blogspot.com), where various film topics are presented.

I am gratified by the faith Peter Lang has shown in my work and I appreciate the positive comments of my colleagues and their students. I leave the reader with this parting thought: may you find this edition worthy of your time.

# Acknowledgments

Many people and institutions assisted in the process of researching and writing four editions of this book. I can only cite a few here.

Reference librarians from the Library of Congress, the University of Wisconsin Film & TV Archives and the UW State Historical Society, the British Film Institute, and librarians at Lycoming, Yavapai and Prescott Colleges all contributed their time and knowledge.

A number of colleagues provided suggestions, comments and feedback from students, including: Jack Schrems, Ron Briley, John Williams, Richard Ostrom, Kevan Yenerall, Barbara Allen, Christa Slaton, David Whiteman, Jay Parker, Jeffrey Sadow, Michael Haas and Thomas Powell. Hollywood also lent a hand: assistance came from Richard Heffner, former head of CARA and Joan Graves, CARA's current head.

I must recognize those who were especially helpful on the fourth edition. First is the encouragement I received from Mary Savigar, Senior Acquisitions Editor, Media and Communications Studies at Peter Lang, who supported another edition of *Here's Looking at You: Hollywood, Film & Politics*. Second, a word of gratitude is due my daughter Elisabeth and her husband Nick, a freelance sound editor for the movies, who gave me "the best room in the house" in which to write while I was teaching at Dutchess Community College. Finally, I am indebted to my assistant, Loryn Isaacs, a Prescott College graduate, who collected and updated the statistics and provided editorial review. Without his contribution, the fourth edition would have remained in draft form.

Finally, to all my colleagues who have used *Here's Looking at You* and all the students who have read the book at some point during the past decade, as well as film aficionados, I appreciated your positive comments.

Prescott, AZ & Staatsburg, NY

Prologue

# President Obama Returns to the White House

President Obama was in the second year of his first term when the third edition of this book went to press, much too early for even a preliminary assessment. This edition continues from where the third ended in early 2010 and traces domestic developments and foreign events into the first year of the president's second term.

In 2008, Democratic presidential candidate Barack Obama appeared to the American public as the patron saint of liberal causes: inclusive and affordable healthcare, green energy policy, regulation of Wall Street and the banking sector and a reasonable immigration policy. No wonder his victory reminded film buffs of Jimmy Stewart's Boy Ranger idealism and his inspiring rhetoric in the Hollywood film *Mr. Smith Goes to Washington* or the promise of John F. Kennedy's New Frontier in the 1960s. Obama's rise to power couldn't have been more of a blockbuster if Hollywood had written the script itself. But the reality of his first term was quite different, with the president spending much of his time deadlocked with the Republican-controlled House of Representatives as he sought to implement his campaign promises. He did manage to secure several stimulus packages to help failing banks, revitalize the American auto industry, and push through the Affordable Care Act to reform the nation's health care system. However, ObamaCare, as the healthcare law came to be called, would prove to be an expensive achievement in terms of the president's prestige and political capital.

## The Two-Year Campaign

Not having to worry about renomination in 2012, the president and vice president, Joe Biden, became spectators to an almost two-year Republican Party primary that saw the Republican candidates engage in campaign rhetoric that eventually eliminated one another. What must the rest of the world think of these American national elections that cost an obscene amount of money yet change the political dynamics very little? American elections are more like running a marathon than standing for public office. This was readily seen in the Republican primary, where there were many candidates seeking to challenge the president in 2012.

As the selection process began, seven men and one woman sought the Republican presidential nomination and were duly dubbed "Snow White and the Seven Dwarfs" by the media. They included Michele Bachman as Snow White and Mitt Romney, Newt Gingrich, Rick Santorum, Ron Paul, Herman Cain, Rick Perry, and Jon Huntsman as the Seven Dwarfs.[1] As the months rolled by, the candidates, one by one, dropped out of the race for a variety of reasons: lack of financial support, personal problems, and, in one case, accusations of improper sexual behavior. It was not until May of 2012 that Governor Romney had the candidates' field to himself wherein he selected Representative Paul Ryan of Wisconsin, a neoconservative, as his vice presidential running mate.

The Republican Presidential Convention met in Tampa, Florida, to formally approve the nomination of Governor Romney as its standard bearer. The highlight of the convention was not the candidate himself nor his wife nor even Ryan. Much to the surprise of the convention delegates and the millions of television viewers, the guest appearance of actor-director Clint Eastwood kept the media humming for days. Eastwood, a conservative Republican and former Mayor of Carmel, California, came to the podium and spent 15 minutes or so talking to an empty chair as if it were occupied by President Obama. The convention crowd was mystified as Eastwood rambled on and they contemplated whether to laugh, clap, or just sit silently. Afterwards, the late-night talk show hosts, cartoonists, and memes had a field day with Eastwood's performance. Although highly respected by his film colleagues for his craft, Eastwood should have known better than to try and duplicate the performance of Jimmy Stewart as the alcoholic Elwood P. Dowd talking to an invisible rabbit in the 1950 film comedy *Harvey*.

By contrast, the Democratic Convention in Charlotte, North Carolina, was a less showy affair, though highlighted with dramatic and passionate speeches by Vice President Biden and Massachusetts Governor Deval Patrick. If the Hollywood crowd was present, it remained in its seats. Both Ann Romney and Michelle Obama, at their respective conventions, gave speeches that were tributes to their husbands. But it was the performance of former President Bill Clinton that electrified the crowd with a stinging attack on Republican obstructionism. He made Eastwood's performance appear amateurish.

Four television debates were scheduled during October, with three involving the presidential candidates and one the vice presidential candidates. By consensus, the pundits agreed that Romney had won the first debate on domestic affairs. He appeared refreshed, confident, and ready for the challenge. In contrast, the president seemed tired and distracted. Speculators saw Obama as being ill like Nixon in the first Kennedy-Nixon 1960 televised debate. The president recovered in the second and third debates, however, by becoming aggressive. Romney held his ground but Obama out-jabbed him.

The vice presidential debate pitted Biden, a veteran politician, against Paul Ryan, a younger, less experienced foe. Biden's objective appeared to be to unnerve his challenger by bullying the young representative, but Ryan remained calm despite Biden's constant interruptions. When the debates finished and the fact checkers recorded the mistakes, exaggerations, misinformation, and false accusations, it left the author wondering what, if anything had been

# President Obama Returns to the White House

gained. Both candidates were guilty of trying to misrepresent their opponent's positions. Add the "dirty tricks" advertisements by both parties to this mass of erroneous information and there were few in the country who were unhappy that the election lead-up was over.

## Victory, But No Slam Dunk

On November 6, 2012, almost 120 million Americans went to the polls to vote for a president who would lead them for the next four years. Normally, the final election results are available late election night or within 24 hours. But not in 2012, as votes were still being counted for the makeup of the 113th U.S. Congress. The president received 51 percent of the popular vote,[2] almost three million more than former Governor Romney, due in large part to the cobbled coalition of Latinos, blacks, Asians, and women. The Electoral College vote showed that Obama had received 332 votes (270 are required to win) to Romney's 206, which might leave those unfamiliar with the American election system with the impression that the president had won handily. But that was not the case. It was a hard-fought battle up to the end. In the American political system the candidate who wins a state's popular vote, even by a single vote, captures all of that state's electoral votes (except for Maine and Nebraska, which split them). This electoral feature made the president's victory appear greater than it was, since his popular vote margin was around 2 percent. The closeness of the election is best understood by looking at the narrow popular vote margins in the important swing states, all won by Obama: Florida by 0.8 percent, Ohio by 1.9 percent, and Virginia by 3 percent. These three states provided Obama with 60 electorate votes and sealed his victory.

Table 0.1. 2012 Presidential Election Profile[3]

|  | Obama | Romney |
|---|---|---|
| Electoral Vote | 332 | 206 |
| Popular Vote | 62,611,250 | 59,134,475 |
| States Won | 27 | 23 |
| **Popular Vote % by Race** | | |
| White | 39 | 59 |
| People of Color | 80 | 20 |
| Black | 93 | 6 |
| Hispanic | 71 | 27 |
| Asian | 73 | 26 |
| **Popular Vote % by Age** | | |
| 18–29 | 60 | 37 |
| 60+ | 45 | 54 |
| **Popular Vote % by Gender** | | |
| Male | 45 | 52 |
| Female | 55 | 44 |

Figure 0.1. Obama's Election Victory: The White, Black, Brown, Yellow and Red House, election cartoon, 2012. Reprinted with permission, Clay Bennett Editorial Cartoon, the Washington Post Writers Group and the Cartoonist Group

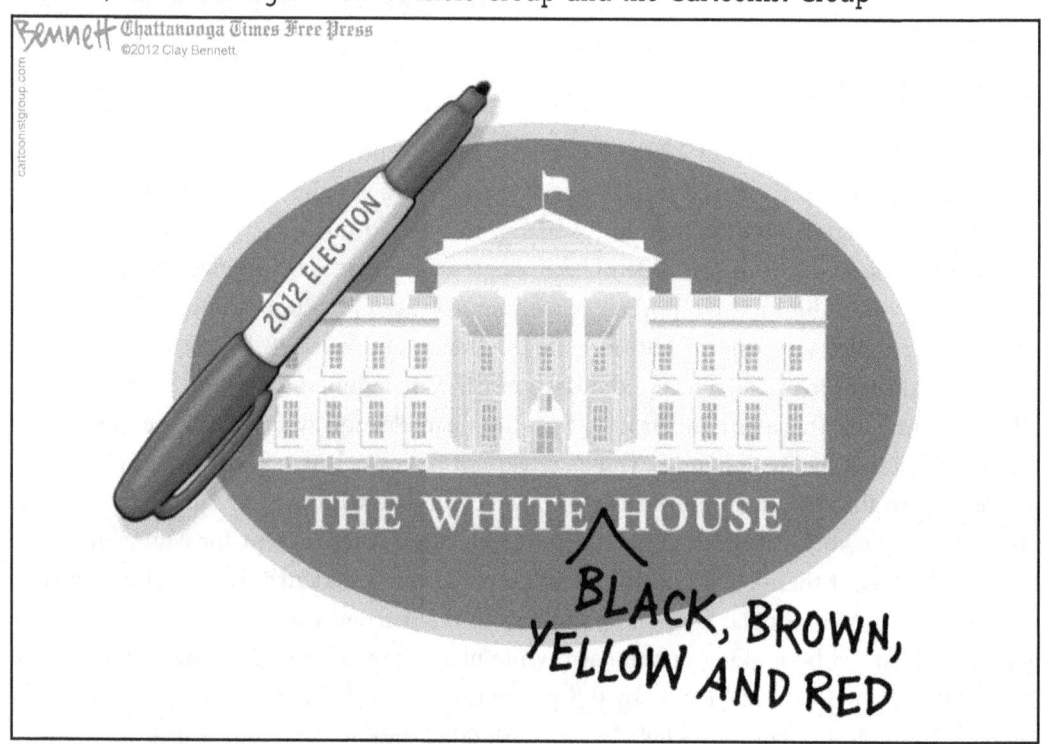

Obama's narrow margin in the popular vote meant there was no coattails effect that would enable the Democrats to control the next Congress. While the Democratic Party continued to hold the Senate, the Republicans emerged with a firm grip on the lower House of Representatives with a 40-seat majority. In summary, the election results showed that after the political parties spent almost $6 billion, the 113th Congress was very much like the gridlocked 112th in political ideology.

## The Second Term

Although the president had won the election, the people had not given him a mandate since the Congress was politically divided. Thus he was left to do battle with the domestic challenges of an underperforming economy, including high unemployment, and a rising poverty level, and with a Congress that wanted to modify his healthcare act and force him to agree to budget cuts to avoid the nation defaulting on its debt.

These serious economic problems were overshadowed in 2011–12 by horrific acts of violence as gunmen engaged in three shooting rampages: one against a Tucson Representative at a constituency meeting, a second at a midnight showing of Hollywood film *The Dark Knight Rises* at a Colorado theater in the summer of 2012, and a third at an elementary school in Connecticut where a gunman killed 26 people, including 20 children. These were not unusual incidents, either, as 33 people were killed in eight other shootings in 2012 alone. These shootings led the president to propose changes to the country's gun laws. But anti-gun advocates wondered why he had not also taken the opportunity to scold Hollywood for the excessive violence in its movies.[4]

Meanwhile, Obama had to contend with notable security issues as well. Terrorist attacks against U.S. citizens occurred in 2013 during the Boston Marathon when two bombs went off near the finish line, killing three people and injuring 170 others, and in Ankara, Turkey, where an attack on the U.S. Embassy killed a Turkish guard and injured a journalist, although no Americans were hurt.

On the foreign affairs front, both Iran and North Korea proved irksome. Iran persisted in developing its nuclear weapons program despite Western sanctions. North Korea continued its belligerent attitude in testing nuclear weapons in the Sea of Japan as part of its campaign to intimidate South Korea. In the Middle East, where the Arab Spring was raging, the president decided against pursuing an aggressive course, refusing to commit U.S. forces in the Syrian civil war and intervene in Egypt as the military toppled the elected government. On a positive note, he kept his promise to withdraw U.S. troops from Iraq and present a drawdown plan for the withdrawal of American troops from Afghanistan.

After enjoying a scandal-free first term, President Obama's second term saw irregularities and improper behavior by the Internal Revenue Service (IRS) and the National Security Administration (NSA) and an investigation into the 2012 Benghazi terrorist attack that killed the U.S. ambassador and three of his staff.

Hollywood, meanwhile, went about its usual business of making films regardless of the party occupying the White House. And rightly so, as it is Congress that the film industry must lobby to protect its global interests and prevent the unlawful piracy of its films. With these interests in mind, Hollywood hired former U.S. Senator Christopher Dodd (Connecticut) to be its new leader. Still, there was reason to wonder whether the election of the first African-American president might not affect the kind of films Hollywood would make. Would it really be business as usual or would having Obama in the White House compel the film industry to become sensitive to minority hiring and racial issues on the big screen? Certainly it seems possible that Dodd, a fellow Democrat, will hasten the making of a movie about the first African-American president, either describing his journey into politics or extolling a legacy still unfinished. The only certainty seems to be that Hollywood's Obama films will never equal the number made about Abraham Lincoln, the president's hero. But then who can ever be sure what will happen when the real world of politics meets the reel world of Hollywood?

Chapter 1

# Film and Politics
## The Hollywood-Washington Connection

"Just because you do not take an interest in politics doesn't mean politics won't take an interest in you."
—Pericles, 430 BC

"The price of apathy towards public affairs is to be ruled by evil men."
—Plato

"For us, the cinema is the most important of the arts."
—Vladimir Ilyich Lenin

"Film is one of the three universal languages, the other two: mathematics and music."
—Filmmaker Frank Capra

In this era of polling and public opinion surveys, suppose the author were to conduct a word association poll asking random people on the street what image came to mind when Hollywood was mentioned? Of course, there would be the usual suspects: entertainment, movies, movie stars, big-budget epics, and so forth. The author is willing to wager, however, that the word "politics" is unlikely to come to mind. And the reason is quite simple: Hollywood wants the public to believe that the industry only makes entertainment pictures. To be sure, in any given year, 90 to 95 percent of what comes out of Hollywood is strictly commercial, designed to bring customers into theaters and make money for the studios and their corporate owners. This book is about the 5 to 10 percent of films where Hollywood's public relations department either denies any political intention or tries to disguise any political message.

Common sense dictates that if entertainment were Hollywood's only focus, then the Motion Picture Association of America's (MPAA) major offices would be located in Los Angeles or New York instead of Washington, D.C. While the film industry has offices in both of those coastal cities, its headquarters is in the nation's capital because, being an international business, the MPAA's concerns are global; it seeks to prevent the piracy of its films, to secure favorable trade agreements with foreign distributors, and to extend its film distribution into the emerging markets of the third world. Indeed, movies are America's second biggest export, after military hardware and equipment. For a good example of what movies mean to our economy, it is instructive to note whom the film industry selects as its leaders: Will Hays, former U.S. Postmaster General, Jack Valenti, assistant to President Lyndon Johnson, Dan Glickman, former Congressman and former U.S. Senator Christopher Dodd, its current president. To the author's knowledge, not one attended film school, directed or produced a movie, or knew anything about the film industry before their appointment. But they all had the kind of knowledge and contacts inside the Beltway that promised success for the industry.

Many Hollywood movies deliver a fantasy world on the big screen, where Americans live in suburban mansions or plush urban apartments. It is an imagined world unknown to the underclass, though such images would be a surprise to many middle-class families as well. Hollywood is very good at creating deceptions in the reel world. But the industry's leaders are also good at tracking domestic legislation and foreign policies that would hurt the industry or its profits. That is why the MPAA does business in Washington while its West Coast offices sell a fantasy world to the American public. When the industry was criticized in the 1920s for its screen content it hired Will Hays, chairman of the Republican National Committee and postmaster general in Warren Harding's administration, as well as a Presbyterian elder, to buffer government and public criticism and to restore the industry's tarnished image. In accepting the position as the MPAA's first president, Hays assured the public that "American motion pictures continue to be free from any but the highest possible entertainment purpose."[1] To this day, Hollywood continues to sell that image to the American people.

## Entertainment Yes, Politics No

Hollywood's public relations portray the industry as a commercial enterprise that produces only entertainment. In his new book, *Hollywood Left and Right*,[2] however, Professor Steven Ross debunks this myth by providing substantial evidence that Hollywood has been turning out political films and engaging in political activities ever since the industry settled in southern California a hundred years ago. He details the historical evidence by examining the activities of a dozen movie stars and studio heads, from Charlie Chaplin through Arnold Schwarzenegger. His research, furthermore, discredits the common perception of Hollywood as a "bastion of liberalism." Rather, Ross contends that Hollywood politics has moved through cyclical periods of both liberalism and conservatism, noting that while liberals draw much of the media attention, conservatives have had a greater political impact due to their election of one California Governor (Arnold Schwarzenegger), one U.S. Senator (George Murphy), and one President (Ronald Reagan).

Ross's thesis is that, at various times, conservatives or liberals dominated the industry's political agenda. He cites, for instance, studio mogul Louis B. Mayer, head of Metro-Goldwyn-Mayer (MGM), as one Hollywood conservative who committed himself to the

Republican Party because he believed it would help his studio and the young film industry. Later, Mayer would become an important campaigner and fund-raiser for Herbert Hoover's 1928 presidential bid. With Hoover's election Mayer became the first studio head to have direct access to a president and his cabinet.

Meanwhile, liberalism was unpopular in Hollywood during and after the Red Scare of the 1950s, and was replaced by a right-of-center movement in the 1960s led by actors George Murphy and Ronald Reagan, two former Democrats who joined the conservative sector within the industry. Both men had made the switch when they thought that left-liberals had taken control of the Democratic Party. Both worked for the election of Richard Nixon in 1960, and thereafter Murphy ran for the U.S. senate in 1964 and Reagan for governor in 1966. While Murphy lost re-election in 1970, Reagan went on to serve two terms as president in the 1980s.

Was there a more unpopular Hollywood actress in the 1970s–80s during the Vietnam War than Jane Fonda? Vietnam divided Hollywood as well as the American people. A novice to politics, Fonda joined the antiwar movement, and aided by her mentor and husband, Students for a Democratic Society (SDS) leader Tom Hayden, she helped create the Indochina Peace Campaign (IPC) and the Campaign for Economic Democracy (CED) in the 1970s. Fonda went so far as to go to North Vietnam in 1972, where she was photographed sitting on top of an anti-aircraft gun. Once the photo was published, her enemies called her "Hanoi Jane" and she became a target of the Federal Bureau of Investigation (FBI) and other government agencies. Ross believes that Fonda's political activities ushered in the era of celebrity politics, which continues to this day. After the shooting of student protesters at Kent State, Fonda moved from liberalism to radicalism. However, her political activities hurt her film career and she had to start her own production company to make political movies like the anti-Vietnam war film *Coming Home* (1978) and *The China Syndrome* (1979), which alerted the country to the potential dangers of nuclear power.

In the 1980s–90s, actors Charlton Heston and Warren Beatty, Hollywood contemporaries, represented opposite ends of the political spectrum. Neither man ran for public office, though Beatty toyed with the idea of a presidential run in 2000. Both were heavily involved in national politics: Beatty with the Democratic Party, Heston with special interest lobby groups like the National Rifle Association (NRA). Heston was closer to a Ron Paul Libertarian than a true Republican, as he believed that, basically, the government should leave the individual alone, with its main function being to protect rights rather than to limit them. His strong belief that the Second Amendment gave citizens the right to own guns led Heston to join the NRA in 1978, and in 1982 he became its president. Heston was a complex political activist even before his NRA leadership days; he had worked for civil rights and, along with Sidney Poitier and Harry Belafonte, led a Hollywood contingent to the 1963 March on Washington. But on the issue of guns, Heston was adamant. He lent his deep baritone voice to advocate for gun rights candidates, campaigning for them, lobbying Congress, and making media ads for the NRA. As keynote speaker at the NRA's annual convention, he delivered a rousing defense of gun ownership as a constitutional right under the Second Amendment to the Constitution, ending his speech with words that became a slogan for the gun organization: "I'll give up my gun when you take it from my cold dead hands."[3]

Beatty, on the other hand, was a left-liberal from the start. As a New Deal Democrat, the actor supported Lyndon Johnson's Great Society program, worked on George McGovern's 1972 presidential campaign, and served as an adviser to Senator Gary Hart in his bids for the presidency in 1984 and 1988. Beatty, the actor, made films with political messages like *The Parallax View* (1974), about a secret organization that hires assassins to take care of trouble-making politicians; *Reds* (1981), which he directed and starred in as Marxist journalist John Reed; and *Bulworth* (1998), where he directed and starred as a depressed U.S. Senator who puts out a contract on his own life, changes his mind about dying, and campaigns against the unregulated amounts of money going into elections.

Joining this group, we have Austrian-born action-adventure star Arnold Schwarzenegger, whose *Terminator* films added as many quotable lines to the Hollywood lexicon as Clint Eastwood's *Dirty Harry* series. Schwarzenegger evolved from a political actor to the governor of California when, in 2003, he seized the opportunity to join the gubernatorial race via the recall election of the incumbent governor. Schwarzenegger had zero political experience but parlayed his screen persona and favorite film lines such as "Hasta la vista, baby" into a winning combination. His election gave credence to the concept of "image politics" where celebrities cash in on their status to run for public office. Schwarzenegger's victory gave hope to other movie stars and to media celebrities in professional sports, broadcasting, and stand-up comedy. In his epilogue, Ross maintains that the ideology of liberals in Hollywood expresses both hope and guilt: hope that the U.S. will live up to the declared ideals and values in our basic documents, and guilt because as a nation we have failed to achieve those goals. Hence the liberal vision tends to look forward to an America with more equality, increased social justice, and greater democratic participation by all citizens. To achieve these goals, more rather than less government is required. This was the message that helped Barack Obama win the presidency in 2008 and 2012.

On the other hand, the conservative story that comes out of Hollywood tends to look backward to America's glorious past and to a continuation of the idea of American exceptionalism. America remains the greatest nation on earth; its wrongs and transgressions have been necessary or minor deviations when compared to its economic achievements such as creating an expansive middle-class society. Conservatives, in short, believe that patriotism requires the defense of the country first, before all else. Conservatives, Ross claims, will always have an advantage over liberals because their message is nationalistic, emotional, and straightforward.[4]

## Into the Political Arena

The existing relationship between film and politics occurs in two contexts. One is played out in the world of practical politics, where film industry members run for office, support candidates, raise and contribute money to political campaigns, lobby governments for special favors, and ask Washington to be the industry's advocate with foreign countries. Others work as activists for a variety of social, economic, and humanitarian causes. The second context occurs on the big screen, where film content often serves to defend the status quo, supports a capitalist economic system, serves as an instrument for government propaganda, and, only occasionally, exposes social and economic ills. Rarely, however, does Hollywood offer radical solutions for the pressing problems of American society.

There are times when the film industry mirrors political reality, as was the case with two films from the 1990s. Both *Wag the Dog* (1997) and *Primary Colors* (1998) were released during the administration of President Bill Clinton and each film centers around an American politician (a president in one and presidential candidate in the other) besieged by charges of improper sexual or ethical behavior. It is not a coincidence that both films were in release when President Clinton faced charges of sexual misbehavior with Paula Jones and Monica Lewinsky. In *Wag the Dog*, the president's political consultants wage a phony television war against Albania as a diversionary tactic. This mirrors President Clinton's campaign of saber-rattling against Saddam Hussein to temporarily displace the sexual accusations against him from the media. As the film's political consultant (played by Robert De Niro) says, "You want to win this election, you better change the subject. You wanna change this subject, you better have a war."[5] Four days after Clinton admitted to the American people that he had an "inappropriate relationship" with Lewinsky, he ordered cruise missile strikes against terrorist camps in Sudan and Afghanistan. Several months later, during his congressional impeachment hearings, Clinton ordered air strikes against Iraq. Was the timing coincidental or was it another effort by the president's spin doctors to divert attention away from his impeachment hearings?

More recently, Oliver Stone omitted all pretenses of "fictitious" politicians and directed his film *W* (2008), about George W. Bush, while the president's term was winding down and his popularity rating was at a low 20 percent. *W* is the first Hollywood movie explicitly about a sitting president. Was Stone admitting that Hollywood's "purely entertainment" mythology was over? Hardly! The films cited above provide the kind of evidence furnished in this book that seriously challenge the veracity of producer Samuel Goldwyn's alleged answer to a film assistant who wanted to make a political film: "If you want to send a message, use Western Union."

The fact is that Hollywood is foremost in the entertainment business, but the industry also delivers political messages in a minority of its films. As one example, the cynical message of *Wag the Dog* seems to be that political spin doctors and second-rate media talent easily deceive the American people. The film wants audiences to accept the image of a gullible American public, easily fooled by emotional and false appeals to nationalism. This attitude is usually associated with fascism rather than the reasoned discourse of democracy. Moreover, the wicked satire in *Wag the Dog* distorts the line between truth and reality when an egotistical Hollywood director (played by Dustin Hoffman) successfully creates a studio war waged on television to save the president's political career, an act that ultimately costs the director his life.

Meanwhile, in *Primary Colors*, John Travolta's Southern governor mounts a campaign for the presidency. Travolta's character is an undisguised imitation of the real Bill Clinton, right down to his philandering and weakness for Krispy Kremes. Coincidental? Not likely, since the film was based on a book written by a member of Clinton's 1992 presidential campaign staff. The film, however, plays like an *apologia* for sleazy and ruthless politicians. It expects audiences to love the womanizing and unscrupulous governor because his public policies are better than those of his opponent. Essentially the movie asks audiences to forgive Travolta's Clinton clone for using damaging personal information to discredit his opponent on the ground that his policies are better for the country. Is the film's message that, in politics, the end justifies the means? Like American football, is winning everything? This may not be the civics lesson American parents want their children to learn. Films like *Primary Colors*, *Wag the Dog*, and *W* remind us that the film industry delivers overt political messages without recourse to Western Union.

As early as D.W. Griffith's *The Birth of a Nation* (1915), a biased presentation of slavery, Reconstruction policies, and the Ku Klux Klan (KKK), filmmakers have viewed the medium as an instrument to communicate stories that express the industry's personal beliefs about love, life, death, and politics. Had the film industry produced exclusively commercial fare, the history of real Hollywood and the America it portrayed would be quite different. The fact is that the industry has been an active player in American politics as demonstrated by its efforts to thwart government attempts to censor and regulate motion pictures, prevent unionization of its employees, and accumulate political goodwill during wartime by producing propaganda films for the government. In supporting the questionable methods used by the House Un-American Activities Committee (HUAC) during the 1950s, the film industry lent validity to the committee's Hollywood hearings, and furthered that relationship by adopting a secret blacklist against suspected communists. Not even George Orwell's Big Brother could have rewritten this history to make Hollywood look heroic.

## From Big Screen to Bigger Stage

In the context of practical politics, the Hollywood-Washington connection is best expressed in terms of political campaigns and elections, support for issue-oriented causes, pragmatic alliances with government during national crises, and lobbying for policies that directly affect the industry and its members.

In the past, entertainers usually did not seek political office, preferring instead to work behind the scenes. Entering politics is essentially a post–World War II development, with the notable exception of P.T. Barnum, the 19th-century showman, who served two terms in the Connecticut state legislature. In recent times, successful candidates tended to be Republicans, like the popular child star Shirley Temple, the 1930s–40s song and dance actor George Murphy, Ronald Reagan, a B-list actor for two decades until he was smitten with the political bug, Arnold Schwarzenegger, the bodybuilder turned actor, television's *Law and Order* actor Fred Thompson, and Sonny Bono, a singer and television personality. Of this group, Reagan, Thompson, and Bono had previous political experience at state or local level before entering the national scene. Temple failed in her bid for Congress but was rewarded with several appointed positions, including a post as delegate to the United Nations (UN). Murphy served one term in the U.S. senate and Bono died while serving in Congress. His widow finished her husband's term and was subsequently reelected. Reagan, of course, was the most notable Hollywood politician, serving two terms as governor of California and two terms as president.[6]

## Providing the Cash

When not running for office, Hollywood actors are inclined to provide encouragement and support to their favorite candidates. What do candidates receive from their connection with Hollywood stars? A very important component of contemporary politics: the ability to raise money, lots of it at one event. Without sufficient funds, a potential campaign will not progress far. This is not a minor concern today, as even state races require millions of dollars. National races are approaching astronomical amounts of money. For instance, in the 2008 presidential campaign Obama spent over $573 million and McCain spent a little more than $293 million.[7] Those amounts increased substantially in 2012 when President Obama and Governor Mitt Romney together spent $2.6 billion.[8]

Hollywood has been particularly generous to Democratic candidates. Obama received considerable financial support from such A-list stars as George Clooney, Tom Hanks, Barbra Streisand, and Denzel Washington. In fact, the entertainment industry (film, television, and music) had already provided $14 million for Obama's 2008 presidential run.[9] The Center for Responsive Politics, a nonpartisan group, reported that since 1990, the entertainment industry had contributed more than $200 million to federal candidates and their parties.[10]

Tom Cruise's character in *Jerry Maguire* (1996) said "show me the money," but it was the Watergate informer "Deep Throat" in the film version of *All the President's Men* (1976) who told *Washington Post* reporters Bob Woodward and Carl Bernstein in a Washington garage to "follow the money" in their investigation of the Watergate break-in. That advice led Woodward and Bernstein to expose the break-in of Democratic Headquarters at the Watergate complex in Washington.[11] Why did Deep Throat offer this advice? In politics, money is the engine that drives election campaigns. Without funding, a campaign will be stillborn. Hollywood plays an important role in the process: first in providing the funding for politicians to run, and second, in permitting film personalities with the financial base to contemplate a run for public office. There is nothing intrinsically wrong with Hollywood fulfilling these functions because it is not a crime for film personalities to run for elective office. Nor is it illegal for Hollywood to protect its economic self-interest by recruiting its leadership elite from White House staff or soliciting political assistance from its Washington friends. What is truly alarming, however, is that Hollywood money gains the industry an unequal amount of access and an inordinate amount of influence. The development and acceptance of a "culture of celebrity" in the U.S. have led one critic to observe that popular entertainment has replaced ideology in American politics. In this regard it seems that political candidates emulate movie stars, that primary campaigns resemble casting calls, that political campaigns are closer to auditions than to the articulation of substantive policy agendas, and that the electorate today behaves as if it were a film audience passively surveying a political performance.[12] This astute observation could apply to the 2012 presidential campaign, where the television debates were short on substance and long on posturing for the camera.

Perhaps equally important as the funds they provide is the additional exposure candidates gain through photo opportunities and their general association with film celebrities. Hobnobbing with prominent Hollywood figures brings a kind of celebrity status to politicians, particularly those who have yet to establish national reputations. The Kennedys did this in the 1950s and 1960s and the Clintons in the 1990s. The question of whether it is profitable for a politician to have friends in Hollywood is no longer raised in a celebrity-obsessed culture where announcements for public office are made on late-night television and where candidates appear regularly on talk shows to raise money and promote their candidacy through indirect appeals. Obama followed this pattern in 2008 and 2012 but his opponents were more reluctant to take that road.

Overall, members of the Hollywood community play perhaps their greatest political role and make their most significant contributions through their status as celebrities. Their standing and their money provide them with the kind of access and influence unavailable to the ordinary citizen. As actress Natalie Portman admitted when she appeared before Congress to plead the cause of FINCA, a micro financial organization that provides small loans to poor women in underdeveloped countries, her celebrity status was instrumental in gaining her an audience.[13]

When actor Robert Redford wanted to restore funding for the arts in the Obama stimulus package, he called Nancy Pelosi. Redford argued that the arts act as an economic engine that employs many people and brings money to states and local areas, citing as evidence that his Sundance Film Festival brought $60 million to Park City, Utah, each January. As a consequence of his phone conversation, $50 million was restored to the recovery package.[14]

## Exercising the Power

Is it profitable for a politician to have friends in Hollywood? Without question! President Obama's super PAC, Priorities USA Action, received $1 million from actor Morgan Freeman.[15] Actor George Clooney sponsored an "Americans Abroad for Obama" event at his Geneva, Switzerland, villa, where he raised $500,000; later he held a gala for Obama where guests paid $15,000 to have dinner with the star. That event raised $15 million.[16] Hollywood has become the Democratic Party's ATM. Sometimes the contributions take on the appearance of gifts to friends. When President Clinton needed cash for his legal defense fund to settle the Paula Jones lawsuit, actor Tom Hanks helped raise more than $2 million.[17] The president returned the favor, allowing Hanks and his wife to stay at the White House. At other times, the Hollywood-Washington friendship can backfire. To cite one example, Warren Beatty's close friendship with Gary Hart cost the senator politically when he fell under the spell of a Hollywood lifestyle at odds with public probity. As a consequence, Hart's promising political career came to a dramatic end.[18] Whether Senator Hart would have won the 1988 presidential race is conjecture, but at the time he was considered to be one of the brightest young candidates on the national political scene.

Occasionally, the benefits work in reverse. That is, the real politician serves as a mentor for the reel politician. This scenario occurred when actor Ben Affleck was selected to play a congressman in the film *State of Play* (2009). To help him prepare for the role, Affleck met with New York Representative Anthony D. Weiner several times, spending hours with Weiner to observe his daily routine. More often than not, these two Democrats engaged in the kind of political banter that proved useful for Affleck's role in the film.[19]

Conversely, is it damaging to run for national or state office when your candidacy is perceived as a threat to the film industry? Without a doubt. In pre–World War I Hollywood, movie moguls like Sam Goldwyn, Louis B. Mayer, and Jack and Harry Warner dominated the industry. But these men would not have thought of running for political office. Instead these European émigrés were gamblers, entrepreneurs at heart, who retaliated whenever their perception of the American dream was threatened. They nurtured favor with Washington politicians but kept vigil over candidates who might alter the status quo.[20] These moguls controlled their film studios with tight fists and they courted the Washington power brokers. The most political of the moguls, Mayer, cultivated a close friendship with Herbert Hoover, first when Hoover served as secretary of commerce and later as president. To garner support for Hoover's run for the presidency in 1928, Mayer intervened to persuade newspaper magnate William Randolph Hearst to put aside his personal aspiration for the White House and instead back Hoover's candidacy. According to Professor Ross, Mayer's political influence is credited with introducing the Republican Party to Hollywood and encouraging film industry people to support it.

When the studio moguls felt threatened, as they did in 1934 with writer Upton Sinclair's bid to become governor of California, they joined ranks to defeat him. Sinclair was one of the journalists at the beginning of the 20th century whose exposés of the meat packing and oil industries earned him the pejorative title of "Muckraker." Sinclair, a socialist trying to win office during the Great Depression, ran his campaign on the slogan of "end poverty in California" (EPIC). Naturally his EPIC platform was designed to promote economic and social justice, including state-run cooperatives and a business tax on the film industry. The longtime critic of capitalism promised to eliminate unemployment, provide monthly pensions of $50 to widows and the poor, drop taxes on homes appraised under $3000, abolish sales taxes, and institute a graduated income tax starting at $5000 and reaching 50 percent of incomes over $50,000.[21]

The moguls began a "Stop Sinclair" drive inside the film industry and, according to one Hollywood source,[22] MGM required every employee who earned more than $150 a week to contribute to Republican candidates.

Sinclair won the Democratic primary and ran a terrific campaign but his EPIC ideas scared the pants off the film studios and the upper class. Fearing Sinclair's possible election, Mayer instituted the first propaganda media campaign in American electoral history when he produced doctored film shorts intended to destroy Sinclair's candidacy. Of course, political "dirty tricks" were not new in American history: their organized usage can be traced back to the control of New York election politics at the end of the 19th century and well into the 20th by the Democratic Party's Tammany Hall machine, which bought votes, largely from immigrants, in return for economic benefits and personal favors.[23] But Mayer was the first to tap into the power of film to persuade and influence the working class by producing five-minute "newsreels" that sought to discredit Sinclair and to frighten the voting public into believing that his election would attract scores of "undesirables"—vagrants and the unemployed—to California. Using bogus news reports, these MGM films implied that tramps and hobos would spend winters basking in the Hollywood sun. In one bogus newsreel, a professional actor playing a Russian immigrant with a thick accent said, "Well, Sinclair's ideas worked in Russia. I don't see why they won't work here." Because many Americans at the time received their information about the world through these newsreels, the masses came to think of them as factual news reports. Although Sinclair received nearly one million votes, he still lost the election.[24]

While the studio heads were political conservatives, many of the actors, writers, technicians, and workers were political liberals and leftists who favored unionization for better wages and benefits. They signed petitions and participated in marches and demonstrations, and some joined the American Communist Party (CPUSA) because it was the only viable radical political movement at the time. Paul Buhle and Dave Wagner, in their book *Radical Hollywood*, estimate that the Hollywood left contained some of the best talent in the industry, including a number of Academy Award winners whose movies were later to be among the American Film Institute's 100 best films.[25] Buhle and Wagner maintain that many of the gangster, western, and film noir movies of the thirties and forties provided a socially acceptable outlet, especially for the leftist screenwriters, to include social and political commentary in their work, including critiques of capitalism. The political irony here is that under the old studio system the moguls had virtually absolute power, which meant that studios like MGM and Warner Bros. had to sign off on these pictures. When you consider gangster movies of this era, where the mobsters are usually poor boys from immigrant families, and when you think about the westerns, where the villains were often the local bankers and railroad barons, it makes you wonder whether the studio moguls understood the subtext of their own movies, particularly since their films were mainly intended for the working class.

The Hollywood-Washington relationship becomes more amicable and cooperative during wartime and during national crises. These were times when the film industry and the government needed each other. World War I presented the industry with an opportunity to develop its relationship and curry favor with Washington. When America finally entered the war in 1917 the government asked the film industry to volunteer its most important stars to aid in the war effort. The studios responded by sending Douglas Fairbanks, Charlie Chaplin, and America's sweetheart, Mary Pickford, on tour to sell Liberty war bonds. This scenario was repeated during World War II when Washington again called on Hollywood to aid the war effort, and the industry responded anew. In one 1942 bond drive, 337 stars participated in selling a staggering $850 million in war bonds. Singer Kate Smith reportedly sold $39 million in war bonds during a single radio marathon.

At other times the cooperation was insidious and unworthy of a democratic state, such as when during the Cold War it was reported that the Central Intelligence Agency (CIA) worked closely with anti-communists in the film industry to spot potentially troubling movie content that portrayed a less than positive image of the United States. That meant

Hollywood was not to dwell on labor problems, the plight of minorities, and social and economic inequality. According to British film producer and historian Frances Saunders,[26] the CIA planted agents inside Hollywood studios to monitor communist activities and leftist themes. One undercover agent filed a critical report on the film *Giant* (1956) because the screenplay contained an unflattering portrayal of rich Texans who had gained their wealth at the expense of exploited Mexican labor.

The cooperative relationship during World War II and its aftermath was nothing short of absolute. (It is treated fully in chapter 8.) That same sort of spirit was resurrected again after the terrorist attack of September 11, 2001. First, Hollywood offered the government positive assistance. Eventually, the industry made a propaganda film that was aired on Middle East television. Then, the studios voluntarily postponed distribution of films with terrorist plots, such as *Bad Company* (2002) and *Collateral Damage* (2002). Both did poorly at the box office, but whether that was due to the postponement or their content is uncertain.

Benefits flow from cooperation with the government, otherwise assistance is withheld. For instance, actor John Wayne secured government assistance that made it possible for him to make his pro-Vietnam war film, *The Green Berets*. Generally, it would be very difficult to make a war film without some cooperation from the military. Similarly, realistic films about space and astronauts would not be possible without the involvement of the National Aeronautics and Space Administration (NASA), which was the situation for two space films, *The Right Stuff* (1983) and *Apollo 13* (1995). Reportedly, NASA offered film companies access to all its facilities—mission control, launch-pads, training services—a considerable savings to the studio, but conditional on the agency approving the script.[27] The point here is that certain films cannot be made convincingly without the cooperation of the government and that support is conditional on satisfying the military, NASA, or any other governmental agency.

But what good is this cooperation and assistance if the film's distribution date is rescheduled to please the military? This is what happened to *Buffalo Soldiers* (2003), the film version of the Robert O'Connor book. The storyline concerns the peacetime U.S. Army in Germany before the fall of the Berlin Wall. The central character is a supply specialist who operates a black market business out of the military depot and manufactures heroin on the side. In the style of irreverent military comedies such as *M\*A\*S\*H* (1970), this satirical and cynical film was completed in the summer of 2001 and scheduled to open in mid-September. The attacks of 9/11 pushed the film back to the following summer, but the beginning of the Afghanistan offensive interfered. The film was rescheduled to open in early 2003 but was delayed again due to the start of the Iraq War. Finally released during the summer of 2003, the film flopped at the box office due to mixed reviews and possibly the two-year delay. Would a more positive military portrayal have allowed the film to open on schedule? No one can say with certainty but, like all bureaucracies, the military is sensitive about its public image and Hollywood is reluctant to offend institutions that it relies on to help produce its films; it is good business sense to please the military.

The symbiotic relationship between government and the film industry has ramifications beyond political campaigns and public relations gambits. Government and special interest groups exploit the reputation and popularity of film stars and Hollywood keeps an eye on state policies that might impact the industry. Specifically, the primary interest of Hollywood is in national and international policies that could affect the acceptance of its films worldwide. The popularity of Hollywood films abroad, shown in venues as diverse as makeshift theaters inside Chinese factories, all the way to glamorous movie palaces installed with stereophonic sound, reinforces the industry's concern with its global image. Back in the thirties the studios worried about the response to its films in countries like Nazi Germany and Fascist Italy. Today, it frets over China's response because that country represents a $2 billion market for Hollywood films. That is why the film studios are producing more 3D and special effects movies that appeal to foreign audiences. The film industry views China as the great Gold Rush of the 21st century. For instance, DreamWorks is actually building a studio in Shanghai to produce animated films, while 20th Century Fox has invested in a Beijing-based film group. The Disney Corporation co-produced the film *Iron Man 3* (2013) in China and, in return, received 38 percent, rather than the normal 25 percent, of its domestic gross.[28]

It is often foreign markets that determine the fiscal fate of a film. The universal appeal of Hollywood movies makes it understandable why the MPAA president's voice is heard in the halls of government. Like Coke and McDonald's, Hollywood is symbolic of the economic rewards of corporate capitalism. For better or worse, Hollywood movies have dominated the world market since the 1920s, overpowering the production capacity and the film budgets of other countries. Beginning in the 1930s, as markets for American movies overseas expanded, the film studios were receiving 30 to 40 percent of their revenue from foreign markets. That percentage continued to rise in the seventies and eighties so that today Hollywood films generate roughly 70 percent of their total revenue abroad.[29] In the past these box office earnings came mostly from Western countries, but that changed in the 1980s and 1990s with the increased interest in American films in Asia. Hollywood films today earn anywhere from 65 to over 90 percent of their overseas box office receipts from just a few Asian countries.[30] Generally, overseas markets especially enjoy the big Hollywood blockbuster and expensive movies like the 2012 films *The Avengers*, *The Dark Knight Rises*, and *The Amazing Spider Man*, which added millions from overseas markets to their strong domestic receipts.[31] It remains to be seen whether this trend will continue, but if it does, what impact will it have on the future content of Hollywood films?

## Film Content

Even though audiences may not be aware of it, the most visible and common occurrence of the Hollywood-Washington connection takes place on the big screen, where Hollywood releases some 500 to 600 films annually. Only a fraction of these contain political messages or present political themes that are ideological, propagandistic, historically misleading, and politically manipulative. Nonetheless, that fraction of 5 to 10 percent results in anywhere from 25 to 30 political films each year.

# Film and Politics

## Film as Ideology

There are so many definitions of ideology that to cite one alone would be useless. The most common usage of the term "ideology" refers to the composite group of beliefs and values that shape our worldview. You might say that in the hands of governments, ideologies are the tool by which those in power try to persuade masses of people to act or behave in a certain way. The reader will notice a similarity with propaganda, which will be discussed later in the chapter.

How do we acquire these core values and beliefs? Individuals acquire them through such primary sources as family, education, and religious affiliation, and by secondary forces such as peer group pressure and mass media exposure. Governments, of course, can manipulate these beliefs and values through control of mass media outlets and indoctrination through the educational system. At some point in our lives, these forces operate to influence our political behavior, that is, determine whether we consider ourselves to be liberals or conservatives, mainstreamers or radicals, while providing us with a rationale for our actions. Professor John Schrems,[32] for example, has listed both economic ideologies like capitalism and socialism and political ideologies like democracy and totalitarianism as forces that have fueled right- and left-wing movements in the Western world.

As part of the mass media, film exerts a secondary influence on shaping our political values. No empirical study exists to prove that merely viewing one or even several political films will affect us enough to shape our political preferences. Films compete with television, print, radio, and the Internet, but with each representing only one variable in our political makeup. How influential film is in developing our political character remains a matter of opinion. Government, however, can affect political behavior, depending on the amount of freedom it allows individuals and the mass media. Ideally, in democratic societies there is a great diversity of opinion and the ability to dissent without fear or punishment. In the U.S. the media often acts as a fourth branch of government, checking on the government and reporting its activities to the people. But there is neither dissent nor diversity in totalitarian states where the government controls the media and the flow of information in and out of the country.

This lesson, taught in any introductory politics class, provides a brief foreword to understanding Hollywood film content. It is safe to state that the mainstream American film industry does not produce overtly ideological films, simply because it strives to please and not offend its customer base. This has been the mantra of the industry for a hundred years. But to say that it is "politically neutral" is incorrect. Since its early history, Hollywood has been making political films and that tradition continues into the present. According to political scientists Mark Sachleben and Kevan Yenerall,[33] Hollywood's most obvious ideological period occurred during the Red Scare of the 1940s and 1950s, when the film industry churned out a number of films like *The Iron Curtain* (1948), *I Married a Communist* (1949), *The Red Menace* (1949), *I Was a Communist for the FBI* (1951), and *Big Jim McLain* (1952), all of which sought to frighten the American public into believing that a communist takeover was imminent. These and similar films supported the right-wing mentality that communism was a global threat, asking citizens at home to be on the watch for subversives everywhere—at work, at school, in the movies, and even in your neighborhood.

As a college student in New York City during the 1950s, the author remembers that several of his professors were in class one day and gone the next, replaced by substitutes without any explanation. Were they communists? Were they part of a group planning to overthrow the government by force and violence? To this day, the author has his doubts. But this incident is a perfect example of how the forces of the Red Scare ideology (to be discussed in chapter 5) enabled college administrators to fire professors suspected of being communists or subversives without due process.

Although the Red Scare is a ghost of America's past, filmmakers who are willing to criticize the status quo, even independent ones like Oliver Stone and George Clooney, are reluctant to take the next step and use the medium as a tool for radical change. Their films may criticize the government's foreign policies, expose flaws in the capitalist, free market system, or denounce the uneven distribution of wealth, but they refrain from advocating radical change. Thus, even independent filmmakers are reduced to being social and political muckrakers rather than militant activists.

There are exceptions, of course. Two are worth noting: Steven Soderbergh's epic biopic of Marxist revolutionary Ernesto "Che" Guevara (*Che*, 2008), a joint American-foreign production, and actor-director Warren Beatty's major studio production of *Reds* (1981), about the American journalist John Reed's admiration for, and involvement in, the Russian Revolution.

Soderbergh's four-hour plus film is divided into two segments: part I focuses on the background to the Cuban Revolution and the events leading to the successful overthrow of the U.S.-backed regime of Fulgencio Batista in 1959, while part II concerns the attempt by Guevara in 1966 to recruit and organize a guerrilla army against the Bolivian government. His unsuccessful efforts led to his capture and death in 1967 at age 39. Soderbergh based his film primarily on Guevara's memoirs and diaries, resulting in a fairly accurate depiction of the physician turned political revolutionary once he joined Fidel Castro's 26th of July Movement. The film is successful in depicting Guevara as an idealist and humanist who advocated land reform and literacy education for rural peasants. Soderbergh's film, however, is not without flaws, particularly in its omissions. For instance, the film omits how Guevara became a Marxist revolutionary after experiencing firsthand the abject poverty of the peasant class in his travels throughout Latin America. Also omitted were his experiences later in Guatemala where he witnessed the CIA's installation of a right-wing dictator as the country's leader. Just as sociologists have exposed the fallacy that "criminals are born," political scientists have determined that revolutionaries are products of their political and economic environments. One other exclusion is worth noting. Whether deliberate or unintentional, Soderbergh omits reference to Guevara's role after the Cuban Revolution as the leader responsible for purging Batista's army of traitors and torturers and in identifying other Cubans as "war criminals." In this capacity, it is alleged that Guevara was brutal and ruthless, executing hundreds without trial or due process of law.[34] Sadly, in the end, Guevara's absolute commitment to force and violence as the only viable means to carry out revolutions against oppressive regimes turned the humanist-writer-poet into the kind of man he went to war against. Yet more than 40 years after his death, Che Guevara remains a symbol against social injustice everywhere in the world. Soderbergh's film was a box office disaster,[35] but the filmmaker can still be proud of his effort to use the medium as an ideological tool to better understand revolutionary movements.

In contrast, Beatty's *Reds*, with an A-list cast and director, diffused the impact of John Reed's admiration for the Russian Revolution and his hopes of achieving something similar in the U.S. by interfacing the political drama with a sappy love story between Reed (Beatty) and his free-thinking lover, Louise Bryant (Diane Keaton), with playwright Eugene O'Neill (Jack Nicholson) as the third party in the love triangle. True, the film does track Reed's career as a left-wing radical and his involvement with CPUSA, but more than half of its three-hour running time is devoted to the romance between Reed and Bryant. *Reds* is a perfect example of Hollywood hedging its bets, in this case by presenting the historic Russian Revolution as secondary to a love story. As a reminder of its original intent, when the 25th anniversary edition of *Reds* was released on DVD in 2006, its cover featured Beatty and Keaton in a passionate embrace.[36] Ah, if only revolutions were so romantic!

## Film as Propaganda

In 1936, the German-Jewish literary critic Walter Benjamin wrote that the film medium had emerged as a significant propaganda tool because of its ability to lend support to, and provide a rationale for, mass movements.[37] He warned that even the weekly newsreel, with its ability to engage the individual in the presentation of big parades and political rallies, had the potential to become an unwitting ally of fascism. Benjamin's essay was published the year after the completion of *Triumph of the Will* (1936), Leni Riefenstahl's homage to Hitler and the Nazi Party.

But what precisely is propaganda? The word originates from the Roman Catholic Church, which in the 17th century created a College of Propaganda to educate its priests. As the term evolved, it came to refer to a deliberate intent to influence attitudes of large crowds or masses by using words and symbols that are highly emotional so as to excite, persuade, and occasionally, move individuals and groups to act. *Triumph of the Will* provides a good example. Riefenstahl herself admitted that the filming of the 1934 Nuremberg Party Convention was more than a straightforward recreation of a historical event, though she denied that it was politically motivated. Commissioned by Hitler himself and approved by Goebbels, the film employed emotional symbols, scenes of mass adoration, and deft camera, sound, lighting, and editing work to create a testimonial to the glory of Nazism.

Similarly, during World War II, the American government asked Frank Capra, the director of *Mr. Smith Goes to Washington* (1939), to produce a series of films on *Why We Fight* (1942–45) to be shown to military personnel. These films were produced under the auspices of the Army Signal Corps, and like *Triumph of the Will*, presented a distorted image of American society in the early forties. Intended by the government to serve as morale boosters for the American soldier, the films made no reference to segregation, discrimination, poverty, labor strife, or class antagonism in the U.S. The *Why We Fight* series portrayed a nation so unspoiled and uncorrupted that it led actor-director John Cassavetes to comment that America might have been the invention of Frank Capra rather than a real place.[38] His remark referred to Hollywood's perpetuation of the cherished myths of an unblemished America. Whether genuine or fake, Capra's representation of America was an idealization of a place that a majority of the public believed, or wished to believe, existed. Certainly the series portrayed a country where the people regarded government as decent and honest, where right would triumph over force, where America's faith and wisdom would overcome adversity, and where the engine of capitalism would deliver the American dream to all people.

Not all political propaganda is overt and government sponsored. There are two other types, one overt but not government sponsored, and the other covert and inserted into commercial films.[39] A good example of the first kind is propaganda disguised as documentaries, such as Michael Moore's *Fahrenheit 9/11* (2004), which tried to dissuade Americans from reelecting President George W. Bush, and Dinesh D'Souza's effort to influence the outcome of the 2012 presidential election in the documentary *2016: Obama's America* (2012), in which D'Souza attempts to scare voters into believing that Obama's election will result in a Socialist America (both films will be discussed in chapter 3).

A second type of propaganda is more likely to be covert and found in commercial films such as the western *High Noon* (1952), released during the Red Scare. On the surface, the film is a standard western with a plot that pits the good sheriff (Gary Cooper), standing alone, against a gang of outlaws he once sent to prison. However, film scholar Dan Nimmo insists that a viewer knowledgeable about the HUAC Hollywood hearings and the subsequent blacklisting could interpret the film as an attack on the hearings and a response to the friendly witnesses who abandoned their colleagues before the committee. Such an interpretation would stamp covert political propaganda on a film that many viewed at the time as simply a lean and tough western. Naturally, it could be interpreted both ways, but Carl Foreman, the film's scriptwriter, admitted its political agenda before he passed away.

Nimmo also treats commercial films coated with a slight indoctrination veneer as "thinly veiled propaganda."[40] Within this category, he places such films about American politicians as *Mr. Smith Goes to Washington* and *The Seduction of Joe Tynan* (1979), which are produced primarily for entertainment purposes but also deliver a little bit of propaganda in the process. In *Mr. Smith*, the film preaches the message that grassroots democracy does work, encouraging the ordinary citizen to participate in the political process. *Joe Tynan*, starring Alan Alda, on the other hand, portrays Washington politics as a game of legislative trade-offs between lobbyists and politicians. Senator Joe Tynan's personal ambition to occupy the White House someday may be attainable, but the film hints that if he becomes president, he will have lost his soul in the process. Films such as these support the argument that propaganda, done covertly or overtly, is found in commercial films.

Film as History

While Hollywood makes historical films the industry often takes liberties with the facts. The books *Past Imperfect* and *History by Hollywood* present examples of Hollywood-made historical films that usually get history wrong, their attempts doing more harm than good. Despite this reservation, film can still be an effective teaching tool in a visually defined age. It can serve many disciplines: literature, drama, science, social sciences, and the arts. Take the discipline of history, as an example. Film has the capacity to recreate historical periods, analyze historical events, and recall the lives of important historical figures. Film is a powerful medium if it is utilized properly and, particularly in the case of historical films, if the content is accurate and objective and any speculation and opinion identified accordingly. Naturally, we have to allow commercial films some leeway as they are not intended as documentaries, so a little dramatic license is acceptable. But this exception is quite different from a distortion of the historical facts to such an extent as to render the film worthless as a teaching tool. Unfortunately, in many of the historical films produced by Hollywood studios, accuracy and objectivity are of secondary importance to commercial values, thereby sacrificing veracity to the demands of drama. Let us examine several films where, either by commission or through omission, the filmmakers took too much liberty with the facts, misrepresented the historical material, or distorted the historical evidence enough to lead the viewer to a false conclusion.

Let us begin with the presidential film biographies *Young Mr. Lincoln* (1939), *Abe Lincoln in Illinois* (1940), *Wilson* (1944), *Sunrise at Campobello* (Franklin Roosevelt, 1960) and *Nixon* (1995). During the 2008 presidential campaign and thereafter, the media often associated President Obama with Lincoln. It was intended as a compliment because Lincoln is consistently ranked among the top five American presidents and is generally well respected by the American public. But what Hollywood did to Lincoln's image would be a major felony if fictitious misrepresentation were a crime. According to historian Mark E. Neely Jr.,[41] John Ford's 1939 film *Young Mr. Lincoln* is very careless with the facts and the lead character bears little resemblance to the young Lincoln. It is true that the young Lincoln progressed from shopkeeper to lawyer to national politician. But the center of Ford's film is the courtroom murder trial in which Lincoln, as defense attorney, discredits the testimony of an eyewitness in order to prove his client's innocence. In fact, that trial occurred much later in Lincoln's career, and was inserted into the film's time frame in order to enhance his stature. This embellishment led one scholar to identify the film as more mythical than historical truth. But it was accepted since movies thrive on myths and the film added to the Lincoln legend.[42] *Abe Lincoln in Illinois*, based on Robert Sherwood's Broadway play, is also concerned with his years as a young lawyer, though not his presidency. In Sherwood's version, Lincoln is presented as a passive and contented lawyer rather than the ambitious lawyer from Springfield that he was. The Sherwood film also has Lincoln saying: "I don't want to be no politician."[43] Nothing was further from the truth.

*Wilson*, Darryl F. Zanuck's labor-of-love biography of Woodrow Wilson, proved to be a disappointment on two levels. First, Zanuck's ambitious project flopped at the box office despite an A-list cast and strong production values. The film ran too long and lacked sufficient drama to hold viewers' interest. The bigger disappointment, however, was its unbalanced portrait of America's 28th president. While Wilson had many fine qualities and genuinely wished for the U.S. to join the League of Nations after World War I, there was a darker side to his character as revealed in his attitude towards women and minorities. He neither supported the suffragette movement nor was he an advocate for racial equality. One scholar has described Wilson as a "racial bigot" because he brought Jim Crow laws to Washington when he became president.[44]

On the other hand, the portrait of Franklin D. Roosevelt (FDR) in *Sunrise at Campobello* is of a courageous and determined man, who with the help of his wife, Eleanor, overcame the debilitating effects of polio to become president. The film, however, neglects any mention of the long affair with Lucy Mercer Rutherford that, according to historian Joseph Persico,[45] began around 1916 and continued through Roosevelt's keynote address at the 1928 Democratic National Convention, where *Sunrise at Campobello* ends. Roosevelt's affairs with his secretary and his distant cousin Daisy Suckley form the basis for another FDR film, *Hyde Park on Hudson* (2012), discussed in chapter 2.

At the 1997 annual meeting of the American Historical Association (AHA), a panel including director Oliver Stone, Senator George McGovern, and historian Arthur Schlesinger Jr. discussed Stone's film *Nixon* (1995).[46] Each panelist had allotted time to speak about the historical accuracy of the film. Surprisingly, McGovern, who lost to Nixon in the 1972 presidential race, liked Stone's film. But Schlesinger did not and noted several historical inaccuracies, primarily Stone's characterization of Nixon. Schlesinger understood the necessity for taking liberty with some of the historical record but he demurred at giving a director a blank check on the use of dramatic license. In historical film biographies, Schlesinger emphasized, what was important was the totality of the characterization, that is, did the film present an honest, accurate picture of Nixon? To Schlesinger, Stone's film made Nixon into a sympathetic character to such an extent that he was reduced to being a victim rather than a complicated and flawed leader. Schlesinger's assessment received support from the AHA panel, particularly in face of the more sympathetic view that Nixon was unloved and this lack of affection affected his political decision-making. The truth was that Nixon was loved by his wife and daughters and his inner circle, though he was constantly searching for more love and came to believe that he never received enough from his family and friends.[47]

Other films released over the past three decades illustrate the pitfalls of reconstructing the past from a contemporary, sometimes biased, viewpoint. Take the following films, for instance. Audiences who viewed Alan Parker's *Mississippi Burning* (1988) without sufficient background knowledge would conclude that only whites played a role in the Civil Rights movement. The film focuses on the role of the two major characters, Gene Hackman and Willem Dafoe as FBI agents, and ignores the role played by African Americans in the struggle for equal rights.[48] Similarly, those who lived through the Cuban missile crisis may want to check their recollections after watching the film version of *Thirteen Days* (2001). The crisis plays out through the perspective of its star, Kevin Costner, who plays Kenneth O'Donnell, a political advisor to the Kennedys. The film embellishes the importance of O'Donnell in the decision-making process that resolved the conflict with the Soviet Union. An even greater distortion lies in the inaccurate portrayals of major participants like McGeorge Bundy, Dean Acheson, and Robert McNamara, as well as the positions taken by the military during the crisis.[49]

Additionally, three World War II pictures raise issues of historical accuracy.[50] In *Saving Private Ryan* (1998), Tom Hank's officer replaces the real-life priest sent to remove the remaining Ryan son from harm's way after the deaths of his two brothers in the service. In this particular case, the substitution does not alter the film's realistic portrayal of the horrors of combat during the Omaha Beach invasion. But it does credit the wrong person for saving the soldier's life. In another WWII movie, the prevailing perspective in the bloated blockbuster *Pearl Harbor* (2001) implies that Japan was deliberately forced into taking steps against the U.S. because of the American oil embargo and other provocative actions.[51] Historians generally agree that FDR believed war with Japan was inevitable and if it were to happen, it would be better if the Japanese were the aggressors. But this is a far cry from a conspiracy theory that posits that Roosevelt purposely set up Pearl Harbor as an attractive target for the Japanese to attack. Furthermore, the film is devoid of the local population. Since the naval base at Pearl Harbor is located in Hawaii, the absence of Hawaiians in the film is curious. Still another WWII example is the film *U-571* (2000), which chronicles the Allies' ability to decipher the German Enigma code and prevent German submarines from sinking merchant ships and other Allied naval vessels. The plot centers on an American submarine crew that boards a damaged German U-boat to remove the Enigma code machine. The ability to decipher enemy messages was crucial for Allied success in the naval war for control of the Atlantic. The film, however, left the mistaken impression that it was the Americans who were solely responsible for the successful mission to capture the code machine. In fact, the British Navy had accomplished the feat before the U.S. entered the war. The substitution of the American Navy for the British Navy cannot be attributed to dramatic license alone but rather to a misplaced spirit of nationalism. *U-571* shouts, "America won the war," ignoring the contribution of our allies.

Unfortunately, these historical blunders persist in films that should have known better. For instance, take Ben Affleck's thrilling reenactment of a little-known secondary story to the 1979 Iranian takeover of the U.S. Embassy in his film *Argo* (2012). When the American Embassy in Tehran was seized by Iranian militants who held 52 employees hostage for 444 days, President Jimmy Carter refused to be blackmailed by the Iranian Revolutionaries, but eventually entered into negotiations for their release. When these efforts failed, Carter agreed to a military rescue operation that ended in failure in the desert, resulting in the deaths of eight servicemen and the destruction of two aircraft. This was the story that received the most media attention and it was a major reason that Carter lost the presidency to Ronald Reagan in 1980. But *Argo* is concerned with the backstory, kept secret until declassified by President Clinton in 1997, of how six Americans escaped during the embassy takeover and took refuge in the Canadian Ambassador's residence. *Argo* describes the implausible escape plan in which the Embassy employees pretended to be a Canadian film crew scouting locations for a sci-fi movie. Affleck's film received strong, critically positive reviews and decent domestic box office returns. But the film had its detractors. Admittedly, some criticisms were picky, like the addition of characters (e.g. Alan Arkin as a Hollywood producer) who were not involved in the fake film plot or the exciting conclusion, when the six are detained by the Iranian guards and just make the flight as the soldiers chase the plane on the runway firing as it takes off. None of this happened. In reality, their departure from the residence to the airport went smoothly. This is where Affleck took advantage of dramatic license to add suspense and excitement to the film's ending. There were other complaints as well. The film altered the character of the real CIA agent, portrayed by Affleck in the film, from a happily married family man with three children to a separated father with one son. The author feels these were all embellishments that did not seriously damage the film's honesty. However, from a purely historical perspective, the significant misrepresentation is the film's undervaluing of the role played by the Canadians in the rescue operation. Ken Taylor, the Canadian Ambassador, put himself and his staff in harm's way because of their involvement in the escape. It was Taylor who pushed Washington to initiate the escape and once it was accepted, the Canadians went to work and scouted the airport, secured copies of entry and exit visas, sent people in and out of Iran to establish random flight patterns, and actually bought the plane tickets. Furthermore, Taylor served as a spy for the U.S. during the hostage crisis, an act that might have cost him his life if he were caught. The real hero of this film is not Affleck's CIA agent, but Canadian Ambassador Taylor.[52] It is true that the CIA did not want its involvement known at the time and so the Canadians received all the credit and the blame by the Iranian revolutionary government. But when *Argo* was premiered in Toronto, Taylor and his friends were upset by their portrayal. To his credit, Affleck added a postscript that the Argo mission was a model of international cooperation, though that hardly makes amends for manipulating the historical record.

The educational value of these films diminishes proportionately to their disregard for the historical record. Good intentions are deceptive when filmmakers tamper with history, converting historical events into fiction. Educators who utilize film need to provide explanations and guidance, lest their students learn the wrong lessons.

## Film as Politicizing Agent

What is the effect, if any, of visual imagery on the development of individual ideology? The process whereby young people acquire their political values and beliefs is known as "political socialization." We know that youngsters are most influenced by their family heritage and political environment, by the strength of their ethnic-religious group affiliation and their socio-economic class. Hence, a youngster raised in a white middle-to-upper-class family that votes Republican consistently and that discusses politics on a regular basis is very likely to become a Republican voter and share the party's values as expressed through its political agenda. The mass media play a role in this process too, but this is ill-defined. For example, it is unclear whether audiences that view a specific political film will be so impressed as to alter their political values, change their party allegiance, or engage in some act of civil disobedience. Thus, describing political film as an agent of political or social change is problematic since the empirical evidence that would indicate a causal relationship between the two variables has yet to be established. Still Stephen Vaughn,[53] in his book on Reagan's Hollywood tenure, presents a convincing argument for adopting a "preponderance of the evidence" approach when the methodology is applied to political figures. Vaughn's analysis of Reagan's film career furnishes clues toward understanding his shifting position on social and political issues while in the White House. Vaughn's research is crucial to understanding Reagan's transformation from a liberal New Deal Democrat to a conservative Cold War warrior.

Speculating on the factors that motivate the policies of political leaders is far different from documenting the influence of films on social and political behavior. This issue was raised as early as the beginning of the last century when the lynching of blacks increased after showings of *The Birth of a Nation*. Did the film's release incite mob violence? Was the film a recruiting tool for the Klan? The research suggests a possible relationship, but not enough to prove causality. This issue of cause-effect has plagued Hollywood since the thirties, when publication of the *Payne Fund Studies*, which linked juvenile delinquency to the Hollywood crime and gangster films of that era, served as a catalyst for establishing tougher regulations on motion pictures. Although the results were methodologically flawed, the film industry and the government interpreted them as proof of a direct connection between film content and criminal and delinquent behavior. These studies lent "scientific respectability" to the industry's establishment of the Production Code, a content-based guideline for the making of movies. The code served as the basis for the industry's regulation over film content for more than 30 years.[54]

The failure by social scientists to document the nexus between film representations and social or political behavior weakens the argument that such a connection exists, particularly the concept that specific films might play a limited, but influential, role in the formation of individual beliefs and values. Much social scientist research today focuses on video games, television programs, and other popular culture media, with little current study being conducted on film and behavior. The subject was in the news again when a shooter entered a Colorado theater during a midnight showing of *The Dark Knight Rises* (2012) and killed 12 people and wounded scores of other patrons. There was an initial suggestion that the action film might have influenced the 24-year-old shooter, but the idea went no further because the shooter's motives remain unknown.[55]

What remains, however, are two attitudinal studies that sought to measure the influence of specific films, both political, on individual attitudes by those who viewed them. One study focused on the impact of the Watergate scandal by collecting data from a viewing of *All the President's Men*.[56] The study found that a substantial attitudinal change occurred in the students who viewed the film, with them exhibiting a marked increase in political alienation and simultaneously displaying a more positive attitude toward the press. The authors concluded that exposure to a clearly delivered political message in a well-crafted film can have a short-term influence on a particular attitude. The long-term impact, however, remains unknown.

In the other study, involving Michael Moore's film *Roger and Me* (1989),[57] the researchers reached similar conclusions in both an American sample and a Japanese comparison group. *Roger and Me* concerns the unsuccessful attempt by filmmaker Michael Moore to locate and interview Roger Smith, the CEO of General Motors (GM), so he can explain on camera why GM was closing plants in Moore's native city of Flint, Michigan. Despite some controversy over whether the film was a documentary or a comedic fable, the study results suggest that the American sample that viewed the film had substantially more negative feelings toward American corporations than the control group that had not seen the film. The Japanese sample group of university students duplicated the American findings except that, in addition to the negative attitudes displayed towards business, the Japanese also expressed more positive feelings towards their home companies.

While these studies are unlikely to end the debate over the influence of the film industry to shape public opinion, their findings add to the body of existing evidence suggesting that films containing political messages are capable of providing audiences with more than harmless diversions. As imaging and media manipulation expand their role in American political culture, the presentation and context of political messages take on greater significance. And as the mediated images proliferate, the bond between the image makers (Hollywood) and the policymakers (Washington) grows stronger.

# Chapter 2

# In Search of the Political Film

In a scene from the film *Casablanca*, Claude Rains, who plays the corrupt Vichy French police chief, Captain Renault, warns Humphrey Bogart, the cynical American owner of Rick's Café:

Renault: We're going to make an arrest in your cafe.

Rick: Again?

Renault: This is no ordinary arrest, a murderer no less. If you're thinking of warning him, don't put yourself out. He cannot possibly escape.

Rick: I stick my neck out for nobody.

Renault: A wise foreign policy.

Does this scene at the beginning of *Casablanca* set up the audience to expect an anti-Nazi, pro-Allies political film? Released to theaters in 1942 to take advantage of the Allied invasion of North Africa, this classic film has earned high praise from screen critics and film buffs alike. Once considered by Warner Brothers to be a B-list production, with a script crafted by four different writers, often on the day of filming, *Casablanca* has become a Hollywood legend. Ranked second only to *Citizen Kane* on the American Film Institute's (AFI) best 100 films list, *Casablanca* has inspired numerous books and articles over the past 70 years.[1] Yet no consensus exists on the question of whether *Casablanca* is essentially a romantic drama, a political film, or both.

What elements are required to make a film political? There is no empirical answer despite many attempts to develop a definition of the genre that appeals to most film scholars. The Library of Congress (LOC), for instance, describes political film as "Fictional work centering on the political milieu, often of candidates, elections, and elective or appointive office. Some of the protagonists may be corrupt or dictatorial."[2] That description may be satisfactory for a library catalogue but it is much too narrow for our purposes. Instead here is one that is generic enough to avoid controversy:

> Political cinema in the narrow sense of the term is a cinema which portrays current or historical events or social conditions in a partisan way in order to inform or agitate the spectator. Political cinema exists in different forms such as documentaries, feature films, or even animated and experimental films.[3]

Definitions are almost always flawed, but rather than analyze those given it is more profitable to first examine why the genre drew interest from scholars and how political science and film studies sought to develop a category where such films could be placed.

The issue was first raised and debated in the 1970s when the American Political Science Association (APSA) published a series of articles on the teaching methodologies of courses that integrated film as part of the curriculum. Historians were utilizing film as a teaching tool since at least World War II, but political scientists were more cautious. Why, they wanted to know, would you examine documentaries and fictional films to explain and understand historical and political events when you could read primary sources instead? What advantages, if any, did visual imagery have over the printed word? How would the use of film in the classroom enhance students' knowledge of the subject matter? Before these questions could be addressed, political scientists and film scholars had to determine whether a separate and distinct genre of "political" film existed and whether it could be readily defined. The effort to identify a distinct genre, however, is so fraught with traps and tricks that scholars and practitioners ought to heed the warning by anthropologist Clifford Geertz,[4] who recounted a Javanese folktale of the legendary "Stupid Boy" to his colleagues as a reminder of their obligation to precisely identify the object of their studies: "Stupid Boy," having been counseled by his mother to seek a quiet wife, returns to his village with a corpse.

Similarly, scholars in identifying the political film had to provide satisfactory answers to the following questions: What distinguishes a political film from other genres? How does the viewer know when a film contains a political agenda or seeks to promote a particular political ideology? The answers are vital to defining the genre. Unfortunately the questions are easier to raise than to answer with any degree of certitude. Instead, what has emerged from the interdisciplinary efforts has been the identification of various schools of thought regarding political film.

## Schools of Thought

### A. The Inclusives

For want of a better descriptive term, I will use the term "inclusives" to refer to those who consider most films to contain some level of political meaning, whether deliberate or inadvertent, brilliant or simple-minded. This group points to a wide range of films that contain a variety of political ideas and concepts, including thematic messages that express ideas and values that reflect the spirit of the government in power, mirror the national mood at the time, or provide support and reinforcement for the status quo.[5] This category contains a wide range of films, from serious dramas to action-adventure movies and comedies. Political scientist Terry Christensen identified 261 films in his 1980s book, *Reel Politics*,[6] including the Errol Flynn swashbuckler *The Sea Hawk* (1940), the film *Country* (1984), about farmers in a struggle with the federal bureaucracy to keep their land, as well as *The Moon Is Blue* (1953), a film featuring two older men in competition to seduce a young virgin. But the expansive nature of the category does not bother the inclusives, who essentially believe that most films contain a political message of some sort, be it to display the opportunities an open society provides for individuals to move up the economic ladder or the freedoms enjoyed by citizens living under a democracy.

Another political scientist, Michael Genovese, built on Christensen's work by putting limits around the inclusives' open-ended category. Genovese developed a taxonomy that requires a film to be classified as "political" if it contains at least *one* of the following criteria:

1. it serves as a vehicle for international propaganda
2. its major intention is to bring about political change or
3. it is designed to support the existing economic, political, and social systems.[7]

The value of Genovese's classification lies in the development of a discriminating category of films with specific characteristics. It thus provides some shape to Christensen's loose classification. His first criterion is fairly obvious, as those in power or those who wield power use the film medium to serve their own propaganda objectives. The subject of propaganda is examined in chapter 3, but here we make sure it is understood as a communication tool used by governments, institutions, organizations and others to promote self-serving ends.

His second requirement, however, is more problematic, as it singles out films that only advocate political change. It thus seems to omit film stories that expose the corruption of political systems or the exploitation of economic systems without mandating their downfall or destruction. Suppose a film scrutinizes the government of the day or the fundamental principles supporting the political system, the unequal distribution of justice within the legal system, the inequality of the social class structure, or the prevailing power relationships without offering a prescription for change? Why should such a film not be included if it merely discloses wrongs without advocating a political solution? Is not a film that educates an audience about a social or political issue, thereby serving as a catalyst for political change, a political film even where change is not its primary purpose? To demonstrate, let us take the 1979 film *The China Syndrome* as an example. It does not preach against the use of nuclear power per se, but it nonetheless demonstrates the potential for nuclear disaster and alerts the audience to expect a possible government cover-up should such a catastrophe befall the country. In light of the Three Mile Island nuclear accident outside of Harrisburg, PA, which coincidentally happened a few weeks after the film's release, why is it not legitimate to state that the film served a political function by informing the public about the negative side of nuclear power as an energy source, a viewpoint unlikely to be publicized by the nuclear power industry or the U.S. government? Since its theatrical release, the U.S., Japan, Russia and other nations (see chapter 11) have experienced just such nuclear accidents at power plants.

Genovese's third criterion restricts itself to films that support the status quo. In one sense, when a film supports the status quo it says that life is good and change is unnecessary. Genovese's contention is that any film that justifies the government in power or supports the existing justice system or the socioeconomic class structure is inherently political because it works against institutional reform and social change. The assertion is correct, but it fails to be bolder and include films that are designed to support or undermine the existing political and socioeconomic systems *at the expense of disadvantaged and deprived groups*. This qualifying adjustment would make the criterion more useful because it would include a host of politically intended movies such as *The Grapes of Wrath* (1940), *Salt of the Earth* (1953), *Norma Rae* (1979), and *Alamo Bay* (1985), among others. These films attacked the uneven distribution of goods and rewards while addressing issues of regional poverty, labor exploitation, and racial and ethnic discrimination.

## B. The Exclusives

At the other end of the spectrum are the "exclusives," comprised mostly of film critics and cinema society members, who consider the very phrase "a political film genre" an oxymoron. To these cinema purists a political film is simply a piece of propaganda. This group argues that filmmaking is essentially a collaborative process, from the banks that provide film studios with the finances to support their projects to the editing process that shapes the film's final narrative style. With so many participants in financing, distribution, and production, it is unlikely that the process could ever deliver ideological or political messages

The exclusives are skeptical that an industry that is devoted almost exclusively to "making money" would turn out a product that offends it audience, insults its leaders, thumbs its nose at the deeply held moral beliefs of its populace or advocates radical changes to its core values. Moreover, the argument goes, whenever Hollywood tackles an obvious political subject, such as election campaigning, the industry dilutes the political message with comedy, romance, or action to subvert the message by distracting attention from it. Warren Beatty's *Bulworth* (1998) is a good example. Here the need for campaign finance reform, a worthy subject of scrutiny, is soft-peddled by general silliness, rap music and an implausible plot.

The exclusives additionally maintain that there is little support today for "political films," as measured by box office earnings. Their contention is supported by the financial returns of a half dozen Hollywood films released in 2011 that, although flawed, nonetheless explored contemporary and historical political issues: Robert Redford's film *The Conspirator*, about Mary Surratt's trial for her part in President Lincoln's assassination; *A Better Life*, in which an illegal immigrant is deported to allow his son to remain in the U.S.; George Clooney's *The Ides of March*, about a Pennsylvania governor running for president; Clint Eastwood's psychological drama *J. Edgar*, about J. Edgar Hoover, the head of the Federal Bureau of Investigation (FBI); and the post 9/11 film *Extremely Loud and Incredibly Close*, in which a son tries to unravel a mystery after his father dies at the World Trade Center. Combined, these five films had a domestic gross of slightly more than $122 million, failing to approach the domestic gross of the 2011 comedy *Bridesmaids*, which grossed $169 million.[8] Of the 20 top grossing films of 2012, *Lincoln*, was the only political film to make the list.[9]

# In Search of the Political Film

Finally, the exclusives believe that Hollywood is incapable of producing a film with a political theme because the industry reduces the subject to easily recognizable clichés and stereotypes. Hollywood thus reduces the complexities of political life to personal stories that are most likely to attract the masses. This tendency to dilute political ideas led film critic John Simon to maintain that Hollywood cannot make commercially successful political films because

> the issues are complex and, to some extent, abstract, and have to be embodied in human antagonists to make them come alive. But then in order to make the characters both dramatic and human in a 90- or 100-minute context, the issues usually have to be foreshortened and oversimplified. In effect, the filmmaker is caught between the Scylla of depersonalization and the Charybdis of over simplification.[10]

This tendency to dilute political ideas led Simon, relying on classical music as a reference point, to remind us that "Beethoven will not sound like Beethoven if played on a kazoo."[11]

Any suggestion that Hollywood only makes entertainment movies for the masses, however, overlooks that small group of films, ranging in any one year from 5 to 10 percent of total output, that probe serious public policy issues despite modest financial returns. Over the last decade Hollywood has produced a list of quality political films, including more than a dozen nominated for best picture. The problem that confronts both the inclusives and the exclusives is not that Hollywood avoids political films altogether but that it is difficult to make a credible argument either way when there are so few movies to cite.

## C. A Third Alternative

Both Christensen and Genovese were pioneers in examining the characteristics that rendered a film "political." Another political scientist, Peter Haas, supports the idea of a political film genre but approaches the subject differently. Since political themes may be conveyed in narratives that are dramatic, comic or thrilling, political films differ in structure and content from other genres since they lack the simplicity of westerns or science fiction, where the forces of good and evil are clearly delineated. By its very nature, politics is more complicated. Films dealing with political issues are peopled with more ambiguous characters, flawed individuals that are closer to reality.

Instead of attempting to define a political film genre, Haas creates a typology to identify four different kinds of political films:[12]

- Pure Political Films: e.g., *Mr. Smith Goes to Washington* and *Frost/Nixon*
- Politically Reflective Films: e.g., *Air Force One* and *Independence Day*
- Auteur Political Films: e.g., the *Godfather* trilogy
- Socially Reflective Films: e.g., *Gone with the Wind*

In Haas's scheme, the "pure" political films are also the most obvious: fictional films whose titles announce their political content. Both the films cited above qualify without a doubt.

What Haas identifies as "politically reflective" films are those in which the political content is used as a plot device but is secondary to the development of a non-political major theme. He cites such films as *Independence Day* (1996) and *Air Force One* (1997), which utilize the institution of the presidency as a contrivance for an action thriller in which Bill Pullman and Harrison Ford respectively are depicted as invincible heroic presidents.

The third category of "auteur" political films refers to a small group of directors whose films impart political meaning, but without the requisite political references. Francis Ford Coppola's *Godfather* films fit here since the American-based mafia is run like an efficient political machine, dispensing rewards and administering punishment.

The last category in Haas's typology, that of "socially reflective" films, is the depository for the vast majority of Hollywood movies that are produced and marketed as entertainment. These films have no political intentions, characters, or events; in some cases; however, they may suggest or infer slight political meanings. The classic and popular *Gone with the Wind* (1939), a romantic drama that takes place during the American Civil War, is a prime example.

## D. A Fourth Gambit: Political Messages

Christensen and Haas teamed up to write *Projecting Politics*[13] a book that attempts to avoid the seemingly insolvable problems inherent in identifying a "political film" genre by concentrating solely on American movies that convey political messages, which the authors define as content "that depicts various aspects of the political system, especially (but not necessarily) political institutions, political actors, and the political system."[14] Both accept the fact that these messages can be of two kinds: overt or explicit and covert or implicit. Obviously, the overt messages are easier to identify than the covert ones, which are more subtle and may turn up in the film's subtext. However the authors soon abandon their objective definition in favor of identifying political films in terms of their political and ideological messages, whether understood by audiences or not.

Taking this approach avoids the frustrations involved in reaching agreement on an established political film genre, but it nonetheless raises several questions of its own. First, if, as the authors maintain, most Hollywood movies contain political content of one kind or another, then how would audiences be able to sort out the more significant messages from the less important ones? How, for example, would audiences distinguish between the serious explicit messages conveyed in D.W. Griffith's *The Birth of a Nation* and another silent film of that era, *The Red Kimona* (1925), that detailed the story of a former prostitute who is involved in a sensational murder trial? The issues are race in the first, the struggle of women for respect in the second. Does the content of these films qualify them for inclusion as political films? Would Christensen and Haas claim both contain political messages of equal importance? This author cannot speak for them but film historian Kevin Brownlow considers the silent film, *The Red Kimona*, as an early plea for women's rights.[15] Both race and gender are considered in later chapters.

Another question that the Christensen and Haas approach raises is the issue of how to measure the significance of the political message among other material in the film? Is there a quantity standard for the political material. Is 10 to 20 minutes of political material in a two-hour film sufficient to make that film political? Apparently, the authors would agree otherwise they would not have included the comedy *Legally Blonde 2: Red, White and Blonde* (2003) in their chapter on "Congressional Acts." This Reese Witherspoon sequel to *Legally*

*Blonde* (2001) has the actress working for a congresswoman intent upon securing legislation to prohibit the testing of cosmetics on animals. While animal rights is a worthy cause, Witherspoon's character is so stupid she has trouble locating the ladies room. She also has a gay dog. So here is a plot involving a dumb lawyer with a gay dog fighting for animal rights simply because she meets the committee chair and their male dogs fall in love. Is this really how legislation gets passed in Congress? Is this a civics lesson we want to convey to our citizens? Additionally, the film exploits the image of *Mr. Smith Goes to Washington* in a scene where Witherspoon goes to the Lincoln Memorial to brood after her animal rights bill fails, reminiscent of the famous Jimmy Stewart scene in the Capra film. Films like *Legally Blonde 2* demonstrate the problem of substituting a political message approach for a definitional approach to political film. In the end, we are no better off.

*Projecting Politics*, published in 2005, includes a political filmography that contains almost 500 films.[16] Many, like *Advise and Consent* (1962), *JFK* (1991) and *The Manchurian Candidate* (2004), are explicitly political, but others like *High Noon* (1952) and *A King in New York* (1956) require knowledge of the historical context to decipher their covert political messages. But there are others on the list such as *Gentlemen Prefer Blondes* (1953), *Attack of the Fifty-Foot Woman* (1958) and *Basic Instinct* (1992) that require more explanatory material to justify their inclusion. Just listing films does not add much to the political film discussion.

E. The Author's Contribution

For what it is worth, the author believes there is a political film genre, even though scholars differ over which films belong in its category. Christensen, Genovese and Haas acknowledge the presence of political content in selected Hollywood films, but each differs over the selection criteria.

Because of his background and interest in constitutional issues, the author created a two-tier test to identify political films: their intent and audience effect. Taking his cue from constitutional law scholar Cass Sunstein, who defined political speech as speech that is "both intended and received as a contribution to public deliberation about some issue,"[17] the author's approach necessitates that both criteria be satisfied before a film qualifies for inclusion in a political film category. Let us now put this scheme to the test.

## Intent

At the production level, the author's definition requires that those involved in the filmmaking process—producer, director, film studio—intend to deliver a political statement and state so either in its advertising or media interviews. Unmistakable examples of intended political films are the propaganda films *Triumph of the Will* (Leni Riefenstahl) and *Why We Fight* (the Frank Capra series). These nonfiction films were made with the support of their respective governments to further a state's interests and to encourage their populations during wartime to make the requisite sacrifices. Two examples drawn from contemporary politics are conservative Dinesh D'Souza's film *2016: Obama's America*, intended to influence the outcome of the 2012 presidential election, and Michael Moore's documentary *Fahrenheit 9/11* (2004), which criticizes President George W. Bush's decision to invade Iraq and was intended to sway audiences to vote against his re-election. When intentions are so blatantly stated by filmmakers, why would viewers question the motives of such ideologues as Moore and D'Souza?

On the other hand, identifying the intent of commercial films like *Che* is more problematic because the director's purpose is ambiguous. Was Soderbergh's intent to glorify the revolutionary hero of the sixties or merely to present a historical portrait? Was it Clint Eastwood's intention to emphasize the personal life of J. Edgar Hoover in *J. Edgar* rather than the role he played as FBI director during the Red Scare of the 1950s? Eastwood devotes only a small percentage of his film to Hoover's obsession with communism and communist sympathizers—more of such content would have moved his film closer to the political category.

However, even in contemporary Hollywood, directors often have to fulfill contractual obligations under which the studios exercise final judgment on their work. Under such conditions, filmmakers first must satisfy the demands of the studio before personalizing the film with any political messages. One relevant example from the 1950s is Carl Foreman's script for the western *High Noon*. Was the film a tribute to the rugged individualism and personal courage of the western lawman or an intended attack on the friendly witnesses, which included the major studio heads, who testified before HUAC during the post–World War II Hollywood hearings on communism in the film industry[18] According to Foreman[19] his original script was a parable of individual decency (Marshall Will Kane) versus the forces of evil (Frank Miller's gang) and an indifferent community. Once HUAC subpoenaed Foreman, the script began to reflect his personal opposition to the HUAC hearings and his anger at the capitulation of the studios. *High Noon* then became a critique of Hollywood cowardice. Had the studio heads understood it as an attack on them and on the HUAC hearings, the film likely would have been shelved.

On other occasions, the initial intention behind a film may change during the course of production. This is what happened to *Force of Evil* (1949)[20] a film about two Jewish brothers coming to terms with crime and greed in a New York City ethnic ghetto. Director Abraham Polonsky, whose name would subsequently be placed on the Hollywood blacklist, wanted to make a traditional gangster film, but was asked to deliver a popular movie that had liberal overtones. During the shooting, the content became more radical as the film reached its conclusion, resulting in a film that challenged the acquisitive and materialistic values of capitalism. Films like *High Noon* and *Force of Evil* are capable of delivering multiple messages to an audience. Which message the audience receives requires the kind of analysis that is often left to the film critic. Further complicating the definition of intentionality is the fact that filmmaking is a collective enterprise, especially when a film is made under contract for a studio. Hollywood journalist Peter Biskind explains the problem inherent in the making of any political film, particularly for a major studio:

> A conservative director may work with a liberal writer, or vice versa, and both, even if they are trying to impose their politics on their films…, may be overruled by the producer who is only trying to make a buck and thus expresses ideology in a different way, not as a personal preference or artistic vision, but as mediated by mainstream institutions like banks and studios, which transmit ideology in the guise of market decisions….[21]

Under these conditions only established auteurs and independent filmmakers have an opportunity to make a political film with few, if any, strings attached. Another necessary consideration is the capital required to finance film projects. The studios borrow millions from banks to finance their projects, and banks are notoriously conservative institutions that minimize risks. Even the independents require national distribution if their films are to compete with the major studios at the box office.

## Effect

If a film's intent is not always discernible to its viewers, its impact on that audience is even more problematic. How to measure the reception of a film's political text raises additional obstacles in defining the genre. An appropriate measuring instrument would gauge an audience's understanding of the film's political text, which is whether the primary story depicts some aspect of political history, promotes a particular ideology, delivers propagandistic messages, advocates political change or reform, and supports the benefits of a capitalist socioeconomic class system that exploits some and disadvantages others. Audiences that saw *Abe Lincoln in Illinois* (1940), *Wilson* (1944), or *Milk* (2008), to cite a few examples, are unlikely to mistake these films for a genre other than political biography. Nor will audiences misconstrue the intent of a film like *Welcome to Sarajevo* (1997), which depicts the plight of two reporters caught up in the Bosnian War. The political nature of the film is reinforced by the inclusion of news reports from Kosovo on the fighting and the ethnic killings.

Hollywood has produced a number of films that examined American institutions and found them lacking in compassion and human justice. For example, some film studios in the thirties specifically produced a number of social message films: audiences empathized with the plight of the Okies during the Great Depression as depicted in John Ford's *The Grapes of Wrath*, a sympathetic story of poor farmers struggling to hold on to their land despite adverse weather conditions, callous banks, and an indifferent federal bureaucracy. Reform of the prison system was the message of *I Am a Fugitive from a Chain Gang* (1932). Prejudice against outsiders and minorities depicted in films like *Fury* (1936) and *They Won't Forget* (1937) cautioned against the injustices of mob violence. Meanwhile, in the post–World War II era, films like *Crossfire* (1947) and *Gentleman's Agreement* (1947) spoke out against anti-Semitism. A cycle of 1949–50 movies such as *Intruder in the Dust* and *No Way Out* confronted racial prejudice and discrimination at a time when segregation was the law of the land. In the post-Vietnam era of the late 1970s–1980s, audiences watching films like *The Deer Hunter* (1978) and *Apocalypse Now* (1979) viewed the conflict in Southeast Asia with ambiguity as to its merits. And in the 21st century, films like *Brokeback Mountain* (2005), *Milk* (2008) and *The Kids Are All Right* (2010) became pleas for tolerance and acceptance of equal rights for gays and lesbians. American audiences could hardly misinterpret the social and political messages expressed in these films.

But film audiences may not always understand or accept the intended messages because these meanings are subject to interpretation. A perfect example was the popular film *Forrest Gump* (1994). Audiences who saw this sentimental film could root for its dim-witted hero as he overcame adversity, while other viewers may have been offended by its celebration of ignorance. *Forrest Gump* is the kind of film Hollywood loves to make because its slick entertainment production offers viewers ambiguous interpretations.

Still another film with an enigmatic message was director Stanley Kramer's *Guess Who's Coming to Dinner* (1967). The storyline for this Spencer Tracy–Katharine Hepburn film centers on the intended marriage of their daughter to a black doctor (Sidney Poitier). Audiences that viewed the film at face value could accept it as another romantic comedy by the popular Hepburn-Tracy team. But viewers who came to the theater with relevant background information on interracial marriages would view the film as a statement against state antimiscegenation laws, albeit packaged in a highly entertaining movie.[22]

Similarly, *Casablanca* is open to dual interpretations. Viewed by millions worldwide since its release, *Casablanca* presents audiences with optional interpretations, depending on the viewer's knowledge. For many, the Rick-Ilsa (Bogart-Bergman) romance remains the quintessential love story. But there are individual scenes with dialogue that would lead other viewers, cognizant of the pre–World War II political climate, to interpret the film's anti-isolationist, pro-democracy message. In this scenario, Rick's neutrality is transformed by his love for Ilsa, a passion so strong it overcomes his cynicism and persuades him to assist her husband, Victor Laszlo, a Resistance leader, in his escape from Nazi-occupied Morocco. On the other hand, if *Casablanca* is really about world politics, why is it that the Victor Laszlo anti-Nazi character is secondary to the Bogart-Bergman love story? Furthermore, had Warner Brothers intended the film to deliver a pro-interventionist message, why was it not made and released a few years earlier, before Pearl Harbor? Then the timing of the film's national distribution, together with Warner Brothers' anti-fascist stand, would have lent credibility to the film's pro-U.S. intervention message. Whether *Casablanca* is a romantic drama or a plea for American intervention in the European War is still debated.

Similarly, Chaplin's *A King in New York* (1957) also can be viewed at face value as one of his lesser comedies or, with additional information, as political satire on HUAC and McCarthyism. One viewer is likely to accept it as a comedy, while another who takes the following background knowledge into the theater surely will view the film differently. English-born Chaplin never became an American citizen. When his loyalty was questioned during the 1950s, Chaplin left the country, eventually residing in Switzerland. Later, when he wanted to return to the States, he discovered that he was *persona non grata* and was refused re-entry by the Immigration and Naturalization Service. *A King in New York*, therefore, was produced in London but not exhibited in the U.S. for two decades.[23] As scriptwriter, director, and star of *A King in New York*, Chaplin exercised complete control over the film, lending support to the view that he sought to critique America because it questioned his loyalty as it embraced mindless conformity and vacuous cultural values.

Likewise, is there a film with greater ambiguity of meaning than *Seabiscuit* (2003)? This 1930s story of an undersized racehorse that is given little chance of outrunning star thoroughbred War Admiral can be viewed as a tribute to a horse with a bigger heart and spirit than the reigning champion. It is a story that applauds the underdog and hence, may be interpreted as a tribute to the spirit of the American people and their disabled president, Franklin Roosevelt, in their desire to overcome the hardships of the Great Depression. To make the parallel between the underdog Seabiscuit and the hard times faced by the American people during the depression, the film strategically intersects the racehorse story with newsreel footage showing breadlines and unemployed workers. Thus, for the common man Seabiscuit represented a symbol of resilience and courage, the very qualities the president said were necessary to restart the engine of American capitalism.

The idea that good films contain several layers of meaning is supported by film scholar Don Morlan, who argues that the popular shorts of the Three Stooges were more than exercises in mindless slapstick; rather they were films of social criticism and pro-World War II interventionism.[24] Morlan discovered that during the period from 1934 to 1958 the Stooges made a total of 190 shorts for Columbia Pictures, of which 34 portrayed conflicts between the upper and lower classes. These included their signature pie-in-the-face routine, where the recipients were the wealthy and snobbish upper classes. Morlan contends that these shorts helped to lift the morale of the working class during hard economic times. He also insists that the Stooges contributed to pro World War II propaganda in several shorts released between 1935 and 1941. One in particular, *You Nazty Spy* (1940), was released to theaters nine months before Chaplin's *The Great Dictator*, leading Morlan to conclude that the Stooges were turning out shorts that, in their slapstick style, warned Americans of the evils of Nazism and fascism before even Chaplin. For Morlan's thesis to be more than mere speculation, tangible evidence of intent and viewer perception is required. Even if we concede that Jules White, the head of Columbia Pictures Short Subjects division, was an admitted interventionist and even if Curly, Larry, and Moe were Popular Front activists (no evidence exists to support this assertion) who abhorred fascism and deliberately poked fun at Hitler and Mussolini in their films, these assumptions would merely satisfy the first requirement of intent. But relying on the author's two-tier definition, political intention alone is not enough. The effective requirement must also be met, and this is where the Morlan thesis about the Three Stooges breaks down. What did the audience at the time think of the Three Stooges and what did the masses make of their films? Were Curly, Larry, and Moe recognizable political activists? Did they appear at public pro-war rallies? Were they outspoken members of the Popular Front movement? The basic question here, which neither Morlan nor this author can answer with authority, is whether audiences who viewed the Stooges in the thirties and early forties accepted their shorts as social criticism and a call for U.S. intervention against the forces of fascism.

To state the question differently, did a consensus exist among critics, film scholars, and movie audiences that these short films preached revolution, the overthrow of government, or reform of the political or socioeconomic class system? Unless such a perception existed at the time, it remains problematic what messages, if any, the Three Stooges were communicating in their slapstick routines.[25] Unlike *The Great Dictator*, which made a statement against anti-Semitism and fascism that angered Hitler and Mussolini, the shorts made by the Three Stooges were generally conceived to be mindless slapstick routines from beginning to end, recycling the same plot in different contexts. If dictators were the patsies in one film, the victims in others were employers, the rich, and the military. In sum, the Stooges' shorts were no more than mass-produced "fillers" to accompany the main feature or to round out a double bill at a Saturday matinee. Political interpretations of these shorts are inconclusive because they do not satisfactorily prove the political intent or the widespread reception of their content as political.

In theory, the author's two-tier requirement to determine whether a film's content qualifies as political film material demands the kind of empirical proof that satisfies scholars. However, as the above discussion demonstrates, the two-tier definition represents an ideal, since serious practical problems arise in its application. Even in those instances when the intent requirement is met, documentation of the effect criterion involving audience perception is close to impossible to determine in films with multiple levels of meaning. Hence, the author realizes that his attempt to identify the political film is just as flawed as those attempts previously described.

To make the point more emphatically, below is a case study of a recent film about President Franklin Roosevelt that on the surface would appear to viewers to be a political biopic—but they would be mistaken.

Figure 2.1. The Roosevelt Clan at Hyde Park, *Hyde Park on Hudson*, 2012. Reprinted with permission, Focus Features/Photofest

## Case Study: *Hyde Park on Hudson*

Hyde Park borders the Hudson River in Dutchess County, New York, about two hours north of Manhattan. It is a largely rural community with a small downtown commercial area that has seen better days. Its primary purpose today is to serve as a tourist attraction for history buffs to visit the homes of Franklin and Eleanor Roosevelt and the FDR museum. It is a place steeped in the history of the 1930s and 1940s when America struggled with the woes of economic depression and the events leading to World War II. But director Roger Mitchell's film depicts only a narrow view into the more mundane aspects of the 32nd president's private life and neglects his substantial achievements. *Hyde Park on Hudson* focuses on one summer when FDR, disabled by the polio he contracted as a young man, is preparing for the visit of King George VI of England and his wife, Queen Elizabeth.

In the film, Roosevelt (played by Bill Murray) is surrounded by four women: his domineering mother, whose home provides a retreat from Washington politics, his wife Eleanor, who is more guest than First Lady, and two mistresses, his secretary Missy and a distant cousin, Daisy Suckley, who provide him with sexual pleasures to ease his headaches and other ailments. The one sex scene is carefully and discreetly staged and the few others are mostly implied. Eleanor, who acted as Roosevelt's social conscience and played a major role in his political life, appears in only a few scenes and disappears into the background.

When the film opens the inhabitants of the Roosevelt home are busily preparing for their royal guests, who are on a diplomatic mission to enlist the assistance and support of FDR in a likely war with Hitler's Germany. Much time is spent on a formal dinner party that goes seriously wrong and an afternoon "hot dog" picnic with the King and Queen that should go wrong but in fact turns out to be unexpectedly right as the royal couple get to behave as ordinary people. But these scenes omit even the slightest hint of politics. In one that occurs late at night the two men retire to Roosevelt's private study with liquor in hand, only to engage in small talk with nary a hint of the war looming on the horizon.

It is disappointing that the director, who shot mostly on location, missed a golden opportunity to add to the memory of one of the country's most admired presidents. Instead this 94-minute film would have the audience believe that all Roosevelt cared about were his stamp collection and fulfilling his sexual needs. The president who gave the U.S. hope during the Great Depression and guided the country through most of World War II is nowhere in sight.

## Factors to Consider in Identifying the Political Film

### Location

Realtors constantly remind us that in purchasing a home the primary consideration should be location, location, location. This is sound advice if buying real estate, but does a Washington, D.C. setting automatically assure audiences they are viewing a political film? A film's location is important because it provides the frame in which the plot is carried out. But can it stand alone in classifying a film as political? Not quite, but it can be a contributing factor in certain films. Let us compare two films set in the nation's capital: Frank Capra's classic, *Mr. Smith Goes to Washington*, and Roger Donaldson's 1987 film, *No Way Out*. In Capra's film, there are numerous shots of the Washington monuments but, more importantly, many scenes of political activities, including a filibuster inside the Senate chamber. It is these scenes that establish the frame in which the narrative of the story takes place because they depict the struggle of a naive young senator using the filibuster as a tool to expose the greedy interests of a corrupt political machine. The Washington background lends authenticity to the story but does not necessarily define it.

On the other hand, in Donaldson's film, Kevin Costner, a naval officer assigned to the secretary of defense (Gene Hackman), becomes romantically involved with Hackman's mistress. When the mistress turns up dead, Costner is put in charge of the investigation, which eventually leads back to Hackman. A good many scenes take place inside the 17-mile Pentagon building in Arlington, Virginia, but the narrative focus is on romance and suspense rather than the workings of the Defense Department. In this case, the location provides legitimacy to the story's framework but is unnecessary to the development of a plot that has the defense secretary unintentionally kill his mistress and then cover up the accident.

A successful political film, then, takes advantage of location and integrates it into the context of the film. A prime example is the 1996 film *City Hall*, shot in New York City, including the working offices of the mayor and the city council and with a plot that involves a besieged mayor (Al Pacino) who is actively engaged in trying to keep racial peace after a black boy is accidentally shot. Pacino's mayor is occupied by politics in virtually every frame. The audience learns little about the mayor's personal life because the focus of the narrative is on his official duties and public activities. Whether the mayor is single or married, a Mets or Yankee fan is of secondary concern. What is important is how he deals with adversity, makes crucial decisions affecting the city, and cuts deals to further his political agenda.

Major Characters

Here again audiences can be misled into thinking that simply because a film's major characters are political leaders or major players in the world of politics, this fact alone would qualify it as a political film. Not necessarily so, as the *Hyde Park on Hudson* case study has demonstrated. While there is no litmus test based upon screen minutes, it is important for the major characters to be actively engaged in their official public and political duties for a significant amount of time. Take, for example, the Geena Davis–Michael Keaton film, *Speechless* (1994), about two speechwriters for opposing candidates in a U.S. senatorial race in New Mexico. The political subject is electioneering, with the story's inspiration coming from the real-life romance of two speechwriters in the 1992 Clinton versus Bush Sr. presidential campaign. While Davis and Keaton supposedly are slaving away writing exciting speeches for their respective candidates, the audience sees only their romantic life. Except for a few brief scenes of campaigning, *Speechless* could have been about two sportswriters who meet, fall in love, have a misunderstanding, but end happily in a romantic embrace at an Albuquerque minor league baseball game. The audience, meanwhile, learns no more about running a U.S. senatorial campaign than if they had stayed at home.

Or take a look at the 1995 film *The American President*. Audiences could reasonably expect a film with such a title to concern itself with a working president. But this president (played by Michael Douglas) is a lonely widower who spends most of the film romancing his new love interest, a lobbyist played by Annette Bening. There is one brief scene in the film where Douglas meets with his cabinet on a foreign policy matter, but the focus then turns quickly to the appropriateness of the president dating Bening, a lobbyist for an environmentalist organization, while he is running for re-election. In the end, the film is a pleasant trifle but hardly takes politics seriously.

A more recent film, *J. Edgar* (2011), demonstrates what can happen when a filmmaker takes a prominent political figure and concentrates more on the personal aspect of his life than on the political role he played in American history. In *J. Edgar*, director Clint Eastwood focuses on Hoover's implied and repressed sexual feelings for his associate FBI director, Clyde Tolson (Armie Hammer), and his tendency towards transvestism rather than on the misuse of his office to carry out his private political agenda. Hoover led the FBI for 48 years during the turbulent Cold War years, Civil Rights Movement, and Vietnam War—all significant political-historical events. Yet these are treated superficially by Eastwood. Leonardo DiCaprio is very credible in his depiction of Hoover as a suppressed and closeted homosexual. But it is a distortion of history by omission to make a film about the famous FBI director and underplay his role as an unscrupulous lawman whose obsession with subversives led him to violate individual rights. Eastwood's misplaced emphasis means the film is on the fringe of historical-political.

## The Narrative

Finally, we come to an overriding factor in the identification of a political film: its dominant theme and prevailing message. Audiences are able to ignore the film's location and even its major characters if the dominant theme of the movie, considered in its entirety, provides insight and understanding of political events, political actors, political institutions, and the workings of the political process. At least these feature films since the third edition qualify: *Fair Game* (2010), *The Ides of March* (2011), *Red Tails* (2012) and *Zero Dark Thirty* (2012), all discussed in later chapters.

Admittedly, this is a subjective judgment, but that evaluation remains the heart of the problem of trying to gauge audience reaction to a film. In theory, it is possible to measure audience feedback, but it is also impractical. To measure a film's effective qualities requires exit-polling and other strategies to survey viewers immediately upon exiting the theater after a film's showing. But who would take on this task? What government agency or private organization would be willing to commit the time and resources to collect the data? Hollywood could do it in conjunction with its "sneak previews" by including specific questions about the film's message, but why would the industry want to? Both Hollywood and the government have the resources, but neither has the motivation or the interest.

In the final analysis, neither the author's attempt to require both production intention and audience effect as essential characteristics of the political film nor Christensen's and Haas's efforts to utilize political content are any more likely to assist audiences and create a viable political film genre than past efforts. This is not a problem for mainstream Hollywood since the major studios mostly deliver commercial entertainment. But for that small minority of films produced mostly by auteurs and independent filmmakers, where the political message is paramount and takes precedence over commercial success, a clearly defined political film genre would be useful.

Can it be that the task of defining the political film is similar to the law's effort to define obscenity? Recall Justice Stewart's famous phrase on obscenity, namely that "I don't know what obscenity is but I know it when I see it."[26] Possibly, political film identification is similar in that we know it when we see it, but we cannot explain the indispensable characteristics of its content. In the end, both obscenity and the political character of a film may rest in the eye of the beholder rather than any textbook definition. Quite possibly nonfiction film, with its less ambiguous intentions, is a better classification to help us understand the nature of political film, even if its effect on audiences remains problematic.

Chapter 3

# Nonfiction Film
Picturing Reality?

"I'm not a fan of Michael Moore's. I think he is an entertainer. I don't think he's interested in complexity."
—Frederick Wiseman

"Propaganda is to a democracy what the bludgeon is to a totalitarian state."
—Noam Chomsky, Professor of Linguistics

"The easiest way to inject a propaganda idea into most people's minds is to let it go in through the medium of an entertainment picture when they do not realize that they are being propagandized."
—Elmer Davis, Office of War Information (OWI) Director during WWII

"If you tell a lie big enough and keep repeating it, people will eventually come to believe it. The lie can be maintained only for such time as the State can shield the people from the political, economic and/or military consequences of the lie. It thus becomes vitally important for the State to use all of its powers to repress dissent, for the truth is the mortal enemy of the lie, and thus by extension, the truth is the greatest enemy of the State."
—Joseph Goebbels, Reich Minister of Propaganda

The opening scene of Leni Riefenstahl's documentary *Triumph of the Will*, depicting the 1934 Nazi Party conference in Nuremberg, pans across the sky as it tracks the landing of a small twin-engine plane. When the plane lands, the door opens and Adolph Hitler emerges triumphant, greeted by the worshiping faces of a crowd waving flags and offering party salutes. It is a dramatic introduction to one of the greatest propaganda films on record, a film where Hitler is portrayed as the benevolent leader, *der Fuhrer*, who has descended, God-like, to restore the German people to their rightful place in history. The film is wonderful theater, but also blatant Nazi propaganda. Propaganda is one film type under the more comprehensive genre known as "nonfiction" film—a category that includes everything from newsreels to documentaries. A relative newcomer to nonfiction is the docudrama, a hybrid of fact and fiction. This chapter examines the effort by filmmakers to investigate aspects of reality and to transfer that reality onto film. Whatever the intention, the evidence indicates that few nonfiction films depict reality or events as they actually occurred.

## Nonfiction Film

It would simplify matters if a consensus existed on an accepted definition of the nonfiction film. Like most attempts at classification, the nonfiction film defies simplistic explanation. This is not surprising since the genre encompasses visual images ranging from newsreels, travelogues, and sports biopics to rock concerts, political campaigns, and Nazi Party rallies. One effort to distinguish the nonfiction film from the commercial feature describes the former as "discourses of sobriety,"[1] that is, films that depict an unedited truth. Critics insist, however, that such films straddle fact and fiction, information and entertainment. Consequently, as a film category, works of nonfiction are tainted because the term implies that the events depicted are true.[2]

While an acceptable definition of nonfiction film cannot marshal a critical consensus, Richard Barsam has nonetheless identified half a dozen characteristics essential for inclusion in the genre.[3] These include the following:

- a focus on a particular event, person, group, or social problem
- the film is shot on location with the actual participants and without costumes, stage sets, or sound effects
- the film has a structured narrative with a beginning and an ending
- historically, the film was photographed in black and white, but color is most common today
- the work typically is filmed without spoken narration, relying on the words of the actual participants, and
- the film is customarily not intended for commercial distribution.

As always, there are exceptions to the last characteristic, notably in Michael Moore's films *Roger and Me* (1989), *The Big One* (1998), *Bowling for Columbine* (2002), *Fahrenheit 9/11* (2004), and *Sicko* (2007), which produced respectable box office returns. *Fahrenheit 9/11*, in fact, broke the box office record for documentaries, earning $119 million.[4]

## The Development of Nonfiction Film

Although film historians are likely to associate the development of the documentary with Robert Flaherty's 1922 recording of the life of Inuit Eskimos, *Nanook of the North*, or with the work of John Grierson in England, the cinematic effort to capture reality began decades earlier when European colonial companies engaged photographers to take pictures of their economic holdings to impress their home governments. By the first decade of the 20th century, all the great European colonial powers employed cameramen to record activities in their overseas colonies and to show these films to private investors and the general public in commercial theaters.[5]

Meanwhile, the desire for pictorial news, particularly of military battles, encouraged filmmakers to take desperate measures. Filmmaker Edward Amet depicted the destruction of Admiral Cervera's fleet at Santiago de Cuba during the Spanish-American war by filming richly detailed ship models floating around inside a bathtub.[6] Such fake battle footage was commonplace during these early years of filmmaking. American filmmakers produced some 68 films of the Spanish-American war and the subsequent Philippine Insurrection for national distribution, making it the first war in American history to employ the camera as a recorder of battle scenes.[7] How much of this footage was real or staged for propaganda purposes remains unclear.

## World War I Era

In the years before World War I when labor unions were struggling to organize and gain public acceptance, the American labor movement decided to use the new medium to educate and politicize the working class and to counter the negative images of the silent films distributed by Hollywood. The American Federation of Labor (AFL) made *A Martyr to His Cause* (1911), a film about the trial of the McNamara brothers, accused of bombing the *Los Angeles Times* office. Two years later the labor movement produced *From Dusk to Dawn* (1913), using professional actors to depict a story about labor strife that eventually ends with a socialist party election victory.[8] These silent films were important recruiting tools, as the labor movement sought to organize unskilled immigrant workers, many unable to understand English. For these workers, a picture was worth a thousand words.

The nonfiction film came of age during World War I because, for the first time, film became an instrument of modern warfare, providing valuable information to the warring nations and a source of propaganda to use against their enemies. The British government, for instance, screened its 1915 film, *Britain Prepared*, to President Wilson and the Congress in an attempt to persuade the U.S. to enter the war. Germany, meanwhile, put its film industry under state control to counter the Allied propaganda.[9] Both Germany and Britain were in competition for American support, but before 1917 few Hollywood films about the war treated the conflict in a way that would offend either side. However, once the U.S. officially entered the hostilities, all films that dealt with the war came under the control of the government's Committee on Public Information (CPI). Furthermore, World War I marked the first official effort by the U.S. to produce its own films; the government created a film section inside the Signal Corps with responsibility for turning out films that would aid the war effort.

## Between the Wars

When World War I ended, the filmmakers returned to recording other subjects. Pare Lorentz, founder and head of the U.S. Film Service, made documentaries underwritten by the government, about the resettlement of the Dust Bowl's dispossessed in *The Plow That Broke the Plains* (1936) and the benefits of the Tennessee Valley Authority in *The River* (1937). Actually, the Department of Agriculture had been making films since the beginning of the century as part of its educational mission. By the thirties, the government had built its own sound stage in the nation's capital to facilitate film production.[10]

Documentary film flourished at this time and led to efforts to improve production and national distribution. To consolidate filmmaking during this period, the labor movement recommended east and west coast production and distribution facilities. Consequently, the Labor Film Services was based in New York and the Federated Film Corporation in Seattle. However, the federal government considered the movement's efforts suspicious; the FBI monitored its activities and watched its films while the postal service denied mailing permits to labor film groups that sought to advertise films in their own magazines. Adding to government concerns, both liberal and leftist films were made of the Spanish Civil War and of the tragic effects of the economic depression. One leftist group, Frontier Films, included among its members such directors and screenwriters as Elia Kazan, John Howard Lawson, and Albert Maltz, all of whom joined the Communist Party and were later called before HUAC. To combat labor's earliest efforts, the corporate sector countered with a stream of its own films designed to portray labor organizers as Bolsheviks and anti-American radicals. This anti-labor viewpoint was portrayed in *Courage of the Commonplace* (1917), *Bolshevism on Trial* (1919), and *Dangerous Hours* (1920). These films depicted union leaders as corrupt Bolshevik agents, intent on generating discontent and subverting American industry.[11] Hollywood, which had its own labor problems during the twenties and thirties, turned out documentaries and feature films intended for use as propaganda weapons in the economic struggle between employers and the working classes.

## World War II Era

Nonfiction films were never intended as popular entertainment. Initially, these travelogues, newsreels, and short documentaries were used by theater owners to supplement the main feature. But in the 1930s, the studios forced theater distributors to rent a "film package" for commercial showing, which generally included a major film, a shorter B-list feature, cartoons, and short subjects. As a consequence, the market for documentaries plummeted.

The German invasion of Poland in 1939 revived interest in documentary film. The U.S. government, although proclaiming neutrality, gave military and economic support to the Allies while it propagandized the war to the American people. For example, Louis de Rochemont's documentary *The Ramparts We Watch* (1940) conveyed the message that the democratic ideals of freedom and justice were not at stake only in Europe. Once America entered the war, the government encouraged the making of films that explicitly served the war effort. Subsequently, a wide range of government films were produced, covering subjects as varied as military training pictures and venereal disease educational films for service personnel, as well as propaganda pieces like Frank Capra's *Why We Fight* series. But unlike during World War I, the government was now better prepared to initiate the propaganda war. The OWI modeled itself on its World War I predecessor. After the war, the duties of the OWI were assigned to the Division of International Information, which later became the U.S. Information Agency (USIA), housed within the State Department.[12]

# Nonfiction Film

## Developments since the End of WWII

Nonfiction films flourished in the post–World War II period as filmmakers began to view the medium as an instrument for journalistic exposé and social reform. Their cameras depicted America with a fresh and often critical eye. Their subjects ranged from contemporary politics to social problems, from union organizing to the evils of the fast-food industry. Former Vice President Al Gore, to cite one example, narrated a documentary on the consequences of global warming, *An Inconvenient Truth* (2006), which received an Oscar.

Some filmmakers, like Frederick Wiseman, remain prolific creators, working almost continuously on projects. Others produced a handful of excellent films over two decades, such as Barbara Kopple, who won Academy Awards for best documentary feature for *Harlan County, USA* (1976) and *American Dream* (1989). A third group of documentarians ventured into commercial features with varying degrees of success. The popular Michael Moore moved from the documentary-style *Roger and Me* to a commercial feature, *Canadian Bacon* (1995), about an attempt by an inept president to begin a war with Canada in an effort to increase his popularity and re-election chances. Moore returned to the documentary form after his film flopped at the box office. Several documentary filmmakers also find steady work in television and others discover an outlet for their talent in state-funded assignments and in projects for educational institutions. The Afghanistan-Iraq wars revived an interest in political documentaries, either those favoring or criticizing the wisdom of these military policies. Despite the variety of uses for nonfiction film, few documentarians retain box office power; many produce one or two films and fade out of sight.

## The Documentary Film

Documentaries are one type of nonfiction film that concerns us in this chapter. Throughout history, the word documentary has referred to the attempt by filmmakers to "document" reality, in one manner or another. The term originally referred to movies shot on film stock but has been expanded to include video and digital productions that are seen in theaters, on television or transferred directly to video. The term itself is continually evolving without any clearly defined boundaries. The first short films (one minute or less) were shots of actual events (primarily scenes) by the French Lumiere brothers at the end of the 19th century. But the word "documentary" was initially used in a review of an early film by American Robert Flaherty in the 1920s. Since then, the documentary form has been utilized by governments for propaganda purposes and by activists as weapons against political institutions and economic systems.[13] More recently, the documentary form has moved from "cinema reality," as in the work of Frederick Wiseman, to a more interpretive style, such as in the work of Michael Moore. Both directors are discussed below.

In theory, the documentary film differs from fiction in several ways. First, it seeks to present the world the way it actually is rather than through imagined representation. Second, if the subject is historical, the documentary tries to recreate an era or a specific factual event without embellishment. Third, the emphasis in the documentary is on fashioning an argument or a point of view through the presentation of images or the testimony of experts or witnesses. Finally, by representing people directly rather than through intermediary actors, the documentary engages the viewer since it is clear the event is real rather than simulated.

## Frederick Wiseman and "Reality Fictions"

In the U.S., documentarian Frederick Wiseman exemplifies the "cinema verité" (direct cinema) style of contemporary filmmaking. He has popularized the style, as his films appear regularly on public television and are made available to educational institutions. Occasionally, one or two of Wiseman's films that have commercial potential, like *La Danse: The Paris Opera Ballet* (2009), which depicts the rehearsals of one of the world's great ballet companies, and *Crazy Horse* (2011), which describes the process of putting on a new show at the famous Parisian cabaret, are shown in commercial theaters. Here we are primarily interested in his work that has antagonized institutions and governments.

Born in Boston to professional parents, Wiseman followed his father's career path after graduation from Yale Law School, He then taught at Boston University before embarking on a film career. His first venture into filmmaking was in 1963 as a producer for the feature film *The Cool World*, an examination into the lives of Harlem teenagers. Wiseman later would return to fictional filmmaking twice more during his career. His major film achievements, however, remain his documentaries.[14] His reputation was established in his first documentary, *Titicut Follies* (1967), where Wiseman took his camera inside the Bridgewater, Massachusetts, State Institution for the Criminally Insane. The idea for the film came to him on a law class visit to the institution, where he became outraged at the conditions inside the prison walls. What he witnessed made him abandon his law books for the camera's eye. His stark depiction of institutional life entangled his film in a controversy with state authorities. Although Wiseman had received permission from state officials, the completed film did not please them and they went to court to prevent its distribution.[15] The state contended that the film violated the privacy rights of the inmates since several were filmed nude, that Wiseman had not received knowledgeable consent from inmates, and that the filmmaker had violated the terms of their oral understanding over editorial rights. Wiseman denied the last charge and rested his case on the First Amendment ground that the public had a right to know of the conditions inside state institutions. After a series of legal decisions, a compromise was reached whereby the film was barred from public release but made available for educational usage. It was under this "limited use" restriction that the author secured the film for showing to his American Institutions television course at the University of Akron during the 1970–71 academic year. This restriction remained in effect for 24 years and was not removed by the court until 1991.[16]

Wiseman encountered problems with institutions, private and public, on two other films. When he decided to do a documentary on an urban public school, he first secured permission from the school district. But once completed, the film apparently offended the sensibilities of the school's middle-class population of administrators, teachers, students, and parents. What upset them were the rather negative comments about the school made by film critics. At that point, Wiseman was threatened with litigation, and since he was still involved in the *Titicut Follies* lawsuit, he withdrew the film from distribution. It was not broadcast or screened until 2001, 33 years after completion. The other problem concerned

Wiseman's filming inside the Yerkes Regional Primate Research Center in Atlanta, Georgia. Once the film was screened for the Center and the public, the negative reaction to it led the Center's director to castigate its contents. In New York the response was worse, with the film's showing generating over 150 negative calls, a threat on Wiseman's life, and a bomb scare. In Boston, the PBS station delayed the broadcast of *Primate*. What was all the fuss about? Wiseman's camera examined the activities inside the Center in explicit detail, much like a doctor performing surgery. In one sequence, the audience sees researchers extracting the contents of a monkey's stomach; in another a gorilla is shaved and cut. And in another sequence, the researchers force the animals to have sex so the process can be observed. All these activities were part of the Center's research and not orchestrated for the camera. This led Wiseman to retort that the Center was responding to the film's negative reviews rather than to the film itself.[17]

Several of Wiseman's documentaries depict individuals in their relationship with public and private institutions in a way that engages the viewer in their emotional plight, as when, in his *Public Housing* (1998) documentary of life inside the Ida Wells Housing development on Chicago's South Side, the director lets us see the pain shown by an old man being evicted from his apartment. There is no denying the strength of his films, which have been characterized as social tracts where the emphasis is on powerful institutions dominating the individuals entrapped within.[18] Wiseman's films often remind audiences of the early 20th-century muckrakers of print fame—writers like Upton Sinclair and Frank Norris. For instance, in films like *Titicut Follies*, *High School I* (1968) and *II* (1994), *Hospital* (1970), and *Juvenile Court* (1973), Wiseman's camera captures public institutions in ways that encourage viewers to question their practices and procedures. One typical example occurs in *Hospital* (1970), where Wiseman takes his camera into New York City's Metropolitan Hospital to describe how American medicine has drifted away from local practice and towards impersonal treatment practices in urban emergency rooms. But not all of his examinations of American institutions are negative. In his 2006 documentary of the Idaho state legislature, aptly titled *State Legislature*, Wiseman portrays ordinary citizens—farmers, ranchers, teachers, salespeople—serving their communities as their elected representatives. Wiseman spent 11 weeks during the 2004 Idaho legislative session shooting over 160 hours of film to depict the democratic process at work. His camera roamed the hallways, went into committee rooms, and listened in on debates and the testimony of witnesses. Nothing was staged in his four-hour film. It is clear, however, that the filmmaker was pleased with the work of these citizen-legislators.

It would be too simplistic to consider Wiseman a social reformer. True, some of his films evolve into critiques of institutions, their employees, clients, and customers, but all through his camera lens rather than through Wiseman's own participation in the film. Rather than draw judgments about the events he records, the director allows the audience to reach its own conclusions.

Now in his eighties, Wiseman remains professionally active. As of 2012, he had 41 films to his credit, including 39 documentaries. What characterize his work best are his nonjudgmental attitude and his willingness to just be an observer of human behavior. Although he dislikes the term, cinema verité, Wiseman's technique follows most of its style: using a lightweight, portable camera and sound equipment, hand-held filming, working without a script or narration, recording events as they develop, and focusing the camera on the hand gestures and body language that accompany dialogue.[19] His usual practice is to use a three-person crew: a cameraman and an assistant, with himself as the sound recorder. Typically he shoots from 50 to 100 hours of film for one documentary, which he edits down to lengths of 90 minutes to six hours. The entire editing process might take up to a year.[20] While Wiseman's films are never staged or rehearsed, the filmmaker puts his stamp on the film during the editing process when he organizes the film footage.

Wiseman is that rare documentarian who is willing to admit the subjectivity of his work in the sense that the notion of objectivity in capturing reality is often lost in the editing process. Hence, he refers to his work as "reality fictions" since he emphasizes the "constructive nature of documentary."[21] He once explained his work this way:

> All aspects of documentary filmmaking involve choice and are therefore manipulative. But the ethical... aspect of it is that you have to make [a film that] is true to the spirit of your sense of what was going on.... My view is that these [my] films are biased, prejudiced, condensed, compressed but fair.[22]

In summary, Wiseman gives meaning to his films during the editing process. He is contemptuous of those colleagues who insist that their work is factual—that the camera never lies, despite evidence to the contrary. What distinguishes Wiseman from other documentarians is his honesty. Unlike others who refuse to admit to the realities of their craft, including staged scenes, misidentified footage, events arranged to misrepresent chronology, and stock film incorporated into authentic footage, Wiseman admits to leaving his footprint on his films. Even the father of American documentary, Robert Flaherty, manipulated actual scenes for dramatic effect. For instance, in *Nanook of the North* (1922), Flaherty would not allow his subjects to shoot a walrus with a shotgun, but had them use a harpoon, a weapon from their past.[23] Even the early *March of Time* newsreels contained staged events and studio reconstructions if genuine footage was unobtainable. Perhaps the worst case of reconstruction occurred in the pre–World War II era when a newsreel supposedly depicting life inside Nazi Germany was actually filmed in the New Jersey farmlands.[24] Frank Capra's *Why We Fight* series also included staged footage and scenes inserted from Hollywood features.

## Michael Moore: Populist Filmmaker or Self-Promoter?

Another contemporary documentarian, Michael Moore, may not be guilty of such deceits but his films raise questions about the integrity of the documentary form. Born in Flint, Michigan, in the 1950s, Moore is the author of four books, seven documentaries, one commercial feature, and one election film, *Slacker Uprising* (2008), which he offered as a free download to fans. While his productivity cannot match Wiseman's prolific output, Moore's films and books have gained a wider popularity with audiences.

Is Michael Moore a true contemporary populist and muckraker or a social satirist more adept at self-promotion than political or social analysis? To answer the question, let us review his documentaries. His first film, *Roger and Me*, in which he attempts to interview the head of General Motors (GM), Roger Smith, drew national attention and became a

Nonfiction Film

popular success when it was released in 1989. Advertised as a documentary about the woes of Moore's hometown, the film became something of a *cause célèbre*. When GM shut down its auto plant in Flint, thousands of workers lost their jobs. At the heart of Moore's film is his attempt to track down GM's chief executive officer at the company's Detroit headquarters to ask him about the plant closings. But the interview never takes place because Smith avoids the confrontation. The elusive CEO is the real star of the film.

*Roger and Me* cost $260,000, a sum befitting a struggling documentarian. But it was later learned that Warner Brothers gave Moore $3 million for the rights to distribute the film, an amount that expressed confidence in its commercial value. When the Motion Picture Academy listed its Oscar nominees for best documentary, Moore's film was omitted because its commercial distribution qualified it for the feature film category. When the film was released on video, however, it was reclassified as a documentary. In some ways, this history of *Roger and Me* is more interesting than the film itself because it questions the arbitrary construction of film categories. Who decides whether Moore's film is a documentary or a commercial venture? The film studio? The Motion Picture Academy? The film critics? Moore himself? What *Roger and Me* demonstrates is the subjective nature of classifying documentary films as authentic depictions of reality.

Ironically, it was the commercial success of *Roger and Me* that led movie critics and film scholars to more closely examine Moore's film. Moore considered his film a documentary,[25] but eventually it was revealed that he had taken liberties even beyond editing and rearranging scenes. For example, Moore charged that the plant closings resulted in 30,000 workers being laid off but the actual figure for the Flint plant was a more modest 5,000. The 30,000 figure actually referred to jobs lost in plant closings in four states over a 12-year period. Furthermore, Moore insinuated that while GM was closing its plant, Flint was wasting millions on city projects that eventually failed. The implication was that the city could have saved some of these jobs by providing incentives to GM. In fact, the three city projects that failed were underway before, rather than after, the 1986 shutdowns. There were other minor discrepancies as well. One scene showed President Reagan touring Flint, sharply contrasting all the hoopla surrounding his visit with the image of a dying city. In actuality, the footage is from Reagan's visit to Flint in 1980 as a presidential candidate rather than as president six years later.[26] But the most egregious error in the film was one of omission. It was later learned that Moore *had* actually interviewed Roger Smith, but left that interview on the cutting room floor.[27] These discrepancies led one film critic to comment that the problem with the film was not that it expressed a personal viewpoint, but rather that it was unfair.[28] Moore had resorted to misrepresentation and dramatic reconstruction, designed to leave the audience with a negative impression of corporate capitalism.

Moore's film should be contrasted with Barbara Kopple's documentary *American Dream*, which was released in the same year as *Roger and Me*. *American Dream* concerned the 1985 strike by the meatpackers' union at the Hormel plant in Austin, Minnesota. Whereas Kopple's film is a traditional documentary, complete with exposition, detailed observation, and support for the strikers' cause, Moore's film, while sympathetic to the plight of his hometown, uses humor and sarcasm as social commentary. The main difference, however, is that Kopple actually failed to gain access to the power brokers—the corporate leaders.[29]

Moore's ego was bruised by the criticism his film received, but his next documentaries were highly regarded by critics and audiences. *The Big One* (1998) is a film record of Moore's national tour to promote his book *Downsize This!*, a critique of corporate capitalism. The camera follows Moore from book signings to plant closings to union-organized strikes as it criticizes American companies that close their factories, throwing thousands out of work, only to open new plants in Mexico and other underdeveloped countries. But Moore offers no solutions to outsourcing. In one scene, he presents a company representative, on camera, with a check for 80 cents to cover the first hour of wages to their Mexican workers. It's a symbolic gesture, good for a quick laugh, but nothing more. Later he confronts Nike chairman and co-founder Phil Knight over the 40 cents an hour the company pays Indonesian workers to make its sneakers, yet fails to mention the millions it pays Michael Jordan to promote them.

In his subsequent documentary, *Bowling for Columbine* (2002), Moore uses the massacre at Columbine High School in Littleton, Colorado, to raise issues related to violence and gun ownership. His film is a devastating indictment of the gun culture in America and includes statistics on shootings in the U.S. compared to other nations, film footage of the Columbine shootings, and commentary on the nature of American violence and the love affair American have with their guns. Once again, however, Moore's tendency to make light of a serious subject is evident. For example, he opens a checking account in a Michigan bank because it advertises that each customer who signs up for a new account receives a free gun. After a quick background check, Moore walks out of the bank holding a rifle. The point that it is as easy in some states to get a gun as a set of dishes is not lost on the viewer. However, the muckrakers of the past—writers like Upton Sinclair, Frank Norris, and Lincoln Steffens—did not settle for a quick laugh, but would have connected the evil under investigation to policy changes that would right the wrong. In his *Shame of the Cities*,[30] Steffens exposed political corruption as a byproduct of the city's power to award public works contracts. Eliminate the ability of government to award jobs to private contractors without oversight and the source of the evil would disappear. About all Moore accomplished was to convince Kmart to stop selling gun ammunition in their stores, a modest change in policy compared to the enormity of the gun problem in America. Nonetheless, his effort was finally recognized by the Motion Picture Academy when *Bowling for Columbine* received an Oscar for best documentary.

Moore followed that success with the documentary *Fahrenheit 9/11*, which caused a storm of controversy even before its release to theaters. Winner of the coveted Palme d'Or, the top prize at the Cannes Film Festival, *Fahrenheit 9/11* is a stinging indictment of the Bush family's relationship with the Saudis, including the bin Laden family, before the terrorist attack on the Twin Towers. The Disney Company, which held the distribution rights to the film, refused to permit its subsidiary, Miramax, to distribute it. Moore labeled the action "censorship" and it looked like the film might not be released. But the Weinstein brothers came to the rescue by buying the distribution rights for $6 million and distributing the film through independents Lionsgate Films and IFC Films. Once released, the film ran into a ratings snafu when its ads wrongly identified the rating as NC-17, which would have prevented teenagers from viewing it. After a few days, the correct R rating replaced NC-17 in the advertisements. Despite these distractions, the film was a box office success.

*Fahrenheit 9/11* generated considerable debate among film critics and scholars. Moore's supporters argued that that the film raised important questions about the Bush administration's decision to go to war with Iraq that were ignored by the mainstream media. His critics, on the other hand, complained about Moore's interpretation of certain facts and the rather obvious intention of the film to deny President Bush a second term in 2004.[31]

The author's view on *Fahrenheit 9/11* is that it is really two films spliced together. During its first half, Moore is at his best in exposing the Bush family's business dealings with the Saudis, covering the disputed 2000 presidential election and the terrorist attack on September 11, 2001. The high point is reached when Moore shows footage of a dazed-looking President Bush sitting in an elementary school continuing to read stories to young children after being informed of the terrorist attack on New York. For some unexplainable reason, Moore turns his attention to Iraq during the film's second hour and the filmmaker is transformed into the partisan ideologue, disputing the decision to invade Iraq. By releasing the film four months before the November presidential election and by openly advocating Bush's defeat, Moore thrust himself into the 2004 campaign. The documentarian became the propagandist. These comments are not meant to disparage the film's intentions but to question Moore's position as an objective filmmaker.

Moore followed up his record-breaking hit with a documentary on the American health care system titled *Sicko* (2007).[32] He certainly had an opportunity here for a serious examination of a health care system that is universally considered to be a mess and in need of reform. But once again the audience does not know whether Moore intends to educate or entertain as he opens his film interviewing people without health insurance, and then follows up with people who have insurance but were still devastated by the costs of their illnesses. These sequences illustrate that the present system affects those both with and without insurance. Moore then shifts gears and examines countries like Canada, England, and France, which have universal coverage. Finally, he takes a group of Americans who have been denied treatment in the U.S. to Cuba, where they receive medical treatment by Castro's government.

Most of the material in *Sicko* is common knowledge to American adults and thus his film is less controversial than *Fahrenheit 9/11*. Health care reform has been a "hot button" subject for at least a decade and President Obama made it a priority on his policy agenda during the 2008 campaign. The basic problem with Moore's film is that it rigorously exposes problems, but offers superficial solutions. His preference for a single-payer system, illustrated by his scenes on the British, Canadian, and French health care systems, represents opinion, not objective criticism, because Moore presents these systems as without flaws. This is not a criticism of universal health care but of the director's failure to provide a more balanced appraisal. He thus misrepresents these health systems through omission, leaving the audience with a biased, fact-selective presentation. It is generally, but not universally accepted, that the American health care system requires an overhaul, but *Sicko* only obfuscates the debate rather than enlightening it.

Moore's next documentary, *Capitalism: A Love Story* (2009), landed in theaters with a thud. After three weeks, its domestic gross was under $10 million despite the timeliness and relevancy of its subject. Part of the reason may be that Moore approached his exposé of capitalism in his too familiar way, collecting bits and pieces and editing them into a somewhat disconnected whole. Along the way, Moore includes some entertaining material, a few funny jokes, statistical charts, interviews, and archival footage. He begins with film footage of ancient Rome and closes with the 2008 financial crisis caused by the collapse of the housing market. Moore blames capitalism (and Republicans) for most of the damage, but a more accurate assessment would acknowledge the role capitalism played in the early development of the U.S., its contribution to industrial and manufacturing progress, and its creation of a healthy middle-class deep into the 20th century. The question which Moore fails to raise is whether capitalism is the right economic engine for the 21st century, given the nation's 2008 economic recession. True, he does take the viewer into several cooperative factories and admires their teamwork and productivity, but he stops short of endorsing these places of "workers' socialism." There is no doubt that Moore sympathizes with the underdog—the poor, the disposed, the powerless, and the victims of the recession who have lost their jobs, homes, and life savings. Once again, however, he is good at descriptive presentation but weak on providing policy alternatives. What the above films indicate is that public exposure alone is insufficient to generate social action.

## The Conservative Backlash against Michael Moore

What do these people have in common: Larry Elder, Jim Hubbard, Evan Coyne Maloney, and Michael Wilson? They all are conservative filmmakers who hate liberalism in general and Michael Moore in particular. Like the lunatic broadcaster played by Peter Finch in the film *Network* (1976), they are "mad as hell and won't take it anymore." They are challenging what they consider to be the left-liberal monopoly over documentaries and have decided to go head-to-head with Moore. Before doing so they had to investigate whether the lack of conservative documentaries was a conspiracy by Hollywood and the independent studios to shut them out of the market. What they discovered is the conventional wisdom that the film industry is first and foremost a business and will therefore work with anyone if it is profitable.

More than any other filmmaker, Michael Moore is probably most responsible for the conservative resurgence. Moore has been identified as the number one target for conservatives, even in films where his ideology is not at issue. Take the case of filmmaker Evan Coyne Maloney. He is being referred to as the "conservative answer to Michael Moore" even though his documentary, *Indoctrinate U* (2007)—a critical response to political correctness on college campuses—is about issues Moore has never tackled. Maloney, a Bucknell University graduate, is angry about campus speech codes, the willingness of administrators to discourage and punish dissent from the prevailing campus viewpoint, and the violation of the academic freedom of students, especially in class, to express their thoughts. He cites one instance where a student at California Polytechnic was disciplined for posting a flyer announcing the campus appearance of a black conservative who had equated welfare with slavery. The charges against the student were eventually dropped after intervention by a civil liberties organization.[33]

Maloney's documentary targeted what he saw as the liberal takeover of college campuses. The following three documentaries are aimed at Moore specifically. The first salvo against Moore came in response to his anti-gun documentary, *Bowling for Columbine*. National syndicated talk show host Larry Elder's reaction was to film *Michael & Me* (2005), a documentary in defense of guns. Elder's pro-gun arguments are fairly standard conservative rhetoric that rest on a favorable interpretation of the Second Amendment that permits citizens to own guns for their protection. Elder proceeds with the corresponding argument that if you take guns away from law-abiding citizens, then only the criminals will have guns, since a huge underground black market will emerge to meet the needs of the criminal class. A third argument that gun control laws lead to an increase in crime is offered but not substantiated. In *Fahrenhype 9/11* (2004), director Alan Peterson and writer Dick Morris, a former Bill Clinton advisor, are engaged in mitigating the damage done to Republicans and the Bush administration as a result of the popular success of *Fahrenheit 9/11*. Like Moore's work, their film relies heavily on opinion and conjecture, with minimal documentation. At its core the film is a tit-for-tat rebuttal of Moore's charges in *Fahrenheit 9/11*. In contrast, Michael Wilson's documentary, *Michael Moore Hates America* (2004), is more thoughtful and less shrill. Wilson takes on Moore's three most successful documentaries—*Roger & Me*, *Bowling for Columbine*, and *Fahrenheit 9/11*—by portraying him as a trickster, a deceptive magician who manipulates facts, takes comments out of context, and engages in misleading editing. But the title alone warns us that this is not an unbiased piece of work. Wilson's aim is to counter what he considers Moore's dishonest portrait of America by presenting a more positive national image. Whether he succeeds or fails is best left to the viewer.

But the most effective piece of work against Moore's films is *Manufacturing Dissent* (2007), by Canadian filmmakers Debbie Melnyk and Rick Caine. Why is this documentary superior to all the others? First, it begins with a balanced portrait of Moore, the filmmaker and personality, and it refrains from accusations and hyperbole. But as the film progresses, disenchantment leads to a more critical view of Moore's work. In many ways, the last half of the film expresses disappointment in Moore's methods rather than his intentions. The catalyst for their disenchantment occurs when Moore refuses to be interviewed for their film and when they discover that he had actually interviewed Roger Smith on two separate occasions, neither of which turns up in Roger & Me. The filmmakers, though initially fans of Moore, then became his adversaries. The reader can sympathize with the disillusionment of filmmakers when they discover that their idolized teacher is exposed as a manipulator at best and a liar at worst.[34]

The conservative backlash against Moore has developed into a movement that has given rise to two film festivals: the American Film Renaissance, run by Jim Hubbard in Dallas, and the Hollywood-based Liberty Film Festival. Only the future will determine how effective the conservative documentarians and their supporters will become in silencing or outshouting Michael Moore.

## The Docudrama

Somewhere between nonfiction films and commercial features lies the "docudrama," a hybrid style that represents a dividing line between the documentary form and dramatic fiction. Of the several definitions available, the following is a fairly comprehensive characterization:

> A unique blend of fact and fiction, which dramatizes events and historic personages from our recent memory.... It is a TV recreation based on fact though it relies on actors, dialogue, sets and costumes to recreate an earlier event. The accuracy and comprehensiveness of such a recreation...can vary widely and is conditioned not only by intent but also by factors such as budget and production time.[35]

A common misperception is that the docudrama originated in the 1970s with the televised "movie of the week" programming. The form actually dates back to the old newsreels that restaged historic events, such as the Spanish-American War and World War I for American audiences. Then in the thirties, the Hollywood studios turned to historic events as the source for epic films like the *Sign of the Cross* (1932) and *The Crusades* (1935), two Cecil B. De Mille stagy productions. Hollywood also found the lives of historical people a good source for re-creation. Warner Brothers in particular became identified with film biographies, as the studio reconstructed the lives of such political figures as Emile Zola and Benito Juarez. Film biographies were so popular with audiences that studios included them in their annual releases for more than 30 years.[36] Hollywood continues to utilize the genre, especially in contemporary biographies, such as the ones on presidents Kennedy and Nixon and in investigative-exposé type films such as *Silkwood* (1983) and *The China Syndrome* (1979).

A significant expansion of the genre occurred in the seventies as the television networks sought to compete with Hollywood for the entertainment dollar. Television, which had been buying Hollywood films to program during primetime, discovered that it was less expensive and a better marketing strategy to produce its own original films. Thus was born the "TV Movie of the Week," with plots lifted from newspaper headlines. The networks competed aggressively for first televising rights to contemporary events that included stories based on real events or programs that used historical themes or personalities. More often, they turned to personal stories of cowardice and heroism, joy and suffering, and criminality and sordid affairs in an attempt to improve ratings. But occasionally, the networks would surprise the viewing public with a film or series of social or political importance as *Roots* (1976–77), the miniseries on slavery, and *Roe v. Wade* (1989), a film on the U.S. Supreme Court's decision permitting abortions.

It needs to be noted that while docudramas have the potential to bring important issues to public attention, the danger is that, in the networks' rush to be first, facts and truth take a back seat to ratings. *D.C. Sniper: 23 Days of Fear* (2003) and *The Perfect Husband* (2004) are good examples of these films' potential harm, in this case their effect on the U.S. legal system. *D.C. Sniper* was a USA network docudrama about the crime wave in the metropolitan Washington, D.C. area, where two snipers shot 13 people, 10 of whom died. The broadcast occurred around the time of the trial of one of the suspects, preceding the verdict in the network's haste to beat the competition. As a result, concerns were raised about interference with the course of justice. Similarly, the same network rushed to document the highly publicized California murder case of pregnant Laci Peterson, whose husband Scott was arrested and charged with murder after she disappeared and was later found dead. While the state was still in the process of jury selection, the USA network televised the docudrama *The Perfect Husband* (2004). Though the film ends with the fictional Scott in jail awaiting trial, it provided him with an opportunity to publicly deny his guilt and to develop a defense. The film, therefore, risked polluting the potential jury pool. Both these exploitation dramas raise questions about the pitfalls of televising contemporary events that are still in the process of unfolding.

Of even greater worry are films that deal with issues like war and terrorism that are of national concern. A prime example was NBC's docudrama *Saving Jessica Lynch* (2003), the story of the American soldier captured during the Iraqi invasion. Since the network failed to receive authorization from Pfc. Lynch, it could not recreate the various versions of her capture, imprisonment, and rescue. Instead, NBC focused its story on the Iraqi who led American forces to Jessica's location. Since the network wanted to be first to televise her story in primetime and since it had not received her authorization, the story it told relied on secondary sources. Eleven American soldiers died in the ambush that led to her capture, yet the film never made it clear to viewers why her story was newsworthy and required special attention. One suggested answer is that the media bought into the Rambo-Pentagon version of her capture and rescue, which encouraged support for the war. Several days after the telecast, Pfc. Lynch told her story on television, which made the docudrama unnecessary. In brief, the mythology initially surrounding Pfc. Lynch's story served as a propaganda tool for the military.

Problems inherent in the docudrama format drew public attention to two films, one concerning the 9/11 terrorist attack on New York City's World Trade Center (WTC) and the other dealing with the intervention by passengers of hijacked United Flight 93 to prevent a suicide attack on Washington, D.C.

The first, *World Trade Center* (2006), directed by Oliver Stone, concentrates on the true story of two Port Authority officers trapped in the rubble under Ground Zero. Stone's film avoids assessing blame and instead concentrates on a few of the many acts of courage performed that day. Actors Nicholas Cage and Michael Pena play Officers McLoughlin and Jimeno, who entered the South Tower before it collapsed and became trapped in the rubble. Much of the movie details the efforts to extract the officers, the only two survivors rescued from the rubble. Why would such a film raise concerns and cause problems? The first criticism concerned the details in the film, which included a number of inaccuracies about the rescue effort. For example, in the actual World Trade Center rescue effort, Chuck Sereika, a paramedic who was not called to duty by his unit, voluntarily crawled into the black hole to rescue Port Authority officer Will Jimeno. What is more amazing is that Sereika had no training in collapsed-building rescue, but he risked his life that day for men he did not know. In Stone's film, however, Sereika's act of courage was assigned to a New York City police officer instead. Stone also distorted another character in the rescue attempt. Dave Karnes, a former marine turned accountant, along with another marine, Sergeant Jason

Thomas, were the first rescuers to locate McLoughlin and Jimeno. In the film, Stone distorts Karnes's character and misrepresents his motivation to join the rescue attempt. Stone made an even greater error when he cast a white actor to play the role of Sgt. Thomas, an African American. Critics noted too that the film misjudged the time and effort it took to dig the men out and underestimated the dangers posed to the rescuers themselves.[37] These errors normally would be forgiven in an ordinary film focused on entertainment, but not in one that sets out to tell a true story of such magnitude.

A different set of complaints came from families whose members did not survive the ordeal. One widow was upset that the real responders in the 9/11 rescue were willing to participate in its production. Meanwhile, another widow thought it unnecessary to make a movie hero out of her husband.[38] These complaints remind filmmakers that they had better consult with, and receive permission from, all participants when dramatizing true events in American history, especially something so momentous and tragic as 9/11. Still another criticism was expressed by a British film critic, who took exception to the character of Dave Karnes, an accountant and former marine. When he hears of the attack, Karnes drives from his home in Connecticut to the WTC site, puts on his uniform, and joins in the search for survivors. At film's end, the fictional Karnes shouts, "They're gonna need some good men out there—to revenge this," proceeds to re-enlist and is shipped directly to Iraq. This led the critic to conclude that Stone was deliberately connecting the 9/11 bombing to Saddam Hussein to provide justification for the Iraq invasion.[39] (Karnes did re-enlist but was apparently sent to the Philippines, though he went on to serve in Iraq.) Whether this connection was intentional or inadvertent is less consequential than the realization that the docudrama format is equivalent to filming in a cinematic minefield. Quite possibly, it is unrealistic to think that any filmmaker can do justice to a re-creation of such a horrific and momentous event as the 9/11 attack without trivializing it.

British director Paul Greengrass's docudrama *United 93* (2006), on the other hand, fared much better than Stone's. In *United 93*, Greengrass re-creates the story of the passengers on United Airlines' flight 93, one of the four planes hijacked on 9/11, who responded to the hijacking by diverting the plane from its intended target, either the White House or the Capitol building in D.C., and causing it to crash in a field near Shanksville, Pennsylvania. By all accounts the victims' families were pleased with the portrayal of their loved ones and the overall tone of the film. Despite a modest budget and a no-name cast, Greengrass still paid attention to details and was able to secure the approval of all but one of the victims' families.[40] Unlike Stone, Greengrass provided a context for his story by detailing what was happening on the ground while the struggle on flight 93 took place in the air. In so doing, the film raised questions about the preparedness and judgment of officials on the ground. For instance, when air controllers learned of a possible hijacking out of Boston's Logan Airport, flight 93 was delayed for 30 minutes. But under the circumstances, why let the plane take off at all? Later, when the air controllers learned of another hijacking and viewed photos of the WTC in flames, they failed to inform flight 93 of these developments. This readiness to raise serious questions without sensationalizing, along with the respect shown for those involved, meant Greengrass's film was well received while reviews for Stone's *World Trade Center* were mixed.[41]

## The Propaganda Film

Propaganda films take several forms. Most frequently, they are masked as documentaries, supposedly objective recordings of actual events, such as the political meeting filmed by Leni Riefenstahl in *Triumph of the Will*. The propaganda in similar films is deceptive because their creators claim neutrality, as if their films were unedited newsreels. Another type of propaganda occurs in commercial films where the message frequently is surreptitiously hidden in the subtext, usually evident only to the scholar or trained viewer.

What exactly is propaganda and why does the term invoke such disdain? It is a term that defies classification since one person's truth may be another's falsehood. No one definition is universally accepted, yet there is general agreement that the term has come to include the twin elements of premeditation and manipulation. Thus David Culbert says that propaganda is "the controlled dissemination of deliberately distorted notions in an effort to induce action favorable to predetermined ends of special interest groups."[42] In other words, propaganda is information that is presented to influence or persuade; with intent that is subjective and filled with provocative symbolism. Culbert's definition is broad enough to encompass the output from state-controlled film industries, political campaign broadcasts, documentaries, and even docudramas.

Propaganda differs from both fact and opinion in that its goal is primarily to present information in such a manner as to influence the intended audience in a particular way. Facts, conversely, are statements whose authenticity is observable by the senses or verifiable by research. All these "facts" are subject to corroboration from other, external sources. Sometimes fact and opinion are blended into one statement, and it is necessary to extract and distinguish one from the other.

In the 20th century, the term propaganda became associated with Nazi Germany. Though it is true that the Nazi Socialists came to power by way of the 1933 elections (with only 44% of the multiparty vote), Hitler then resorted to force to eliminate his opponents and to mass manipulation and intimidation to consolidate that power. The Nazis systemically eliminated their opponents via assassinations, cold-blooded murders, and terrorist threats, so that when Hitler became chancellor, the Nazis had already eliminated or frightened most of the political opposition. Once in command, they sought to mobilize the German people through a campaign of emotional and patriotic appeals. This campaign to capture the hearts and minds of the German people was entrusted to Joseph Goebbels, Hitler's Minister of Propaganda. Nazi propaganda had two objectives: to enlist support for Hitler's global plans for a Third Reich that "would last a thousand years" and to weaken the morale and the resistance of those who stood in the way. Goebbels' efforts were directed at solidifying support at home by re-establishing the German film industry, which had dominated Europe prior to World War I. He disdained the overt propaganda film replete with swastikas, SS uniforms, and "Heil Hitler" salutes, preferring instead historical dramas that heralded mythic heroes. Of the 1,097 feature films produced under Goebbels' orders between 1933 and 1945, only 183, or one-sixth, were overtly propagandistic.[43] Actually, the Nazis produced fewer wartime propaganda films than either the Americans or the British.

The Nazis were ingenious and crafty manipulators. A third propaganda objective during the war was to disguise several of their concentration camps for the benefit of international investigators. For example, the author has visited one of these so-called "show camps", in the Czech Republic at Terezin, that were created specifically to impress the International Red Cross. Terezin had been a fortress and was converted in 1941 to house Jewish prisoners. Eventually, the camp expanded to such an extent that the local German inhabitants had to relocate. The camp fulfilled three functions: (1) it served as a transit camp for Jewish prisoners who were sent later to termination camps like Auschwitz; (2) it became a deathtrap for the inmates since 20 percent of them died there from natural causes or from the gas chamber; and (3) it had great propaganda value since Red Cross officials could report that the prisoners were being treated decently and had amenities like a symphony orchestra, an active theater group, and a playground area for children.[44] The reality, of course, was starkly different. Of the 87,000 Jewish prisoners who passed through Terezin, only 4,000 survived the Holocaust. The Red Cross investigations notwithstanding, Terezin was a death camp.

Goebbels sparred with Riefenstahl over the content of her films which he viewed as too propagandistic. But he usually lost the argument since the director was a Hitler favorite. Riefenstahl insisted that *Triumph of the Will* was merely a recording of a historic event by an artist rather than a piece of propaganda, but she failed to satisfactorily explain why her film contained restaged scenes, some included Hitler even when he was not present.[45] Other scenes were rearranged so as to give coherence to the series of events, thus "dramatizing" the film footage. *Triumph* took months of planning, shooting, and editing in order for Riefenstahl to present a view of a united Nazi Party when, in fact, Hitler had ordered the assassination of a rival faction the night before the Nuremberg Party Congress scene depicted in the film.

Riefenstahl always maintained that she was an artist, not a political figure, a claim at odds with the tone of her congratulatory telegram to Hitler when France surrendered:

> Adolf Hitler—Fuehrer Headquarters. With indescribable joy, deeply moved and full of gratitude, we now bear witness to your, my Fuehrer, and the Germans' great victory—the entry of German troops into Paris. You achieve feats that have been unimaginable so far, unprecedented in the history of mankind. How can I thank you? Expressing congratulations is much too little to show you the emotions that move me. —Leni Riefenstahl[46]

True, Riefenstahl did not join the Nazi Party, nor is there evidence that she was anti-Semitic. Yet she was a favorite of Hitler and so one would assume that she supported his cause as well. Apparently, she had unlimited budgets for her films and she was granted unrestricted access to the elite corps within the Nazi command bureaucracy.[47] Given the structure of the Nazi Party, with its emphasis on loyalty and submission, an intelligent woman like Riefenstahl, who had access to the top echelon of party leadership, presumably did not have to become an official party member to know what was happening. Riefenstahl could hardly claim independence as a filmmaker, since under Goebbels' command all film producers and artists had to register with the propaganda ministry and all scripts were subject to review and party clearance. Working within this hierarchical structure, Riefenstahl was as much a civil servant as Pare Lorentz was in Depression-era America. Moreover, two recent books on Riefenstahl provide documented evidence that the filmmaker was more than an innocent bystander. Documents reveal that Riefenstahl was present at the Polish town of Konskie when Jews were massacred in the town square. Other documents disclose that she used gypsies from the camps as forced laborers on her films.[48]

Riefenstahl, who died at the age of 101, spent the years after World War II reinventing herself as a photographer. Arrested and held by the Allies for three years, she was subsequently cleared of any wrongdoing during the de-Nazification process. But her film career was finished. Riefenstahl defiantly asserted her neutrality until her death. Still, her life and work resurrect the eternal question of whether it is possible to separate art from politics.

The Nazis were not alone in manufacturing propaganda during World War II. The U.S. had cranked up its own propaganda machine under the auspices of the OWI to coordinate film activities with Hollywood. Actually, there was a propaganda campaign at work in Hollywood long before Pearl Harbor. Professor Don Morlan notes that in the five years leading up to America's entrance into WWII, the industry was busy producing both anti-Nazi and war preparedness films.[49]

The U.S. also had to adjust its attitude toward one of its allies—Soviet Russia. After the Nazi invasion of Russia, Hollywood supported the Allies' newest member in the most glowing terms. At least four features released in 1943 and 1944 glorified Stalin, the Russian military, and the courage of the Russian people. Two war films, *The North Star* (1943) and *Days of Glory* (1944), paid tribute to the heroism of Russian partisans and guerrillas in their fight against overwhelming German forces. Reportedly, the Russians loved *The North Star*, a big hit in Siberia, where it played to 50,000 people.[50] Meanwhile, MGM's *Song of Russia* primarily portrayed a love affair between an American conductor (Robert Taylor) and a Russian concert pianist (Susan Peters). When the Germans invade Russia, the lovers exchange their musical talents for military weapons and join the partisans in their fight against the advancing Nazis. Although a love story set against a war background, *Song of Russia* abounds with praise for collectivism, comparing, for example, the Soviet collective farms with those in Midwestern America. Its pro-Soviet ideology put the film on HUAC's subversive list, even though the patriotism of MGM or actor Taylor was never questioned during his appearance before the committee. But the most egregious piece of pro-Soviet propaganda to come out of Hollywood was the film *Mission to Moscow* (1943), a box office fiasco released after the Battle of Stalingrad to drum up American support for the Russians. *Mission to Moscow* purported to be a factual record of Ambassador Joseph Davies' three years of service (1936–38) in the Soviet Union. But it turned out to be an overt piece of pro-Soviet propaganda, opening with the real Ambassador Davies saying directly to the audience:

> While in Russia, I came to have a very high respect for the integrity and the honesty of the Soviet leaders. I respected the honesty of their convictions and they respected mine. I also came back with a firm conviction that these people were sincerely devoted to world peace.[51]

The film proved to be such an exaggerated glorification of Stalinist Russia that its credibility was seriously damaged.[52] For example, condensing the four Stalinist purge trials into one may be forgiven, but not at the expense of historical accuracy. For the film to present the Moscow trials as justification for Stalin to remove traitors plotting against him is pure fiction and content manipulation to serve political ends. According to Soviet historian Roy Aleksandrovich Medvedev,[53] whose figures are considered to be conservative estimates, Stalin was directly responsible for at least 20 million non-war related deaths as follows: one million imprisoned or exiled between 1927–29; 9–11 million peasants forced off their land, resulting in many deaths from starvation; 2–3 million peasants killed or imprisoned during the collectivization program; 1 million executed during the party purges of 1937–38; 4–6 million dispatched to forced labor camps; and 1 million arrested for "political crimes" from 1946–53. Yet *Mission to Moscow* portrayed Stalin as a friendly, smiling "Uncle Joe" character; this was equivalent to Riefenstahl showing Hitler in *Triumph of the Will* as a kindly grandfather figure, rather than the monster who would be directly responsible for some 11 million deaths. After the war, HUAC considered these four pro-Soviet films "un-American."

During the so-called Cold War between the U.S. and Soviet Union that followed the end of World War II, Hollywood responded to the Red Scare hysteria by releasing a number of anti-communist films. The most blatant of the group was a low-budget B-film called *The Red Menace* (1949), intended as a warning to discontented Americans who might be tempted to join a communist cell. The amateurish plot relates the story of a war veteran duped by the communists. The irony is that the communists in the film are portrayed as much smarter than the decent but weak and naive American followers. *Red Menace* is the classic, although sophomoric, propaganda film of the postwar era. The movie's ads warned that the subject was so important it had to be filmed in secret. Fourteen years later, Warner Brothers (perhaps as self-imposed penance for producing *Mission to Moscow*) made a film entitled *Red Nightmare* (1962) following the Cuban missile crisis. The plot unfolds in flashback as the major American character wakes up from his dream to discover that his town has been taken over by communists. For the next hour, the film depicts what life would be like under Soviet domination. Salvation arrives just in time to spare the life of the major character as he wakes from his horrible dream. Despite the anti-communist theme, the film was an embarrassment and never released to theaters. Thus, the reputation of *The Red Menace* as the most overt piece of Cold War propaganda remained intact.

Another propaganda film from that era, but from an entirely different perspective, was *Salt of the Earth*. This fictional recreation of a successful strike in the zinc mines of the American Southwest in the early 1950s was denied commercial distribution in the U.S.[54] Dismissed as a piece of "communist propaganda" by film critic Pauline Kael and blacklisted nationally, the film remained a source of controversy for many years. The movie starred a few professional actors and was produced, written, and directed by blacklisted filmmakers. The real union organizer actually was a member of the Communist Party. The film nonetheless depicted, in gritty black and white, corporate violence and a disregard for the health and safety of the mostly Chicano mine workers. When the mine owners succeed in securing an injunction to stop the workers from picketing, wives and mothers take their places on the picket line. Indeed, as described in a later chapter, the film underrepresents the real amount of violence that occurred during the actual strike when 62 women were arrested and several shot by company guards and local police. The cast of professional actors and local citizens and members of the crew were subjected to physical abuse and death threats in the wake of the Red Scare hysteria. Furthermore, the filmmakers were denied technical facilities and the lead actress was deported, requiring that the film be finished in Mexico. Looking back, the movie can be perceived as a piece of anti-capitalist propaganda, but it also can be viewed as a piece of social muckraking and as an early feminist tract, since the strongest characters in the film are women. *Salt of the Earth* is a good illustration of a film that is multilayered: a piece of "communist propaganda," a promotional for the trade union movement, an argument against laissez-faire capitalism, a consciousness-raising precursor to the women's movement. *Salt of the Earth* was hardly the traditional Hollywood film fare.

### The New War Documentaries: Hard News or Propaganda?

The U.S. military action in Afghanistan and Iraq has motivated documentarians to film various aspects of the wars. More than four dozen documentaries already have been produced and more are expected. The media interest in these wars is not surprising, since the reasons for going to war and the military strategy supporting them were questionable. But a review of these films raises the question of whether their intention is to inform the American public or to manipulate the news to support an ideological agenda for or against these wars. In short, are these objective documentaries or are they ideological tracts?

Several of these documentaries were released to theaters, but many more went directly to video or to the Internet to later surface on websites like YouTube. Essentially the question is: how do we determine the legitimacy and veracity of these war-in-progress documentaries? Take the case of veteran filmmaker Robert Greenwald. Greenwald has been producing and making movies for television, theatrical release, and cable miniseries for 30 years, but particularly since 9/11 he has concentrated on social and political issues, such as the wars in Afghanistan and Iraq. His 2004 documentary *Uncovered: The War on Iraq* is a detailed accounting of the alleged lies, deceptions, and manipulations of the Bush government to create just cause for the 2003 pre-emptive strike. Greenwald released his film a month before the 2004 presidential election, presumably to influence the outcome. His film demonstrates how the Bush administration's rhetoric was designed to tie 9/11 to Iraq and to present the Saddam Hussein regime as a threat to the U.S. because of its accumulation of weapons of mass destruction (WMDs). The American public learned from the release of the "torture memos" that their primary purpose was not to collect intelligence but to secure evidence for the Bush administration that would justify the invasion. It is to Greenwald's credit that he refrained from editorializing but let the recounting come from the mouths of the people he interviewed and from archives of the Bush government.

In another war documentary, *Rethink Afghanistan* (2009), Greenwald cobbled together a series of short film segments into one feature-length documentary designed to present opposition to the decision of the Obama administration to escalate the American military presence in Afghanistan. Each segment has a distinct subject: a historical recounting of past failures by invaders of Afghanistan like the British and the Soviets; an examination of U.S.-Pakistan relations, citing the importance of Pakistan, which has nuclear weapons, to the future of Afghanistan; a third segment on the cost of the war, both in terms of life and property; and a final segment that asks viewers to become proactive and sign petitions to

Congress against the military escalation and in favor of peaceful negotiations and an exit strategy out of the country.

On the other hand, Charles Ferguson's Oscar-nominated documentary *No End in Sight* explicitly questions the conduct of the war in Iraq. As the title suggests, Ferguson is critical of the American occupation for the following reasons:

- the lack of preparation by the Bush government for the occupation of the country following the downfall of Saddam
- the destruction of the country's infrastructure
- the failure by the military to establish control after the collapse of the Saddam regime
- the lack of control over the 45,000 private contractors and their dealings with the civilian population, and
- the sending of government administrators to Iraq who had no post-reconstruction experience, no understanding of the culture, and no language skills.

Ferguson's film summarized information already in the public domain when his film was released in 2007. But if his documentary appears unbalanced it is because key administration people like Secretary of Defense Donald Rumsfeld refused to be interviewed. At least Ferguson refrained from turning his film into a proactive exercise in politicizing the war.

Other noteworthy documentaries on the Afghan-Iraqi wars cover a wide range of subjects and formats. Director Alex Gibney looked at these wars through the eyes of its victims in his 2007 Oscar-winning documentary *Taxi to the Dark Side*. Gibney's film examines the torture practices endorsed by the Bush administration in Bagram prison (Afghanistan), Abu Ghraib prison (Iraq), and Guantanamo prison (Cuba) by focusing on an innocent Afghan taxi driver who is imprisoned, tortured, and killed while in detention. The film is not for the squeamish, as it details the various torture techniques used on prisoners. But what is most depressing about this horrible situation is that the crimes were committed by lower-ranking soldiers following ambiguous orders issued by senior military and political officials. This film challenged President Bush's statement that "we do not torture."

Two other documentaries, *Gunner Palace* (2004) and *The War Tapes* (2006), are similar in the sense that the Iraq war is viewed through the eyes and words of the soldiers who are on the ground and in harm's way. In *Gunner Palace*, director Michael Tucker spent two months embedded with the 400 soldiers in the 2-3 Field Artillery unit who were living in Uday Hussein's bombed-out palace in Baghdad. Tucker records the unit's night patrols, house raids, and weapon searches, which place both soldiers and civilians at risk, but he also records the unit's leisure activities, as the soldiers swim in the palace pool and dance and sing to hip hop and rap music. It is a strange juxtaposition that will puzzle older veterans of WWII and Korea.

Director Deborah Scranton takes a similar approach in her documentary, *The War Tapes*. But unlike Tucker, Scranton's film is an edited version of more than 1,000 hours of footage shot by three National Guardsmen serving in Iraq. The soldiers record their basic training at Fort Dix, New Jersey, and their subsequent deployment to Iraq. There they are assigned to escort Halliburton trucks delivering food to military units. Their convoy missions subject them to sniper and motor fire and to the danger of improvised explosive devices (IEDs).

What is bizarre about the film is that soldiers are filming it while under fire. The process gives the film a surreal quality since the soldiers interpret the war they are fighting in as if they were shooting a home movie.

Another Afghanistan-Iraq war documentary, but one that treats war as serious business without the bravado, is *The Ground Truth* (2006). Director Patricia Foulkrod focuses her camera on the ordinary men and women who are persuaded by recruiters to sign up for military duty, survive boot camp, are deployed to Iraq, and return home severely affected by their tour of duty. All this is covered in a compact 72 minutes, mostly through interviews and archival footage. No politicians or military brass appear in the film. First, Foulkrod explores the reasons given for their enlistment: travel opportunities, escape from the limitations of rural and small towns, money for college, health and other benefits. A few express the desire to serve their country after the attack on 9/11. But these motives are all but forgotten once they land in Iraq and discover they are in a constant war zone where the enemy combatants are often invisible, not unlike the situation faced by Vietnam veterans. The reality of their environment soon leads to tragic consequences, as innocent civilians are mistaken for enemy insurgents and the young soldiers discover that their protective armor cannot shield their extremities from IEDs, mortars, and sniper fire. The injured return home as damaged goods—minus limbs and with scarred bodies and tortured souls. Some suffer from undetected Post Traumatic Stress Disorder (PTSD) and succumb to depression, alcoholism, suicide, and fits of violent rage at provocations, real or imagined. Some sleep with their guns; others carry them around for protection against an enemy that exists only in their minds. As one marine told Foulkrod, "we all became casualties of war." *The Ground Truth* is one unembellished war film that rings true. Foulkrod presents an antiwar message at film's end in scenes of Iraqi veterans bonding with Vietnam Veterans for Peace, but her overall theme is that the consequences of war remain long after the gunfire ends.

## Case Study: Women in the Military—*The Invisible War*

In early 2013 the Pentagon announced that women were no longer prohibited from serving in combat zones. This represents a significant shift in policy from the Gulf War, where women were kept out of combat. Since the Afghan-Iraqi wars, however, women have served as medics, military police, and intelligence operators and a number have died in fulfilling those roles. The new directive makes women eligible for such elite units as the Navy SEALs and Delta Force.[55] In effect, the U.S. is simply catching up with countries like Canada, Australia, New Zealand, and the Scandinavian countries that allow women in front-line combat roles.[56]

Interestingly, there has been little debate about this new policy, which will put more women in harm's way. The change occurs, coincidentally, during an era when sexual assault against women in the military has increased at an alarming rate. Their stories of rape, sexual harassment, and sexual humiliation at the hands of their trainers, supervisors, and senior officers bring back memories of the lurid paperbacks of the 1950s. A case in point is that of Air Force Tech Sgt. Jennifer Smith, who told *The New York*

*Times* that when she walked into the office of her senior officer at their air base in South Korea with paperwork that had to be signed, he told her to sit down and then said, "It's Friday afternoon, why don't you take off your blouse and get comfortable."[57] Another woman described an incident during her service tour in Germany where her sergeant tried to assault her, but was prevented by co-workers. Yet another recounted her experience at an air base in South Carolina where she was told to keep quiet about the pornography stored on the unit's computers.[58]

These were incidents of sexual harassment, bad enough, but even more serious charges have been detailed in the 2012 Oscar-nominated documentary by Kirby Dick and Amy Ziering, *The Invisible War*. Their investigative fieldwork uncovered evidence of sexual misdeeds from all branches of the military. The filmmakers not only interviewed the victims of sexual abuse but military psychologists, members of the Advocate-General's Office, and the families of the victims. Since much of the evidence is anecdotal, how reliable is it?

As it turns out, past evidence coupled with recent events makes the case against military sexual abuse very convincing. The victims of rape and assault recount their stories of fear and reprisal, harassment and threats of physical bodily harm by male warrant officers and senior military officers. For instance, a former coast guard seaman told of having her jaw dislocated from a blow by her superior, followed by being raped after she rejected his advances. Several women from the navy and air force told of having .45 caliber pistols put against their heads if they refused to provide sexual favors. When these women filed charges, their complaints were not heard for more than a year. Other women told the filmmakers that they were punished for reporting their rapes, while still others were accused by their superiors of being consensual partners in their sexual encounters. Unbelievably, one victim disclosed that after she complained of being raped, she was charged with adultery even though she was unmarried.

If all the stories by victims of sexual abuse were told, the film would have lasted hours. What the film showed conclusively was that the hierarchical system of military service virtually renders female trainees and recruits under male superiors as fair game for sexual exploitation. Women were placed in the Hobson's choice of filing charges and being punished for their action in one way or another, or remaining silent and having their reputations on base sullied to the point where they would be more vulnerable rather than less. It is apparent that the military is a male preserve where those accused close ranks and protect each other. It is not surprising, therefore, that no one in authority knew anything about the sexual assaults or had been informed of such attacks. When confronted, each military service pointed to their policy of "zero tolerance" for such behavior, making the military a safe haven for sexual predators where it is the victims who bear the burden of proof.

The Department of Defense (DOD) has statistics, of course, but sex crimes are generally underreported anyway. Dick's film claims 20 percent of military women are sexually assaulted while in service and as many as 200,000 have reported such offences. Convictions are rare, however. The documentary claims that 2,500 complaints were sent to the DOD's Inspector-General for review and not one was accepted. Data from the DOD 2011 fiscal year (October 1, 2010 to September 30, 2011) indicates that 3,192 sexual assaults were reported out of an estimated 19,000 allegations, which represents only 14 percent of the assaults. Hence, all the military's known data is largely meaningless if underreported. When one adds the number of unreported assaults to the number not prosecuted, prospects for corrective action appear dismal despite the mind-numbing 734-page annual sexual assault report that cost taxpayers $578,000.[59]

What provides *The Invisible War* with credibility is the documented past record of sexual misbehavior by members of the armed services. Just in the past two decades, five major sex scandals were uncovered, two in the air force, one in the army, one in the marines, and one featuring both naval and air force personnel. The film touches on these events but not in detail. Let's take them in chronological order, dating from 1991 through 2012.

In 1991, at the annual convention of the Tailhook Association (a group of active and retired naval aviators) in Las Vegas, scores of drunken officers assaulted at least 26 women by forming a gauntlet from the elevator down the corridor and groping and disrobing the unfortunate women who got off on the third floor of the hotel. From the military investigation that followed, it was clear that senior officers knew about the unruly behavior but refused to intervene. The media referred to it as "the animal house off the high seas."[60]

Five years later, 12 commissioned and non-commissioned male officers were charged with sexual assault of female trainees under their command at the Army's Aberdeen Proving Ground in Maryland. The charges, among others, included sodomy, disobeying orders, obstructing justice, and adultery.[61] Then in 2003 the U.S. Air Force Academy at Colorado Springs was hit with a scandal involving sexual assaults of female recruits. What the subsequent investigation uncovered was an astounding pattern of sexual abuse: 12 percent of the women who had graduated from the Air Force Academy reported that they were victims of rape or attempted rape, and of the 659 women enrolled at the Academy, some 70 percent said they were victims of sexual harassment that included "pressure for sexual favors."[62]

More recently, charges of sexual assault have been filed against Lackland Air Force Base in Texas, a basic training camp for new recruits, and the prestigious marine barracks in Washington, D.C. In 2012, at the Lackland base, Staff Sgt. Luis Walker was found guilty on 28 counts for committing sexual crimes against female trainees. Eleven other instructors were under investigation for sexual crimes against 31 female recruits.[63] The same year the spotlight fell on the D.C. marine barracks, home of the ceremonial guard for the president and the security force at the White House and Camp David. In March 2012, lawsuits were filed in federal court by eight military women—four marines and four navy members, including two assigned to the D.C. marine barracks—who claimed they were raped while in the service. Their chances for success are problematic, since previous courts have ruled that such crimes are best left to the military justice system.[64]

> As the military adjusts to women in combat zones, the evidence of sexual abuse and harassment exposed in *The Invisible War*, together with the past history of sexual assaults that were often ignored or shielded by senior officers, raises several concerns about the new military directive that allows women to fight. These concerns are not about the ability or courage of women in combat. Rather the red flag warnings concern how the male members of a unit at the front will respond to women in close proximity and under combat conditions. Will it encourage respect for their female buddies or will it be seen as another opportunity to view women as sexual objects to be further exploited? Past history does not support the assumption that gender differences will be accepted and respected by men. The answers to these concerns must await the future.

## Categories of Propaganda

Political Scientist Dan Nimmo identifies four distinct forms of film propaganda, but we are only concerned with two: overt and covert. Documentary movies that serve the interests of the government in power, such as *Why We Fight* and *Triumph of the Will*, fall into the first category. So also do commercial films loosely based on actual political figures and events that utilize the form to recreate those events with political intentions, such as *Mission to Moscow* and *Salt of the Earth*. The second category consists of covert propaganda films that require audiences to possess relevant factual knowledge if they are to understand the film's hidden message. These messages are much harder for audiences to detect. One example would be the 1950s western *High Noon*, where the backstory was set against the HUAC's Hollywood hearings. [65]

Using Nimmo's typology, where would he place a film like D.W. Griffith's *The Birth of a Nation*? It is not a piece of government-sponsored propaganda, although the film's content criticized Reconstruction policies. While *The Birth of a Nation* depicts a specific period in American history, it is unclear whether its director intended to make an epic film or deliver a racial political opinion. Hence, the film fits best in Nimmo's category of a covert piece of racial propaganda, whether intended or not, that implied that the post–Civil War black population was ill-suited for citizenship. In portraying them as undisciplined beasts, lusting after white women and easily duped by northern carpetbaggers, it justified the existence of the Klan as a necessary instrument to keep blacks in a subservient place within the social structure. Its portrayal of black men as either evil beasts or as lazy, ignorant beings advanced the racial stereotype of African-American males and set back civil rights for the entire race for half a century.

Nimmo's typology was published around the time that strategists for political candidates in the U.S. saw the value of utilizing media outlets as primary sources for communicating their campaign messages to the general public. As political campaigns moved from street corners and train-stop speeches to TV ads, video clips and social media outlets, campaign rhetoric concentrated more on negativism and raising doubts about the ability and personal life of their opponents. Although propaganda as a campaign tool was not new in American elections, its utilization became more frequent in political campaigns. And filmmakers saw in political campaigns opportunities for future subjects. Let us consider, for example, the contrasting portrayals depicted in the documentaries *The War Room* (1993) and *A Perfect Candidate* (1996). The first is an upbeat presentation of the successful 1992 Clinton campaign for the presidency, while the other paints a dark picture of the electoral process as it follows Oliver North's 1994 unsuccessful bid for a senate seat. Which film more accurately depicts American politics? How does the public sort through this barrage of visual and textual material in an effort to uncover the truth as measured by confirmed facts?

Another development in using the film medium as a propaganda tool in political campaigns saw Michael Moore time the release of his anti-Bush documentary, *Fahrenheit 9/11*, so as to have maximum impact on the 2004 presidential election. Liberals praised the film while conservatives hated it. Subsequently, it was *déjà vu* during the 2012 campaign between President Obama and his Republican challenger Mitt Romney when conservative political writer Dinesh D'Souza sought to repeat Moore's campaign intervention by releasing his documentary, *2016: Obama's America*, two months before Election Day. The film's intent was to answer this question: What would America be like in 2016 after an Obama second term? According to D'Souza, the question needed to be answered because the American people did not know the "real Obama."

D'Souza does not get to the question right away. First, he does a personal comparison of himself and the president and finds that both were born in the same year, attended Ivy League schools, graduated from college at the same time, were married in the same year, and, holding up his hand, D'Souza says rather joyously, we both have the same skin color. The author assumes that the latter fact is meant to diffuse any cries of racism. But D'Souza is not finished with his comparison; he wants to know how it came to be that with similar backgrounds, he is a grateful American while the president developed into an anti-American, anti-colonial, anti-Western, anti-capitalist radical liberal? D'Souza spends a good deal of the middle of the film in analyzing Obama's autobiography, *Dreams From My Father*, where the president explains his Kenyan father's opposition to Western colonialism in terms of his African nationalism. Even if D'Souza's negative characterizations of Obama are accurate, the fact remains that the president hardly knew his father because he left the family when Obama was two and the son did not see him again until he was 10. The president, in fact, was raised by his white mother and grandparents.

Who else was a mentor or influence in Obama's life? Here D'Souza engages in a bit of 1950s "guilty by association" character assassination by implying that Obama's mentors included the Reverend Jeremiah Wright, the president's former pastor at Trinity United Church of Christ in Chicago, and former domestic terrorist, William Ayers, who was one of the founders of the radical Weather Underground group during the 1960s. No one knows what influence, if any, the Reverend Wright had on Obama when the president lived and worked in Chicago and attended church services. Bill Ayers met Obama when he was running for the Illinois state senate and their relationship is characterized as an acquaintanceship rather than a close friendship.[66] Yet in cobbling the president's father together with Wright and Ayers, D'Souza's intention is to warn the American public that an Obama victory will mean a socialist America, anti-Western and pro-Muslim.

But does this kind of propaganda alter the outcome of political campaigns? Here is another question that social scientists have yet to answer definitively. For the present we have to be satisfied with probabilities. To broaden the question somewhat: Do propaganda films change minds? Much of the evidence above would seem to support the conventional wisdom that persistent and continuous exposure to effective lies and distortions can serve as a powerful weapon to influence individual and mass behavior. But Professor Sean Heuston argues that the effect on public opinion and behavior is exaggerated, especially as it pertains to visual images.[67] He reasons that in the contemporary world we are subjected to so much information that is delivered instantly and from such a wide variety of sources that propaganda films have lost their emotional impact. When the public is able to view events on the Internet and respond to blogs and chat sites instantly after an event has taken place, then the effect of a subsequent propaganda film on the same subject is mediated by previous information. It is an interesting theory, but one that requires further study.

Surely, political films are more readily recognized in the nonfiction genre than in purely commercial entertainment. But political content, whether encased in fictionalized stories or in documentaries, does not ensure the delivery of truthful messages to audiences. At the end of the day, truth is a hard commodity to ascertain in any media form.

Chapter 4

# Kiss, Kiss, Bang, Bang
Hollywood, Sex and Violence

"My constituents can't read but they can understand pictures."
—Boss Tweed of Tammany Hall

"There were a lot of things the censors wouldn't let me do in the movies that I had done on stage. They wouldn't even let me sit on a guy's lap and I'd been on more laps than a napkin."
—Mae West

"We went back four times before we got an R.... We had to get rid of a few thrusts when he's having sex with the apple pie. The MPAA was like 'Can he thrust two times instead of four?'"
—Warren Zide, producer of *American Pie*

"I think it's unfortunate that the value judgments by the MPAA allow for graphic violence, homophobia, and aggression against women.... All the things we see in a PG-13 film and are acceptable. This just typifies how our rating system is broken."
—Lee Hirsch, director of the documentary *Bully*

When the author was growing up in New York in the 1940s–50s, my parents could send me to the neighborhood movie theater with little, if any, anxiety. Saturday matinees were reserved for youngsters, and attendants were present in the theater. Parents relied more or less on appropriate film content since movies in those days were under the supervision of the Production Code, an industry-wide set of guidelines that controlled the making of Hollywood films. Parents were secure in knowing that their youngsters were not going to see films like *Spring Breakers* (2012) with sexual content and the very violent *Django Unchained* (2012). Moreover, local theaters then had one screen, unlike modern movie multiplexes, so that parents were assured that their children would see the film that was advertised.

All that changed with the demise of the Production Code and the creation of the industry-administered film rating system, together with the growth of multiplex theaters. Selecting an appropriate movie for children, especially teenagers, has become a more serious parental concern. How that change occurred, its detrimental effect on film content, and what Hollywood can do to restore parental confidence in the film industry is the subject of this chapter.

## The Film Industry: From Censorship to Regulation

Virtually every new form of popular entertainment has at one time been a target of public criticism; movies were no exception.[1] From the first protests in 1896 of the popular peep show *Dolorita's Passion Dance*, playing on the Atlantic City boardwalk, movies have evoked strong moral feelings that in some cases have led to police action. Apparently, Dolorita's "Houchi Kouchi" dance was too risqué for public taste.[2]

Efforts to control film content evolved through three often overlapping stages in cinema history. In its formative years, federal, state, and local governments tried, and some succeeded, to censor film content. In an effort to prevent government regulation, the film industry in the 1930s first adopted a form of self-regulation with the Production Code and later replaced it with a film rating system, which had the effect of shifting the burden of film selection from the industry to parents and adult guardians. In this latest stage, pressure groups, which formerly negotiated with the industry over film content during the code years, have had to resort to the use of economic boycotts and threatened sanctions against the showing of specific films that offended their particular religious, racial, or sexual/gender sensibilities.[3]

Pressure group activity and government intervention during the film industry's early years led to the passage of city censorship ordinances, state censorship statutes, and the creation of state and local censor boards that required a permit or license from the censors prior to the film's public exhibition. Whether the silent films and early talkies were so immoral and socially dangerous as to warrant such regulation is open to question. The negative influence and social harm attributed to these early films were grossly exaggerated: they were charged with everything from causing juvenile crime to corrupting public morals with lurid and sensational titles, even though the films failed to deliver what was advertised. Nonetheless, this did not deter state and local governments from enacting regulatory legislation.

It would be a mistake, however, to think that pre-Code Hollywood was entirely innocent. From the silent era of films to the early thirties,[4] for example, films were often suggestive, provocative and violent, replete with double entendres, fallen women, and vicious criminals. Moviegoers during these early Depression years viewed James Cagney smash a grapefruit in Mae Clarke's face (*The Public Enemy*, 1931) and watched Edward G. Robinson (*Little Caesar*, 1930) and Paul Muni (*Scarface*, 1930) shoot and maim their way up the crime ladder. Nor did these early films spare women, as when Barbara Stanwyck slept her way to the top of the New York business community in *Baby Face* (1933) and Jean Harlow exploited her sexuality in *Red-Headed Woman* (1932) to gain entrance into the world of the rich and famous. Harlow's film was particularly singled out for rebuke; protesters picketed it where it was shown and it was denounced from the pulpit by Catholic churches.[5] Harlow and Stanwyck were but two of the many amoral screen women that populated the movies in the earlier 1930s.

Criticism against such content was reinforced by media reports of Hollywood as "sin city," a place of wild sexual orgies, bootleg whiskey, studio call girls, and drug abuse. The industry was beset with negative publicity about its stars' depraved conduct, drug use, and, in the case of comedian Fatty Arbuckle, criminal charges of manslaughter and possible rape. Such stories, coupled with public complaints, led U.S. Senator Henry Myers of Montana to indict Hollywood as a place "where debauchery, riotous living, drunkenness, ribaldry, dissipation, free love, seem to be conspicuous."[6]

At first, the film studios tried to discourage government censorship and to quiet public criticism by hiring former U.S. Postmaster General Will Hays in 1922 to head the industry. Hays became the first president of the Motion Picture Producers and Distributors of America, later the Motion Picture Association of America (MPAA). He saw his job as twofold: clean up film content and polish the industry's tarnished image. To achieve these goals, Hays sought to weed out undesirables from the film industry, discourage migration of young people to Hollywood, and persuade the major film studios to make movies acceptable to civic and religious leaders. He also took a step toward self-regulation by encouraging the studios to permit his staff to review scripts for objectionable material. Later, he sought to control screen content by convincing producers to accept his list of "Don'ts" and "Be Carefuls" in the making of their films. This was to be accomplished first through avoidance of certain subjects and second by treating particular topics with special care. For example, under Hays's direction even married screen couples were prevented from sharing the same bed. Profanity, nudity, white slavery, miscegenation, and ridicule of the clergy were to be avoided at all cost. Traditional social institutions like marriage and family were to be properly presented, while religion and symbols of authority, such as the clergy and the police, were to be respected at all times. But Hays soon discovered that verbal acceptance of the guidelines by studio executives did not guarantee compliance. By 1930, he had become disenchanted with efforts to improve screen morality.

Discouraged by the ineffectiveness of his office to control film content and apprehensive about the Catholic Church's formation of a National Legion of Decency to monitor movies, and in some cases, to forbid parishioners to see condemned movies on pain of mortal sin, Hays convinced the major studios that a code of moral principles, enforced by his office, was necessary to ensure the making of respectable motion pictures. Consequently, a set of guidelines, developed by a Catholic priest and a trade paper journalist and strongly supported by the Catholic Church, was instituted to guide the studios in the production of their films. Labeled the Production Code by the industry,[7] these guidelines served as an internal regulating mechanism for more than three decades.

## The Production Code

Making movies under the code was a game of barter and exchange between three participants: the major film studios, the Production Code Administration (PCA) headed by Catholic Joseph Breen, and the Legion of Decency. Not only did the code contain a list of prohibited subjects, but it also defined basic moral principles and applied these to inappropriate screen material: crime, sex, disrespect toward religion and authority, vulgarity, obscenity, revealing costumes, and offensive material. A separate section dealt with the treatment of special subjects, such as bedroom scenes, surgeries and childbirth, alcohol and drinking, and hangings and electrocutions. Strict application of the code often made the honest treatment of certain adult material on the screen virtually impossible.

When box office receipts were good, the studios were more likely to faithfully abide by the code. But as the Depression deepened and receipts declined, studios were more interested in filling theaters than in promoting public virtue. For example, gangster films were popular with Depression audiences. The box office success of *Little Caesar*, *Public Enemy*, and *Scarface* encouraged the studios to promote screen violence, as long as the criminals were punished in the end. The criminals in the above films all paid with their lives for their crimes, but not before they did their share of killing. Nor could adultery be presented without redemption or punishment. A film like *Unfaithful* (2002), with a plot in which a married woman has a torrid love affair with a younger man, could not have been made under the code because there was no punishment at the end. When the woman's husband discovers the affair, he confronts his wife's lover and then kills him. But instead of apprehension and guilt, the husband and wife flee to the safety of Mexico. Some scholars even suggested that the code was enforced more strictly against sexual conduct than violence,[8] a criticism that persists under today's rating system.

One piece of evidence to support this assertion is the PCA's treatment of Mae West. West's films, with their suggestive dialogue and implied immorality, proved very popular at the box office and posed a challenge to local censors and later to code administrators, because even her most innocent line of dialogue could be interpreted as innuendo. Born in Brooklyn to immigrant parents, West spent two decades performing in vaudeville, burlesque, and legitimate theater before reaching stardom in 1930s Hollywood, where she wrote most of her material and learned to exploit her sexuality to further her career. Her first two starring films, *She Done Him Wrong* and *I'm No Angel*, both released in 1933 before the implementation of the code, tested the resolve of the Hays Office and the local censors. For instance, in *She Done Him Wrong*, West plays Lady Lou, a barroom entertainer who tries to seduce the head of the Salvation Army. In one scene she invites him to "come up sometime and see me," and in another scene she flaunts her sexuality in this song:

> A guy what takes his time
> I'll go for any time.
> A hasty job really spoils the master's touch
> I don't like a big commotion.
> I'm a demon for slow motion or such
> Why should I deny
> That I would die
> To know a guy what takes his time?[9]

Then there is a scene in *I'm No Angel* where West, dressed in her usual low-cut form-fitting sequin gown, rubs up against her male co-star, who naively praises her good behavior, to which she replies: "When I'm good, I'm very good, but when I'm bad, I'm better."[10] Everyone in the audience howled, the censors seethed, and West took the money to the bank because she understood that a provocative scene lies in the delivery and the context. As the trade paper *Variety* noted, the actress could not sing a "lullaby without making it sexy."[11]

Film historian Gregory Black maintains that the code, in addition to defining the treatment of sex and violence, served a conservative political agenda.[12] This is apparent in guidelines that required studio movies to show respect for government and all authority figures, to present only acceptable social behavior in films, and to adhere to Judeo-Christian morality before they could receive a certificate for public exhibition. Whether Hollywood adopted the code because it believed in its moral precepts or because it proved a useful instrument to fend off government regulation and economic boycotts is debatable. More likely, adherence was sound economics and good business practice. The code provided the industry with a tool to regulate its own product, mitigating the risk of state and local censors making their own film deletions and preempting a potential boycott by the Catholic Legion of Decency and other pressure groups. The Production Code, therefore, bought the film industry some much-needed public goodwill, staved off any threat of federal intervention, and provided an economic benefit as well.

Much has been made of the economic clout wielded by the Legion of Decency as a moral player in content negotiations with the PCA. Created by the Catholic hierarchy and armed with its concomitant threat of a boycott, the Legion supported the code's moral principles with an economic hammer. Its power lay in the pledge that Catholics took to boycott films condemned by the Church. However, the force of the boycotts often depended on the strength of the Catholic presence in the community. Where there was a strong Catholic population, as in cities such as Cincinnati, Philadelphia, St. Louis, and San Francisco, the Church's tactics were effective. But where Catholics were a minority, its censorship directives had little impact.[13]

But even when the Church could not deliver an effective boycott on every film it condemned, the Legion could still exert pressure on the industry to make cuts and alter scenes, especially since it had an ally in Joseph Breen, the Catholic leader of the PCA. The effectiveness of the relationship between the Legion and the PCA is evidenced by the fact that only five films out of the more than 5,000 released with a PCA certificate during 1934–68 were condemned by the Catholic Church.[14] Most contemporary interest groups would consider what the Legion achieved as a model in effective lobbying. However, contrary to popular opinion, the Catholic Church is not a monolithic institution in practice. Divisions exist among the clergy as well as the laity. Catholic bishops occasionally disagreed with the Legion over the ratings assigned to specific films and over the action that should be taken against condemned films. Still, a combination of economic forces, state and local censors and Catholic pressure led Hollywood to produce more musical comedies, children's pictures, and family movies in the decades prior to World War II.

Movies under the Code

The major problem with the Production Code was that it depended on its application by Breen and his PCA staff. Breen had been given virtually dictatorial power: in the initial stages of production, his office had approval over all scripts and musical lyrics. Once completed, the film had to receive authorization in the form of a certificate from his office before it could be shown in theaters. Since the major studios controlled a majority of the theaters at that time, a film released without a certificate was unlikely to find a distributor.[15]

Breen's staff, meanwhile, often applied the narrowest interpretation possible to Code guidelines, turning film production into a series of obstacles to overcome through negotiation and circumvention. First, Breen applied the Code strictly to prohibit the filming of certain subjects, whether the story derived from commercial hacks or established authors such as Leo Tolstoy, William Faulkner, and Sinclair Lewis. Lewis's novel *It Can't Happen Here*, for instance, was prevented from reaching the screen because of PCA objections. Additionally, strictly enforcing the code requirements led to absurd results. For example, the code permitted the treatment of sex on screen as long as the participants were punished for it. Naturally, nudity and explicit sex were forbidden and divorce was a taboo subject per se under the "sanctity of marriage" provision in the code, even though, according to film historian Jeanine Basinger, Hollywood was ambiguous about the institution of marriage.[16] Basinger claims that the film industry refused to use the word "marriage" in its ads and posters, preferring to promote a film as a romance because audiences thought love was exciting and married life boring. If divorce was not an option, how could a screenwriter get rid of a movie spouse except through death by accident and natural causes or through annulment and murder?[17]

Breen also had the authority to demand cuts and eliminate or edit dialogue. Possibly the silliest example of code application occurred during the filming of *Gone With the Wind*, when Breen's staff sought to rewrite the following dialogue between Scarlett O'Hara and Rhett Butler:

Scarlett: "Oh, my darling, if you go, what shall I do?"
Rhett: "Frankly, my dear, I don't give a damn."[18]

The code administrators wanted to change the last line to "My dear, I don't care." Only the persuasion of the producer, David O. Selznick, preserved one of the classic lines in screen history. The code was particularly sensitive to suggestive lyrics. In the 1959 remake of *Imitation of Life*, the code office had actress Susan Kohner, playing a black woman passing as white, cut the following lyrics from a song she sings at a local nightclub:

Although my equipment is fine
Hate to complain but will you explain
Why nobody's using mine?[19]

While the original intention of the code to place sensible restraints on screen material may have been laudable, its implementation was often arbitrary and unreasonable.

As the film industry recovered from World War II, Breen and his office became involved in numerous censorship controversies. At least six major films in the 1950s challenged the authority of the PCA. In rapid succession, Breen's office was confronted with films that violated the code in terms of subject matter and treatment. The film adaptation of the successful Broadway play *The Moon Is Blue* (1953) was considered too risqué and the drug use and addiction in *The Man with the Golden Arm* (1956) too explicit; both were released without a PCA certificate. Cuts and dialogue changes had to be made in two 1954 films: *The Wild One*, starring Marlon Brando as the leader of a motorcycle gang, and *From Here to Eternity*, the film version of James Jones's novel of army life in Hawaii before Pearl Harbor. Other major productions that ran into trouble with the Breen office included *A Streetcar Named Desire* (1951) and *Baby Doll*, (1956) two films based on the plays of Tennessee Williams. To Hollywood insiders, the Breen Office appeared under siege.

The constant squabbling over code violations, together with the growth of independent producers, the divorce of film studios from theater ownership,[20] and the Supreme Court's decision in *Burstyn v. Wilson*,[21] which included movies under the protection of the First Amendment, led ultimately to the code's demise.[22] Decades of discontent reached a climax in the 1960s with the selection in 1966 of Jack Valenti, former administrative aide to President Lyndon Johnson, to head the MPAA.[23] After a few weeks on the job, Valenti was faced with several major challenges to the code that would finally determine its fate.[24] The first dispute involved the film version of Edward Albee's play *Who's Afraid of Virginia Woolf?* (1966), where the words "screw" and "hump the hostess" were retained from the stage production. Both raised problems under code guidelines and the resolution, worked out after hours of negotiation, resulted in the exclusion of the word "screw" but retention of "hump the hostess." Hence you could "hump the hostess" but you couldn't screw her even though both terms represent similar sexual activity. The second incident proved more serious. Director Michelangelo Antonioni's British-Italian production, *Blow-Up* (1966), contained scenes of nudity, strictly prohibited by the code. The PCA denied the film an exhibition certificate. However, MGM defied the code by distributing the film through a subsidiary company, making it the first time that a major studio had exhibited a film without PCA approval. Encouraged by MGM's rebelliousness, other producers followed suit and within two years Valenti replaced the code with a film rating system that classifies films according to audience suitability.

## The Hollywood Movie Rating System

The rating system that Valenti persuaded the Hollywood moguls to adopt was a stroke of administrative genius. The old Production Code clearly was dysfunctional, yet the prospect of external censorship by government or capitulation to the economic threats of pressure groups was totally unacceptable to the industry. Hence, Valenti was able to sell the new rating system to the studios as a reasonable compromise. The film classification system adopted by the industry is age-based and intended for parents; its sole purpose, according to Valenti, is in "giving advance cautionary warnings to parents so that parents could make the decision about the movie going of their young children."[25] These sentiments were reaffirmed by Valenti's successors, Dan Glickman[26] and current MPAA President and former senator Christopher Dodd. In effect, the application of the rating system is intended for film patrons 17 and younger.

The Hollywood classification system has undergone several revisions over the years. New categories have been added and the former X category has been replaced by NC-17. The present rating system, in effect since 1990, requires films to be placed in one of five categories based upon audience suitability:

> **G:** A G-rated movie admits all ages. It contains nothing in theme, language, nudity, sex, or violence that would offend young children. No bad language, drug use, or sex scenes. Violence is minimal.
>
> **PG:** A PG movie means that some material may be unsuitable for children. Parents are advised to investigate the film. The movie may contain some profanity, violence, and brief nudity but no drug use.
>
> **PG-13:** A PG-13 rating means that parents need to determine whether their children under 13 should view the film because its content falls somewhere between the R-restricted rating and the PG rating. Hence, it may contain inappropriate material such as drug use, nudity, persistent violence, and at least one expletive (e.g., fuck). However, the rating does allow for some flexibility in the use and manner of such words.
>
> **R:** An R-rated movie contains some adult material and is not intended for children under 17 unless accompanied by a parent or adult guardian. A restricted film contains all adult material—hard language, sexually oriented nudity, persistent violence, and drug use. Parents are informed that it is generally not appropriate to take their young children to such films.
>
> **NC-17:** This rating requires that the person be at least 17 years old. These films are rated as too adult for those under 17. The rating indicates that its content includes behavior—drug, sex, or violence—that is too strong for children. However, the rating does not mean the film is obscene or pornographic.[27]

In response to prodding by the Federal Trade Commission (FTC), anti-smoking groups, various parent groups, and an assortment of critics, the MPAA in 2007 instituted the following changes in its film rating system. First, it added descriptors (specific information) to its age-based ratings. Second, it included an additional warning to parents that R-rated movies were not appropriate for young children. Third, in a concession to the medical profession and anti-smoking groups, it promised to consider smoking in films as a rating factor. Other changes included placing rating reasons in all film ads and on websites and posters and requiring that all movie trailers shown before the feature presentation be compatible with the film's rating. For example, R-rated trailers should not precede a PG-rated feature.[28]

The ratings applied to Hollywood films are the result of the deliberations of a Los Angeles-based group of reviewers who work for the Code and Rating Administration (CARA) under the supervision of a leader appointed by the MPAA president. Prior to filmmaker Kirby Dick's 2006 documentary, *This Film Is Not Yet Rated*, the CARA reviewers were anonymous except for their present chairwoman, Joan Graves. Dick's film, however, exposed their identities. Their basic qualification seems to be as parents of children under 17 because, as the reasoning goes, they would best know what material is suitable for the various age groups. Its head, Ms. Graves, has been with CARA for more than 2 decades.[29]

The rating process begins with a producer submitting his or her film, together with a fee, to CARA to be reviewed prior to national exhibition. The producer voluntarily submits to the rating process because as a matter of policy non-rated films, along with NC-17 rated films, are unable to be booked into the large theater chains like Regal Entertainment Group, AMC, Cinemark, Carmike, and National Amusements. To receive a desirable rating (at least PG-13, but R acceptable) from CARA is a sound business decision by the studios and distributors because it assures that such films will have access to the multiplexes located in shopping malls. After CARA reviews a film, each reviewer assigns an appropriate rating accompanied by a justification. They then meet to discuss the initial ratings. The final rating is the result of a majority vote. A producer who is unhappy with the assigned rating has the option of re-editing and resubmitting the film or appealing the decision to the Rating Appeals Board, a group of reviewers from within the film industry. After listening to arguments to overturn the initial rating, the appeals group will decide either to uphold the assigned rating or overturn it, based on a two-thirds majority vote. Their decision is final and not subject to further appeal. In order to render some semblance of objectivity, the MPAA president is not involved in the rating process at any stage of the proceedings.

## Putting Hollywood to the Test: The Rating System Assessed

Before beginning an assessment of the Hollywood film rating system, it is necessary to note that all evaluations contain an element of subjectivity that is inherent in any judgmental process. But simply because these judgments are imperfect does not reduce them to useless exercises. On the contrary, when done with care and the application of standards that are adaptable and flexible and supported by available evidence, evaluations provide a useful service.

Hence there will always be films with more complicated content whose ratings can legitimately be challenged because a reasoned case can be made both for and against the assigned rating. Does it make a difference whether CARA assigns, say, an R-rating rather than a PG-13 to a film? Most definitely. A PG-13 film has access to the multiplexes, located in huge malls frequented by teenagers. An R-rated film, meanwhile, is restricted to those 17+ or to those under 17 accompanied by a parent or adult guardian and, at least in theory if not execution, would limit the audience for that film. This is not a hypothetical situation for the film industry because money and, in some respects, power are involved. Both these factors came into play when the Weinstein Company sought to distribute its documentary on school bullying.

Figure 4.1. BULLY Poster, 2011. Reprinted with permission, The Weinstein Company/Photofest

## Case Study: *Bully*—A Challenge for CARA

Bullying, in one form or another, is as old as civilization itself. Those who are powerful use that advantage to physically or psychologically dominate those who are weaker and vulnerable. Bullies have resorted to teasing, rejection, verbal threats, insults and physical abuse to frighten, control, or punish those who are most susceptible to being hurt. Bullying is a form of meanness that often was tolerated in the past because it was considered a stage in the developmental process.

Definitions of bullying abound in the behavioral literature; still no consensus exists as to its components. Some include only physical abuse, others expand the abuse into verbal name-calling and still others require the bullies to harm the victim through social isolation and rejection. The federal government, meanwhile, emphasizes that for behavior to be considered bullying it must be aggressive and repetitive with intent to exercise control over others, who are usually weaker and more vulnerable.[30]

Bullying caught the nation's attention when the media reported a series of suicides that began in 2009 and were blamed on acts of bullying. The first death was particularly upsetting because it was shown that 17-year-old student Tyler Long killed himself after enduring years of torment from his Georgia classmates. Tyler suffered from Asperger's Syndrome, a form of autism which causes personality changes. He believed in adhering to school rules, and so when students were talking in class he would shout out that that behavior was against the rules. Apparently his classmates were angered by these outbursts and a group of them decided to harass him by stealing his school property, spitting in his food, and calling him names like "faggot." Despite his parents' complaints to school officials, the harassment continued until one day Tyler hanged himself from the top shelf in his bedroom.[31]

In 2010, student Tyler Clementi jumped off the George Washington Bridge after his Rutgers University roommate surreptitiously filmed him having sex with another male. In that same year, 15-year-old Phoebe Prince, an Irish girl who emigrated to the U.S., hanged herself after being bullied by her Massachusetts classmates. Thereafter, in 2012, a Staten Island teen, Amanda Cummings, jumped in front of a bus after relentless bullying.[32] While these are tragic events, some researchers claim it is a mistake to consider suicides in terms of a one-to-one correlation between cause (bullying) and effect (taking one's life). Research by the American Foundation for Suicide Prevention indicates that many of those who commit suicide were suffering from mental illness of some sort at the time of their death, and in the case of three of the above suicides, there were other causes at work besides bullying. In Tyler Clementi's case, he had told his family of his sexual orientation a few days before he entered Rutgers and they did not respond well to the news. After her death, it was revealed that Phoebe Prince had attempted suicide before and that she had a history of cutting herself. While Amanda Cummings' family attributed her death to bullying, a follow-up police investigation discovered that Amanda was devastated at the break-up of her relationship with an older boy. In brief, social researchers today treat suicide deaths as tragic but complicated events that are likely due to multiple causes.[33]

But this is not to minimize the seriousness of the bullying problem for many school youngsters, particularly at the junior-senior high school level. Data from the Center for Disease Control reveal that during the years 2000–09, suicides among these students averaged around eight per 100,000.[34] Statistics notwithstanding, the U.S. Department of Education noted that some 160,000 children stay home from school each day because they fear being bullied,[35] while another school organization estimated that some 3 million schoolchildren are victims of bullying during the school year.[36]

This background introduction to bullying, especially among schoolchildren, is necessary to fully understand the problem confronting CARA when the Weinstein Company bought the distribution rights to *Bully* (2011), a documentary by director Lee Hirsch. The film examines how bullying affected five school victims, three boys and two girls, and their families over the course of one year. Told as a series of interrelated case studies, the film depicts the tragic consequences of bullying. Two of the victims could no longer tolerate the harassment and pain and killed themselves. The third boy, Alex, age 12, was harassed on a daily basis, both physically and verbally. On the school bus, he was punched, hit, stabbed with a pencil, and choked while the bus driver stared straight ahead and the other students watched but did not interfere. It is not surprising, then, that Alex spent much of his day alone, without friends, watching trains pull in and out of the train yard. Another victim, Kelby, was a 16-year-old girl who announced her lesbianism to the small Oklahoma town where she lived and was immediately shunned and made unwelcome at her school, church, and other places in the community. Isolated and persecuted, she attempted suicide three times. The other girl, 14-year-old Ja'Maya, became so tired and fearful of the bullying that she took her mother's gun on the school bus. For that infraction she was incarcerated in the county's juvenile detention center.

*Bully* delivers a powerful message on the harm done to its victims. Its only flaw is that we learn nothing about the bullies: what motivates them, what stimulates their antisocial behavior, and what characteristics they share, if any. Regardless, most educators and film critics supported the film as bringing a social problem into the spotlight. CARA, on the other hand, did not see it quite that way. As with all films that seek national distribution, *Bully* was submitted to CARA for classification prior to national release. Both the director and the distributor expected a PG-13 rating because of several F-words, but they were shocked and dismayed when the film received an R-rating, which meant it could not be shown in schools, nor could youngsters under 17 see the film in theaters without a parent or guardian. Hirsch and the Weinstein Company challenged the rating in an appeal that included an appearance by one of the bullied victims, but to no avail. CARA's head, Joan Graves justified the decision in this statement:

> Bullying is a serious issue and is a subject that parents should discuss with their children. The MPAA agrees with the Weinstein Company that *Bully* can serve as a vehicle for such important discussions. The MPAA also has the responsibility, however, to acknowledge and represent the strong feedback from parents throughout the country who want to be informed about content in movies, including language. The rating and rating descriptor of "some language" indicates to parents that this movie contains certain language. With that, some parents may choose to take their kids to this movie and others may not, but it is their choice and not ours to make for them.[37]

With their appeal denied, Hirsch and Weinstein had to decide whether to release the film as "unrated," which would have restricted its theatrical distribution and limited its audience, or to utilize the power and influence of public opinion to force CARA to change its mind. Fortunately for them, they decided to fight the R-rating, and within weeks CARA agreed to a PG-13 rating in exchange for elimination of three F-words used by youngsters. Later, Weinstein thanked Christopher Dodd, the new MPAA president, for his intervention while proclaiming the turnaround a moral victory because CARA originally asked that one scene be cut from the film along with several more F-words.[38]

The *Bully* case study is instructive for two reasons. On the negative side, CARA remains an insular organization, sensitive to criticism but unwilling to consult outside experts for assistance in problem cases. No serious reforms will ever occur unless CARA's underlying secrecy and its "us vs. them" attitude changes. On the positive side, the *Bully* negotiations demonstrate that although CARA can be stubborn, it still respects public sentiment and can change its mind if enough outside pressure is applied.

Any classification system is subjective in practice and open to criticism. Categorizing subjects and assigning them ratings are vulnerable to charges of arbitrariness and favoritism. CARA's critics range from film critics to academic scholars and their complaints fall into one of three broadly designated objections: (1) the rating system is arbitrary in its application, (2) assigned ratings discriminate because preference is awarded to the major studios over independents, and (3) the rating system operates largely in secret, is resistant to change, and its ratings are laxly enforced, if at all, at theaters. How valid are these charges?

The arbitrariness charge is usually linked to the accusation that CARA applies a stricter standard to sexual content than it does to film violence. As one example, consider Quentin Tarantino's western, *Django Unchained*, which won the director an Oscar. *Django* competes in body count with Brian De Palma's remake of the Depression-era gangster classic *Scarface* (1983), starring Al Pacino as a Cuban drug dealer. Tarantino vividly depicts every act of violence, torture, degradation and humiliation, leaving nothing to the imagination. For Tarantino, the screaming must be seen as well as heard. His blood-splattered film is an exercise in unrestrained excess, yet it received an R-restricted rating, which means youngsters under 17 are able to see it with an adult parent or guardian.

But is it accurate to state that the ratings favor violence over sex? There is insufficient empirical evidence to support the accusation, but anecdotal signs point in that direction. Take the case of the 2003 independent (indie) film *The Cooler*. This movie, about a Las Vegas loser (William Macy), received an initial NC-17 rating largely due to one lovemaking scene where the actors' genitals are briefly visible. After a protracted battle with CARA, the film was granted an R-rating with the scene virtually unchanged. During the ratings negotiations, actress Maria Bello argued that her love scene with Macy was tender and gentle, as befitting two adults engaged in an act of passion. Does tender sex with nudity warrant the same rating as the explicit blood-soaked violence of *Django*? The reader should view both films back-to-back before answering.

Arbitrariness to the point of absurdity can be found in the R-rating assigned to *Hyde Park on Hudson*, the film about President Roosevelt previously discussed in chapter 2. It depicts a sexual encountered between the president and his cousin but it is filmed very discreetly. The sexual act is done gently without any of the explicitness and violence in many R-rated movies. So why did CARA make a fuss? Its restricted rating was based on sexuality when, in fact, the sex is implied. There is one scene where the president takes his cousin Daisy for a drive in the country and once parked, a sexual act is being performed, but the activity is viewed from the back of the automobile. Very likely teens will understand the implications behind several scenes where Roosevelt summons either Daisy or his secretary, Missy, to inspect his stamp collection or meet him late at night in his private lodge. But these scenes are shot discreetly and there is no nudity or vulgarity in the film. For contrast compare the sexuality in *Hyde Park* with the explicit sex, nudity and drug scenes in *Spring Breakers*,[39] also an R-rated film, that approach the soft-porn films of the past. It is difficult to see the justification for placing these two films in the same category.

*Hyde Park on Hudson* fared better in other countries. It was rated PG in Canada and suitable for 12 and above in the UK and Ireland.[40] It is this kind of inconsistency that fuels CARA's critics, who also claim that CARA treats gay sex scenes more harshly than heterosexual sex scenes, though the evidence remains sketchy.[41] In defense of its ratings decisions, CARA asserts that it all depends on the context, explicitness and severity of the scene. Possibly CARA could mitigate this complaint if it paid more attention to the "totality" of a film rather than the content in one scene or several scenes.

The second accusation is that CARA shows preference to the major studios in assigning ratings over the indies. Filmmaker Kirby Dick makes this charge in his documentary *This Film Is Not Yet Rated*, to which CARA assigned an NC-17 rating. Dick appealed the decision, believing that the NC-17 designation was due to the film's critique of the rating system itself rather than its content. After all, the documentary's content had to include restricted and NC-17 material to make its point. Dick lost the appeal and the film was released without a rating, which severely limited its distribution.[42]

This charge of discrimination against indie films is also difficult to substantiate. We can cite the problems encountered by Dick and films like *The Cooler* but there is simply not enough information to support the accusation. However, evidence of assigning questionable ratings to indie films persists. Take the case of *Frozen River* (2007), a film about poverty, Native Americans, and the measures taken by desperate people. The plot involves two women who smuggle undocumented immigrants across the frozen river between Messina, New York, and Canada during the winter months. Each journey puts their lives at risk or, if caught by the police, assures them of jail time. The film is a sad commentary on the drastic choices desperate people make and their consequences. The film contained four "fucks" and was R-rated. But it contained no sex, scenes of extreme violence, or acts of meanness. A viewer could legitimately question why this serious drama about ordinary but desperate people deserves a restricted rating that places it in the same category as major studio movies containing vicious violence and scenes of degrading sexuality. Even more puzzling is the R-rating (for language) given to the Kelly Reichardt indie film *Wendy and Lucy* (2008), which tells the story of a young woman and her dog trying to reach Alaska in search of a better life. True, it does contain a few swear words and a brief shot of drug use, but again there is no nudity, sex or explicit violence. It is a sweet but sad film about loneliness and the hard realities of life, one that would resonate with teenagers.

Such questionable ratings lead to the third accusation: that CARA is a secret organization, hostile to challengers and resistant to change. It is true that CARA's internal policy is to protect the identities of its reviewers and to keep information about its operation from public scrutiny, and as a private organization it has no legal obligation to provide transparency. But a more transparent rating process would benefit both CARA and the public interest. After all, the purpose of the rating system is to assist parents in selecting appropriate movie fare for their children. Any inconvenience or distress accompanying a more open policy on CARA's part would be offset by a greater appreciation for the trials and tribulations of its reviewing staff and result in more public support for the organization. In addition, a more diversified group of reviewers would instill more confidence in the ratings process, such as the expertise that practitioners in the fields of child psychology and pediatrics could add. When CARA is unsure of how to classify a troublesome film, why not have it call in outside experts for assistance, as the British Board of Film Classification (BBFC) is permitted to do? Why is CARA such an insular body that shuns outsiders? When director David Cronenberg's disturbing film *Crash* (1996), about people who receive sexual stimulation from auto crashes, came before CARA, it originally received a NC-17 rating. After approximately 10 minutes from the film was cut, an R-version was approved. In England, where the film's anticipated distribution led to government opposition and public indignation, the BBFC assigned the film an 18 rating after consultation with a psychologist and feedback from disabled people who attended a special screening.[43]

Two modifications would help alleviate the "resistance to change" argument. First, the appeals process might benefit from an infusion of fresh blood from outside the industry. Second, a two-thirds majority to change a rating practically guarantees that few appeals will succeed. In fact, from 1984, when the PG-13 rating was introduced, to 2004 only 38 appeals out of 81 R-rated films were successful in moving up to PG-13.[44] Lowering the vote to a simple majority would increase flexibility in the appeals process.

The reality, however, is that even if the MPAA implemented all of the above suggestions and adopted the recommended changes, its rating system would fall short of its promise to parents, and by extension, to the movie-going public in three respects: articulating the standards by which CARA assigns its rating, applying the assigned rating to each patron, and enforcing the rating at the box office.

## Film Content

What does CARA consider in classifying film content? Does the organization worry about the politics of a film? The impact of a particular rating on the box office? Or is it concerned with what the public response will be to the assigned rating? These are all rhetorical questions since CARA does its work behind closed doors, its reviewers are prohibited from giving interviews, and when they leave their job, they are forbidden to discuss or write about their work. Because their ratings are made public, CARA reviewers prefer to remain anonymous. That is why CARA was angry that Dick's film exposed them. CARA expects outsiders to accept its ratings on good faith.

But people within the industry have to do the same. Scriptwriters, directors, and producers know that what CARA decides will likely affect their product. An NC-17 is significant because it severely limits the number of theater bookings and restricts advertising opportunities for the film, which will adversely impact box office receipts. That is why the studios often make it a contractual obligation for a filmmaker to deliver a movie with a specific rating. For instance, director Paul Verhoeven was required by distributor TriStar Pictures to secure at most no more than an R-rating for his sex-violence thriller, *Basic Instinct* (1992).[45] Verhoeven was unhappy with the cuts CARA required, but in the end the studio and CARA had the necessary leverage. The economic factor is so important that even highly respected directors, such as Stanley Kubrick (*Eyes Wide Shut*, 1999) and Brian De Palma (*Dressed to Kill*, 1980), eventually had to agree to the required deletions and dialogue changes to avoid an NC-17 rating. The 2010 indie movie *Blue Valentine*, which chronicles the end of a relationship that both parties know is heading toward dissolution, contained scenes of sex and nudity which normally earn an R-rating. Instead CARA assigned the NC-17 rating to the film because it contained one very graphic sex scene and another scene of physical violence. In this case the studio won the appeal and the rating change was announced.[46]

Which film ratings have dominated over the last decade? The following chart clearly shows that almost two-thirds of all released films classified by CARA received the R-restricted rating, followed by PG-13 with 23 percent, leaving the G and PG categories underutilized. NC-17 is so small that it is a non-factor statistically.[47]

Table 4.1. CARA's Ratings Assigned to Films, 2000-11

|      | G   | PG    | PG-13 | R     | NC-17 |
|------|-----|-------|-------|-------|-------|
| 2000 | 36  | 51    | 146   | 528   | 1     |
| 2001 | 30  | 55    | 163   | 490   | 1     |
| 2002 | 30  | 71    | 145   | 539   | 1     |
| 2003 | 29  | 79    | 186   | 645   | 1     |
| 2004 | 29  | 110   | 187   | 540   | 5     |
| 2005 | 33  | 109   | 232   | 551   | 6     |
| 2006 | 29  | 93    | 191   | 539   | 1     |
| 2007 | 29  | 105   | 206   | 495   | 1     |
| 2008 | 37  | 107   | 201   | 551   | 4     |
| 2009 | 22  | 101   | 191   | 478   | 1     |
| 2010 | 27  | 93    | 177   | 408   | 0     |
| 2011 | 43  | 102   | 200   | 422   | 3     |
|      | 374 | 1,076 | 2,225 | 6,186 | 25    |

The preponderance of the R-rating continued in 2012 as 177 features received the restricted rating while 119 received PG-13. What is unusual and mystifying is that the PG-13 movies brought in more money at the box office. According to the National Association of Theatre Owners (NATO), the 177 R-rated films grossed almost $3 billion domestically, for an average of $16.8 million per film. But the 119 PG-13 rated films earned $5.6 billion at the domestic box office, for an average of $47.3 million a film.[48] What these statistics reveal is that Hollywood continues to make films that receive restricted ratings even though these movies earn less at the box office than those rated PG-13.

How to explain this puzzling phenomenon in a high-risk industry where success is measured at the box office? Unfortunately, the author can only speculate on the reasons. A relevant observation that the film industry was not engaged in good business practices came from a study by two California economists[49] that showed that G, PG, and PG-13 films were financially more successful during the 1985–96 decade than R-rated films. Then why does the film industry continue to over-produce such films? The economists said one possible explanation could be a result of studio error, that is, ticket sales were less than projected against the costs of production and advertising. But this is not an R-specific scenario: witness the 2012 PG-13-rated blockbuster films *John Carter* and *Battleship*, whose worldwide ticket sales of $302 million and $282 million respectively proved a poor return on their $200+ million production budgets, increased by marketing budgets of $100 million or more.[50]

The author offers a different explanation. While studio CEOs strive and hope for maximum profits on one of their films, they also desire respectability and status among their peers. To acquire such acclaim some studio heads may seek Oscars and bragging rights as much as financial success. In such situations, they succumb to approving R-rated projects because Julia Roberts or Tom Hanks wants to play a particular character or Steven Spielberg wants to take on the challenge of a certain script. In other words, some R-rated film projects may be approved on the basis of vanity and ego enhancement rather than sound economics. In the end, only insiders who understand the workings of the film industry can provide a more knowledgeable reason for why the R-restricted ratings dominate the film classification system despite common sense and good business practice.[51]

If the present R-rated preference continues in Hollywood, the film industry can relieve the anxiety of parents with youngsters under 17 by replacing both the R and the NC-17 classifications in favor of an adult 18 category. Why 18? Why not 21 or 17? Admitting that any designated age representing a level of maturity is arbitrary, 18 is a recognized benchmark in the U.S. as the legal demarcation line for being treated as an adult. At age 18, most American youngsters will have graduated from high school, joined the workforce, entered the military, or begun their college careers. They will be able to vote, and with a few exceptions, to marry without parental consent, make a valid will, and serve on a jury. An 18 classification also would eliminate much of the bartering and bickering between filmmakers and the rating system since the studios will be able to make the kind of films they want and take their chances with adult audiences in the free market.

## Internal Integrity

No film classification system is of any value unless it has internal integrity and public respect. Two more changes to the present rating system would achieve both. The first is to require that each patron entering the theater meets the age requirement. The present policy allows parents or an adult guardian to bring young people aged 17 or younger with them to view an R-rated film. This questionable policy rests on the principle that parents have exclusive rights over their children even when they exhibit a lack of common sense and exercise poor judgment. Common sense dictates that an R-rated movie contains material inappropriate for youngsters. How does the material change because a parent is sitting next to them? Therefore, Hollywood needs to adopt the BBFC practice of applying the film rating to every patron who enters the theater. Even the Queen of England could not bring her grandchildren into a theater where the film rating is unsuitable for their age group. There is common sense to the British practice since the content of a film does not magically change simply because a parent or guardian has purchased the tickets. The current Hollywood rating system not only defies logic but encourages deception and circumvention.

## Box Office Enforcement

The next step is to ensure that the age requirement is consistently enforced at the theater, particularly if an adult 18 rating category is adopted. Unfortunately, no systematic study pertaining to the level of enforcement of film ratings at the box office has been undertaken. The MPAA claims that 85 percent of the theater owners in the nation voluntarily subscribe to the rating system, which obligates the theaters to make certain that underage patrons are not admitted to restricted film fare.[52] Theater owners insist that they are adhering to the rules. If that were the case, no youngsters would be viewing restricted films. Yet a 2009 follow-up study to the 2000 Federal Trade Commission (FTC) report *Marketing Violent Entertainment to Children*[53] found mixed results on rating enforcement. The commission discovered that theaters allow about three in 10 children under age 17 to gain admission, unaccompanied, to R-rated films.

In another inquiry the FTC recruited a group of 13- to 16-year-old teens to attempt to purchase tickets to R-rated movies. The 2010 study discovered that 33 percent of these undercover teenagers were able to buy a ticket.[54] The enforcement problem is exacerbated at the mall multiplex theaters with their dozen or more screens where underage teens may have older patrons buy their tickets for them. Another tactic is for teens to buy tickets for a PG or PG-13 movie and then sneak into an R-rated one when the ushers are preoccupied or for a 17-year-old to purchase multiple tickets, which they then distribute to underage teens when theaters are especially busy. Of course, there may also be parents and guardians who buy tickets for their children but not for themselves.[55]

A proposed solution is to require a photo-ID akin to an adult driving license. But multiple problems exist with this proposal. First, it likely will delay the admission process and cause long lines at particular times and for very popular movies. Another problem is that children grow quickly and their photo-IDs will have to be changed regularly, possibly every year. And unless the government or school systems require such an ID, children from poorer families or immigrant families may not have one unless they are provided free. Even though a photo-ID system may not resolve the enforcement issue totally, it may address the more blatant attempts to gain admission to restricted film fare. A foolproof way to ensure box office enforcement probably does not exist. Still, a cooperative effort by the MPAA, theater owners, and parents working together could diminish the circumvention problem.

## Censorship vs. Classification

What options exist for a democratic society, such as the U.S. with a strong commitment to the First Amendment rights of speech and press, to regulate screen sex and violence? A democratic country is presented with only two choices since government censorship is severely limited in a free society. First, it may take a laissez-faire attitude toward popular entertainment, leaving the choice entirely up to market forces and responsible parents. Under a "hands-off" policy, sex and violent films could be shown to any audience. Government would abstain from playing a regulatory role. Many politicians and parents would consider such a laissez-faire policy irresponsible.

Furthermore, government censorship, where the state either owns and controls the production and distribution of films or has the authority to exercise final approval prior to general exhibition, is anathema to First Amendment theory and unacceptable to a free society. Such action is what legal scholars consider "prior restraint." When Muslim states in the Middle East would not permit the gay film *Brokeback Mountain* (2005) to be shown, the film's distributor had to cancel its bookings. When Pakistan banned *The Da Vinci Code* (2006) and Middle Eastern governments cut scenes from *Syriana* (2005) for political reasons, these countries were exercising "prior restraint" or censorship.[56]

If these actions had been committed by an American government, they would have run counter to Supreme Court decisions dating back to the 1920s, since the Justices consistently have ruled against government efforts at censorship, except for national security reasons and for the distribution of obscene material.[57] No Washington administration could impose such content restrictions even if it had the desire.

Common sense rules out a laissez-faire policy and democratic theory repudiates government censorship. Wherever feasible, self-regulation is preferred over government control, and this is the path taken by the film industry with the creation of the rating system. In its present form, however, the Hollywood-based age classification system fails to either shield children from adult material or reassure parents that their children are viewing films appropriate to their respective age group.

While the author supports self-regulation, the Hollywood application of the rating process to motion pictures is flawed in three respects. Adapting the three BBFC reforms proposed by the author:

- Replace the current R and NC-17 categories with an 18 classification
- Apply the film rating to each theater patron
- Devise effective enforcement procedures at the box office

should restore integrity, honesty, and common sense to the Hollywood rating system.

## Hollywood's Social Responsibility

If Hollywood were in the business of selling tobacco and alcohol to youngsters or dispensing prescription drugs instead of providing entertainment, the American public would expect some sort of regulation to protect children and the public interest. The use of tobacco, alcohol, and drugs has been demonstrated to be harmful to individual health, and their abuse may pose a serious danger to public safety. Entertainment, specifically film, is not harmful per se, but is it harmless? Even though social science research has failed to prove a causal connection between exposure to screen violence and the perpetuation of real violence, this does not absolve the film industry of all social responsibility, nor should it serve as an obstruction to reform.

The results of the first FTC report into Hollywood's marketing practices in 2000 exposed the industry as indifferent to the welfare of children when profits are at stake. The commission's review of the entertainment industries revealed, not surprisingly, that Hollywood was in the practice of marketing violent fare to children. Specifically, the FTC report uncovered the following wrongdoings: (1) previewing R-rated (for violence) films during the showing of G-rated movies, (2) using youngsters (9–12 years old) to test market their R-rated films, (3) targeting R-rated films to youngsters under 17, and (4) at least half of the theaters reviewed at the time admitted underage children to R-rated films that required an accompanying adult.[58] Despite these findings, Congress failed to take any legislative action and, after days of hearings, could solicit only a promise from several film studios to cease the above practices. Whether the failure to act was due to congressional First Amendment concerns, the strength of the Hollywood lobby, a lack of any visible interest on the part of parents, or a combination of these factors, the film industry escaped sanctions and departed Washington chastised but undeterred.

The question of the effects of film images on social behavior is still under scrutiny. Powerful organizations such as the American Medical Association, American Psychological Association, American Academy of Pediatrics, and the National Institutes of Mental Health maintain that a limited and circumstantial linkage exists between violent images and behavior, especially among the young and impressionable. In the first longitudinal study of the long-term effects of media violence on youngsters,[59] University of Michigan researchers examined aggressive behavior of children exposed to media violence in 1977 and then reexamined them 15 years later. While the researchers admitted that aggression is the product of complex variables, they nonetheless concluded that, other factors being equal, children who view a substantial amount of media violence are more likely to express aggressive behavior later as adults, particularly when children identify with an aggressor who is rewarded for his or her bad behavior. Even though most of the exposure was to television violence, the study implied an extension to film violence as well. More recently, studies by the Academy of Pediatrics support previous research that indicates a causal relationship between media violence and aggressive behavior. The Academy noted that of 1,000 research studies conducted on the causal relationship, only roughly 3 percent could find no relationship between the two variables. The Academy concluded that the evidence linking media violence and aggression is almost as strong as the connection between smoking and lung cancer. Admittedly, media violence is not the main cause for societal violence, but it is believed to be a contributing factor.[60]

Other research studies, here and abroad, refute these findings and argue that real violence, rather than fictional violence, is the culprit. The debate is similar to the one fought over pornography in the seventies and eighties and is unlikely to be resolved empirically. Moreover, attempts by plaintiffs to use the courts to win damages against particular films that allegedly caused harm to them or others have been unsuccessful.[61] Therefore, the real issue should be whether the film industry, like other businesses, has an obligation to act with greater circumspection and concern for the public welfare. In fact, is this not what Hollywood did after the 9/11 terrorist attacks when the studios delayed the distribution of films with terrorist themes? If film lacks the power to persuade or influence, why postpone the scheduled openings? Could it be that the distribution of these films so soon after 9/11 would demonstrate that art and reality had the potential to be disturbingly similar?

Fortunately, parents today have access to help from sources other than Hollywood. There are Internet sources to assist them by providing content information. Several Internet sites provide film reviews from a religious perspective. Chuck Colson, a born-again former Watergate participant, includes a list of recommended films with Christian themes on his *breakpoint.com* website. Another Christian web site is *movieguide.org*, which rates films on their "redemptive themes and inspiration." Parents also may consult *www.moviemom.com*, a website which reviews films specifically for children. Another website, *kids-in-mind.com*, provides parents with a 0 to 10 scale to indicate the amount and context of sex, nudity, violence, gore, and profanity in a film. For example, in the teen-marketed film *Fired Up!* (2009), two high school football players decide to attend cheerleader camp rather than football camp. Any parent with imagination can readily see the sexual possibilities of two young teenage boys among 300 female cheerleaders. In its review, using a 0 to 10 scale with 10 as the highest rating, *kids-in-mind* assigned a 7 for sex or nudity, 4 for violence, and 5 for profanity. *Kids-in-mind* also provided details of at least 10 scenes in which sex (usually implied) or nudity were involved and left it up to parents to determine the film's suitability for their children.[62] Two other web sites, *screenit.com* and *filmvalues.com*, also provide fairly comprehensive and useful film guides for parents. For instance, *screenit.com*'s review of *American Pie 2* runs nine pages, informing parents that the film contains a heavy dose of profanity, sex or nudity, and alcohol and drug use. This may be more than parents want to read, but at least there is no longer an excuse for parents to claim ignorance about the content of a particular film.

The Catholic Church, which initiated its Legion of Decency in the 1930s to influence film content, today offers its faithful a classification system based on moral values to compare with the Hollywood version offered by CARA. The Church's film classification ratings, provided by its Catholic News Service (CNS) at *http://www.usccb.org/movies* and sponsored by the U.S. Catholic Bishops' Office of Film and Broadcasting, largely parallels CARA's film ratings. Catholic parents, as well as other denominations, may find it useful in selecting films for their children's viewing. Below is a side-by-side comparison:

Table 4.2. CARA Ratings and Catholic Church Classifications

| CARA ratings | Catholic Church classifications |
|---|---|
| **G:** General Audiences | **A-I:** General Patronage |
| **PG:** Parental Guidance Suggested | **A-II:** Adults & Adolescents |
| **PG-13:** Parents Strongly Cautioned | **A-III:** Adults |
| **R:** Restricted for under 17<br>**NC-17:** No one under 17 admitted | **A-IV:** Adults, with reservations (films that require analysis & explanation) |
| | **L:** Limited Adult Audiences (films that contain problematic content that many adults would find troubling) |
| | **O:** Morally Offensive (films that previously might have been condemned by the Church or found morally objectionable) |

When the author compared ratings assigned by CARA and the Catholic Church to a few recent films, there were agreements and differences. Take the film *Hyde Park on Hudson*, about FDR's personal life. CARA gave it an R-rating while CNS gave it its O-rating. Essentially, both systems found the film "offensive." Two other examples are instructive. CARA applied its R-rating to the controversial *Zero Dark Thirty* (2012), but the Church placed it in the L-rating rather than applying its O-rating. *Zero* contains no sex, but it does have violence and roughly 30 minutes of torture scenes. The film presented the Church with an opportunity to express its moral objection to torture. Instead, it relied on the L-rating, a weak, ambiguous rebuke. Finally, the documentary *Bully* presents an interesting contrast in classifying films. Initially CARA assigned a restricted rating, which would have prevented teenagers from viewing the film. On appeal, CARA recanted and gave it a PG-13 after a few cuts. On the other hand, the Church, which could have placed it in its A-11 category, decided to give it an A-111, making it objectionable for teenagers, the film's target audience, to view it or for the film to be shown in Catholic schools. In the documentary a 16-year-old girl is subjected to persecution in her Oklahoma town for being an avowed lesbian. Here is a teenager being treated cruelly because of her sexual orientation. Instead of seizing this opportunity to speak out strongly against such behavior, the Church failed to find the courage to support a victim of incessant bullying.

In order for any rating system to gain respectability, its application must be logical and executed with common sense, compassion, and understanding. Parents and the film industry have an opportunity to transform self-regulation into an effective instrument to protect children from adult material and to ward off any government intervention. The potential exists for a meaningful film rating system if parents exert their will and if Hollywood accepts its social responsibility.

# Chapter 5

# HUAC and the Blacklist
## The Red Scare Comes to Hollywood

"I could answer the question…but if I did I would hate myself in the morning."
—Ring Lardner Jr. before HUAC

"I cannot and will not cut my conscience to fit this year's fashions."
—Lillian Hellman on "naming names" to HUAC

"Joe couldn't find a Communist in Red Square—he didn't know Karl Marx from Groucho."
—George Reedy on McCarthy

"There was bad faith and good, honesty and dishonesty, courage and cowardice, selflessness and opportunism, wisdom and stupidity, good and bad on both sides…in the end…we were all victims…no one emerged from that long nightmare without sin."
—Dalton Trumbo, on the HUAC hearings

In a scene at the end of Irwin Winkler's 1991 film, *Guilty by Suspicion*, actor Robert De Niro, playing a prominent film director falsely accused of being a communist, rises from his chair and shouts at the members of the congressional committee interrogating him: "Shame on you! Shame on you!" Television viewers old enough to remember the Army-McCarthy hearings might recall a similar scene where special counsel for the army, Joseph Welch, turns to the senator from Wisconsin and says, "Have you no sense of decency, sir, at long last? Have you left no sense of decency?"

Unfortunately, that final scene in *Suspicion* is the highlight of a rather lackluster film about life in post-World War II Hollywood where the real drama being played out was far more exciting and tumultuous than anything portrayed on screen. The industry was so embarrassed by its performance during the HUAC hearings that *Guilty by Suspicion* represents only one of four major feature films that Hollywood has released about that dark period in film history when friends turned against friends, colleagues accused other colleagues, and the studios, succumbing to the political pressure of the day, instituted an industry-wide blacklist in an effort to demonstrate their loyalty and patriotism. Of course, a few filmmakers masked their insinuations behind the façade of western melodramas such as *High Noon* and *Johnny Guitar* (1953). Although both these films had western narratives, insiders recognized them as metaphors for HUAC and the blacklist.[1]

Of the four films with explicit blacklist plots, the first, *The Way We Were* (1973), and the most recent, *The Majestic* (2001), are essentially love stories sugar-coated with nostalgia for the good old days of the 1950s. In *The Way We Were*, a WASPish Robert Redford falls in love with leftist radical Barbra Streisand. This two-hour film portrays their wavering romance and marriage as they relocate from New York to Hollywood, where Redford works as a screenwriter and Streisand embarrasses him with her leftist politics. During its second hour the film focuses on the HUAC hearings, with Redford's character choosing not to get involved while Streisand supports the Hollywood Ten, members of the film industry who refused to testify and instead publicly denounced the committee. Eventually the pair split and go their separate ways, although it is clear to the audience that they still love each other. Arthur Laurents, who wrote the screenplay, later would claim that the film was altered to soften the politics and emphasize the love story.[2] *The Majestic* is an overlong dramatic vehicle for actor Jim Carrey, who stars as a Hollywood writer blacklisted for communist activities during his college years. Depressed and drunk, Carrey is involved in an auto accident, loses his memory, settles in a small coastal town, and is mistaken by the local theater owner for his lost son. The bulk of the film concerns the renovation of the town's old movie theater and a budding romance. Eventually the FBI catches up with Carrey and he is subpoenaed to appear before HUAC. His memory restored, Carrey's character rejects his previous willingness to testify and "name names" in favor of a heroic stand that challenges the committee on First Amendment grounds, a position which was never accepted either by Congress or the courts. Carrey walks out of the committee a hero, rejects Hollywood, and returns to the small town where he is last seen selling tickets for the movie *Invasion of the Body Snatchers*.

At least in *The Front* (1976) and *Guilty by Suspicion* HUAC and the blacklist were dealt with more directly. *The Front* is the first feature film that compelled Hollywood to confront its past. In the film, Woody Allen plays a cashier/bookie who lends his name to blacklisted writers, a tactic actually used by several of the Hollywood Ten. Allen's character is apolitical but his willingness to serve as a "front" has more to do with paying off his gambling debts than principle. When he is discovered and called to testify, Allen does a Hollywood turnabout, develops a political conscience, and refuses to "name names." He defiantly walks out of the hearings, telling the committee members "you can go fuck yourselves." Possibly to protect itself, the film concerned blacklisting in the television industry rather than the movies, surprising since the screen credits listed half-a-dozen Hollywood artists who had suffered through the real blacklist. Still, the film comes closest to showing the tragic effects of blacklisting, which the film industry refused to acknowledge for many years.

*Guilty by Suspicion* touches on the effect the blacklist had on people in the industry. It could have expressed stronger sentiments against HUAC and the blacklist except for the fact that even after 40 years Hollywood lacked the courage to face up to its past. In the original screenplay by blacklisted writer Abraham Polonsky, the De Niro character was supposed to be a former party member called before HUAC, a situation closer to the real events played out in 1947. When director Irwin Winkler changed the status of the De Niro character from party member to non-communist, Polonsky had his name removed from the film credits.[3] Though Polonsky's stand may have been a victory for the integrity of the creative process, it also was a tacit admission that communists had worked in the film industry.

The truth of the matter is that the film industry succumbed to the Red Scare hysteria that engulfed America in the 1950s. The one significant resistance to the HUAC hearings was the failure of the Screen Directors Guild (SDG) to impose a loyalty oath on all filmmakers, a proposal that would have barred a director with communist membership or affiliation from making any more films in Hollywood.[4] The truth is that the industry resorted to blacklisting as an industrial weapon, first against the trade unions and later against employees named during the HUAC investigations. To put the Hollywood blacklist in perspective, a brief summary of the post–World War II period is in order.

## Cold War America, 1945-55

In retrospect, the decade following the end of World War II might best be described as another watershed in American history. The U.S. emerged as the economic and political leader of the democratic West in a bipolarized world fraught with danger, where a wrong decision or misunderstood movement could trigger nuclear war. That fear of total destruction hung like Damocles' sword over the decade, leading schools to prepare children for a possible atomic attack and frightening some people into building bomb shelters in their backyards.

Culturally, the more interesting projects of the decade were being created for the new medium of television, while Hollywood retreated into producing predictable dramas, inane comedies, and musicals as the studios sought to meet the challenge of TV with gimmicks (3-D movies) and new technology (cinemascope projection). A few "message" films about racism and bigotry were made at this time but in the wake of the prison sentences handed out to the Hollywood Ten and the blacklisting of unfriendly witnesses, the studios played it safe by also releasing a number of films that warned of the communist menace.

As the fifties approached, Americans had settled down in their suburban homes, content to enjoy their new consumer goods. But the break with the Soviet Union over numerous postwar issues provided the catalyst for the anti-communism campaign that erupted in the country. This campaign of fear was manipulated by a political opportunist named Joseph McCarthy, the junior senator from Wisconsin, whose wild assertions and unsubstantiated charges created an atmosphere of such terror that the term "McCarthyism" came to define the decade.

## McCarthyism and the Red Scare

In truth, there were two "Red Scares" in American history. The first occurred after the World War I, when Attorney-General Palmer in the Wilson administration conducted a series of "roundup raids," led by a young FBI agent named J. Edgar Hoover. This was in response to the Bolshevik victory in Russia and attacks at home against prominent capitalists, government officials, and public figures. The raids took on the character of "collective sweeps" common to totalitarian regimes, where the government arrests political activists, suspected radicals, and "outsiders" with the wrong religion or ethnicity and places them into one generic category labeled "subversive" and "dangerous" to national security. In 1919, during one 12-city sweep against the Union of Russian Workers, the federal government made 300 arrests, resulting in the deportation of 199 workers. The following year, raids in 33 cities led to 591 deportations and over 4,000 arrests; more than half of those arrested were subsequently released.[5] This fear of subversion from within led to the imposition of immigration quotas in the 1920s and helped to create the atmosphere of intolerance that led to the injustices that tainted the Sacco and Vanzetti trial, the Italian-born anarchists who were executed for the deaths of two men during a robbery. Historians today believe that the men were convicted primarily because of their political beliefs.

There was no middle ground in this internal war: you were either for America or against it, either a patriot or a traitor. The seeds of nativism and anti-radical hysteria, planted after World War I, were waiting to resurface when the "right person at the right time" appeared. That person turned out to be the junior senator from Wisconsin.

## McCarthyism

So much has been written about Joe McCarthy that his life story is easily accessible:[6] his early childhood in Appleton, Wisconsin, his rather humble beginnings, his decision to quit school and go to work, his subsequent return to education to complete law school, and finally, his determination to enter politics. What is remarkable about McCarthy's early career is its lack of any discernible characteristics: he loses some electoral races and wins others. His military service record is also undistinguished. His first significant electoral victory came in 1946 when he defeated the popular senator Robert Lafollette for the Republican nomination and went on to whip his Democratic opponent in the general election.

After three years in the U.S. Senate, McCarthy had a moderate voting record: in foreign affairs, he voted in favor of the North Atlantic Treaty Organization (NATO), the Marshall Plan, and aid to Greece and Turkey; in domestic matters he voted for high price supports for farmers and followed the advice of Republican Party leaders on other issues. His political career languishing, McCarthy seized the opportunity presented during the traditional Lincoln Day Birthday address and turned it into political capital when he discarded his prepared speech on housing in favor of one on communism.

The rest is history. McCarthy never had a list of State Department employees who were communists nor did he have any plan in mind. He was an astute politician, grabbing headlines by announcing daily charges of new communists discovered in the government, academia, and the military. His accusation that there were 205 communists in the State Department would be pared down to 57 and eventually reduced to four names supplied by his staff. McCarthy had a knack for manipulating the media, providing newspapers and broadcasters with tomorrow's headlines. At the same time he was as much a creation of the media as any contemporary rock star, whose entourage of reporters printed accusations without checking or verifying them first. McCarthy was instant news, driving even President Eisenhower off the front page. The senator came to dominate the news during the five years of his ascendancy (1950–54) to such an extent that historians refer to this period as "McCarthyism," adding a new word to the American political vocabulary. That word became synonymous with "the practice of publicizing accusations of political disloyalty or subversion with insufficient regard to evidence."[7]

In sum, McCarthy exploited the political situation and capitalized on weakness and vulnerability. Recently released documents from the fifties reveal that McCarthy held secret examinations of witnesses as a sort of dress rehearsal for his subcommittee's public hearings.[8] The results of these quasi-official hearings determined whether the witness would be subpoenaed to appear before the whole committee. As a consequence, some witnesses like writer Dashiell Hammett were recalled, while others, like composer Aaron Copland, were excused, apparently on the basis of their resistance to McCarthy's bullying tactics or their perceived inability to provide dramatic theater for his media appearances. Hammett, for instance, took on the persona of his tough guy fictional detective, Sam Spade, when he remarked after being sentenced for his refusal to give up names: "If it were more than jail, if it were my life, I would give it for what I think democracy is, and I don't let cops or judges tell me what I think democracy is."[9]

Historian Albert Fried maintains that McCarthyism cannot be adequately understood by a simple explanation.[10] Instead Fried offers a more complex definition and demonstrates that, unlike previous brief Red Scares, the effects of McCarthyism lasted for decades. For example, Hollywood refused until recently to acknowledge the wrong done to blacklisted writers and directors; only in 1997 were the pseudonyms and "fronts" removed from 47 films produced during the Red Scare era and replaced by the names of their creators.[11] Second, Fried holds McCarthy responsible for creating anxiety in the hearts of 1960s liberal democrats at any sign of weakness toward communism during the Cold War. This fear, according to Fried, supposedly drove the administrations of John Kennedy and Lyndon Johnson into the Bay of Pigs and Vietnam. Finally, Fried believes McCarthyism illustrates the abuse of power by the government and its agents, encouraging errant behavior on the part of the FBI and the Justice Department.

McCarthyism was not nurtured in a vacuum. Its context is best understood as a mixture of fact and fiction stimulated by public fear and intolerance and promoted by the media. McCarthy was good copy, and by making him front-page news, the media provided credibility to his accusations. One journalist who stood up to McCarthy, Edward R. Murrow, challenged him on his CBS TV News program, *See it Now*. That pivotal clash is depicted in George Clooney's film *Good Night, and Good Luck* (2005), which received six Oscar nominations but won none. As one reviewer noted, what the film proved is that "television…can be both a potent vehicle for demagoguery and a weapon in the fight against it."[12]

While an active CPUSA did exist, the U.S. government could only speculate on the actual number of hardcore Stalinists dedicated to overthrowing the institutions of government by force and violence. It seems fruitless to guess that there were 100,000 or 10,000 members because joiners moved in and out of the party and others attended local meetings without becoming members. What is much easier to account for in the Cold War hysteria was Soviet imperialism in eastern Europe, the fall of China, the outbreak of the Korean War, the disclosure of the Amerasis spy ring that left the Foreign Service vulnerable to accusations, the passing of atomic secrets to the Soviets by the Rosenbergs, and the subsequent Soviet detonation of a nuclear device. These political realities provided substance to the perception of a legitimate communist threat; opinion polls overwhelmingly showed that the public would allow the government to outlaw the Communist Party, force communists to register, and bar them from college and university teaching.[13] In other words, current events and public opinion lent comfort and support to McCarthy and his political allies. Biographer Ted Morgan insists, however, that the most sordid aspect of McCarthyism was the failure and cowardice of his Senate colleagues, who knew him best, to stand up and expose him for what he was—a bully and a drunk.[14] Instead, Washington encouraged him by its silence.

As a political phenomenon, McCarthyism may be interpreted in three ways. One is to see it as the articulation of working-class intolerance, a sort of lower class reaction against intellectualism, as McCarthy regularly railed against academics and intellectuals. Another is to place it within a historical line of American paranoia that exhibits a deep distrust of elites and strangers, a suspicion ripe for exploitation by an adept demagogue, dating back to the nativism and populism of the 19th century. Third, and more positively, his downfall after the Army-McCarthy hearings represents a national rejection of extremism. Simply put, McCarthy had gone too far in his accusations and had exceeded American limits of tolerance.[15] On the negative side, Americans also had to share in the blame for their public support of his methods. Quite possibly Shakespeare summed it up best in *Julius Caesar* when he wrote, "The fault, dear Brutus, lies not in our stars but in ourselves."

## A Conservative Dream: Redeeming McCarthy

Fifty years after the junior senator from Wisconsin died of liver failure at the age of 48, neo-conservatives are trying to restore creditability to McCarthy's anti-communist crusade and, in the process, redeem his political reputation. The task is daunting, but journalist M. Stanton Evans makes a valiant effort to defend McCarthy against his critics.[16] Evans's thesis is straightforward: communism in the fifties posed a real threat to the U.S. and McCarthy alerted the country to the danger. Using new information from FBI files as well as evidence from Soviet sources, Evans presents a revisionist portrait of the junior senator that contradicts the image of the modern demagogue whose name became synonymous with witch-hunting, slander, innuendo, and the clever manipulation of facts and rumors from which to draw communist inferences. Instead, Evans insists that McCarthy was victimized by the liberal left for warning Americans of the conspiracy in the administrations of FDR and Truman that allowed China and parts of Europe to fall under communist control and that permitted spies, secret agents, and fellow travelers to infiltrate the government.

Evans believes that McCarthy served his country well by exposing suspected communists and spies. It was up to law enforcement and the legal system to arrest, convict, and imprison such persons. But that was precisely the point expressed by attorney Joseph Welsh at the Army-McCarthy hearings when he challenged Roy Cohn, a McCarthy aide, to turn over the names of all the communists working in defense plants to the FBI so the agency could do its job. As usual, those suspected "commies" never materialized. This was a customary McCarthy tactic, that is, to warn that there were 200 communists in the State Department or that our overseas facilities contained 30,000 pro-Red books without providing any hard evidence. His strategy was to insinuate, suggest, and make inferences rather than supply specific documentation. When all of McCarthy's accusations and investigations are analyzed, the results are rather paltry. Citing Soviet sources, the best Evans can do in McCarthy's defense is to justify the 10 names of communists who worked in the federal government. Even if these 10 were documented as legitimate communists, the price America paid for "McCarthyism" was extravagantly high.

On the other charge, that the policies of the Democratic administrations of Roosevelt and Truman "lost" China to the communists and allowed the Soviets to dominate Eastern Europe after World War II, most American historians, like David Oshinsky,[17] disagree. China was lost despite billions of dollars in aid due to the corruption of the Chiang Kai-shek government, and Soviet penetration into Europe was, at best, a mistake in judgment extended to an ally who had suffered greatly from the war. Allowing the Russian Army to enter triumphantly into Eastern Europe, where they remained to rig elections, was a wartime mistake rather than a pro-communist conspiracy on the part of the Allies. Besides, Oshinsky points out, the Truman administration's policy of aid to Greece and Turkey prevented those countries from falling under Soviet domination. Mistakes were made, but to label it "a conspiracy so immense" is to grant McCarthy more credit than he deserves.

## Hollywood and the Blacklist

### Against Labor

Hollywood has never admitted to the practice of "blacklisting," an underhanded way of depriving a person of his/her livelihood without formal acknowledgment. Those blacklisted are frequently locked out of a whole industry or line of work as employers conspire against them. It is a form of punishment without trial and Hollywood has used it twice against its artists and employees. Years before HUAC came to Hollywood and McCarthyism became a national phenomenon, the film industry resorted to the blacklist in an attempt to prevent unionization.

Mike Nielsen and Gene Mailes have documented the complete story of early blacklisting in the film industry.[18] The authors argue that Hollywood was not only anti-communist, it was also anti-union. The industry fought unionization in the courts and on the streets.[19] Labor organizing in the entertainment industry began in the 1890s when stagehands sought to protect themselves against exploitation by theater managers. The organizing process eventually would reach the motion picture industry, involving all craft workers (carpenters, electricians, and painters) employed in film production. These laborers worked long hours under poor conditions and without benefits. While the studios employed a hardcore of regular workers, most of the laborers had to "shape-up" every day, similar to conditions on the waterfront. Apparently, the industry had a "sweetheart" arrangement with organized crime whereby mob bosses "fronted" for the company union, keeping wages and benefits low in return for payoffs from the studios. This is not a story likely to show up in any Hollywood film.

Not until 1926 did the International Alliance of Theatrical & Stage Employees (IA) and the studios sign the first labor agreement that provided for negotiations over wages, hours, working conditions, and grievances. Referred to as the Studio Basic Agreement, it became the cornerstone for labor relations within the film industry. In the thirties, discontent over labor conditions led the professional employees—the writers, actors and directors—to create their own unions along the lines of the medieval guilds. Later these active leaders in the labor movement were the ones called to appear before HUAC, where they learned that their names appeared on the industry's blacklist.

As elsewhere, labor organizing in Hollywood did not come easily or peacefully. In fact, labor unrest and violence cover three decades of Hollywood history; this was a labor-management war every bit as intense as any military engagement, with reports of arbitrary firings, beatings by goon squads, mob murders, violent clashes on picket lines, and collusion of the studios with organized crime figures like Chicago gangster Frank Nitti. It is also a story of jurisdictional strikes and clashes within the labor movement for control of the film industry. Although several strikes occurred in the thirties, labor was committed to its "no strike" pledge during World War II, a pledge that the CPUSA endorsed against the wishes of a few labor leaders. But it was during the postwar strikes from 1945 to 1947 that union-studio confrontations became quite nasty. One 1945 strike at Warner Brothers, in particular, was so vicious that it earned the label "Bloody Friday." Some 1,000 strikers set up a mass picket line around Warner Studios and were confronted by company security, non-strikers, and local police. The ensuing two-hour melee resulted in 40 injuries when the picketers were dispersed with tear gas, clubs, and fire hoses. Screenwriter Dalton Trumbo, one of the Hollywood Ten, described the day as "fascism in action."[20] The following Monday, the picket line was broken by police and non-strikers using metal chains, clubs, and battery cables, resulting in more bloodshed. Additional injuries occurred when Warner Brothers had its security cops drop heavy bolts on unsuspecting picketers from a five-story sound stage. To make sure that strikers did not return the next day, the studio hired a private "goon squad" to beat up those who were still walking the picket lines. In total, almost 150 persons required hospitalization or suffered physical injuries during the course of the strike.

Even more insidious than the physical violence was the conspiracy by the major studios to "blackball" the participating strikers by placing the names of union activists on a sheet of unsigned paper, which circulated among the film studios and the independents. The Hollywood blacklist indicated that the persons named should be fired if they were working or not hired if they applied for work. For example, labor organizer Irv Hentschel, who formed the IA Progressives, lost his job because of his union activities. Under union rules, Hentschel, a machinist by trade, was listed as eligible to work, but he received zero calls from the studios. He finally decided to call the studios directly and was told that the word around the industry was not to hire him.[21] Hentschel's name had landed on the "invisible" blacklist.

Another tactic used by the film studios and their mobster henchmen at this time was to label union organizers and activists as "communists." This strategy aimed to discredit union advocates, isolate studio dissenters, and label them as "un-American" workers. When the union bosses who fronted for the mob and the film studios wanted to purge the IA of local troublemakers, they filed "conduct unbecoming a loyal member of the union" charges,

# HUAC and the Blacklist

which required a union trial. All the IA progressives were cited as "communists," even though only one of the five local leaders was a party member at the time.[22]

The Hollywood blacklist, then, was a product of the early labor wars in the industry; this strategy of labeling foes as "communists" or "un-American" was later used during the HUAC hearings to discredit both the post–World War II peace movement and the promotion of civil rights. Discrediting a foe or a movement by labeling was still in vogue in the 1980s, as evidenced by President Reagan's characterization of nuclear freeze proponents as "communists."[23] When HUAC came to town in 1947, the atmosphere in Hollywood was conducive to a public trial that would expose, and then exorcise, the evil forces that plagued the industry after WWII, including the new competitor—television. The hearings provided an opportunity for the studios to silence activists, for individuals to pay back personal grudges, and for politicians to exploit patriotism to advance their careers.

## Against Communists, Radicals, and Liberals

The HUAC investigation of the film industry occurred in three stages. Initially, HUAC met informally with studio heads and individual actors, many of whom were members of the conservative Motion Picture Alliance for the Preservation of American Ideals (the Alliance), an organization that worked with the committee to cleanse Hollywood of communists and other radicals. These were the so-called "friendly" witnesses, who provided the committee with names of communists or reinforced the suspicion already held by the committee about particular colleagues.[24] Often their testimony was based on rumor and gossip. For example, Walt Disney named the League of Women Voters as a communist group without proof or fear of cross-examination. Film stars Adolphe Menjou, Robert Taylor, and Gary Cooper[25] cited persons who associated with actor-singer Paul Robeson or others who had criticized the U.S. Constitution and the government in Washington. Based on this sort of testimony, HUAC created a list of 79 "named communists" scheduled to be called before the committee. In October 1947, HUAC narrowed the list to 19 Hollywood writers, directors, producers, and actors, issuing them subpoenas to appear before the committee. Of those subpoenaed, 11 appeared (Bertolt Brecht, the last to appear, claimed that he was not a communist and departed for Europe), leaving the 10 "unfriendly" witnesses (the Hollywood Ten) to be cited for contempt. As punishment they were sent to prison for their refusal to answer the committee's questions. The final act in the drama occurred during the second round of hearings between 1951 and 1953, when HUAC subpoenaed the remaining eight people on the original list in addition to others identified during the hearings. It was during this stage that witnesses broke down (actor Larry Parks begged the committee not to force him to "name names"), others recanted (director Edward Dmytryk, one of the original Hollywood Ten, admitted his communist past and named 26 of his colleagues as communists), while still others purged themselves of their radical pasts by reciting every conceivable name they could remember. According to one source, 58 informers recited 902 names before the committee, an average of 29 names per witness.[26] Some witnesses, like former communist turned FBI informer Harvey Matusow, provided hundreds of names to the committee but later recanted and admitted most were lies.[27] If the reader discounts duplications, the informers identified roughly 200 Hollywood artists as "communists" associated with the film industry. The total blacklisted probably exceeded the 200, since the ones with valid passports left the country to seek work elsewhere and others who remained were "graylisted." That is, they found work in the industry scarce because they had supported the Hollywood Ten or worked for left-liberal causes. The "graylisted" were victims of "guilt by association," best illustrated on screen by the De Niro character in *Guilty by Suspicion*. The exact number of film industry people blacklisted is unlikely to be ever publicized but estimates range as high as 250.[28] A few like Trumbo, John Howard Lawson, and Polonsky eventually would resume their film careers, while others were less fortunate and often forced to take odd jobs to survive. It is estimated that only 10 percent of those blacklisted returned to work in the film industry.[29] Possibly the saddest aspect of the HUAC hearings was that the committee already had knowledge of the activities of many of those named. What the committee wanted from witnesses was a public confession, similar to the Stalinist purges of the 1930s. This aspect of the Hollywood investigations caused its critics to claim that the purpose of the hearings was for public entertainment staged by members of the committee to further their political careers.

## The Hollywood Ten: Heroes or Villains?

The drama that unfolded during the hearings of the original 10 "unfriendly witnesses" was not accidental or even spontaneous. HUAC singled out the most professionally successful Hollywood liberals and radicals to interrogate, the implication being that while the 1947 hearings were about communism, some of the politicians and friendly witnesses took the opportunity to strike a blow against aggressive trade unionism and left-liberal political activism. Membership in Popular Front, radical, and peace organizations automatically placed an individual under HUAC's suspicion.[30] A majority of the Hollywood Ten, who were or had been members of CPUSA, adopted the strategy of attacking the committee's authority and its constitutionality under the First Amendment. But they faced a "catch-22" situation because if any one of them had answered "no" to the question, "Are you now or have you ever been a member of the Communist Party?", he would have been subject to perjury charges. On the other hand, by answering "yes" to the question, the witness was subjected to even more intensive questioning, increasing the chances of breaking down and "naming names." To the political left, the Hollywood Ten were heroes, standing up to demagogues and fascists. They drew support from their liberal colleagues, many of whom formed the Committee for the First Amendment and traveled to Washington to support the Ten during the hearings. The group petitioned Congress to disband HUAC and its members donated their time and celebrity status to fund-raising campaigns. However, most of the studio heads, the leadership of the various screen acting and writing guilds, and the members of the Alliance believed the Ten were everything from dangerous to naive. Actor Ward Bond, a leader in the Alliance and a close friend of John Wayne, lobbied the Motion Picture Academy not to give an Oscar to actor José Ferrer, whom Bond considered to be a communist well *before* the actor was subpoenaed to appear before the committee.[31]

Those who informed were either praised or despised. Some former party members, like director Edward Dmytryk, finally testified because they did not want to be punished for

# HUAC and the Blacklist

their past associations, especially since they no longer believed in the cause.[32] Dmytryk, in fact, had left the party before the hearings but still joined the Ten in their united strategy against HUAC and went to jail with them before deciding to testify. Others, such as screenwriter Leo Townsend, admitted their communist past and repented, seeking salvation through public confession. To Albert Maltz, one of the Hollywood Ten, there was no justification for "naming names." He considered the informers to be rats and he hated their guts. Trumbo, on the other hand, was more conciliatory, citing both "friendly" and "unfriendly" witnesses as victims of the postwar hysteria.[33]

To liberals, the Hollywood Ten were heroes for standing up to HUAC. To conservatives they were either gullible fools or enemies of the state. More than six decades later, time has not ended the debate. Film historian Richard Schickel decided to revisit the whole HUAC episode in Hollywood with more objectivity than the committee's supporters and detractors.[34] While Schickel makes it clear that he neither defends HUAC's performance nor the actions of the studio moguls who capitulated to the committee, he goes on record as confirming the wrong done to the Ten. He likens the whole episode to the line in the film *The Man Who Shot Liberty Valance*: "When the truth becomes legend, print the legend." It is time to set the record straight. Schickel makes the following points:

- The Hollywood Ten were either active members of the Communist Party or former members at the time of the hearings. But they had little, if any, influence over the films they wrote or directed. Moreover, while it is true that some of them were involved in a handful of pro-Soviet films (*Song of Russia*, *Mission to Moscow*), they did not initiate these projects.
- The Ten's strategy was to present a united front against HUAC by refusing to testify on free speech grounds, citing the First Amendment. But had they used the self-incrimination clause of the Fifth Amendment, it may have saved their careers. The Ten sought to make a political statement rather than a defense.
- The studio heads were wrong in imposing an industry-wide blacklist that affected hundreds of Hollywood people and that haunted the industry for decades.
- Not all the Ten held similar political beliefs; some like John Howard Lawson and Albert Maltz were zealous and dedicated communists while others like Edward Dmytrk and Adrian Scott were less enthusiastic followers. Lawson and Maltz remained bitter towards and unforgiving against those who "named names" or recanted. Afterwards, it was left to Dalton Trumbo to be more compassionate and conciliatory by characterizing all those involved in the hearings as "victims."

To Schickel, the real villains were HUAC and the studio moguls who aided and abetted them in their work. A generous heart could forgive the Ten for putting their faith in the theoretical dream of an equalitarian society. Might it be said of the Ten that they were idealists who believed in a false dream but were not evil men themselves? Their sin was to hold on to a misguided dream against all the evidence.

# Chapter Five

## The Unfriendly Witnesses

### The Original 11 Witnesses

**Alvah Bessie**: novelist and screenwriter; author of *Bread in the Stone*; wrote a screenplay (with Lester Cole) for two Errol Flynn World War II movies (*Northern Pursuit* and *Objective Burma*), supported the Spanish Republic, and served in the International Brigade and later in World War II.

**Herbert Biberman**: director and producer; co-produced the film *New Orleans* and directed the film *The Master Race*; married to blacklisted actress Gale Sondergaard; directed *Salt of the Earth*, a film project of blacklisted writers, directors, and actors.

**Lester Cole**: writer of 40 screenplays, including *None Shall Escape* and *Blood on the Sun* and co-author of *Objective Burma*; founder of the Screen Writer's Guild (SWG).*

**Edward Dmytryk**: noted director of such films as *Hitler's Children*, *Back to Bataan*, *Tender Comrade*, and *Crossfire*; resumed his career after becoming an informer.*

**Ring Lardner, Jr.**: writer, author of the screenplays for *Woman of the Year* and *Forever Amber*; co-author with Albert Maltz of the film *Cloak and Dagger*; served as officer of SWG; did not write under his own name until the 1965 script for *The Cincinnati Kid*.*

**John Howard Lawson**: critic and writer; author of numerous screenplays, including two Humphrey Bogart World War II films, *Action in the North Atlantic* and *Sahara*; served as president of SWG.*

**Albert Maltz**: novelist, playwright, and screenwriter; wrote scripts for *Destination Tokyo* and *Pride of the Marines* and the award-winning documentary *The House I Live In*; was "ghost writer" on film scripts for *The Robe* and *Broken Arrow*, receiving no screen credits.

**Samuel Ornitz**: novelist and author; wrote screenplays for *The Man Who Reclaimed His Head* and *Three Faces West*; after prison he turned his attention to research and writing.*

**Adrian Scott**: screenwriter and film producer of such films as *Crossfire* and *Murder My Sweet*; also wrote the script for the film *Mr. Lucky*.*

**Dalton Trumbo**: novelist and screenwriter; author of the anti-war novel *Johnny Got His Gun*; wrote scripts for *Thirty Seconds Over Tokyo*, *A Guy Named Joe*, and *Our Vines Have Tender Grapes*; also active in Hollywood trade union movement and SWG; wrote 30 scripts under pseudonyms during the blacklist.*

**Bertolt Brecht**: novelist, poet, and playwright. After his HUAC appearance, fled to Europe, thereby avoiding further interrogation and possible prosecution.

### The Remaining Eight Witnesses

**Richard Collins**: screenwriter for *Song of Russia*; served on the executive board of the SWG; turned informer during second round of HUAC hearings, 1951–53.*

**Gordon Kahn**: author and correspondent for *The Atlantic Monthly*; managing editor of *The Screen Writer*; served on SWG executive board.*

**Howard Koch**: scriptwriter for *Casablanca*, *Sergeant York*, and *Mission to Moscow*; served on SWG executive board.*

**Lewis Milestone**: film director of *All Quiet on the Western Front*, *A Walk in the Sun*, *Arch of Triumph*, and *Of Mice and Men*.

**Irving Pichel**: actor and director of *The Moon Is Down*, *OSS*, and *A Medal for Benny*.

**Larry Parks**: actor on verge of stardom after playing the lead in *The Jolson Story*; became an informer, which ruined his film career.

**Robert Rossen**: author and director; wrote screenplays for the World War II films *Edge of Darkness* and *A Walk in the Sun*; directed *Body and Soul* and *Johnny O'Clock*; served as officer in SWG; later became an informer.*

**Waldo Salt**: screenwriter for films like *Shopworn Angel* and *Mr. Winkle Goes to War*.*

\* Self-confessed or named as member of CPUSA.

## The Communist Threat in Hollywood

The search for communists, real and imagined, by HUAC and McCarthy's Senate Committee took a wide swipe through the unions, academia, the legal profession, the military, and even the clergy. Few occupations were spared during this national campaign allegedly designed to protect America's internal security from its enemies. But how strong was the CPUSA? The estimates of party membership ranged from J. Edgar Hoover's exaggerated half million to several thousand. As mentioned earlier, the exact number is impossible to determine since people moved freely in and out of the party. For example, writer and director Cy Endfield, named in the 1951 HUAC hearings, attended communist meetings during the thirties and forties but actually never joined the party.[35] Were people like Endfield included? Playwright Clifford Odets only spent six months in the party and then left. Was he among those included in the membership statistic? The best estimate of CPUSA membership at this time ranged anywhere from 10,000 to 100,000 members, most likely fluctuating between 30,000 and 50,000.[36] In addition to the transitory nature of party membership, left-liberals joined communists in a number of Popular Front causes against fascism during this period. One example was Charlie Chaplin. The actor was accused of being a communist for his leftist speeches and political activities. Congress even considered deporting him. Along with his political problems, Chaplin faced charges of tax evasion and paternity suits. He fled to his native England in 1952, eventually establishing residency in Switzerland. He did not return to the U.S. until 20 years later when Hollywood honored him for his lifetime achievement in cinema.[37] However, Chaplin's politics were inconsistent. He flirted with communism in the 1920s, deserted the cause in the thirties, and returned to the party when he believed that the Soviets were the singular anti-Nazi power in Europe.[38] Should people like Chaplin have been counted in the membership statistics? How many other Hollywood entertainment figures besides Chaplin pursued politically erratic paths but were counted as committed communists?

While the Red Scare dragnet snared many, the logical question remains: why focus on the entertainment industry? What harm could communists do in Hollywood? There are two very plausible reasons why HUAC considered Hollywood an attractive venue. First, and of paramount importance, was the obvious publicity that the discovery of communists active in the film industry would provide to the committee and its members. The Hollywood hearings had the potential to be as dramatic as anything on the silver screen since the appearance of recognized stars lent an air of show business to the entire proceedings. As it turned out, the hearings had the effect of furthering the political career of a young California representative named Richard Nixon.[39] The second reason is that the film industry, like all the popular arts, is vulnerable to public scrutiny. The arts attract creative people, free spirits who often ignore the rules of social conventions; artists are particularly drawn to new ideas and to critical analysis of the existing order. HUAC's focus on Hollywood is not surprising when the vulnerability of the arts is combined with whispered allegations by the American Legion[40] and printed accusations in publications like *Red Stars* and *Fellow Travelers in Hollywood*,[41] which listed some 200 Hollywood celebrities as "reds" and partners in a fifth column aimed at overthrowing the government.

How strong was the Communist Party in Hollywood? Out of thousands of studio employees, one source estimates local party membership at around 300 between 1936 and 1949.[42] Another assessment corroborates these statistics but breaks down party members according to their work in the film industry: 145 screenwriters, some 50–60 actors, 15–20 producers and directors, and another 60–90 back lot workers and office staff.[43] That figure totals 315, using the maximum estimates. But in 1952 HUAC announced that their investigations uncovered only 222 movie employees or their spouses who were or had been party members; this represented less than 1 percent of the film industry's entire workforce.[44] Like McCarthy, HUAC made a lot of noise but its results were less than impressive.

Regardless of their number, how influential were these party members? Their greatest effectiveness seemed to be in the trade union movement and in the SWG. HUAC focused in on the latter group since 16 of the first 19 witnesses were writers. This was likely due to the assumption that the scripts written by these writers were tainted with communist propaganda or else compromised American security. While it is true that the Ten and other party members and sympathizers wrote many film scripts in the thirties and forties, the reality of moviemaking under the old studio system was similar to a system of checks and balances; all film scripts were subject to internal review by studio heads and producers. Screenwriters never had the last word. As Dorothy B. Jones confirmed in her study of film content, it was virtually impossible to incorporate Marxist ideology into films produced by the major studios because

> the very nature of the film-making process which divides creative responsibility among a number of different people and which keeps ultimate control of content in the hands of top studio executives; the habitual caution of moviemakers with respect to film content; and the self-regulating practices of the motion picture industry prevented such propaganda from reaching the screen in all but possibly rare instances.[45]

# HUAC and the Blacklist

What is surprising is the fact that if HUAC considered the films themselves to be "subversive" or "dangerous to American security," would the committee not have wanted to examine their content firsthand? Instead, the committee rejected Dalton Trumbo's offer to view 18 of his film scripts, including several written for movies about World War II.[46] Had they accepted Trumbo's challenge, the committee would have discovered that the Hollywood Ten and the unfriendly witnesses had worked on many film favorites, including *The Wizard of Oz* (1939), *Lassie Come Home* (1943) and *It's a Wonderful Life* (1946).[47] Furthermore, subjecting the films involving the Hollywood Ten to content analysis reveals that the majority of their projects included topics that were strictly nonpolitical. For example, between 1929 and 1949 the Hollywood Ten participated in the making of 159 feature films in the following subject categories:

- 45 were a combination of biography and historical films, romances, love stories, and comedies;
- 28 were murder, mystery, and espionage films;
- 23 were war or military service films;
- 22 were social message films;
- 17 were westerns and action/adventure films; and
- 15 were gangster, crime, and prison films.[48]

Combining the above film subjects with strict studio supervision confirms that the bulk of the films made by the Ten were typical Hollywood entertainment fare, free from political ideology with the exception of war films.

History has brought the HUAC hearings into perspective. The committee could not have been interested in film content per se because if it had been, the studio heads would have been held accountable rather than the writers, directors, and actors. Films like *Song of Russia* and *Mission to Moscow*, for instance, were considered by HUAC's "friendly witnesses" to be pro-Red despite the fact that they were made with the blessing of MGM and Warner Brothers. Louis Mayer told HUAC he made *Song of Russia* because "Russia was an ally. It seemed the patriotic thing to do."[49]

Meanwhile, producer Jack Warner agreed to do *Mission to Moscow* at the request of the Roosevelt administration despite his concern that the film would not be attractive box office fare. There is a backstory to the making of *Mission to Moscow* that is recounted by T. Bennett in his 2001 historical article.[50] In 1943, President Franklin Roosevelt sent former ambassador Joseph E. Davies to the Soviet Union to arrange a meeting with Josef Stalin. Davies had written his memoir of his experience, which provided a favorable impression of Stalin and the Russian people and Warner Bros. had made it into a film. According to Bennett, FDR's plan was to use the flattering film to persuade Stalin not to enter into separate negotiations with Hitler and at the same time drum up support for the Soviets at home. It was a sound plan because Davies had approved the script and the final cut. Bennett reports that Davies was on the movie set almost daily. But because Jack Warner had business reservations about the film, FDR arranged a deal that would protect the industry from antitrust legislation (that would come later in 1948) in return for Warner Bros.' pledge to support the administration's foreign policies. Thus, the film was made without criticism of the purges or of the Soviet invasion of Finland, and it portrayed the Soviet Union as a non-totalitarian state. The president's strategy backfired, as it failed to halt Soviet aggression after the war.

Furthermore, both these films, as well as the pro-Soviet movie scripted by Lillian Hellman, *The North Star*, had to be vetted through the OWI. Ironically, two of HUAC's friendliest witnesses, director Sam Wood (first president of the Alliance) and actor Gary Cooper, both involved in *For Whom the Bell Tolls*, the pro-Republican film of the Spanish Civil War, never had their loyalty or patriotism questioned despite the film's admiration for the popular Spanish government instead of the U.S.-supported invaders of Generalissimo Franco. Clearly, film content was not what most concerned HUAC.

Suppose the Ten and the other unfriendly witnesses were all committed Stalinists who attended every cell meeting and followed every communist command—still their films required executive approval. It is now clear that the Ten and the other blacklisted victims were singled out because of their pro-union and off-screen political activities rather than for the content of their work. Possibly Ronald Reagan, head of the Screen Actors Guild (SAG) at the time, hit the nail on the head when he characterized the risk of having communists and subversives in the film industry in these terms: "The danger is not what is on the screen. It is what these people do behind the scenes to gain power in organizations to further their beliefs."[51] Thus, HUAC, with the collaboration of the film studios, some union leaders, and the Alliance, appears to have intended the 1947 Hollywood hearings and those held from 1951 to 1953 to put an end to what they considered to be radical unionism and leftist-liberal politics.

## The Impact of the Red Scare and the Blacklist

### Personal Harm

The Hollywood hearings had personal and professional repercussions, both on the informers and on those named. Which group had the heaviest burden to bear? In economic terms, all the unfriendly witnesses suffered personal loss and endured economic hardship through blacklisting. The informers, on the other hand, carried the mark of Judas around with them throughout the remainder of their careers. Trumbo was right when he characterized the informers and the blacklisted as victims because both were shunned by former friends and despised by their enemies. Blacklisted actors, directors, and producers were hardest hit because they were visible to their enemies. However, writers like Trumbo, Michael Wilson, and Ned Young could still work under pseudonyms. Even though they were paid for their scripts, these blacklisted writers worked without recognition. Trumbo, for example, could not collect his Oscar for *The Brave One* since he wrote the script under the pseudonym Robert Rich. Furthermore, blacklisting was open-ended: there was no deadline or date when redemption began and careers resumed. Actress Lee Grant spent 16 years on the blacklist and Herbert Biberman's wife, actress Gale Sondergaard, went seven years without a paid acting job. Trumbo was not publicly recognized for his work until 1960 when producer Kirk Douglas gave him credit for working on the screenplay of *Spartacus* (1960). That same year, Otto Preminger gave Trumbo credit for writing the screenplay for *Exodus*, thus breaking the stranglehold of the blacklist. On the other hand, turning informer did not provide actor Larry Parks with salvation; he played a supporting role in only one major Hollywood film after his HUAC appearance. His actress wife, Betty Garrett, also found work in the industry hard to come by.[52]

Blacklisted director Abraham Polonsky would not direct another film for 20 years and screenwriter Samuel Ornitz deserted the film industry altogether for lack of work.[53] Others, like Albert Maltz, had screen projects pulled out from underneath them. Maltz was hired by Frank Sinatra to do the screenplay for *The Execution of Eddie Slovak* (1974), a story about an American deserter in World War II. Maltz claims that he did considerable research on the script and even wrote a first draft when Sinatra fired him, presumably because of intense pressure from the Alliance and the Kennedy White House.[54]

Those writers who were unable to find work even under pseudonyms and those who were unsuccessful in locating "fronts" for submitting their scripts to the studios resorted to any kind of work just to survive. Ned Young was forced to work as a bartender, salesman, and junkman. Meanwhile, others left the country to pursue their film work in England (Joseph Losey, Carl Foreman, Adrian Scott), France (Jules Dassin, John Howard Lawson), and Mexico (Maltz, Trumbo). Others formed the Blacklist Company to produce their own films, but the failure of their first feature, *Salt of the Earth*, caused them to abandon the effort.

There were personal casualties as well. Betsy Blair, Gene Kelly's wife, had her career cut short by the blacklist. Although not a party member, Blair was sympathetic to left-wing causes and worked on behalf of the National Association for Colored People (NAACP) and the Independent Progressive Party. After not being able to get work, she left Kelly and went to live in Paris and London.[55] Ned Young's wife, blacklisted along with her husband, committed suicide after years of depression. There is some suggestion that at least half a dozen Hollywood deaths, including actors John Garfield, J. Edward Bromberg, and Canada Lee, can be attributed directly to the hearings and the blacklist.[56] Garfield, for example, was rejected for military service because of heart trouble. He was not a communist but worried that HUAC would ask him about his wife, who had been a party member. Regardless, *Red Channels* named him as a communist sympathizer in 1950. The following year, HUAC subpoenaed him to appear before the committee. He never appeared because he died from a heart attack at 39 and his family and friends blamed HUAC, citing the stress associated with his subpoena. A tough New Yorker, Garfield once said, "Where I come from, we don't snitch on friends."[57]

That there were marriage breakups and divorces and negative effects on the children of those blacklisted has only now been recognized. The children of the blacklist, middle-aged at the time of the interviews, were gathered together to make a documentary during which they offered bittersweet recollections of their parents, with occasional reproaches against their accusers. Julie Garfield described the studio heads as "racists" who went after her father because he was Jewish; Joshua Mostel claimed his father, Zero, was apolitical, or more likely an anarchist; Martha Randolph recalled how her father was permitted to work in the theater but not on radio or film; Liz Schwartz talked about her mother's suicide; others remembered being prohibited to play with or socialize with the children of informers; still others had memories of fleeing California in the middle of the night and hiding out in desert motels. Although their evidence is largely anecdotal, these personal stories reveal a second generation scarred by the blacklist.[58]

## The Defiant Ones

Several of the blacklisted sought to continue their professional careers by forming the independent Blacklist Company to produce their own films. Led by Herbert Biberman, Paul Jarrico, and Michael Wilson, the newly formed Independent Productions Corporation searched for stories to transfer to the big screen. When the group learned of a year-long labor strike in southwestern New Mexico between Local 890 of the International Union of Mine, Mill, and Smelter Workers (IUMMSW) and Empire Zinc Corporation, writer Michael Wilson was sent to investigate. The miners walked out after negotiations with the owners broke down. They started a picket line but were prohibited by the Taft-Hartley Act, and so their wives picketed instead. The labor dispute turned ugly after the local sheriff used tear gas to disperse the women. In all, three women were injured on the picket line, including one who had been hit by a truck, and 62 others were arrested and jailed.

After discussions with union leaders, mine workers from the IUMMSW, and local citizens, Wilson drafted a fictional account of the actual events. The completed film, entitled *Salt of the Earth*, starred five professionals, including Mexican actress Rosaura Revueltas and blacklisted American actor Will Geer, but the majority of the cast roles were filled with non-professionals, including the union president, Juan Chacón, as the lead actor. Shot on location and in black and white, the Wilson script integrated three plots into its story line. As mentioned in chapter 3, the dominant narrative featured the labor-management dispute over wage discrimination, worker benefits, and mine safety conditions that precipitated the strike. This is the heart of the film and provides its dramatic center. But two subplots involving class and gender took on greater significance in retrospect. The union leaders were white and middle class, the miners largely Mexican and lower class. The workers' families lived in abominable conditions without adequate sanitation and hot running water. After 15 months both sides agreed to end the walkout, with the workers receiving several concessions involving wages, fringe benefits, and security protection for the strikers. And the women got hot running water in their homes.

The story behind the making of the film proved more dramatic than the events depicted on screen.[59] *Salt of the Earth* encountered opposition at every stage during production, post-production, and distribution. The mine owners received support from the big labor unions and from the film industry. During filming, Revueltas, who played the main female character, was arrested by immigration authorities and deported. Filming was constantly interrupted by physical threats from local vigilante groups. When shooting was finished and the film was ready for final editing, it was locked out of Hollywood's technical facilities. Roy Brewer, head of the IA, told the film company that it would receive no help from the union. In addition, the SAG forwarded information about the film and its personnel to HUAC, the FBI, and the State Department. Howard Hughes sent a letter to Congress detailing how to stop the production of the film and, failing that, how the government could curtail its distribution. Historian James Lorence claims that Hughes's letter would be the cause of Revueltas's deportation. In fact, every dirty trick was used to prevent the making and showing of *Salt of the Earth*.

The final blow was struck by the reviewers, who were generally negative about the film. Critic Pauline Kael labeled it "communist propaganda."[60] And theater exhibitors put the last nail in the coffin when they boycotted the film's release in 1954. As a consequence, *Salt of the Earth* played briefly in only 13 theaters in the entire country. Denied commercial exhibition in the U.S., the film was praised in Europe and became a cult favorite on American college campuses. In 2003, on the film's 50th anniversary, the College of Santa Fe paid tribute to its legacy by hosting a national conference that included several of the original participants along with noted scholars, artists, filmmakers, and labor organizers. But an announced remake never materialized.

## Professional Consequences

Many of the participants in the HUAC proceedings—friendly witnesses, informers, unfriendly witnesses—not only knew each other but worked together on film projects, belonged to the same guilds, and occasionally joined the same Popular Front organizations. Their political and working association possibly explains the depth of the unfriendly witnesses' bitterness toward the informers.

The personal conflict between informer and unfriendly witness ultimately moved from the congressional hearing room to the big screen and is best epitomized in the dispute between film director Elia Kazan and playwright Arthur Miller. Witnesses before HUAC were limited to three choices: talk, as the friendly witnesses did, or remain silent, which was the tactic of the unfriendly witnesses. The third option, a compromised position whereby the witness speaks about him/herself but not about others, is best exemplified by the testimonies of Lillian Hellman and Miller. Kazan, however, was a willing witness before HUAC, talking freely about the political activities of himself and his colleagues.[61] Years later, Miller confessed that he could have escaped the committee hearing altogether if he had persuaded his wife at the time, actress Marilyn Monroe, to have her photo taken with HUAC's chairman, Representative Francis Walters.[62] Miller declined the offer and the charade continued. Miller's revelation supports the assertion that the HUAC hearings were about performance rather than substance.

Prior to the hearings, Kazan and Miller talked of collaborating on a film about longshoremen and their life on the docks. When Kazan became a friendly witness before HUAC, Miller broke off their relationship. Kazan, meanwhile, went ahead with the project, which became the critically acclaimed film *On the Waterfront* (1954). Kazan persuaded Marlon Brando to play the main character, washed-up fighter Terry Malloy, who through the efforts of the local priest (Karl Malden) and the love of a good woman (Eva Marie Saint) turns into a state informer against the organized crime mob that controls the waterfront. In a dramatic ending, Terry receives a vicious beating from the mob but still leads the strikers back to work against the wishes of the crime boss (Lee J. Cobb). In *On the Waterfront*, the informer is transformed into a hero by cooperating with the authorities. Kazan used the film to justify his decision to "name names."[63] Budd Schulberg, who wrote the screenplay for the film, claimed that the story was inspired by Reverend John Corridon (played by

Malden in the film), a Catholic priest who persuaded a contingent of honest longshoremen to testify to the Waterfront Commission against the mob that controlled the union.[64]

Miller, meanwhile, countered with *The Crucible*,[65] a play about the Salem witch trials, which was clearly intended to demonstrate the evils associated with paranoia and public hysteria. Miller's play argues that the informer is a villain whose action supports and encourages wrongdoing. Because Miller's play took place in 17th century New England, it could be viewed as a historical recreation. But in order to directly confront Kazan's "informer as hero," Miller wrote *A View from the Bridge*, a play about the Brooklyn waterfront that subsequently became a motion picture in 1962. In this answer to *On the Waterfront*, Miller's hero Eddie Carbone, a longshoreman who lives with his wife and his sister's daughter, Catherine, agrees to hide illegal immigrants (called "submarines") from the immigration authorities. Eddie understands the law of the waterfront: act deaf, dumb and blind. But when he takes in these two illegal immigrants, the pieces for a Greek tragedy are in place. When the younger of the two falls in love with Catherine, Eddie becomes jealous because he also harbors suppressed feelings for his niece. These feelings lead Eddie to inform, to break the unwritten code of silence on the waterfront, by reporting the location of the two submarines to immigration. It is this act of betrayal that the Miller play dramatizes; this treacherous deed results in Eddie's death, since there is no honor in informing.

The Kazan-Miller clash was but one piece of personal drama played out as a result of the HUAC hearings and the subsequent blacklisting. Although neither Kazan nor Miller had their careers destroyed by the blacklist, each suffered from its effects. Miller felt betrayed by a friend and colleague; Kazan's career continued but not without retribution from his peers in the industry who denied him professional recognition.[66] As Dalton Trumbo might have observed, both Kazan and Miller were victims of the Hollywood blacklist.

The initial use of the blacklist in the twenties and thirties was to curb union organizing and threaten the jobs of Hollywood workers. Then in the fifties, the industry sought to impress the government with its patriotism by refusing to hire named "communists" and by insisting that anyone named by HUAC pass a loyalty clearance before being employed. The studios also sought to illustrate their allegiance by making over 40 anti-communist films between 1949 and 1953.[67] Films like *The Red Menace* (1949), *I Married a Communist* (1950), *I Was a Communist for the FBI* (1951), *My Son John* (1952), and *Big Jim McLain* (1952) were blatant pieces of patriotic propaganda that would hardly qualify for Academy Awards in any era. In *The Red Menace*, for example, an ex-serviceman joins a local Communist Party cell with the assistance of a seductive woman. If all Americans were as naive as the main character, the U.S. would have voted for the Communist Party in 1952 instead of Eisenhower. Similarly, the film *Big Jim McLain* has John Wayne smashing a communist cell in Hawaii, thereby preventing a takeover of the island. Actually, the film adhered to a formulaic plot that would have enabled the producers to substitute the Nazis, Japanese, or cattle rustlers for the communists without too many script changes. It so happened that the communists were the villains of the era and Hollywood capitalized on the current mood in the country. As late as 1958, Hollywood was turning out low-budget anti-communist movies like *The Fearmakers*, which warned the American public to be wary of lobby groups, like the film's Committee for the Abolition of Nuclear Warfare, because they might be communist-front organizations.

Few films dared to criticize the anti-communist message directly. Instead a smattering challenged the communist paranoia and the effects of McCarthyism allegorically, expressing their condemnation of HUAC and the blacklist in plots that dealt with subjects ranging from space aliens to westerns. *The Thing* (1951), for example, a film about a frozen creature that comes to life and threatens an Arctic expedition, was interpreted as a metaphor for the spate of communist invasion movies; one scriptwriter insisted that the evil creature in *The Thing* represented McCarthy(ism).[68] Another film released in 1951, *The Day the Earth Stood Still*, concerned a flying saucer that lands in Washington, D.C. The two aliens aboard have come to the nation's capital on a peace mission, to warn planet Earth against a global nuclear war. As could be anticipated, no one in government pays any attention to the peace message and, subsequently, events turn ugly as the alien leader is shot due to public fear and ignorance. Eventually the aliens return to their own planet. Certainly, the pro-peace message of *The Day the Earth Stood Still* was a daring theme in an age when atom bombs and nuclear weapons were part of military strategy and when the release of the film coincided with McCarthy's announcement about communists in the State Department.[69]

Meanwhile, another film, *Invasion of the Body Snatchers* (1956), dealt with giant seedpods that take over the bodies of people and turn them into cold, Godless creatures similar to the Soviets. Supposedly the pods represented the three dominant forces of the fifties: conformity, paranoia, and alienation. The film was designed to confront America for exhibiting similar characteristics during the Cold War.[70] A Nicholas Ray western, *Johnny Guitar* (1953), featured a guitar-playing drifter (HUAC informer Sterling Hayden), in the middle of a town feud between two women, saloon owner Joan Crawford, who befriends outlaws, and upright citizen and banker Mercedes McCambridge. Was the film intended to be a western parody or a political allegory about McCarthyism? If you accept the latter interpretation, then the outlaws represent the communists, Hayden is the former communist, Crawford the fellow traveler, and McCambridge the McCarthy clone who manipulates the townspeople into "naming names," converting their fear and ignorance into an ugly lynch mob.[71] When the mob turns on the Crawford character, the script gives the actress an opportunity to address the crowd and deliver a speech against the making of false accusations (friendly witnesses and informers) and against the making of guilty judgments on the basis of the company she keeps (guilt by association). These films at least reveal that there were a few in the industry who tried to counter the propaganda of the studios' anti-communist films.

## Film Content

Except for a handful of serious films that confronted American racism and prejudice, Hollywood played it safe in the fifties, concentrating on musicals, Doris Day-Rock Hudson romantic comedies, crime thrillers, and westerns. This rather bland film diet is not so surprising since some of the very best Hollywood writers were on the blacklist. Between 1938 and the 1947 HUAC hearings the eight major Hollywood studios released over 3,100 films, with about 600 or one-fifth scripted by radicals or leftists. It is this group of writers who combined to win four Oscars and receive 19 Academy Award nominations. No wonder the studios considered them a valuable commodity, paid them well (Dalton Trumbo received $3,000 per week from MGM and Ring Lardner Jr. received a salary of $2,000 per week from 20th Century Fox), and agreed to let some of them write under pseudonyms or use "fronts" to submit their work.[72]

Why did these talented artists turn to the left? What attracted them to Marx and the Communist Party? Perhaps author Vivian Gornick, reminiscing about her own life in New York, expressed it best when she wrote,

> It was characteristic of that world that during those hours at the kitchen table I didn't know we were poor. I didn't know that in those places beyond the streets of my Bronx neighborhood we were without power, position, material or social existence. I only knew that I felt the same electric thrill as when Rouben, my Yiddish teacher, pressed my upper arm between two bony fingers and, his eyes shining behind thick glasses, said to me: "Ideas, dolly, ideas. Without them, life is nothing. With them, life is everything." For the people among whom I grew this intensity of feeling was transmitted through Marxism as interpreted by the CPUSA. At the indisputable center of their world stood the Communist Party. It was the Party whose awesome structure harnessed that inchoate emotion which, with the force of a tidal wave, drove millions of people around the globe toward Marxism. It was the Party whose moral authority gave shape and substance to the abstractions. It was the Party that brought to life a remarkably far-reaching sense of comradeship. For of this Party it could rightly be said, as Richard Wright in his bitterest moment did say, "There was no agency in the world so capable of making men feel the earth and the people upon it as the Communist Party."[73]

Hollywood released more than 2,500 movies during the fifties; less than 1 percent were serious dramas that confronted the important social problems of that time. The witch hunt in Hollywood had succeeded in silencing dissent and stifling creativity. It would not be until the mid-sixties that Hollywood returned to the exploration of contemporary social issues.[74] Two decades would pass before the film industry recovered from the wounds inflicted by the Red Scare hysteria.

Chapter 6

# Real to Reel Politicians
Idealists, Saviors and Scoundrels

"It could probably be shown by facts and figures that there is no distinctly native American criminal class except Congress."
—Mark Twain

"Those who are too smart to engage in politics are punished by being governed by those who are dumber."
—Plato

"Nearly all men can stand adversity, but if you want to test a man's character, give him power."
—Abraham Lincoln

"Politics is supposed to be the second oldest profession. I have come to realize that it bears a very close resemblance to the first."
—President Ronald Reagan

"When the President does it that means that it is not illegal."
—Former President Nixon to David Frost May 1977 TV interview

"Politics is just like show business.... You begin with a hell of an opening, you coast for a while, and you end with a hell of a closing."
—Ronald Reagan, running for Governor of California, 1965

There is a marvelous scene at the end of Robert Redford's *The Candidate* (1972) where he is sitting in his hotel suite surrounded by staff and friends in celebration of his election to the U.S. Senate. In walks his father (Melvyn Douglas), the former Governor of California and consummate wheeler-dealer. Douglas approaches Redford, who is seated on the bed looking rather glum, and with a quizzical grin that runs from ear to ear, says, "Congratulations, son. You're a politician now." If there is one scene in all the films on American politics that would discourage, if not seriously damage, the interest of young people to run for political office, this is it. The scene's cynicism offends two vital concepts in a democratic society: first is the notion that the electorate believes politicians hold office as a public trust, and second that politics is an honorable and commendable profession. But does the scene represent reality or Hollywood's version of the U.S. Congress?

On second thought, Hollywood has not always been kind to the presidency either. Recent Hollywood presidents, such as Bill Pullman fighting alien invaders in *Independence Day* (1996) or Harrison Ford socking it to hijackers who have taken over his plane in *Air Force One* (1997), reinforce a macho image that defies credibility as well as historical accuracy. Americans expect their presidents to reside in Camelot, but also mingle with common folk, be compassionate but act tough against external enemies, be human but not too seriously flawed. The reel presidents—Pullman and Ford—however, are glamorous heroes, creative inventions rather than real people. Most American presidents have understood the difference between fact and fantasy, but occasionally a Nixon or a Reagan is inspired by the fictions on the screen: Nixon bombing Cambodia the day after viewing *Patton* (1970), Reagan watching *Rambo: First Blood, Part II* (1985) to reinforce his "evil empire" foreign policy against the old Soviet Union.[1]

Since Hollywood deals in illusions and fantasies, the industry should find politics an attractive partner in the entertainment business. Not true. Only a fraction of the 150,000 films[2] turned out by Hollywood over the past century actually feature American politics as the primary subject and politicians as the central characters. Historically, the studios decided that serious films on politics would not fill theater seats. Whenever a studio disregarded the conventional wisdom and made a film depicting American politics, either the finished product was accorded a bland treatment or the plot took liberties with the facts and the historical record. Moreover, in films that attempt to present serious domestic or foreign policy issues, the script is likely to focus on the personal foibles of the political characters, dwell on their private lives rather than the actual workings of the legislative process, and ignore the means by which the president reaches a policy decision.[3] Seldom does the industry portray evil politicians as expressions of institutional wrongdoing or virtuous politicians as defenders of constitutional principles.[4]

However, the film industry has not ignored American politics completely. A few political films were released during the silent era, but interest in the subject revived again in the thirties as Hollywood turned out several political biographies, including three on Lincoln. The presidency interested Hollywood again in the sixties, particularly in portraying presidents under stress from internal and external enemies. The industry returned to the presidency in the 1990s with a vengeance, placing the Oval Office center stage in over two dozen major features. These screen presidents were a varied bunch: romantically involved lovers, womanizers and sex abusers, macho patriots, enigmatic political figures, fatherly figures, wimpy impostors, calculating politicians, decisive leaders, and political hacks. Quite a mélange.

Despite these periodic bursts of interest, Hollywood typically avoids the treatment of American politicians because of the fear that partisan politics or hardline ideological political figures will affect box office receipts. Even when politics is the dominant theme, the subject is often diluted. Essentially, what happens in a Hollywood film where politics is the central focus is that it serves as a framework for more familiar plots such as assassination thrillers, or as a backdrop for romance.

## American Politics on Screen

When Hollywood enters the world of politics, it often does so through the back door. Political activities in feature films frequently express individual behavior that is motivated by self-interest: bad politicians act out of greed and ambition while good politicians act in response to the deeds of bad politicians. Few act out of a deep commitment to democratic principles. Observe the intentions of the screen politicians below and draw your own conclusion.

### Political Campaigns and Conventions

The film industry has been churning out political films since the silent era. But these early movies were mostly about class and the struggle between capitalists and the working classes.[5] The direction changed in the 1930s when political elections provided material for the new "talkies." And why not? Movies are a terrific venue for depicting political campaigns and elections that surprise us (Truman vs. Dewey, 1948), that keep us in suspense (Bush vs. Gore, 2000), that break tradition (Obama vs. McCain, 2008), and that affect the course of history (Lincoln vs. Douglas, 1860). It is not surprising, then, that the film industry has tapped into the topic, often hitting gold.

Besides being a solid source for screen stories, elections and political campaigns provide scriptwriters with a dramatized event around which to develop a narrative that can be melodramatic, exciting, and even amusing. Several British scholars who have studied the American electoral process in Hollywood films found that they shared elements of greed, unfettered individual political ambition, and close alliances with the moneyed classes.[6] These scholars maintain that some of Hollywood's finest political films have depicted all or many of these elements.

Hollywood turned its attention to political elections as screen fare in the 1930s, with the release of several films on campaign politics, including *Judge Priest* (1934), a star vehicle for humorist Will Rogers. This early John Ford film has Rogers playing a small-town magistrate in 1890s Kentucky, dispensing justice and wisdom equally from his courtroom seat and his front porch. Although up for reelection, Rogers' judge seldom leaves his home or works up a sweat campaigning. The film is best viewed for contrast with contemporary elections dominated by high technology and media promotion.

Hollywood took a hiatus from the political campaign film until the post-World War II era when three features, *The Dark Horse* (1946), *The Farmer's Daughter* (1947), and *State of the Union* (1948), hit theater screens. *The Dark Horse* is a serious political drama about a veteran of World War II who runs for city alderman only to discover that the local political machine is exploiting his war record for personal gain. In *The Farmer's Daughter*, a young Swedish woman (Loretta Young) goes to work as a maid for a wealthy family and falls in love with their congressman son (Joseph Cotton). Billed as a comedy in the advertisements, most of the screen action concerns the budding romance between the two stars. When a local congressman dies in office, Young decides to run for the vacant seat even though her lover's family supports her opponent. She is successful despite an attempted smear by the opposition. The script, however, avoids the details of a real election. The film's political campaign consumes about five minutes of screen time with a majority of the important political events occurring off-camera and the most impressive political speech given by a supporting actor rather than the candidate herself.

Frank Capra's *State of the Union* features Spencer Tracy and Katharine Hepburn in one of their nine films together. The plot has Tracy playing Grant Matthews, a successful and idealistic industrialist, persuaded by an ambitious newspaper owner to run for the presidential nomination on the Republican ticket. Mary (Hepburn), his estranged wife, reluctantly agrees to accompany her husband on the campaign trail. Except for one or two unnecessary scenes in an airplane, the film sticks to the business of electioneering, which allows the major characters to make speeches expressing Capra's liberal philosophy and general belief in the wisdom and essential decency of the common man. When Grant discovers that the party bosses are using him, he withdraws from the race but not from politics. Reunited with his wife at the end, he intends to go to the convention and influence the selection of the Republican candidate. The film is best remembered today for the one-liner "Politics makes strange bedfellows."

During the days of the Red Scare, Hollywood was too preoccupied with the HUAC hearings and Cold War themes to be concerned with political elections. The industry returned to the subject in the sixties. On the surface, John Ford's *The Man Who Shot Liberty Valance* (1962) appears to be a traditional western with John Wayne playing rancher-gunman Tom Doniphon. But the story quickly shifts to the other major character, a tenderfoot Eastern lawyer named Ransom Stoddard (James Stewart), who, in contrast to Doniphon's penchant for violence, believes the West can be civilized by adherence to the rule of law rather than the gun. When Stoddard is beaten and threatened by the town bully and outlaw, Liberty Valance (Lee Marvin), it is Doniphon who comes to his rescue in the climactic shootout. The town folks, however, believe it was Stoddard's gun that rid the community of Valance, an act that makes Stoddard the town hero and catapults him into politics, first as a representative to the territorial legislature and later as one of the state's U.S. senators. Ford intends Stoddard's political career to parallel the development of the West from a lawless frontier into statehood and civilization. While Stoddard goes east to civilized Washington, Doniphon remains in the West. Doniphon's death signals the passing of the Old West as well, its future development delivered into the hands of businessmen, railroaders, shopkeepers, and law-abiding citizens like Ransom Stoddard. The fact that Stoddard profited from a lie should not be overlooked: his political career was built on a false legend of heroism. The local editor, who knows the truth about Stoddard, refuses to print the true story, preferring to keep the legend alive. Released at a time when campaign managers, public relation specialists, and media experts had begun to market candidates as commodities to be sold to the public like commercial products, Ford's film is a reminder of the significant role that myth plays in American politics.

The first Hollywood entry into convention politics, *The Best Man* (1964), was based on the Gore Vidal play. The action revolves around the politics of a presidential nominating convention. The film studios, apparently, were so apprehensive about offending Democrats or Republicans that the convention depicted in *The Best Man* remains unidentified. The narrative has two candidates seeking the endorsement of the incumbent president, who is dying of cancer. William Russell (Henry Fonda), the principled secretary of state, is seeking the nomination against a rival candidate, the ambitious and unscrupulous U.S. Senator Dan Cantwell (Cliff Robertson). The president's endorsement will virtually guarantee the nomination. Which one will the president select? That question lies at the heart of the drama because each candidate has a flawed past—Russell's bout with depression raises questions of his competency under stress and Cantwell's homosexual affair fosters concerns about his electability. In the end, the president selects neither, throwing his support instead behind a third candidate who goes on to win the nomination. *The Best Man* is rich in backroom convention politics, as it explores the characteristics that make for an "ideal" presidential candidate. It also proved prescient, since during the 1972 campaign Senator Tom Eagleton's vice presidential candidacy was derailed when the media revealed that he had suffered a nervous breakdown and received electro-shock therapy.

One film concerned with political campaigning, *The Candidate* (1972), is usually singled out for acclamation. Scripted by a former staffer for Eugene McCarthy's 1968 presidential race, the film concerns a liberal antipoverty lawyer, Bill McKay (played by Robert Redford), son of the former Governor of California. When the Democrats ask him to run against the incumbent Republican U.S. senator, McKay is reluctant to join the race. He finally consents after receiving assurance that he can discuss the real issues and run his own campaign, even if doing so will guarantee his defeat. Since he is expected to lose, McKay enters the race discussing the issues to bored audiences. When he outperforms his opponent in a televised debate and the polls show his election chances improving, McKay relinquishes more and more of the control over his campaign to his managers, who exploit his good looks and charisma. On the campaign trail, McKay begins to spout ready-made slogans and clichés and accepts the support of his father's old cronies. To illustrate that he has become a media-managed candidate, the film contains a scene at a women's luncheon where McKay's speech is reduced to the apology, "I'm sorry, ladies, that I ate all the shrimp." McKay smiles, the women laugh. Removed from his ideals, McKay succumbs to the manipulation of his campaign managers and wins the election. In the fade-out scene, McKay asks his manager, "What do we do now?" Criticized by some as lacking substance, *The Candidate*, on the contrary, warns the audience of the pitfalls of contemporary electioneering, where superficiality is preferred over hard content, personal appeal is celebrated over intelligence and ethical principles, and 30-second campaign sound bites are favored over detailed analysis of complex issues. Can an image-created candidate win a national election? After the two terms of Ronald Reagan, is there anyone today who would wager against a successful race by a George Clooney or a Tom Hanks? The successful elections of pro-wrestler Jessie Ventura and movie star Arnold Schwarzenegger to governorships remind us that politics is as much a celebrity game today as popular entertainment.

Actor Tim Robbins depicted a 1990s version of a political campaign in his film *Bob Roberts* (1992). Whereas Redford's film was a commercial and critical success, *Bob Roberts* failed at the box office. Robbins, who wrote the script and served as director, plays the title character, a self-made, guitar-playing right-wing conservative millionaire from Pennsylvania who runs for the U.S. Senate. Filmed in mock documentary style, *Bob Roberts* unfolds as a diary of a political campaign, from the initial announcement to Election Day victory.

Roberts' campaign slogan is PRIDE, which he displays on his motorbus as he tours the state campaigning against drugs, sexual promiscuity, and wasteful social programs. On the surface, Roberts is a sincere charmer who preaches family values and national pride, but off-camera he is prone to dirty campaign tricks. When a local reporter threatens to expose him as a fraud, Roberts and his staff fake an assassination attempt on the candidate's life. The strategy works, as the troublesome reporter is killed and Roberts is shown in a wheelchair, seriously wounded. But in the ironic conclusion, the audience sees Roberts tapping his feet under the blanket that covers his legs as he celebrates his election victory with a song. This deception and its portrayal of a gullible electorate proved too harsh for American audiences to accept.

Two 1990s entries in the political campaigning mold include Mike Nichols' *Primary Colors* and Warren Beatty's *Bulworth*. *Primary Colors*, based on the book by a former Clinton staffer, makes no attempt to hide the fact that it is a re-creation of the Clinton 1992 presidential campaign. The John Travolta character is a southern governor with a weakness for Krispy Kremes and women, not necessarily in that order. *Bulworth*, however, is quite different. In this film, Beatty plays a despondent U.S. senator whose life is transformed after he falls in love with a political activist. He changes the campaign strategy in his re-election bid and adopts rap music to express his ideas on campaign financing and race relations. Knowing that he has sold out to corporate interests, Bulworth expresses his dismay in rapper style:

> One man, one vote/now izzat real?
> The name of our game is/let's make a deal
> Now the people got their problems/the haves and have-nots
> But the ones that make me listen/pay for 30-second spots…
> You've been taught in this country/there's speech that is free
> But free do not get you/no spots on tv
> If you want to have senators/not on the take
> Then give them free airtime/they won't have to fake…
> We got factories closin' down/where the hell did all the good jobs go?
> Well, I'll tell you where they went
> My contributors make more profits/hiring kids in Mexico
> Yo, everybody gonna get sick someday/but nobody knows how they gonna pay
> Health care, managed care, HMOs/ain't gonna work, no sir, not those
> Cause the thing that's the same in every one of these
> Is these motherfuckers there, the insurance companies!
> Yeah, yeah/you can call it single payer or Canadian way
> Only socialized medicine will ever save the day!
> Come on now. Lemma hear that dirty word—
> Socialism!

*Bulworth* has many of the attributes of *Bob Roberts*, particularly in using comedy to deliver its timely political message of the necessity for campaign finance reform, an overhaul of our health care system, and a raillery against U.S. corporations for outsourcing jobs. Beatty, a life-long liberal who worked with the Democratic Party and the McGovern, Bobby Kennedy, and Gary Hart campaigns, could not, however, deliver a political film that audiences wanted to see.

Probably the most realistic presentation of a political campaign remains *Tanner '88* (1988), the result of the collaboration of director Robert Altman and cartoonist Gary Trudeau. The film was never shown in theaters but aired originally as a miniseries on cable television. *Tanner '88* runs six hours and depicts in documentary style the story of the 1988 presidential race, from the New Hampshire primary to the convention in Atlanta, as viewed through the eyes of one Democratic hopeful, Jack Tanner. Tanner is a divorced former congressman with a college-aged daughter and a lover whom he meets occasionally for trysts while on the campaign trail. Despite his academic credentials (he holds a Ph.D. in economics) Tanner is very much a manufactured candidate, the product of his campaign staff. The film weaves a rich tapestry of American electioneering that includes attempted assassinations, dirty tricks, media-styled campaign slogans, and appearances by real presidential candidates Bob Dole, Gary Hart, Bruce Babbitt, and Pat Robertson. Whether some mistook the series as the actual campaign or whether some voters decided to play a prank, the fact remains that the fictitious Jack Tanner actually received write-in votes in the November election. By interweaving Tanner together with the real candidates in the New Hampshire and Tennessee primaries, Altman was able to depict the grungy work of running a major campaign, along with the gaffes and disasters. For instance, when Tanner is speaking to an outdoor rally in New Hampshire he is upstaged by a group of snowmobilers. Later, when he attends a quilting party with his daughter, the women are more interested in his daughter than in his prepared remarks. As the campaign moves toward the convention and Democratic candidates begin to drop out of the race, Tanner's remaining opponents are Michael Dukakis and Jesse Jackson. In an effort to influence convention delegates, Tanner announces his Cabinet choices, which include, among others, Ralph Nader, Gloria Steinem, Barbara Jordan, and Robert Redford. But when Jackson releases his votes to Dukakis at the convention, Tanner's chances for the nomination are squashed. At film's end, Tanner turns down a Cabinet post in the Dukakis administration while he ponders a presidential race as an independent. Taking full advantage of the expanded running time, Altman produced a commercial film on political campaigns that is the equal of political documentaries like *The War Room* and *A Perfect Candidate*. Altman's film was so good that the Sundance channel aired an updated version during the spring of 2004 when the Democratic primaries were running in many states.

Four recent 21st-century entries into political campaigns and elections, *Recount, Swing Vote, The Campaign,* and *The Ides of March*, differ in presentation and delivery. *Recount* (2008) is a serious, if somewhat complicated, depiction of the infamous 2000 presidential election between Democratic Vice President Al Gore and his Republican challenger, George W. Bush, the son of President George H.W. Bush. Aired on the HBO Cable network, the film adheres closely to the actual events in Florida as the outcome of the election rests on the results from that state. Unfortunately, the state has an archaic voting process which confuses Florida's elderly population, destroys their paper ballots, negates their votes because of dangling chads caught in the tabulating machines, and disfranchises many black voters. And that's without the dirty tricks! After viewing the film twice, it still is unclear who is responsible for the fiasco—the political parties, the voters, or the U.S. Supreme Court. To complicate matters further, Gore captures the national popular vote but is shy of the required 270 electoral votes to be declared president. Thus, whichever candidate wins Florida's 25 electoral votes will win the election. Bush has a slight lead in the Florida popular vote but the Democrats claim that all the votes had not been counted and ask for a recount. Meanwhile, the major TV networks predict Bush as the winner and Gore concedes but then retracts his concession. At that moment, the election is in limbo. Enter Katherine Harris (played as a real flake by Laura Dern), Florida's secretary of state, who maintains that the election must be certified within six days. Gore's camp argues that a recount is mandatory if an error occurs in the vote tabulation and requests an extension to permit all votes to be counted. Harris refuses. The Democrats take their case to the Florida Supreme Court, which agrees that all ballots must be counted. Not to be outdone, the Republicans appeal the decision to the U.S. Supreme Court. Thirty-six days after the election, the Highest Court in the U.S. rules in *Bush v. Gore* (2000)[7] that since the certification deadline has passed, the state does not have to continue the recount. This is how George W. Bush became president.

In theory, democracies require an enlightened and dedicated citizenry who are well informed on issues and are consistent voters. Not many Hollywood movies scrutinize the American voter under a microscope. The reader who views the 2008 comedy *Swing Vote*, starring Kevin Costner, may want to thank Hollywood for its neglect after seeing this film. *Swing Vote* requires the audience to suspend disbelief since the plot is crammed with implausibility. Costner is Bud Johnson, a beer-drinking couch potato and single father who lives with his young daughter in New Mexico. He spends most of his time sleeping and drinking, especially after he is fired from his low-level job. He has absolutely zero interest in politics and when asked about his political affiliation responds, "I'm a conscientious objector." It happens to be a presidential election year and even with his daughter's reminder to vote, Bud gets drunk instead and passes out. Since the polls are still open, his daughter sneaks in, signs his name, and votes for him (implausibility #1). But the machine malfunctions and the vote fails to record (despite efforts to correct unrecorded votes after 2000), which becomes implausibility #2. As a result, Bud's unrecorded vote will determine the outcome in New Mexico and, hence, the presidential election.

Bud becomes a national celebrity and is courted by both presidential candidates. The incumbent president invites him for a tour of Air Force One and offers him a beer and a lecture on the responsibilities of being the commander-in-chief in the nuclear age, using the game of football as a metaphor. Bud is clueless. Meanwhile, the challenger throws Bud a party where he reunites with his old country western band, giving Costner a chance to sing a ditty. But in typical Hollywood style, Bud sobers up in the last reel, is coached on the campaign issues, undergoes a complete transformation from slob to clean-shaven respectable adult, and attends the presidential debate, where he delivers a redeeming speech in which he admits all his faults and promises to clean up his act. The film ends as the reinvented Bud casts the deciding ballot. Who does he vote for? The film rightly leaves that to our imagination because that fact is unnecessary, since *Swing Vote* is really about us—the American electorate. But the lesson to be learned from this PG-13 rated film is the wrong one to emulate. Bud is precisely the kind of citizen Thomas Jefferson warned us about, namely, one ignorant of the issues and indifferent to the responsibilities of citizenship. The film's poster should have read, "TWO THUMBS DOWN!"

Satire at its best represents a challenge even to the gifted writer. It requires subtlety and a light hand to be successful, particularly if its subject is politics. The screenwriters for *The Campaign*, a film which opened in August, 2012 to take advantage of the presidential conventions and the November election, failed to heed this warning. The film was billed as a "comedy" starring Will Ferrell and Zach Galifianakis. What there is of a plot concerns an attempt by two businessmen to oust their long-term local congressman, Ferrell, by selecting the naive political novice, Galifianakis, head of the local Tourism Bureau, to run against him. Their intention is to buy up land in Ferrell's district in order to build three factories that will employ cheap Chinese labor, a kind of "insourcing" rather than outsourcing. From that point on, the political campaign becomes a shambles as the film tries to get laughs from visual jokes (Ferrell punching a kid in the face by mistake and later repeating the punch on a dog) and sad jokes about "asses, tits, and penises" that fall flat. To do political comedy requires a deft, satirical touch à la Preston Sturgis rather than the heavy-handed sophomoric humor found in *The Campaign*. One critic succinctly encapsulated the film's plot as "Two nincompoops run against each other for a seat in Congress. It's not a documentary…"[8] Enough said!

However, there are talented people in Hollywood, like George Clooney, who know how to make a serious film about political campaigns. I want the reader to imagine that you are a dedicated liberal campaign staffer who works for a candidate you admire and respect and whose policies you support, such as pro-environment, gun control, and energy independence while opposing capital punishment. But what do you do when you discover that your ideal politician is flawed, like everyone else? This is the dilemma for Ryan Gosling's campaign staffer in *The Ides of March* (2011), George Clooney's presidential campaign film. Gosling idolizes Clooney, the Governor of Pennsylvania, who is running in the Ohio Democratic Party primary in his bid for the presidency. Gosling's idealistic image is shattered when he discovers that Clooney has had an affair with one of the campaign interns, who happens to be Gosling's girlfriend. When the intern realizes she is pregnant, Gosling gives her money to have an abortion. Instead, for reasons too complicated to detail here, the intern kills herself by overdosing on the pre-abortion meds.

Running alongside this personal track, a second storyline emerges in the film. Gosling's character, who appears to be self-assured, even cocky, is a novice compared to his boss, Clooney's, campaign manager (Philip Seymour Hoffman). This is also true with the opposing candidate's manager (Paul Giamatti), since both managers exhibit the tough attitudes of seasoned campaigners for whom winning is everything, regardless of the cost. They would do anything to help their candidate win, including bribing a U.S. senator for his delegates in exchange for the post of secretary of state in the new administration. When Hoffman discovers that Gosling had an interview with Giamatti, he fires him. Stung by his dismissal, Gosling offers his services to Giamatti's candidate, but is rebuffed. It is at this point in the film that nice guy Gosling realizes that backroom politics is a dirty business. Putting aside his principles, Gosling adopts the unwritten rule of "Do unto others before they do it to you" and confronts Clooney about his affair with the intern. Gosling threatens to go to the media with the information, but Clooney believes he is bluffing until Gosling says the intern left a letter that would implicate Clooney and damage his career. Now Clooney must decide whether to believe Gosling's claim. But being a pragmatic politician, Clooney accepts Gosling's offer to remain silent in exchange for Hoffman's job as campaign manager. In the final scene, Gosling is busy preparing before one of Clooney's campaign appearances. The audience knows that the team of Clooney and Gosling will win the Democratic nomination, and then the election, because they are willing to do whatever it takes to win in November. *The Ides of March* does not offer a positive example of the practical experience most students receive as interns in a political campaign, but given the reported scandals and corruption associated with recent election campaigns, it may not be too far off the mark.

## Political Machines

Hollywood movies about political machines usually depict two very different attitudes about politics. On the one hand, the films portray the machine as a monolithic force that controls votes and remains in power through corrupt deals made by self-serving politicians and justified on grounds of political necessity. On the other hand, the existing machine becomes the target of reform politicians who overthrow it, only to succumb to the temptations awarded to those with absolute power.

What exactly is a political machine? Most political scientists agree that any acceptable definition must include a political party organization, longevity, and the exchange of patronage and social services for votes. In the U.S. the machine is historically associated with big cities and with the arrival of an immigrant population that required jobs, housing, and assistance with the English language. Ellis Island became the primary arrival point for immigrants from Europe, met at the Customs House by Tammany Hall bosses who helped with their assimilation into their new environment. In exchange for this assistance, immigrants were asked to vote for Democratic candidates, an arrangement that kept Tammany Hall in control of New York City for virtually 80 years. George Washington Plunkitt, ward boss for the city's Fifteenth Assembly District, explained the secret of Tammany's power: understand human nature, familiarize yourself with the local neighborhood, and make government friendly and personal.[9]

Films that depict a cynical view of machine politics include Preston Sturges' *The Great McGinty* (1940) and *The Glass Key* (1942), based on the Dashiell Hammett novel. *The Great McGinty* is a satirical look at big city politics with the moral message that honesty in politics does not pay. On the other hand, *The Glass Key* depicts both reformers and machine bosses as double-crossing, unscrupulous politicians, reducing political reform to changing personnel but not policies. Another film, Frank Capra's *Meet John Doe* (1941) has a happy ending but the film's message is also that the masses are easily swayed by sentimentality and democratic clichés, weaknesses that leave the people vulnerable to domination by political machines.

Can there be a decent political boss? Novelist Edwin O'Connor thought so in *The Last Hurrah* (1958), which John Ford transferred to the big screen. In this paean to Irish politics, Spencer Tracy plays Frank Skeffington, a Boston political boss who resembles the charismatic Beantown Mayor James Michael Curley. Skeffington is a wily old politician, ruthless yet charming, whose power base rests on personal favors and debts collected at election time. He is the consummate politician, even campaigning at the wake of Jocko, a not particularly admired constituent. Skeffington makes sure, however, that a crowd shows up at the wake to pay tribute to Jocko, who now has more friends in death than he ever had in life. But in the new era of media-based campaigns, personal politics are no match for a sophisticated television crusade by his opponent. Skeffington loses his bid for a fourth term as a victim of mediated politics. While *The Last Hurrah* is a nostalgic and romantic examination of machine politics, it does serve as an indictment of contemporary media-created politicians. After viewing *The Last Hurrah*, audiences may wonder whether the replacement of the political machine by reform candidates without character or concern for individual welfare has actually improved the public good.

Two decent politicians who are corrupted by machine politics turn up in *All the King's Men* (1949) and *City Hall* (1996). The former film was based on Robert Penn Warren's Pulitzer Prize–winning novel and transferred to the screen with the message that unchecked power can destroy political reformers. Warren's novel is a thinly disguised biography of the political career of Louisiana Governor Huey Long. In the film version, Broderick Crawford plays Willie Stark, a poor backwoods Southern lawyer who gains political power through a populist attack on state corruption. But once in office, Stark becomes as ruthless and corrupt as the political machine he ousted. Although Stark sets up a fascist government, complete with thugs and goons, and resorts to blackmail, beatings, and even murder, he remains popular with the masses because of his building projects, which create jobs, result in school improvements, and advance social programs. Stark's popularity reaches its peak after an unsuccessful impeachment attempt by the state legislature. Like the real Huey Long, Stark has his eye on the White House, but an assassin's bullet cuts his political career short. After more than two hundred years of American politics, Huey Long's regime in 1930s Louisiana came closest to homegrown fascism and a threat to democratic state government.[10]

Al Pacino plays a beleaguered mayor in the other film, *City Hall*, scripted by Ken Lipper, former deputy mayor in the Ed Koch administration, and filmed on location in New York City. *City Hall* relates the story of Mayor John Pappas (Pacino), a popular and liberal mayor, who has had to make deals with the county political bosses, especially Frank Anselmo (Danny Aiello), the political leader of Kings County, in order to rebuild the city, create jobs, and foster race relations. This richly detailed film portrays the political process as a series of compromises and tradeoffs. Pacino's mayor plays this game until one unacceptable deal is struck that comes back to haunt him and the other politicians and judges involved. The film's location shots and finely detailed characters are recognizable to New Yorkers with memories of city politics in the 1980s, complete with revelations of political cover-ups, shady deals, and personal corruption. *City Hall* brings back to mind the scandal-ridden Koch administration in the eighties that sent one political boss to prison and led another to commit suicide.[11] Pacino's alter-ego and conscience is the deputy mayor, Kevin Calhoun (John Cusack), whose investigation uncovers murder and drug deals that ultimately destroy the political aspirations of his boss. At its center *City Hall* questions whether any elected official, however decent, can be an effective politician without support from the power brokers. This film comes closest to challenging the simplistic textbook explanation of machine politics as evil per se and reformers as "white knight" politicians. It does so in depicting the realities of governing our cities, where policy choices are reduced to compromises among legitimate but competing interests.

Present-day Hollywood seems to have lost interest in mining the richness of plots involving urban political machines that dominated major American cities in the past. Yet for many years major cities like Boston, Chicago, New York, Philadelphia, and Providence were governed by machines representing both political parties. And in the case of the 1960 presidential election, machines helped to elect John Kennedy. Too bad Hollywood has deserted such a valuable source for stories that represent a uniquely American phenomenon.

## Capital Crimes and Misdemeanors

A number of very good dramatic films exploit the Washington, D.C., location in narratives that both praise and damn the federal government. Foremost among this group is Frank Capra's film *Mr. Smith Goes to Washington*. Jimmy Stewart's character, Jefferson Smith, boy ranger and ingenuous idealist, is appointed to the Senate because he is expected to serve as a patsy for his state's corrupt political machine, headed by Jim Taylor (Edward Arnold). Capra's movies often revolve around decent common men exploited by the rich and the powerful who, nonetheless, manage to triumph over their adversaries in the final reel. In order for Smith to win his battle against the political bosses, however, he must engage in a filibuster. While Capra utilizes this political tactic for a good cause in the film, historically the filibuster has been employed to defeat and delay liberal legislation such as civil rights. But an intriguing question was raised in the documentary, *Can Mr. Smith Get to Washington, Anymore?* (2006) as it followed the campaign of Jeff Smith, a young adjunct political science instructor at Washington University of St. Louis, in his bid to win the House seat held by Dick Gephardt. Smith is a novice to politics, as is his young staff, and his campaign is short on money and endorsements. Yet he is confident that he can beat state representative Russ Carnahan, son of a prominent political family, in the Democratic primary by running a grassroots campaign including door-to-door canvassing, yard signs, direct mail flyers and a home-made video. Despite his efforts, however, Jeff Smith loses to Carnahan in a close race. What the film demonstrates is that political machines, family dynasties and wealth are formidable political advantages to overcome.

Meanwhile, in *Advise and Consent* (1962), the film version of the Allen Drury novel, the appointment of a secretary of state provides the basis for the drama. In the American political system the presidential appointment of a Cabinet-level post, federal judgeship, and an ambassadorship requires senatorial approval. When the film president (Franchot Tone) nominates the controversial Robert Leffingwell (Henry Fonda) to be secretary of state, the Senate divides over his selection. Foes of the president take the appointment as an opportunity to settle old scores. Dixiecrats (Southern Democrats) object to Leffingwell's liberalism while conservatives are concerned that he is soft on communism. To neutralize one of Leffingwell's Senate supporters (Don Murray), the opposition threatens to expose a homosexual incident in his past, which leads the young senator to commit suicide. At the end, the president dies and the vice president decides to name his own candidate. While the film reflects America's Cold War concern of Soviet expansion and the need for policy-making officials to be committed to the containment of communism as the cornerstone of foreign policy, it also exposes Capitol Hill as a ruthlessly competitive place.

*The Seduction of Joe Tynan* (1979), scripted by and starring Alan Alda, is another film with a plot grounded in the politics of the U.S. Senate. Alda plays the title character, a young liberal senator and contented family man. The political issue at the forefront of this film is a presidential appointment to the U.S. Supreme Court, which requires Senate confirmation. Southern senators, led by senior Senator Birney (Melvyn Douglas), favor a candidate that the NAACP characterizes as "racist" and unacceptable. Both sides lobby for Tynan's support. Should he side with the black lobby or should he do the expedient thing and promote his career by standing with the Southern coalition? Tynan decides to oppose the Southerners' candidate; a decision that rewards him with the political plum of making the presidential nominating speech at the convention, an honor normally reserved for potential presidential candidates.[12] Although Tynan makes the right choice politically, he makes the wrong choice morally when he has an affair with a Southern lobbyist (Meryl Streep) that almost destroys his marriage. But true to Hollywood form, reconciliation, if not repentance, is implied at the end along with fulfillment of presidential ambitions.

*Legally Blonde 2* (2003) aspires to duplicate the "Capra-esque" world of Jefferson Smith, but is merely a poor substitute. In this sequel to *Legally Blonde* (2001), Elle Woods (Reese Witherspoon) has graduated from Harvard Law and becomes an advocate for animal rights when she discovers that her pet chihuahua's mother is being used to test cosmetics at a Boston research lab. Shocked by this revelation, Elle goes to Washington to persuade Congress to enact animal rights legislation. Although she is successful in protecting animals, the movie's simplistic approach to politics led one film scholar to observe: "The film's preposterous premise that silly costuming and naïve rhetorical masturbation will win the day is a disservice to those who seek real change."[13] That assessment is much too polite for this ridiculous film. For instance, one scene has Elle bringing cheerleaders to Washington to have them perform a rock 'n' roll song about her dog on the steps of the Capitol to the delight of the Congressmen, who join in the festivities. This is definitely not a film to show to Congress.

Political skullduggery is at the heart of a couple of films about Washington politics that deal with the abuse of political power. *True Colors* (1991) tracks the careers of two bright law school students, Peter Burton (John Cusack) and Tim Garrity (James Spader). Burton is an ambitious manipulator with a Nixon-type personality who chooses politics as a career, while his law school friend, Garrity, joins the Justice Department. Burton romances and marries the daughter of an influential senator (Richard Widmark) and becomes his father-in-law's aide as part of his ambitious political scheme. Using an assortment of dirty tricks, blackmail, and his father-in-law's money and influence, Burton decides to run for Congress. Meanwhile, Garrity is content to prosecute cases for the government. Their paths cross when Burton involves Garrity in a shady deal with a land developer, which guarantees Burton the developer's financial support. To save his job and his reputation, Garrity turns informer, becoming Burton's campaign manager in a plan to secure incriminating evidence for a Justice Department prosecution. At the end, Burton wins his congressional seat but loses his wife and is likely headed to prison. Still, the final scene implies that an unrepentant Burton is ready to resume his political career after serving his prison term, which is not an encouraging assessment of what Hollywood thinks of the American electorate.

A portrait of political infighting is at the heart of Rod Lurie's film *The Contender* (2000), deliberately released one month before the presidential election. Democratic president Jackson Evans (Jeff Bridges), a good ole boy who loves to eat, bowl, and smoke tobacco, nominates the female senator from Ohio (Joan Allen) to fill the vacant vice presidency position. However, the villainous chair of the House Judiciary Committee, Republican Shelly Runyon (Gary Oldman) opposes her nomination and sets out to destroy her candidacy through the release of photos that supposedly show Allen involved in a college sex orgy. Although the charges are false and the president urges her to fight back, Allen refuses to respond to them or to withdraw her candidacy. Runyon is depicted as such a mean-spirited, evil character that Joe McCarthy would have been proud of him. After the film's release, Oldman, who also was one of the producers, accused Dream-Works, Steven Spielberg's company, of deliberately changing the film's emphasis to support a Democratic agenda.[14] The true story of the backstage politicking is unlikely to be made public, but the incident demonstrates that at least some people in Hollywood take their politics seriously.

## Reel Presidents: Heroes, Hapless Fools and Villains

With few exceptions, the film industry has treated the American presidency with respect and dignity, if not reverence. The honorable screen presidents of the past—Henry Fonda and Raymond Massey as Lincoln, Alexander Knox as Wilson, Ralph Bellamy as FDR, and Gary Sinise as Truman—featured in historical biographies in which sitting and future presidents were portrayed as statesmen and men of integrity. Together with the political media, the film industry acted as co-conspirators in protecting the public image of the early presidents. In pre-WWII Hollywood, the studios made only two kinds of films involving presidents: biographical and fictional. For the first half-century, historical-biographical films dominated the studio output. From 1908 until the 1950s, more than half of the presidential films were biographies of some sort. Although many film historians consider these factually inaccurate in detail, they treated the president and the office with respect.[15] The fact that Hollywood produced over 130 films, many respectful of the presidency, reflects on the industry's requirements under the old Production Code regarding authority figures and on the patriotism of the early studio heads.

Lincoln is a perfect example. There were at least four silent films about the 16th president and three more with sound in the 1930s–40s. The latter were about Lincoln's life before his ascendancy to the presidency and in each one he is depicted as humble, modest, even saintly. This screen image of Lincoln as a one-dimensional character led Americans to believe the president lacked personal ambition, political skills, and human flaws. The latest addition to the Lincoln legend tells a different story, however.

Figure 6.1. A Pensive Lincoln in Steven Spielberg's Film, *Lincoln*, 2012. Reprinted with permission, Walt Disney Studios Motion Pictures/Photofest

## Case Study: Spielberg's *Lincoln*

Director Steven Spielberg's *Lincoln* (2012) rejects the former imagery, portraying the president as a shrewd politician not above using the power of his office to achieve his objective. Spielberg's *Lincoln* is not a biopic but rather an issue-oriented examination of the president's quandary after his re-election in 1864. The film opens in January 1865, when a Union victory appears imminent and a lame duck Congress is considering passage of the 13th Amendment, which would abolish slavery. The U.S. Senate had already adopted the amendment and Lincoln supported it but the House of Representatives is some 20 votes short of the two-thirds necessary for adoption. The focus of the movie, then, is the effort by Lincoln and the abolitionists to secure those necessary votes from conservative Republicans of their own party and several politically vulnerable Democrats. The president's dilemma is this: he must secure those 20 votes and the adoption of the amendment before the war with the Confederacy ends. Peace would bring the seceding southern states back into the Union, giving them an opportunity to vote against the amendment. Once an amendment to the Constitution has been adopted by both houses of Congress, it still must be approved by three-quarters of the states. Hence, Lincoln decides to delay the peace process, buying time in order to secure the necessary votes, but at the cost of many lives. Put bluntly, what is more important: lives or the end of slavery? This is the political and moral issue facing Lincoln in Spielberg's film.

*Lincoln* was well received by the critics but historians and others had complaints about its accuracy. One complaint was that the film mentioned only three children, Robert and Tad (living) and Willie (dead before the film begins). But the Lincolns had a fourth son, Eddie, who died as an infant. Hence, the two children not present in the film were dead before the plot of the movie unfolds. The second criticism is that the film wrongly polarized the slavery issue as between Southern Democrats and Northern Abolitionists. The House vote on adoption was 119 in favor and 56 opposed but among the latter group were Democrats from New York and New Jersey. While the South wanted to retain slavery, there were interests in the North who found the slave trade a lucrative profession. It is also true that there were a number of proposals put forth to abolish slavery, including one by Senator John Henderson of Missouri, a War Democrat.[16] A more serious mistake occurs in the voting by the four Connecticut representatives. The error occurs in the important scene in which the House is voting on the 13th Amendment to abolish slavery. The film shows two Connecticut lawmakers voting "no" when in fact all four House representatives voted in favor of the amendment.[17]

These are other mistakes of omission and commission that are relatively minor errors. However, the substantive issue that bothered historians the most was the portrayal of Lincoln as an abolitionist who went to war to end slavery. The traditional view presented previously was that the Civil War was fought by the Union over secession. Slavery, of course, was the overwhelming reason for the Confederacy. The traditionalist long relied on Lincoln's own words written in 1862:

> My paramount object in this struggle is to save the Union, and is not either to save or to destroy slavery. If I could save the Union without freeing any slave I would do it, and if I could save it by freeing all the slaves I would do it; and if I could save it by freeing some and leaving others alone I would also do that. What I do about slavery, and the colored race, I do because I believe it helps to save the Union...[18]

Lincoln wrote these words in a private letter to Horace Greeley in an attempt to explain the difference between his personal views and his actions as president. Spielberg's film, on the other hand, portrays Lincoln as a man who could not abide slavery and was willing to trade lives to defend the moral imperative that inequality was incompatible with democratic government. Which viewpoint is more accurate? Possibly both if you see Lincoln as a transformative figure who placed the Union above abolition at the beginning of the war but after 600,000 deaths felt the human cost demanded the end of slavery.[19] It is the author's conjecture that at this point Lincoln believed the abolishment of slavery was the greater good.

Spielberg's *Lincoln* is the eighth film about our 16th president and the most balanced. Lincoln is no longer an icon spouting lofty speeches but a tortured, flawed human being, troubled at home and at work. It is true that Spielberg's Lincoln loves to tell stories and talk in parables, but he is also not above deceiving his own party, buying votes through patronage jobs, and twisting arms when necessary. Columnist David Brooks noted that the film was a good lesson in the art of legislating, that is, in how laws get passed in the American system.[20] The author would like to add to that lesson his suggestion that *Lincoln* be shown to every new president and Congress to remind them that, as public servants, they are in Washington to serve the public good.

Hollywood portrayed real presidents with respect and deference, but its fictional presidents in pre-WWII movies were also men of action who took political risks, sometimes stretching the boundaries of constitutionality. As one illustration, take the screen president Judd Hammond (Walter Houston) in *Gabriel Over the White House* (1933). He begins as an indifferent and corrupt politician who is transformed into a decent and caring leader after a visit from the angel Gabriel. At the beginning of the film, Hammond acts like the real President Hoover, expressing political platitudes but doing nothing to meet the challenge of the Depression. When the angel Gabriel visits him after a serious automobile accident puts him at death's door, Hammond is miraculously converted into a political activist, taking steps to bring about economic recovery, rooting out political corruption, and supporting efforts to achieve world peace.[21] His methods, however, border on the dictatorial—dismissing the legislature, creating military tribunals, and organizing the unemployed into a brown shirt cadre. The public, meanwhile, saw the screen Hammond as a welcome relief from the actual do-nothing Hoover.[22]

After WWII, Hollywood continued to occasionally turn out screen biographies of presidents, with old-fashioned screen biographies made of Wilson, Franklin Roosevelt, and Harry Truman (cable TV). *Wilson* (1944) followed the president from his early years into the White House. *Sunrise at Campobello* (1960) focused on FDR's battle with polio and ends with his nomination speech at the 1928 Democratic Convention. On the other hand, *Truman* (1995) is more interested in the decisions that president faced during his time in office. These three films were respectful toward their subjects. Usually the action unfolded chronologically and these screen biographies were intended to be mythic personal stories of human courage and sacrifice rather than controversial political tracts. What moviegoer will forget President Wilson's stirring speeches or FDR's efforts to overcome polio? These were uplifting film moments, yet they were biased presentations because *Wilson* ignored the president's prejudicial views on race and gender and Roosevelt's sexual liaisons were omitted from *Sunrise at Campobello*.

However, the presidential biography of Harry Truman, made for cable distribution rather than commercial theaters, was more honest than most. The film reverts to the format of the pre–World War II biography, with the intent to elevate Truman's presidency above the 32 percent approval rating his administration received in 1952 at the end of its second term. Gary Sinise is a very credible Truman, in both appearance and mannerisms. Beginning with the 1948 campaign, the film unfolds in a series of flashbacks, commencing in 1917 with the young Truman volunteering to serve in World War I and ending with the second term of his presidency. Between these two events, Truman enters politics with the support of the Prendergast Kansas City machine and ascends to the presidency upon the death of FDR. The second half concentrates on the difficult issues Truman faced in the White House: namely, whether to use the atom bomb during World War II, how to desegregate the military, how to thwart Soviet aggression, whether to seize the steel mills during the Korean War, whether to recognize the new state of Israel, and whether he should fire the popular General MacArthur over issues of authority and command during the Korean conflict. These momentous political issues, as usual in commercial films, are treated superficially during the 135-minute running time. Still, *Truman* represents a more balanced approach to political biography.

The "hands-off" treatment previously accorded presidents changed dramatically in the 1990s when Hollywood presented audiences with a series of larger-than-life leaders veering from comic book heroes to foolish buffoons and dastardly villains. The filmic assault on the office escalated to such a degree that a couple of political scientists described the representations as a collection of "shysters, sycophants, and sexual deviants."[23]

Two popular films of the nineties depicted their presidents as strong and decisive leaders, but in an unrealistic fashion usually found in comic books. Both Bill Pullman's president in *Independence Day* and Harrison Ford's president in *Air Force One* are action adventure, over-the-top heroes. Both films appealed to the American public, as *Air Force One* had a domestic gross of $172 million and *Independence Day* exceeded $300 million. Pullman's president almost single-handedly takes on and defeats invading aliens in outer space combat and Ford's president engages in hand-to-hand combat to save his wife and family. When Air Force One is taken over by Russian terrorists, Ford chooses to stay on the plane rather than take the safety chute. As a combat veteran and Medal of Honor winner who refuses to negotiate with terrorists, Ford as president is the right person to handle this situation. In short order, he kills all the terrorists and recaptures the plane. He is certainly no middle-aged, soft-bellied wimp of a president. During the struggle with the terrorist leader, Ford overpowers him and shoves him out the open door yelling, "Get off my plane!" Audiences clapped and cheered, demonstrating that Americans fantasize that their presidents are like their superhero reel impersonators.

Other 1990s activist screen presidents include Stanley Anderson (*Armageddon*, 1998) and Morgan Freeman (*Deep Impact*, 1998), who try to save the U.S. and the world from an asteroid, and Kevin Pollak (*Deterrence*, 2000), who exercises firm leadership in a foreign policy crisis despite being trapped in a blizzard. Of the three, Pollak's president, Walter Emerson, is presented with the most compelling dilemma. While campaigning in Colorado, Emerson and his staff get caught in a snowstorm and take refuge in a local diner. When Emerson learns that Saddam's son has reinvaded Kuwait and overrun UN and American forces, he is faced with a major international crisis. Turning the diner into a mini-war room, Emerson and his staff discuss their options, which are limited because the majority of American troops are stationed far away from Iraq. At this point, Emerson decides that his only recourse is to threaten the Iraqis with a nuclear attack unless their armies withdraw from Kuwaiti soil. On the surface, Emerson appears to be a resolute leader who refuses to negotiate with terrorists. But his decision to bomb Baghdad brings the world to the brink of nuclear war. These strong fictional presidents may help to explain the rising popularity of macho men in American political life. President Obama's election, however, may force Hollywood to rethink its ultra-heroic occupants of the Oval Office.

Comedy has always been a favorite genre of the Hollywood studios, but in the nineties the laughs appeared to be at the expense of the presidency. At least four major productions poked fun at both the institution and the occupant of the office. The most ridiculous of the lot was Tim Burton's *Mars Attacks!* (1996), where the U.S. is invaded by little technicolored aliens sporting heavy firepower. What must have seemed funny to Burton on the printed page fizzled on the big screen, as special effects and an A-list cast failed to attract an audience. Jack Nicholson plays a dim-witted president who welcomes the "little creatures" from outer space until they annihilate the entire U.S. Congress. Nicholson relies for advice upon a pipe-smoking professor who is out of touch with reality and constantly spouts nonsensical advice such as that all advanced civilizations are friendly and peace loving. In the end, earth is saved from the foolishness of Nicholson's moronic president and even dumber professorial advisor when a demented old woman and her grandson discover that the aliens cannot stand the song "Indian Love Call." Only older viewers will recognize it and scratch their heads.

A less ridiculous approach to the presidency is taken in the 1996 comedy *My Fellow Americans*, where Jack Lemmon and James Garner play two former presidents who are framed by the incumbent occupant of the White House. Lemmon (Republican) and Garner (Democrat) hate each other and spend most of the film bickering even when on the run from agents who want to kill them. The plot is preposterous and obviously intended for laughs, as these two hapless and cranky guys escape shootings, bombings, and one misadventure after another. In one scene, for instance, they rent a car but forget how to drive it. In another they borrow a car from a family only to discover that its baby is in the backseat. Can these be our fearless leaders? More likely, these nitwits would never survive the primary.

On the other hand, both *Dave* (1993) and *Dick* (1999) are more subtle comedies involving the office of the presidency. The screen president in *Dave* is engaged in extracurricular sexual activities. Except here, the philandering president suffers a stroke during a sexual encounter with one of the White House secretaries and is hidden in the White House basement. His wicked chief of staff decides to cover up the incident by recruiting a look-alike, Dave Kovic (Kevin Kline), to impersonate the dead president as part of a devious plot to deny the executive office to the liberal vice president.[24] Being a comedy the plan naturally fails, as the impostor Kovic becomes a more compassionate president than the one he replaced. With the assistance of the First Lady and some White House staffers, he pulls off a palace coup, allowing the liberal vice president to take office. *Dave* is a Hollywood fairy tale, as Kovic returns to his real job at the end and also wins the heart of the president's wife. Here the imposter president turns out to be an improvement over the real president and his Machiavellian chief of staff.

*Dick*, not surprisingly, is President Richard Nixon during the Watergate scandal. Two Washington teenage girls are suspected by Nixon's staff of having learned details of the Watergate break-in after meeting G. Gordon Liddy. While staffers debrief the girls to determine how much they know, Nixon's dog, Checkers, takes to the girls, so Nixon hires them as the White House dog walkers. Eventually, the girls do learn the truth of the break-in and the subsequent cover-up, hear the break-in tapes, and witness the shredding of documents. This information leads them to contact Woodward and Bernstein, who proceed to write the story that brings down Nixon. Contrary to actuality, the girls are the real "deep throats" that lead to Nixon's exposure. As the president resigns and leaves the White House in disgrace, the girls hold up a banner that reads: "YOU SUCK DICK." The comedy is facetious and understated, but the characterizations are well developed and neatly played. The film is farce, with Nixon the president part of the fun.

Comic book heroics and bumbling and foolish presidents may test the boundaries of reality and good taste, but screen presidents as dastardly men pushes the limits of public acceptability. Two films in particular portray the presidency in terms not previously seen in the movies. Coincidentally, both films use the word "power" in their titles, were produced in the same year, and open with the president engaged in a sexual encounter that leads to death, followed by an elaborate cover-up.

The president in *Executive Power* (1999) has the Secret Service sneak women into the Oval Office on a regular basis. On one particular night a woman dies in the course of having sex on top of the presidential seal, an act witnessed by three agents. The White House chief of staff puts into motion a cover-up that protects the president from public exposure. But three years later, during the presidential election campaign, one witness is found dead. That triggers an investigation by the two remaining agents that eventually puts their lives in danger. At this point, the film deteriorates into a standard chase flick, with the bad guys pursuing the good guys. By film's end, there are at least 16 dead bodies. While the president in this film is no saint, his wife turns out to be even worse, as she is behind all these killings in an attempt to recover an incriminating sex video.

In Clint Eastwood's *Absolute Power* (1997) the president (Gene Hackman) is portrayed as a boozy womanizer who enjoys rough sex and lacks even one redeeming quality. During one sexual encounter with his mistress, the president's penchant for rough sexual foreplay goes too far and the pair engage in a violent struggle. As she gets the upper hand and is about to stab the president with a letter opener, the Secret Service break in, opening fire and killing her instantly. As the story unfolds, the president's staff devises a convoluted cover-up scheme to hide the murder from the Washington police. But unknown to the president and his staff, a burglar (Eastwood) has witnessed the whole affair from his hiding place inside a bedroom closet (he can see them, but they can't see him). Subsequently, Eastwood becomes the chief suspect but is saved from arrest when the dead woman's husband discovers the truth and kills Hackman. These two screen presidents are scoundrels in the worst sense of the word.

Is there an explanation to account for this shift from favorable to negative presidential imagery? Yenerall and Kelley acknowledge the defining influence of Watergate in the transformation, but believe other factors also contributed.[25] For instance, the end of the Cold War encouraged screenwriters to look for new villains at the same time that the Watergate scandal allowed them to fantasize about internal enemies. Another factor to consider, according to Yenerall and Kelley, is that after Watergate, the media felt free to focus on the character of the president, a subject once thought to be taboo. The sexual scandals of presidential candidate Gary Hart and the White House shenanigans of Bill Clinton left the presidency vulnerable to personal attack. Communications professor Ralph Donald makes the case for the Watergate scandal as the catalyst for the predominately negative view of presidents and the presidential office.[26] While Donald focuses on Watergate, he suggests that public disillusionment after media revelations about the late President Kennedy's proclivities and the series of lies about Vietnam told to the American people by President Lyndon Johnson were also factors. In any event, Professor Donald envisions Hollywood movies about the presidency as reflecting the antihero era that dominated American politics until President Obama's election.

Screen portrayals of Nixon and George W. Bush require separate consideration since both are depicted as neither heroes nor fools, but rather as problematic presidents. Each had character flaws that hindered their leadership performance. Nixon lacked the temperament for the office, was at times venal and self-loathing, this being nurtured by feelings of distrust and envy. Bush lacked the self-confidence and the commitment to the responsibilities of the office. He appeared at times to be the mouthpiece of his advisors.

Three films feature Nixon as president. Two of these would likely not have been made by pre–World War II Hollywood. Oliver Stone's *Nixon* (1995) reconstructs the presidency as a dark and secret place inhabited by an unstable leader. Stone's three-hour film is a psychological study of a tortured and lonely man whose insecurity consistently required social acceptance and public adoration. Although the Nixon family found fault with the portrayal, George McGovern, Nixon's Democratic opponent in the 1972 presidential race, considered Stone's treatment to be balanced.[27] Stone himself thought Nixon a tragic figure, incapable of taming a system dominated by power elites, corporate greed, and political intrigue.[28] This idea is dramatically portrayed in the night scene at the Lincoln Memorial where Nixon is confronted by student protesters. When Nixon tells the students that he wants to end the war, one protester replies, "The system won't let you stop it." Nixon is stunned by this observation as the Secret Service leads him away from the group. Stone tells Nixon's story in flashback, culminating in the Watergate break-in and the subsequent resignation. Despite his personal fall from grace, Nixon remains an important political player in the 20th century, particularly in foreign affairs. Although he left office in disgrace, recent history has been kinder and remembers Nixon as the president who brought Vietnam to closure, opened China to the West, and improved relations with the old Soviet Union. Nevertheless, a 2009 C-Span poll of historians placed Nixon's presidency in the bottom half of the 43 presidents that were ranked.[29]

If Stone's film is considered harsh, Robert Altman's view of Nixon in *Secret Honor* (1985) is absolutely devastating. Although not a screen biography per se, *Secret Honor* is a 90-minute monologue filmed on a set designed to represent Nixon's private White House quarters, where actor Philip Baker Hall paces, raves, and curses his fate. Altman's Nixon is a sad, lonely figure who drinks too much and blames everyone else—Kennedy, Eisenhower, his mother—for his misfortune. This Nixon is a foul-mouthed whiner continually conjuring up enemies, real and imagined, and searching for scapegoats. The only prop missing from the film is a straightjacket.

Director Ron Howard edited the 30 hours of televised interviews in 1977 between David Frost and ex-President Nixon and then fictionalized an intense two-hour movie out of their content in his film *Frost/Nixon* (2008). Frost was an ambitious BBC performer anxious for glory, while Nixon was seeking to reshape his image and restore his reputation three years after his resignation from the presidency. In this verbal boxing match, each man feinted and jabbed for three days, as if they were sparring partners. Nixon cleverly dominated the discourse and was clearly ahead on talking points until the last interview, when each man fought with no holds barred. On that final day, Frost had finally done his homework and was prepared to deliver the knockout punch. After listening to the Watergate tapes for the first time, he confronts Nixon on the cover-up. Caught off-guard, Nixon admits on TV that "when the president does it [orders the Watergate break-in], that means it's not illegal." Reeling from that sucker punch, Nixon admits he made horrendous mistakes and apologizes for the cover-up, confessing that "I brought myself down. I let down the country. I let down our system of government.... I let the American people down." As played by Frank Langella, this Nixon is a complex character—sly, humorous, arrogant, and at the end, sad and beaten. Although he does not resemble Nixon in physical appearance, Langella's Nixon is the best screen characterization of the former president.

Oliver Stone's *W.* opens in 2002 with the Bush administration struggling for a slogan that represents their foreign policy thinking, finally settling on "Axis of Evil." Stone then backtracks to examine G.W.'s life, from his early years through his college days at Yale, his disinterest in working in the family oil business, his election as Governor of Texas, and his tainted victory over Al Gore in the 2000 presidential election. Stone spends most of his film time on G.W. growing into manhood; yet nothing new is revealed. Most Americans already knew G.W. as the college frat boy more interested in partying and drinking than in academics, a lifestyle that displeased his father. In 1977 G.W. meets Laura Welch, his future wife, and runs for Congress, only to lose the election. According to the film, he sees the light as he works on his father's next campaign, gives up drinking, and becomes a born-again Christian. These events seemingly altered the course of G.W.'s political career. Thereafter, his political fortunes brighten as he becomes the Governor of Texas in 1994 with the aid of his campaign manager, Karl Rove, and is reelected in 1998. Stone does not spend much time on the 2000 presidential election but instead moves forward to 2003 and the decision to invade Iraq. But underneath the biographical benchmarks that mark G.W.'s life is his obvious inadequacy when compared to his father and younger brother, Jeb. G.W's father repeatedly expresses his disappointment with his oldest son for his lack of ambition and seriousness of purpose, and unwillingness to become an adult. In a scene toward the end of the film, his father tells G.W, "You ruined it for us," a reference to the damage done to Jeb's political future. The film concludes with a puzzled President Bush at his final press conference, unable to respond to such questions as "What were your biggest mistakes?" and "What lessons did you learn?" Dazed, Bush just stares into the abyss.

The problem with Stone's film is that it is boring because Bush Jr. is such an ordinary guy, dull and uninteresting, and it is clear to the audience that without his family's money and power, G.W. would have spent his life associated with the Texas Rangers baseball team. In the 2009 presidential ranking poll by historians,[30] George W. Bush is grouped with the likes of James Buchanan, Millard Fillmore, and Warren Harding, at 36th among the 43 presidents ranked. His father, President George H.W. Bush, was ranked 18 places higher.[31]

This brief overview of Hollywood's treatment of the presidency confirms an attitudinal shift away from respect and a movement towards irreverence. But whether the Watergate scandal was responsible for the change or merely contributed to it is a question best left to the historians. Any student of history, however, will come to realize that since the end of World War II, America has undergone a vast transformation in values and policies. In this sense, Hollywood's view of the presidency mirrors that change.

## Political Assassinations

Conspiracies abound in the minds of Hollywood screenwriters because films about assassinations make highly dramatic movies, full of suspense and action sequences that draw well at the box office. History and cultural factors provide another reason why political assassinations interest the film studios. The U.S. is a country with a violent past, from the war for independence to the institution of slavery, the winning of the West, the systemic extermination of Native American tribes, the exploitation of women and children as cheap labor (many of them immigrants), the birth of organized crime during Prohibition, the development of urban street gangs in the post–World War II era, and the increasing use of guns in shooting rampages throughout the country. These historical benchmarks provide context for the crime rate in the U.S. today, including a higher murder rate compared to other Western industrial nations.

Political figures have not escaped becoming victims of violence. Of the 44 American presidents (including President Obama), 10 have had attempts made on their lives. Four presidents actually died at the hands of assassins: Lincoln, Garfield, McKinley, and Kennedy. Six unsuccessful attempts were made on Presidents Jackson, Teddy Roosevelt, Franklin Roosevelt, Truman, Ford, and Reagan. Added to this list are the assassinations of such prominent political figures as Martin Luther King Jr., Medgar Evers, Bobby Kennedy, and Malcolm X. It is a sobering statistic that almost a quarter of American presidents have been the target of assassins.

The author wonders what other nations must think of us. Do they believe violence is inherent in America's genetic makeup? Is it perhaps due to racial and socioeconomic class differences which breed discontent and hate? Or might it be the increasingly gratuitous violence found in Hollywood films? Regardless of the reasons cited for this violence, public officials and political figures in contemporary America perform their public duties at considerable personal risk.

Virtually all of Hollywood's assassination films have focused on the presidency, including John Frankenheimer's *The Manchurian Candidate* (1962), a film about a conspiracy to plant a communist functionary inside the White House. Although the final assassination attempt on the life of a U.S. senator is thwarted, the film's conspiracy theory preceded Oliver Stone's *JFK* film by almost three decades. The film stars Laurence Harvey as prisoner of war Raymond Shaw, who is brainwashed by the North Koreans and their communist allies into becoming a sleeper assassin. He returns to the U.S. to be reunited with his mother, the politically ambitious wife of a right-wing, McCarthy-type senator. Her intention is to promote her husband as vice president as a ruse to infiltrate communists into the White House. The plan is to have the president assassinated so her doltish husband would move into the Oval Office and she would be the power behind the throne. Her scheme is foiled by Harvey's former army commander, Lt. Bennett Marco (Frank Sinatra). The 1960s *Manchurian Candidate* explored the new brainwashing technique of the fifties, practiced by the Chinese communists in the Korean War as they experimented on prisoners using mind-altering drugs, deprivation techniques, water boarding, and other forms of torture. Ironically, when the Obama administration made public the "torture memos," they revealed that U.S. intelligence had studied, applied, and incorporated these same communist techniques on suspected Islamic terrorists after 9/11.[32]

The original *Manchurian Candidate*'s paranoia resonated with the reality of the Cuban Missile Crisis. But the 2004 version is not really a remake since the plot and some characters have changed. The villains here include an incestuous mother and her corporate power base, Manchurian Global, a multinational equity fund. This time around, Marco (Denzel Washington) and Shaw (Liev Schreiber) are soldiers in the 1991 Persian Gulf War. Captured, they become unwitting resources for Manchurian Global: once implanted with command chips, they will serve as sleeper assassins. The scheme is to have Shaw enter national politics, aided by his mother (Meryl Streep), a powerful and influential U.S. senator. Streep maneuvers her son onto the national ticket as vice president with the intention of having the president assassinated, allowing Shaw to move into the Oval Office, where mother and Manchurian Global can control him. With the assistance of an F.B.I. agent, Marco fortunately uncovers the conspiracy in time. The film contains timely references to terrorists, terror alerts, and intense security measures, but its paranoia of total control by a vague equity fund may no longer frighten audiences accustomed to the machinations of a Halliburton.

Frank Sinatra figured prominently in another assassination film, *Suddenly* (1954), where he plays the role of a presidential assassin. Sinatra portrays a disgruntled war veteran turned professional assassin, John Baron, who arrives in the small town of Suddenly, California, to wait for the president to appear on his scheduled whistle-stop tour. To carry out the planned assassination, Baron and his gang take over a strategically located home, hold the family hostage, and set up headquarters in a second floor room with a good vantage point from which to shoot the president. The motivation for the assassination attempt in this film is more personal than political: Baron believes that only by killing the president will he "become somebody." Because Baron's character slightly matched that of Lee Harvey Oswald, the film was temporarily withdrawn from television after 1963.[33]

A number of films have dealt directly with President Kennedy's assassination and its aftermath. Other films used the assassination as a reference point from which to develop the assassination plot. For instance, in the culmination of Robert Altman's *Nashville* (1975) all the characters are assembled for the grand finale—an outdoor country-western show as a prelude to a political rally for fictitious presidential candidate Hal Phillip Walker. Before Walker's motorcar reaches the Nashville Parthenon Theater where the rally is being held, a disturbed young man shoots the lead singer, Barbara Jean,[34] frightening off the Walker cavalcade. As the shooter is subdued, the audience is persuaded to remain calm by the master of ceremonies, Haven Hamilton, who reminds the crowd, "This isn't Dallas, this is Nashville." Although candidate Walker is never seen in the film, his name, nonetheless, ended up on several write-in ballots in 1976, just as the fictitious Jack Tanner, from the *Tanner '88* film, received votes in the 1988 presidential election.

Since the Kennedy assassination, five feature films have used this tragic event as the basis for screen material involving conspiracies of one kind or another. Robert Robins and Jerrold Post maintain that the conspiracy theme is attractive to filmmakers because such plots appeal to the political paranoia of the public seeking to explain tragedies that appear incomprehensible.[35] An early entry into political paranoia, *Executive Action* (1973), is pure speculation, as screenwriter Dalton Trumbo reconstructs a conspiracy theory in which a group of millionaires, joined by military leaders, plot to kill Kennedy and use Oswald as the patsy. To give the appearance of being a documentary, the film is constructed around a daily log of events, leading up to the assassination day, and supported by newsreels from the Kennedy era that are interspersed with fictitious characters. To further enhance its appearance of authenticity, the film's prologue contends that the evidence supports its conspiracy conclusion, which is based on Mark Lane's book *Rush to Judgment*, an attempt to provide a more plausible explanation than the "lone assassin" theory accepted by the Warren Commission. *Executive Action* would have the audience believe that Kennedy was targeted for death because of three fears: that he would withdraw the U.S. from Vietnam, that he would eventually end nuclear testing, and that he would encourage the civil rights revolution. There is not one shred of evidence to support these accusations. The film advances a three-gunmen theory rather than the Commission's "lone assassin" or the alternative, the two-gunmen theory. In the film's scenario, Oswald is guilty of murderous intentions, but innocent of the deed itself.

Two subsequent films, *The Parallax View* (1974) and *Winter Kills* (1979), have scenarios that parallel the Kennedy assassination. In *The Parallax View*, Joseph Frady (Warren Beatty) is a Seattle television reporter who stumbles onto an old political assassination story. When Frady digs deeper into the mystery, he discovers parallels with the Kennedy assassination, such as the lone assassin being killed by the police and several eyewitnesses dying under mysterious circumstances. Frady's investigation leads him to the monolithic Parallax Corporation, an organization that specializes in political assassinations. This discovery puts his life in danger. In *Winter Kills*, Jeff Bridges is Nick Kegan, the younger brother of an assassinated president. Based on the Richard Condon novel, Kegan's investigation into his brother's death uncovers an implausible conspiracy. This time the assassination occurs in Philadelphia rather than Dallas. However, the convicted assassin is shot dead by a nightclub owner prior to trial. Why did the president have to be killed? The film script wants the audience to believe that the president had taken money from the mob but had failed to deliver favors as his part of the bargain. Kegan's family is obscenely rich and conspicuously dysfunctional—a womanizing bully of a father, an alcoholic mother, a weak older brother, and the dead president, who had a madame supply him with an endless array of women. If all this sounds too familiar, the similarities with the real Kennedys are meant to be intentional.

Like *Executive Action*, Oliver Stone's conspiracy version of the Kennedy assassination depicted in *JFK* deals directly with the subject and the personalities involved. Based on several books, including one by New Orleans District Attorney Jim Garrison (played by Kevin Costner), Stone's film, however, mixes fact with fiction, interfaces historical newsreel footage with filmed events, and includes a "deep throat" informer to weave a sweeping conspiracy tale that embraces the military, the Dallas police, the intelligence community, and multinational corporations.[36] Stone's film centers on Garrison's efforts to prosecute businessman Clay Shaw (Tommy Lee Jones) for complicity in Kennedy's assassination. The actual legal record indicates that the trial was a fraud, an attempt by Garrison to blame Kennedy's death on a small group of homosexuals, including Shaw, together with an unidentified military-industrial complex. Shaw's jury took just 45 minutes to acquit him, while Stone took over three hours on screen to convict him. Stone's supposed "documented evidence" neglected to include Shaw's trial record.[37] The film's distributor, Warner Brothers, contributed to the deception by promoting the film as if the contents were the truth rather than Stone's version of events.[38] Stone's film deceptively intertwines the two worlds of illusion—Washington and Hollywood—to propagandize an unsubstantiated theory.

Political scientist Ray Pratt views the JFK assassination as the motivation for the government's obsession with secrecy.[39] Thereafter, government agencies adopted stricter policies that led to the withholding of information, the reclassification of documents to limit their accessibility, to limit disclosure, and generally deny all allegations and rumors. Rather than reassure the public by affirming the seven-member Warren Commission's conclusion that Oswald was the lone gunman, these restrictive policies only fed the rumor mill. A good example is Mark Sobel's film version of the Warren Commission hearings, simply entitled *The Commission*.[40] The film starred Sam Waterston, Martin Sheen, Ed Asner, and Martin Landau and supposedly took eight years to complete. Using transcripts from the Warren report, the film concluded that a cover-up of the assassination had, in fact, occurred. At the time of President Ford's death in 2006, no members of the Warren Commission were alive to be interviewed. Afterward, the archivist for the Ford Presidential Library discovered the existence of the Sobel film, but his internet search failed to uncover additional information on the film except that it was shown at the American Film Institute's festival in 2003. The author's follow-up research revealed that the film was apparently shown at the Los Angeles Film Festival in 2007, but whether it was ever distributed to theaters or made available on DVD remains a mystery. Was the film suppressed? Was there a conspiracy among distributors to deny the film exhibition play dates, similar to the situation with *Salt of the Earth*? Here is a good example of how secrecy fuels controversy and encourages rumors where transparency would have provided more light.

Another film with a plot involving the assassination of a president by a gunman who acts alone is not technically part of the conspiracy genre because it represents a discontented gunman striking back at those who have injured him. Sean Penn is the potential assassin in *The Assassination of Richard Nixon* (2004) who dies during a failed attempt to hijack a plane and fly it into the White House. Penn's character is not politically motivated in the sense that his actions are ideologically driven. Rather, he is a loser, a social misfit who cannot keep a job or a wife. He blames others for his misfortunes—the business community, the rich, the government, and while the film's intent is to demonstrate the growing inequality between the rich and the poor, it lacks conviction largely because Penn is a totally unsympathetic character. The film wants the audience to believe that it is "the system" that has beaten him, when in fact he has done that to himself. It is not surprising, therefore, that it flopped at the box office.[41]

Conspiracy theories appear to be the most recent fad in American popular culture, as evidenced by Stone's *JFK*, Mel Gibson's *Conspiracy Theory* (1997), and the popular television series *The X-Files*. The attack on 9/11 has encouraged the formation of conspiracy organizations, such as the International Education and Strategy group for 9/11 that met in Chicago in 2006. The more than 500 attendees heard speeches and received literature accusing the Bush administration of plotting the 9/11 terrorists attacks. The evidence given for the accusation involves the easy collapse of the WTC, the failure of the air defense network to prevent the attacks, and the rather large number of short-sell bids on airline stocks that day.[42] While the factual evidence reported by the 9/11 Commission, like the findings of the Warren Commission, convinced most Americans, the conspiracy theorists prefer to create their own villains.

Why this fascination with conspiracy theories today? Political Scientist Michael Barkun believes that there are two reasons for this attraction.[43] First, Barkun suggests that in the human need to make sense of the world, conspiracy theories greatly simplify reality, which appears inordinately complex. The end of the Cold War and the dissolution of the old Soviet Union, for instance, removed an identifiable enemy that could be blamed for world problems. Hollywood is in a continuous search for screen villains, vacillating between aliens and a variety of terrorists bent on destroying the U.S. and its allies. Second, Barkun speculates that the millennium is often associated with a literal or metaphysical Armageddon—a New World Order—ranging from religious fundamentalists preaching against the Antichrist to UFO enthusiasts who believe the government deliberately hides the truth about extraterrestrial life. Hollywood conspiracy films, therefore, provide us with convenient scapegoats to blame for the troubles in the world.

Historian Robert Alan Goldberg goes further than Barkun, blaming Hollywood for validating conspiracy theories in such major films as *JFK*, *The Manchurian Candidate*, and *Wag the Dog*.[44] These films serve as catalysts for skeptics, the gullible and misinformed, and antigovernment groups. Credibility of conspiracy theories is aided, sometimes unintentionally, by government denials and cover-ups, mainstream media's often unquestioned acceptance of the official government line, and by governmental attempts to discredit or silence its critics. In an effort to provide greater public access to governmental actions, President

Obama instituted a transparency policy that led to the release of the "torture memos" that documented the abuse and torture of prisoners and detainees in the war on terror.

## Reel Politicians: From Saints to Sinners?

What generalization can be derived from this overview of American politics and politicians as portrayed in Hollywood feature films? Some moviegoers who remember the early days of Hollywood might be tempted to answer that the film industry made a 180-degree turnabout in its attitude toward American politics. While there is a kernel of truth to that observation, particularly as applied to political biographies, it is seriously flawed historically because it wrongly suggests that Hollywood treated politicians with more respect and depicted political institutions in the past with greater deference than the present. The truth is more complicated. American politicians have been depicted as less than honorable figures as early as the silent era. Rather it is more accurate to state that the film industry continues to take a critical look at its political leaders and institutions. In fact, Hollywood has frequently depicted politicians as screen villains. What separates the present from the past is that pre-WWII Hollywood sought to balance the negative portrayals with more positive attributes of political honesty and integrity. Recall that in *Gabriel Over the White House*, crooked president Judd Hammond (Walter Huston) is redeemed and transformed into a man of the people after a visit from the angel Gabriel. Meanwhile, Jefferson Smith's idealistic freshman senator triumphs at the end of the film over the weak and flawed Senator Paine and the corrupt political machine he represents. Capra was willing to criticize the political system and point a disapproving finger at some of the people in it, but he never attributed their flaws and failures to representative government.[45] And Loretta Young's resourceful farmer's daughter wins her novice congressional race despite the opposition's attempt to smear her reputation.

However, there have been few Jefferson Smith–type "white knight" heroes on the silver screen since the sixties. In recent decades, the fictional political characters are more than flawed human beings. They seem to lack any redeeming personal qualities. Instead, they are depicted as political opportunists interested more in personal advancement and rewards than the public good, willing to cheat on their spouses, and not above abusing their friends and colleagues—sometimes without having to pay the price of disgrace and rejection. As a scheming and ambitious political animal in *True Colors*, the John Cusack character shows little remorse for his criminal behavior. Instead of displaying shame and disgrace for his misdeeds, he defiantly intends to remain in politics. Less than a decade after the film's release, President Clinton lied about his affair with Monica Lewinsky, and even when the lie was disclosed, he refused to admit it or to consider that he owed the American people a public apology. Clinton did not hesitate to announce to the American public that "I have not had sex with that woman," but he refused to go on television to apologize for the lie. Although Alan Alda's philandering Joe Tynan reconciles with his wife at the end of *The Seduction of Joe Tynan*, it is less a case of regenerated love than it is pragmatic politics because he needs her for his run for the presidency. Tim Robbins' *Bob Roberts* schemes and tricks his way into the U.S. Senate, raising questions as to what nefarious political plans he has for the future. Even Robert Redford's Bill McKay is a victorious but imperfect senator, unsure of himself after suppressing his political values in order to win the election. Warren Beatty's Senator Bulworth raises some serious questions about class and race in America, yet tempers them with tongue-in-cheek comedy. And *Wag the Dog* presents a Clintonesque clone in the White House with an eye for young girls.

Hollywood has not been shy about featuring politicians as despicable characters, like the womanizing governor in *Primary Colors*, the president as sex maniac in *Executive Power*, and the rough sex/rapist president in *Absolute Power*. In the few films where the major political character is portrayed in a totally positive light, he is apt to be cast in the unlikely role of action-hero. Even the comedic film presidents are flawed characters. In an age when the average film budget exceeds $60–70 million, major studios are unlikely to take risks with multidimensional politicians and complex political issues. The president in *Deterrence* threatens the city of Baghdad with nuclear annihilation after five minutes of reflection when, in the real political world, President Kennedy and his staff spent days negotiating with the Soviets during the Cuban missile crisis. Oversimplification and violent solutions are the buzzwords in the entertainment industry today, where human characteristics and people-oriented plots are replaced by special effects featuring the latest destructive weapons. The trend is possibly inevitable. In studying feature films on the Congress, one scholar concluded that Hollywood's need for simplification is irrevocably at odds with the complexities of life on Capitol Hill, where cooperation and compromise are often necessary for the passage of legislation or the enactment of a balanced budget.[46] This process is impossible to portray in a two-hour film.

Admittedly, the working life of a politician is routine and lacking in high drama, much like police work, where most police officers never fire their weapons. Hollywood and the public may fantasize that the life of a politician is exciting because he/she is involved in making important decisions every day. More often than not, the days of politicians are filled with committee meetings, reading reports, talking on the phone, listening to speeches, responding to constituents, and interacting with lobbyists and colleagues. This is the stuff of ordinary life. Because Hollywood's purpose is to entertain rather than to educate, its films dare not focus on the intricacies of the political process or the ordinary routine of political life. The studios prefer to provide audiences with an imaginary political world, filled with unlikely characters engaged in behavior that is sheer fantasy. Since these negative views often are reinforced by other social institutions and by the news media, the end result has been a complete debunking of American politics, defined on screen as a corrupting process fit only for villains.[47] No wonder many American students reject politics as a career choice. Possibly this contributes as well to the failure of young people to vote—more so than any other age group—at least as was the case until the 2008 presidential election.

The political world depicted in Hollywood films is a misrepresentation of the majority of decent, honest, hard-working people who work in government. The current climate recalls the time when a young Harry Truman told his disapproving mother that he intended to run for political office. Her response was terse: "Politics cheapens a man." Recent Hollywood films reinforce that view.

# Chapter 7

# Picturing Justice
## The Law and Lawyers in Hollywood Films

"The first thing we do, let's kill all the lawyers."
—Shakespeare, *Henry VI, Part II*

"Lawyers are the only persons in whom ignorance of the law is not punished."
—Jeremy Bentham

"When the 30-year old lawyer died he complained to St. Peter: How can you do this to me? A heart attack at my age? I'm only 30! Replied St. Peter: When we looked at your total hours billed we figured you were 95."
—Anonymous

"When I go to a party and people ask me what I do and I tell them I'm a lawyer, they seem shocked; as if I said I was a topless dancer."
—Woman lawyer

"If there were no bad people there would be no good lawyers."
—Charles Dickens

"It is the trade of lawyers to question everything, yield nothing, and talk by the hour."
—Thomas Jefferson

"The life of the law has not been logic; it has been experience."
—Justice Oliver Wendell Holmes

"Scarcely any political question arises in the United States that is not resolved, sooner or later, into a judicial one."
—Alexis de Tocqueville

## Law and Popular Culture

Lawyers, like politicians, make dramatic film subjects because their characters have the capacity for both good and evil. Furthermore, their actions affect the lives of others in significant ways. The good lawyer insures a client's personal freedom or economic security; the client who has a mediocre lawyer may end up in prison or the poorhouse. Moreover, lawyers, judges, and the police are perceived by the citizenry to be representatives of the country's values as expressed through its legal system. That system is supposed to dispense justice in every case; failure to provide a right decision adversely affects the system's credibility. Therefore, images that represent the legal culture can reinforce its authority or undermine its popular support.

According to law professor Stewart Macaulay, representations of the legal culture are present in everyday life, from the schoolroom to the sports arena.[1] Particularly important to Macaulay is the contribution of the entertainment arts because, as he correctly suggests, the visual media formulate an especially significant image of the law and the legal profession. Why is media influence so compelling? The legal culture consists of statutes, case law, and scholarly essays on jurisprudence—all of which shape and affect ordinary life. Yet as Macaulay observes, relatively few Americans read the legal literature and only a smaller number are involved in litigation or see the inside of a courtroom. He cites the study by the Hearst Corporation which ascertained that only 20 percent of the survey population had ever been a party in a civil suit, that only 16 percent had actually served on a jury, that 15 percent had been witnesses in a personal injury suit, and that as few as 10 percent had been victims.[2] Therefore, where do Americans learn about the law? Macaulay's response is that they learn the law from the experiences of ordinary life—work, school, sports, and entertainment. He reasons that more Americans learn about the legal system from the visual arts, especially film and television, than from any firsthand experience.[3]

To legal scholars Michael Asimow and Shannon Mader,[4] the legal culture represents what the public thinks it knows about the law, the legal profession, and the justice system. That legal culture is influenced by its portrayal in the venue of commercial entertainment, particularly in contemporary America, which is inundated by a "multiplicity of media outlets" and an endless variety of information available from such cyberspace sources as internet blogs, chat rooms, and twitters. Individuals are also able to distribute their own videos on YouTube, an outlet that has played an important role since the 2008 presidential election.

Asimow and Mader concur with Macaulay that the legal culture portrayed in popular culture outlets like movies may provide insights into the public's thinking about the law. The film *All the President's Men* focused on the two *Washington Post* reporters, Bernstein and Woodward, whose investigation exposed the Watergate scandal. In real life, their investigation brought down President Nixon and led to the indictment of 40 government officials, many of whom were lawyers. Public surveys and polls conducted after Watergate revealed public disenchantment with both government and lawyers. Lawyers became the butt of jokes on late-night TV and the profession's reputation suffered. Asimow and Mader believe that portrayals in the popular culture provide a legal realist perspective—that is, commercial entertainment portrays what lawyers, judges, jurors, and police actually do, rather than what they are supposed to do as detailed in legal texts. Although fictional works, do these movie portrayals influence how the public perceives the legal system? For instance, does the public perceive the insanity defense in a different light after viewing a film like *Anatomy of a Murder* (1959)? Would people view jury duty differently after seeing a film like *Suspect*

(1987)? What effect, if any, would a film like *The Paper Chase* (1973) have on college students contemplating law school?

These are relevant questions which have yet to be answered empirically. But the reader first may wish to consider Hollywood's response to Supreme Court decisions such as *Miranda v. Arizona*,[5] where the court held that persons in police custody have a right to remain silent and to consult an attorney. In a series of *Dirty Harry* movies in the seventies, Clint Eastwood, playing Lt. Harry Callahan, generally disregarded all of the so-called *Miranda* requirements. Harry had no use for them and he made sure they did not interfere with his police work. Moreover, he actually was contemptuous of the *Miranda* ruling and other legal requirements that he felt interfered with his job. His attitude irked the district attorney, who delivered this lecture to him:

> Where does it say that you have the right to kick down doors, torture suspects, deny medical attention and legal counsel? Where have you been? Does *Escobedo* ring a bell? *Miranda*? Why surely you have heard of the Fourth Amendment? What I'm saying is—that man had rights.

The *Miranda* ruling became an issue in the 2013 Boston Marathon bombings allegedly perpetrated by two terrorists, Tamerlan and Dzhokhar Tsarnaev. Tamerlan, the older brother, had been killed by police in a shootout after the bombing but his brother, Dzhokhar, was only wounded and taken captive. When Dzhokhar, an American citizen, was taken into custody as a suspect in the bombing, the Boston police invoked an exception to the *Miranda* rule laid down by the Supreme Court in *New York v. Quarles* (1984)[6] that allows a suspect to be interrogated without being informed of the right to be silent and to have an attorney present. In effect, the court had placed the protection and safety of the country's citizens over the individual rights of the suspect.[7]

Another legal scholar, John Denvir, explains how using court cases and legal issues such as abortion and capital punishment as film material can shed light on changes in current law or even serve as challenges to existing laws.[8] According to Denvir, films like *The Godfather* (1972) serve as legal texts, supplementing material found in the law reports. He believes that films describing the legal culture help shape popular perceptions about the law. Analyzing movies is a way to study one aspect of the legal culture.

Still the question remains: why study films about the law or fictitious plots involving courts, judges, and lawyers in movies when newspapers and television provide extensive coverage of actual events? There are three good reasons, according to Professor Timothy Lenz.[9] First, much of what appears in legal fiction is often related to the facts and the storylines are perused by specialists for accuracy about the law. Second, fictionalized versions about the law center around the search by individuals or groups to achieve justice for themselves or their loved ones, and finally, films provide models for an ideal justice system, reflecting the public's preference for a just society. He is of the opinion that some good can even come from viewing "legal nonsense," fictitious stories about the law that are exaggerated for dramatic effect, such as the two film versions of *Cape Fear*, involving a psychopathic character stalking and threatening the lives of a family because the father had sent him to prison. In the original 1961 version, the psychopath, Max Cady, upon his release from prison is determined to seek revenge against the former prosecutor who convicted him. Cady, however, is a wily convict who understands enough about the legal rules to use the law in his favor. He threatens the prosecutor and his family, always making sure that he is within the legal boundaries to prevent the police from arresting him. The film, then, touches on the due process rights of criminals, a perennial issue before the U.S. Supreme Court. This film version focuses on convicts who menace but do no physical harm. What action can a prosecutor, acting as an ordinary citizen, take against such a person? At the film's end, the prosecutor wounds Cady in a physical confrontation but does not kill him. Cady stands trial again and is returned to prison.

Thirty years later, director Martin Scorsese did a remake of *Cape Fear* (1991). In this version Cady plots vengeance against his negligent public defender after being released from prison because his lawyer refused to introduce evidence that Cady's rape victim was promiscuous, resulting in Cady's conviction. Lenz reminds us, however, that rape shield laws prohibit the use of such evidence in a criminal trial. In the Scorsese version, Cady is killed in a violent struggle with his lawyer rather than arrested and processed through the criminal justice system. In the context of the 1990s, the film relayed the message that Cady had to die because the legal system no longer could be trusted to deliver justice. If you want justice, Scorsese's film says, do it yourself.[10]

These are the not the worst examples of legal fictions, however. In *Runaway Jury* (2003), based on the John Grisham bestseller, a woman sues a gun manufacturer after her husband is killed in an office shooting. The gun manufacturer brings in a noted jury consultant to help select a jury favorable to the defense. In a convoluted plot development that hinges on an event 30 years before, a juror on the inside and a woman on the outside work to manipulate the jury verdict and deliver it to the highest bidder. The legal nonsense is considerable when the audience is asked to believe that a sequestered juror is easily able to sneak out of his motel room and receive outside phone calls. Even more implausible is the alcoholic juror who sneaks a whiskey bottle into the jury room without being detected. Finally, the jury consultant, who is the villain of the piece, hires thugs to trash the corrupt juror's home and set it on fire. These are major felonies that carry prison time. It is unlikely viewers will learn anything from this film except a completely ill-founded disdain for the jury system, an integral part of the American justice system.

## The Reel World of the Law

All the scholars above contend that movies reflect the legal culture, contradictions and all. On the one hand, there are the "legal texts" in films that reinforce existing principles, which lend support to the ruling authority and foster compliance with the established law. Yet there are legal texts in films that challenge those in control and portray public officials and authority figures as dishonest and corrupt. Similarly, in films on American politics, Hollywood movies often try to avoid direct attacks on the institutions of government, including the justice system, preferring instead to present the imperfections in a context that blames human weakness rather than a flawed legal system. Exceptions exist, like the final scene in Al Pacino's film *And Justice for All* (1979). Pacino is assigned to defend a judge accused of the rape and assault of a young woman. Pacino knows his client is guilty but lacks enough evidence to prove it. Instead he accuses his client in his opening statement to the jury and pandemonium breaks out in the courtroom:

> Pacino: "And ladies and gentlemen of the jury, the prosecution is not going to get that man today, no, because I'm gonna'get him! My client…should go right to fucking jail! That man is guilty.…Judge: "Mr. Kirkland, you are out of order!" Pacino: "You're out of order! You're out of order! The whole trial is out of order! That man…raped and beat that woman there, and he'd like to do it again!… (to the defendant): "You son-of-a-bitch. You're supposed to protect people! But instead you rape and murder them!"

Pacino is dragged out of the courtroom and is likely to be disbarred, his law career finished. And while such a scene is unlikely to happen in an American courtroom, the film puts the whole criminal justice system on trial.

Law professor David Ray Papke makes the cogent point that prior to WWII, the film industry generally portrayed the legal system and its practitioners positively.[11] Law films glorified lawyers, courtroom trials were presented deferentially, and the rule of law not only prevailed, but was respected. As evidence, he lists nine films of the 1950s and 1960s that present legal institutions as objective bodies and their practitioners as neutral players devoted to achieving fairness and securing justice for their clients.[12] Law was king then on the big screen and in real life, its practitioners admired and respected. Papke notes that the year following Senator McCarthy's death, President Eisenhower proclaimed May 1 of each year as "law day," a day to celebrate the virtues of the American legal system in contrast to the perverted system of law under communism.

As with cinematic politicians, the defining change in lawyer imaging occurred with Watergate. Trial lawyer William G. Hyland Jr. points out the negative images presented in the legal films of the 1980s and 1990s,[13] a trend that continues into the 21st century. From *The Verdict* to *Michael Clayton*, Hyland details the portrayal of lawyers as substance abusers (drugs and alcohol), immoral and unprofessional (sleeping with clients), corrupt (working for the mob), and driven by greed and personal ambition to advance themselves, regardless of the cost to their clients. Why the 180-degree change in imagery? In Hyland's opinion, the Watergate scandal tarnished lawyers so completely that the public came to not only distrust them, but to develop a permanent dislike for the whole profession. In support of this view, Hyland cites a 2005 Gallup poll that showed that only 18 percent of the public considered lawyers to be ethical.

The following discussion examines Hollywood movies as legal texts in different circumstances. But what constitutes a legal text? Criminal Justice lecturer Stefan Machura describes a law film as one having these four characteristics:

- it must include the "geography of law," such as scenes involving trials and courtrooms, juries and jury rooms, law offices, lawyers and clients, and sometimes prisons
- it must use the language of the law, that is, the legal terminology, and if required by the legal culture, the necessary dress, such as wigs and gowns required in English courtrooms
- its major characters must work in the legal system, practicing law or attending law school

- it must express the "authority of law," namely, that its treatment of the law and its practitioners be authentic and pay due respect to the law's power and responsibilities.[14]

## Frontier Violence

Historians describe the frontier as the demarcation line that divides civilization from the wilderness. In the American past, the frontier's edge moved westward from Pittsburgh until it met the Pacific. Historian Frederick Jackson Turner believed that those pioneers who settled the West shaped the American character.[15]

Hollywood exploited the dramatic potential of the Turner thesis in its visual exploration of the migration westward. Thus, it should not come as a surprise that the first narrative to come out of Hollywood, *The Great Train Robbery* (1903), had a western action plot. Thereafter, westerns became a staple of the film industry well into the sixties. Hollywood's version of the western genre often reduced the plots to simplified morality tales in which the forces of evil are dispatched, usually violently, after the climactic barroom brawl or street shootout with the noble lawman. Frontier justice was normally achieved by brute strength and the quick draw rather than by persuasion or the appeal to reason.

Occasionally the western film served as a legal text,[16] as exemplified by James Stewart's lawyer (Ransome Stoddard) in *The Man Who Shot Liberty Valance* (1972), who eventually proved that in the new West the law book would replace Tom Doniphon's (John Wayne) six-shooter. Remember that Wayne began his film career in the thirties by appearing in a series of short westerns for Republic Pictures. In one such film set in the 1870s, *King of the Pecos* (1936), Wayne plays John Clayborn, a young lawyer out to avenge his parents' murder at the hands of the local cattle baron, Alexander Stiles. Stiles' strategy is to claim most of the open range for himself, either through buying out deceived ranchers or killing those, like Clayborn's parents, that refuse to sell. Stiles, however, fails to file legal claim to the land, preferring instead to control the water rights. Unless ranchers sell their cattle to him at a low price, Stiles threatens to cut off their water supply. Ten years pass and the grown-up Clayborn returns to town as a lawyer and persuades the court to accept the waterholes as property held in the public domain. When the legal system rules against him, Stiles resorts to violence. Although Clayborn is committed to using the law to settle disputes, he comes to realize that his law books are no match for Stiles' guns. Reluctantly, Clayborn straps on his gun belt and, after a fierce shootout, kills Stiles and most of his gang in the climactic gunfight. Afterward, Clayborn throws away his guns, an act symbolic of his new commitment to the law.

*King of the Pecos* relied on the legal system and the use of force to achieve justice. Sometimes, however, frontier justice on the big screen meant vigilantism and mob rule.[17] In *The Ox-Bow Incident* (1943), a pair of saddle tramps, played by Henry Fonda and Harry Morgan, reluctantly join a posse in search of cattle rustlers who are accused of killing a local rancher. Disregarding the instructions of the sheriff, the posse, led by an ex-Confederate major, stumbles onto three men, who are quickly given a kangaroo trial and lynched. Fonda and Morgan try to persuade the men to wait for the sheriff but they are overruled by the mob. On their way back to town, the posse meets the sheriff, who informs them that the real culprits are in custody and that the rancher who was shot is very much alive. When the sheriff learns about the lynching, he promises to hold those involved accountable. Back in town, the major commits suicide and the rest of the posse gathers in the local saloon to drown their guilt. Fonda, however, reads aloud the letter one of the victims had written to his wife in which he refers to the law as the "conscience of humanity." In taking the lives of three innocent men, the posse had become judge and jury, losing its humanity and retrogressing into an uncivilized mob.

A variation on the mob vigilantism theme, but still within the western genre, is found in the film story of *The Life and Times of Judge Roy Bean* (1972). Paul Newman plays the title character, a drifter who declares himself "the law" in a small town west of the Pecos. There he dispenses his brand of justice, usually at the end of a rope. Based on an actual post-Civil War character, Bean comes into the frontier town of Vinegaroon, Texas, where there is neither law nor order. He proceeds to kill or drive out all the outlaws and, relying on a copy of *The Revised Statutes of Texas*, proclaims himself "judge of the territory." Converting the town brothel into a saloon/courthouse, he dispenses justice so harshly that he acquires a reputation as the "hanging judge." In the film version, the law literally is what Bean says it is. When the statute book fails to conform to his concept of the law, Bean rips that page out of the law book. When an outlaw is brought before Bean for killing a Chinese man, Bean's jurisdiction is challenged because "Chinks, Niggers, and Injuns" are excluded as "persons" in the statute books. Judge Bean will not hear of it; regardless of what the statute book contains, all persons are considered equal before him. Hence Bean and the law become one. The outlaw does not have a chance and is hanged. Part history and part legend,[18] the film constructs an idol out of an outlaw who tried and sentenced his victims arbitrarily, sometimes on the basis of personal whim. Roy Bean had to be the worst kind of judge to represent the legal system. His story demonstrated what happened in territories where official authority had yet to be established.

While hangings, lynchings, and shootouts fit the mythology of the old West, such violence in the 20th century is more likely to arouse public wrath. Yet lynching and mob brutality continued well into the 1930s, especially in certain sections of the country. While lynchings occurred throughout the U.S., the deed was most common in the South and used against the black population. Studies indicate that almost 4,000 lynchings took place in the South between 1880 and 1930; the vast majority of the victims were blacks.[19] A correlation usually occurred between economic conditions in an area and the prevalence of lynching. When economic times were good lynching decreased. When prices paid to white farmers dropped, lynching increased. Economically distressed whites found blacks to be convenient scapegoats on which to take out their aggression and frustration.

During the Depression era, Hollywood produced several social message films, including two on mob rule. Both director Fritz Lang's *Fury* and Warner Brothers' *They Won't Forget* confronted the issue of mob violence directly. *Fury* starred Spencer Tracy as an innocent young man mistakenly arrested for a fugitive kidnapper. Tracy is arrested on the basis of circumstantial evidence, exacerbated by his being an outsider unknown to the townsfolk. While he languishes in the local jail, a large angry mob develops outside. The sheriff asks for state assistance but the governor is up for re-election and reluctant to intervene. The self-appointed vigilantes, unable to break into the jail to lynch Tracy, set it on fire instead and presume Tracy to have died. However, he manages to escape and goes into hiding. Meanwhile, the real kidnappers are captured and the local district attorney brings murder charges against 22 identified members of the lynch mob. Angry and bitter toward those accused, Tracy refuses to reveal himself and is content to allow his persecutors be tried for a murder they did not commit. After the defendants are found guilty, Tracy has a change of heart and walks into the courtroom in the final scene while the trial judge is handing out the sentences. Although Tracy's reappearance saves the defendants from certain death, he tells the court that he has lost faith in the ability of the legal system to deliver justice. Lang's film failed at the box office, but it did help to establish his reputation in Hollywood.

Unlike *Fury*, *They Won't Forget* is a fictionalized account of actual events: the historic 1913 Leo Frank case. Set in a Southern town, *They Won't Forget* retells the story of a teenage secretarial student found murdered in her school building. The politically ambitious district attorney pounces on the case as a potential springboard into the U.S. Senate. He needs to make an arrest and secure a conviction if the crime is to advance his career. The D.A. narrows his suspects to a young teacher, a Northerner and outsider who was inside the school building on the day the dead student was found. The teacher is quickly arrested and convicted, largely on the basis of circumstantial evidence. The governor, however, commutes his sentence from death to life imprisonment. On his way to prison, the teacher is taken off the train by a vicious mob and lynched. As was true in the actual case, the accumulation of circumstantial evidence supported by anti-Yankee prejudice, yellow journalism, and political ambition led to Leo Frank's conviction and eventual death because it was felt that "we can lynch a nigger anytime but when do we get the chance to hang a Yankee Jew?"[20] Georgia Governor John Slaton commuted the real Leo Frank's sentence but a few months later, Frank was taken from the prison farm and lynched.[21] His killers were not prosecuted even though several were identified. Films like *Fury* and *They Won't Forget* serve as reminders that prejudice and violence did not disappear with the end of the frontier.

## Urban Vigilantism: Dirty Harry & Paul Kersey Meet Jodie Foster

In 1968 criminologist Herbert Packer explained his dual model for the U.S criminal justice system.[22] One model, the due process model, resonated with liberals since it was predicated on the presumption of innocence, advocated rights for those accused and charged, and prescribed treatment and rehabilitation for those convicted. Its opposite, the crime control model, appealed to conservatives because it expressed confidence that, unfettered, law enforcement personnel could apprehend criminals and reduce street crime. The crime control model favored community security over individual rights and punishment over treatment. Like most social science models, Packer's represented "ideal types" rather than the prevailing legal reality. At the time, the escalating crime rate and U.S. Supreme Court decisions[23] that created protective rights for those accused of crimes fueled public disaffection with the courts and support for the crime control advocates. Public opinion surveys conducted during the decade, from 1972 to 1983, consistently revealed that Americans believed the courts were much too lenient with criminals. The prevalent impression was that the courts had handcuffed the police in dealing with crime and that judges were dispensing light sentences to those convicted.

Hollywood, always ready to capitalize on the prevailing public mood, responded by creating two film characters in the seventies: Lt. Harry Callahan (Clint Eastwood) in *Dirty Harry* (1971) and New York City businessman Paul Kersey (Charles Bronson) in *Death Wish* (1974). Both screen characters reflected the popular sentiment that criminals had taken over the cities thanks to a liberal Supreme Court under Chief Justice Earl Warren. While Callahan was a rogue cop operating under the color of law, Kersey represented the ordinary citizen driven by circumstances into becoming an urban vigilante. The popularity of these two screen vigilantes led Hollywood to produce five films in each series—the *Dirty Harry* films covered 1971 to 1988 and the *Death Wish* films from 1974 through 1994. Both series testify to the traditional Hollywood rule to continue producing similar kind of films until patronage declines.

Vigilantism is part of the American tradition, according to Lenz.[24] He traces its roots to the concept of popular sovereignty in a culture where the people, not the government, represent the ultimate authority. Vigilantism occurs when an individual or a mob decides to dispense justice without consideration for due process and other legal requirements. If government is a social contract between the people and the ruling authority, then the latter has the responsibility to protect the people in return for their relinquishing certain rights to the government. Should the government fail in its responsibility, the people have the right to take the law into their own hands. At least, that is the theory justifying vigilantism. More often than not, it is a charade to mask underlying reasons of hatred, prejudice, and personal vengeance.

Lt. Callahan has no use for criminals or for what he sarcastically considers "legal technicalities" like due process of law, the exclusionary rule of evidence, or the Miranda warning read to those apprehended. In *Dirty Harry*, Callahan is after a serial killer named Scorpio who kidnaps victims and extorts money for their release. He is a thoroughly despicable character, a sociopath who shows his victims no mercy. Callahan is a dedicated officer who has little regard for police rules or constitutional rights. He disdains the Fourth, Sixth, and Fourteenth Amendments if they hinder his ability to apprehend criminals. Moreover, he has a mean streak and likes to bait criminals, tempting them with lines like: "Do you feel lucky—well, do you, punk?" and "Go ahead, make my day" before he shoots them between the eyes. The *Dirty Harry* character appealed to an America tired of criminals like Scorpio, street gangs, and urban punks. And the public seemed to enjoy it more because Harry did his killing under the authority of law.

Paul Kersey is a decent family man, and according to the *Death Wish* films, a bleeding-heart liberal. He is transformed into an urban killing machine after his wife and daughter are brutally attacked. His wife dies from the assault and his daughter is so traumatized that she requires institutional care. The police inform him that the attackers are unlikely to be apprehended. On a business trip to Arizona, Kersey is given a handgun as a gift. Returning to New York, he begins to roam the streets at night, gun in pocket. One night he shoots a man who intends to rob him. Later he shoots three thugs who threaten him. The New York City public likes this urban avenger so much that when the police discover his identity, he is asked to leave town rather than be arrested. In *Death Wish II* (1982) Kersey resurfaces in Los Angeles, where he pursues a gang of thugs who rape and murder his housekeeper.

The rape scenes were considered so brutal that the BBFC ordered the scene cut from the film. Kersey continues his manhunt until he has killed each member of the gang, the last one under treatment in a mental hospital. Once again, the film ends with Kersey escaping punishment so he can pursue his vigilantism in three more *Death Wish* movies.

The public spotlight shone on the *Death Wish* motif of unpunished urban vigilantism when life imitated art on the New York subway in the 1980s. There is a scene in the first *Death Wish* film where Kersey shoots three black youths who threaten him on a New York subway car. A decade later, a real New Yorker named Bernard Goetz—a white man who had previously been mugged—shot and seriously wounded four black youths who approached him on a subway car and asked him for money. Goetz was charged with several felonies, but he contended that his actions were justified because he felt threatened he would be robbed and mugged again. Through their lawyers, the black youths said that panhandling and robbery was not their intention. In a celebrated trial, the jury acquitted Goetz on the felonies but convicted him on the illegal weapon charge, for which he received six months in jail. Had the crime been committed during a more liberal era when criminals were considered products of societal dysfunction, his sentence might have been longer. But a crime-weary New York jury could not find it in its heart to punish a mild-mannered shooter who carried a gun for protection in the urban jungle.

In traditional Hollywood movies, the typical vigilantes are male. That is what made Jodie Foster's film *The Brave One* (2007) unique in that the avenger here is a woman. The plot is similar to the *Death Wish* series, where an act of violence converts an ordinary citizen into a modern-day vigilante. Foster is a radio personality working in an urban environment that looks like New York City. One night, she and her fiancé are beaten by thugs; she survives but her fiancé dies from his wounds. When Foster recovers and is told by the police that her assailants may not be caught, she buys an illegal gun and, like Paul Kersey, goes on a shooting spree killing bad guys—potential robbers, muggers, and rapists—even in situations where she is able to walk away without doing violence. One scene in particular stands out. Foster is riding the city subway late at night when two mean-looking dudes enter the train. They immediately begin to harass the few passengers. When the train pulls into the next station, all the passengers leave—except Foster. Why not get off and wait for the next train? That certainly would be the smart strategy, and as a New Yorker, that is what the author would have done. But Foster is packing her gun and when the doors close and she is alone with the two menacing guys, she shoots them dead at the first opportunity and then leaves the train at the next station.

At this point in the film, the audience realizes that Foster enjoys the killing and the empowerment that the gun gives her. The film's scenario further endorses the acceptability of unprovoked vigilantism when it becomes clear that a police detective, who has been trailing her, knows exactly what Foster is doing and still fails to arrest her despite six killings. The intent of the film is to encourage the audience to sympathize with Foster as a wronged woman who is driven by circumstances to become an avenging angel. But that is not one of the functions of citizenship. The protector role is assigned to the police, not to ordinary citizens. The film's title is enigmatic: is Foster supposed to be the brave one? Is carrying a concealed weapon, waiting, even wishing for the slightest pretext—"Go ahead, punk, make my day"—to use it for personal vengeance really heroic? What would city life be like if all citizens were armed? Political scientists refer to that state of being as anarchy—where each person lives in constant fear of his neighbors, fearful to walk the streets without protection. In such an environment, would anyone really be free?

## Military Justice

Because the U.S. government is a federal system with powers shared by both the national and state governments, the country has 51 legal systems—one for the federal government and one for each of the 50 states. In addition, two types of courts distinguish the federal court system: constitutional and legislative. Constitutional courts are created under the language of Article III of the U.S. Constitution, which authorizes Congress to establish courts inferior to the Supreme Court. Legislative courts, on the other hand, are created pursuant to a congressional legislative function. For example, under Article I Congress has the power to organize, arm, and discipline the militia. Discipline is held so vital for military success that even the U.S. Supreme Court has ruled that an orthodox Jew cannot wear his yarmulke instead of regulation headgear.[25] The Congress, therefore, has the power to establish military tribunals to discipline soldiers.

One example of a legislative court is the U.S. Court of Military Appeals, which reviews the decisions of courts-martial. Its caseload consists primarily of military personnel discharged for bad conduct or sentenced to the stockade for violations of the Uniform Code of Military Justice. Offenses while in the military service, crimes committed on military bases, and other infractions that are "service connected" fall within the jurisdiction of the Uniform Code. Though military personnel do not forfeit their constitutional rights while in the service, the application of the code differs from legal practices in civilian life. For instance, while the Fourth Amendment protection against "unreasonable searches and seizures" applies to service personnel, routine inspections and shakedowns are not considered searches and are therefore permissible. Nor do military personnel accused of a crime have a right to post bail. Military courts substitute military personnel, appointed by commanding officers, for jurors in civilian trials. And while a unanimous verdict is required in civilian criminal trials, courts-martial permit a two-thirds vote to convict in noncapital cases. Only in cases where conviction requires the death penalty is a unanimous verdict required in military trials. The justification for these differences in the Uniform Code is that military necessity requires absolute discipline and adherence to the chain of command.

Hollywood has ignored military trials as screen material except for several notable post–World War II films on the subject. In *The Court Martial of Billy Mitchell* (1955), Gary Cooper plays the title role of the Brigadier General who commanded the American Expeditionary Air Force during the First World War, and later served as assistant chief of the Army Air Service. He clashed with his superiors over the role of air power in future wars, including the military potential of strategic bombing, airborne forces, and polar air routes. His incessant and sharp criticism of military leaders led to his court-martial in 1925. The film recounts Mitchell's advocacy of a strong air force, opposing military leaders who were committed to naval power and the infantry. When one of Mitchell's friends dies in an air crash, he accuses the war and navy departments of incompetence and negligence. His accusations and insubordination led to his court-martial under Article 134 of the Uniform Code, which prohibits conduct that discredits the armed forces or is prejudicial to order and discipline. Mitchell's legal strategy was to use the courtroom as a public forum, a place where he could expound his ideas, including the vulnerability of Pearl Harbor to air attack. Mitchell is found guilty because, as a maverick, he dared to question the entrenched establishment. What the trial demonstrates is that the military chain of command requires blind obedience to orders regardless of the consequences. As punishment, the real Mitchell was suspended for five years. He subsequently resigned from the army, but continued to lecture on the use of air power until his death. Unfortunately, his ideas were not accepted by the military until after the attack on Pearl Harbor.

Mutiny, rather than insubordination, is at the heart of the 1955 film *The Caine Mutiny*. Article 184 of the Uniform Code defines mutiny as the refusal to obey orders from a proper authority in concert with others with the intention to override military orders. Mutiny is one of the most serious offenses under the Military Code and is punishable by death. The mutiny in the film occurs during World War II when the *Caine*, an old minesweeper, encounters a Pacific typhoon and its commanding officer, Captain Queeg (Humphrey Bogart), fails to take charge. At that point his naval officers, led by Lt. Maryk (Van Johnson) and Ensign Keith (Robert Francis), seize control of the *Caine*.

Queeg, a strict disciplinarian, had assumed command of the *Caine* from a lackadaisical officer and managed to get the ship back in shape, but had become increasingly paranoid as a result of too many combat missions. Queeg became preoccupied with unimportant details, like improper dress on board the ship. His erratic behavior comes to a climax in his obsession with locating a box of missing strawberries from the mess hall. He orders a thorough investigation for the strawberries, even though it is obvious to the other officers that they had been eaten and were no longer available to be produced. When Queeg stalls during the typhoon and hesitates to take action, Maryk and Keith assume command. Both are subsequently charged with mutiny. Their military lawyer, Barney Greenwald (José Ferrer) reluctantly defends them at their court-martial by attempting to destroy Queeg's credibility. Under intense questioning, Queeg breaks down on the stand, violently rolling the steel balls in his hands as the cross-examination intensifies. Greenwald's strategy works as Queeg cracks under pressure and Maryk and Keith are cleared of all charges. Later, at a post-victory celebration, Greenwald defends Queeg as a good officer who was worn down by the stress of command. In return for the cooperation of the U.S. Navy, changes had to be made to the film, which is based on the Herman Wouk novel, to direct blame for the mutiny on the conduct of individuals rather than on the military establishment. Still, the film conveys both a sense of the importance of hierarchical decision-making for military effectiveness and a perception of fairness within the military justice system.

Severe hazing (known as Code Red) that leads to murder on a military base forms the basis for the film *A Few Good Men* (1992). Loosely based on an incident at the marine base in Guantanamo Bay in the 1980s, *A Few Good Men* recounts the story of Pvt. Santiago, an unhappy marine intent on snitching to the authorities that two fellow marines were shooting on the fence line in Cuba. To frighten him into silence, the two marines initiate Code Red when they stuff a rag down Santiago's throat and tape his mouth shut. As a consequence, Santiago dies and the two marines are charged with his murder. Their base commander, Col. Nathan Jessep (Jack Nicholson), a gung-ho marine, who had denied Santiago a transfer, tries to minimize the incident as an accident. The U.S. Navy also would like to whitewash the incident. It therefore appoints a young and brash but untested trial lawyer, Lt. Daniel Kaffe (Tom Cruise), to head the court-martial defense team. Initially Kaffe is willing to accept the prosecutor's plea bargain because he has never tried a case. He changes his mind after meeting with Jessep and after the constant goading of his colleague, Lt. Cmdr. JoAnne Galloway (Demi Moore). Kaffe and Galloway come to believe their clients did not act alone, but on orders, and to substantiate their suspicions they subpoena Jessep. The strategy works, as Jessep, under intense examination, admits to giving the Code Red order. During the heated exchange, Jessep defends the hazing order because Santiago was a whiner, a weakling and not a true marine. He berates Kaffe as well, arguing that when the U.S. goes to war it calls upon men like him—real marines—instead of the soft, bookish lawyers in white dress uniforms like Kaffe, to do the dirty work. He tells the courtroom that when the country faces a crisis, discipline and strength, not weakness and self-indulgence, are required of the military services. As he is being led out of the courtroom by Military Police, Jessep screams that men like Kaffe undermine the strength of the military. From one perspective, Kaffe's first trial is a success; his clients are acquitted of the murder charge. But since they are dishonorably discharged from the corps, their punishment raises the question of whether it is fair to punish lower echelon military personnel for carrying out a crime under orders from a superior officer. The Nuremberg War Crimes Trial after World War II established the principle that military personnel cannot rely on illegal orders, such as a Code Red, to absolve them of wrongdoing.[26] However, for subordinates to disobey an order is a serious offense under military law. Within the context of the film, the two marines would have had to pass judgment on Jessep's order—which was not to kill Santiago but simply to toughen him up, frighten him into becoming a real marine. For military personnel who apply the Uniform Code to preserve discipline and obedience rather than the attainment of just ends, it is a no-win situation.

## Trials and Tribulations: Lawyers on the Big Screen

In the American legal system it is the lawyer who is the pivotal character in the resolution of legal contests. Having an adversarial legal system places the lawyer center stage. Hollywood films about the law tend to portray lawyers in three contexts: as larger-than-life heroes, as sleazy shysters available for hire, or as fallen idols seeking redemption through their clients.

### Heroic Lawyers

A hero or heroine is usually characterized as a person who has committed an act of courage or bravery without regard for personal consequences. Heroes are admired and held in high esteem by the rest of society. Hollywood action-adventure films consistently feature characters who perform heroic deeds or overcome extreme obstacles to right a wrong. Such heroes usually cannot serve as role models because their escapades are often implausible and belong more to the realm of the imagination than to real life.

Courtroom movies, however, can utilize the trial as a paradigm for the confrontation between good and evil. Trial movies provide opportunities for lawyers to become heroic figures when their legal strategy saves the life of an innocent client or delivers just compensation to the plaintiff in a civil suit. For more than half a century the film industry exploited the dramatic potential of the heroic lawyer in pursuit of truth and justice. What young person would not want to grow up to be like Abe Lincoln, the advocate with a social conscience, in *Young Mr. Lincoln* (1939)? Not only does the Springfield lawyer prove the innocence of two brothers accused of murder, but he saves them from a lynch mob and then exposes the real killer in the final scene. Nor is this Lincoln reluctant to engage in courtroom tricks, including reliance on the *Farmers' Almanac* to identify the real killer.

Could there be a more heroic lawyer than Atticus Finch in *To Kill a Mockingbird* (1962)? Gregory Peck plays Finch in the film adaptation of the Harper Lee novel about a small-town Southern lawyer who defends a black man accused of raping a white woman. Finch, a widower and a respected lawyer, is struggling to raise his two children during the Depression years. When asked by the local judge to accept the rape case, he never hesitates even though his client's case appears hopeless. Finch's acceptance is a lesson to audiences that even marginalized groups are entitled to the best defense possible under the American legal system. Like the young Lincoln, Finch also faces down a lynch mob. Yet despite an impassioned closing argument in which he asks the all-white jury to lay aside their racial prejudices, his client is convicted. Historically, in segregated Alabama in the 1930s, a black man accused of raping a white woman had no chance whatsoever. Blacks were sent to prison just for "leering" at white women. While it is unlikely that any lawyer could have saved Finch's client, his insistence on uncovering the truth despite the personal consequences represents the best tradition of defense lawyers.

Lincoln and Atticus Finch are noble characters, fighting for justice in the courtroom. They symbolize Hollywood's most ideal representation of lawyers on the big screen. They are flawless characters, a credit to the legal profession. Other screen lawyers who fit this mold to a lesser degree include Humphrey Bogart in *Knock on Any Door* (1949) and Glenn Ford in *Trial* (1955): both represent minority defendants in trials permeated with prejudice and ethnic hostility.

In *Knock on Any Door*, attorney Andrew Morton (Bogart) defends a young Italian-American hoodlum, Nick Romano (John Derek), accused of murdering a policeman during a robbery. Morton takes the case despite a warning that his acceptance jeopardizes his chance for a full partnership in the law firm where he practices. Morton identifies with Romano because both were products of the urban slum and he believes that Romano, the son of immigrant parents, can become a useful citizen. However, Romano is too weak to stay out of trouble, flaunting an attitude of "Live fast, die young, and have a good-looking corpse." Morton's defense strategy is to put society on trial, to have the jury believe that Romano is a decent kid who never had a chance to go straight. But when cross-examined on the stand, the D.A. provokes Romano into confessing to the crime. Morton, then, has no choice but to make an impassioned plea to the judge to save Romano's life, citing the arguments of the social determinists that environment is the real culprit responsible for crime. If Romano is guilty, Morton pleads, then so is society because it failed to provide him with a decent home and a good neighborhood. Despite his passionate defense, Romano is sentenced to death in the electric chair, thereby making his prophecy of dying young and having a good-looking corpse come true.

In *Trial*, David Blake's (Glenn Ford) client, Angel Chavez, is a Mexican-American high school student accused of murdering his girlfriend. Blake is a law professor on the verge of getting fired because he lacks trial experience. To save his job, Blake accepts an offer to spend the summer as an assistant to local attorney Barney Castle (Arthur Kennedy). Castle convinces Chavez's mother to let him handle the case. Instead of doing the trial work he assigns it to Blake on the pretense that he will be too busy raising the funds for the defense. Unknown to Blake, Castle actively promotes the Chavez case, turning it into a cause célèbre for the Communist Party because the party needs a martyr (Chavez) and an inexperienced trial lawyer like Blake is the perfect patsy to lose the case. Meanwhile, local bigots surround the courthouse, anxious to dispense with the trial altogether and lynch Chavez on the spot. The threat of a possible lynching brings in the National Guard to keep order and the local sheriff finally dissuades the crowd from committing violence. Back in the courtroom, Blake is learning the law on the job, his mistakes corrected by the patient trial judge. At least Blake has enough sense not to put Chavez on the stand. Castle, who has the support of Chavez's mother, overrules him on this matter. As expected, the vulnerable Chavez crumbles under cross-examination and the jury finds him guilty. Blake is devastated by the verdict. Nonetheless, because he believes that somewhere in the law, "where there is a wrong, there is a remedy," he decides to try one last legal tactic. During the sentencing hearing, Blake convinces the judge, with the consent of the prosecution, to send Chavez to reform school rather than the gas chamber. In order to save Chavez, however, Blake must confess to his incompetence and admit that Castle had tricked him to further the communist cause. The film concludes at this point with the implication that while Blake did the right thing, he should return to the classroom and avoid the courtroom at all cost.

Al Pacino plays beleaguered Baltimore criminal defense attorney Arthur Kirkland in *And Justice for All*. The opening scene finds Kirkland in jail for contempt after he takes a punch at his nemesis, Judge Fleming (John Forsythe). Kirkland represents the sensitive lawyer with a conscience. He is angry with Fleming for refusing to reopen the case of a wrongly convicted client. In addition to the jail time, Kirkland is under investigation by the judicial ethics committee to determine whether he is fit to continue practicing law. After his release from jail, Kirkland is asked by Fleming to defend him against a rape charge. This puts Kirkland in a catch-22 situation since he despises the judge, yet if he refuses to take the case he most likely will be disbarred. Laying aside his personal feelings, Kirkland accepts the case and provides an aggressive defense until he discovers that Fleming committed the rape. In the final scene, Kirkland confesses his client's guilt to the stunned courtroom, an act that leads to his disbarment.

While Kirkland is an improbable lawyer, *And Justice for All* is the rare Hollywood film that is willing to cast aspersions on the criminal justice system itself rather than on the individual participants, it presents an unending parade of corrupt officials, scenes of judicial abuse of power, and questionable plea bargain deals. Although it tends toward exaggeration, the audience is left with the feeling that the urban legal system demands compromise and expediency rather than truth in order to survive. Kirkland represents the idealistic and ethical lawyer trying to exist in an irrational system that overwhelms and eventually destroys him.

Michigan attorney Paul Biegler, Jimmy Stewart's character in *Anatomy of a Murder*, would rather fish for trout and play jazz on the piano than practice law. Based on the bestselling novel that recounts an actual Michigan case, *Anatomy of a Murder* is an ironic depiction of the criminal law in practice. Paul Biegler is less the heroic lawyer than the duped attorney similar to the one depicted in Harvard law professor Alan Dershowitz's novel, *The Best Defense*. In the book Dershowitz recounts the story of a lawyer who cables his client that "justice has prevailed." His client responds quickly, "Appeal immediately."[27] Biegler agrees to handle the case of an army officer, Lt. Manion (Ben Gazzara), charged with killing the man who allegedly raped his wife. When Biegler interviews Manion at the local jail, he tells his client that there is no such thing in law as an unwritten rule that acquits a husband who protects his wife's honor. In desperate need of a viable defense, Biegler skirts the code of ethics when he lays out the various excuses for such a crime and, after repeated questioning, gets Manion to admit that he "must have been crazy" when he shot and killed his wife's attacker. The admission allows Biegler to develop the "irresistible impulse" strategy, a defense permitted under Michigan law. Legal scholars contend that Biegler's coaching is just one of several legal improprieties evident in the film.[28] Biegler's legal tactics prove successful and Manion is acquitted. Afterward, Biegler goes to the Manions' trailer court to collect his fee, only to discover that the couple had an "irresistible impulse" to skip town. Like the client in the Dershowitz story, Manion was guilty as sin.

Occasionally, Hollywood will take a real lawyer or a famous case to dramatize on the big screen. In one example, actor Ron Silver portrayed attorney Alan Dershowitz in *Reversal of Fortune* (1990), the film version of the Claus von Bulow case. Dershowitz and his Harvard law students were successful in convincing the Rhode Island Supreme Court to reverse von Bulow's attempted murder conviction. In another, noted criminal lawyer Clarence Darrow is represented on screen in the famous "Monkey Trial," where Darrow was retained by the American Civil Liberties Union (ACLU) to defend teacher John T. Scopes for teaching the theory of evolution, an offense under Tennessee state law. The film version of the Scopes trial, *Inherit the Wind* (1960), had Spencer Tracy playing Darrow and Fredric March playing William Jennings Bryan. What is often not known about the real trial (and omitted from the film) is that the Scopes trial represents a legal "test case" because the ACLU sought to challenge the Tennessee anti-evolution statute and needed a teacher willing to volunteer to break the law. Scopes answered the ACLU advertisement. Moreover, unlike the rest of the fundamentalist Dayton, Tennessee, community, the town merchants actually believed that a national trial would be good for business.[29]

In *Compulsion* (1959), Orson Welles plays Darrow in a fictionalized account of the famous 1920s Leopold-Loeb murder case. The film story concerns two brilliant law students who want to commit the "perfect crime" and plot to kidnap and kill a young boy. Arrested for the crime, their families hire Darrow to defend them. While his bravado courtroom performance failed to win an acquittal, Darrow's two-day closing argument saved the teenagers from the death penalty by depicting them as mentally disturbed and unable to comprehend the enormity of their crime. Darrow's summation, in which he asked the court to be more compassionate and kinder than his clients, still resonates today as a convincing argument against capital punishment. These two cases secured Darrow's reputation as America's most outstanding criminal lawyer at the time.

Denzel Washington's lawyer (Joe Miller), in Jonathan Demme's film *Philadelphia* (1993), is heroic only in the negative sense that despite being homophobic, he is willing to defend a homosexual. When Tom Hanks, an associate in a Main Line Philadelphia law firm, is fired because he has AIDS, he cannot find a lawyer to take his discrimination suit until Washington is willing to file a wrongful dismissal suit against Hanks's prestigious law firm. His courtroom strategy wins the civil suit for Hanks, who dies soon thereafter. Washington's lawyer should not receive too much credit. Although lawyers in the private sector are not obligated to take every client, except upon court appointment, once a client is accepted he/she is entitled to the best possible defense regardless of race, religion, gender, or sexual orientation.[30]

## Grisham's Lawyers vs. Connelly's Lincoln Lawyer

The film studios are enamored with John Grisham's novels, having made screen adaptations of his first seven books. There are two apparent reasons for Hollywood's interest. The Grisham books are popular bestsellers with a substantial readership that forms an established audience for the film versions of his novels. One source claims Grisham's books have been translated into 31 languages and have sold some 87 million copies.[31] When adapted for the big screen, Grisham's novels have done well at the box office. Another explanation for Hollywood's interest is that Grisham's fiction contains at least one good lawyer, a hero or heroine, who fights for the underdog, the disenfranchised, and the wrongfully accused. Even though the novels contain bad lawyers, they are usually on the losing side and their characters are balanced by opposition lawyers intent on seeing that justice is done.

However, not all actual lawyers appreciate Grisham's portrayals. Trial attorney William Hyland claims the lawyers in Grisham's books are arrogant, greedy, and unethical and his prosecutors are treated with disrespect.[32] While Harland may have a point, a majority of Grisham's lawyers are portrayed positively. Take, for example, the Matthew McConaughey character in *A Time to Kill* (1996), Grisham's first novel. McConaughey's liberal lawyer, Jake Brigance, has the formidable task of defending Carl Lee Hailey, the black Mississippi farmer accused of killing the two rednecks who raped and beat his 10-year-old daughter. That Brigance does it successfully in a Southern town renders his victory even more heroic.

In Grisham's *The Firm* (1993), Tom Cruise's young lawyer, fresh out of law school, is seduced by the money and gifts showered on him by "the Firm" and appears oblivious to the company's association with organized crime. Then two law associates are murdered and Cruise, working with the FBI, must help expose the firm's shady dealings. In *The Pelican Brief* (1993) Julia Roberts plays a law student who stumbles into a plot involving the deaths of two Supreme Court justices. It seems a friend of the president is trying to manipulate the outcome of a trial before the Supreme Court and Roberts is drawn into this unlikely scenario through her law professor, with whom she is having an affair. Roberts solves the mystery and satisfactorily resolves the case by the final reel with the help of an investigative reporter (Denzel Washington). Meanwhile, Reggie Love (Susan Sarandon) is another heroine in a Grisham novel, *The Client* (1994), who tries to help a young boy being pursued by the Mafia and harassed by the local prosecutor. Although obviously out of her league, Reggie manages to protect the boy from both dangers. Like Roberts, the Reggie Love character is a larger-than-life heroine.

Then there is another overmatched young lawyer (Matt Damon), who takes on corporate America in Grisham's *The Rainmaker* (1997), and in true Hollywood fashion, wins his case with the aid of an assistant who never passed the state bar exam. As they used to say in Brooklyn, "if you believe that, I have a bridge to sell you." Damon's case involves a woman suing a large insurance company that refused to pay her son's medical bills. Now the boy is terminally ill and Damon and his assistant are locked in a struggle with a high-powered law firm that represents the interests of the insurance company. It is the familiar Hollywood scenario of David versus Goliath and the film's happy ending complies with the fantasy world created in Hollywood movies. These Grisham characters may not be perfect lawyers, but they represent a more positive view of the profession than is normally found in the popular culture.

However, what separates these heroic Grisham lawyers from the young Abe Lincoln and the idealistic Atticus Finch is their total lack of believability. Grisham's lawyers are usually overmatched upstarts, with limited resources and staff, who achieve the impossible for their clients against powerful interests that employ expensive law firms with huge staffs to ensure success. The fact that Grisham's lawyers always are victorious is what appeals to both Hollywood and a compliant American public that believes in miracles.

In contrast, mystery writer Michael Connelly is best known for his Harry Bosch detective novels, based on stories that he learned as a police reporter early in his journalistic career. Of his many novels, four have lawyer Mickey Haller as their key character. Haller plays a secondary role to Harry Bosch in both *The Brass Verdict* (2008) and *The Reversal* (2010), and he shows up as a minor character in one or two other Bosch books. Connelly introduced Haller to his readers as a main character in *The Lincoln Lawyer* (2005) and followed that with his second work of legal fiction, *The Fifth Witness* (2011). Connelly has shaped Haller into a charming but somewhat sleazy solo practitioner who works out of the back of his Lincoln Town Car.

Hollywood prefers Grisham's fiction as more adaptable to film since only two of Connelly's books have been transferred to the big screen. Also, Grisham is the more popular writer and his movies have performed better at the box office. In the first film, based on an early Connelly book, *Blood Work* (2002), the hero is a former FBI agent. Despite the fact that Clint Eastwood was the star and director, the film flopped at the box office, earning about half of its budget in the domestic market.[33] It took nine years for Hollywood to take a chance on another Connelly vehicle, *The Lincoln Lawyer* (2011), as a suitable movie property. By that time, seven Grisham books had already been adapted to the screen.

Mickey Haller, the *Lincoln Lawyer* of the title, will take just about anybody on as a client: accused murderers, drug dealers, con artists, and DUI drunks. The reader might imagine

Haller as a small, unshaven, rumpled-looking guy in a cheap suit. Instead he is played by the smooth-talking, charming and impeccably dressed Matthew McConaughey so that when he lies to his clients, refuses to work without cash up front, and scams his chauffeur, his sins are immediately forgiven. The client he comes to defend in *The Lincoln Lawyer* is a wealthy playboy (Ryan Phillippe) who is accused of assaulting and raping a prostitute. Phillippe insists that he is innocent, that he will take the stand, and adamantly denies he would accept a plea bargain should it be offered. On the surface, Haller's client has all the advantages over the word of a prostitute and it seems as though this is an easy case of a woman-for-hire who aims to get money out of her rich client. But when Haller, with the aid of his field investigator, uncovers evidence that links Phillippe to a previous sexual murder, Haller is faced with the defense lawyer's greatest challenge: loyalty to a potential murderer who may be guilty as charged. The American Bar Association (ABA) code requires that attorneys owe allegiance to their clients, guilt or innocence notwithstanding.

This dilemma reminds the author of Terence Rattigan's 1946 play, *The Winslow Boy*, where a young navel cadet is expelled from the British Naval Academy over a petty theft. The boy's middle-class family believes in his innocence and, despite the odds, decides to challenge the British Navy by requesting a trial. To exonerate their son and defend the family's honor, the family engages a prominent barrister, Sir Robert Morton, to represent its interests. After interviewing the boy, Morton is convinced of his innocence and decides to take the case even though it may adversely affect his political career. When Morton succeeds in clearing the boy and preserving the family's name, the daughter thanks him for seeing that justice was done. But the lawyer demurs:

> Sir Morton: I wept today because right had been done.
> Catherine Winslow: Not justice?
> Sir Morton: No, not justice. Right. Easy to do justice. Very hard to do right.[34]

What Morton meant was that since the boy was innocent, justice would prevail regardless. But doing the right thing was hard because Morton knew that if he won, it would ruin his political future.

Connelly's lawyer, Mickey Haller, is neither Sir Robert Morton nor Atticus Finch, lawyers who placed their principles above personal gain. Mickey Haller is no "white knight" of the legal profession but rather an ambiguous moral character who does right by his clients even if his methods skirt the letter of the law. On the other hand, Grisham's lawyers are mostly larger-than-life heroic types, possibly with minor flaws. Maybe that explains why Hollywood prefers Grisham's lawyers.

## Shyster Lawyers

Unlike the serious heroic lawyers of the Grisham-based films, the movies where lawyers are portrayed as disreputable characters are either silly comedies or crime and gangster movies. There are few exceptions to that generalization. The most common portrayals of shyster lawyers occur in Hollywood comedies where the laughs are at the expense of an incompetent or unscrupulous lawyer. A case in point is the Joe Pesci character, Vincent

Gambini, in the 1992 film *My Cousin Vinny*. Vinny is a recent graduate from a not surprisingly unidentified law school who travels to the Deep South to defend his nephew against a wrongful murder charge. Armed with his fiancée, Mona Lisa Vito, and his cowboy boots, Vinny is the kind of relative most people would like to disown. He is brash, vulgar, ostentatiously dressed in black leather and chains of jewelry, and has failed the bar exam six times. Nonetheless, he still manages to get his cousin acquitted in a silly but harmless film.

Decidedly funnier, but not quite as harmless, is Willie Gingrich (Walter Matthau), the lawyer character that Billy Wilder created for his film *The Fortune Cookie* (1966). If you would not want Vinny Gambini as a cousin, you certainly would not want Willie Gingrich as a brother-in-law. Willie is an ambulance-chasing personal injury lawyer who richly deserves his nickname: "Whiplash Willie." When his brother-in-law, Harry Hinkle (Jack Lemmon), a CBS sportscaster, is run over by a Cleveland Browns running back and ends up in the hospital, Willie sees an opportunity for a megabuck insurance settlement. Harry, of course, is not seriously injured, but Willie convinces him to accept the splints, neck braces, and wheelchair charade, at least until the insurance settlement. The scam almost works until Harry's conscience upsets the fraudulent scheme. With Willie Gingrich, Wilder created one of the funniest lawyers in film history but also one of the sleaziest. Willie is an unprincipled opportunist whose philosophy is summed up in the phrase, "life is a racket." Matthau's performance won him an Oscar because, in the opinion of one reviewer, it came close to the truth.[35]

While the origin for "shyster" remains unclear,[36] the word found its way into Hollywood gangster movies in the thirties. The lawyers in these crime films worked for the mob and valued money and power over the legal code of ethics. Illustrations of the shyster lawyer can be found in two 1932 films, *The Mouthpiece* and *Lawyer Man*. As their titles suggest, these are portraits of charming rogues who either work for the underworld or for crooked politicians.[37] The attorney in *The Mouthpiece* is an assistant D.A. who turns to drink when he discovers that the defendant he convicted, who later was executed, was innocent of the crime. Unable to overcome his guilt, he becomes an attorney for hire, even to the criminal class. He receives his just desserts when mobsters shoot him down at film's end. The fortunes of unscrupulous lawyers like that in *The Mouthpiece* were usually tied to the mobsters they defended.[38] The lawyer (William Powell) in *The Lawyer Man* begins as a decent but poor attorney working in the New York slums. But he becomes an overnight celebrity when he wins an important case and gains the attention of a corrupt politician. When Powell refuses to work for him, the political boss destroys Powell's reputation on a trumped-up charge. Ruined, Powell seeks revenge, not by playing square and fair, but resorting to dirty tricks himself.[39]

The importance of the lawyer to the criminal class and to organized crime is best exemplified by *The Godfather* trilogy (1972, 1974, and 1990). The collaborative work of writer Mario Puzo and director Francis Ford Coppola, *The Godfather* films tell the saga of the "Corleones," Vito and Michael—two generations of Mafia chieftains. A key figure in this intergenerational story of a Mafia family is the "consigliore," the Corleones' adopted son and legal advisor. The consigliore acted in the same capacity as the legal department in modern corporations. As the Corleones' illegal business empire grows, the greater the need the Don,

# Picturing Justice

"the Godfather," has for legal advice and counsel. It is inconceivable that the lawyer acting as a consigliore in real life could later deny knowledge of the organization's illegal activities. To make that point clear, the Puzo novel included a line, cut from the film version, where Don Corleone says, "A lawyer with his briefcase can steal more than a hundred men with guns."[40] To the Mafia leadership, lawyers were "hired guns," important players within the organizational structure. In every sense of the word, they were lawyers for the mob.

## Fallen Idols

A common theme in the entertainment arts is the concept of redemption: narratives built around a major character who falls from a position of prestige to the lower depths, usually due to alcohol, drugs, or bad women (restricted to women since men dominate positions of power in the film industry). Hollywood has applied this traditional plot idea in its films to all sorts of occupations, including the legal profession.

As early as the thirties, the studios began to grind out films where prominent lawyers succumb to the pleasures of the flesh. Occasionally, Hollywood produced a film where the lawyer's descent was not due to a "femme fatale" or to substance abuse but to a failure to live up to personal ideals. Two films involving Jewish lawyers concern characters who lost their souls to greed and succumb to temptations that only money can provide. Elmer Rice's stage play, *Counsellor At Law*, was adapted for the screen in 1933 and starred John Barrymore as George Simon, a successful Jewish lawyer with an office in the Empire State Building. Simon has progressed from a humble boyhood on the lower East Side ghetto to become a highly respected and successful attorney. From all outward appearances, Simon has a flourishing practice. Yet he has a troubled soul. His socialite wife and her two children from a previous marriage look down on him because of his humble background, while his mother reprimands him for rejecting his heritage. For example, his mother embarrasses Simon into defending the son of a Jewish woman from the old neighborhood, a communist arrested for making speeches in Union Square. The young man is completely out of place in Simon's plush offices, and during their consultation, he refuses to listen to Simon's advice that he refrain from making future speeches. The disparity between Simon's wealth and the young man's Marxist ideals are so obvious to Simon that all the attorney can do is shrug his shoulders. Simon's descent begins when a rival lawyer threatens to expose some wrongdoing in Simon's past, knowledge of a false alibi provided to a former client. To add even more misery to his possible disbarment, Simon discovers that his wife has been unfaithful. In a moment of utter despair, he considers jumping out his office window, but is prevented by his loyal secretary, who adores him. With new inspiration and true love, Simon decides to fight the disbarment charge rather than commit suicide.

John Garfield is another beleaguered Jewish lawyer, Joe Morse, who has climbed his way out of the New York slums and into a plush Wall Street office in *Force of Evil* (1948). Joe's decision to make lots of money by working for Tucker, a racketeer and mobster, has made him a successful lawyer, albeit one without scruples. In contrast, Joe's older brother, Leo (Thomas Gomez), sacrificed to put him through college and law school, a familiar scenario among lower-class immigrant families. Without an education, Leo tries his hand at several businesses that fail. Eventually, he goes to work in the illegal numbers policy racket as an independent operator. When Joe's boss, Tucker, has a scheme to control the numbers racket, Joe tries to warn Leo, but his brother refuses his help. In a plot too complicated to detail here, Tucker's men kidnap Leo and his bookkeeper. In the process, the bookkeeper is killed and Leo dies from a heart attack brought on by shock. Joe learns of Leo's death and takes revenge on Tucker in a dramatic shootout. At film's end, Joe decides to turn himself in to the special prosecutor who has been appointed to investigate the numbers racket. Looking at Leo's body on the banks of the Hudson River, Joe's voice-over expresses his remorse and his hope for redemption:

> I found my brother's body at the bottom there, like an old dirty rag nobody wants. He was dead and I felt that I had killed him. I turned back to give myself up to Hall. Because if a man's life can be lived so long and come out this way, like rubbish, it's something that is horrible and has to be ended one way or another. And I decided to help.

*Force of Evil* is one of those multifaceted films that operate on several levels. At its most obvious level of understanding, it is a gangster story. On a second level, it is a retelling of the story of Cain and Abel. At a third level, it is also a story of personal redemption. Finally, at its highest level of understanding, it can be construed as a critique of the capitalist system. The story of Joe Morse's rise from ghetto to Wall Street raises the moral question of whether it is possible to become financially successful within the capitalist system without becoming corrupted by it.[41] This is not an inappropriate interpretation of the film since it was the collaboration of political leftist Abraham Polonsky, who directed and did the screenplay, and liberal actor John Garfield's independent company, Enterprise Productions. Both men came under the scrutiny of HUAC during the Hollywood hearings. Polonsky would be blacklisted by Hollywood and Garfield died before his scheduled HUAC appearance.

*Counsellor At Law* and *Force of Evil* were not typical Hollywood redemption films. More common within the industry were films where the major character's fall from grace is due to a personal flaw or addiction. For instance, alcoholism is the cause of the descent in films like *The People Against O'Hara* (1951) and *The Verdict* (1982). In the first, Spencer Tracy plays a noted criminal attorney who is forced to retire because of alcoholism. He agrees to defend young O'Hara on a murder charge because the family is poor and can only afford to pay a fee of $325 for legal services (a situation rectified by the creation of the public defender system in the 1960s). Unfortunately, due to inebriation, carelessness, and old age, Tracy loses the case. He still believes O'Hara is innocent, however, and launches his own investigation, which leads him to the real killer. Although he secures sufficient evidence to free O'Hara, Tracy is killed in the process, thus providing redemption through death.

Alcoholism also is the downfall of attorney Frank Gavin (Paul Newman) in *The Verdict*. Gavin is a shabby, alcoholic lawyer who begins his day with a shot and a beer chaser. He has few, if any, clients and is reduced to ambulance chasing and hustling up business at wakes. His career is at rock bottom and he is one step from disbarment when he is given a medical malpractice suit by default. Since the suit is against a Catholic hospital, few lawyers in Irish-Catholic Boston are willing to take a case where the Catholic Church is the defendant. Gavin rejects an out-of-court settlement by the Boston Archdiocese after he visits the comatose victim in the hospital and decides to go to trial and to secure a larger settlement. He sobers up and his pre-alcoholic legal skills return. Meanwhile, the archdiocese has hired a high-priced law firm to defend its case. Gavin once again proves his competence as an attorney, but he must contend with considerable opposition: the defense team has put a corporate spy (Charlotte Rampling) onto him, many of his witnesses are discredited, and the rulings of a prejudicial judge eliminate most of his evidence. A surprise witness—a hospital nurse—saves his case when her testimony establishes the negligence Gavin requires for a victorious verdict. At film's end, Gavin is sober, has won his big case to restore his reputation, and his clients have received substantial personal injury damages. While it is true that almost half the lawyers who are disbarred or disciplined are alcoholics or drug addicts, the legal community was most unhappy with the film for its erroneous presentation of tort law, trial lawyering, and judicial behavior. The film's legal lapses led two law professors to complain, "If justice is blind, justice got lucky in *The Verdict*."[42]

The substance that brings down Eddie Dodd in *True Believer* (1989) is drugs, not alcohol. Eddie (James Woods) is a former civil rights activist turned drug addict and ambulance chaser. A fighter for liberal causes in the sixties, Eddie's law practice has been neglected due to his addiction, and as a result, his clients are mostly drug dealers and dope pushers. He has become so disillusioned by the legal system that he accepts the injustice of the system since "everybody's guilty of something," and justice becomes an irrelevant commodity. Goaded by his young protégé, Eddie is pressured to take one last "lost cause"—the kind of hopeless cause Jefferson Smith reminds Senator Paine of in *Mr. Smith Goes to Washington*. Eddie agrees to defend Kim, an Asian-American inmate accused of murdering another prisoner. Supported by his protégé, who reminds Eddie of himself in his early years, and the legitimacy of his client's self-defense claim, Eddie's investigation reveals that his client is innocent of the crime that sent him to prison in the first place. In the final scene, Kim's family meets him as he leaves prison while Eddie looks on, his confidence renewed and his faith in the justice system restored.

A new twist on the redemption plot is found in *The Devil's Advocate* (1997). Keanu Reeves goes to work for a prestigious New York law firm headed by a slick lawyer (Al Pacino) who serves as a metaphor for Satan. Pacino recruits Reeves after the young lawyer has successfully defended a child molester he knew to be guilty of the crime. In fact, Reeves has a perfect record as both prosecutor and defense counsel. It is his desire to win regardless of whether justice is done that makes him the perfect candidate for Pacino's firm. Thus, blind ambition and the lure of financial success seduce Reeves into joining the New York law firm where he learns what it means to work for the devil. During the fiery climax, Reeves asks Pacino why he selected lawyers to do his bidding. Pacino's answer is similar to the reason Macaulay gave: the law touches everyone at some point in life.

Another overly ambitious personal injury lawyer (John Travolta) takes on the case of eight families in Woburn, Massachusetts, whose household members contract leukemia and die. Based on the Jonathan Harr bestselling book, *A Civil Action* (1998) recounts an actual legal case where two large corporate giants, W.R. Grace and Beatrice Foods, are the industrial polluters who poison the town's water supply. Travolta plays real-life Boston attorney Jan Schlichtmann, who initially refuses to take the case because he cannot locate the identity of the polluters and the case will eat up too much of the firm's assets. But Schlichtmann receives a speeding ticket as he is leaving town near the industrial waste dump site. It is at this point that he discovers that he has hit pay dirt since both defendants have what is known in the trade as "deep pockets." The case, however, drags on as neither Grace nor Beatrice is willing to settle out of court and Schlichtmann sees the firm's funds dwindle to the point of bankruptcy. When the case goes to the jury, the attorney for Beatrice offers him $20 million to settle. Without consulting his clients, Schlichtmann declines the offer. The jury exonerates Beatrice but holds that the case against W.R. Grace should go forward. Schlichtmann has lost $20 million for his clients. Despite being heavily in debt and without other clients, Schlichtmann later turns down an $8 million settlement offer from Grace. But after his partners leave the firm, Schlichtmann is forced to accept the offer. Due to his personal greed, oversized ego, and legal mistakes, Schlichtmann's law firm went bankrupt, his clients received unsatisfactory compensation, and Grace continued to dump waste into the Woburn river and did not even apologize to the victims' families. At this point, Schlichtmann turns the case over to the Environmental Protection Agency, which eventually shuts down the waste dump.

George Clooney plays the title character in *Michael Clayton* (2007), a "fixer" for his prestigious law firm. Clayton's job is to resolve troublesome problems, such as a client's hit-and-run accident. As Clayton describes himself to the client, "I'm a janitor. I clean up the mess." The firm assigns Clayton to watch one of its lawyers (Tom Wilkinson), who has a breakdown while representing a chemical company, U/North, that he knows is guilty of using poisonous pesticides. U/North is the defendant in a multibillion-dollar class action suit and the law firm cannot allow their maverick attorney to ruin their defense. But Clooney is a flawed individual—divorced, heavily in debt, with a gambling and alcohol problem. His major concern is to get out from under his own personal problems and he refuses to believe Wilkinson until he is found dead. In true Hollywood fashion, Clayton comes to realize that Wilkinson was telling the truth and then he goes about securing the necessary evidence to bring down U/North and its unscrupulous legal counsel. Lawyer Michael Clayton is also not a "white knight," but a troubled soul who must be shocked into taking action and doing the right thing. He is not the stuff of heroes.

Ambition, not drugs, alcohol, or sex, is the downfall of Michael Douglas's district attorney in *Beyond a Reasonable Doubt* (2009), a remake of a 1956 Fritz Lang film. Douglas is a high-profile prosecutor with a reputation for securing convictions in criminal cases who has his eye on the governorship and who believes that his good looks, positive media exposure, and high conviction rate will make him a lock for the party's nomination. That is the plan until a young journalist suspects that the D.A. is tampering with the evidence to exaggerate his record and impress the public. In an implausible plot twist, the reporter frames himself as a murder suspect in the hope of exposing Douglas for the corrupt lawyer that he is. Given that it is a Hollywood movie, it is not surprising that Douglas receives his just desserts at the end.

## Family Law

How many of us go to see a movie where the storyline involves romance, marriage, and family life and think about the laws that govern such ancillary issues as marriage, divorce, child custody, and adoption? The author is willing to bet that at some point in our lives many of us had to contend with one or another of these matters. Certainly, Hollywood has often relied upon these family-related issues as the basis for countless film narratives. The increasing demand for lawyers who specialize in such matters has led several law schools to offer a course in "family law in the cinema" as part of the student's legal education.[43]

While Marquette law professor David Ray Papke teaches such a course, he remains skeptical of its educational value.[44] He reminds us that Hollywood films are a double-edged sword: they can enlighten and educate but they can provide misinformation and cause more harm than good. He cites as an example the 1989 film *The War of the Roses*, which details the marriage of a once happy couple, Oliver (Michael Douglas) and Barbara (Kathleen Turner). The Roses' marriage turns sour and eventually downright nasty. Barbara begins to imagine a life without Oliver and the fulfillment of her desire to open a catering business. She asks for a divorce, including the beautiful house she designed, but Oliver refuses. Instead he hires a divorce lawyer (Danny DeVito) to protect his interests. While doing research, DeVito discovers a state law (fictional) which permits divorcing parties to live under the same roof as long as they lead separate lives. The arrangement is possible in their very large house where Oliver lives in one wing and Barbara lives in another. But the arrangement gets on their nerves and the Roses begin a war of attrition to see who will capitulate first and move out. They do spiteful and unimaginable things to each other. One example will suffice. Barbara is giving a dinner party to promote her catering business and the "piece de resistance" is the fish entrée laid out on this large board. While the guests are dining, Oliver sneaks into the kitchen and urinates on the fish. As their war escalates, the Roses end up crushed under the weight of their humongous chandelier. This film, obviously, is not an endorsement for the institution of marriage.

Is it coincidental that the release of this movie coincides with the declining marriage rate in the U.S.? The percentage of adults 18 and older who were married in 2010 was 51 percent, down from 72 percent in 1972. This decline is attributed to the increase in cohabitation, single-person households, and single parenthood. At the same time, the number of new marriages has fallen as well, especially in the 18–29 age group. If the trend continues, the percentage of unmarried women will soon surpass the percentage of married women.[45] Whether this decline is due to economic conditions, a rejection of marriage or both is unclear.

Professor Papke also cites several films as useful tools to teach about child custody and adoption laws, including *Kramer vs. Kramer* (1979) and *The Good Mother* (1988). He found that in most child custody films the major focus is on the adults rather than the children. While child custody films portray a wide range of parental responses, he cites these two film dramas to show that perfect endings are not the norm.

The very popular *Kramer vs. Kramer* garnered four Oscars for best actor, supporting actor, director, and screenplay for its story of a child custody controversy. Joanna Kramer (Meryl Streep) leaves her six-year-old son and her husband Ted (Dustin Hoffman) to find herself. The film was released in the midst of the wave of feminism which consumed the country for several decades. Ted, who left the parenting to Joanna while he went off to work, eventually develops a warm and loving relationship with his son. But after a year or so, Joanna returns and seeks custody. Because Joanna left the marriage, Ted was given custody but, as Ted's lawyer warns, the courts favor a maternal preference role. When Joanna regains custody, Ted's lawyer provides some bad advice by telling him that if he decides to appeal, his son would have to testify in open court. He decides not to contest the judgment. Papke points out that these misrepresentations make Joanna the "villain" in the piece when, in his opinion, justice would require that the son stay with Ted or that he be shared with both parents, but with the father having custody. The screenplay, however, has Joanna giving up her custody so that Ted and son can stay together at the end.

Another sad custody battle is portrayed in *The Good Mother*, where Anna Dunlop (Diane Keaton) is a loving, caring mother to her six-year-old daughter, Molly. After her divorce, Anna takes a job in a medical lab while Molly attends daycare. Anna leads a quiet, rather dull, life until she meets artist Leo Cutter (Liam Neeson) in a laundromat and they begin a relationship. As the weeks pass, the three function as a normal family as Molly takes to the free-spirited and charming Leo. But one night Molly wakes and sees Cutter come out of the shower, naked and without a towel. Since Anna had previously used books to illustrate aspects of the human body, Molly asks Leo about his penis. Without thinking, Cutter allows the girl to touch it and this indiscretion, along with others (such as allowing Molly to share their bed while they are having intercourse), leads Anna's ex-husband to seek custody of his daughter. During the custody hearing, it becomes obvious how difficult it is to explain such a situation in a legal hearing where the parties involved are restricted largely to "yes" and "no" answers. The lawyer for Anna's ex-husband (who is not a bad man but socially conservative) plots out a strategy to prove that Anna is an unfit mother, the best chance to win the custody battle. Although Anna admits that she and Leo made "mistakes" and that these would not be repeated and even though she is supported by a court-appointed child psychologist, the judge awards Molly to her ex-husband. In the end, she has lost both Molly and Leo. *The Good Mother* illustrates that even in Hollywood's fantasy world, the law occasionally produces painfully sad endings.

The number of child adoptions in the U.S. remains stable but the publicity about them has increased due to the media coverage of celebrities like Madonna, Angelina Jolie, and Sandra Bullock. Adoption stories may make for solid dramatic plots but their endings are usually always happy. As an example of a less than happy ending, let us look at the 1995 film *Losing Isaiah*, about an interracial adoption, starring Halle Berry as an African-American mother and Jessica Lange as a white social worker. When sanitation workers find crackhead Berry's baby, Isaiah, on a trash pile, Lange and her husband become his temporary foster parents until Isaiah's mother can be found. Berry, meanwhile, believes Isaiah is dead and stops looking for him. Eventually, Lange and husband happily adopt Isaiah. Years pass, Berry is rehabilitated, and when she learns that her son is alive, she desperately wants him back. What follows is an extended legal battle that is made more sensitive by the race issue. Do black children belong to black parents regardless of other considerations? Berry's lawyer (Samuel L. Jackson) gets Lange to admit that she only reads to Isaiah books with white characters. In the end, the judge invalidates the adoption and returns Isaiah to Berry because it is best for a child to be with his "natural mother," particularly where race is an issue. Like Professor Papke, the reader may want to question the judge's decision because Berry, given her drug-related past and her lack of help in raising Isaiah, is a greater parental risk that Lange.[46] When Isaiah does not get along with his "new mother," Berry realizes she needs help and goes to Lange for assistance. The film leaves the audience with an open-ended conclusion as the final scene shows both women on the floor playing with Isaiah. Will they unofficially share custody? Or will Berry return Isaiah to Lange? According to one family law specialist, the film's ending is a better result for the child that both love, an arrangement that a good mediator might have facilitated.[47]

A happier adoption ending is found in *The Blind Side* (2009), which dramatizes the real-life story of Michael Oher, an African-American boy from the underclass who, against all odds, goes on to become a left tackle for the Baltimore Ravens of the National Football League. When the film opens, Michael (Quinton Aaron), who is called "Big Mike" because of his size, is a ward of the state because his crack-addicted mother cannot take care of him. Mike is accepted, with reservations, to the Wingate Christian Academy in Memphis, Tennessee, where he meets the white Tuohy family: mother Leigh Anne (Sandra Bullock), father Sean (Tim McGraw), daughter Collins (Lily Collins), and son S.J. (Jae Head). The Tuohy family takes him in, at first as a temporary measure until he can find a home, but eventually as a permanent guest. However, the film is not technically about an adoption even though Leigh Anne refers to Michael as her "son" and he calls her "Mama," because Michael is approaching adult status at 18. Instead, Leigh Anne and Sean petition the state to have them named as guardians.[48] Due to his size, Michael is recruited for the academy's football team and with patience and coaching he becomes an outstanding left tackle. Under the Tuohys' care, and with the help of a private tutor, he improves his high school grades and receives football scholarships from the powerhouse colleges of the southeastern conference. To illustrate that point, the film has a parade of coaches, like Nick Saban of Alabama, in cameo roles. Mike likes Tennessee but since the Tuohys are Ole Miss graduates, he chooses Mississippi University. In the last scene, the viewer sees the real Michael Oher being called to the podium as a first-round draft pick of the Baltimore Ravens. While the film won a best actor award for Sandra Bullock and did well at the box office, Papke has reservations about the legal guardian process it portrays. The author, meanwhile, has serious concerns about the film's racial attitudes, which he examines in chapter 12.

The author also is concerned that Hollywood plots revolving around family law issues reduce the legal questions to minor points in films where the law described is more likely to cause problems rather than resolve them; these include issues such as blocking or restricting interracial marriages, causing pain and complications in divorce proceedings, and rendering more wrong decisions than right ones.

## Women Trial Lawyers

With the exception of the 1930s, women trial lawyers were not major characters in Hollywood films until the eighties. Contrary to popular belief, Hollywood churned out a dozen or more films in the thirties that featured women lawyers.[49] This is somewhat surprising since at the time women comprised 24 percent of the workforce but only 3 percent of the national bar.[50] Why so few? One reason is that the law schools refused to admit them. Another is that even when a law school accepted them, their numbers were restricted. Still, the film industry turned to depicting female lawyers for screen plots in the thirties and forties. Some of these movies were "B" films like *Scarlet Pages* (1930), where actress Elsie Ferguson defends a murderess who turns out to be her illegitimate daughter. Others, however, featured established female stars like Fay Wray (*Ann Carver's Profession*, 1933), Jean Arthur (*The Defense Rests*, 1934), and Claire Trevor (*Career Woman*, 1936). The trend continued until World War II put a halt to women-centered films. But what distinguishes these films from the ones that will reappear in the 1980s is the pre-feminist message that women lawyers cannot have both successful professional careers and happy personal lives. For instance, Fay Wray's character in *Ann Carver's Profession* wins an important murder case but relinquishes her career to save her marriage.

Plots involving women lawyers largely disappeared from the screen over the next four decades, due largely to the industry's interest in war movies, westerns, and musicals. The one notable exception is Katharine Hepburn's character, Amanda Bonner, in the 1950 film *Adam's Rib*, where she co-starred with Spencer Tracy. *Adam's Rib* is a romantic comedy where Hepburn and Tracy are practicing attorneys, with Amanda a solo practitioner and Tracy (Adam Bonner) an assistant D.A. When Amanda takes the case of a ditzy blonde (Judy Holliday) charged with the attempted murder of her unfaithful spouse, she is unaware that Adam has been assigned to prosecute. The comedy comes from the complications caused by spouses representing different sides of the law. What provides the film with substance is the fact that Amanda sees in the case an opportunity to criticize the prevailing moral double standard and preach the cause of legal equality. Adam views the case differently, as the facts, which are not in dispute, show that the defendant did shoot at her husband. In her client's defense Amanda maintains that if she were a man, her actions would be excused under the "unwritten law" that married men have a right to protect their home and their honor. In her summation, Amanda tells the jury that equality is on trial, rather than her client, who had just as much right to defend her family and home as her husband. The argument proves persuasive and Amanda wins the case. Although the trial has caused domestic problems, Adam and Amanda are reconciled at the end. It is not hyperbole to suggest that Amanda Bonner is an early feminist who would have made an excellent screen attorney for the 21st century.[51]

The film industry awoke from its slumber in the 1980s to resume making movies featuring women trial lawyers. Whether this was in response to the feminist movement, a desire to be politically correct, or an attempt to lure women into movie theaters, is a question best left to Hollywood insiders. What is obvious to even the most casual Hollywood follower is the fact that the industry could hardly continue to ignore the significant gains made by women in law school admissions and enrollments, private sector practice, and judicial prominence. One notable statistical trend involved applications to law school. Women applicants went from 3 percent of the total law school roll in the late 1940s to 34 percent in the 1980s. By the first decade of the 21st century, women comprised 53 percent of the law school population. Meanwhile, the number of women practicing law moved from pre–World War II single digits to almost one-third of the more than one million practicing lawyers in the U.S. Women, moreover, had made gains in the number of judicial appointments to state and national courts as cited below.

Table 7.1. Women in the Judiciary[52]

| COURT | % FEMALE JUDGES |
| --- | --- |
| District Courts | 25 % |
| Circuit Courts | 27 % |
| State Courts of Last Appeal | 32 % |
| U.S. Supreme Court | 3 % |

Males, however, are entrenched in the majority of leadership positions in law firms and also far surpass women in compensation. Women have made the most gains in the federal judiciary.

Beginning in the mid-eighties, Hollywood recognized the change in the legal demographics by releasing more than half-a-dozen feature films with major actresses portraying women lawyers as central characters. Glenn Close, Barbara Hershey, and Jessica Lange played defense lawyers in *Jagged Edge* (1985), *Defenseless* (1991), and *Music Box* (1989); Debra Winger and Kelly McGillis were district attorneys in *Legal Eagles* (1986) and *The Accused* (1988); Cher portrayed a public defender in *Suspect*; and Mary Elizabeth Mastrantonio a corporate lawyer in *Class Action* (1991).

Hollywood is to be commended for producing films that provide starring roles previously reserved almost exclusively for male actors. Even so, the female lawyer characters in the films cited above raise serious questions regarding screen depictions. The acceptance of women in professional roles is offset by the manner in which these screen women conduct their professional and personal lives. On a personal level, women lawyers in films are portrayed as either unmarried or divorced, lonely, and frequently without children. Their private lives are often out of sync, giving the appearance of an unfulfilled life. When children are present, the relationship with their mother is often estranged. Glenn Close's defense lawyer, for instance, has a son who resents her practicing law.[53]

As members of the legal profession, women trial lawyers are depicted in stereotypical terms as either incompetent or unethical attorneys who often exercise poor judgment. For example, Glenn Close (*Jagged Edge*) sleeps with her client during his murder trial and Barbara Hershey (*Defenseless*) has an ongoing affair with her married client. Both women breach professional ethics and contradict the conventional wisdom that in order to maintain objectivity, a lawyer should never become involved with a client. Jessica Lange violates a corollary of that principle in *Music Box* when she unwisely decides to represent her father against charges that he had been a war criminal. In law and medicine, the general rule is that lawyers and doctors should not represent or treat family members.

Meanwhile, Mary Elizabeth Mastrantonio (*Class Action*) carries on an office affair with her superior, which clouds her judgment in a civil suit where her father represents the plaintiff. Worse yet, she later conspires with her father, counsel for the opposition, in a civil case to destroy her own client.[54] Moreover, she commits several serious legal blunders, including committing a conflict of interest by defending a client who is being sued by her father's client and knowingly allowing her bed partner boss to perjure himself on the stand without objecting. In *Suspect*, Cher allows a juror to provide her with clues in a murder case. In real life, consorting with a juror, for whatever reason, is grounds for disbarment. In *Defenseless*, Hershey defends a client in a murder case without informing her or the police that she is a material witness to the crime. Kelly McGillis's district attorney does a disservice to a crime victim (Jodie Foster) in *The Accused* when she plea-bargains away those responsible for the gang rape in favor of prosecuting the witnesses who encouraged and supported the rape.

The examples of outright negative screen portrayals of women lawyers are too numerous to document here. A few examples will have to suffice. Take the film adaptation of Scott Turow's novel *Presumed Innocent* (1990), where D.A. Harrison Ford is having an affair with one of the female assistants in his office. The movie leads the audience to believe that this woman has slept her way up the career ladder, since she previously had been the mistress of the chief district attorney. Christine Lahti's character in *And Justice for All* is having an affair with attorney Al Pacino while she sits on the ethics panel that will decide whether he should be disbarred. Charlotte Rampling's ambitious lawyer, seeking to restart her career after a failed marriage, allows herself to be exploited by the legal team representing the Boston Archdiocese in *The Verdict*. She agrees to seduce the opposition lawyer, Frank Gavin (Paul Newman), and spy on him, feeding information back to her boss. Once Rebecca De Mornay's criminal defense lawyer in *Guilty as Sin* (1993) suspects that her client has murdered his wife, she plants evidence that secures his conviction. Her actions violate professional ethics. Finally, has Hollywood ever produced a more unscrupulous lawyer than Karen Crowder (Tilda Swinton) in *Michael Clayton*? Her task is to prevent damaging evidence against her corporate employer, U/North, from coming to light. She hires goons to tail, ransack, and eventually kill one of the defense attorneys (Tom Wilkinson) before he reveals the truth about U/North's use of pesticides. And after Wilkinson is silenced, she turns her goons onto George Clooney, who escapes a car bombing when he stops to watch horses grazing in an open field. Crowder is a female shark without a conscience or an ounce of human decency. All the actions of these women lawyers violate the ethical rules of the profession and are grounds for disbarment. Crowder goes further; she is so desperate that she resorts to murder. These are certainly not the kind of lawyers to recommend to your friends. Feminists might disagree with the above analysis by citing Steven Soderbergh's hugely popular film *Erin Brockovich* (2000), which won an Academy Award for actress Julia Roberts. Technically, Brockovich is not a lawyer but a paralegal, that is, a person who has received some legal training but is not licensed to practice law. The film is based on an actual person, a single mother, who goes after a large corporation, Pacific Gas & Electric, after she discovers that the utility is poisoning the water supply of a small California town. Brockovich works in a North Hollywood law office, where she is shunned by the other office workers and spends her lunch hour perusing the firm's files. One day she discovers a *pro bono* case involving a Hinkley, California, woman who is suing the electric company because of health problems caused by the company's toxic waste dump. On her own initiative, Brockovich visits the town, interviews the woman, and is convinced that the utility is culpable. She convinces 634 town residents to initiate a class action suit and persuades the law firm she works for to take the case. Doing most of the legwork herself in gathering the evidence, Brockovich and the townspeople are rewarded when an arbitration panel awards a $333 million settlement. Brockovich is given a $2 million bonus and a new job; the law firm receives $133 million for its services, while the residents receive the remainder. It is the typical Hollywood fairy tale of how one ordinary individual overcomes the odds, brings a large corporation to its knees, and secures justice for the underdog. Brockovich became a media celebrity after Hollywood brought her story to the big screen. Afterward, she became a motivational speaker on the lecture circuit, inspiring women to reach higher achievement goals. She then went to work for a Manhattan personal injury law firm and later opened her own research and consulting firm to become involved in major environmental cases.[55]

Rumors about Brockovich persisted long after the film was relegated to DVD. An Internet report claims the film misrepresented the facts.[56] While the story cannot be substantiated because, unlike trials, arbitration proceedings are secret, a number of client complaints were registered concerning the awards. First, there was unhappiness that the award money was held for six months without interest added to the distribution. Other complaints involved the questioning of the unequal distribution of award monies without regard to medical histories. For example, the average award divided among the plaintiffs came to roughly $300,000 each, but some residents received only $50,000 to $60,000, including one man who was awarded $80,000 despite surgery to remove 17 tumors from his throat. Since no reasons were provided for the individual awards and the amounts were kept secret, several residents filed lawsuits against the firm that won them their awards. Besides, 400 of Hinckley's residents received zero from the $333 million settlement. Admittedly, the law firm had $12 million in expenses but it did receive 40 percent of the award, leaving the plaintiffs, who were the victims of the corporate polluter, to share $196 million or $300,000 each.[57] Lawyers, of course, are entitled to receive compensation for their work. But the sense of equity in this case is badly skewed.

Possibly someday the full Erin Brockovich story will become part of the public record while, as the newspaper editor in John Ford's *The Man Who Shot Liberty Valence* remarks when questioned about the truth behind the shooting of Valence, "When the truth becomes legend, print the legend." Hollywood loves to film legends.

Betty Anne Waters is not a legend but a loving sister who is dedicated to seeing that justice is done. In *Conviction*, a 2010 film, Hilary Swank plays Waters, a working-class woman raised in foster homes along with her brother, Kenny (Sam Rockwell). Their difficult childhood forged a strong bond between sister and brother. That bond is sorely tested when Kenny, a hothead and a drunk, is arrested for murdering a local woman. Kenny is convicted largely on the basis of his character traits, a few questionable eyewitnesses, and a vengeful cop. After the trial, Betty dedicates her life to proving her brother's innocence. She returns to high school to get her diploma and then her college degree. She enrolls in law school, where she bonds with another student and both pursue an investigation into Kenny's conviction. Thanks to DNA evidence, Kenny is cleared to resume his normal life. Based on a true story, the film is a testimony to familial love, hard work and dedication, and the admission of DNA testing at trial. How many of us would wish for a sister like Betty Anne Waters?[58]

In the real world of the law, the status of women in the profession has improved but has yet to reach parity with men. Some law firms have instituted flex hours to accommodate their employees with children. Other firms have provided for parental leave for both sexes after the birth of a child. Still others are willing to reduce the firm's quota for billable hours for those employees who prefer to spend more time with their families in exchange for reduced pay.[59]

But problems persist for women in the profession. These include, among others, sexual harassment, a hostile work environment, and stereotyping. While details on sexual harassment are unavailable for the legal profession, the ABA reported that women initiate 85 percent of all the sexual harassment complaints filed with the Equal Employment Opportunity Commission (EEOC). What is more worrisome is the fact that these complaints have increased 20 percent since 1992. Additionally, some law firms have reacted badly to the filing of sexual harassment complaints and have retaliated against the filers. Hence, the number of retaliation complaints has doubled since 1992. Furthermore, women remain the recipients of sexual jokes and innuendo and other forms of inappropriate behavior in the workplace, and many of these incidents never reach the complaint stage. This form of disrespect and male stereotyping even pervades the courtroom, as there are sitting judges who continue to refer to women lawyers as "honey" and "baby."[60] Stereotypes die hard, especially in the male-dominated bastion of the law.

## Doing Justice, Hollywood Style

At this point, the reader may wonder why any rational person would want to join the legal profession. But data from the ABA would likely confuse you even more, since law school enrollments have skyrocketed over the past 40 years.

Table 7.2. Law School Enrollment[61]

| Academic Year | Male | Female | Minority | Total Enrollment |
|---|---|---|---|---|
| 1967–68 | 58,315 | 2,769 | n/a | 61,084 |
| 1977–78 | 81,430 | 31,650 | 9,580 | 113,080 |
| 1987–88 | 69,077 | 48,920 | 13,250 | 117,997 |
| 1997–98 | 68,971 | 56,915 | 24,685 | 125,886 |
| 2007–08 | 75,523 | 66,196 | 30,598 | 141,719 |
| 2011–12 | 78,026 | 68,262 | 35,859 | 146,288 |
|  | 431,342 | 274,712 | 113,972 | 706,054 |

These statistics show that law school enrollments have more than doubled in 40 years and that the number of women admitted to law school has increased almost 25 times. Minorities have also gained as well, increasing their law school enrollment fourfold in 30 years. But the aftermath of the 2008 economic downturn has caught up with the law schools as both applications and enrollments declined in both 2012 and 2013. While the slow economy and soft job market are factors, the fact that recent law school graduates are carrying loans of $120,000 must cast doubt on whether a law degree is still worth the effort and money.[62]

Why this persistent attraction to the law despite the Watergate scandal, low public esteem, long hours, constant stress, harassment, an uncomfortable work environment (mostly for women and minorities), and a largely negative cinematic image? There are two possible explanations. First, in the U.S. law is a very viable profession because it allows one to venture into other work areas besides practicing law. Today, you will find lawyers working in the fields of government, sports, entertainment, broadcasting, teaching, and writing. I bet Grisham does not regret giving up the law for writing. A second reason is pure speculation but still plausible, namely that young people contemplating law as a career are unfazed by the jokes, low public esteem, derision, and negative media images. This is a subject that warrants further inquiry.

Meanwhile, the U.S. remains a litigious society where alleged wrongs are settled by the law, rather than through mediation or arbitration. The commonly heard joke, "If one lawyer is in town, he/she will starve to death. But if a second lawyer comes to town, both will flourish," is no longer considered funny. Statistics reveal that there are more practicing lawyers in the U.S. than in any other country in the world. There is one lawyer for every 300 Americans. Considering the popularity in the U.S. of law as a career and the number of practicing lawyers, it is surprising to discover that Hollywood has not found the subject more interesting as screen fare. Yet just roughly 6 percent of feature films produced since the industry's beginning have lawyers as major characters.[63]

One observation to be drawn from the evidence presented here is that Hollywood is just as ambivalent about lawyers as it is toward politicians. On the one hand, Hollywood tends to under-represent lawyers and politicians as screen material. On the other hand, when the industry portrays the law and lawyers in films, it either gets the legal facts wrong or it portrays lawyers as one-dimensional, usually unsavory, characters. Up to this point, Hollywood has had an aversion to presenting a balanced, objective view of the profession. Screen lawyers are more likely to be ready for sainthood (*Young Mr. Lincoln*, *To Kill a Mockingbird*), candidates for prison (*True Believer*), Gamblers Anonymous members (*Michael Clayton*), Alcoholics Anonymous members (*The Verdict*), or on the unemployment line (*A Civil Action*), than ordinary professionals working within the law. Additionally, screen lawyers behave as if they flunked law school, repeating the kind of mistakes that are usually corrected during moot court. Even if we grant dramatic license to the filmmaker, lawyers as a distinct class are no more likely to be one-dimensional characters than politicians, teachers, or doctors.

What does Hollywood have against lawyers? The answer is "nothing" because the studios hire many and rely upon them for their legal advice. How, then, to explain their screen portrayals? One explanation is that the entertainment media has turned lawyering into a performance art.[64] In a culture dominated by the visual media, the screen courtroom no longer is a venue for sifting through the facts to discover the truth. Rather it is an opportunity for lawyers to sway jurors with emotional appeals, bombastic rhetoric, and courtroom tricks. The public, so the argument goes, has come to expect lawyers to behave badly.

Law Professor Michael Asimow agrees and sees the portrayal transition in Hollywood between the more positive image of lawyers in 1930s and 1940s films with the more negative, unpleasant representations today as occurring in the seventies.[65] The shift reflects a change in public attitudes that is reinforced by the largely negative stereotypes portrayed in Hollywood films, according to Asimow. In a content analysis of 284 Hollywood films in which lawyers are significant characters, he found around two-thirds contained at least one bad lawyer. Were the earlier positive portrayals due to the requirements of the old Production Code? Asimow does not think so, but the code did require respect for the law, authority figures, and practicing professionals.

Asimow is not the only lawyer concerned with the profession's public image. The negative screen portrayals have distressed the ABA as well. In a report delivered at the 2002 ABA conference, it was noted that a survey of public confidence in 10 American institutions and their practitioners ranked lawyers ninth. Doctors were first, while only the news media kept lawyers out of last place.[66] In a Harris Poll conducted about the same time, people were asked a question about who could be trusted to tell the truth.[67] Doctors, teachers, and college professors were held to be most trustworthy, while lawyers were at the bottom of the list—along with members of Congress and trade union leaders. Two-thirds of the respondents, in fact, would not trust lawyers to tell the truth. Admittedly, part of the public negativity is understandable because unlike doctors and teachers, lawyers interact with people when they are in crisis and most vulnerable—sorting through a messy divorce, trying to reach agreement in a nasty custody battle, handling the probate and estate taxes when a loved one has died. These are traumatic experiences for people and it is at these times that individuals rely upon lawyers. Still, the excessive negativity is hard to accept. After all, doctors lose patients and teachers fail students. It is conceivable that the public's love-hate relationship with the law and its practitioners has always existed, but the dominance of the negative relationship beginning in the mid-seventies is due to factors beyond the control of the profession. Remember that of the 40 individuals charged in the Watergate scandal, 30 pleaded guilty or were found guilty and 19 went to prison. Many involved in the crime and cover-up had studied and practiced law, including the president of the United States. The legal profession and their political counterparts have not recovered from that debacle.

Hollywood has been especially unkind to women lawyers in this regard. Their depictions convey the impression that modern women who opt for legal careers are likely to end up unhappy and alone and sometimes indebted to a male colleague. Mary Elizabeth Mastrantonio's lawyer in *Class Action*, for example, defends an automaker in a personal injury suit whose car self-destructs on impact due to a faulty design. Her father (Gene Hackman), a famous liberal attorney, represents the plaintiff. The script discriminates against Mastrantonio's character because she works for a law firm that hides damaging evidence, steals documents, and generally lies to cover up its illegal activities. At the end, Mastrantonio has a change of heart and works with her father (against her client, the automaker) to achieve a settlement for the plaintiff. At a victory party in a local hangout, father and daughter dance and reconcile; daughter will join dad's law firm and work for the good guys. This sappy ending reinforced the film's message that "father still knows best."[68] Forget about Tilda Swinton's murderous lawyer, Karen Crowder, in *Michael Clayton*—she may prove to be an apparition. It is no surprise that she is unmarried and without a family since in real life, 40 percent of women lawyers are unmarried. But unlike Swinton's character in the film, approximately seven out of 10 women lawyers work as sole practitioners rather than for law firms.[69]

Film depictions of women lawyers also have had an influence on the real world expectations, particularly regarding appropriate dress, demeanor, and lifestyle. According to one source, these screen portrayals have led to the "androgynous female attorney" who wears pants suits and adopts other male characteristics in order to avoid appearing too feminine.[70] Rather than view these characterizations as a conspiracy of the male power structure within the film industry,[71] a more plausible scenario has to do with box office receipts. The discussion in this chapter indicates that male lawyers on screen are often just as flawed as their female counterparts. Spencer Tracy and Paul Newman portrayed alcoholic lawyers, James Woods's attorney was a drug addict, and George Clooney had a gambling problem. In addition, no female screen lawyer yet has even come close to Walter Matthau's unscrupulous sleazy lawyer, "Whiplash Willie," although Tilda Swinton's corporate shark gives it a good shot.

What is of greater concern for the legal profession than gender representation is the question of how justice is achieved in Hollywood films. Aristotle considers two kinds of justice in his *Nicomachean Ethics*: distributive and corrective. Distributive justice concerns how honor, prestige, and material goods are distributed throughout society. Hollywood virtually never constructs a film plot around the unequal share of the goods and rewards of society. *Force of Evil* is the rare exception that challenges the economics and the morality of the capitalist system. However, it was not a conventional film for its time because an independent company owned by a Marxist writer-director and a leftist-liberal actor produced it.

Aristotle's second kind of justice is corrective, where the law is used as an instrument to provide remedies for those wrongly victimized. Hence, Aristotle's concept of corrective justice requires both an injury and a wrongdoing. The party that has committed the wrong should be identified and punished for it. Here the law is much more interested in the wrongful injury than in the character of the parties involved. Hollywood films usually achieve justice through unlawful procedures, a timely accident, or last-minute evidentiary discovery. This unrealistic depiction serves to remind us once again that Hollywood is in the business of marketing products that sell at the box office. In so doing, the film industry has done a disservice to the moral principles underlying the American legal system and to the men and women who serve as its practitioners.

Chapter 8

# Hollywood Goes to War
## From the Great War to the Good War to the Forgotten War

"In peace, sons bury their fathers. In war, fathers bury their sons."
—Herodotus

"The only glory in war is surviving."
—Samuel Fuller, director and WWII infantryman

"The object of war is not to die for your country but to make the other bastard die for his."
—General George S. Patton

"The real heroes of Iwo Jima are the guys who didn't come back."
—John "Doc" Bradley, who helped raise the flag on Iwo Jima.

"War does not determine who is right—only who is left."
—Bertrand Russell

## Overview: War Is Hell

When the author was teaching his film and politics course, invariably a student would ask why the subject of war takes up almost one quarter of his book. It is a legitimate question that deserves a reflective response. As I thought about the question, two possible replies came to mind. For one, is it possible that being male I was simply reflecting Hollywood's paean to the testosterone that drives the action-adventure emphasis of the marketplace? Could I have succumbed to the excitement and violence of the war movies that played at least once or twice a month at my local theater during WWII when I was a teenager? But, truthfully, the author's interest in war movies waned like the rest of the nation's once hostilities ceased. Being shipped to Korea after receiving my degree dispelled any fantasy images from Hollywood war movies. As a young man, I had no real affection for war movies of any kind. Hence, this would not be the answer to the student's question. Further reflection and reviewing the historical data led to a more factual response that had escaped my attention, namely that the U.S. has been involved in a war about every quarter-of-a-century: beginning with colonial involvement in the French and Indian Wars and the American Revolution in the 18th century, and on into the 19th century with the Indian Wars, the Mexican War, the Civil War, and the Spanish-American War, and continuing with WWI and II, the Korean War, Vietnam, and a host of small wars like Grenada and the Persian Gulf War in the 20th century, and extending into the 21st century with the wars in Afghanistan and Iraq. Students are always amazed by this sobering fact.

When General William Tecumseh Sherman coined the phrase "War is hell" he was right, but up to a point, because the scars of war, both physical and mental, remain long after the conflict is over. The effects of war extend beyond those who wage it, affecting families, children, innocent civilians, and entire nations, both victorious and defeated. So often, those who were enemies on the battlefield become trading partners afterward as peacetime restores a sense of normalcy to daily life. But for the combatants and their victims, wars never end, and the horrors of war return anew in a lonely moment or dream. And in the 21st century, nuclear war will have no real victors—only the remains of what was once civilization. Put in this context, Sherman's phrase is truly an understatement.

War films are of two kinds: pro-war, propagandistic, patriotic flag-waving tracts and anti-war stories aimed at changing the hearts and minds of combatants and civilians. War as a film genre encompasses several sub-categories, including those about the horror and heartbreak of combat, and then those about the effects of war on the home front and society. Beginning with D.W. Griffith's Civil War masterpiece, *The Birth of a Nation* (1915), to the latest film stories emanating out of the Afghan-Iraqi wars, Hollywood has mined war for its narratives. How can we explain Hollywood's attraction for this brutal and violent subject?

War has been a staple of the film industry for much of its history. The straightforward reason is that the war genre is interchangeable with westerns and action-adventure films—the type of movies that bring men and teenage boys into theaters. It may surprise the reader to learn that more than 5,000 war-related film titles were released during Hollywood's first century.[1] War movies with both combat and home front themes have done well in two manners: as award recipients at Oscar time and as financial winners at the box office. Since the inception of the Academy Awards in 1928, up to 2011, 15 war movies have won Oscars for best picture and at least two dozen more were nominated for the award. Since 1915, seven war films, silent and talkies, have the distinction of being the top grosses for the year in which they were released. These seven films include ones with anti-war messages, like *The Big Parade* (1925), and patriotic ones, like *The Longest Day* (1962), which paid tribute to the valor and bravery of those involved in the Allied invasion of Normandy during WWII. However, since 1998 when *Saving Private Ryan* earned over $216 million at the box office, no other war film has been so successful.[2] In chapter 10 we will examine films from the Afghan-Iraqi wars and try to explain the reasons they fail to attract audiences. However, one fact is clear: the days of the war movie are numbered.

## World War I: The Great War

2014 will mark a hundred years since the beginning of World War I, a horrible war that saw casualties that were unimaginable at the time. Yet despite the passage of time and the fact that few, if any, witnesses remain, the last decade has seen renewed interest by film and television media in this ghastly war with its staggering human cost. Films like Steven Spielberg's Oscar-nominated *War Horse* (2011) and PBS's mini-series *Downton Abbey* have enjoyed considerable popularity and have renewed public interest in the so-called Great War, which took over eight million lives and wounded more than 21 million soldiers. The statistics are staggering: the combined casualties of both dead and wounded of the Allies and the opposing forces of the Central Powers totaled almost 30 million. The war left almost one and a half million Russian soldiers permanently disabled, while 240,000 British soldiers became war amputees. Over its 19-month participation, the U.S. lost 126,000 men, twice as many as in Vietnam and more than 20 times the casualties suffered in the Afghan-Iraqi wars. What is so mind-numbing is the fact that much of the war was fought in trenches on the Western Front, a stretch of land 500 miles long with Belgium at one end and Switzerland at the other. The over eight million dead were the victims of mustard gas, machine gun fire, tanks, and artillery shells. Soldiers advanced into enemy trenches one day only to retreat the next. In one day, at the Battle of the Somme, the British Army suffered 60,000 dead and wounded—one of the worst slaughters in military history. French casualties numbered more than 200,000, but the German casualties for this piece of land in northern France totaled a staggering 450,000–600,000.[3] And the irony is that on Armistice Day, which brought hostilities to an end, the opposing sides were pretty much in the same places as when the war began. The senseless carnage led one writer-director to characterize World War I as "19th century armies equipped with 20th century weapons."[4]

Historians consider World War I as the first modern war where the number of battle-related casualties exceeded those from disease. It was also the first war to use modern weapons of destruction such as artillery, tanks, airplanes, and poison gas. In human terms, it was a slaughterhouse where soldiers became disposable commodities in a senseless chess match to see which side could capture and hold the trench ahead. Historians have come to believe that those living today underestimate the brutality and tremendous human cost of the war. This would show us that the renewed interest today is due more to a lack of knowledge rather than the war's value as entertainment.

One area where modernity played an important factor was in portraying the war on film. The technology and economics of the motion picture business were sufficiently advanced by the time war broke out in Europe in 1914 for many of the countries involved—particularly Germany, France, and Britain—to have established film industries. Hollywood, however, was still preoccupied with the growing pains associated with the development of a new industry. Prior to 1917, when the U.S. entered the European war, the U.S. film industry imitated the "official" government neutrality policy by making films that would appease both isolationists and interventionists. Films like J. Stuart Blackton's *Battle Cry of Peace* (1915) and Thomas Ince's *Civilization* (1916) cancelled each other out, preaching warmongering and pacifism respectively. Hollywood produced films that characterized the Germans as "Huns" and brutes, alternating these with anti-war movies that cautioned Americans against becoming cannon fodder in a predominately European conflict.

The situation changed dramatically after President Wilson's 1916 election to a second term. Wilson appointed George Creel to head the CPI with authority to oversee all propaganda activities, including a special department "to sell the war to America" once the U.S. officially joined the Allied side. The Creel Committee was responsible for the distribution of official army and navy war footage and for the production of such films as *Pershing's Crusaders*, about the Army Expeditionary Forces, *America's Answer*, which dealt with mobilization efforts, and *Under Four Flags*, which promoted the role of the Allies in the war—all released in 1918. Since U.S. involvement in the war was relatively brief, little documentary footage was shot of trench warfare involving American troops.[5] Hollywood neglected the European war until after 1917, when 23 feature films on the war were released, amounting to almost one-quarter of total film production for that year. With the arrival of the armistice in November 1918, however, Hollywood was left with a plethora of war movies that American audiences largely ignored.[6]

When the mood of the country turned toward isolationism under the presidencies of Harding and Coolidge, the film industry abandoned idealistic images of war in favor of narratives that depicted the futility of war and the virtues of pacifism. Consequently, for two decades Hollywood made films about the war that were skeptical or ambivalent about its necessity. Unlike previous patriotic World War I films, *The Big Parade* (1925), *What Price Glory?* (1926), and *Wings* (1928) questioned the virtues of dying and suffering for one's country. Disillusionment with the war is the theme of *The Big Parade*, where silent screen star John Gilbert played a wounded veteran returning to an indifferent and even callous home front. Then in *All Quiet on the Western Front* (1930), the classic anti-war film of trench combat presented from the German point of view, a young recruit (Lew Ayers) is killed by a sniper's bullet as he reaches over a parapet for a butterfly in the closing days of the war. This scene epitomized the futility of war for almost all the participants. Nor can a moviegoer find a stronger anti-war sentiment than the one expressed in *The Eagle and the Hawk* (1933), where a burnt-out pilot (Fredric March) regrets shooting down German planes during air combat. In a scene filled with sarcasm and self-loathing, he raises his glass in a toast, saying, "I give you war," before he goes off and shoots himself.[7]

When war swept across Europe and Asia in the 1930s, Hollywood reacted cautiously. The industry continued to sell mostly entertainment to American audiences while the interventionist-isolationist scenario repeated itself to another generation. But as fascism gained a stronghold in Europe and Japan waged an imperialist war in Asia, several film studios sought to reverse the demythologization of World War I as meaningless slaughter and wasted idealism in a series of pre-World War II films that warned the country against the threat of fascism and that justified war as a necessary means to protect democracy. Between 1939 and 1941, the studios turned out 14 anti-Nazi films, six military preparedness movies, and two World War I films that glorified wartime heroics.[8]

One anti-Nazi movie was Warner Brothers' *Confessions of a Nazi Spy* (1939), which brought the threat of fascism close to home by depicting the FBI crackdown on a German spy ring in America. The film's message was clear: America was not immune against Nazi subversion. The film, however, drew the ire of Father Charles Coughlin and was picketed by the priest's followers, who saw it as a Jewish plot to lure America into the European war. The following year, Alfred Hitchcock's *Foreign Correspondent* (1940) reiterated the warning to an indifferent America when the film's hero, an American correspondent based in London, broadcasts a message in terms reminiscent of Edward R. Murrow: "The lights have gone out in Europe! Hang on to your lights, America—they're the only lights still on in the world!" Meanwhile, MGM's *The Mortal Storm* (1940) portrayed the evils of Nazism in personal terms when a university professor is sent to a concentration camp for his anti-Nazi opposition and his daughter is killed trying to escape to Switzerland. In that same year, Charlie Chaplin used satire and comedy to poke fun at Hitler and Mussolini in *The Great Dictator*, but turned quite serious in the final scene where Hynkel, Chaplin's alter ego, asks the army to overthrow the dictators and restore power to the people. Even Bogart's character in *Casablanca*, the disillusioned owner of "Rick's Cafe," comes to realize that the threat of fascism takes precedence over his love for Ingrid Bergman. By giving his visa papers to Bergman and her husband, a leader of the Resistance, Bogart facilitates their escape from North Africa to continue the fight against fascism.

Still it would be misleading to conclude that all the studios were turning out pro-interventionist films. Although many of the studios were headed by Jewish émigrés, the major film companies did not overemphasize the war in Europe. During the period of 1937–41, slightly more than half of the films produced by the nine major Hollywood studios had a connection to the conflicts raging in Europe and the Far East. Fearful that Germany, Italy, and Spain would boycott their films, the Hollywood studios encouraged nonpolitical screen plots and an attitude of neutrality toward the warring sides.[9]

Only Warner Brothers, the producers of *Casablanca*, continued its enthusiasm for war by portraying death in combat as a form of personal redemption. In both *The Fighting 69th* (1940) and *Sergeant York* (1941), the major characters are transformed by their war experiences. Both films sought to revive positive memories of the "Great War" despite statistics that proved the First World War to be the costliest war in human history up to that time. *The Fighting 69th* confined itself to recounting the adventures of a tough New York kid (James Cagney) assigned to an Irish regiment that acquitted itself nobly in battle. The story centers on the Cagney character as he goes from cowardly under fire to dying a heroic death. The actual New York regiment suffered heavy casualties, but the film neglected the pain and suffering in favor of the value of wartime camaraderie.

In contrast to Cagney's tough Irish New Yorker, the major character in *Sergeant York* is a poor Tennessee country boy who is transformed from Christian pacifist to combat hero while serving in the trenches. The film biography of Alvin York (Gary Cooper) allowed Warner Brothers to glorify war and make it morally respectable when fought for honorable ends. In the film York becomes a one-man army after he concludes that killing Germans would help to end the war and bring about peace. In this sense, *Sergeant York* represents an attempt to erase the memory of those anti-war films of the twenties and early thirties.

The Japanese attack on Pearl Harbor altered the course of world events and transformed Hollywood along with the rest of the country. President Roosevelt followed the lead of his predecessor, President Wilson, by creating the OWI as a successor to the Creel Committee. The administration later established a Bureau of Motion Pictures within the OWI to provide leadership and guidance on how the industry could best contribute to the war effort. Between Hitler's invasion of Poland in 1939 and the Japanese surrender in September 1945, Hollywood released a significant number of motion pictures that touched on the war, either directly through films of military training and combat, or through stories that dealt with the hardships of life at home.

## World War II: The Good War

If World War I was dubbed the "Great War", in part because of the tremendous human cost in waging it, these losses pale in comparison to the millions of lives lost in World War II.[10] It was considered by Americans to be a "good war" in the sense that it both unified the nation to wage a successful battle against a fascist ideology that sought world domination and it stimulated a depressed economy at home, providing jobs and opportunities for women and minorities that could not be denied in the future. And these objectives were achieved without physical damage to the country. Yet describing World War II as the "good war" is an oxymoron for the rest of the world when the actual damage of the war is disclosed: more than 45 million dead, including 20 million Russians, whole cities like London and Dresden virtually leveled by systematic bombing, six million Jews and another five million gentiles, Jehovah's Witnesses, gypsies, and homosexuals victim to the European holocaust, the cities of Hiroshima and Nagasaki demolished by atomic bombs, and much of Europe and Asia left in ruins that required decades to rebuild.[11]

The war proved advantageous for some Americans who traded in the black market or for corporations that enjoyed surplus profits from the war machine. Corporations and businesses that were converted to war production or engaged in the manufacture of war-related goods enjoyed soaring profits. The shift from civilian goods to war production created jobs in defense plants and war factories that were filled by women and minorities, complemented by 4-F (unfit for military service) men.

The film industry also profited from the war financially, but not without paying a price. Some of its most established male stars—Eddie Albert, Douglas Fairbanks Jr., Henry Fonda, Clark Gable, Robert Montgomery, Tyrone Power, James Stewart, and Robert Taylor—entered the military, with many seeing combat duty.[12] For their service, 18 Hollywood actors earned 70 medals during the war, including Bronze and Silver Stars, Purple Hearts, and a Distinguished Service Cross. Actor Audie Murphy, all 5'5" and 110 pounds, became the most decorated serviceman of WWII. What the American public may not have realized at the time was that these actors left promising careers to serve, many even volunteered for duty, and their war exploits largely remained private once they return to their work. On the other hand, declaring oneself a conscientious objector could ruin a film career, as happened with actor Lew Ayers.[13] Several movie stars lost their lives during the war years. British actor Leslie Howard (*Gone with the Wind*), allegedly on assignment for the British Government, had his plane shot down by the Germans over Portugal, and actress Carole Lombard died in a plane crash on her return home from a war bond drive. Many entertainers toured with the United Service Organization (USO) or worked in local service canteens. Other Hollywood stars were active in raising money for the war or in supporting rationing efforts.

The film industry also profited because going to the local movie theater weekly became a diversion from the war. Movie attendance skyrocketed, resulting in the doubling of box-office receipts.[14] Defense plant workers, often working overtime shifts, looked forward to the weekly three hours of relaxation at the movies. Parents and spouses sought respite from the boredom and anxiety of waiting for their loved ones to return home. School-aged youngsters eagerly awaited the Saturday matinee, where their heroes outwitted and defeated the enemy on a weekly basis. For these youngsters, the lessons of war were learned from films and newsreels.

Hollywood responded to the public demand for entertainment by grinding out almost 400 films a year to meet the needs of all age groups. While the film industry continued to churn out musicals, comedies, and westerns, still, it is estimated that one-fifth to one-quarter of the 1,500 films released between 1942 and 1945 were movies with war-related themes.[15] The government contributed to the mix with its own documentaries and propaganda films. All shared a common purpose, namely to depict the world as divided into good versus evil forces, free versus totalitarian states, as well as to unify the country behind the war effort.

## Combat Films

World War II movies fall into four categories: the pure combat film, the hybrid training-battle action film, the resistance of our Allies film, and the home front film—when men were away in the service and women entered the workforce. Jeanine Basinger, in her seminal work on World War II movies, claims that Hollywood produced few pure combat films before 1943.[16] According to Basinger, the industry produced many more films where combat was secondary to military training or preparation for battle. These hybrid films—part training, part combat—were less expensive to shoot and often did not require government assistance. The formula was successful because it could be recycled, substituting one branch of the service for another. For example, *Crash Dive* (1943) depicts naval training before the crew engages in combat and *Sands of Iwo Jima* (1949) depicts a similar preparation-combat scenario for the marines.

*Wake Island* (1942) has the distinction of being the first World War II combat film distributed to movie theaters. The film deposits the audience on a small Pacific island where a marine detachment's job is to protect the island because it serves as a refueling base for flights from the U.S. to Asia. After the attack on Pearl Harbor, the Japanese fleet bombarded the island, softening it up for a land invasion. Although outnumbered, the marines refuse to surrender, holding the enemy at bay for 16 days. No American soldier is alive at film's end. Although U.S. forces suffered a military defeat at Wake Island, Hollywood, with the assistance of the OWI, still turned the film into a positive propaganda piece by having the commanding officer send this final message to headquarters: "The enemy has landed; the issue is still in doubt." The DOD thought so highly of the film that it became an integral part of military training, providing a rationale for the value of human sacrifice against what the film described as "the forces of destruction."

The pace picked up considerably in 1943 when Hollywood released 13 combat films to theaters. Several, like *Bataan* and *Action in the North Atlantic*, depicted American defeats or unsuccessful forays against the enemy similar to *Wake Island*. Such films disappeared once the war turned in favor of the Allies; in the Pacific the U.S. victory in the Battle of Midway proved decisive, while in Europe the surrender of Italy not only took the Italians out of the war but also paved the way for the Normandy invasion. The American defeat suffered at Wake Island was reversed in *Guadalcanal Diary*, which glorified the marines' victory over the Japanese in several battles in the Solomon Islands. The film was based on an eyewitness account, yet it contained stock characters that appeared in most war movies: the stereotypical group of tough sergeants, sensitive chaplains, and the typical melting-pot G.I. platoon featuring rural Southerners, ethnic and racial minorities, and the always-present wise guy from Brooklyn. Fifty years later, Terrence Malick's *The Thin Red Line* revisited Guadalcanal for a new generation of moviegoers. In depicting the fierce battle between American and Japanese forces for control of this strategic island, Malick's film preaches that war dehumanizes its participants. It remains unclear whether *The Thin Red Line* would have been made while the U.S. was engaged in World War II.

Combat movies after *Guadalcanal Diary* featured established male stars like John Wayne in predictable plots that depicted successful combat missions against the enemy. Wayne was kept busy during the war years because he did not qualify for military duty and leading men were in demand. Wayne played a PT commander fighting the Japanese in John Ford's *They Were Expendable* (1945) and also portrayed an American officer working with the Filipino resistance movement in *Back to Bataan* (1945). Wayne did not star in the first *Bataan* film (1943) but headed the cast of the sequel. By re-creating MacArthur's return to the islands, the sequel sought to reverse the demoralizing effect of the infamous Bataan death march where over 600 U.S. soldiers and 5,000–10,000 Filipino troops, captured by the Japanese in the early days of the war, died as a result of the forced march through the jungle.[17] Made with the full cooperation of the U.S. government, *Back to Bataan* describes the almost three-year guerrilla war waged by the Filipino resistance against the Japanese invaders. Wayne is cast in his traditional heroic role, leading his undermanned and poorly armed Filipino fighters against the superior Japanese forces. Though the two *Bataan* films depict the Japanese in particularly brutal terms, including scenes that detail the hanging of a school principal for refusing to take down the American flag, the beating of a young boy to extract information, and the shooting, stabbing, and inhumane treatment of the death marchers, it did not replicate all the horrors of the real experience. There is one scene where Wayne tries to explain the war to a young Filipino boy by saying, "You're the guy we're fighting this for." It is a line that Wayne would reuse 30 years later at the end of his pro-Vietnam film, *Green Berets*. Meanwhile, another Hollywood leading man, Errol Flynn, portrayed a leader of an American paratroop battalion dropped behind enemy lines on a mission to disable a Japanese radio station in *Objective Burma* (1945). After completing their mission Flynn and his men are cut off by Japanese forces and must fight their way back to Allied lines. The remainder of the film describes their escape from enemy forces.

On the European front, movies like *The Story of GI Joe* (1945), about war correspondent Ernie Pyle, and *A Walk in the Sun* (1946), about an infantry platoon in Italy that achieves its mission despite the loss of its officers, extolled the virtues of the foot soldier. Pyle is the centerpiece of *The Story of GI Joe*, a modest war film that concentrates on the ordeals of the infantry soldiers—the soldiers that would be characterized as the "grunts" of the Vietnam War. Although the real Pyle was middle-aged at the time, he insisted on walking along with the army infantry unit during the Italian campaign. It was said that 40 million Americans back home read his column. Pyle served as technical advisor on the film, and then returned to the front, where he was killed by a sniper. He never did see the completed film. *A Walk in the Sun* also views war on a small scale as the film follows the adventures of one platoon in achieving its modest objective—the capture, but not without significant casualties, of a strategic farmhouse held by the Germans. War is hell for the infantrymen in these two films.

Hybrid World War II films usually began in boot camp as the military trains and prepares its troops for battle. This preparedness sequence may take up to half of a film's running time, as it did in *Crash Dive*, where actors Tyrone Power and Dana Andrews play submarine commanders who complete a successful raid against a Japanese installation. But as was common in these hybrid war films, the two men spend most of their time competing for the love of a woman back home. Meanwhile, in *Gung Ho!* (1943) Randolph Scott is placed in charge of a specially created marine battalion, Carlson's Raiders, that destroys the Japanese installation at Makin Island, signaling the beginning of the American offensive in the Pacific.

Another favorite wartime movie subject had to do with the resistance of our Allies against the Axis powers. These films portrayed ordinary people as heroes engaged in extraordinary and courageous feats against an invading enemy. The Russians were portrayed heroically in two 1943 films, *The North Star* and *Days of Glory*. Both films extolled the virtues of the Russian people and the love expressed for their homeland. *The North Star* was the work of a talented group: writer Lillian Hellman, composers Aaron Copland and Ira Gershwin, and director Lewis Milestone. The film focused on a battle of wits between a German commander and the village leader. *Days of Glory*, on the other hand, was a B-movie with a cast of unknowns. The film was dedicated to the bravery of the Russian people, especially peasants. The film starred Gregory Peck (in his film debut) as the leader of a small group of guerrillas who fight valiantly but are nonetheless overwhelmed by German forces. *Days of Glory* is an obvious effort to drum up American support for its Russian allies, but Hollywood could not resist the temptation to romanticize the war. While the Russians suffered tremendous losses, the film failed to do justice to their cause. Although there are enough "comrade" greetings in the film to fill Red Square, Hollywood dealt in cliché characterizations (Germans as brutes, Russians as happy peace-loving people who sing, dance, and quote Pushkin) and unrealistic images of the war on the Russian front. Ironically, some of the people involved in these sympathetic screen portrayals would later come under the scrutiny of HUAC, even though these pro-Russian films received OWI approval.

Meanwhile, the exploits of the Norwegians during World War II were also depicted in two 1943 films: *Commandos Strike at Dawn* and *Edge of Darkness*. The question of Norwegian resistance, however, is equivocal. When war broke out in Europe, Norway proclaimed its neutrality and continued to trade iron ore to the Germans. It was in 1940 after Churchill ordered the Norwegian waters to be mined to prevent the Germans from reaching their iron ore supply that the Nazis responded by invading Norway. Haakon VII, King of Norway at the time, refused to abdicate despite German pressure and his action inspired a resistance movement against German occupation.[18] It is the resistance of ordinary people that is celebrated in these two films. Made before the attack on Pearl Harbor, *Commandos Strike at Dawn* was filmed with the cooperation of the Canadian and British governments and starred a contingent of American and British actors. On the other hand, *Edge of Darkness* was strictly Hollywood, as Errol Flynn played a local fisherman who leads the Norwegian underground against the Nazis. Meant as a tribute to the Norwegian resistance, the film was cast with stock actors from the Warner Brothers studio and looked like it was filmed on the back lot. The film contains two scenes of German brutality, one involving the beating and public humiliation of the town's intellectual, and the other the rape of a resistance woman, which had to be implied rather than depicted under the Production Code. Both crimes are revenged in typical Hollywood fashion.

While men saw combat duty, women joined the armed services as nurses and as noncombatant replacements for the men at the front. Almost 400,000 women, including nurses, saw military service during the war; some lost their lives in performing their duty. The Army Air Force, for example, commissioned over 1,800 women as pilots in the newly formed Women Air Force Service Pilots (WASP) unit to fly ferry planes, tow gunnery targets, and serve as test pilots and flight instructors in an effort to release men for combat duty overseas. The government did not officially recognize this secret unit as military personnel, even though 38 women died in plane crashes in the course of flying 60 million miles, until Congress disbanded the unit in December 1944.[19]

Regrettably, Hollywood chose to ignore these women and others like them. When women appeared in World War II films they usually were cast in the roles of USO entertainers, home front workers, and, sometimes, as spies. Mainly, however, Hollywood minimized their contribution by portraying them as romantic interests or as volunteers and workers in field hospitals. There were several notable exceptions to this generalization: a 1943 film, *Ladies Courageous*, starred Loretta Young and told the story of the first group of women pilots that later became the WASPs.[20] Both *So Proudly We Hail* (1943) and *Cry Havoc* (1944) depicted nurses under combat conditions. An estimated 50,000 nurses served in the military during World War II, receiving military as well as medical training. Nurses served in all military branches and in all the war zones; some became prisoners of war when Corregidor fell, others were killed when the enemy shelled field hospitals.[21] Both Paramount's *So Proudly We Hail* and MGM's *Cry Havoc* paid tribute to Red Cross nurses. In *So Proudly We Hail* an all-star cast of actresses is trapped in the early days of the Pacific war. The film depicts their daily hardships, including several encounters with the enemy. In one such confrontation, a nurse sacrifices herself by becoming a human bomb, permitting the other nurses to escape from the advancing Japanese. The storyline requires virtually non-stop combat conditions, though Paramount, bowing to projected market demand, permitted a few romantic interludes. The film concludes with the fall of Bataan; despite that defeat, the film remains more optimistic than is warranted by the actual status of the war at the time. Like the patriotism of the marines in *Wake Island*, the nurses in *So Proudly We Hail* represent an American confidence that democracy will prevail over the forces of evil.

MGM's *Cry Havoc*, another token effort by a major Hollywood film studio regarding the role of women during World War II, also relates the plight of nurses caught behind enemy lines during the American retreat from Bataan,[22] including one casualty when a nurse is machine-gunned to death while swimming. It remains a mystery why the two film studios made *Cry Havoc* and *So Proudly We Hail*, identical movies on a similar subject, and released them during the same year. Whether by accident or design, these films influenced the federal government to recognize the heroism of the women who served in WWII. Washington eventually erected a Women's Memorial at the entrance to Arlington National Cemetery to commemorate the contribution of women to the country's military service, beginning with the American Revolution and continuing through the Persian Gulf War.[23]

Hollywood did not do right by women or minorities during World War II,[24] but the film studios certainly knew how to churn out hate propaganda against the enemy. No one expected Hollywood to present heroic images of the enemy, but the studios took every opportunity to inject propaganda into their screenplays. The war, of course, was being fought at home as well as at the front. The research of film scholars in applying content analysis to World War II movies reveals a strong film bias against the Japanese, relative to the other two Axis Powers, Germany and Italy.[25] The bias against the Japanese encouraged Hollywood to depict racist images in its Pacific war films. This was less true of films involving the Germans because the war with Germany was being waged ideologically in wartime movies, that is, it was being waged against the German government—the Nazis—and not necessarily against the German people. As a matter of fact, even before *Schindler's List*, there were a few films where Germans befriend Allied soldiers or protect civilians from potential harm. Such an event occurs in *Desperate Journey* (1942), where some "good" Germans aid Errol Flynn and his squadron. Again, in *The Moon Is Down* (1943), a film about the Nazi occupation of Norway, one of the German officers is portrayed rather sympathetically. He is tired of the war and is homesick. His softness leads to his death, but not before his character has the opportunity to voice the sentiments of a sane Germany.

This is definitely not the case for the Japanese, who fared so badly in these war movies as to suggest a more deeply held racist bias. Take the 1942 B-movie *Little Tokyo, U.S.A.*, for instance. In this story of domestic espionage in Southern California, the film implied that any person of Japanese ancestry was a spy or saboteur. All of the Japanese characters were portrayed as treacherous and not to be trusted. The movie was considered so prejudicial that even the War Relocation Authority, the government agency that administered the internment camps, complained to the OWI about the film.[26] The following year, RKO Pictures released *Behind the Rising Sun* (1943), a piece of anti-Japanese propaganda that concerned the efforts of a Japanese father to persuade his Americanized son to join the Sino-Japanese war. In approximately 90 minutes of running time, the film contains scenes of Japanese raping women, bayoneting children, and torturing prisoners by placing needles under their fingernails, burning them with cigarettes, and hanging them by their wrists until they die.[27] While it is true that these were primarily low-budget B-films rushed into release after Pearl Harbor and could be excused on that account, the depictions of Japanese soldiers in feature films like *Wake Island* and *Guadalcanal Diary* also were overtly racist. Derogatory terms like "Nips," "monkeys," and "apes" were used to refer to the Japanese. Nor did Japanese soldiers fight by the rules in Hollywood films. In contrast, American soldiers were portrayed as harboring little hatred toward their enemies; their feelings were not personal. On the screen, the Japanese had no redeeming qualities.[28] These negative depictions of the Japanese can be considered part of a continuous line of racial stereotypes of Asians, historically traceable to the Philippine insurgency following the Spanish-American War, and reinforced during the war in Vietnam described in the next chapter.

Whatever misgivings film scholars and historians had regarding Hollywood war movies, they were generally good box office for several decades after the end of World War II. To test the market, Hollywood released nine combat films in 1949 alone, including *Sands of Iwo Jima*, which grossed $25 million, a considerable figure at the time. The financial success of these war films a few years after the end of hostilities encouraged the industry to generate more movies in the same genre over the next four decades. Combat films included *The Longest Day* (1962), *Battle of the Bulge* (1965), and *Patton* (1970); prison camps were featured in *Stalag 17* (1953), *The Bridge on the River Kwai* (1957), and *The Great Escape* (1963). In fact, Hollywood released at least one World War II combat film each year from 1948 through 1970.[29] Even into the nineties, the studios continued to find the World War II good box office, with several major films' critical and financial successes, including Steven Spielberg's *Schindler's List* and *Saving Private Ryan*.[30]

Recent World War II combat films have been more critical and analytical of the war and of the government's treatment of minorities. The original film about the battle of Iwo Jima was a pumped-up, heroic poster for the U.S. marines without regard to the carnage and historical facts. But Iwo Jima was one of the fiercest battles of the Pacific War, costing 29,000 lives, including 7,000 G.I.s. Director Clint Eastwood remedied that with two films depicting the battle to control the strategic island. What Americans tend to remember today is the raising of the flag on Mt. Suribachi, brilliantly retold in James Bradley's book *Flags of our Fathers*.[31] Bradley's father was one of the six marines from Easy Company that raised the second, replacement flag. Three of the men died in the flag raising. The remaining three, including Bradley's father, played small roles in Eastwood's film. However, what Hollywood had failed to depict in the original film was the personal cost, not only of those who died but also of the three survivors. That attitude changed in 2006 when Eastwood undertook to film the battle from both the viewpoint of the American and Japanese forces. In Eastwood's *Flags of Our Fathers*, the struggle to secure the island and raise the flag consumes only the first half of the film. Eastwood devotes the remainder to the Marine Corps' use of the three survivors (one navy, two marines) to help sell war bonds back home. The marketing of these men as war heroes embarrassed and humiliated them for two reasons. One was because they were in the second flag raising, the one for the photographers rather than in the original raising of the flag on Mt. Suribachi. The other reason was the guilt they felt for being treated as heroes when so many of their comrades had died or were wounded. Of the three survivors, only navy corpsman James (Doc) Bradley resumed his regular life after the war. Despite all the publicity, Rene Gagnon, a marine from New Hampshire, spent the rest of his life as a janitor. And Ira Hayes, a Pima Indian, fell into poverty and alcoholism. As Bradley noted, "The real heroes are dead on that island." Maybe that is why Hollywood made less than two dozen films where the action centers around combat fought on the ground, in the air, or on the sea and where the armed forces face death and destruction in reaching, or holding, a military objective. Basinger considers these films "special" because many included actual newsreel footage that added to the realism of the action scenes and because most required the support of the DOD to be made.

Eastwood's treatment of the battle for Iwo Jima in his companion film, *Letters from Iwo Jima*, retells the battle mainly from letters written by Japanese soldiers to their family and friends. The commanding general, played by Japanese actor Ken Watanabe, is portrayed humanely rather than as the stereotypical fanatic seen in many WWII movies about the Pacific theater. When he warns his troops that "none of you will leave here alive," his statement represents a realistic assessment of the situation where his forces are outnumbered, lack air or ground power, and are low on ammunition, food, and water. His forces are doomed, yet many fight valiantly. What Eastwood has done in this film is to put a human face on the Japanese infantry-soldier, who like his American counterpart, fights wars up close where he can see the enemies' faces and hear their screams. In this sense, *Letters from Iwo Jima* is an anti-war film for all nations.

The most recent entry into the World War II combat film genre caused not one but two controversies. One dispute, concerning race, will be discussed in a later chapter, but Spike Lee's flap with the Italian partisans requires immediate attention. Lee has been angry with Hollywood for ignoring the contributions of African Americans to World War II. While it is a fact that many blacks in the military were assigned to transportation units, mess hall duties, and other menial tasks, at least two black units were active on the European front: the 92nd Infantry Division (featured in Lee's film) and the 320th Antiaircraft Barrage Balloon Battalion that landed on the D-Day beaches at Omaha and Utah.[32] Lee's film *Miracle at St. Anna* (2008), about four black soldiers trapped behind German lines in 1944 Italy, is his effort to rectify history. His film is based on a novel by author James McBride, and while the narrative details the struggle of these four men—Buffalo Soldiers from the 92nd infantry division—to return to their company, a subplot involving the role of Italian partisans initiated the dispute.

One scene in the film reveals in great detail the real-life Nazi SS massacre of a small town where more than 500 villagers—elderly men, women, and 116 children—were slaughtered because they refused to identify the location of the resistance leader. Lee's portrayal upset the surviving partisans because it depicts one of their own resistance fighters as a Nazi collaborator who informs on the village. The partisans saw this as a slur on the courage of the Italian partisan movement during WWII. Lee defiantly stuck by his account, which is true to McBride's novel. However, the partisans had history on their side, as the proof of their version of events was supported by the 2005 convictions of 10 former members of the SS for their part in the massacre.[33] Unfortunately, the controversy was the most interesting aspect of Lee's film, as the plot follows the conventional formula adhered to by combat movies of the 1940s. And the film did poorly at the box office, continuing the recent pattern of American audiences' lack of interest in war movies.[34]

Thus, it was surprising to discover that George Lucas, of *Star Wars* fame, had decided to take on the financing of a film about the Tuskegee Airmen of the 332nd Fighter Group since none of the major studios was willing to support a project they considered a bad business risk. Why was Lucas willing to take on a project about the so-called "Tuskegee Experiment," where the U.S. Army Air Corps established a training program to integrate African American pilots into its fighter pilot program? All he would tell the media was that it was a personal decision.

*Red Tails* (2012) cost $58 million to produce but took in $50 million in the domestic market, a surprisingly decent box office for a WWII war movie. The film received mixed reviews: the critics liked the digital aerial dogfight scenes but found the dialogue and characterizations at comic book level.[35] Despite these flaws, the little known story of the Tuskegee Airmen needed to be dramatized to contradict the findings of a 1925 study by the U.S. Army War College that labeled blacks as not intelligent, ambitious, or courageous enough to serve in combat.[36] In fact, African Americans were barred from flying for the U.S. military before 1940 on the grounds that they lacked the "qualifications" for combat duty.[37] This fact helps to explain why black soldiers were assigned to transportation and service units during the war, a racial stain that *Red Tails* sought to erase. The film also serves to remind us that the U.S. fought WWII as a segregated country where "people of color" were subject to racial prejudice and abuse. There is one particular scene in the film where one of the Tuskegee officers walks into the all-white Officers Club and is told to "Go home, nigger." Admittedly, *Red Tails* is not the best film to restore to the Tuskegee Airmen their respect and honor, but if nothing else, it reminds us that 66 of these airmen were killed in action and 96 received the Distinguished Flying Cross. Not a shabby war record once the U.S. military allowed these men to see combat.

## Homefront

Combat films remained in the Hollywood repertory for a good 40 years after World War II. A few Hollywood films had plots that revolved around life at home during the war, showing the housing shortage, scarcity of consumer goods, and food rationing. Hollywood produced just two major feature films about the home front during the war, *Tender Comrade* (1943) and *Since You Went Away* (1944). In *Tender Comrade*, five women (girlfriends, wives, and mothers) live together while their men are in the service.[38] Ginger Rogers stars as a woman who decides to share a house with three other women who work with her in the same defense plant after her husband is drafted. The fifth member of the group is a German woman who, because she is not a citizen and cannot work in the defense plant, serves as cook and housemaid for the others. The women in *Tender Comrade* are depicted as independent characters and not mere extensions of their menfolk. The film was considered a "woman's" picture because the audience learns details about the war off-camera. *Tender Comrade* was written by Dalton Trumbo and directed by Edward Dmytryk, to be identified later as members of the Hollywood Ten. Their involvement with the film, coupled with its communal living arrangements ("share and share alike") and a short monologue in which Rogers talks to her infant son about her husband who has been killed in action, "No million dollars or country clubs or long shining cars for you, little guy. He only left you the best world a boy could ever grow up in. He bought it for you with his life,"[39] led HUAC to label it "un-American" after the war.

In *Since You Went Away* (1944), Claudette Colbert's husband is called to military duty, leaving her to care for their two children. The film focuses on the plight of a middle-class family struggling to survive the war years. Money becomes a primary concern and the family is forced to take in a boarder. The film features major female characters (even Colbert's children in the film are girls), with the studio's intention to appeal to women in the audience who could relate to the situation on the screen. Much like the World War II combat film, home front movies glorified individual sacrifice for the good of the country; Colbert's character is compelled to enter the workforce as a welder (aka Rosie the Riveter) in a defense plant.

However, the most honored film about the home front turned out to be *The Best Years of Our Lives* (1946), based on a story published in 1944 about problems veterans faced in adjusting to civilian life. Production was delayed for two years and the film was not released until the war had ended. The film follows three vets: Al Stephenson (Fredric March), a middle-aged banker turned army sergeant, Fred Derry (Dana Andrews), an air force hero and former drugstore clerk, and Homer Parrish (non-actor Harold Russell in his debut film role), a navy vet who lost both hands in combat, as they try to adjust to civilian life. These reel veterans faced the same issues as the real newly discharged veterans: unemployment, interrupted marriages, and acceptance of their war disabilities.[40] The film was a box office hit and proved to be an artistic success, as it won seven Oscars, including best picture.

Contrary to popular belief, Hollywood films about the civilian population during World War II did not imitate government propaganda slogans promoting duty, obligation, and patriotic responsibility. Instead the home front movies emphasized democratic values and they encouraged civilians to protect their home and family. These wholesome themes contributed to the mythology that World War II was a "good war" fought by the "greatest generation," as described by Tom Brokaw in his book.[41] That generation, Brokaw reminds us, survived the Great Depression and went on to defeat the Axis Powers.

The popularity of World War II spurred interest in building monuments to the men and women who fought "the good war." The World War II Memorial, lying between the Washington Monument and the Lincoln Memorial, opened to the public in April 2004. It contains a garden, fountain, and waterfall, which surrounds a wall containing 4,000 gold stars, each one representing 100 U.S. deaths in the war.[42] Meanwhile, historian Stephen Ambrose established the National World War II Foundation to secure funds for a D-Day museum in New Orleans. The museum, dedicated to all those who took part in the amphibious invasions, opened in June 2000. In 2003 the Congress designated the museum as the National WWII Museum. Thereafter, plans were soon in progress to expand the museum, and celebrities like Tom Hanks were soliciting additional funds to include the Pacific and other war areas. The expanded museum opened on June 6, 2009 to celebrate the 65th anniversary of D-Day.[43]

While credit is due to the generation who, although ordinary people, managed to perform extraordinary feats of courage and self-sacrifice, still Brokaw failed to mention that these same decent people lived in (and possibly contributed to) a racist and sexist society, and generally supported McCarthyism, HUAC, and the anti-communist hysteria in the 1950s as well as the Vietnam War in the sixties. Possibly Hollywood has contributed to the hype, but as James Bradley noted in *Flags of Our Fathers*, the Iwo Jima veterans never talked about themselves or the war. Maybe, unlike Hollywood, these veterans understood that media labels do not always reflect the whole truth.

Documentaries

Possibly, Hollywood could be excused for glamorizing the war film, exploiting the setting to depict acts of heroism and self-sacrifice, and showing individual deeds of glory as the means to build character and test manhood. But the federal government cannot be absolved from treating the film medium as another weapon of war. The OWI had primary responsibility for oversight of Hollywood films produced during the war years, but it also commissioned war movies of its own for the armed forces and the general public. The U.S. government distributed 164 films between 1941 and 1945, with 13 pre–Pearl Harbor films enlisting support for the USO and the Red Cross.[44] Commencing in 1942, however, the emphasis shifted to films that would directly aid the war effort through recruitment in the Coast Guard and through special pleadings to women to consider working in defense plants. For instance, government-made movies appealed to feelings of patriotism in soliciting war bonds sales, conserving resources, and planting victory gardens. On the other hand, some government films served as warnings against profiting from the war (black marketeering) and illustrating the dangers of loose lips and careless talk.

The government sought to offset the more romantic and fantasized images of the Hollywood war film by shooting its own combat footage. These films were commercially distributed through five newsreel companies, including MGM's News of the Day, Paramount News, RKO-Pathe News, 20th Century-Fox's Movietone News, and Universal Newsreel, and were shown as part of the weekly movie program in at least two-thirds of the nation's theaters.[45] These government-produced films, known as official reports, supposedly cost the government $50 million a year to produce and distribute. Many are still available in the National Archives. The government was fortunate to have the services of such prominent Hollywood directors as John Ford, Frank Capra, George Stevens, William Wyler, and John Huston at its disposal, either as civilians under contract or as military personnel assigned to a combat unit. Some of the more important documentaries made by these men included *The Memphis Belle* (1943), in which Wyler depicted the last mission of a B-17 bomber, part of the Eighth U.S. Air Force Command, from ground crew preparation to its return from a bombing mission over Germany. John Huston was commissioned by the War Department to make two films, *Report from the Aleutians* (1943), about a bombing raid, and *The Battle of San Pietro* (1944), about the Italian campaign. To capture the sense of combat, Huston accompanied a front-line unit and shot footage while the battle raged. Because it shattered the warrior myth the army disliked the film and gave it a "secret" classification, ensuring that it would be kept out of public circulation. Huston's documentary was not distributed to the public until almost one-third of its footage was cut from the original.[46]

Another Hollywood director, John Ford, re-created the attack on Pearl Harbor in *December 7th: The Movie* (1943).[47] Previously, Lt. Commander Ford, on duty in the Pacific, shot film during the fierce naval and air war being waged at the time. Ford filmed as the battle raged and then edited and released the result as *The Battle of Midway* (1942). The navy was so impressed with the film that it was used to stimulate war bond sales.[48] Films like *The Battle of Midway* and commercial newsreels containing actual footage depicted the war in terms that even Hollywood, with all its money, talent, and technical resources, could not replicate. Although edited in some cases, these documentaries portrayed World War II in more realistic terms than the traditional Hollywood version, except perhaps the first half-hour of *Saving Private Ryan*.[49] In order to get the gritty feel of Omaha Beach on D-Day, Spielberg stripped the coating off the lenses on his Panasonic cameras, adjusted the shutter openings, and then attached blood packs to handheld cameras during the filming.[50] Audiences agreed that he had succeeded in capturing the true atmosphere of battle.

## To Use or Not to Use: The A-Bomb as a Weapon of Mass Destruction

World War II came to a conclusion after the U.S. dropped atomic bombs on the cities of Hiroshima and Nagasaki. Yet 70 years later scholars continue to debate the wisdom and necessity of their use. The discussion usually centers around three questions: was it necessary? Was its use strictly a military decision or was it meant as a political statement? And lastly, was it meant as payback for the Japanese bombing of Pearl Harbor?

Was the dropping of the atomic bomb on Hiroshima necessary, that is, was it approved by President Truman because the military consensus at the time indicated that it was the best option? Truman maintained that his military advisors thought it would end the war and avoid the thousands of American and Japanese deaths that would have resulted from a land invasion. General George Marshall reportedly told the president that a land invasion of the Japanese islands had the potential to cost almost one million U.S. and Japanese casualties. Moreover, the U.S. knew that the Japanese government had ordered the execution of 400,000 Allied POWs interned in Japanese camps.[51] Why not bluff the Japanese with the A-bomb and hope that it would scare them into surrendering, however? The fact of the matter is that the Japanese had proved that they would "fight to the last man," as their army did on Iwo Jima, rather than surrender. When U.S. bombers dropped warning leaflets over Hiroshima, the Japanese government dismissed them as propaganda. And it took a second A-bomb on Nagasaki to get the Japanese to finally accept the surrender terms. While the estimates of total casualties from the atomic bombings differ, the figures seem to range from 135,000 to 150,000 for Hiroshima and 64,000 to 75,000 for Nagasaki;[52] it can never be established with certainty that these casualties, horrific as they were, were lower than those that would have resulted from a land invasion of the Japanese islands.

As for the second consideration, was the primary end of the atomic bombings to serve notice on the Soviets that the U.S. had the power to neutralize Stalin's postwar ambitions? After the 1945 Potsdam meeting, Truman was cognizant of Soviet expansionist demands. Did the president envision the bomb as a duel weapon to both bring the war to an end and provide a warning against Soviet expansionism? Revisionist historians like Gar Alperovitz argue that this was the case, that Truman saw the bomb as a political tool as well as a military weapon.[53] Alperovitz claims that Truman primarily used the bomb as a bargaining chip in future negotiations with the Soviets and only secondarily did the president consider it as a means to save lives, both Japanese and American. Whatever the motivation, once the Soviets developed nuclear capability, the U.S. lost its leverage. Consequently, the Soviets marched into Eastern Europe, established a communist regime in North Korea and became a major player in the postwar era.

What is not in dispute is that President Truman's decision had the support of the American people. A Roper poll taken in the fall of 1945 revealed that three-quarters of Americans approved of the president's decision. In fact, more than one-fifth thought more atomic bombs should have been dropped. Only 5 percent disapproved of the use of the bomb.[54] As it turns out, new research proves that the revisionists and the militarists who thought the atomic bomb was necessary were wrong. Having access to Japanese and Russian sources, historian Tsuyoshi Hasegawa disputes the notion that the bombing of Hiroshima and Nagasaki were instrumental in the Japanese decision to surrender.[55] Instead, Professor Hasegawa says that the decision to surrender was made independent of the bombings. However, he does agree that President Truman had reason to fear Soviet expansionism—but so did the Japanese government. When the Soviet Union declared war on August 8, 1945, two days after the Hiroshima bombing, the Japanese feared that Manchuria and their other possessions in the Pacific region would fall to the Soviets. Three days later, the Soviets invaded Sakhalin Island, and after fierce resistance Japanese forces requested a truce. Hasegawa makes a strong case that it was the Soviet declaration of war and not the atomic bombs that compelled the Japanese government to surrender to the Allied Forces.

Lastly, was the destruction of Hiroshima and Nagasaki a conscious decision by the Truman administration to exact some revenge for the Japanese "sneak attack" on Pearl Harbor while its ambassadors were negotiating in Washington, D.C.? There is no doubt that a hard core of Americans was bitter and angry over the attack on Pearl Harbor and the news of Japanese atrocities elsewhere, but there is no evidence that the U.S. government included payback or revenge in its use of atomic bombs on Japanese civilians.

Which explanation the reader accepts as bona fide is strictly an individual matter, although more scholars are beginning to accept the view that not one, but several factors may have played a part in America's momentous decision to be the first nation to use nuclear weapons in wartime.

## Korea: The Forgotten War

There are many reasons why the Korean War (1950–53) (athough "war" was the term used by the media and the public, the term "conflict" was used officially because Congress never declared war) has been dubbed "the forgotten war." One explanation is that the war was fought under the auspices of the United Nations (UN), even though the U.S. contributed a majority of the troops and supplies. In effect, the UN sanctioned the sending of troops as part of America's right to meet its treaty obligations since the North Koreans were the aggressors. Eventually other UN members contributed troops to what was referred to as an "international police action." Moreover, it was a war fought for limited objectives. From the UN viewpoint, the war was not about gaining territory or furthering political or military objectives. The sole purpose of the UN action was to drive the North Koreans back over

Figure 8.1. Korean War Memorial, Olympia, Washington, 2009.
Reprinted with permission, David Giglio

the 38th parallel and restore the territorial status quo. Meanwhile, the fighting between North and South waged for three years and included Chinese and U.S. intervention. A year after the initial clash between North and South Korean troops, cease-fire talks were initiated, though sporadic fighting continued for two more years until an armistice was signed in 1953. The war also lacked visibility because, unlike Vietnam, Korea was not a television war. Instead, the networks continued to rely on government reports for their news rather than journalists in the field, a facsimile of the way news was collected during World War II. Therefore, the Korean War was not filmed as it happened.

Nor did the war affect the collective conscience of the nation as its predecessor did. A memorial to its veterans was not constructed in Washington until 1995, more than 40 years after the armistice and 13 years after the erection of the Vietnam Wall, despite the more than 33,000 deaths suffered in the conflict. Finally, Hollywood did not seem terribly interested in the war; it failed to stir the patriotism of the stars or serve as a resource for screen stories. Possibly because the war in Korea was one of attrition and stalemate rather than liberation and military victory, the film studios believed they could not duplicate the patriotism and idealism of the World War II movies.

A reliable indication of how Hollywood neglected Korea is found in the production statistics covering the years between 1950 and 1970, when the industry released four times as many World War II movies as films on the Korean conflict. The two most popular war movies during this period were films about World War II: *From Here to Eternity* (1953) and *The Bridge on the River Kwai* (1957). Also, no film on the Korean War has won an Oscar in any of the major categories, in contrast to the number of awards presented to World War II and Vietnam War films. And to support this point, a military history magazine in 2007 included only two films from the Korean War out of its "100 greatest war movies" compilation, a number easily surpassed by the foreign war movies on the list.[56]

However, there was one major Hollywood production, *The Bridges at Toko-Ri* (1954), with an A-list cast, which told the story of a war-weary navy pilot (William Holden) who is called back into service during the Korean War and has ambivalent feelings about the recall.[57] Holden, a WW II vet, has to leave his Denver law practice and his family to fly carrier-based jets bombing targets in North Korea and wonders what he has done to deserve two wars. He is reassured by the carrier's commander (Fredric March), who tells him we do not choose our wars but simply fight in the wars we are stuck with. Holden's misgivings deepen when he learns that his squadron's assignment is to destroy the bridges at Toko-Ri which will force the North Koreans to end the war. On the bombing mission, his plane has to make a forced landing in enemy territory. While he waits for the carrier's helicopter to rescue him, he is temporarily protected from Korean ground troops by his fellow jets. Armed only with his pistol, Holden sits in a ditch watching the jets, low on fuel, leave but the rescue helicopter (piloted by Mickey Rooney) arrives to pick him up. However, the North Koreans shoot and disable the helicopter as Rooney joins Holden in the muddy ditch, where both are killed. Despite the heroic finale, the film certainly was not an endorsement of the American involvement in the conflict five years after the conclusion of WWII, despite being an A-list production.

When Hollywood did address the Korean War, it usually was in low budget B-movies without production values and minus strong marketing campaigns. Basinger reports that many of the Korean War films were replays of World War II combat films in terms of narrative development, characterizations, and symbolic events.[58] For example, the Korean War films continued to utilize the composite combat group, including ethnic diversity, as the basis for plot development. The film's hero was still the tough officer or sergeant and the central action was a "single mission" to knock out an enemy objective or to make a last stand against overwhelming enemy forces. To make the films more plausible, Hollywood updated its military hardware to match the requirements of the new conflict: the M1 carbine was added alongside the M1 rifle, the helicopter was used for medical evacuations, jet aircraft played a central role in aerial warfare, and the Mobile Army Surgical Hospital (MASH) units replaced base hospitals.

In addition to the updated military hardware, Hollywood differentiated Korean War films from those of World War II in another significant way. In the prisoner of war films from World War II, the American captives were defiant and heroic and usually plotted to escape from their camps. With a few exceptions, such as in *Stalag 17* (1953), World War II POWs were always patriotic and loyal to the U.S. Not so in Korean War films, where the POWs were often portrayed as "brainwashed victims" or worse, as traitors. At least in a half-dozen films, the POWs cooperated and even collaborated with their captors. It is true that after the war, 14 POWs were officially tried as collaborators and 11 were convicted of collaborating with the enemy. Yet this is a small number compared to the more than 7,000 POWs interned during the war, half of whom did not survive their captivity.[59]

Hollywood exploited this fact in a series of POW-type films. The most prominent of its type, *The Manchurian Candidate*, is not a Korean combat film but rather a study of communist brainwashing. As discussed in chapter 6, this film was concerned with the new brainwashing techniques used by the Chinese to create "sleeper assassins" who could be planted in another country and placed into action later on. Whether or not this aspect of the film's plot was factual, the term "brainwashing" entered the U. S. military's lexicon thereafter. The plot concerns a non-commissioned officer, captured in Korea, who is taken to China and programmed to carry out political assassinations. At the end, he deliberately avoids his intended target (a presidential candidate) and shoots his conniving mother and McCarthy-type stepfather (the VP candidate) instead. Released two days before the Cuban Missile Crisis, the film became a cult classic, with viewers intrigued by conspiracy theories and Hollywood mythology. Not overly popular with audiences during its initial run, the film was shelved after President Kennedy's assassination, partly out of respect. But recent evidence seems to indicate that the withdrawal had more to do with the ownership of the film rights.

Another Korean POW film, *Prisoner of War* (1954), starred Ronald Reagan as an Army Intelligence officer who allows himself to be captured by the North Koreans. He avoids the torture and brainwashing administered to the other prisoners by pretending to cooperate with the communists. In this way, he is able to collect evidence on the mistreatment of American POWs. Brainwashing was a major concern during the Korean War and it proved a sticking point during the two years of peace talks because the North Koreans insisted on a return of all their prisoners while the U.S. and its UN allies wanted POWs to have freedom of choice.

But another POW film resonates more closely with contemporary events. In the 1956 film *The Rack*, Paul Newman plays Capt. Edward Hall, a POW who returns home after two years in a North Korean prison camp. Hall is a decorated hero but suffers from a psychological disorder. While watching a movie in an army hospital, another veteran sneaks up behind him and places a TRAITOR sign around his neck. Soon thereafter, Capt. Hall discovers that the army intends to court-martial him for "collaborating with the enemy." At the trial, Hall takes the stand, admits the charges, but provides an explanation that his actions were not committed willingly and knowingly. At this point, Hall describes the method used by the Chinese to "break" the will of their captives. Unlike the POWs in *The Manchurian Candidate*, Hall is not "brainwashed," drugged, or physically tortured, but broken mentally through deprivation, isolation, and manipulation. Despite these justifications, the court-martial finds him guilty. Another prisoner testifies to his physical torture through being hung naked upside down, beaten, and burned with cigarettes. It was too early in the fifties to discuss "water boarding," slapping, and humiliation, as identified in the Bush administration's "torture memos," because these techniques were developed later. But the memos reveal that the American CIA had studied the Chinese interrogation methods and applied them to detainees at Guantanamo, including sleep deprivation, degradation, isolation, and death threats to secure confessions. Ironically, *The Rack* is ambivalent in its attitude toward excessive interrogation techniques. The film is sympathetic to the suffering endured by Newman's character, yet the military jury considers him a traitor. Fifty years later, the American public learned that the U.S. used disputed interrogation methods after 9/11, apparently with the tacit approval of the Oval Office.[60]

Several films on the combat aspects of the Korean War deserve consideration. Two, *The Steel Helmet* and *Fixed Bayonets*, were made by the decorated World War II combat veteran Samuel Fuller, and were released in 1951 during the early stages of the war; a third by director Anthony Mann, *Men in War* (1957), and a fourth, *Pork Chop Hill* (1959), were released on the eve of the growing American presence in Vietnam. Like most of Fuller's war movies, *Steel Helmet* and *Fixed Bayonets* were lean, tough films, shot in black and white, with their focus on the foot soldier, reminiscent of World War II combat movies. In *Fixed Bayonets*, Fuller's drama centers on a 48-man platoon left behind during a Korean winter to fight a rearguard action against the enemy in order to save the 15,000 members of the battalion. Made with the cooperation of the War Department, *Fixed Bayonets* had a formula familiar to film audiences that remembered World War II's *Bataan* and *Wake Island*. It included acts of courage and self-sacrifice and the major character, a non-commissioned officer who must lead his platoon back to its regiment, displays the kind of courage under fire that symbolized the coming of manhood in World War II movies.

*The Steel Helmet* was Fuller's first war film and a *tour de force*, since he wrote the screenplay and served as producer and director. The film was completed in 10 days and dedicated to the U.S. infantry. Like many of Fuller's films, it has a straightforward plot but its strength lies in its characterizations. The simple story concerns a tough, experienced sergeant and his platoon who are ordered to capture and hold a Buddhist temple to serve as an observation post for directing artillery fire. Most of the action takes place within the temple. The film ends with a fierce battle between the handful of American troops and hundreds of communist forces. Aside from the fighting, this B-movie raised the racial issue, a subject considered taboo by the traditional film studios at the time. The issue arises when the platoon discovers a North Korean major hiding inside the temple. The major wants to know why the black medic and the Japanese-American (Nisei) soldier are fighting with white men against the oppressed peoples of color. The North Korean reminds the black medic that his platoon members are unlikely to eat with him in civilian life. Addressing the soldier, the major cannot understand why the Nisei would be fighting in Korea when his family had been interned in a relocation camp during WWII.[61] Although Fuller's characters provide unsatisfactory answers, raising the racial question in a film that was released three years before the *Brown v. Board of Education*[62] desegregation decision was symbolic of the director's personal sympathies toward the world's "underdogs," whether they are minorities mistreated by their homeland or infantry soldiers resigned to doing the dirty work of war.

A minor work in the combat genre, *Men in War* takes place in the early stage of the war and at its core explores the question of who is the better soldier for command—a lieutenant whose value system may be too gentle for combat or the hardened sergeant whose driving force is survival at any cost. At the film's end, the audience is convinced that it is men like the sergeant who are necessary in wartime. The question is universal and could have been pursued in almost any war.

*Pork Chop Hill* had the sound and smell of combat, not surprising since it was directed by Lewis Milestone of *All Quiet on the Western Front*, based on essays written by a veteran, S.L.A. Marshall, and made with the cooperation of the U.S. Army. Lt. Clemons' (Gregory Peck) outfit is ordered to retake Chinese-held Pork Chop Hill and hold the position until reinforcements arrive. His men suffer tremendous casualties before reaching the top of a hill that has no military value. Outnumbered by overwhelming Chinese forces, Clemons asks headquarters for reinforcements or permission to withdraw. He is ordered to hold the hill at all costs. Later on he learns that his platoon was used as a bargaining chip at the negotiating table at Panmunjom. As one U.S. general at the peace talks put it, "Are we as willing as the Chinese to spend lives for nothing?" The answer is a qualified "yes," as reinforcements finally arrive, but only after 80 percent of Peck's unit has been sacrificed as political pawns. Although there were rumors that the film had been edited, what remains clearly illustrates the complexity of combining military and political ends. *Pork Chop Hill* serves to bridge the gap between the heroics of the World War II combat films and the later disillusionment of American involvement in Vietnam.

Hollywood made very few films about the impact of the Korean War at home. One exception was *I Want You* (1951), starring Dana Andrews, who had appeared in *The Best Years of Our Lives* and a number of other World War II movies. Andrews plays an ex-GI, married and with a family and living in small-town America. His father had served in the First World War and he had seen action in the Second. Andrews has a younger brother and when the Korean War begins, the key plot issue involves the draft and military service. Should Andrews write a letter to the local draft board asking for a deferment for his brother, who works in the family architectural firm? Examining his conscience, Andrews decides against asking for special privileges for his brother, which leads to his induction into the army. The draft issue during the Korean conflict was not as dramatic or divisive as in the sixties with Vietnam, yet college-age males received automatic deferments until graduation. The author received a college deferment and experienced hostility for not being in the military. An anonymous source complained to the local draft board but I was allowed to graduate regardless. This special treatment of college students would reach a climax during the Vietnam era, when men who sought refuge from the draft either bought time in college or skipped to Canada. In *I Want You*, complaints to draft boards about why a particular young man was not in the service came from the parents of those already drafted into military duty; whispers and gossip around town meanwhile questioned the fairness of the selective service system. The issue is conveniently resolved in the film, as Andrews' brother is assigned to Germany rather than Korea and he therefore escapes combat duty. But when Andrews is asked by his former commanding officer to rejoin his old World War II outfit to help build airfields in Korea, Andrews chooses to reenter the military rather than seek a military exemption. Their mother has the best line in the film when she declares to her family, "It seems all my life I've been saying goodbye to my sons."

Most Americans born after World War II learned about the Korean War from *M\*A\*S\*H*, the popular seventies television series that was based on the 1970 Robert Altman film of the same title. The television show about a mobile medical unit in Korea became one of the most successful shows on air, running for 11 seasons and many years of reruns. Considered irreverent toward the military and strongly anti-war in its sentiments, the TV show provided an opportunity to comment and express anti-war views during the Vietnam War. Its relationship to battlefield conditions in Korea, however, existed mostly in the imagination of the sitcom's writers. Though MASH units did provide medical facilities for battlefield surgeries, a whole generation of Americans viewed the Korean conflict through the antics of fictional characters like Hawkeye, Radar, Trapper John, and "Hot lips" Houlihan. Only occasionally did the series tackle a serious subject, such as deaths caused by friendly fire that were covered up by the military.

## Just Wars and Wars of Necessity

Nations use propaganda and patriotic appeals to rationalize their wars and the U.S. is no exception. Of its many wars, historian Arthur Schlesinger Jr. singled out only three as necessary: the Revolutionary War, the Civil War, and World War II because they were "driven by decent purposes and produced beneficial results."[63] Although we have been allies for 200 years, the British would not consider our war for independence as one that was inevitable and absolutely necessary. The logical extension of Schlesinger's statement is that all colonial wars are justified on the grounds of self-determination. It represents the viewpoint of the colonial subjects and while the author is happy to be under the American flag, it is questionable whether the Revolutionary War was absolutely necessary. On the other hand, Schlesinger is right concerning the Civil War and World War II. While President Lincoln did not fight the war to end slavery, it was necessary to bury the issue of secession and keep the union intact. The end of slavery, although laudatory, was a byproduct of the Union victory. The U.S.'s entrance into WWII two years after it had been raging in Europe helped to ensure an Allied victory over the expansionist ambitions of the Axis Powers. The reader need only imagine what life would have been like under Nazis and Japanese rule. World War II was a war that had to be fought and had to be won, regardless of the cost.

Schlesinger excluded Korea from his "wars of necessity" list, presumably because these wars are waged for just reasons. But Professor Michael Walzer, in his book *Just and Unjust Wars*, disagrees and categorizes Korea as a "just war" for three reasons.[64] First, U.S. involvement rested on assisting South Korea against a full-scale invasion by 60,000 North Korean troops. Second, the UN authorized the American participation. Third, the military objective underneath the intervention was to restore the *status quo ante bellum* and reestablish the 38th parallel as the demarcation line between North and South as defined by treaty. It is the nature of a "just war" that precludes a nation from bragging over the war's events; in fighting "just wars" nations do not punish their enemies or celebrate military victories, two necessary dramatic effects in any combat war movie.

After years of decisive World War II films where the enemy was clearly defined and where commitment to total victory was absolute, it was understandable that the ambiguity of the Korean "police action" discouraged the making of salutary films about the war. The Korean War was not so much forgotten as ignored by Hollywood and the American people. One aspect of the conflict that was deliberately forgotten by the military until 1999 were atrocities committed during the war. Several news stories revealed two such incidents early in the war.[65] The first involved the massacre of South Korean civilians, mostly refugees, at No Gun Ri. Apparently inexperienced American troops fired upon hundreds of these refugees in July 1950, mistakenly believing them to be North Korean infiltrators. The second incident did not directly involve American troops. Instead, U.S. Army officers stood by while the South Korean military executed more than 2,000 political prisoners during the early days of the war. There is some evidence that the North Koreans did the same when they occupied territory in the south, but, of course, they were not our allies.

Would Michael Walzer still consider Korea as a just war had he had the advantage of reading historian Bruce Cumings' revisionist view of the war in his book *The Korean War*?[66] Cumings argues that the Korean War was a civil war with historical roots dating back to the Japanese occupation of the country in 1910. Americans tend to look at the war as beginning in 1950 and ending in 1953 in a stalemate. But by examining Korea's history as a colony of Japan, apparently with America's blessing, animosity toward the U.S. is better understood. Japan treated the Koreans as inferior people, establishing Japanese as the official language, and later, during WWII, the Japanese Army forcibly recruited thousands of Korean women to be sex slaves or comfort women. Apparently North Korea remains upset and bitter about it and is opposed to joining the South because its leaders have past ties to Japan. But even more upsetting to the North is the U.S.'s saturation bombing of its civilian population. According to Cumings, the U.S. "carpet bombing" of the north dropped more bombs on Korea than in the Pacific theater of WWII. Another source claims that the carpet bombing destroyed 75 percent of North Korea's cities and villages.[67] Cumings at least admits that the North Koreans mistreated POWs and engaged in summary executions and other atrocities. But he faults the U.S. for "mythologizing" the war and hypocritically taking the moral high ground. In short, Korea was a "dirty war" filled with atrocities and mistreatment by all sides.

Such unpleasant aspects of the Korean War were largely omitted from journalist David Halberstam's last book before his death, a comprehensive military and political account of the war.[68] Halberstam did not address the question of whether Korea was a war of necessity or a just war. Instead his book pays tribute to the soldiers who fight the wars, the foot soldiers who became the "grunts" of the Vietnam War, and who bear the full brunt of military blunders and miscalculations. He reminds us that Korea was the first of three similar ground wars the U.S. would pursue in Vietnam, Iraq, and Afghanistan. Writing from the perspective of those who fought it, Halberstam notes that the U.S. government was asking its troops to suffer and "die for a tie," restoring the original boundary line between North and South Korea. All sports enthusiasts know that most Americans hate ties—only wins count for something. But if Americans were frustrated by the political stalemate in Korea that ended the fighting, their discontent was barely visible. On the horizon loomed another conflict in Southeast Asia that would prove as divisive at home as the Civil War.

Chapter 9

# Remembering Vietnam on Film
## Lessons Learned and Forgotten

"I love the smell of napalm in the morning…smells like…victory."
—Col. Kilgore, *Apocalypse Now*

"The Oriental doesn't put the value on human life as we do in the West."
—General William Westmoreland

"Everything depends on the Americans. If they want to make war for 20 years then we shall make war for 20 years. If they want to make peace, we shall make peace and invite them to tea afterwards."
—North Vietnamese leader Ho Chi Minh, December 1966

"Television brought the brutality of war into the comfort of the living room. Vietnam was lost in the living rooms of America—not on the battlefields of Vietnam."
—Marshall McLuhan

Unlike the Korean conflict, Vietnam was very much a television war, with the fighting and dying vividly displayed on the evening news. Bringing the war into the home was best expressed in a scene from the film *Summertree* (1971), where actor Michael Douglas drops out of college and is shipped to Vietnam. The poignant moment occurs in the final scene when his parents, watching the late night television news in their bedroom, click off the set just as their son's body bag is being loaded onto a helicopter. This dramatic scene depicts the pervasiveness of the war, from the soldiers at the front to civilians in the comfort of their homes. To avoid its presence would have required a life of isolation, a monk's existence without access to the daily newspaper or television set. In urban centers and on university campuses, the war often preempted academic studies when picketers waved their placards, demonstrators' chanted anti-war slogans, protesters blocked the entrances into campus buildings, and police clashed with students. In short, the spirit of the war permeated the country and its presence was felt even when its effects were not always visible.

Figure 9.1. Vietnam Wall Memorial, Washington, D.C., 1985.
Reprinted with permission, Michael Roskin

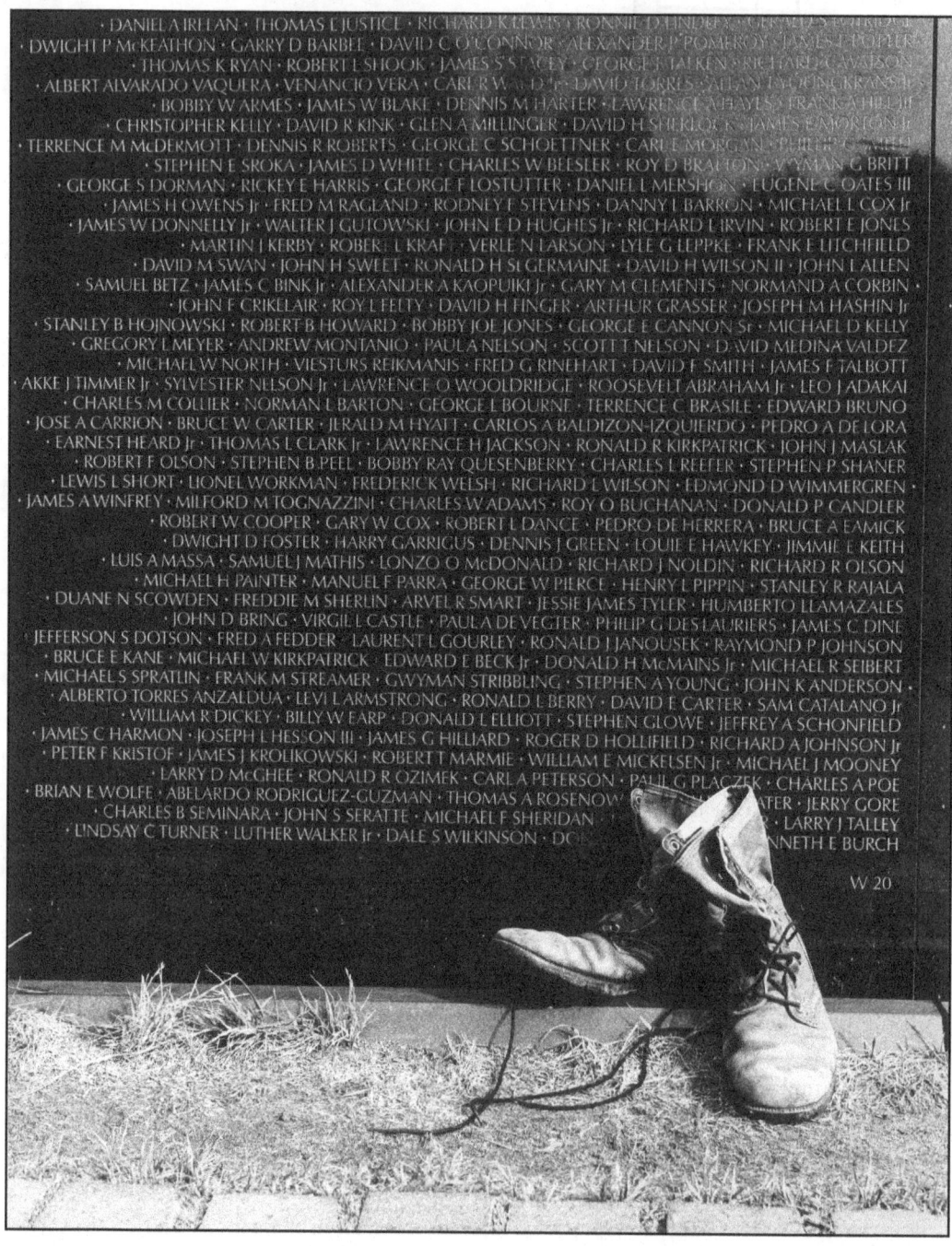

The Vietnam War era was a time of affliction for the U.S., generating pain and suffering at home and abroad. The war cost the U.S. an estimated $165 billion. The number of American dead exceeded 58,000, with another 300,000 wounded. A considerable number of veterans returned home either physically disabled or mentally impaired. The number of suicides among Vietnam vets was proportionally higher than among other segments of the population. Often neglected by those in the U.S. are the casualties suffered by the Vietnamese people; over one million South Vietnamese troops, North Vietnamese Army regulars, and Vietcong (VC) guerrillas were killed, together with an additional one million civilian casualties. The bombing and napalm destroyed more than 5.2 million acres of Vietnamese land.[1] These are tremendous losses for what correspondent Bernard Fall once characterized as "a small war."[2] Fall had placed Vietnam within the post–World War II era characterization of a period of modest revolutionary wars. Once the casualties from these 48 minor wars were computed, Fall acknowledged that they would equal losses suffered in either of the two world wars.

The setback in Vietnam was difficult for Americans to accept since the American national character is preconditioned to military victories rather negotiated settlements. The Korean conflict, conducted under UN authority, was accepted by the country, albeit reluctantly, as a bona fide stalemate. At least after the Panmunjom negotiations, Korea remained a divided country with the communists in control of the northern half only. But in Vietnam, the entire country was lost to the communists once the U.S. withdrew its armed forces as part of the Paris Accords; the fall of Saigon in 1975 marked the official end of South Vietnam. Moreover the conclusion of this divisive war left thousands of loyal South Vietnamese to the mercy of the enemy. Critics of Vietnam policy considered this decision by the U.S. a shameful act of betrayal.

As the war escalated and dragged on, the increasing Americanization of the conflict caused havoc at home, dividing generations, families, races, and socioeconomic classes. Fathers who served in the "Good War" clashed with their sons over the merits of the war just as actor Michael Douglas did with his father in *Summertree*. Laborers and the working class generally supported the war, while intellectuals, academics, and college students opposed it. Civil rights leaders argued that young black men were being sent to Vietnam to fight against another minority while the smart, rich white boys retreated to the security of a college or university campus and proceeded to protest the war from within their safe haven. Police entered college campuses to quell student demonstrations. Students, in turn, boycotted classes, harassed pro-war professors, and locked administrators in their offices. Anti-war students literally shut down colleges and universities. When the author was teaching at Villanova in the sixties, a campus rally by Tom Hayden and the Students for a Democratic Society (SDS) closed down the university for five days. It seemed at the time that America was a fractured society, one part at war against a foreign foe, another segment at odds against the government in power and authority in general. In his book *In the New World*, Author Lawrence Wright eloquently expressed one aspect of the intergenerational clash caused by the war:

> Each year, as the war dragged on and I came closer to the end of my deferment, the arguments between my father and me became more heated.... What made this generational contest greater than any in our country's history was the lack of balance between the Baby Boomers of my generation and the Depression and war-seared generation that gave birth to us.... It was not Vietnam we were arguing about, but America. In our polarized state, my father saw America as all good and I saw it as all bad.... The war was dividing the country along lines of race and class, as well as age. I knew the weight of the

war was falling heaviest on the poor and the minorities…and yet like most middle-class white boys I hid behind my II-S deferment, which was out of reach of those who couldn't afford a college education… the war between my father and me was fought in other households all over the country, tearing the generations apart.³

Vietnam was not a war that could be ignored. Taking a neutral position was virtually indefensible, politically or philosophically; one was either for the war or against it. Also, unlike World War II soldiers, the Vietnam veterans did not receive a warm homecoming; there were few parades or marching bands to greet them. Instead they returned to an America that ignored or scorned them. Vietnam had become as divisive and unpopular as the Civil War.

The national feeling of ambivalence toward Vietnam was reflected in the films of the era. While the war movie genre continued to do well at the box office, the studios doubted that there was much commercial value in Vietnam films during the early stages of the conflict. Eventually, Vietnam films would surpass the number of films on the Korean conflict, although the studios proceeded cautiously. An early B-movie entry, *To the Shores of Hell* (1965), proved a commercial failure despite its gung-ho storyline about the efforts of marines to free one of their comrades captured by the Vietcong. Perhaps its failure was predictable given its low-budget production and unknown cast.

The film's poor reception, however, did not deter John Wayne, who with the assistance of the U.S. military produced, directed, and starred in *The Green Berets* (1968). It turned out to be the only American film to unequivocally support U.S. involvement in the war. The major film studios were reluctant to fund such a project but Wayne was willing to risk his money and his considerable reputation. Supposedly, Wayne wrote to President Johnson that it was "extremely important that not only the people of the U.S. but those all over the world should know why it is necessary for us to be there [Vietnam]," and that furthermore the "most effective way to accomplish this is through the motion picture medium." Wayne told LBJ that the film "would inspire a patriotic attitude on the part of fellow Americans."⁴ Jack Valenti, LBJ's aide, was receptive to Wayne's request for government support and persuaded the president to grant the actor the military assistance required to complete the project. The aid included arms and equipment, as well as advisors and permission to shoot the film at Fort Benning, Georgia. *The Green Berets* turned out to be a commercial for the Special Forces and an apologia for the Johnson administration's war policy. The film's rhetoric flaunted a Cold War mentality since its message was that Vietnam was one small part of the worldwide communist conspiracy; therefore the American presence was required. Similar to many of the World War II combat movies, *The Green Berets* is a hybrid film with both training and battle scenes. Using a skeptical journalist (David Janssen) as a convenient plot device, Wayne took every script opportunity to articulate the government's position that Vietnam was not a civil war since the North received aid from the Chinese and the Russians. America is in Vietnam, Wayne's film insisted, because the U.S. had to protect the Vietnamese people from communist domination. For the film's finale, Wayne would repeat almost verbatim the line he used in *Back to Bataan* almost three decades before, but this time to a Vietnamese orphan, explaining that the U.S. was fighting the war for children like him. *The Green Berets* turned a profit despite poor reviews, anti-war protests, and an ill-timed theatrical release during the year of the Tet Offensive and the My Lai massacre. Its box office success was testimony to Wayne's star power, but the film was recognized as an attempt by the actor to structure the film as if it were a formulaic western or World War II movie with clear heroes and villains. Hence, *The Green Berets* proved to be nothing more than the standard action yarn about good guys (cowboys, U.S. cavalry, U.S. military) versus bad guys (Indians, North Vietnamese Army, Vietcong).[5] Its poor reception by critics and public alike ensured that it would garner no awards and have no imitators.

Hollywood ignored the Vietnam War movie during the turbulent sixties. But when the film industry decided to utilize the war as screen material, it did so with a vengeance. In the late seventies, the studios renewed their interest in the topic after the Tet Offensive and the fall of Saigon. By 1975, the literature on the war was extensive and scholars from several fields, among them history, politics, and film studies, wrote scripts and directed films and a few documentaries of the war from their respective disciplines. Their scholarship, although overlapping in analysis, is best understood as two contrasting perspectives on Hollywood's version of the war, with each outlook reflecting the methodology of their particular discipline merged with their respective personal reflection.

## The Wave Theory

Several scholars[6] characterized the Vietnam War films in terms of marketing saturation or "wave theory" analysis, where Hollywood releases a batch of films within a concentrated time span. According to this theory, the film industry dealt with the war in clusters, releasing films about the war in two distinct waves; the first grouping was released to theaters in the years 1978 and 1979 and the second appeared between 1985 and 1989.

The first wave of Vietnam War movies includes two combat (in country) films, *Go Tell the Spartans* (1978) and *Apocalypse Now* (1979), one hybrid training-combat film, *The Boys in Company C* (1977), one hybrid combat-returning veteran film, *The Deer Hunter* (1978), and one film, *Coming Home* (1978), that concerns the adjustment of the returning veteran.

Contrary to World War II movies, the Vietnam combat films differ considerably from their predecessors in two respects: they refused to reconstruct a false image of American unity and military competence in Vietnam and they avoided the unequivocal acts of courage by individual soldiers. It is rare to find heroic acts in Vietnam-era films. In fact these foot soldiers or "grunts" commit acts of cowardice and participate in unspeakable crimes. In Vietnam and more recently in Abu Ghraib prison in Baghdad, revelations of torture and abuse of detainees' raises the fundamental question of whether war itself changes the nature of its participants. This moral question reverberates throughout many Vietnam era films.

In *Go Tell the Spartans*, a film that represents the early years of the war when the American military served primarily as advisors to the South Vietnamese government, the major characters explicitly criticize the strategy of the high command in fighting the war. When a seasoned U.S. major (Burt Lancaster) is ordered to defend an isolated outpost, he reluctantly obeys the command despite reservations about holding a military position that is vulnerable to attack and is of no strategic importance. True to his prediction, Lancaster's troops, composed of raw recruits and South Vietnamese militia, are overrun and killed by the Vietcong. Only one soldier, an idealistic volunteer, survives to relate the tragedy to headquarters. As a consequence his idealism is destroyed along with his fallen comrades. To add insult to injury, the Vietcong strip the bodies, leaving the naked soldiers as a symbol that the Americans will be unable to accomplish what the French and other invaders had failed to achieve since 200 B.C.

The other combat film, *Apocalypse Now*, could belong in a category of its own because it contains both positive (pro-war) and negative (anti-war) images of fighting an insurgency war where the enemy appears as an old farmer, innocent mother, or young child. Drawing from Joseph Conrad's early 20th-century novella, *Heart of Darkness*,[7] the film relates the CIA-directed mission of Captain Willard (Martin Sheen) to locate the renegade ex-Special Forces Colonel Kurtz (Marlon Brando) and terminate him "with extreme prejudice." Kurtz has taken his army of Montagnards into Cambodia and established a camp from which his forces engage in indiscriminate killing. Willard's journey upriver into Cambodia, where he locates Kurtz, is meant to represent America's intervention in Vietnam. The film's commercial and artistic failure proved to be a perfect metaphor for the war itself. At some point, Kurtz has realized that the war cannot be fought by conventional means, nor can it be won by adherence to the traditional code of warfare. Before Willard carries out his termination order, Kurtz tells him:

> I've seen horrors…horrors that you've seen. But you have no right to call me a murderer. You have a right to kill me. You have a right to do that…but you have no right to judge me. It's impossible to describe what is necessary to those who do not know what horror means.… Horror and moral terror are your friends. If they are not then they are enemies to be feared.… I remember when I was with Special Forces.… We went into a camp to inoculate the children. We left the camp after we had inoculated the children for Polio, and this old man came running after us and he was crying.… We went back there and they had come and hacked off every inoculated arm. They were in a pile, a pile of little arms. And I remember…I cried…I wanted to tear my teeth out…I never want to forget it.… And then I realized… And I thought: My God…the genius of that.…the will to do that.… And then I realized they were stronger than we. Because they could stand that these were not monsters. These were men…trained cadres. These men who fought with their hearts, who had families, who had children, who were filled with love…but they had the strength…to do that.… You have to have men who are moral…and at the same time who are able to utilize their primordial instincts to kill without feeling…without passion… without judgment…without judgment. Because it's judgment that defeats us.

Kurtz adopted brutality and then imposed it upon the enemy with one horrific act that led to others, even greater horrors, until the excesses of war changed the humanity of those who waged it. Whether meant as a metaphor for the end of civilization or a depiction of America's descent into hell, Coppola's *Apocalypse Now* would never be mistaken for a World War II film where the forces of good and evil are explicitly delineated.

On the other hand, *The Boys in Company C* is the type of hybrid combat film that was familiar to World War II audiences. It traces the fortunes of five recruits, from marine boot camp to combat in Vietnam. The contrast between the competence and efficiency of their drill sergeant (portrayed by a real marine DI) and the incompetence of their field commanders is not coincidental. Field officers put their troops at risk in order to deliver booze and other supplies to the commanding general's birthday party, leading their convoy into an ambush. Constant bickering among the company's officers over strategy needlessly costs the lives of their men. As further evidence of military corruption, the American forces are ordered to "lose" a soccer match with the South Vietnamese, an action the team rejects even though it would guarantee that their remaining days in Vietnam were spent in the relative safety at base headquarters rather than on jungle patrol. Hence, the soccer match becomes a metaphor for the senselessness of the war itself.

Both Michael Cimino's *The Deer Hunter* and Hal Ashby's *Coming Home* confront the physical and psychological problems that faced the Vietnam veteran on his return home. Cimino's film focuses on three working-class men—Michael (Robert De Niro), Nick (Christopher Walken), and Steven (John Savage)—living in a small Pennsylvania steel town that believes in God and country. The three enlist and are sent to Vietnam, where the Vietcong capture them. During their imprisonment, they are subjected to the torture of playing Russian roulette for the enjoyment of their captors. In one intense scene De Niro challenges the Vietcong to play Russian roulette as part of his escape plan. After putting one bullet in the revolver's chamber and succeeding, he next puts in two cartridges, and when the first fails to fire, he uses the remaining bullets to escape in a bloody shootout with the guards. The three friends successfully escape from the prison camp, but their experience in Vietnam has permanently altered their lives. Steven is wounded in the escape and returns home a paraplegic who prefers to remain in the VA hospital rather than go home to his wife. Nick stays in Vietnam, becoming a drug addict with such low self-esteem that he gambles and loses his life playing Russian roulette. Michael is the only survivor who returns home physically whole, but he is psychologically damaged. This bleak portrait of the harm done to those who served in Vietnam is offset by the final scene at Nick's wake where, despite their personal suffering, the mourners are still able to sing "God Bless America." Conversely, at the heart of *Coming Home* are the veterans who regret their Vietnam experience and are transformed into anti-war activists. Different though these films may be from each other, what they share in common is an ambiguity toward the war and America's involvement in it.

The films of the second wave (1985–89) are more explicitly critical of the war and symbolize greater cynicism about American involvement. Films such as Oliver Stone's *Platoon* (1986), Stanley Kubrick's *Full Metal Jacket* (1987), John Irvin's *Hamburger Hill* (1987), and Brian De Palma's *Casualties of War* (1989) express dismay, if not disgust, at American militarism. The soldiers in these films would not qualify for good conduct medals. Instead they are presented as cowards, murderers, and rapists. These films are revisionist exercises that indict the U.S. for its wrongful intervention in the war. One hybrid training-combat film, Stone's *Born on the Fourth of July* (1989), follows real-life Vietnam veteran Ron Kovic, from gung-ho marine to anti-war activist. Kovic returns home, physically and emotionally scarred. He is consumed with guilt for atrocities over which he had little control. When his platoon invades a village and riddles it with gunfire, the company inadvertently kills women and children. Kovic and several of his buddies try to assist the wounded but are ordered to withdraw as an artillery strike is planned against the village.

These Vietnam combat films were flawed in two significant respects. First, they focused on the grunts—the infantry soldiers—who fought the ground war in villages and jungle terrain, leading audiences to believe that the foot soldiers were the heroic figures in Vietnam when most of the damage, in lives and property, resulted from air and artillery strikes. Second, these films presented an American perspective on the war where the Vietnamese people are portrayed as Vietcong or as victims of the carnage.[8] The second-wave films, therefore, are symbolic of the Americanization of the war.

Films that also would fit within the timeframe of the second wave include the first two Rambo (Sylvester Stallone) films, *First Blood* (1982) and *Rambo: First Blood 2* (1985), and the Braddock (Chuck Norris) trilogy, *Missing in Action* (1984), *Missing in Action 2: The Beginning* (1985), and *Braddock: Missing in Action III* (1988). These films present a view of the war that places the blame for its failure squarely on politicians and civilian bureaucrats at home.[9] When in *Rambo: First Blood, Part 2* ex-green beret John Rambo is asked by his former commanding officer Colonel Trautman to return to Vietnam to rescue American POWs, Rambo replies, "Do we get to win this time?"[10] The question is rhetorical but the film answers it anyway. The Stallone character had an immediate impact on the public, with visitors to the Vietnam Memorial Wall even searching for the name "Arthur John Rambo" to make rubbings as a souvenir.[11]

## The Phase Analysis

Social historian William Palmer has a different take on Vietnam War movies.[12] He views them as progressive stages in the filmic representation of the war as a visual text, evolving from an epic phase (1976–79) to two overlapping phases in the 1980s—the comic book and the symbolic nihilist. Palmer's theory is that the Vietnam films are best understood as a series of evolving texts related to political and social developments. In the epic phase (1976–79) such films as *The Deer Hunter*, *Apocalypse Now*, and *Coming Home* renewed America's interest in the war, since each film acted as consciousness-raising stimuli on film audiences. Palmer views these films as "the publicists of a Vietnam War consciousness that was abroad in the country yet dormant for various reasons: bitterness, shame, depression, decompression, inarticulateness."[13] He considers these films to be traditional narratives that are related to such previous literary texts as Stephen Crane's *Red Badge of Courage* and World War II movies like *Sergeant York* and *Sands of Iwo Jima*.

The initial stage of the second phase of the Vietnam War films, the comic book period, occurred, not surprisingly, during the renascent nationalism of the Reagan administration. Films like the Rambo series and the Braddock trilogy supported the president's belief that America did not lose the war in Vietnam. Moreover, the Reagan administration implied that similar "small wars" could be fought and won in places like Grenada, the Middle East, and Central America. Palmer notes the similarities between the popular comic book figure at the time Sergeant Rock and the Rambo film character. As Rambo's picture appeared on magazines and in newspapers throughout the country, he became the icon for the restoration of American military power in the world. Stallone was even invited to dine with the Reagans at the White House and was treated as if he were a Congressional Medal of Honor recipient.[14]

The other part of the second phase (1987–88), identified as the symbolic nihilist stage, includes films like *Platoon*, *Full Metal Jacket*, and *Hamburger Hill*: visual attempts to capture the disorder, chaos, and futility of the war. Within a 16-month timeframe, Hollywood released six major features on the war, all except one set in Vietnam. Two films, *Platoon* and *Hamburger Hill*, were inspired by Vietnam veterans who saw combat in the war and who centered the action on the hardships endured by the foot soldiers—the "grunts"—who come to view the war as senseless. If Vietnam is commonly identified with the swish, swish, swish of the helicopter and the sound of artillery fire and aerial bombing, its "dirty war" was fought on the ground. In *Hamburger Hill*, for example, the 101st Airborne unit's objective is to take a hill away from the enemy. After a fierce 10-day firefight where the outfit suffered 70 percent casualties, the Americans secure the hill, but then are ordered to abandon it as the fighting moves forward. Much like the hill in the Korean War film *Pork Chop Hill*, the territory fought over in *Hamburger Hill* was of psychological rather than strategic importance.

The second half of Kubrick's *Full Metal Jacket* takes place in Vietnam during the 1968 Tet Offensive, where a squad of marines is picked off one by one by a Vietcong sniper. The marines have been so thoroughly indoctrinated with the "born to kill" mentality that they become as brutal as the enemy. At film's end only a handful has survived the ordeal. Similarly, the Everyman character in Stone's *Platoon*, Chris Taylor (Charlie Sheen), arrives in Vietnam a naive recruit and leaves three months later, alive but with a damaged soul. The film is as much a rite of passage story as a war movie where Taylor loses his innocence and his idealism. During his short tour of duty, Taylor experiences the anguish of trying to survive in a war where the enemy lacks an identifiable face. This sobering realization has the effect of transforming him into a cold-blooded killer as he revenges the death of his compassionate sergeant. After the burning of a local village and the gang rape of a young Vietnamese girl, Taylor writes home, "I don't know right from wrong anymore." If Taylor represents Everyman, then America lost its soul in Vietnam.

## The Political Expediency Factor

These interpretations of Vietnam War films are valid as explanations for how the war was presented to the American public. There is a third perspective that also is worth considering. Historically, the film industry has been politically bifurcated; select executives and movie stars tend to be more liberal, while many of the studio heads see themselves as conservatives who view movies predominately as a business. Hollywood neglected the Vietnam War movie because no consensus existed in the country on the war. That would also explain why the major studios avoided treating Vietnam as source material until it was relatively safe to tackle the subject once American troops left Saigon.

Examination of those late seventies films reveals Hollywood's practice of hedging its bets. What is *The Deer Hunter* save an affirmation of the attitude "my country right or wrong"? Although the lives of the three major characters have been irrevocably altered by Vietnam, they and their friends can still pay homage to flag and country in the final scene. *Apocalypse Now*, on the other hand, is more ambiguous since it lends support for both pro-war and anti-war interpretations.[15] The battle at Charlie's Point, for instance, where gung-ho Colonel Kilgore (Robert Duvall) destroys a Vietnamese village, demonstrates the superiority of American firepower. But Kilgore's helicopter assault, to the sound of loudspeakers blasting Wagner's "Ride of the Valkyries" and mainly because he wants access to a prime surf spot, also reveals the madness, the total insanity, of the war long before Willard and the audience meet Kurtz. Even the returning veteran film *Coming Home* is more believable as a love story between a marine officer's wife (Jane Fonda) and a wounded veteran turned anti-war activist (Jon Voight) than as an anti-war polemic. The film conveniently neglected several important issues associated with the Vietnam veteran, namely the government's denial of the effect of Agent Orange on troops and civilians alike, the difficulty of dealing with the veterans' administration bureaucracy, and the problem of post-traumatic stress disorder (PTSD) and survivor guilt syndrome.

One issue that Hollywood did exploit for screen material was the returning veteran as a "walking time bomb"—sick, angry, and even psychotic.[16] The Travis Bickle (Robert De Niro) character in *Taxi Driver* (1976) is an unstable veteran whose outburst of violence against urban immorality escalates into murder and attempted assassination. A year later, *Rolling Thunder* (1977) reached the screen with a plot that had a Vietnam POW return home to an unloving wife and unfriendly son. When thieves rob his prized coin collection, disfigure him, and kill his family, the veteran extracts his own brand of revenge. Revenge is the motive, also, in a number of B-movies about returning Vietnam veterans. For example, in *Angels from Hell* (1968) a Vietnam veteran returns home to organize his own motorcycle gang and tangles with both rival bikers and the police. In *Chrome and Hot Leather* (1971), an ex-green beret seeks to extract his own brand of justice from bikers who are responsible for his fiancée's death. Contrary to the World War II veterans in *The Best Years of Our Lives*, these Vietnam vets are often portrayed as a menace to the community and a danger to society. The only comforting news about these B-films is that few Americans saw them.

With President Reagan's election in 1980, the film studios acknowledged a change in government attitude and in the national mood and sought to take advantage of the transformation. What were described as the comic book phase representations of the war were also political tracts and propaganda pieces that tried to blame misguided bureaucrats and impotent politicians, rather than the American military, for what happened in Vietnam. The "winning the war" syndrome films focused on the exploits of individual superheroes—Rambo and Braddock—who single-handedly locate the missing-in-action (MIAs), rescue the POWs, and do considerable damage to the life and property of the enemy. A near-perfect illustration of this bravado can be found in *Uncommon Valor* (1983), where the super-heroics are supplied by a commando team of experts and specialists put together by a former Vietnam officer (Gene Hackman) and supported with funds from private sources. Their objective is to return to Vietnam and Laos to find POWs, including Hackman's son, despite objections from the CIA and Congress. Hackman tells his group of six that there are 2,500 soldiers still missing and that the U.S. government either refuses or is unable to bring them home. Thus, this rogue band of misfits (most of the six recruits cannot adjust to civilian life), with the help of local guides, penetrate into Laos, locate the prison camp, and rescue a handful of prisoners. But Hackman's son is not among the group, having died in the camp. The mission, though, costs the lives of two guides and two Vietnam vets, hardly a cost-effective undertaking. However, the film preaches that the U.S. remains a commanding military power to be reckoned with despite the fact that its heroics are done by a private army rather than sanctioned government forces. The film's message seems to be that private armies can accomplish successful missions by force rather than wait for diplomatic negotiations. It is a lesson not lost on active paramilitary groups scattered across the U.S.

Admittedly, the period from 1985 to 1989 also saw the release of films like *Platoon* and *Hamburger Hill*, which came from independent filmmakers. These films, as well as *Casualties of War* (1989) also can be legitimately viewed as personal statements since *Platoon's* Oliver Stone, *Hamburger Hill's* Jim Carabatsos and, *Casualties of War's* David Rabe were Vietnam veterans whose scripts were memory plays. These films, together with *Full Metal Jacket*, share important similarities to the war-is-hell combat movies of the Second World War. The significant difference, of course, is that the World War II soldier was always cast as the hero.

Thus, Vietnam War films can be viewed as reflecting the political expediency factor in Hollywood that requires that a film never alienate its audience, especially by challenging the dominant political ideology. While these interpretations may claim some modicum of validity, there is one criticism of the Vietnam War film that they all share, namely that Hollywood focused on the American presence rather than on the Vietnamese people who endured and suffered through the war. Laying our political ideology aside, there is no denying that the war was fought in their country—on their land, in their villages, and rice paddies. What is largely missing from Hollywood's versions of the war are the Vietnamese. Not one Hollywood Vietnam film raised the fundamental question of who was morally responsible for all the human suffering and property damage.[17] Even left-liberal directors like Stone avoided the issue of American involvement in the war, preferring instead to dramatize the plight of the ordinary soldier.

On the Vietnam War Hollywood churned out roughly four dozen feature films, six dozen documentaries, PBS specials such as *Vietnam: A Television History*, and several television series, like *China Beach*; the vast majority were made before the dawn of the new century. The film industry then lost interest in the subject despite the collateral damage suffered by both Americans and Vietnamese, particularly after the terrorist attacks on September 11, 2001.

Hollywood has made only two major motion pictures about Vietnam since 9/11. One, *We Were Soldiers* (2002), is a combat film, the other, *Rescue Dawn* (2007), has a POW escape plot. *We Were Soldiers* presents a revisionist view toward Vietnam while retelling the true story of Lt. Colonel Harold Moore's (Mel Gibson) experience in Vietnam. Moore is commander of the First Battalion, Seventh Cavalry, and is assigned during the early days of the war to action in the La Drang Valley, an area overrun with North Vietnamese troops. His outfit is soon hemmed in by 2,000 enemy troops in an area the size of an American football field. There, in the first major battle of the war, Moore's forces hold and refuse to yield ground to the North Vietnamese. The film recreates the three-day battle at what came to be known as the "Valley of Death" in the central highlands, where both sides suffered tremendous losses. But instead of restricting itself to the heroism of the U.S. forces alone, the film pays tribute to the bravery of the North Vietnamese as well. This bloody battle claimed 50 percent of Moore's battalion and 90 percent of the Vietnamese troops. When the battle is ended, it is the leader of the Vietnamese forces who praises the American victory, but warns that the final result will be the same as it was for all the previous invaders. He knew the history of his country; the Americans did not.

*Rescue Dawn* (2007), was made by German director Werner Herzog, although it starred American actors Christian Bale, Jeremy Davies, and Steve Zahn. The film depicts the true story of navy pilot Dieter Dengler, a German-American, who is shot down over Laos during the Vietnam War, captured, and sent to a Laotian prison camp. Once there, Dengler refuses to give up hope and accept his fate and begins to plot his daring escape. There are few political overtones in the film, which details the extraordinary strength of the human spirit to survive despite overwhelming obstacles. The film has a happy ending, with Dengler rescued and returned to safety.

## Could the U.S. Have Won the Vietnam War?

Is it conceivable that a reasoned brief can be made for viewing the Vietnam War as a military and political success? At first glance, it appears to be an improbable task given the consequences of the U.S. intervention:

- More than 58,000 American soldiers killed, with another 300,000 wounded. An estimated 830,000 Vietnam veterans suffer from symptoms of PTSD
- An estimated two million Vietnamese dead, including 1.3 million civilian casualties
- Approximately $168 billion total cost of the war to the U.S. government
- The U.S. dropped more than 15 tons of firepower in Vietnam as well as two million gallons of chemical defoliation (including Agent Orange) to destroy food crops
- One year after the U.S. left Saigon, North Vietnam took over the whole country; today Laos is a Marxist-Leninist state while the government in Cambodia gives the appearance of a multiparty democracy but has been controlled by Prime Minister Hun Sen and his Cambodian People's Party[18]

Yet Professor James Kurth maintains that, in fact, the U.S. could have won the Vietnam War had it ended in 1973.[19] Professor Kurth takes the position that, unlike Korea, the outcome in Vietnam would have had no impact on the Cold War between the U.S. and the Soviet Union. The key to understanding his position is the Tet Offensive of 1968, which Kurth describes as a military victory but a political defeat. It was a military victory because the American counterattack had seriously damaged both the NVA and the Vietcong. However, Kurth maintains that the protests at home were so intense in 1968 that they limited the options of the incoming president. Thus, when the Nixon administration assumed power, it devised a strategy that would provide the U.S. with greater bargaining power to negotiate with the North Vietnamese and eventually end the war. One part of the strategy was to separate North Vietnam from its two protectors: China and the Soviet Union. This was achieved by offering China diplomatic recognition and the Soviet Union an arms control agreement. The second step was to slowly withdraw U.S. ground forces while fortifying the South Vietnamese Army in what came to be known as the "Vietnamization" program. When North Vietnam's spring offensive in 1972 failed, the Nixon administration countered with an intensive "Christmas bombing" of both Hanoi and Haiphong. This action brought the North Vietnamese to the negotiating table to sign the Paris Peace Accords. Hence, Kurth concludes that the Nixon administration's strategy had enabled the U.S. to win its war in Vietnam by leaving South Vietnam with some semblance of "peace with honor": American troops could go home and the territorial integrity of the South was preserved. What undid this "victory" were the Watergate scandal and the control of Congress by the anti-war Democrats, the so-called "doves." With a weakened president and the Democratic doves in control, Congress passed the War Powers Act of 1973 that limited the president's ability to use force without the approval of the Congress. With Nixon's resignation in 1974, Gerald Ford moved into the White House. When the North Vietnamese leadership decided to move against the South, Congress would not permit President Ford to resume the bombing of the North. Without that threat, the South was soon overrun and defeated.

This is Professor Kurth's thesis in a nutshell. It boils down to blaming the failure of the U.S. intervention in Vietnam on a combination of Watergate (which the Democrats had nothing to do with) and the control of the Congress by anti-war activists. While Kurth makes a reasonable "what if" case, does the so-called "political victory" attained by the Nixon administration really overcome the tremendous losses from the war? Professor Kurth may think so but the author disagrees.

Another way of looking at this question sheds an entirely different light on it. Conservative columnist George Will, writing in 2009, reminds us of the testimony by diplomat and historian George F. Kennan before the Senate Relations Committee in 1966, where he spoke against the Vietnam intervention and told the committee that "I don't think we can do it successfully."[20] When Kennan testified, Will notes that there were some 200,000 U.S. troops in Vietnam—by the Tet Offensive of 1968 that number would reach 537,000. Will's point is that had the committee listened to Kennan, some 55,000 of the 58,000 deaths would not have occurred. Had the U.S. followed Kennan's advice, it would have reached some agreement in 1966, saving these American lives as well as many Vietnamese ones. Would that not have been an even better victory? Sometimes it is better to abandon an unsound position than to blindly hold on to it. This issue is revisited in 2003 with the U.S. invasion of Iraq.

## Post-Vietnam Interventions

Since the evacuation of Saigon in 1975, the U.S. has committed its troops to some dozen military operations around the world, with mixed results.[21] Several were military failures: the aborted Iranian hostage rescue, the intervention in Lebanon, and the disastrous firefight on the streets of Mogadishu. But there were some military victories and operational successes scored in Grenada, Panama, the Persian Gulf, and Afghanistan. Limited troops were utilized in the skirmishes and military actions in Lebanon, Grenada, Panama, and Somalia, but the Persian Gulf and Iraqi wars involved full-scale military operations.

The American government used military force after Vietnam for three reasons: to evacuate or rescue its citizens from foreign countries under siege or caught in the midst of civil wars (Iran, Grenada, Panama), to act as peacekeepers on behalf of the UN or provide humanitarian relief from mass killings and starvation (Lebanon, Somalia, the Balkans), and to liberate occupied lands at the request of friendly nations or as part of a coalition force (Persian Gulf, Iraq). The political reasons for intervention, however, do not lend themselves to neat compartmentalization. In politics, the motivation for military intervention is usually never singular. The invasion of Grenada, for example, was designed not only to protect 1,000 American medical students but also to topple the Marxist government. Similarly, the purpose in Panama was to depose General Noriega before the Canal was turned over to Panama, although the administration stressed the security threat to the 34,000 Americans residing in the country at the time. The fact that the Panamanian dictator had ties to Columbian drug cartels sealed the case for intervention.

For whatever reasons, Hollywood ignored these post-Vietnam military interventions as suitable screen fare. Only a handful of films were produced on these interventions. Perhaps the studios thought audiences had been saturated with war films, even though the industry continued to churn out WWII movies. Perhaps in some cases the obvious superiority of American military power would diminish the dramatic interest for American viewers. Another reason to consider is that after Vietnam the major studios also may have wished to avoid military interventions that ended badly.

The disastrous 1982 U.S. involvement in Lebanon, where an 18-month peacekeeping mission ended in failure, with 266 military dead and 151 wounded, was ignored completely by the film industry. The same could be said for the botched Iranian hostage rescue during President Carter's administration. However, the Grenada intervention, although a minor military operation, turned out quite well for the Reagan administration. In October 1983, the Reagan White House responded to a request from the Organization of Eastern Caribbean States to invade the tiny island of Grenada to ensure the safety of American students attending the local medical college. Within three days, the combined strength of 15,000 U.S. Marines and Army Rangers, joined by a token force from six Caribbean nations, overwhelmed the local militia and their "Cuban advisors," evacuated American citizens, and deposed the Marxist government. It was a quick victory, with 19 American soldiers killed in action. Politically, the Grenada invasion was to President Reagan what the Falkland Islands war was to Mrs. Thatcher—an opportunity to reassert military superiority at the expense of an inferior opponent.

With the exception of one major film, Hollywood overlooked the Grenada military success. Actor-director Clint Eastwood, an admirer of Sam Fuller's work, directed a hybrid WWII-type movie about the Grenada invasion, entitled *Heartbreak Ridge* (1986).[22] Eastwood hired Jim Carabatsos, the Vietnam veteran and writer of *Hamburger Hill*, to write the screenplay, while Eastwood starred as a tough, anti-establishment drill sergeant who had previously seen action in Korea and Vietnam and was having problems adjusting to the new civilian volunteer army. Following the hybrid WWII formula, Eastwood devoted two-thirds of the film to the preparation of his green recruits. As a consequence, *Heartbreak Ridge*, like many of its predecessors, failed to meet the criteria for a combat film and did poorly at the box office.

A second intervention—really a limited "police action"—occurred in December 1989 when President George H.W. Bush sent 4,000 U.S. troops into Panama to drive General Manuel Noriega from power. The brief military action led to Noriega's capture and deportation to the U.S. to stand trial, where he was convicted and sent to prison. The four-day invasion cost 23 American lives, with an additional 300 wounded. The U.S. action was criticized in Latin America and other parts of the world. Hollywood preferred to ignore the episode altogether.

The film studios, however, expressed some interest in stories where American military forces assumed the role of peacekeepers. Operating under a 1992 UN resolution to provide humanitarian relief to Somalia's starving population by ensuring the safety and distribution of food shipments, U.S. forces moved from peacekeeping to military action against the local warlord, Mohamed Aidid. In retaliation, Somali forces targeted Westerners when open warfare raged on the streets of Mogadishu, the capital city. While U.S. ground forces were in the process of rounding up prisoners, a rocket-propelled grenade brought down a Black Hawk helicopter. During a fierce firefight, 18 Americans were killed along with several hundred Somalis. U.S. forces subsequently withdrew from Somalia without capturing Aidid. The lasting image of dead American pilots being dragged through the streets of Mogadishu raised serious questions as to the wisdom of interventionist policies. When the Clinton administration took office in 1993, the situation in Somalia had deteriorated to such an extent that America's role as a super power was tarnished because of this inability to bring a local warlord to justice. Did this incident provide encouragement to local thugs and international terrorists? The question was never answered in the film reenactment directed by Ridley Scott and produced by Jerry Bruckheimer, although *Black Hawk Down* (2001) wants audiences to leave theaters impressed with American troops "kicking ass." True, 100 Army Rangers, together with a Delta Force team, killed hundreds of Somalis. But the U.S. neither won the battle nor accomplished its humanitarian mission. The film poses none of the serious interventionist questions, demonstrating once again that Hollywood is primarily in the business of selling tickets and avoiding political issues.

Another peacekeeping mission that drew some interest from Hollywood concerned the decade-long struggle in the Balkans, first in Bosnia and later in Kosovo. Neither the first President Bush nor President Clinton wanted to intervene in the war that developed among Serbs, Croats, and Muslims until the horrors and brutality of the savagery were reported in the daily press and appeared on the nightly newscasts. The Bush administration's failure to adopt a hard-line policy encouraged Yugoslavian President Slobodan Milosevic to use force to keep the various ethnic groups from seceding. After Slovenia and Croatia declared their independence in 1991, three bloody wars began that would claim more than 100,000 lives and compel millions more to flee.

Four films have been made about the Bosnian War. Each one focused on different aspects of the conflict. The first was an English-American production, *Welcome to Sarajevo* (1997), which focused on journalists covering the beginning of the war. The film's intention was to show the horrors of a city under siege, intercutting the lives of the fictional reporters with actual news footage. The second film, *Savior* (1998), was an Oliver Stone production and starred American actor Dennis Quaid as a mercenary in the Foreign Legion sent to

Bosnia to fight with Serbian forces against Muslims. Although the film adequately represents the brutality and senselessness of the war, the narrative seems more concerned with Quaid's personal redemption. Quaid had joined the Legion after his wife and son were killed by Islamic terrorists, and in his grief and anger, he becomes an inhuman killing machine until one day he befriends a Serbian woman and her baby. The third film, *Behind Enemy Lines* (2001), portrays the ethnic conflict through the eyes of an American pilot shot down over Bosnia and pursued by Serbian troops while his commanding officer attempts to rescue him. The pilot, part of an American peacekeeping operation, is in the process of photographing Serbian ground movements when his plane is downed. Before he is rescued, the audience has an opportunity to speculate on the horrors that could result once the peacekeepers leave. While each film involves Americans in some active role, in actuality the U.S. government was a spectator to the conflict until President Clinton committed American airpower to NATO forces in an effort to protect UN peacekeepers on the ground. In 1999 the U.S. again participated in air strikes in Kosovo against Serb forces until Milosevic agreed to the peace accords that ended the fighting. Although the Balkan wars contained enough dramatic material for several films, Hollywood adopted a "not interested" policy, similar to the U.S. government.

That is why it was a complete surprise when actress-turned-director Angelina Jolie decided to reexamine the Bosnian War as a variation on the Romeo and Juliet story. Her *In the Land of Blood and Honey* (2011) begins in 1992 when Ajla, a Muslim woman, falls for Danijel, a Bosnian police captain. Their brief romance is interrupted when a bomb explosion inside a disco marks the beginning of the attempt by the Bosnian Serbs to seize power and end the mixed-ethnic socialization that had previously characterized the region. Responsibility for the bomb is never revealed, but the Serbs begin a campaign of intimidation, rape, and bloodletting. Muslims are rounded up and separated by gender; the men are executed or shipped off to labor camps, the women become captives who cook and serve meals during the day and become sex slaves at night. When Danijel, now commander of a labor camp, learns that Ajla is one of his captives, he tries to protect her by moving her to a private room, where she is saved from sexual assault because she is now his property. However, Danijel's father, a Serbian general and hard-line Muslim hater, warns his son to get rid of her. When Danijel, who has begun a sexual relationship with Ajla, refuses, his father has one of his aides sexually assault her in one of the film's more brutal scenes. The film has several such scenes: one where a woman is raped in public, another where women are used by the Serbs as human shields during an attack. Jolie looks at the war from the perspective of women who became the victims of its extreme violence. *In the Land of Blood and Honey* graphically depicts a war where old wounds and personal scores are settled against innocent bystanders and not only those fighting. It is the best film on the Bosnian War and a stark reminder that war also brutalizes the civilian population.

The U.S. has fought two brief but full-scale wars in the Middle East since the end of the Vietnam hostilities. Both involved the father-son presidencies of George H.W. and George W. Bush. The first war began rather suddenly in August 1990 when the Iraqi forces of Saddam Hussein invaded Kuwait. President Bush Sr. acted quickly to organize American military forces to protect Saudi Arabia as part of Operation Desert Shield. By the end of

January 1991, the defensive objective of the initial operation was replaced by the offensive firepower of Desert Storm with the intention of toppling Hussein and initiating a "New World Order" in the area. The Persian Gulf War, the president assured the nation, would not be another Vietnam. That promise was kept, as the war was over within months after U.S. military firepower reduced Iraq's infrastructure to the "preindustrial age." Hussein, however, was permitted to remain in power and the new world order was more slogan than reality. President Bush was delighted with the victory, exclaiming, "By God, we've kicked the Vietnam syndrome once and for all."[23] In the flush of military victory, the president could be forgiven for engaging in a bit of hyperbole, but the war did serve to ease, if not erase, the memory of Vietnam.

Like Vietnam, the Persian Gulf War lent itself to television, as CNN filed nightly reports directly from the front. It was also a war that proved attractive to the video market and made celebrities out of Generals Schwarzkopf and Powell. At least a dozen videos were produced on various aspects of the war. Additionally, several documentaries were released about the war, with such titles as *Desert Storm: Eagles over the Gulf* (1991) and *Sandstorm in the Gulf: Digging Out* (1991). One documentary video, *Desert Storm: Cockpit Videos of Bomb Runs* (1992), places the viewer in the pilot's seat on bombing missions. Television journalists also secured a piece of the action, as Dan Rather narrated the war from beginning to end in the three-volume set *Desert Triumph* and Diane Sawyer and Barbara Walters conducted interviews and provided commentary in a four-volume series, entitled *Persian Gulf: The Images of a Conflict*.

But Hollywood refused to join in the national hoopla by flooding the theater screens with films about the war. Except for a couple of quickie B-films released in 1991, *The Finest Hour* and *The Heroes of Desert Storm*, the major studios largely ignored the war. By the mid-nineties, Hollywood had released only one feature film, *Courage under Fire* (1996) that concerned the conduct of the war. In this film, Denzel Washington stars as an officer assigned the task of investigating the merits of awarding the Congressional Medal of Honor to helicopter pilot Meg Ryan, the first woman in U.S. history to be so designated. Ryan is in charge of a flight rescue mission when her helicopter is shot down over Kuwait. The crew manages to hold off the Iraqis until another chopper arrives and most return to base safely, except for Ryan, whose body is left behind. After interviewing the crew survivors and receiving conflicting versions of what happened in the field under fire, the question for Washington is to uncover the truth, that is, whether Ryan was a hero or a coward. Although the film contains occasional combat scenes, *Courage under Fire* is more a mystery about the discovery of the truth than a conventional combat film. As one reviewer observed, film is the worst possible medium to discuss truth honestly since it is edited, cut, and reshot so as to construct a logical story that an audience will accept.[24] War, on the other hand, is neither sensible nor logical.

In 1999, director David O. Russell, working from his own screenplay, made the second major Gulf War film, *Three Kings*, a quixotic, baffling movie that puzzled critics and audiences alike. Though it starred popular actor George Clooney from television's *ER*, the film disappointed at the box office. One reason for the poor showing is its ambiguous dramatic focus. It was unclear as to whether the film was supposed to be a satiric action-adventure feature or whether it was intended as a critique of American indifference to the suffering of the Iraqi people. The narrative involves four U.S. soldiers at the end of the Gulf War, who find a map that purportedly identifies the place where Saddam Hussein has hid gold bullion stolen from Kuwait. Being resourceful Americans, the soldiers devise a plan to find the gold and steal it for themselves. During their quest, they encounter Iraqi resistance forces that are waging war against Hussein's elite Republican Guards. The resisters mistakenly believe that the soldiers have come to help them depose Hussein. But Clooney and his pals are intent on thievery until, in typical Hollywood style, they undergo a change of heart and decide to help the resisters reach the safety of the Iranian border. At the film's climax, the gold is turned over to the American military in exchange for allowing the Iraqis to enter Iran. Despite several funny scenes, the film is filled with violence, torture, gas attacks, and other atrocities. Possibly, this mixture of comedy and war-inflicted suffering turned off American audiences. Certainly, Iraqis living under Hussein's reign of terror would not have found the film amusing.

British director Sam Mendes's 2005 film, *Jarhead*, is based on the memoir by ex-marine Anthony Swofford (Jake Gyllenhaal), who had joined Desert Storm to continue his family's tradition of "attaining manhood through combat," only to discover, like Milton, that heroes "also serve who only stand and wait." The film's title refers to the traditional marine haircut, but it also serves as a metaphor for the marines' training process where new recruits are perceived as empty vessels to be filled with the discipline and mythology of the corps. At its core, *Jarhead* is a clone of the World War II hybrid training-combat film, but with minimal combat. Most of the film dwells on the preparation and the boredom prior to battle action. Swofford spent six months in the first Gulf War as a marine scout and sniper and never fired his rifle. He returned home bitter and disillusioned over his failure to see combat.[25] As one disappointed marine asks a buddy in the film, "Are we ever going to kill anyone?" That question is answered affirmatively in Iraq a decade later.

American losses in the Persian Gulf War totaled 148 dead, including 15 women, and 467 wounded. The Iraqis paid a much heavier price. Their losses are estimates: Iraqi soldiers killed range from 75,000 to 100,000 and civilian casualties due to Allied bombing range from 35,000 to 40,000. In addition, the civilian population suffered considerably from imposed sanctions. Under UN Security Council Resolution 661, comprehensive international sanctions were imposed on Iraq and all its foreign assets were frozen. Although it had considerable oil reserves, Iraq could not feed itself and had to import about 70 percent of its food and medicine. Supposedly, the imposed sanctions served as both punishment and as an incentive for the Iraqi people to overthrow Hussein. Unfortunately, after 13 years of sanctions, Hussein, his family, and his henchmen remained firmly entrenched while the sanctioned policy resulted in the deaths of roughly 500,000 children due to starvation and lack of medical supplies.[26]

Saddam Hussein remained in power until March 2003, when Coalition Forces led by the U.S. and Great Britain deposed him. This aspect of the war lasted three weeks and was initiated because Hussein refused to turn over its suspected nuclear and biological weapons to the UN. Consequently, the U.S. and the U.K. governments invaded Iraq in a preemptive strike to protect their security from a potential enemy that supposedly had weapons of mass destruction (WMDs). This second Iraqi war was very much a television war. Unlike the Gulf War, when reporters were limited in their movements, the 2003 version embedded reporters with specific regiments. The result was 24-hour coverage, with every battle detailed and with constant commentary by what seemed to be every general who ever wore a uniform. The 2003 version was so extensive that the viewing and listening public may have wanted to shout, "War is not a spectator sport." Nonetheless, the American public seemed to embrace this extensive media coverage as vicarious "recreational violence."[27]

While the intense fighting lasted three weeks, the guerrilla warfare against coalition forces persisted, but no nuclear or biological weapons were uncovered. Since the war dragged on into the new Obama administration, the comparison with Vietnam deserves at least a cursory consideration. Was Iraq becoming America's second Vietnam? A brief analysis indicates that there are both parallels and differences.[28] One similarity is that the justifications and reasoning for going to war in the first place have been discredited. In Vietnam, the U.S. became a replacement for French colonialism, supporting an unpopular and corrupt regime without an understanding of Vietnamese resiliency against outsiders, whether Chinese, Japanese, French, or American. In Iraq, no weapons of mass destruction were ever discovered, and as the "torture memos" later revealed, the Bush administration coerced confessions from Iraqi prisoners in an effort to justify the invasion. Also, in both instances, public support for the wars diminished considerably as the deaths, bombings, dwindling allied support, financial drain, and apparent lack of an exit strategy led to decreasingly low popularity numbers for both Presidents Johnson and Bush. Other similarities include the government's systematic use of lies, deception, and the manipulation of information, reports of prisoner abuse, and the devastation of civilian life and property.

On the other hand, several factors distinguish the two wars. First is the military distinction between the two conflicts. American troops reached half a million in Vietnam but roughly one-fifth that number in Iraq. The war in Vietnam began as an insurgency but escalated into a conventional war, while Iraq began with a preemptive invasion that toppled the Hussein government but ignited a growing insurgency. Also the Iraqi casualties, while deplorable, are much fewer than those incurred in Vietnam. One other important distinction to be noted is that Iraq is being fought by volunteers (National Guard and enlistees); whereas draftees outnumbered the regular army in the Vietnam War. So is Iraq another Vietnam? The reader will have to decide. But remember that America lost the Vietnam War despite John Wayne and the Johnson administration.

## Post 9/11: Just Wars, Reel Wars

President Bush's preemptive strike against Iraq raised serious questions over just war theory, which permits intervention but on a limited, justifiable basis.[29] Under just war theory, intervention is justifiable on three grounds: self-defense, to prevent genocide or flagrant human rights violations, and to serve humanitarian reasons. A preemptive strike to ward off a potential attack does not fit into any of these categories. The Bush administration sought to link the 9/11 terrorist attack to an organized, if not always identifiable, enemy—al Qaeda, supported in Afghanistan and Iraq by the Taliban and local militants. The U.S. and its allies are in a war against terrorism—an ideology that transcends national boundaries. The 9/11 assault on U.S. soil was not an attack by one or several countries against the U.S. but rather a strike by Islamic terrorists, independent of country. Furthermore, the argument by the Bush government that a first strike is justified on "probability" grounds without substantial and positive proof runs counter to Professor Walzer's definition of a just war discussed in chapter 8. Remember Walzer's theory requires that most just wars are fought to restore the *status quo ante* before the aggression took place. His theory is not meant to justify unwarranted acts of aggression. In Korea, the objectives were to repel North Korean aggression and restore the 38th parallel as the legitimate boundary line. But in Vietnam, for example, the U.S. lent assistance to a government that lacked popular support and whose legitimacy was questioned.[30]

Similar reasoning was used by the Bush administration in Afghanistan. The U.S. government demanded that the Taliban regime turn over al Qaeda members and their camp locations or the whereabouts of Osama bin Laden. When the Taliban refused to comply, President Bush ordered a bombing as a prelude to a military assault. Under this scenario, any government can justify its aggression against another government.

This helps to explain why Hollywood was reluctant to deal with such material in its films. Hardly ever has the industry used the medium to deliver ideological messages or ask hard questions about the justifiability of war. Instead, Hollywood war films emphasize the plight of the soldiers fighting it and avoid the basic political questions.

The Vietnam combat films described earlier were praised for their gritty realism, but they remain representations and creative inventions of war.[31] These films come close to letting the audience "experience Vietnam," yet they are still works of fiction. Films about the grunts did not spare the realism of fighting a guerrilla war in the jungle, where the foot soldiers were subject to leeches, snakes, and heavy rains while slogging through mud and rice paddies in search of an invisible enemy disguised as a local farmer, peasant, or fisherman. No audience would ever understand the disappointment, which intensified into anger and hatred, when the endurance of these conditions failed to secure local loyalty and gratitude. Imagine the shock in the scene from *Go Tell the Spartans* when an idealistic soldier discovers the Vietnamese family he befriended has betrayed him. Or take the disk jockey character Robin Williams portrays in *Good Morning, Vietnam* (1987), who comes to realize that the brother of the Vietnamese woman he loves is a Vietcong terrorist.

Yet despite their attempts at authenticity, these Hollywood war films remain fantasies, unsuccessful imitations of the realities of actual combat, where air strikes are errant and artillery fire often goes astray, killing friend and foe alike. Helicopters, which appear on cue in the movies to pick up the wounded, do not always arrive on time under battle conditions. Armies and troops may not be where they are supposed to be and, especially in a place like Vietnam, battles with the enemy are often characterized by confusion, disorder, and chaos. With the notable exception of *Saving Private Ryan*, what war film has had the courage to depict a sense of fear before battle so strong that soldiers vomit and soil their pants? As one veteran in a VA hospital put it in the documentary *Dear America: Letters Home from Vietnam* (1988), "Heroes are for the late show."

Maybe Hollywood will never get it right because no one, save the soldier, can understand the true nature of combat. As former marine sniper Anthony Swofford wrote:

> The warrior becomes the hero, and the society celebrates the death and destruction of war, two things the warrior never celebrates. The warrior celebrates the fact of having survived, not of killing Japs or Krauts or gooks or Russkies or ragheads. That large and complex emotional mess called national victory holds no sway for the warrior. It is necessary to remind civilians of this fact, to make them hear the voice of the warrior.[32]

When World War II veteran Samuel Fuller was asked about the honesty in his combat films *The Steel Helmet* (Korean) and *The Big Red One* (World War II), he supposedly replied that the only way to get at the truth in a war film is to put a machine gun behind the camera and gun down the audience.[33] No doubt Fuller's reply was not intended to be taken literally, but it reminded moviegoers that viewing "war in the dark" is a vastly different experience from being there.

Chapter 10

# Mission Accomplished?
Hollywood and the Afghanistan-Iraq War Films

"All wars are fought three times. There is the political struggle over whether to go to war. There is the physical war itself. And then there is the struggle over differing interpretations of what was accomplished and the lessons of it all."
  —Richard N. Haass, former State Department official and author of *War of Necessity, War of Choice*

"These guys have no problem with killing."
  —1st Recon marine to embedded reporter Evan Wright during the invasion of Iraq

"I try not to cry. I have never cried this much in my entire life. Two great men got taken from us too soon. I wonder why it was them n' not me.... I try every night to count my blessings that I made it another day but why are we in this hell over here? Why? I can't stop askin' why?"
  —Pvt. Ryan Hill, MySpace Blog from Iraq, November 1, 2006

"Major combat operations in Iraq have ended. In the battle of Iraq, the United States and our allies have prevailed."
  —President George W. Bush on the USS *Abraham Lincoln*, May 1, 2003.

The purpose of this third war chapter is to cover America's latest wars in Afghanistan and Iraq, including Hollywood's response to these events, as well as to examine President Obama's intervention policy and conclude with an assessment of the future of the war film genre. Admittedly, this is a comprehensive and complex collection of topics to cover in one chapter, but hopefully, its content will bring the war film subject to its logical conclusion.

## America's Interventions in Iraq & Afghanistan

On May 1, 2003, President George W. Bush, standing on the deck of the aircraft carrier USS *Abraham Lincoln*, made his historic pronouncement that "major combat operations in Iraq have ended" and that what remained was to "secure and reconstruct the country."[1] In a triumphant mood, the president assured the American people that the military victory in Iraq demonstrated that the U.S. had the power to free a nation from tyranny, relying on the use of precision weapons to minimize civilian casualties. After the speech, the president posed in his flight jacket for a victory photo-op.

In retrospect, Bush's announcement was a bit of hyperbole and certainly premature, as the U.S. continued to wage war in Iraq and Afghanistan for the next decade. Shortly after the terrorist attacks on September 11, 2001, the Bush administration and its coalition allies pursued military action against the Taliban in Afghanistan in an attempt to capture Osama bin Laden, destroy the training ground for al Qaeda forces and remove the Taliban from power. Only the last objective was achieved. Having reached its twelfth year, the war in Afghanistan persists without any visible signs American objectives have been achieved. President Bush's foreign policy advisors chose to ignore the past lessons taught to foreign invaders: the British failure in 1842 to retain *their* ruler in power and the withdrawal of the Soviets from Afghan soil in the 20th century. The Soviet withdrawal provides a sound history lesson in the futility of attempting to conquer and then govern Afghanistan's mountainous terrain where tribal leaders are in control. Despite superior military equipment and manpower, the Soviets capitulated after 10 years of guerrilla warfare (1979–89) waged by the mujahedeen.[2]

In the midst of pursuing military action against the Taliban, the Bush government rushed into an invasion of Iraq in March 2003 that was based on dubious intelligence, misinformation, and a predetermined commitment to force regime change by ousting Saddam Hussein from power. Six weeks later, a triumphant President Bush proclaimed military victory. Rather than signaling the end of hostilities, it proved to be just the opposite as U.S. forces encountered stiff resistance from insurgents. The Iraq War cost the U.S. over 4,400 in casualties and billions of dollars.[3] U.S. troops left Iraq under President Obama's plan to withdraw American forces by the end of 2011. The president, however, had wanted Iraq's President Jalal Talabani to step down in favor of a Shiite leader more acceptable to the Sunni minority. But Talabani refused to comply; he also rejected a plan to have 5,000 American troops remain as training officers for the Iraqi military.[4]

It may be unfair to make an assessment of Iraq so soon after the U.S. military withdrawal at the end of 2011. Still, some preliminary observations might be in order. No one believed that Iraq would become a democratic society in just one year. But the Shiite coalition dominates the government and the Sunni Arabs and other minorities feel excluded. Economically, oil production is still under prewar levels. Abu Ghraib has been renovated and is now the Baghdad Central Prison. All of Hussein's palaces are back in Iraqi hands. The Green Zone inside Baghdad, which houses the Iraqi government and the U.S. Embassy, is protected by several rings of checkpoints. The airport is open and the road to it is safer than in the past. However, the Mahdi Army of Shiite cleric Moktada al-Sadr controls Sadr City and the Kurds still want to acquire northern areas of Iraq.[5]

Meanwhile in Afghanistan, President Obama has ordered the U.S. military to prepare for the eventual withdrawal of troops, although it is likely some 16,000 State Department personnel will remain. What is the state of Afghanistan as the U.S. prepares to withdraw its troops? A report by the Council on Foreign Relations at the end of 2011 concluded that despite the casualties and billions spent, the outlook for a stable, unified, democratically elected government in Kabul is poor.[6] The Karzai government is generally considered to be corrupt, its posts filled with family and friends. Its banking system cannot attract investors. Its American-trained forces are considered unreliable and some of its members may in fact favor the Taliban. There is little guarantee that the Karzai government can control and stabilize the country once outside forces leave.[7] Anti-American sentiment remains high, but the Taliban have decided to target their aggression against Afghan military and police, killing 26,000 since 2011, largely using improvised explosive devices (IEDs).[8] In sum, the U.S. has little to show for the billions spent and thousands of lives lost.[9] The war in Afghanistan has now surpassed Vietnam as the longest war in American history.[10]

## The Costs of War

Can the horrors of war ever be compiled, totaled and summarized? Certainly statisticians are able to compute the numbers and tally the figures. The U.S. lost over 6,600 soldiers in both wars.[11] More than 50,000 U.S. soldiers were wounded.[12] These veterans require treatment, many for the remainder of their lives. In 2013, over one million veterans or 56 percent of those returning from Afghanistan and Iraq were receiving medical treatment from VA facilities.[13] A Harvard University study on the potential total costs of the two wars reported that this could range from $4 to $6 trillion, a sum that included the long-term medical costs of treating injured soldiers.[14]

These estimates do not include coalition troops killed and wounded. Nor do they include the extraordinary costs inflicted on the Afghan-Iraqi populations. It is estimated that at least 134,000 Iraqis, including civilians, have died as a direct result of the war as of spring 2013.[15] These deaths occurred when people were in their homes, marketplaces or on roadways. They were killed by cluster and other type bombs, drones, IEDs, bullets and fire by American and coalition forces on the one side, and by insurgents and sectarians on the other. These are the innocent victims of war.

But beyond casualties and economic costs, as horrific as they are, there exist human costs for the living that can best be understood on an individual basis. For those in combat there is death, bodily harm, psychological trauma, depression, and suicide. For their families, loved ones, and friends, there is grief, emotional loss, dysfunctional family life, divorce, and, sometimes, abuse and death. Their stories are recorded in the daily newspapers and reported on television and the Internet in tragic descriptions of violent and anti-social behavior, self-destruction through alcohol abuse and drug addiction, often a prelude to spousal abuse. Here is a sample of their stories: 25-year-old Staff Sergeant Calvin Gibbs was convicted of exhorting his five-man squad to kill Afghans as sport; 38-year-old Staff Sergeant Robert Bales, father of two, serving in his fourth deployment, left his outpost in Kandahar Province one Sunday morning, walked into two Afghan villages, and murdered 16 people, nine of them children; and Staff Sergeant Dwight L. Smith, a decorated combat veteran, returned from Afghanistan brain damaged and one day out of the blue ran down, raped and murdered a 65-year-old woman.[16] Then there is the tragic case of Major Ben Richards, who returned home to his wife after two concussions from roadside IEDs only to learn that he had suffered traumatic brain injury (TBI) as a result and wished that he had lost a leg instead.[17] Yet another Afghanistan veteran, 26-year-old Specialist Joey Paulk, returned home so badly burned that he was wrapped in bandages from head to toe. Paulk required cosmetic surgery to realign his face and skin grafts to restore his burnt arms, hands, and legs.[18] These are some of the events, crimes and abuses that turn up in Hollywood films under fictitious names.

But as horrific as these individual stories appear, they pale compared to the collateral damage resulting from these two wars; namely, suicide rates among returned veterans have jumped dramatically, exceeding the rates for the civilian population, violent sex crimes among active duty military have escalated as have addictions to prescription drugs and alcohol abuse. The last two appear to have become staples of military life.[19] Many more military suffer from PTSD and will require medical and psychological help from their families and assistance from the Veterans Administration to endure an uncertain future.

Possibly the combination of waning public support for the two wars, coupled with the discouraging economic prospects that the U.S. faces in the future sheds some light on Hollywood's reaction to these events and the public's rejection of the war films the industry made in response to them.

## Hollywood's Response to the Afghanistan-Iraq Wars

More than four dozen American-produced films and documentaries focusing on some aspect of the war on terror have been released since September 11, 2001. Most were distributed by the major Hollywood studios, but others were made by independent and freelance filmmakers. Many were released while the wars were still in progress. This deviates from the film industry's strategy since World War II to delay the production and distribution of such films until the war is officially over or there is an end to the fighting. Thus, the release of the Afghanistan-Iraq films to be discussed in this chapter represents a significant change in Hollywood policy.

Hollywood released six films during the 2007–08 U.S. surge in Iraq. All had one factor in common: they did poorly at the domestic box office. Four had high expectations due to their A-list cast, prominent directors, noted screenwriters, and superior production values. A fifth, *Redacted*, was a low-budget docudrama. The sixth, *Stop-Loss*, had an Oscar-winning director but a meager $15 million budget. The combined domestic gross of these six films, *In the Valley of Elah*, *Lions for Lambs*, *Redacted*, *Rendition*, *Charlie Wilson's War*—all released in 2007—and *Stop-Loss* (2008), was under $110 million.[20] In comparison, during this same time period, the fourth Indiana Jones film, *Indiana Jones and the Kingdom of the Crystal Skull* (2008), racked up a whopping $145 million during its first week in national release. Even more stunning was the record-breaking opening of the sixth film in the Batman series, *The Dark Knight* (2008), which grossed $238 million in its first week and went on to earn $533 million in the domestic market.[21]

Also released during the summer of 2008 was the HBO TV miniseries *Generation Kill*, in which embedded journalist Evan Wright follows the marines of the 1st Recon Battalion during the first days of the 2003 Iraqi invasion. The series was based on Wright's real-life account and received positive reviews, especially from marines who watched the show, because it avoided the political aspects of the invasion and stuck to presenting it from the viewpoint of the participants themselves.[22]

A second wave of Afghanistan-Iraq war films included four commercial features released to theaters and one original movie made for cable TV. The four commercial films were released in 2009, along with the cable film, *Taking Chance*. These warrant examination too, because these commercial features also did poorly at the box office despite some positive reviews. After these two waves, however, films that featured the wars as their dominant theme were released only occasionally to theaters or sent directly to DVD.

What should we make of these two waves of films from an industry where money is traditionally the bottom line? First, we should discount the idea that they were all "business mistakes" because in the film industry you are not going to secure financing if your films consistently lose money. Hence, what was the film industry thinking? Was it patriotism? Was it venting by anti-war liberals? Was it due to a spate of poor business decisions? Or was it a combination of factors that seduced Hollywood into producing a number of box office duds?

One possible explanation has to do with a lesson Hollywood learned after Vietnam, and that is not to allow other media, particularly television and now the Internet, to dominate coverage. Hollywood ignored the fact that by 2007 public interest in the Afghanistan-Iraq wars had waned considerably. According to Lara Logan, chief foreign correspondent for CNN, the network news programs had already started to reduce the amount of television time devoted to the war on terror. For instance, the three major networks devoted 1,157 weekday minutes in 2007 to coverage on Iraq, but from January through June, 2008, that number had dwindled to 181 minutes a week. Meanwhile, the three networks devoted 83 minutes in all of 2007 to the conflict in Afghanistan. The fact that the three major news networks did not have a full-time correspondent in Afghanistan and that CBS News had eliminated its correspondent in Iraq were signs that the networks had decided to further diminish their coverage.[23] Yet Hollywood persisted in turning out films about wars that had lost the interest of the public.

Another factor besides the declining public interest in the wars was the heated primary races for the 2008 presidential election, particularly the contest between the two Democratic candidates, Senators Hillary Clinton and Barack Obama, which drew strong television audiences and often dominated the media news. This fact is particularly significant since five of the six films during the first wave were released in the fall of 2007 when the political rivalry involving Clinton and Obama intensified. Thus the new political news pushed the old news from the two wars to the back pages of the print media and reduced their coverage on the electronic media.

Another factor to consider is the greater freedom within the industry that has encouraged more artistic creativity and risk-taking among established stars and independent filmmakers. Consequently, certain films are made because a bankable actor like Tom Hanks is interested in the starring role or Robert Redford yearns to direct a particular project. This is especially true if the star or director is also one of the producers and provides financial support. If you tie the rise of artistic independence to a political agenda, then the release of these war films at this time would make more sense.

## The First Wave of War Films: 2007-2008

The first wave of war films arrived in 2007 and was led by director Paul Haggis, whose 2005 film *Crash* won an Oscar. His war film, *In the Valley of Elah* (2007), describes the residual damage inflicted on the soldiers who fight in a war that lacks popular support and is fought without clearly defined objectives. The film's plot centers around the discovery by former military officer Tommy Lee Jones that his son has been murdered by fellow soldiers after their return home from a tour of duty in Iraq. Jones sets about discovering why his son was beaten to death by his comrades, and he is devastated by the senselessness of his death. Distraught and disillusioned, he commits an act of civil disobedience by flying the American flag upside down at the local school. This act of defiance takes on greater significance when committed by a patriotic former soldier whose personal loss turns him against his country. Is Haggis making a statement about the senselessness of all wars or just the one in Iraq? Or is the film a comment on the indifference to life expressed by the new American military composed of professionals and reservists?

Actor-director Robert Redford, long associated with environmental causes and liberal political issues, possibly saw in the script for his *Lions into Lambs* an opportunity to express his personal views on contemporary events. Playing the part of a California political science professor, Redford admonishes one of his brightest students for his political apathy, as he recounts the experience of two former students killed in Afghanistan. Featuring an A-list cast that includes Meryl Streep and Tom Cruise, *Lions for Lambs* weaves together three stories into one narrative. Cruise plays a hawkish U.S. senator who advocates "staying the course" in Afghanistan, while Streep plays a reporter assigned to write a story about Cruise, even though she disagrees with his politics. At the end, she decides that her principles are more important than a news story. Meanwhile, Redford's professor, a former Vietnam veteran and anti-war activist, counsels two of his students against volunteering for active duty. Is Redford's film delivering an anti-war message? Or were his dead former students making the announcement that a democratic society demands citizen participation if its core political values are to be protected?

Critics complained that Redford's film was "too preachy," and that is why the public disliked it, even though it delivered contradictory messages. In contrast, Brian De Palma's *Redacted* is a blistering exposé of the brutal rape of a 15-year-old Iraqi girl by American soldiers, after which she and her family are murdered and their house set on fire. De Palma explored a similar theme in his Vietnam War film, *Casualties of War* (1989). In both films, the soldiers who witness the crime are threatened into silence. These two De Palma films show us how war alters human behavior and causes certain acts to be committed that might not occur under normal circumstances.

*Rendition* has Reese Witherspoon's Egyptian husband detained by the CIA after returning from a conference in South Africa. Thereafter, he is shipped to a secret detention facility overseas where he is interrogated and tortured. Director Gavin Hood's film is explicit in its torture details; Witherspoon's husband is taken to a foreign location (unidentified), shackled naked in an underground prison, beaten, waterboarded, and subjected to electric shocks while dangling from chains. It seems obvious that these scenes are meant to reflect on the torture scenes reported at Abu Ghraib and Guantanamo prisons. Of South African birth,

# Mission Accomplished?

Hood knows what it is like to live in a country where "suspects," real or imagined, are taken by the authorities and virtually disappear into another world. Reportedly, the rendition process, whereby the U.S. allows suspected terrorists to be taken to foreign countries to be interrogated and abused, was authorized on a limited basis during the Clinton administration, but used extensively after 9/11 despite official pronouncements that "America does not torture."[24] More on this subject later in the chapter.

At first viewing, *Charlie Wilson's War* does not seem to fit the pattern of war stories coming out of the conflicts in Afghanistan and Iraq. The film did have two bankable stars in Tom Hanks and Julia Roberts, a screenplay by Aaron Sorkin of *The West Wing*, and Oscar-winning director Mike Nichols. But the film treated its overtly political subject lightly. From its opening scene of Hanks cavorting with a bevy of nude women in a Vegas hot tub, the audience is primed to see a film that its cast and crew desired to make and that they thought would be financially profitable—for them and Universal Pictures. The film, however, proved to be a big box office disappointment. The "based on a true story" plot is a fictional account of former Texas congressman Charlie Wilson, a 24-year veteran of the House of Representatives whose claim to fame is his involvement in a covert CIA operation to help the mujahedeen oust the Soviets from Afghanistan in 1989. This entertaining Hollywood film, however, conveniently omits that previously Wilson had been a staunch supporter of the 1970s right-wing Somoza regime in Nicaragua and that after his retirement from Congress, he began a lucrative career as a lobbyist for Pakistan.[25] And while Wilson's efforts may have hastened the Soviet defeat, the film totally neglects the involvement and contribution of the Afghans themselves. In his recent book, *The Great Gamble*, NPR correspondent Gregory Feiffer makes a convincing case that the Soviets were defeated by a combination of a hostile terrain, a formidable adversary, a nationalistic desire to drive all foreigners out of the country, and enough Afghan intelligence to introduce the enemy to drugs. The Afghans were willing to lose 1.3 million lives rather than capitulate to outsiders.[26] This is the more plausible account of the Soviet defeat in Afghanistan.

The last of the 2007–08 Afghanistan-Iraq commercial war movies tackled the controversial military "stop-loss" policy authorized by the Bush White House. This policy permitted the return to combat of veterans after completion of their initial tour of duty. This so-called "stop-loss" policy went into effect in November 2002, and since then more than 100,000 troops have been subjected to its enforcement, which prohibited them from leaving the military until their units returned from Afghanistan or Iraq. The stop-loss policy went unchallenged until 2004, when Sgt. Emiliano Santiago of the Oregon National Guard filed suit in federal court. Court records show that Santiago joined the Guard for an eight-year term as an 18-year old recruit on June 28, 1996. Two weeks before his discharge, however, Santiago was informed that his termination date had been extended. A few months later, his army unit was mobilized for active duty, destined for deployment to Afghanistan after six weeks of training. Santiago sought judicial relief on the grounds that implementation of the "stop-loss" policy was a breach of contract. The district court denied relief. Santiago then appealed the decision, claiming denial of due process in addition to breach of contract. The veteran argued that the Bush administration, in effect, had subjected him to an illegal "backdoor draft" by extending his eight-year enlistment. But in *Santiago v. Rumsfeld*,[27] the

Ninth Circuit Court of Appeals affirmed the lower court's ruling under U.S.C. sec. 12305, which allows the president to suspend retirement or separation from the armed forces if he determines it to be essential to the country's national security. Santiago shipped out to join his unit in Afghanistan the following day. While he lost the legal battle, he was vindicated when the Pentagon announced that the "stop-loss" policy was destined for termination, but the announcement was premature despite the fact that candidate Obama in 2008 promised to end it if elected. The "stop-loss" program was not terminated until June 2011.[28]

The controversial military policy caught the attention of film director Kimberley Peirce (*Boys Don't Cry*), who co-wrote the script *Stop-Loss* with Mark Richards. Peirce learned from her half-brother, who was serving in Iraq at the time, that some of his buddies were serving in combat zones "for their third, fourth and fifth tours of duty."[29] Her script focused on a group of Iraqi veterans—Brandon, Steve, and Tommy—who return to their small Texas town as "war heroes." But instead of adjusting to civilian life, they drink, refight the war and scare the hell out of anyone around. Steve, for example, cannot stop "fighting the war" and after a night of heavy drinking, finishes off the evening by trashing his girlfriend's house and beating her before he goes outside, digs a foxhole on her front lawn, and protects it with his army pistol from an invisible enemy. Tommy, on the other hand, gets thrown out of his house on his wedding night and, in a drunken rage, uses the wedding presents for target practice. Later, unable to re-enlist or find work, an alcoholic Tommy kills himself. The third member of the group, Brandon, is looking forward to working his family's ranch, but discovers that he has been subjected to the "stop-loss" policy when his unit is deployed back to Iraq. Refusing to report, Brandon goes AWOL and becomes a fugitive. Unable to get help from his senator and rejecting asylum in Canada or Mexico as an alternative, Brandon reluctantly returns to his unit. Defeated by forces beyond his control, Brandon joins Steve in the final scene as their bus leaves base for deployment to Iraq. While one of the better films under discussion, nonetheless, *Stop-Loss* did poorly at the box office with an anemic domestic gross of slightly under $11 million, another casualty of American indifference to the Afghanistan-Iraq wars and the reluctance of American audiences to accept films that confront serious political issues.

The seventh offering of the first wave, the docudrama miniseries *Generation Kill*, takes the viewer into the heart of the military action by following *Rolling Stone* reporter Evan Wright, who was embedded with the 1st Recon Marine Battalion during the first 40 days of the Iraqi invasion. Wright's book was a war journal of the actual invasion but the TV miniseries follows Wright as he accompanies the battalion from a training camp in Kuwait through the occupation of Baghdad. The strength of the series was due to the time the director had to detail the myriad problems faced by the invading forces, which may help explain why the U.S. became bogged down in these wars. *Generation Kill* proffers a litany of political and military mistakes made by the U.S. and its coalition, including the failure of the Bush administration to prepare for the occupation of the country, resulting in food and water shortages for the civilian population; several incompetent command decisions such as the one to provide a single translator for the entire battalion, with the consequence that there were communication problems with Iraqis at checkpoints; faulty equipment that often malfunctioned and left ground forces at the mercy of sand and wind as deadly as enemy snipers and roadside bombs; and a complete lack of any understanding among American troops of the local culture and customs. The series also confirms military deaths by "friendly fire," such as the death of NFL football player Pat Tillman,[30] who was killed in Afghanistan in 2004. The military presented his death as "heroic," when in fact he was killed by friendly fire. It took years for the Tillman family to expose the cover-up. *Generation Kill* neither sentimentalizes war nor promotes a jingoistic portrait of American forces. However, to the veterans of World War II and Korea, its portrait of a new generation of soldiers would strike the old, drafted veterans as virtually unrecognizable. As depicted here they show little respect for authority and even less regard for human life. At times, the war is presented as if it were a video game, where killing is done so matter-of-factly that it appears unreal, as though the victims were characters in the video rather than the Iraqi people.

## The Second Wave: 2009-2010

With the box office failures of all of the first wave's six commercial features, it would have been understandable if Hollywood had temporarily ceased using the wars as film narratives. But that was not the case. Over the next two years, the film industry continued to release five more commercial films that all lost money, including *Taking Chance*, made for cable television. How can we understand the second wave? A plausible explanation is to look at these war movies, released while the fighting raged on in Iraq and Afghanistan, as metaphors for America's global decline as a major power. But this is pure speculation.

Certainly, these five features exhibit little hope or optimism on the state of the wars being portrayed or the soldiers who fight them. A good example is Neil Burger's *The Lucky Ones* (2009), which examines how the government's stop-loss policy at the time affected its three military protagonists. Meanwhile, Kathryn Bigelow's *The Hurt Locker* (2009) dispassionately examines the work of a detonation squad in Iraq without politicizing the process. The film *Brothers* (2009) depicts the war's effect on two bothers whose lives are headed in opposite directions. And *The Messenger* (2009) portrays the emotionally draining job of informing the next of kin of the death of a loved one. These films are not exercises in assigning blame or advancing a personal political agenda; rather they are visual essays on the consequences of the wars' damage to soldiers and their families. The cable film *Taking Chance* resonates with the storyline of *The Messenger* in that it portrays the experience of a marine officer who accompanies the body of an enlisted man home to his family. The wars are not at issue here, except for the feeling of guilt that consumes one of the "messenger" officers for not having experienced combat.

Of these five films, *The Lucky Ones* is the only one that received military assistance. The army has been providing assistance to the film industry since the 1927 World War I film *Wings*, which won an Academy Award. Many of the Afghanistan-Iraq war films did not seek military assistance and those that did usually were denied it by a new post-Vietnam military screening office led by Lt. Colonel J. Todd Breasseale. Located in downtown Los Angeles, Breasseale's office reviews scripts of Hollywood war movies and makes a determination on whether to provide military assistance, in the form of equipment or advice on military matters. How does Breasseale's office decide which film projects to assist? Apparently, assistance is forthcoming if the script provides fair and equal treatment toward the military or if the filmmaker is willing to address any problems Breasseale's staff has with the script or the filming. Filmmakers like Paul Haggis consider the process akin to censorship, but Breasseale disagrees, contending that the army merely seeks to ensure that the portrayal is authentic and not didactic.[31] What is ironic is that *The Lucky Ones* received military assistance even though its star, Tim Robbins, is a noted anti-war activist.

Robbins plays Sgt. Fred Cheever, one of three soldiers in *The Lucky Ones* returning home to his family after his tour of duty in Iraq. The other two major characters are T.K. Poole (Michael Pena), on leave following a gunshot wound to the groin that leaves him impotent, and Pvt. Colee Dunn (Rachel McAdams), on leave after suffering a thigh wound. The latter two are on temporary leave, whereas Cheever is going home for good since his recruitment period has ended. These three physically and emotionally wounded soldiers meet on the plane, but when it lands at New York's Kennedy Airport, they discover that all domestic flights have been cancelled. They rent a car and start on a road trip filled with misadventures and emotional heartbreaks. Cheever is distraught when he discovers that his wife wants a divorce. Colee is upset when she discovers that her boyfriend in Iraq, who died saving her life, has told her nothing but lies. And T.K., regaining his sexual virility, struggles with the dilemma of whether to flee to Canada rather than return to Iraq for his fourth tour of duty. The story, which refrains from taking a position on the war, takes place mostly in America, with just one combat scene at the beginning of the film. At film's end, the audience sees all three boarding a plane headed for another tour in Iraq. The film's distributor, Lionsgate, possibly sensing public hostility or indifference to the wars, waited until the fall of 2008 to release the film even though it had been completed earlier. No matter, since *The Lucky Ones* had a miserable opening weekend and its box office did not improve in the following weeks.[32]

Another film that examines the plight of the returning combat soldier is Jim Sheridan's *Brothers* (2009), which tells the story of two brothers who undergo 360-degree life changes. Captain Sam Cahill (Tobey Maguire) is a career marine officer headed to Afghanistan at the same time that his ne'er-do-well brother, Tommy (Jake Gyllenhaal), is being released from prison. Sam appears to be a good husband and father, but a strict disciplinarian to his two daughters. Tommy, meanwhile, is a shiftless character, a heavy drinker and roustabout quick to use his fists. When Sam is declared missing and presumed dead, Tommy becomes a surrogate father to his nieces and a comfort to Sam's wife. As it turns out, Sam is not dead but imprisoned by the Taliban, who subject him to both physical and psychological abuse. When the Taliban force Sam to choose between beating another prisoner to death or his own immediate execution, Sam does the former, an act that haunts and changes him drastically. Eventually freed by American ground forces and sent home, Sam is a different person to his wife and daughters, who now prefer their uncle Tommy to their dad. Meanwhile, Sam cannot overcome the enormity of what he has done and is tormented by feelings of guilt. Each day he becomes more isolated, suspicious, and paranoid, until one night he goes over the edge in a confrontation with the police. In one of the film's more frightening scenes, Sam aims his pistol at the police, hoping they will shoot him; when that does not happen, he turns the gun on himself, barrel to head. Fortunately, Tommy talks him out of pulling the trigger. The film ends on a muted upbeat note of rehabilitation and family reconciliation.

The harrowing scene in *Brothers* reminds us again of the human costs of war. As the wars in Afghanistan and Iraq dragged on, media stories documented the psychological toll on combatants and their families after their return home. Reports of suicide, violent behavior, family abuse, marital breakdowns, and stories of PTSD appeared in the daily press and on the electronic media. Statistics on the emotional and mental breakdown of post-combat veterans is sketchy at best, but a clue as to their number comes from an understaffed VA that declared it was unable to cope with the number of returning veterans requiring help. The military are reluctant to offer possible explanations for the increase, but several reasons come to mind: repeat deployments of military personnel, along with alcohol and drug abuse, depression, PTSD, brain damage due to extreme shocks from IEDs and a myriad of family and economic problems that confront the returned soldier.

Why are combat soldiers experiencing such problems? The question is beyond the scope of this chapter but one possible explanation is that they are fighting a non-traditional enemy, often clothed in their customary dress rather than in uniform, in skirmishes in neighborhoods where the ensuing gunfire often results in civilian casualties. Another factor is the character of current military personnel. Without a draft to provide a continuous supply of new recruits and with voluntary enlistments lagging, the military reached into a previously "undesirable" pool of ex-convicts in 2007 to furnish soldiers for the surge. Many of these recruits had committed serious crimes such as armed robbery, aggravated assault and burglary.[33]

Put in that context, the scenarios depicted on screen may not be too far-fetched. Does the rape and murder of an Iraqi family in De Palma's *Redacted*, for example, have its roots in the quality of military recruits, the rigors of military training or the anger of the combat soldier fighting an insurgency war where the enemy wears civilian clothes that may hide an explosive device? Can it help explain the murder and butchering of Tommy Lee Jones's son by his army buddies in the aftermath of a personal fight in *In the Valley of Elah*? Are the conditions of imprisonment in Iraq and Afghanistan so brutal and inhuman, as described in the film *Brothers*, that veterans return home so traumatized by what they have done or experienced that they have lost their humanity? There is evidence such scenes may be grounded in reality. In 2008 a leading newspaper reported that at least 121 Afghanistan-Iraq war veterans had committed a killing or were charged with one after returning home. The statistics reveal that in the six years prior to the Afghanistan invasion (1995–2001), 184 homicides were committed by military personnel, while in the six years after 2001, the number of homicides had increased 89 percent to 349. One-fourth of these killings were of other soldiers,[34] as depicted in *In the Valley of Elah*. Unfortunately, Haggis's film does not provide enough information to determine whether the brutality of the murder was due to the felon status of the soldiers, their psychological trauma from combat, or revenge for a deed committed against them. What made the killing of Jones's son so horrific was the complete lack of remorse afterward. The fact is that behavioral motivations are complex and often difficult to sort out. Take the case of Maj. Nidal Hasan, a Muslim, who went on a shooting rampage at Fort Hood, Texas, killing 13 soldiers and wounding dozens more. The motivation behind the attack stimulated plenty of media speculation.[35]

The problem with recruiting felons and persons with behavioral problems as soldiers is their unpredictability. In that sense, they can become "walking time bombs" ready to explode at any moment, often without provocation. That likelihood is not totally without merit. During the Korean War, President Eisenhower instituted a policy of shipping so-called "bad boys" directly from the stockade to Korea, based on the reasoning that if these guys were intent on fighting and brawling, then they might as well take out their aggression on the North Koreans and the Chinese. The author recalls a night in his tent south of Seoul when one of these "stockade boys" went berserk. Fortunately, no harm was done, but with weapons readily at hand, a potential killing was not out of the question. At another time during the author's tour of duty, some of these "stockade boys," joined by a few others, plotted to kill a company officer. Although the attempt failed, it reinforced concerns about the government's policy because, in combat, the individual soldier relies upon the support of his buddies to stay alive. Hollywood notwithstanding, survival, rather than flag and country, is the main objective of the ordinary soldier.

Two 2009 films, *Taking Chance* and *The Messenger*, confront the onerous military task of accompanying the dead home and delivering notification to the next of kin. In the wake of the nightly TV images of body bags being loaded onto helicopters, the Bush administration sought to diffuse public criticism of the Afghanistan-Iraq wars by hiding coffins containing dead soldiers in unmarked cardboard cartons aboard commercial passenger flights. Jim Sheeler's book *Final Salute* describes scenes of horrified plane passengers peering down from their cabin windows before take-off from Reno-Tahoe International Airport to witness marine honor guards preparing the flags to lay on the coffins of their fallen comrades.[36] HBO Films tried to re-create this piece of government deception in *Taking Chance*, a film based on the experience of Marine Lt. Colonel Michael Strobl (Kevin Bacon). Strobl is doing desk work stateside and, despite being a family man, regrets not having seen combat. Consequently, when Chance Phelps, an enlisted soldier from his hometown is killed, Strobl volunteers to accompany the body, an unusual request from an officer. The film proceeds to detail each step of the process, from body preparation at Dover Air Force Base to the commercial flight home for burial. Government regulation 638-2 describes the process for the "Care and Disposition of Remains and Disposition of Personal Effects" and runs some 147 pages.[37] A scene that portrays one segment of the government regulation occurs at the airport when the plane lands and the casket is unloaded onto the conveyor belt. Strobl, in dress uniform and at attention, stands at salute as the casket is loaded onto the waiting hearse. The camera then spans to the plane to show the sadness on the faces of the onlooking passengers. *Taking Chance* personalizes the war and makes it visible to those at home. Strobl is ordered by his superiors not to provide Phelps' family with the details and the circumstances of their son's death, but to simply present the personal effects to the family. In a gut-wrenching scene, Strobl hands these over—dog tags, a watch, a medal, and a wooden cross—and the viewer is left to wonder: is this all that remains of a life? The televising of *Taking Chance* coincided with the Obama administration's reversal of the Bush policy to prohibit media coverage of the coffins of military soldiers arriving from Afghanistan and Iraq. The present policy now leaves that decision to the families of the deceased.[38]

*The Messenger* covers similar ground, but from a different perspective. Captain Tony Stone (Woody Harrelson) and his partner, Sgt. Will Montgomery (Ben Foster), have one of the toughest jobs in the military: they are officially known as the "Casualty Notification Officers" and have the task of informing the next of kin of the death of a loved one. Stone is a recovering alcoholic and Montgomery is recovering from wounds suffered in an explosion that killed most of his squad. To add to his pain, Montgomery discovers that his girlfriend is set to marry someone else. These two psychologically damaged soldiers are the most unlikely persons to provide comfort to the families of the deceased. In fact, the military cautions them that this is not part of their job. Like Lt. Colonel Mike Strobl in *Taking Chance*, their orders are to meet with the next of kin, deliver the personal effects, and dispassionately relate the government's gratitude and condolences. Sometimes the news is received with abuse, other times with howls of pain and anguish. Occasionally, the messengers are greeted with silence or with compassion for the work they have to do. In one particularly upsetting scene, Montgomery has the task of informing a distraught father that his only son is dead. The father (Steve Buscemi) is so angry and outraged that he spits in Montgomery's face and then walks away. This understated film conveys the harsh realities of warfare and, in so doing, a message against wars of any kind.

Kathryn Bigelow's Oscar-winning film, *The Hurt Locker*, is a harrowing war thriller about an army unit whose job it is to detect, defuse—and in some cases, detonate—the IEDs that appear to be everywhere on the streets of Baghdad and the surrounding desert. The film focuses on one three-man team that works in the "kill zone"—the term for the bomb area. Its leader is Staff Sgt. Will James (Jeremy Renner), a fearless, methodical, but reckless specialist. The other two squad members are Eldridge (Brian Geraghty), a frightened and confused young soldier, and the experienced Sgt. Sanborn (Anthony Mackie), a professional soldier who follows procedure as the surest way to stay alive. Except for one combat scene in the desert, Bigelow films her soldiers in close, tight quarters so as to force the audience to feel the suspense and anxiety of the job. Can the reader imagine doing this work; not knowing whether that abandoned car is empty or filled with explosives? Never to be certain that an Iraqi man with a cell phone near the bomb site is placing a call or using it as a detonating device? Not sure whether the Iraqis watching from nearby windows and rooftops are merely curious bystanders or bombers assessing their work? Imagine the emotional stress of going to work every day and being subjected to the unpredictability of those around you? When Sgt. James's commanding officer asks him how he decides the best way to defuse a bomb, James matter-of-factly replies: "The way you don't die, sir." *The Hurt Locker* is neither a conventional combat film nor a polemic. Rather it is an examination of soldiers doing a dangerous, but necessary, job without fanfare or heroics. Despite favorable reviews, *The Hurt Locker* had difficulty in attracting an audience. It was first marketed in limited release and later opened at the movie chains, yet it grossed only $17 million.[39]

## Drawing Down: The Residual Afghanistan-Iraq War Films, 2010-2012

Director Paul Greengrass and actor Matt Damon teamed up to make *Green Zone* (2010), a film that looks as though it was made earlier but put on the shelf for later release. Damon is a chief warrant officer sent to Baghdad to search for Saddam Hussein's hidden cache of WMDs. Once Damon discovers he has been duped, in fact there were no WMDs to be found, the storyline evolves into another action-thriller conspiracy plot, with the U.S. government and the CIA involved in the cover-up. At that point, Greengrass uses firefights and explosions to keep viewers interested. Could this film have been completed in, say, 2004, but kept on the shelf for political reasons?

In the same year that *Green Zone* was released, directors Tim Hetherington and Sebastian Junger released their documentary, *Restrepo*, about the members of a platoon engaged in the building and maintaining of a U.S. outpost in the deadly Korengal Valley in Afghanistan. Hetherington and Junger spent the entire 2007 year embedded with the men of Battle Company 2nd of the 503rd Infantry Regiment as the soldiers fought the Taliban, did chores, and tried to relax. *Restrepo* is unique because there is no commentary and no interviews with the 15-man outfit that defends this isolated outpost. There are no heroics, no embellished action scenes, only daily boredom and the eternal wait for the next attack by an unseen Taliban. This is the real face of war in Afghanistan and Iraq. What the filmmakers have done is to allow the audience to experience what life is like in this godforsaken place where the soldiers are under daily threat of fire from an invisible enemy. Three years after the filmmakers left, the U.S. withdrew from Restrepo. The men named the outpost in honor of their medic who had been killed. Unlike *Green Zone*, *Restrepo* is the real deal and delivers a punch to the gut that no fictionalized film can duplicate.

Figure 10.1. The Hunt for Osama bin Laden in *Zero Dark Thirty*, 2012. Reprinted with permission, Columbia Pictures/Photofest

## Case Study: *Zero Dark Thirty*

Is there anyone left in the U.S. who still believes in the truth of that presidential pronouncement that "America does not torture?" Apparently not, because the fuss caused by director Kathryn Bigelow's *Zero Dark Thirty* (2012) was not about denying the use of torture by U.S. military to extract information but whether the film represented such activities as justifiable. *Zero Dark Thirty* details the CIA's decade-long hunt for Osama bin Laden, who masterminded the 9/11 terrorist attacks, and implies that it was the application of torture that led the U.S. to the Abbottabad compound in Pakistan where Navy SEALs found and killed bin Laden.

*Zero Dark Thirty*, which received five Oscar nominations, but won only one award, has been criticized for three content issues: first, for exaggerating the role of the female agent Maya (played by Jessica Chastain) in bin Laden's capture. The criticism is partially warranted. Mark Boal, the film's screenwriter, admitted that the Maya character, based on an actual CIA operative, was dramatically embellished. Actually Boal's screenplay combined material from the SEAL Team Six memoir *No Easy Day* and interviews with the team's members and CIA staff, who verified that a female agent was among the intelligence operatives involved in the hunt. When questioned about Maya, Boal responded that the film was fiction, although based on historical research.[40] Another minor criticism was raised by Republicans, because they felt that the movie served to enhance the stature of the Obama administration (the president was on screen for only 30 seconds).

But the complaint that caused most of the controversy centered around the use of various torture techniques for intelligence gathering, as the film implies that bin Laden's location was secured through the use of "enhanced interrogation techniques"(EITs). The assertion received an immediate denial from the CIA, which claimed that bin Laden was found by the use of "multiple streams of intelligence."[41] The CIA statement was mild compared to the ire of three members of the Senate Intelligence Committee Dianne Feinstein, John McCain and Carl Levin, who forwarded their objections to Sony Pictures on the grounds that the film implied that intelligence derived from the use of torture led eventually to bin Laden's compound. Sony was further advised that the Senate committee would open an investigation into the film's facts and the filmmakers' association with the CIA.[42] While Bigelow and Boal continued to deny they were given access to classified information, they received support from MPAA President Christopher Dodd.[43] Both conservative and liberal media sources joined the controversy. A *Wall Street Journal* editorial called Senators Feinstein, McCain, and Levin "censors," whose letters to Sony intimidated the Academy into denying Bigelow a nomination for best director and denying *Zero Dark Thirty* an Oscar for best picture. The *Journal* noted that once the Oscar ceremony was over, Senator Feinstein ended her investigation.[44] At the opposite end of the political spectrum, on the *Common Dreams* website, New York University Professor Karen Greenberg argued that the film provided support for the Bush administration view that torture is an effective tool in the war on terror. She further noted that torture is illegal under American and international law, and that President Obama had decided not to bring charges against members of the previous administration for its use.[45]

Although torture violates international law, it is universally practiced. Its use by Western democracies that support human rights is particularly egregious. But what precisely constitutes torture? Sleep and food deprivation? Being placed in isolation cells and in total darkness for days? Or does it have to be physical abuse? In the film, the emphasis is on the physical abuse as the CIA seeks to secure information on planned terror attacks. During the interrogation, the U.S. agent repeatedly tells the prisoner, "Tell me the truth or I will hurt you." As I watched the film, I kept asking myself: how does the agent know if the prisoner is lying? The agent must have had previous information that either corroborates or contradicts what he was being told. But the logic here is circular because it rests on the reliability of previous information which may also have been gathered through torture. In American constitutional law, coerced confessions are not admissible as evidence on the same unreliability basis.[46] Why would the information be more reliable coming from an enemy source? If looked at in this way, torture as an initial step probably does not work. And its continuous use over long periods of time may bring forth totally useless information in order to stop the pain. At some point in the process, the prisoner may give the interrogator something of value or die during the torturing. Because *Zero Dark Thirty* opens with torture and closes with the capture and death of bin Laden, it could lead audiences to assume a cause and effect relationship where none existed.

With the exception of *Zero Dark Thirty*, which had a domestic gross of $95 million,[47] more than twice its budget, the remaining films dealing with American involvement in Afghanistan and Iraq were box office losers or disappointments. That is not surprising, for even well-crafted films that are perceived as conveying political messages of one kind or another, ideological in content or delivering a political science lecture to the audience, are high-risk ventures destined to underperform at the box office. Not all film scholars would concur with this assessment, though the evidence for it is substantial.[48] Of course, there are exceptions like *Fahrenheit 9/11*, but the film industry considers these to be anomalies.

Another factor to consider in the poor performance of these films is related to their time of distribution. By 2007 the American public had grown tired of these wars, impatient with their apparent endlessness and their cost in human life and economic resources, and had already "tuned out" their depiction on CNN. Unlike Vietnam, the soldiers fighting in the Afghanistan-Iraq wars are volunteers and National Guardsmen. Were there a draft in place as in the 1960–70s, public reaction to these wars would be much different. It would have been interesting to see how these Afghanistan-Iraq war films would have done financially had the studios and filmmakers waited another decade to release them. But regardless of the merits or flaws of the films discussed, releasing them during 2007–09 proved to be a major marketing mistake. Did the film industry think that the American public would pay to see a film like *Rendition* that reminded them of the torture and mistreatment of prisoners at Abu Ghraib and Guantanamo Bay? Likewise, did the makers of *Redacted* believe that portraying the American military as rapists and murderers, without one bit of remorse, would encourage citizens to rush to the theater? And was it a bit too close to home for Americans to watch a film like *Lions for Lambs*, in which Tom Cruise, playing a gung-ho U.S. senator with presidential ambitions, uses the occasion of the war in Afghanistan to advance his political career? Even critically praised films like *In the Valley of Elah*, *Stop-Loss*, and *The Hurt Locker* failed to catch on with the American public. The sad moral here is that Americans do not like bad news, even less if they have to pay for it.

## Obama's Non-Intervention Gambit

If we were to draw a spectrum of American wars, starting with the War of Independence, we would discover that the U.S has been involved in wars, minor and major, about every quarter of a century. Certainly, that would be the case since WWII, when it seems the U.S. tumbled into one war after another. No sooner had the country reverted back to peacetime than it became involved in the Korean conflict. A few years later, the U.S. virtually supplanted the French in Indochina. The ensuing Vietnam War lasted almost a decade and the peaceful interlude afterward was short-lived, as the invasion of Kuwait by Saddam Hussein saw the U.S. join a military contingent aimed at driving the invading Iraqis back across their own border. The attempt to oust Hussein from the Persian Gulf was left to another day. Thereafter, American forces were deployed around the world in such places as Kosovo and Yemen (after the USS *Cole* was bombed), but these were relatively minor engagements until the 9/11 terrorist attacks on American soil.

Since then the U.S. has intervened in foreign countries at least a dozen times. A majority of these were either minor engagements or situations where American aid was largely advisory, such as training the Philippine military in their fight against rebels in Mindanao in 2002 or providing U.S. Special Forces as advisers to Ethiopia before it invaded Somalia in 2006 to topple the Islamist government. None, however, compared to the Bush administration's interventions in Afghanistan to overthrow the Taliban and the preemptive invasion in Iraq to bring down Saddam Hussein. In contrast, during his first term President Obama instituted a draw-down plan that left only advisors and a small military contingency remaining in Iraq after American troops withdrew in 2011.

When mass protests in Tunisia and Egypt spread across North Africa into Libya, the political pundits in the U.S. wondered how the president would react to the "Arab Spring" movement. Adopting a wait-and-see attitude, Obama spoke encouragingly of the pro-democracy movements, but offered no substantive assistance. Only when the protestors in Tunisia and Egypt brought down their respective governments did Obama extend recognition to them. When these populist movements stretched into Libya, external pressure was exerted on the U.S. to do more than recognize the rebels who were fighting against Muammar al-Qaddafi, but to provide military support as well. Yet the Obama administration did neither. Instead the U.S. told Qaddafi that it was time for him to step down. When the dictator refused to abdicate, resorting instead to military force against his own people, the Arab League requested international intervention. In response, the U.N. Security Council established a "no-fly zone" over the country to protect civilian lives. At this point, the

Obama administration responded by cutting off funding to the Libyan government, freezing its assets in the U.S., and taking a leadership position in a coalition to oust Qaddafi through air and missile strikes against his supporters. Once this intervention was successful, the U.S. turned over control of the operation to its NATO partners. As a result, within two months, Qaddafi was dead and his regime destroyed—all without the loss of one American life and at the modest cost of several billion.[49]

In the debates leading up to the 2012 presidential election, Mitt Romney, the Republican challenger, talked like a hawk but it was Obama who, despite his non-intervention policies, had Osama bin Laden found and killed. Did this indicate a more aggressive foreign policy should Obama win a second term? Or had the political pundits misread his toughness?

Prior to Election Day, political analyst and former CIA intelligence officer Michael Scheuer wrote on his website: "No matter who wins, the next president will—without question—be an interventionist war president."[50] Scheuer supported his assessment by citing the following evidence:

- First, despite full-fledged wars in Afghanistan and Iraq, Islamic militants remain a potent force to strike at America as they did in Benghazi, Libya, where they killed the U.S. ambassador and three of his staff;
- Second, Islamic militants remain entrenched in Yemen, North Caucasus, Northern Africa, and other sections of the continent; and
- Third, once American forces depart from Afghanistan at the end of 2014, both Afghanistan and Iraq will stand on their own despite being characterized as unstable, weak, and vulnerable governments that have yet to unite their countries and win public support.[51]

Contrary to Scheuer's predictions, President Obama so far has refrained from pursuing a more aggressive interventionist course. In the early months of his second term, he has avoided providing more than moral support and minimal assistance, mostly of the technological-communication kind, to the French fighting Islamic militants in and around Mali and to the Syrian Coalition in its struggle against President Bashar al-Assad.[52]

Still, has Scheuer raised a valid point? Did it really matter whether Romney or Obama won in 2012, since American leadership of the Western world requires it to strike against terrorism and insurgency wherever it occurs? The answer, according to Max Boot, military historian and senior fellow at the Council on Foreign Relations, is that it depends on whether one views terrorists and insurgents as guerrillas rather than as conventional war enemies.[53] Boot's thesis is that guerrilla wars have a long historical record, dating back to the first century when the Jewish population revolted against the Romans. He considers the American Revolution to be a guerrilla war or insurgency as well, but admits that such wars have become even more successful, especially since the end of WWII. Boot identifies such wars of insurgency as having the following characteristics: there are neither front lines nor soldiers in uniform; their target is the civilian population, with the objective to destroy morale so as to encourage pressure on their government to negotiate; and insurgency tactics usually include sneak attacks and hit-and-run strikes because the insurgents are too weak to compete with their stronger adversaries. Insurgencies such as in Vietnam and recent interventions elsewhere are not traditional wars and, according to Boot, to treat them as such is a mistake. But, then, how should the U.S. and its NATO allies have responded to the situations in Afghanistan and Iraq? Instead of looking for a quick victory through deployment of massive troops, Boot would have counseled a long-term military plan to allow for the civilian population to come to accept the inevitable frustrations inherent in drawn-out wars. Time, Boot advises, is against insurgencies despite their more recent successes.

There is no doubt that Boot's analysis is a critique of U.S. interventions in Afghanistan and Iraq, where the military strategy aimed for a quick victory. Certainly, this was the objective of the Bush administration, particularly in its March 2003 preemptive invasion of Iraq while the UN search for WMDs was still in progress. The Obama administration, especially after the surge in 2007, with the military under the leadership of commander David Petraeus, instituted a counterinsurgency doctrine that sought to punish the militants while it attempted to protect the civilian population and win support for the American mission.[54] This shift in military strategy eventually enabled the U.S. to withdraw its troops from Iraq.

By the end of 2014, Afghanistan supposedly will join Iraq as American allies in the struggle against the Taliban, al Qaeda, and global terrorism. Will they be able to stand alone against the insurgents in their respective countries while instituting the kind of reforms required to sustain democratic government? Will Pakistan, another U.S. ally in the region, join forces with the governments of Afghanistan and Iraq in an economic and political partnership to strengthen democratic institutions and win popular support against the extremists within? It is too early to write the last chapter in the war against terrorism and radical militancy that escalated after the 9/11 attacks. Nor can we confidently articulate what lessons, if any, the U.S. and its Western allies have learned from these costly interventions.

Maybe it would be well to recall the judgment expressed by Hollywood Ten writer Dalton Trumbo, who, commenting on the consequences of HUAC's investigation into communism in the film industry after World War II, described the hearings as having no victors, only victims. Quite possibly Hollywood, remembering the dark days of the Red Scare, sought to purge past ghosts and demonstrate its newfound courage by aggressively portraying the wars in Afghanistan and Iraq in more critical and questioning films, despite their poor reception at the box office. *Zero Dark Thirty* remains the lone exception to the string of Afghanistan-Iraq war films that disappointed at the box office. Alternatively, it is possible that these failures signify a prelude to the dance of death for war films in Hollywood.

## Is This the End of Hollywood War Films?

War films suffer from the same fate as "political films," namely, there is little agreement as to what content should be included in the genre. According to the Library of Congress, the American Film Institute lists 1,195 titles as war films while the Internet Movie Database, using a broader definition of war, cites 1,729 feature films, beginning with *The Birth of a Nation*. For our purposes, it is enough to state that Hollywood has released thousands of war films since 1915, with the greatest number released during World War II.[55]

Hollywood war films are divided into two groups: those released through WWII were overwhelmingly positive and supportive of the American cause; those released since Vietnam, however, have been critical of American intervention, the U.S. military establishment, and even those fighting the wars, *The Green Berets* notwithstanding. Moreover, with a few exceptions like Steven Spielberg's *Saving Private Ryan*, a majority of post-WWII war films were box office disappointments.

Why this turnabout in the film industry? There are several possibilities. One is that the wars after WWII were conflicts without clear goals and were media-characterized as ambivalent (Korea) or controversial (Vietnam), and the public was either indifferent to the struggle or the conflict caused such divisiveness that a resistance movement developed to oppose it. Another is that a post-Vietnam generation has been reluctant to accept an unconditional commitment to American interventions abroad, often challenging the wisdom and necessity of military involvement. U.S. filmgoers may also have become exhausted with the war genre when the bad news coming out of Afghanistan and Iraq overlapped with the economic downturn.

Another explanation lies in the demographics. There are 1.2 million World War II veterans still living but they are dying at the rate of 18,000 each month.[56] Korean War veterans, meanwhile, are in their seventies and eighties. It is just a matter of time, possibly as soon as a decade, when these two groups will fade into American history, leaving the Vietnam veterans as the remaining military draftees. With the passing of these old soldiers, the concept of war becomes much less personal.

Another factor to consider is the absence of real heroes in post-World War II war films. This statement excludes a few films like *Saving Private Ryan* that portray fictional accounts of real heroes. The lack of similar stories today raises the question of why Hollywood has abandoned the cinematic heroes of earlier wars like Sgt. York (WWI) and Audie Murphy (WWII), ordinary men who performed extraordinary feats during wartime. The straightforward answer is that there have been very few real heroes since World War II, as measured by the number of Congressional Medals of Honor awarded. The prestigious Medal of Honor dates to 1861 and is the highest honor awarded by the American government. The U.S. Congress awarded 464 medals of honor during World War II, 133 during the Korean War, and 248 during Vietnam, but less than a dozen since the start of military operations in Afghanistan and Iraq.[57] Of course, the wars are different in scale; still the number awarded during the recent wars is rather low. Might the reason for the scarcity of contemporary war heroes have something to do with the ambiguous military and political goals and the corresponding ambivalence of the public regarding the wisdom and motivation behind their undertaking? It is a formidable feat, no doubt, to produce real heroes under such circumstances.

Finally, audience perception of war films as political films that contain propaganda or overt government messages is at odds with the conventional wisdom that Americans go to the movies to be "entertained" rather than be subjected to a public lecture or an unwanted history lesson. It is a sad but true fact that contemporary American film audiences prefer fantasy over realism, special effects over interesting stories, and visual imagery over the spoken word. Thus the declining interest in war films over the past 70 years signifies that films of this genre will become scarcer in the future. Looking back, film historians may identify the commercial failure of the Afghanistan-Iraq war movies as the death knell of the Hollywood war film.

Chapter 11

# Hollywood Confronts Nuclear War and Global Terrorism

"The discovery of nuclear chain reactions need not bring about the destruction of mankind any more than the discovery of matches. We only must do everything in our power to safeguard against its abuses."
—Albert Einstein

"Just as we stood for freedom in the 20th century, we must stand together for the right of people everywhere to live free from fear in the 21st century.... As a nuclear power—as the only nuclear power to have used a nuclear weapon—the United States has a moral responsibility to act."
—President Barack Obama, April 2009

*An exchange of dialogue between a California couple awakened from a sound sleep:*

Wife: "What's that?"
Husband: "Oh, go back to sleep. It's only an atomic bomb test."
Wife: "All right. I was afraid one of the kids had fallen out of bed." 1952 issue of the *Reader's Digest*

In accepting the Nobel Prize, French philosopher and World War II resistance fighter Albert Camus referred to the 20th century as the "century of fear" due to the new weapon of mass destruction—the atom bomb. August 6, 1945, is often cited as the beginning of the nuclear age when "Little Boy," the code name for the uranium bomb, was dropped on Hiroshima. Three days later, "Fat Man," the plutonium bomb, leveled Nagasaki and persuaded the Japanese to surrender, thus bringing World War II to its conclusion.

The atomic era actually began three years earlier when President Roosevelt gave approval in 1942 to the Manhattan Project, the code name assigned to the secret development of the atom bomb. As it turned out, the code name could not have been more appropriate, since the first headquarters of the nation's effort to build such a bomb was located in the borough of Manhattan, in New York City, where scientists at Columbia University used a cyclotron machine to split the atom and conduct similar experiments. In fact, there were 10 sites in Manhattan that were involved in some aspect of the Manhattan Project.[1]

The atomic project brought together a number of European émigrés and American scientists to produce the bomb. It was a cold December day in 1942 at the University of Chicago when Enrico Fermi and his team of scientists achieved the first sustained nuclear reaction, which altered the course of human history. The initial atomic chain reaction lasted only a few minutes but the demonstration showed enough promise to warrant the movement of the Manhattan Project to Los Alamos, New Mexico, where it was placed under the leadership of General Leslie Groves and physicist J. Robert Oppenheimer to head the scientific team. Under Groves' command, the U.S. Army appropriated over 54,000 acres and built an entire self-contained community and military compound. To build the bomb cost more than $2 billion, and the coordination of plants that stretched from Tennessee to New Mexico involved some 200,000 workers who were under strict orders to keep their work secret.[2] Secrecy was so tight that all incoming mail was sent to the same Post Office box number, 1663 Santa Fe, New Mexico, and all incoming and outgoing mail was censored by the government.[3]

Work on the bomb was anything but serene. A difference of opinion developed between physicist Edward Teller, who advocated building a hydrogen bomb, and Oppenheimer, who thought that an atomic bomb had to be built first. Although security was supposed to be tight, declassified U.S. documents and personal recollections by Russian scientists after the collapse of the Soviet Union confirmed that spies had infiltrated Los Alamos. These included Klaus Fuchs and David Greenglass, who passed on atomic secrets to the Soviets.[4] A sleeper agent named Abram Koval, who worked for the Soviets, also passed on information from the atomic laboratories at Oak Ridge, Tennessee, that eventually landed in the hands of Fuchs at Los Alamos, who sent it on to the Russians. How important was Koval to the Soviets? When Russian President Vladimir Putin posthumously awarded Koval the highest Soviet honor for his spying, he revealed that "his work helped speed up considerably the time it took for the Soviet Union to develop an atomic bomb of its own."[5] Clearly there was more ideological sympathy for the Soviets at Los Alamos than anyone suspected at the time.

While the atomic lab was situated at Los Alamos, the actual testing ground, code name "Trinity," was set 60 miles south at the White Sands Missile Range near Alamogordo. There, on July 16, 1945, a successful nuclear bomb was detonated in the New Mexico desert as a prelude to Hiroshima. As Paul Boyer observes in his book *By the Bomb's Early Light*, once news of the bomb became public, people realized that life on earth would never be the same.[6] The bomb's devastation far exceeded the scientific estimates. Oppenheimer, for example, thought the death toll in Japan would be under 20,000. The actual figures proved to be much higher: 80,000 people were killed immediately at Hiroshima, with another 60,000 deaths caused by radiation and other illnesses attributed to the fallout. At Nagasaki, 35,000 died immediately and another 35,000 died from the effects of the blast.[7]

While these statistics are appalling, the fatalities from the atomic bombs rank 10th among the worst accidents and disasters in human history, far below the 75 million deaths attributed to the bubonic plague (Black Death) in 14th century Eurasia, the 35 million Chinese slaughtered during the Mongol genocide in the same century, and the 21 million deaths attributed to the 1918 worldwide influenza epidemic. And for comparison purposes, the deaths attributed to the dropping of nuclear bombs on Hiroshima and Nagasaki are slightly less than the 225,000 deaths caused by the Indian Ocean tsunami in 2004. Another consideration, often forgotten, is that the two bombs persuaded the Japanese government to surrender, possibly saving a million Allied and Japanese lives that would have been lost in an invasion of the islands.[8]

Statistics alone do not define the aftermath of the atomic blasts. Boyer cites the dropping of the atom bombs as a benchmark for the 20th century, setting off what came to be identified in the popular culture as the "nuclear age," an era marked by both public apprehension and post-World War II consumer euphoria. Once the Soviets acquired the bomb, however, the world was divided into East (Soviet) and West (led by the U.S.) blocs, each suspicious of the other. For more than 40 years, these ideological blocs kept the rest of the world on edge, fearing that at any moment the "cold war" of words would turn into a hot war of nuclear destruction.

## Films of the Nuclear Age

Hollywood was quick to exploit the nuclear technology as a base for its post-WW II screen plots. Within 18 months after "Little Boy" was dropped on Hiroshima, MGM studios released *The Beginning or the End?*, a docudrama on the making and deployment of the first atom bomb.[9] But the 1947 film was an artistic disaster and a box office failure. The entire project was plagued from the beginning by internal and external squabbles, several revisions, and the final version that landed on the screen was a blend of fact and fiction. The whole process may have discouraged other studios from dealing with the subject in a scientific or historical approach.

Nevertheless, Hollywood tackled the subject again in 1952 with another A-bomb film, *Above and Beyond*. The film focused on Colonel Paul Tibbets, the pilot of the *Enola Gay*, the plane that dropped the bomb on Hiroshima.[10] *Above and Beyond* became a personal story about Tibbets, his family, and the events leading up to the August 6th bombing. Hollywood did not produce another film on the subject until the 1980s, when it released *The Manhattan Project* (1986) and *Fat Man and Little Boy* (1989). Neither film made much of an impact, even though the latter's political message questioned the wisdom of using the bomb. Actor Paul Newman, a committed antinuclear activist, accepted the role of General Groves. His concern about playing Groves was justified, as the film directed most of the blame on the military rather than the scientific community. While the film accurately depicts the team of scientists working to develop the bomb, there were a number of serious omissions: it was Groves who manipulated Oppenheimer to remain on the project and bring it to a successful conclusion; both Klaus Fuchs and David Greenglass (Julius Rosenberg's brother-in-law) were Los Alamos employees who passed information on the bomb to the Soviets; Rosenberg and his wife Ethel were convicted on spy charges and later executed; and while Oppenheimer lost his security clearance during the Red Scare hysteria of the 1950s due to his past communist association and his having a Russian mistress, General Groves' loyalty was never questioned, even though he was responsible for security at the Los Alamos facility. *Fat Man and Little Boy* (1989) placed the blame for the bomb entirely on the military, even though it was the scientists who urged Roosevelt to support the project lest the Germans develop the weapon before the U.S. The urgency felt by the scientists, some of whom were émigrés from fascism, made the Manhattan Project a moral as well as a scientific challenge.[11] Both of these films were commercial failures, reinforcing the conventional wisdom that the public goes to the movies to be entertained, not informed. Their failure also signaled that the American public had lost interest in the topic. Certainly by the mid-1980s, liberals in the film industry had deserted the nuclear disarmament/nuclear freeze campaign in favor of AIDS research and environmental causes.[12]

In the immediate aftermath of the Japan bombings, however, Hollywood latched onto nuclear technology as a new source of numerous dramatic plots. The Nazis and Japanese were replaced by the new Cold War enemies—the Soviets and communist agents—and the scripts converted weapon blueprints and war plans into spies and atomic secrets. One filmography on nuclear movies lists some 874 films released in 36 countries, with almost two-thirds having been produced in the U.S.[13] Their themes involved nuclear war, nuclear accidents, or the after-effects of an atomic blast, including trying to survive the radioactive fallout from a nuclear bomb. Not surprisingly, most of these films were distributed after the end of World War II, with more than one-third released in the 1980s. Included in the filmography are a dozen *Godzilla* movies and various clones of the "atomic monster" variety in films that dealt with annihilation and world destruction. At least a dozen of the James Bond films employed scenarios of nuclear technology as well, including conflicts over possession of nuclear weapons and efforts to secure the materials to manufacture nuclear armaments.[14]

The new technology also proved a script bonanza for the weekly serials, which continued to be a staple of the Saturday afternoon matinee well into the 1950s. At least a dozen serials, some with exotic titles like *Zombies of the Stratosphere* and *Radar Men from the Moon*, included the atom bomb or nuclear weaponry in their narratives. Naturally, a popular Saturday serial favorite like *Superman* did not ignore the potential scripts that could be culled from the new scientific discoveries. For instance, in 1950, Columbia Pictures produced 15 episodes of the serial *Atom Man versus Superman*, in which the comic book hero saves Metropolis from an arsenal of atomic weapons and other gadgets of the space age, such as thermal guns, flying saucers, and stratospheric vehicles. Earlier, Universal-International had released a 13-week serial entitled *Lost City of the Jungle* (1946), in which an FBI agent battled a villain who had discovered a metal in the lost city that could be used against atomic bombs and who planned to sell the discovery to the highest bidder. Some of the serial villains speak with a German accent, an obvious reference to Nazi war criminals not prosecuted at Nuremberg and other war crimes trials. While the crude "special effects" would not fool any contemporary youngster with access to a computer, still, nuclear technology provided Hollywood writers with an opportunity to recycle the old formulas by merely substituting the A-bomb for previous weaponry.

The decline of the Saturday matinee serials did not deter the studios from producing feature films about the atomic age well into the 1980s since the subject had the potential to be recycled—in the aforementioned Bond movies, for example, or in Cold War action thrillers like *The Fourth Protocol* (1987) and *The Package* (1989), where control of the new technology serves as the source for the plot.

Regardless, the hundreds of movies that comprise a nuclear film genre can be topically subdivided into five distinct categories:

- science-fiction/horror films, where nuclear power has released an assortment of beasts on the civilized world
- nuclear war/attack films, where warring governments unleash disaster on the world
- nuclear accident or disaster films, where human or mechanical error has caused a threat to both life and the environment
- nuclear survival films, where the world has been destroyed and those left alive after the blast or those who have survived the radioactive fallout struggle to remain alive, and
- nuclear terrorist films, where evil men (Russians, Arabs, Muslims) pose a serious threat to the rest of the world.

## Nuclear Age Science Fiction Films

The fifties has been characterized as a decade of paranoia and mass hysteria brought on by the creation of the atom bomb and the subsequent arms race competition between East and West that typified the Cold War. The science fiction films of this era reflected the national mood at the time, since Hollywood had made few such films before 1950.[15] Many of these science fiction films were low-budget B-flicks, "monster" movies where atomic testing or radioactivity produces mutations like giant grasshoppers, huge ants and overgrown spiders, or where the atomic explosions awaken long-buried beasts that proceed to wreak havoc on the human population.[16] What these films have in common is a presentment of what is possible when science and technology transcend the boundaries of humanity by manufacturing weapons of mass destruction. One of the earliest of this type was the 1951 film *The Thing*, featuring actor James Arness playing a carrot-topped creature that is defrosted as a result of nuclear testing. In order to survive, the creature apparently requires human blood. During the course of the film, "the Thing" creates carnage and mayhem on an Arctic military base as it searches for human victims.

But the best of the 1950s science fiction films is Don Siegel's *Invasion of the Body Snatchers* (1956), which became a cult classic because its ambiguous message about alien pods inhabiting sleeping bodies and transforming them into living robots could be interpreted in two ways: as a warning against communist infiltration and subsequent takeover of the U.S. from within, as Senator McCarthy predicted, or as a sign that the Red Scare of the fifties was in danger of converting the American people into a bunch of conforming, non-thinking sheep. *Body Snatchers* is among the few films that involved creatures from outer space or aliens from another planet. More often the evil forces came from below the earth or from under the sea in films with titles like *Them!* (1954), *Tarantula* (1955), *It Came from Beneath the Sea* (1955), and *The Beast from 20,000 Fathoms* (1953).

A few science fiction films of this period, such as *The Day the Earth Stood Still* (1951) and *It Came from Outer Space* (1953), feature aliens that are friendly creatures—in contrast to the harmful pods that take over human bodies in *Invasion of the Body Snatchers*. Klaatu (Michael Rennie), the alien leader in *The Day the Earth Stood Still*, has a powerful weapon of destruction (aka: an atom bomb) but comes to earth to further interplanetary peace. He is met, however, by government mistrust, public fear, and accusations of being a communist agent.[17] Shot by the police, Klaatu warns earth that unless it ceases its nuclear arms race, his planet will destroy it. Ray Bradbury wrote the script for *It Came from Outer Space*, another story about peace-loving aliens whose spacecraft crashes in the Arizona desert. At first misunderstood by the local townsfolk, the benign aliens and the local population come to a peaceful resolution. Regrettably, such serious science fiction films out of Hollywood were rare.

Nuclear War Films

A few films delivered apocalyptic visions of a nuclear holocaust brought on by scheming politicians, deranged military commanders, and public officials who misjudge their ability to control modern technology. What these films express is a view of the bomb as a catastrophic force with the capability to destroy the entire world. In this sense, these films present the same kind of negative "end of civilization" scenario as found in the earlier science fiction films. An initial entry in this category was Stanley Kramer's 1959 film, *On the Beach*, based on the Neville Shute novel. The film opens with an unidentified nuclear war resulting in the destruction of much of the world except for Australia, where the survivors await the inevitable sickness and death brought on by radioactive dust ("Black Rain") carried by the winds to the South Pacific. Kramer's film featured an all-star cast and was a major production, unlike the typical low-budget science fiction films. With the exception of one scene where the scientists and military blame each other for what has happened, the film presents a sanitized version of world extinction. While Kramer's film may have been intended as a warning to the nuclear powers that the next war would be the last for mankind, it never assigns responsibility for the bomb's deployment, nor does it depict the end of civilization in a horrific manner. Essentially, *On the Beach* is an old-fashioned romance, a love story involving married Gregory Peck, an American submarine commander, and Ava Gardner, the single woman he meets and falls in love with while his sub is stranded in Australia. *On the Beach* is no nuclear horror show, because it lacks even one scene of death or destruction. While Kramer's end message is for mankind to reform before it is too late, the dramatic impact of the final scene as the characters wait for the nuclear fallout to reach them is minimized because of the romanticized treatment that dominates the film. Here is a film about nuclear holocaust without pain or suffering. In light of the film's romanticism, why the Pentagon refused to provide Kramer with assistance on the film remains a mystery.[18]

Sidney Lumet's 1964 film, *Fail Safe*, concerns a limited nuclear war between the U.S. and the Soviets caused by a mechanical malfunction. The film could easily fit into the category of a nuclear accident, except that it focuses on the decision-making process by which political leaders control the damage inflicted by nuclear technology. The plot has the U.S. president (played by Henry Fonda) offering to give the Soviet premier permission to bomb New York City as a way to avoid World War III after an American plane breaks through the "fail-safe" security system and mistakenly drops a nuclear bomb on Moscow—a kind of tit-for-tat political arrangement. Lumet's film is a well-crafted exercise in presidential decision-making. Purposely confining the action of the film to three interior sets, Lumet wants the audience to concentrate on the president's dilemma, that is, risk total nuclear war or permit the Soviets to drop a bomb (unannounced) on a major American city. This may have been the only film during the Cold War where the audience was encouraged to cheer when the U.S. military shoots down its own planes.

Like *Fail Safe*, Stanley Kubrick's *Dr. Strangelove or: How I Learned to Stop Worrying and Love the Bomb*, is also about the inadequacies of mechanical safeguards, military control, and communication devices to prevent unauthorized preemptive nuclear strikes against a political enemy. Contrary to the serious drama presented in *Fail Safe*, Kubrick's 1964 film is a satirical comedy populated with exaggerated characters: a lunatic officer (General Jack D. Ripper) who is convinced the communists are destroying our "precious bodily fluids" through fluoridation of the country's water supply and orders an unauthorized nuclear strike against the Soviets; a right-wing cold war "nuke'em dead" chief of staff (General Buck Turgidson) who acts more like an ape than a human being; a presidential advisor (Dr. Strangelove) whose bionic arm cannot stop giving the Nazi salute; and a cowboy air force pilot (Major Kong) who straddles a nuclear bomb like a bronco as it descends on the Soviet Union while the soundtrack sings, "We'll meet again, don't know where, don't know when."

Kubrick took a serious suspense story, *Red Alert* by Peter George, and turned it into a black comedy about the nuclear apocalypse. He was denied assistance from the U.S. Air Force and shot the film in England, where he enjoyed greater artistic freedom. The result is a believable yet devastatingly funny film fantasy on how the world could end. There are many hilarious scenes in the film but one in particular stands out. It takes place in the American war room as the world teeters on the brink of atomic annihilation and the U.S. president tries valiantly to reach his Soviet counterpart, Dmitri, on the red phone hotline:

> Hello, Dmitri? Listen, I can't hear too well. Do you suppose you could turn the music down just a little? Oh, that's much better. Yes, fine. I can hear you now, Dmitri, clear and plain and coming through fine. I'm coming through fine too, eh? Good, then. Well, then, as you say, we're both coming through fine. Good. Well, it's good that you're fine and I'm fine. I agree with you. It's great to be fine. Now then, Dmitri, you know how we've always talked about the possibility of something going wrong with the bomb? The *bomb*, Dmitri. The *hydrogen bomb*. Well, now what happened, is, um, one of our base commanders, he had a sort of...well, he went a little funny in the head. You know, just a little *funny* and he went and did a silly thing. Well, I'll tell you what he did: He ordered his planes to attack your country. Well, let me finish, Dmitri. Let me finish, Dmitri. Well, listen, how do you think I feel about it? Can you imagine how I feel about it, Dmitri? Why do you think I'm calling you? Just to say hello? Of course, I like to speak to you. Of course, I like to say hello. Not now but anytime, Dmitri. I'm just calling up to tell you something terrible has happened. It's a friendly call, of course, it's a friendly call. Listen, if it wasn't friendly, you probably wouldn't have even got it.

Today, after the end of the Cold War and the dissolution of the old Soviet Union, the film's scenario may strike viewers as dated. But how far-fetched was the film in the 1960s? Political scientist Richard Ostrom maintains that what audiences considered hilarious were the very ideas and equipment that were most based on reality.[19] For example, loony General Ripper's paranoia over fluoridation as part of a Soviet plot to destroy the U.S. could be found in the literature of the right-wing John Birch Society that flourished in the country for more than two decades. And the Russians apparently explored the development of a Doomsday Machine that could destroy everything on earth, an idea based on a cobalt-thorium G bomb that was advanced by nuclear pioneer Leo Szilard. Additionally, Ostrom claims that a number of actual scientists could have been the inspiration for the reel Dr.

Strangelove, including Edward Teller, Werner Von Braun, and Herman Kahn, although consensus among film scholars is that Strangelove was a composite character.

Unfortunately the nuclear threat is greater today due to the proliferation of nuclear weapons and the addition of Third World powers to the nuclear arms race. The fact that India, Pakistan, Israel, and North Korea have the bomb and that Iran has refused to suspend its pursuit of developing nuclear power (as a prelude to nuclear weapons), increases rather than diminishes the prospects of a nuclear holocaust. If anything, Kubrick's film is more relevant today than when it was originally released in the 1960s.

At least five nuclear war scenarios are plausible, with one or two more likely than the rest.[20] One possibility is that terrorists will ignite a nuclear war. A second potential cause is a mechanical failure due to shoddy or improper equipment. Human error could lead to the catastrophe in a third scenario. A fourth likelihood would revolve around a misunderstanding or miscommunication among nuclear club members, such as the confrontation between the U.S. and the Soviets during the 1963 Cuban Missile Crisis. Finally, computer error could lead to a false alert that subsequently triggers a real nuclear reaction. Hollywood explored the latter scenario in the film *War Games* (1983). Based on the premise that machines are not infallible, the film's scenario envisions a foul-up in the attack-alert warning system, which mistakenly indicates that the U.S. is under attack, thereby precipitating a retaliatory strike. The film contends that a young computer hacker (Matthew Broderick) could bring the country to the brink of thermonuclear war through accidental access into the command room of the North American Radar Air Defense (NORAD). Although the premise may have seemed implausible in the 1980s, the subsequent revelation that in 2011 a British teenager was able to break into U.S. government files from his home computer makes *War Games* less entertaining and more frightening. At the film's end, the computer is asked to imagine the outcome of a nuclear war and determine a "game winner." The computer flashes out the words, "There is no winner."

The plot of *War Games* and similar films is predicated on the likelihood of nuclear war. But is nuclear war possible today or just a screenwriter's fantasy? The threat was taken seriously during the Cold War when the U.S. government prepared for just such an eventuality in its secret Outpost Mission project, which trained and prepared an elite corps of helicopter pilots to rescue the president from the White House in the event of a nuclear attack. Other so-called "doomsday" operations include saving important historical documents, such as the Declaration of Independence and priceless works of art from the National Gallery in Washington. The Outpost Mission operation consumed 20 years of government preparation in the event of a nuclear strike against the U.S.[21]

Nuclear Accidents

Ironically, Hollywood has made only two serious films about nuclear accidents, although a significant number of incidents and mishaps have actually occurred.[22] With the release of *The China Syndrome* (1979) and *Silkwood* (1983), an ecological dimension was added to the nuclear war-doomsday threat. *The China Syndrome* explored the issue of death at the hands of an invisible force—radiation. This perceptive film details an attempted cover-up of a nuclear accident at a California power plant. The plant manager (Jack Lemmon) realizes that the radiation leak could trigger a core meltdown—the "China Syndrome" of the film title—and tries to prevent the facility from reopening. He manages to take over the control room, which leads the nuclear power company to call in the authorities to subdue Lemmon, described as an emotionally disturbed employee. The power company hopes Lemmon will be killed in the confrontation. Lemmon's plea falls on deaf ears; instead the SWAT team breaks into the control room and shoots him. What Lemmon was trying to do was to prevent a core meltdown which would cause more people to be killed from the radiation leak than from any bomb blast. The film could not have been timelier, since it was released to theaters two weeks before the leak at the Three Mile Island nuclear plant near Harrisburg, Pennsylvania. In this case, life imitated art.

The film was even more prescient than first suspected. The situation in *The China Syndrome* was virtually duplicated in real life in the April 1986 accident at the Chernobyl nuclear plant in the Soviet Ukraine. The explosion at Chernobyl was due to a combination of faulty design and human error when workers were testing one of the four reactors. It appears that the test was improperly conducted, because the number of rods in place to maintain control was less than the minimum required to ensure safety. The result was a series of massive explosions that destroyed the reactor core and then blew apart the containment structure, which caused an estimated 6,000 deaths, numerous cases of thyroid cancer, birth deformities, and the contamination of some 16,000 square miles of fertile land in Ukraine, Belarus, and Russia. The health consequences of the Chernobyl explosions are likely to never be fully known. But data collected in 2000 indicated that 300,000 had died in Ukraine alone from radiation sickness, some 1.8 million people in the three republics remain contaminated, and 143,000 people in these areas had to be evacuated from their homes. It is estimated that some 17 million people have been affected to some degree from the Chernobyl accident.[23] Chernobyl remained the worst nuclear accident in the world until the 2011 Fukushima Daiichi disaster in Japan.[24]

The Fukushima Daiichi Nuclear Power Plant is located 180 miles north of Tokyo. On March 11, 2011, the eastern coast of Japan experienced a massive 9.0 magnitude earthquake, followed by a 14–15 magnitude tsunami that caused thousands of deaths and damage to three of the plant's four reactors. While the Japanese government evacuated the area and restricted air traffic, it underestimated the long-term environmental effects resulting from the accidents. Later reports indicated that future earthquakes could lead to more radiation fire than Chernobyl. Even more distressing was the news that tons of contaminated groundwater from the Fukushima nuclear plant, containing the strontium isotope, were emptying into the Pacific Ocean.[25]

At the other end of the nuclear holocaust spectrum, a comparatively minor incident is at the heart of Mike Nichols's 1983 film, *Silkwood*, based on a true story. Nichols's film is a reenactment of the real case of Karen Silkwood, a blue-collar worker in a plutonium plant who died under mysterious circumstances while on her way to deliver incriminating evidence to a *New York Times* reporter. Supposedly, the documents, which were never found, would verify the unsafe conditions at the Kerr-McGee factory where plutonium rods for nuclear weapons were being manufactured. Nichols's film is multidimensional, because at one level it is a mystery story that concerns itself with Silkwood's strange death. Did the corporate leaders at Kerr-McGee have Karen eliminated because she intended to blow the whistle on the dangerous working conditions at their plant? Or was her death in a car accident merely a coincidence? At another level, *Silkwood* serves as a reminder that nuclear age weapons are unlike conventional weapons and require greater care. It also demonstrates the importance of ensuring that the people who work with nuclear materials receive the highest level of protection and concern for their personal safety.

## Nuclear Survival Films

Another category of nuclear age films includes those that primarily concern themselves with survival after an atomic explosion or nuclear attack. These films focus on individuals or families who must adjust to an entirely different, and often hostile, environment and overcome new challenges in order to stay alive. In some ways, the origin of such films is traceable to stories featuring the settlement of the frontier or the taming of the wilderness, except that in westerns individuals had a chance against a human enemy or a wild beast. In nuclear films, death from a bomb explosion or radiation exposure is inescapable.

The nuclear survival film and its derivations proved to be a popular subject with the film studios, quite possibly because of their similarity to science fiction movies. The topic of nuclear survival is morbid and an unlikely source for commercial entertainment, but the plot variations of the subject are endless. Three such films—*Five* (1951), *Panic in Year Zero!* (1962), and *The World, the Flesh, and the Devil* (1959)—had optimistic endings. Two films, the made-for television *The Day After* (1983) and *Testament* (1983), were both more pessimistic and provided little comfort to viewers. Meanwhile, Roger Corman's B-film *The Last Woman on Earth* (1961) promised more intrigue and excitement in its title than it delivered on the screen.

The plots of *Five* and *The World* are similar. *Five* is the first survivor film of the nuclear age, and it and *The World* both take place in contained environments where the survivors, groups of five and three persons, respectively, each contain one woman. This fact is crucial to plot development because each film finds hope through the reproductive organs of the surviving female. Both flirt with the issue of sexuality and race but are too timid to pursue that subject with any conviction. Also, the two films present fairly romanticized versions of a post-holocaust world, one without horror, pain, or human suffering.

The location for director Roger Corman's film *The Last Woman on Earth* is Puerto Rico, and while the viewer is shown dead bodies lying in streets, inside cars, and on jungle ground, they are posed so peacefully as to suggest an afternoon siesta rather than a horrible death from nuclear radiation. Here the plot revolves around a married couple and the husband's lawyer (male), who survive the nuclear holocaust because they were deep-sea diving at the time of the blast. Once it is established that they are the sole survivors on the island, the film sinks to a formulaic romantic love triangle and is unintentionally funny. For example, after the trio has learned of their rather desperate situation, they return to their hotel rooms and very carefully pack all their nice suits and dresses as if preparing for a holiday rather than certain death.

*Panic in Year Zero!* is another variation on the nuclear survival film. Actor-director Ray Milland focuses on the struggle for survival of a single family fleeing Los Angeles after a nuclear attack. There are plenty of other survivors, and it is these people who pose more of a threat to this family than any nuclear bomb or radioactive material. Theirs is a conventional middle-class family that adopts Herbert Spencer's principle of "survival of the fittest."[26] In order to protect his family, the father (Milland) takes guns and ammunition from a hardware store and gasoline from a service station. When three young thugs assault the father, the son comes to his rescue by wounding one of the hoodlums. Later, when the daughter is raped by this trio, the father and son track the three down and kill two of them in cold blood. The film is filled with mixed messages. On the one hand, it supports individualism over cooperation in a crisis and promotes the idea that the ends justify the means. On the other hand, the film occasionally stops to allow the family members (primarily the mother) to engage in moralistic speeches whenever the family performs an act of kindness. At the end, when the unnamed warring powers have agreed to a truce and the family is headed home, Milland comes to realize that he has changed and that a future incident may force him to resort to similar behavior in order to survive. It becomes clear that this film is less about the horror of nuclear war and more about what happens to human behavior when societal norms have broken down. An earthquake or tornado might have produced similar results.

Two films, *The Day After* and *Testament*, treat the subject of nuclear attack quite differently. Both personalize the experience, focusing on the impact of the attack on one family (*Testament*) and on several major characters (*The Day After*). The ABC network turned *The Day After* into a media event by promoting the film's showing as an educational opportunity and encouraging teachers, students and their schools, churches and their congregations, and families to share the experience together.[27] Before the film's showing, the network announced that while the film was based on scientific fact, it nevertheless was a work of fiction. After the screening, the network presented a discussion panel of experts to critique the film. The story of ordinary people caught up in an unexpected nuclear attack contained many expected images: dead bodies, radiation sickness, virulent epidemics, a scarce supply of uncontaminated food and water, and outbreaks of violence and lawlessness. Still, the film seems to want to shock its audience through special effects and gruesome makeup rather than to enlighten it. *Testament*, on the other hand, was a low-budget, 90-minute film about the effect of a nuclear attack on one California middle-class family. The opening scene finds the father away on business, leaving the mother and children to face the nuclear holocaust alone. After the initial blast, the film moves quickly to show their community covered by radioactive dust as a result of World War III. The remainder of the film describes how the family and the community cope with the aftermath of such a catastrophe. There are no special effects or expensive makeup requirements in *Testament*. The emphasis is on the personal drama. For instance, in the final scene, when the mother, her son, and his friend await certain death, it is clear that the end of the family is a metaphor for the end of civilization. As T.S. Eliot wrote, the end is likely to come "not with a bang but a whimper."

While the flashier *The Day After* drew a viewing audience of 100 million, *Testament* virtually disappeared from sight. The film had a strange history. Originally produced for Paramount Pictures and first screened at the New York Film Festival, it starred stage actress Jane Alexander as the mother, a role that brought her an Academy Award nomination. Nonetheless, the film had a limited theatrical release and eventually was shown on PBS as part of its American Playhouse television series. Unlike *The Day After*, the rather unemotional but more realistic ending of life as depicted in *Testament* failed to capture the public's imagination and the film went virtually unnoticed.

A derivation of the nuclear survival genre can be found in films like *A Boy and His Dog* (1975) and also the *Mad Max* trilogy, starring Mel Gibson, both of which take place in a post-apocalyptic world—an arid wasteland—inhabited by a population whose major preoccupation is with survival. While the dramatic situations in these films are byproducts of nuclear war, their narratives concern a future where the characters confront the immediate aftermath of nuclear destruction.

## Nuclear Terrorist Films: The Arabs Are Coming! The Muslims Are Coming!

At the height of the Cold War, director Norman Jewison made a spoof of the East-West political situation in a film titled *The Russians Are Coming, the Russians Are Coming*. The improbable plot has a Russian submarine accidentally grounded off the coast of a small New England village, causing the locals to mistakenly believe the Soviets are invading the U.S. When a contingent of Russian sailors leaves the sub and comes on land to seek help, the villagers are ready to start World War III. Much hilarity follows, including the local police chief giving the sub a traffic violation for illegal parking, before all the misunderstandings are resolved peacefully.

But with the dissolution of the old Soviet Union and the end of the Cold War, Hollywood had to invent new film enemies for American audiences. In the 1990s, that dubious distinction fell, although not exclusively, on Arabs and Muslims. In these films, the "bad guys" often are seeking nuclear weapons to use against the West. The following seven films, three released in the 1990s, one in 2000, and the remaining three after 9/11, offer a sampling of how present-day Hollywood has separated itself from the nuclear films of the 1950s.

An early entry in the nuclear terrorist subgenre was director James Cameron's *True Lies* (1994), a star vehicle for Arnold Schwarzenegger. Schwarzenegger plays CIA agent Harry Tasker, a composite character of Rambo, James Bond, and Chuck Norris welded together in one body. His assignment is to track down an Arab terrorist group known as the Crimson Jihad, whose leader is played by Pakistani actor Art Malik. Malik and his gang have acquired several nuclear warheads and plan to fire them on major American cities in a show of power. The numerous improbabilities in this financially successful film[28] start at the very beginning, when within the first 10 minutes Schwarzenegger emerges from a Swiss lake, changes into a tuxedo, crashes a party for Arab terrorists, speaks fluent French and Arabic, dances a mean tango with a gorgeous woman, and then, when his cover is blown, makes an improbable escape, leaving a trail of dead bodies behind. By film's end, Schwarzenegger single-handedly has killed hundreds of the bad guys and virtually destroyed the Florida Keys all by himself. What purpose this film served other than to introduce Arabs as the new "bad guys" in Hollywood is hard to fathom.

Next up was a film with serious intentions. Director Mimi Leder's *The Peacemaker* (1997) teams George Clooney as an Army Special Forces Colonel with Nicole Kidman as a nuclear scientist in pursuit of rogue terrorists (Muslim, Serb, and Chechen) who have stolen 10 nuclear warheads from the Russians. The film's premise of the dangers posed by the apparent lack of security over nuclear weapons was sound, as Russia acknowledged in

1997 that some 68 such weapons were missing.²⁹ Similarly, in the summer of 2011 a freight train from Romania guarded with armed troops had 64 nuclear missiles stolen by the time it arrived in Bulgaria. The Romanian government offered several explanations as to why the warheads posed no danger to the public but more problematic was that the thieves knew which one of the eight cars on the 27-car train contained the missiles.³⁰ Whether the 64 missiles were functional or could become operational was a secondary concern to the clear breach of security.

The last of the three pre-9/11 films involving terrorists, *The Siege* (1998), flopped at the domestic box office. Starring Denzel Washington as an FBI agent and Bruce Willis as a villainous army general, the plot pivots around the imposition of martial law in the wake of a series of radical Islamic attacks in New York City, leading to the internment of Arab Americans. Older readers will recall a similar situation after Pearl Harbor when the federal government rounded up some 115,000 Japanese Americans living on the West Coast and sent them to internment camps. In *The Siege* Willis orders prisoners tortured for information, foreshadowing similar abuses at the Abu Ghraib and Guantanamo detention centers. The Council on American-Islamic Relations criticized the film for perpetuating Arab stereotypes and distorting the religious teachings of Islam. On the other hand, the film's supporters argued that the true meaning of the movie lay in its depiction of how a knee-jerk reaction to terror can lead to wrong decisions.³¹ Audiences were left to decide which view was the more accurate.

The plot of the fourth film, *Rules of Engagement* (2000), does not involve a nuclear threat. But it does exhibit a strong negative attitude toward Arabs and Muslims even before 9/11. When Colonel Childers (Samuel L. Jackson) orders his troops to fire on a crowd of civilians storming the U.S. Embassy in Yemen, he is court-martialed for his action. His friend and Vietnam buddy, Colonel Hodges (Tommy Lee Jones), serves as his defense attorney in a film that turns into a courtroom thriller about military strategy and its subsequent consequences. Childers's order results in the deaths of some 83 civilians. Why the film is included here has little to do with the issue of military accountability and morality. Rather it is because the firing order Childers shouts out is accompanied by the words "waste the motherfuckers," language that implies rage and hatred rather than military necessity. Is the film's underlying message supposed to be that "the only good Muslim is a dead one?"

The three post-9/11 films are of interest, each for a different reason. The 2002 film *The Sum of All Fears* is based on a Tom Clancy novel that has Palestinians selling a nuclear device to al Qaeda, which uses it to blow up the city of Denver. But in the movie version, Clancy's hero, CIA agent Jack Ryan (Ben Affleck), is assigned to foil a terrorist plot intended to initiate a war between Russia and the U.S. after a nuclear bomb is detonated during a football game in Baltimore. As the plot develops, it turns out that the terrorists are not Arabs but central European neo-Nazis. The interesting question here is: why did Hollywood change the Clancy novel, particularly after 9/11? Was it fearful that the film would enrage Americans to act against all Arabs? Did it not want to offend the Muslim community in the U.S.? Was Hollywood concerned about the film's reception overseas? The answer is not readily available, but the plot switch is a reason to ponder.³²

In Peter Berg's 2007 Middle East action film, *The Kingdom*, the bad guys are Arabs but the FBI "good guys" are aided by a Saudi colonel in their pursuit of terrorists who bombed an American compound. Here is another improbable and implausible Hollywood film stocked with stereotypical characters. The FBI agents have five days to find the culprits, although none speak or understand Arabic and are clueless about Arab culture. The Saudi colonel continuously admonishes them for swearing and cursing because it offends the host country. Many of the Arabs are depicted as incompetent and totally useless. At the end, the film dissolves into the typical bloodbath, with the four agents killing hundreds of terrorists and destroying half of Baghdad. It also flopped at the American box office.

Figure 11.1. *Unthinkable*, 2010. Reprinted with permission, Sidney Kimmel Entertainment/Photofest

## Case Study: *Unthinkable*

The latest entry into the nuclear terror category had an unusual film history. *Unthinkable* (2010) featured Samuel L. Jackson and Michael Sheen and a $15 million production budget, but was saddled with a familiar nuclear terrorist plot where U.S. authorities are trying to locate three nuclear bombs before they are detonated. What is different in this scenario, however, are the extreme (and very explicit) methods used to discover these locations.

In outline, an American-born terrorist (Sheen), a convert to Islam, has placed nuclear bombs in three U.S. cities: New York, Los Angeles, and Dallas. The terrorist, using his Muslim name, Yusuf, sends a videotape to U.S. authorities vowing to detonate the bombs unless his demands are met. These include the removal of an American presence in all Muslim countries, an ultimatum unlikely to succeed since the U.S. has a declared policy not to negotiate with terrorists. Yusuf, who appears to be intelligent and well informed, allows himself to be captured, knowing that he will likely be tortured and possibly killed. In fact, he has prepared himself to withstand the pain and suffering that will be inflicted on him. The question, which is never fully explored in the film, is why he accepts this painful route. Is Yusuf a variant of a "suicide bomber?" Or does he envision himself as a modern-day Jesus on the road to Calvary?

The remainder of the film details Yusuf's treatment while in U.S. custody. He is interrogated by an FBI agent (Carrie-Anne Moss) but mostly by a special-ops agent (Jackson) whose job it is to get Yusuf to divulge the locations of the three bombs. Moss plays the "good cop" role in her efforts to break Yusuf down, but she refuses to use more persuasive methods. Jackson has no such constraints. For him, the answer is simple: is one life (Yusuf's) worth more than the estimated 10 million lives that will be lost should the bombs go off? Jackson doesn't even ponder the question but determinedly goes to work. When Yusuf refuses to provide the location of even one bomb, Jackson chops off one of his fingers. When Yusuf continues his silence, Jackson takes out his bag of torture tools and does the following: attempts to suffocate Yusuf by tying a plastic bag over his head, cuts his genitals, beats him with a whip, pulls off his fingernails, drills into his teeth, and stabs a knife into various parts of his body. Still, Yusuf refuses to talk except to scream. Enter the FBI agent, who is appalled by Jackson's methods. Using her feminine charms and promises of ending the torture, Moss gets Yusuf to admit the bombs are a hoax to embarrass the U.S. as a country that tortures at home as well as outsourcing the task to foreign countries, known as rendition. But when the FBI investigates and goes to one of the bomb sites, there is an explosion that kills 53 people. Jackson is infuriated and is now convinced that Yusuf will never tell them anything as long as only he is tortured. So Jackson tries a new tactic: bring Yusuf's Muslim wife into the interrogation room and ask him the question again. When Yusuf refuses to answer once again, Jackson slits his wife's throat. Yusuf is horrified but remains defiant. With only hours left before the remaining bombs are set to detonate, Jackson decides to do the "unthinkable": kill Yusuf's two children. Believing that Jackson will carry out

> his threat, Yusuf identifies the locations of these bombs. There is a genuine sigh of relief in the interrogation room, except Jackson suspects that Yusuf, who has enough nuclear material for four bombs, has a fourth one hidden somewhere else. Of course, no one believes him and the film ends as Yusuf grabs a gun, asks Moss to care for his children, and shoots himself. At the fadeout, the audience sees Moss walking out with Yusuf's children. But when the film was shown to preview audiences, their responses indicated confusion over the ending. So the producers had an alternative ending shot with the fourth bomb detonating as the screen goes to black. This ending is on the DVD version.
>
> The oddity here is that despite its two stars and its $15 million production values, the producers decided to release the film directly to video, with the alternate ending included. What are viewers to make of this brutal, horrifying film? Film critics were divided as to its merits, or lack thereof. Conservatives were against it because they thought the film was a left-wing rant against U.S. interrogation methods after 9/11 and that the revered FBI is characterized as an organization that would cover up government torture. Liberals found the film offensive because the torture scenes reached the porn level of violent obscenity. Maybe both sides are right: this is a film that never should have been made.

All of the above films dealt with terrorists, four explicitly with Arab-Muslim terrorists. What conclusions, if any, can we draw from this small sample? The answer is none, but Professor Jack Shaheen in his book *Reel Bad Arabs: How Hollywood Vilifies a People* concludes, after analyzing over 900 feature films, that Hollywood has "degraded and dehumanized a people." He identifies five Arab stereotypes in Hollywood films: villains (including fanatics and terrorists), sheikhs (including lechers and hedonists), maidens (including harem dwellers and belly dancers), Egyptians (including Jew haters and souk swindlers), and Palestinians (terrorists). Shaheen's point is that Hollywood has indicted a whole group of people for the crimes of a few.[33] Is his thesis valid? That depends on two factors: the reader's level of sensitivity to stereotypes and the reader's ethnicity and cultural affiliation. Admittedly, the American film industry, at various times in its history, has engaged in stereotyping most every race, ethnicity and minority group. What is more disturbing, however, is to see that the practice persists. The reader has to wonder whether the continual negative depiction of "foreigners" by Hollywood is intentional, inadvertent, or simply a case of inattentiveness. It would be a sad day indeed if the film industry were to cater to the prejudices of America's worst representatives rather than its best.

## The Second Nuclear Age

The atomic era began in 1942 on a squash court at the University of Chicago, where the first nuclear reaction occurred. More than seven decades later, it appears that the energy released by the atom has brought mankind greater prospects for destruction than life improvement. It no longer matters who is responsible because all the participants in the development of the bomb should be held accountable: the scientists laid the foundation by splitting the atom, the military used that knowledge to develop weapons of mass destruction, and the politicians made the decisions as to when, how, and under what circumstances these weapons would be utilized. Later, scientists like Oppenheimer regretted what they had done. Teller also had misgivings about the hydrogen bomb. By then it was too late. Had World War II continued, the Germans might have developed the bomb and used it against the Allies. Would the Japanese not have done so too, had they had the capability? Scientific progress cannot be contained, only delayed. The real problem with atomic energy lies not so much in its discovery, but in its utilization. As Einstein remarked after the bombing of Hiroshima and Nagasaki, "The release of atom power has changed everything except our way of thinking."[34]

Concerned scientists agreed with Einstein and in 1945, under the leadership of biophysicist Eugene Rabinowitch, founded the *Bulletin of Atomic Scientists* as a means of keeping the public informed about nuclear power and of lobbying for the international control of nuclear energy. Einstein had warned that the thinking of the world's leaders had to be adjusted for the nuclear age. But apparently few, if any, politicians paid attention. Revisionist historians now claim that Truman used the A-bomb primarily as a future bargaining chip in negotiations with the Soviet Union, rather than as a calculated means of saving lives (American and Japanese) by bringing World War II to an end. Clearly President Truman had the support of the American people to use the bomb. A Roper poll taken in the fall of 1945 revealed that three-fourths of Americans approved of the president's decision. In fact, more than one-fifth thought more atomic bombs should have been dropped. Only 5 percent disapproved of the use of the bomb.[35]

Eisenhower, Truman's successor in the White House, also saw the bomb as a political rather than a purely military weapon, a means to regain the Cold War initiative from the Soviets. Reportedly, Eisenhower moved atomic warheads to Okinawa to impress the Chinese, and later, during the Formosa Straits confrontation, ordered the military to be in a state of nuclear readiness. At one point in his administration, Eisenhower reportedly said, "I see no reason why they [nuclear weapons] shouldn't be used just exactly as you would use a bullet or anything else."[36] As Einstein had predicted, Eisenhower, as president, failed to distinguish conventional armaments from nuclear weapons.

Fortunately, some international cooperation has occurred since the 1963 Partial Test Ban Treaty banned atmospheric nuclear testing. The five major nuclear powers (U.S., Russia, China, France, and the UK) have agreed to prohibit aboveground testing and to limit underground tests. The 1996 Comprehensive Nuclear Test Ban Treaty banned all nuclear explosions on earth, but it has yet to be ratified by the U.S. Meanwhile, the 1968 Non-Proliferation Treaty was intended to restrict the spread of nuclear weapons. But India, Pakistan, and North Korea have tested nuclear weapons and Iran seems determined to join that group as well. On the positive side, a number of countries, including Brazil, South Africa, South Korea, and Libya have either dismantled or relinquished their nuclear arsenals.[37]

Since 1945, more than 2,000 atmospheric and underground nuclear tests have been conducted worldwide, with 1,032 by the U.S. and 715 by the Soviet Union/Russia.[38] Of the 193 UN members,[39] all but three—India, Pakistan, and North Korea—have signed the Comprehensive Nuclear Test Ban Treaty, which provides for worldwide monitoring as well as on-site inspections to ensure compliance. The failure of the U.S. Senate to ratify the test ban treaty damages America's world image and remains an obstacle to world peace. To offset its rejection, the American government pointed to previous agreements, like the Start Treaties with the old Soviet Union to reduce their nuclear stockpiles to no more than 2,200 "operational" nuclear weapons.[40] Recently, Russia and the U.S. reached agreement to further reduce the ceiling on strategic weapons from 2,200 to between 1,500 and 1,675.[41] Both *The New York Times* and General James E. Cartwright, former Commander of U.S. Nuclear Forces, have called for further drastic reductions of nuclear warheads, even below those agreed upon by Russia and the U.S., because such reductions would not jeopardize American nuclear deterrence capability.[42] While reductions in nuclear weapons are laudable, the power of these weapons as measured by kilotons (1 kiloton has an explosive force of 1,000 tons of TNT), has multiplied 20 to 30 times since the Hiroshima bomb. Even a few of these bombs would cause considerable damage.

The first nuclear age initiated by the Hiroshima and Nagasaki bombing reached a stalemate when the Soviets leveled the playing field with their own nuclear arsenal. But scientific secrets do not remain undisclosed for long. Soon China, France, and the United Kingdom joined the U.S. and the Soviets. The Big Five powers, regardless of political and ideological differences, understood that nuclear weapons were the real weapons of mass destruction and had to be brought under some semblance of control. Scientists mark 1998, when India and Pakistan detonated nuclear weapons, as the dawn of the second nuclear age.[43] Since then, North Korea has developed and tested nuclear weapons and the present government in Iran has the materials to make nuclear weapons. Any addition to the present nuclear club exponentially multiplies the risk of a nuclear holocaust.

## The Three Nuclear Question Marks: Iran, North Korea, and Pakistan

The present regimes in Iran and North Korea espouse ideologies and political values different from those of the U.S. and the West and are characterized by the West as "unfriendly nations." Pakistan, on the other hand, has had a love-hate relationship with the U.S. since the end of WWII, when the U.S. chose to support it rather than India with economic and military aid. America became Pakistan's benefactor, providing billions of dollars in the hope it would become an ally with a modern democratic government. Seventy years later, however, India is the rising economic star with a democratic government, while Pakistan is a "failed state" economically, politically, and as an ally against terrorism. It secretly built a uranium enrichment facility in 1979 after India had established its nuclear weapons program and, under the command of the military, began to support radical Islamic organizations. The military, fed by American money, grew in power so that by the 1980s it had become an entity unto itself. The military openly aided the Taliban until 9/11 when the government disavowed the group. Still U.S. intelligence believes that the country provides a safe haven for Taliban leaders in the areas along its border with Afghanistan. And despite its denials, Pakistan allowed Osama bin Laden to live undisturbed outside of Islamabad, its capital, until Navy Seals tracked him down and killed him in May of 2011.[44]

In summary, Pakistan is a nuclear power with conflicting allegiances, an unstable government, and a checkered history with the U.S. What makes the situation troubling is that it has replaced the UK as the world's fifth largest nuclear power, having, according to U.S. intelligence, the ability to deploy more than 100 nuclear weapons. Many of these weapons are miniaturized so they can be mounted on ballistic missiles with ranges exceeding 1,000 miles, enough to reach many Indian cities, because India, not the Taliban or al Qaeda, is Pakistan's major concern.[45] These facts raise grave concerns about Pakistan's intentions and allegiances as a nuclear power. What if the Afghan Taliban steals or manages to come into possession of some of Pakistan's nuclear weapons? Although this scenario remains a possibility, what is more likely to happen is that terrorists acquire the necessary fissile material to produce their own bomb, probably from an outside source. Additionally, Pakistan is not a party to the Nuclear Non-Proliferation Treaty and has resisted international inspections of its enrichment activities. It is not a comforting thought to the U.S. and its allies that the Pakistani military exercise considerable power and are willing to play politics with nuclear weapons.

At present, Iran and North Korea both possess the nuclear potential to cause damage in the future. Of the two, North Korea is presently more of a "pretender" to the nuclear club, while Iran's nuclear program is much further advanced. But it would be a mistake to take North Korea lightly simply because its 2012 nuclear missile test landed in the ocean and became the butt of cartoons and late night television jokes. Its first bomb blast in 2006 had a small yield of 1 kiloton and the second one in 2009 was estimated at 2 kilotons, puny compared to the fire power of the major nuclear powers. But the U.S. and the West should remain vigilant for several reasons. First, after using plutonium in the 2006 blast, the North Korean regime converted to enriched uranium, the material in the atom bombs that destroyed Hiroshima and Nagasaki. This indicates that the present regime has raised the ante in its efforts to bully South Korea, a U.S. ally. Second, North Korea has been under the dictatorial rule of the Kim family since the end of hostilities between the North and South in 1953. The two countries are technically still at war since no peace treaty was signed and they remain in a tense relationship that occasionally erupts into violence—as seen when North Korea provokes the South with assassination attempts against its presidents and occasionally fires missiles over the border. The relationship was further tested in 2010 when the North sank a South Korean warship, killing 46 men, and also later that year when the North shelled a border island, killing four South Koreans. Finally, the North has amassed an army of one million to intimidate the South and to put boots on the ground as a warning to its neighbor, which depends on the U.S. for support. In short, North Korea is an unpredictable regime that cannot be trusted to abide by its word, given that it has repeatedly promised the U.S. it would cease its nuclear activities in exchange for food, only to resume testing again. So far, the present regime of Kim Jong-un has given no indication that it will deviate from the tactics of his father, Kim Jung-il, or alter its bad behavior through inducements and persuasion.[46] Iran is the "wild card" of the three because it is firmly committed to developing nuclear power which it insists will be used for peaceful purposes. However, Iran considers Israel and the U.S. its enemies, and it soon will have nuclear bomb capability.[47] Iran has made it clear that it intends to play a more dominant role in the Middle East, and in order to do so the present government believes that its enemies must come to fear and respect it. Saudi Arabia has no nuclear ambitions, while Iraq and Afghanistan are not likely to have them, if at all, until sometime in the future. That leaves Pakistan as the main challenger to Iran for influence over Iraq and Afghanistan.

Iran's urgency to develop nuclear capability is in response to Israel's nuclear stockpile. Israel has played a cat-and-mouse game with the U.S. since the 1960s, assuring the American government that its nuclear program was meant for peaceful purposes while simultaneously acquiring the materials to make nuclear weapons. After the Kennedy assassination, the Johnson administration was willing to accept Israel's nuclear plans as long as they were not made public. By the time of the Nixon administration, the Israeli charade was over and the media had declared Israel a nuclear power. By the 1980s, Israel had acquired a considerable stockpile of nuclear weapons, which the Iranian leaders viewed as a threat to the country's security.[48] And similar to the India-Pakistan rivalry, the country that did not have the bomb sought to level the playing field against the country that did.

But even if Iran intends to develop nuclear weapons to annihilate Israel, does it have the capability? On that question there is a difference of opinion. Conservatives in the Israeli government insist that since Iran's intention is clear, Israel should make a preemptive strike to destroy Iran's underground facilities for making nuclear weapons and its subsidiary plants and laboratories. To delay would give Iran a first-strike advantage. The U.S. claims that its intelligence confirms Iran's intentions but that it does not yet have the capability, and therefore diplomacy should be given a chance to work out a peaceful solution. However, the Institute for Science and International Security (ISIS), a U.S. think-tank, discovered that Iran has upgraded its low-enriched uranium to give it the capability to produce at least five nuclear bombs.[49] While disagreements among Israel, the U.S., and Western Europe exist, all acknowledge that Iran's objective is to secure nuclear weapons—and quickly. The potential for a nuclear WWIII lies dormant, but what if the religious theocracy that is the ultimate governing power in Iran comes to believe that its existence depends on the destruction of Israel? What if Israel decides to make a preemptive strike but fails to take out Iran's nuclear reactor? Surely Iran would retaliate and inflict considerable damage on Israel. In return, Israel would still have its nuclear submarines to provide a second strike. In the final analysis, even a limited regional nuclear war would result in a nuclear winter that would kill millions.[50] To consider even a "controlled" nuclear war in conventional terms verges on madness.

On a less apocalyptic note, suppose that states such as North Korea and Iran develop radiation dispersal devices, so-called "dirty bombs" that can be used to demoralize and weaken their enemies? Such bombs produce less damage than nuclear weapons but might have the effect of toppling weak governments, opening opportunities for terrorist groups to take over control. All these "what if" scenarios are frightening to contemplate but need to be considered. The application of any one could bring mankind to the brink of a nuclear catastrophe.

Former Secretary of State Henry Kissinger contends that proliferation of nuclear weapons, particularly among rogue and volatile regimes, must be prevented and explains why the U.S. should work more closely with Russia to reduce the risk of nuclear strikes from such unstable governments. At home, Kissinger suggests that the pro- and anti-nuclear forces reach a mutually agreed-upon consensus to assist the present administration in forging a global nuclear policy.[51]

Additionally, Kissinger and four other so-called "Cold War Warriors" (lifelong Republicans and Democrats) are engaged in an endeavor to abolish nuclear weapons altogether out of concern that nuclear material will fall into the hands of terrorist organizations like al Qaeda, noting that nuclear deterrence will not work with stateless terrorists. Their concern is also with incidents where people have smuggled out nuclear material from facilities in the former Soviet Union. They fear, as well, an accidental launch by missiles and bombers on hair-trigger alert in the U.S. and other nuclear states. Hence, the group proposes concrete steps to reduce the threat of both nuclear war and terrorism:

- Secure poorly guarded stockpiles of enriched uranium around the world
- Reduce uranium in nuclear reactors to a grade that renders it useless for weapons but still viable for the production of nuclear power
- Provide assistance to global nuclear facilities to secure their stocks, and
- Replace existing nuclear weapons with sophisticated, precision-guided conventional weapons.[52]

Is a nuclear-free world attainable? Perhaps not, but government leaders must come to accept the fact that the world faces a greater risk to its survival today than it did 70 years ago after the bombings of Hiroshima and Nagasaki. One thing, however, is certain: nuclear technology, whether designed to produce domestic energy or weapons of war, is a permanent fixture of modern life. The challenge facing political decision-makers is daunting: how to harness nuclear energy to improve the quality of life rather than to use it to destroy the very existence of life. Maybe the UN should screen the end of *On the Beach* and make the film mandatory viewing at its opening session so that its members can focus on the final scene where the radioactive dust has extinguished all life on earth and a draped banner reads, "There is still time, brother."

Chapter 12

# Hollywood, Race and Obama
## Feel-Good Racism

"I have a dream that my four little children will one day live in a nation where they will not be judged by the color of their skin but by the content of their character."
—Martin Luther King Jr.

"The emotions between the races could never be pure; even love was tarnished by the desire to find in the other some element that was missing in ourselves. Whether we sought out our demons or salvation, the other race would always remain just that: menacing, alien, and apart."
—Barack Obama, *Dreams from My Father*

"Until justice is blind to color, until education is unaware of race, until opportunity is unconcerned with the color of men's skins, emancipation will be a proclamation but not a fact."
—Lyndon Baines Johnson

With the election of Barack Obama to the presidency in 2008, liberal pundits proclaimed that the United States had reached the promised land of equality, with Obama's victory signaling America's entrance into a "post-racial society" where skin color would no longer be taken into account. But the political events, media representations, and highly publicized interracial encounters during the past few years indicate that that judgment was premature.

The focus of this chapter is on the film industry's treatment of race in its motion pictures, from the silent era to the present day, including films released since President Obama's election in 2008. Did his election alter or shape the film representation of race? That is one of the questions examined in the chapter. But first an examination of Hollywood's racial history is in order.

### Early Hollywood: Race in the Past

In the industry's early years, movie studios treated issues of race in several ways. When the script required non-white characters, they simply used white actors and relied on makeup and costuming. In *The Birth of a Nation*, for example, D.W. Griffith blackened the faces of white actors while Al Jolson played *The Jazz Singer* (1927) in blackface. In the 1930s, Hollywood did produce several pictures that included African-Americans actors, but they were restricted to minor roles or musicals. Some African Americans found employment in the small black film market.

Other racial/ethnic groups were treated in similar fashion. In 1919 D.W. Griffith cast white actor Richard Barthelmess as a Chinese aristocrat in *Broken Blossoms*. In the 1930s, English actor Boris Karloff played a Chinese villain in *The Mask of Fu Manchu* (1932) and German-born actress Luise Rainer won an Oscar for playing a Chinese peasant in the film *The Good Earth* (1937). Raised eyebrows may occur when the reader discovers that a young Katharine Hepburn played a Chinese woman who rallies villagers against the invading Japanese in the World War II film *Dragon Seed* (1944). The very popular Charlie Chan B-movies, which were staples of the 1940s double features, had white actors playing the Chinese detective. For instance, Swedish actor Warner Oland played the first Charlie Chan, and when he died he was replaced by Kansas-born Sidney Toler. Hollywood's penchant for casting white actors in Asian roles extended well into the post-World War II era. For example, Marlon Brando played an Okinawan interpreter in the film *The Teahouse of the August Moon* (1956). And as late as 1962, Chuck "Rifleman" Connors played the Apache warrior Geronimo. There were a few notable exceptions to this trend. Chinese-American Anna May Wong was the first Asian actress to achieve stardom in 1930s Hollywood and later, in the 1960s, Asian-American actor James Shigeta became a leading man in studio-made films.[1] But Japanese-American actor Sessue Hayakawa is acknowledged as the first Asian actor to find stardom in the U.S. as he began his American acting career in 1914 and continued it into the 1960s, even though he largely performed outside the U.S. during most of his career [2] These few exceptions aside, early Hollywood consistently refused to use minorities in its films.

For minority actors, rejection was only half the insult. The other half occurred when the studios began to cast minorities in demeaning roles. To say that Hollywood portrayed minorities as stereotypes hardly needs to be argued. That happened with some frequency in the 1930s and 1940s when the only roles available to African-American actors, except in specific racially filled musicals, were supporting roles as servants, chauffeurs, janitors, and other workers in menial jobs. When the studios were not using African Americans in a singing and dancing capacity, they showed up in comedies as foils to the white lead—as Willie Best did in films like *The Ghost Breakers* (1940). Later, Latinos would replace African Americans in some of these roles. Asian Americans, like Hayakawa, were often utilized as screen villains.

What is especially unfortunate about black stereotyping is that it ignored the talented and gifted African-American film entertainers. Artists like director Oscar Micheaux and actor-singer Paul Robeson were not accepted by the major studios that controlled the film industry before World War II. Oscar Micheaux, who was born into a family of former slaves, began his professional career as a writer, but soon moved into the new medium of motion pictures.[3] In 1919, Micheaux formed his own production company, thus becoming the first African-American filmmaker in the U.S. His initial venture was the silent picture *The Homesteader* (1919), which he wrote, directed, and produced. *Within Our Gates* (1919) followed shortly thereafter and served as his response to Griffith's racial stereotyping in *The Birth of a Nation*. *Within Our Gates* counters Griffith's portrayal of the black rapist with a more historically accurate depiction of the white man's raping of black women with impunity. The complex plot of *Within Our Gates*, told in flashback, relates the story of Sylvia, a black Boston schoolteacher, who takes a job teaching in rural Mississippi. She is soon asked to return to Boston to raise money for the almost bankrupt school where she teaches and there falls in love with a black physician. But a secret in her past prevents her from pursuing this romance. A flashback sequence reveals that her mother was impregnated by one of the white plantation owners, who abandons the child (Sylvia) on the porch of one of his sharecroppers. Years later, the plantation owner is killed along with the sharecropper and his family. Sylvia manages to escape but is caught by another plantation owner, the brother of the slain plantation owner, who attempts to rape her until he discovers a scar on her chest that he recognizes as belonging to his daughter. The film ends happily as the remorseful brother takes Sylvia to Boston to complete her education.

From 1919 to 1947 Micheaux made 41 films, 18 of them with sound. Although his race films played mostly in segregated movie theaters, they eventually were accepted in white theaters as well. Because many of his films were lost or destroyed, not played on television or cable, and unavailable for rental in 16mm format, Micheaux remained forgotten until the 1960s–70s.

In addition to his unique achievement as a writer and film director, Micheaux is to be remembered as the filmmaker who introduced actor-singer Paul Robeson to film audiences. The two artists were very different men. Micheaux was basically self-taught and worked at menial jobs until he started his writing career. Robeson was born in Princeton, New Jersey, to middle-class parents. An excellent student, he won a scholarship to Rutgers University, where he became an All-American football player and a member of Phi Beta Kappa Honor Society. He was the only African American on campus and was occasionally subjected to harassment. However, Robeson was capable of taking care of himself and after knocking a few heads during football practice he was left alone. After graduation he took an interest in law and entered Columbia University Law School. Later Robeson joined a law firm, where an office secretary told him, "I ain't taking dictation from a nigger." His law firm suggested that he might want to manage a branch in Harlem. Taking the hint, Robeson, who had an excellent voice, decided to pursue a career in stage acting and concert singing. With his wife as his stage manager and promoter, he soon became known as an outstanding actor-singer, starring in two works by Eugene O'Neill, *The Emperor Jones* and *All God's Chillun' Got Wings*, both in 1924.

Robeson also was a political activist, fighting at home for trade unionism and civil rights, campaigning abroad against colonialism in Africa and India, and speaking out against Fascism in Spain and Nazism in Germany. He later became an admirer of the Soviet Union and traveled there several times. After World War II he promoted world peace and spoke against the Cold War and the nuclear arms race. His political activities led the U.S. government in 1950 to revoke his passport. He subsequently was subpoenaed to appear before HUAC in 1956 despite his never having joined the Community Party. Proud and stubborn, Robeson refused to take a non-communist oath as a step toward regaining his passport.

Consequently, his name was put on the blacklist and he had a hard time getting work. He thus became another victim of the Red Scare.

Despite his stage work and concert performances, Robeson found time to make 11 films between 1935 and 1942, mostly British productions. His best known films were *Body and Soul* (1924), where he worked with Micheaux and played the part of a minister who was both good and evil, and a reprise of O'Neill's play *The Emperor Jones* (1933).[4] Unfortunately, Robeson's genius is often overshadowed by his politics. Although he showed some naiveté about the prospects of the Soviet Union under Stalin and was stubborn in his refusal to admit the abuses of the Stalinist purges of the 1930s, he was right on the mistreatment of his race at the hands of white America. Early black artists like Micheaux and Robeson should be celebrated and studied because black actors and directors who followed them owe a debt to those who paved the way for their acceptance by the film industry.

## Race in Post-World War II Hollywood

During World War II, the film industry, partly for propaganda reasons, used an all-black cast in two 1943 musicals, *Cabin in the Sky* and *Stormy Weather*, which were intended to promote wartime unity but instead featured a segregated America. Black soldiers were segregated in the military and rarely seen in combat movies, leaving the impression that African-American men sat out the war. The reality, however, is that more than one million such soldiers were inducted into the armed forces, constituting about 11 percent of the military. Even though a majority were assigned to transportation and "behind the line units," a considerable number fought in combat units in Europe. One outfit, the Buffalo Soldiers of the 92nd Infantry Division, was featured in Spike Lee's film *Miracle at St. Anna* (2008). Another unit, the all-black 24th Infantry Regiment, became the last segregated unit to see combat during the Korean War.[5] Thereafter, all military units were integrated.

Admittedly, Hollywood did make a few "racial message" films after World War II. For instance, *Pinky* (1949) tells the story of a light-skinned black woman (played by white actress Jeanne Crain) who tries to pass for white but, in the end, returns home to her own people. Another of these message films was *Home of the Brave* (1949), about a black soldier becoming psychologically paralyzed after his only white buddy is killed. Told in flashback, the audience discovers that the paralysis is due less to the trauma than to the accumulation of racial bigotry suffered by soldiers like him. Considered fairly liberal at the time, the film had an overly optimistic ending, with ex-soldiers of both races planning to open a business together, that is out of harmony with the reality of that time. However, neither of these films nor the historic 1954 desegregation decision in *Brown v. Board of Education*[6] advanced the cause of integration within the film industry as much as did the arrival in Hollywood of a young actor named Sidney Poitier. Born in Miami but raised in the Bahamas, Poitier grew up with no electricity or indoor plumbing. As a boy he received an elementary education that allowed him to read at a fourth grade level, which makes his rise to stardom even more impressive. At age 15 Poitier left the Bahamas for new prospects in Miami, but his encounter with racial discrimination left him dismayed. He was working as a delivery boy in a white neighborhood when one day he rang the doorbell of a large home to deliver a package and was told to go to the back entrance as the door slammed in his face. That unhappy experience encouraged him to leave the south for New York and Harlem, where he survived for a while on odd jobs. One day he answered a theater audition call, but was not offered a part. He spent the next six months reading and studying before his next audition landed him a role. Like many show business tales, Poitier's lucky break came when the leading actor, Harry Belafonte, was not available for the evening performance and Poitier filled in for him. Eventually, Poitier left the lights of Broadway for Hollywood, where he would make nine movies in the 1950s, followed by 16 more the following decade, including three box office hits in 1967, and an Oscar for his performance in *Lilies of the Field* (1964). Ultimately, Poitier would make 56 movies, direct nine others, and become a co-producer with his friend Harry Belafonte.

The height of Poitier's film career coincided with the civil rights era. Poitier, however, was criticized by some in the civil rights movement as an "Uncle Tom," a term that refers to any black man who is deferential and subservient to whites, similar to the slave character in Harriet Beecher Stowe's 19th-century novel *Uncle Tom's Cabin*. It is an unfair designation because, in his own way, Poitier was an important catalyst in fostering racial integration and respect for African Americans. This was especially true early in his career when he chose his parts carefully, refusing to be cast in the racially stereotyped roles that often were assigned to persons of color. He refused certain film roles and even balked at doing particular scenes that he found demeaning. For example, in one of his 1967 films, *In the Heat of the Night*, Poitier plays a Philadelphia detective assisting a southern sheriff in solving a local murder. In this particular scene, the script called for an important white character in the community to slap Poitier across the face for something he said. The scene was written for Poitier to simply turn and walk away. But he refused to do it that way and persuaded the director to allow his character, a proud northern black man, to smack the bigot back. The scene works wonderfully and is even more powerful than the one in the original script. By the mid-sixties, Poitier had enough leverage to refuse roles that were demeaning or disrespectful to his race because he had become the top box office star of 1967. Thirty years later, the American Film Institute (AFI) designated him as one of the "greatest male stars of all time" in recognition of his 30-year film career.

Poitier remains a proud, dignified family man. His gentle demeanor and his preference for the quiet life misrepresented the strength of his moral principles. In the 1950s, for example, he refused to sign a loyalty oath in deference to his friends—Paul Robeson and Canada Lee, even though he was apolitical. In the 1960s he was criticized for not being more aggressive and militant during the civil rights movement, although he joined Belafonte and Charlton Heston in the 1963 March on Washington. As he explains in his memoir, he did what he could with his limited power and his quiet personality to serve as an example of how blacks should be portrayed on screen, regardless of what the white male power structure that controlled Hollywood or the black militants thought about him.[7] Poitier paved the way within the film industry for future stars like Denzel Washington and Will Smith. His career is a fine example of how race relations in Hollywood were improved by quiet actions instead of mass demonstrations.

Poitier was still working when a young director, Sheldon Jackson "Spike" Lee, arrived on the film scene in the mid-1980s. Like Poitier's, Lee's career includes acting, writing, directing, and producing.[8] His production company, 40 Acres and a Mule, has turned out some 3 dozen films to date. Born in Atlanta but raised in Brooklyn, Lee considers New York his home and it is here where his film production company is presently located. Talented African-American directors like John Singleton (*Boyz n the Hood*, 1991), Robert Townsend (*The Five Heartbeats*, 1991), and Carl Franklin (*Dead in a Blue Dress*, 1995), all emerged in the nineties, but it is Lee who has produced the greatest body of work and received the most acclaim. The bulk of Lee's films concern various aspects of being black in white America. In *Mo' Better Blues* (1990), Denzel Washington plays a troubled jazz trumpeter (supposedly modeled after Lee's father, Bill Lee); in *Malcolm X* (1992) Washington recreates the life of the controversial black activist; in *Jungle Fever* (1991) Lee examines the pitfalls of an interracial love affair between a married black man and his white secretary; and in his 1989 hit, *Do the Right Thing*, Lee deals openly with the issue of how latent bigotry and prejudice can escalate into racial violence. Lee's films are not always financial or critical successes, but he remains one of the few filmmakers willing to challenge American audiences with the realities of racism in the U.S.

In the second decade of the 21st century, Hollywood looks quite different than it did a hundred years ago. It is no longer exclusively white and people of color have made inroads into the film business, except in executive positions. One barometer of this improvement is the success of a dozen black actors and actresses, including Denzel Washington and Halle Berry, who have received Oscars for their work. Another sign of progress is the half-dozen or so directors, besides Lee, who have become successful filmmakers. Progress for African-Americans in Hollywood needs to be seen against the wider context of race relations in the U.S., however, not least because of the role that the media, including film, has on developing and perpetuating discrimination. Three recent incidents illustrate the potential damage when latent racism flares.

## Race Outside of Hollywood

The first episode, during the summer of 2009, came to be referred to by the media as the "incident at Cambridge."[9] Harvard professor Henry Louis Gates Jr., returning to his home in Harvard Square, had difficulty opening his front door and asked his driver to assist him. A passerby thought the men might be breaking in and called 911. Gates was inside his house when Sgt. James Crowley, a veteran police officer who leads racial sensitivity training in his department, arrived. Crowley asked Gates to provide identification; mindful of police race relations in the U.S., Gates countered with a request for Crowley to do the same. Words were exchanged and Gates was arrested for disorderly conduct. That charge was subsequently dropped but the exchange escalated via the media, with both sides demanding an apology. President Obama intervened after a week and invited the men to the White House for a "beer summit." Still no apologies ensued from either side and eventually the story petered out.

The second incident took place three years later in Sanford, Florida, and was much more serious. As with the Gates-Crowley episode, it has been well reported but briefly the circumstances, as reported by the media, were as follows.[10] Trayvon Martin, a black 17-year-old boy, was walking back from his local 7-Eleven store when he was spotted by Hispanic neighborhood watch volunteer George Zimmerman. Zimmerman rang the police and reported the boy, who had his hoodie up, as looking "suspicious." He was told to sit and wait for the police. Ignoring that directive, he pursued Martin and confronted him. The boy was holding a bag of Skittles and a can of iced tea while Zimmerman was carrying a 9-mm handgun. From this point, events are in dispute. Zimmerman claims Martin punched him and knocked him to the ground whereby, reportedly fearing for his life, Zimmerman shot the boy at close range and killed him. The Sanford police department initially chose to accept Zimmerman's explanation and, applying Florida's "stand your ground" law, did not charge him.[11] The decision sparked a national outcry and after 44 days of protests, Zimmerman was finally charged with 2nd degree murder. After a two-week trial in July 2013, a jury acquitted Zimmerman of the murder charge. At the time of writing, the incident and outcome were still under fierce debate.

The third episode also involved Florida's "stand your ground" law. Two cars were parked outside a Jacksonville convenience store, with 46-year-old Michael Dunn in one and a group of black youths, including 17-year-old Jordan Davis, in another. Dunn allegedly asked the boys to turn down their loud music, an argument broke out and Dunn, claiming he saw a shotgun pointed at him, took out his handgun and fired into the car. Davis was killed. The police found no shotgun in the boys' car, while Davis's father said his son did not own a weapon and he had no criminal record.[12] At the time of writing, Dunn was in a Florida jail awaiting charges of first-degree murder and three counts of attempted murder.[13]

At first glance, these incidents appear to have little if anything to do with Hollywood. But the common factor in all three scenarios was the way each protagonist was perceived by the other party. When Crowley appeared on Gates' porch, he saw a black man and worried that his life was at risk. When Professor Gates saw Crowley, his memory recalled the police racial conflicts of the past and he feared for his life. Zimmerman and Dunn also invoked this fear of the other in defending their violent response to a perceived threat. Each participant distrusted the other, based on what Professor Thomas Powell has documented as "the persistence of racism in America," the kind of racism that percolates just below the surface of civility.[14] Do these incidents show that Americans in general still fear "people of color" and view them as threats to their security? If there is any truth whatsoever to this assertion, then even the accomplishments of a minority president will not reverse the course of more than 200 years of racial violence, bigotry, and prejudice. Whites better look at the demographics and racial intermarriage rates. Certainly by 2050, if not sooner, the U.S. will become a multiracial society where those who characterize themselves as "white" will be in the minority. The Census Bureau reported that by 2043, no single ethnic group will constitute a majority of the U.S.[15] But back to Hollywood, which, while not directly responsible for any of the three incidents above, has certainly played its part in perpetuating racism by supporting racial stereotyping and by reinforcing negative and false images of minority groups in its films. These racial practices, even if unintentional, have permeated Hollywood films since the industry's beginning and, as the next section shows, Hollywood still gets race wrong as often as it gets it right.

## Presenting Race on Screen

It would take a separate book to present a comprehensive examination of how the film industry has treated race during its long history. Like other businesses in the private sector, the film industry concerned itself with its own product, rather than breaking social or racial barriers in its films and employment practices. The author is not accusing Hollywood of intentional racism for the simple reason that while the studios held a monopoly of various aspects of film production there was room for individual filmmakers to express their own views if they could secure financing. Rather the industry's neglect of minority interests in employment and films was due more to insensitivity and indifference than ideological racism. Below are samples of where Hollywood got race right and wrong in the films it produced.

### Getting Race Right

Nothing Hollywood has achieved during the past half-century can mitigate the harm done to the image of "persons of color" portrayed on the big screen during the industry's early history. In retrospect, what is surprising is that as early as the forties there were race-sensitive people in the industry. Take director Clarence Brown as an example. Five years before the *Brown* desegregation decision, director Clarence Brown took William Faulkner's novel *Intruder in the Dust*, set in the Jim Crow South, and turned it into a racial lesson for a segregated America. An elderly black man (Juano Hernández) is charged with the murder of a white man in Mississippi. As depicted, Hernández is represented in court by a reluctant white lawyer, reluctant because his client refuses to explain that the killing was an accident. Meanwhile, an angry mob gathers around the jailhouse, wanting to lynch Hernández rather than wait for a trial. Luckily, through the efforts of the lawyer and his nephew, Hernández is released from jail and the truth is divulged to the community. In the final scene, the lawyer asks Hernández why he refused to tell him the facts of what had really happened. Being a proud man, Hernández looks at him and says: "Would you have believed me?" The lawyer doesn't answer as the film ends. Why the silence? In 1940s Mississippi, no white man would take the word of a black man.

Another African-American man is the center of an early independent film, *Nothing But a Man* (1964), which relates a tale of what it meant to be a proud black man in a country where segregation is now illegal but prejudice and bigotry persevere. Ivan Dixon plays a laborer who falls for a preacher's daughter, but his demand for respect angers his employers and scares his minister father-in-law. Dixon bristles at being called "boy" by the white community, but resents it even more when it comes from his wife's father. And his on-the-job talk of "organizing" gets him fired from his job. Hired as a gas station attendant, he is harassed by a group of white men and is fired once again because he is "bad for business." At film's end, he and his wife leave town to face an uncertain future.

Sidney Poitier made two films in the sixties that dealt with race in a realistic and intelligent manner. In the first, *A Raisin in the Sun* (1961), based on Lorraine Hansberry's play, Poitier is a discontented young family man living with his wife, son, sister, and mother in a cramped apartment. He dreams of a three-bedroom house with a backyard where his son can play. But he works in a low-paying job as a chauffeur to a rich white man and is unlikely to be able to afford a home of his own. When his father dies and his mother receives her husband's $10,000 insurance policy, the sister dreams of medical school tuition, the mother of a house and Poitier of partnering with his friend to buy a liquor store. Without telling her family, the mother puts a down payment on a house in a white neighborhood. Meanwhile, Poitier hands the $6,500 his mother has given him to save for his sister's education to his partner for a share of the liquor store, only to discover that his partner has run off with the money. At this point, Poitier is ready to take money from the white homeowners association to *not* move into the neighborhood. But he comes to realize that money alone cannot bring self-respect, so he and his family pack up their goods and move to their new home in the white neighborhood.

In another Poitier film, *In the Heat of the Night* (1967), he plays a Philadelphia detective who helps a Mississippi sheriff (Rod Steiger) solve a local murder. Throughout the film, Poitier is subjected to verbal abuse ("hey *boy*"), physical threats (by a gang of white trash), and humiliation (denied service in a luncheonette), but remains the professional police officer. The actor refused in one scene to be slapped by a white man without retaliation. His persistence won the day and the scene was changed. At film's end, he solves the crime and returns to Philadelphia. Poitier was anything but an "Uncle Tom" on or off the screen.

Director Edward Zwick's *Glory* (1989) recounts the story of Colonel Robert Gould Shaw, who led the all-black 54th Massachusetts Infantry Regiment during the Civil War.[16] Shaw is the only historical figure in the film, but the 54th regiment, composed mostly of free black volunteers, was real. This is the unit that turned back Confederate troops twice in and around Charleston, South Carolina. The 54th sustained significant casualties during the battle, while at the same time rioters in New York City formed mobs that beat, tortured, and lynched blacks in the mistaken belief that they, rather than the preservation of the Union, were responsible for the onset of the Civil War.

Back in the 1930s and 1940s, the film industry frequently turned to historical biographies of famous scientists, artists, and political leaders such as Émile Zola, Louis Pasteur, Benito Juárez, and Marie Curie as inspiration for its screenplays. These so-called "biopics" have been a staple of the industry, except that recently their emphasis has been on celebrities and entertainers. This is particularly true of biopics of famous black personalities such as Ray Charles, Tina Turner, Dorothy Dandridge, Billie Holiday, and Charlie Parker.

That renders the recent HBO film *Thurgood* (2011) a pleasant surprise, despite its format as a filmed presentation of a staged play performed before a live audience at the Kennedy Center in Washington, D.C. Actor Lawrence Fishburne portrays Thurgood Marshall, the first African American on the U.S. Supreme Court, in a one-man presentation of Marshall's life filled with humorous anecdotes, outbursts of passion and anger ("nigger, nigger"), and acts of courageous perseverance. Fishburne is spellbinding as he retells Marshall's story, beginning with his early life in Baltimore, his education at the all-black schools of Lincoln

University and Howard School of Law, his work as Chief Counsel for the NAACP, his appointment to the U.S. Court of Appeals by the Kennedy administration, and his appointment by President Lyndon Johnson, first as U.S. Solicitor-General, and later to the High Court in 1967.

Fishburne overcomes the static nature of the film's presentation by his energy, wit, and sly humor to provide a valuable history lesson, showing how Marshall had to survive the humiliation of living under segregation and Jim Crow laws. Fishburne illustrates this fact when Thurgood, on assignment for the NAACP, travels from New York to Washington and is forced to change to the "colored" car when the train crosses the Mason-Dixon Line. This is but one example of Thurgood's subjection to racism, which only strengthens his determination to change the "separate but equal" rule laid down by the High Court in *Plessy v. Ferguson* (1896). Marshall changed the course of civil rights in America by his successful arguments before the court in two important cases: *Smith v. Allwright* (1944), which struck down the white primary in Texas, thereby allowing blacks to vote in the state primary elections, and *Brown v. Board of Education* (1954), which declared all segregation laws to be unconstitutional.

HBO Films is to be commended for its straightforward and honest portrayal of the struggle for equality without succumbing to political correctness. Thurgood's story reveals what it was like to be black in America before desegregation and the passage of civil rights laws. This stage play/film is not shy about use of the word "nigger" nor about the shamefulness of playing the subservient role in a segregated society. Thurgood's friend, poet Langston Hughes, once admitted to him that he was humiliated "by the color of my skin."

Why did all these films get race right? First, the African-American characters are depicted as ordinary people from several social classes. The black characters in these films resonate with audiences because they could be members of any other ethnic or racial group. They are recognizable people—friends and neighbors—that could live in your community. Simply put, these black characters represent mainstream America. Second, the problems that Sidney Poitier, Juano Hernández, or Ivan Dixon confront in these films are similar to difficulties encountered by people of all races. Poitier wants a larger and better home for his family, Hernández wants to receive a fair trial, and Dixon wants his employers to treat him like a man. These are universal human needs that resonate with all audiences. And their responses to the dramatic situations they face are realistic rather than exaggerated; they act and behave in a fashion that is recognizable to most adult Americans. Even *Thurgood* depicts an Associate Justice of the Supreme Court as a determined fighter for equality, but not without human flaws. In brief, these are people that receive our empathy because as an audience we can relate to their dreams, desires, and fears.

## Getting Race Wrong

Hollywood gets race wrong in films when it persists in presenting minority characters in demeaning and humiliating roles. Fortunately, stereotyping has declined during the last half-century, but remnants remain. All Latinas are not maids or housekeepers. All African-Americans are not drug dealers and abusers. All minority members do not live below the poverty line. These stereotypical screen characters are one-dimensional cutouts, rather than the real people we know.

But what is more irritating and alarming is the practice within the industry to engage in what Professor Powell describes as "feel-good" racism that allows both Hollywood and the movie audience to leave the theater satisfied with their gesture of tolerance.[17] According to Powell's concept, "feel-good" racism is characterized by film plots where:

- the predominant white character helps to solve or improve the lives of the minority characters in the film, who appear to be incapable or helpless without that assistance
- the bigoted white leads undergo a last minute, 180-degree turnabout in attitude and behavior towards the members of other races, and
- the dramatic focus of the story concerns a substantial racial issue, say interracial marriage, that is readily resolved in the film, but the resolution ignores or omits the larger, more substantive questions.

Here are a few examples of "feel-good" racism evident in Hollywood movies that got race wrong.

Although released 20 years apart, both *Mississippi Burning* (1988) and *Gran Torino* (2008) share a common Hollywood flaw of making members of a minority group dependent on the heroics of the white characters. Such dependence represents a variation on the "white man's burden" ideology, which justified Western colonialism of Third World countries. *Mississippi Burning*'s plot was inspired by the civil rights movement of the 1960s when black and white volunteers traveled south in the summer of 1964 to assist and support local blacks in their struggle for racial justice and equality. Three of these volunteers (two white, one black) arrived in Mississippi, were stopped allegedly for speeding, taken to jail, and then disappeared. Their bodies were discovered buried in an earthen dam near Philadelphia, Mississippi, six weeks later. In this film, director Alan Parker accurately captures the terroristic atmosphere in which blacks lived under the control of white supremacists. But as historian William Chafe notes, the focus of Parker's film is on the conflict between the two white FBI agents (Gene Hackman, playing a former Southern sheriff, and Willem Dafoe, as a young Northern agent) as to the best way to uncover what happened to the three civil rights activists.[18] Dafoe is the gentle moralist, Hackman the savvy and tough southerner who, in one scene, squeezes the testicles of a local redneck to prove a point. Hackman eventually secures the necessary information on the murders from the wife of a Klan sheriff after a carefully planned seduction. But as Chafe points out, where are the black activists in the film? Did blacks play no role in the civil rights movement? Chafe documents the "reign of terror" in Mississippi where 600 blacks were lynched between 1880 and 1940, yet not one person was arrested for these crimes. He also notes that in 1963, one year before the incident portrayed in the film, 85,000 black Mississippians cast symbolic "freedom ballots" to demonstrate their determination to vote despite threats, church burnings, and murders. Blacks prevailed in Mississippi mostly due to their own effort, but audiences would not know that from this film.

Similarly, in *Gran Torino*, director Clint Eastwood plays a grumpy and ill Korean War veteran, a retired Ford auto worker, who is estranged from his own children and generally dislikes everybody he meets. His only joy seems to be his 1972 Gran Torino car, but when Thao, his Hmong neighbor's son, tries to steal it under pressure from local gangbangers, Eastwood is first angry and then sympathetic as he becomes a surrogate father to the boy. The Hmong people came from the mountainous and hilly regions of Southeast Asia and many of them emigrated to the U.S. in the 1970s when the communist Pathet Lao took over their governments. Thao gives the dying Eastwood a purpose in his life as the curmudgeon takes the boy under his wing. When Eastwood's children want to put him in a nursing home, he is further alienated from them. Meanwhile, Eastwood warms to his Hmong neighbors, especially to Thao's sister, Sue, who apologizes for her brother's bad behavior. The audience senses that Eastwood likes Sue because she is among the privileged few he allows to step on his property. Despite their budding friendship, Eastwood continues to disrespect Thao by calling him a "gook" (a favorite term used by G.I.s in Korea), along with "toad," "slope," and "zipperhead." It is ironic that Eastwood's racist epithets are directed toward a people who supported the U.S. in Vietnam. When Thao's cousin's gang roughs him up, burning his face and raping his sister, the police are not informed. Feeling somewhat responsible for these violent acts, the "Dirty Harry" persona of Eastwood's character emerges and he swings into action to save the boy and revenge the sister's rape. He dupes Thao into a showdown with the gang, but instead locks him away and proceeds, unarmed, to call out the gangbangers. During the confrontation, Eastwood is killed and the police arrest the gang members. At the reading of the will, Eastwood has left his prized Gran Torino to Thao, much to the chagrin of his granddaughter.

The problem with the film is that, once again, it is the white man who rescues his minority neighbors from physical harm. Why do the Hmong people not defend themselves? Why is the solution not left to local authorities? Why is the resolution left to a dying 78-year-old white guy? The ending of this film encourages white adult males to feel good about the outcome because it fulfills their heroic fantasies, but it has little to do with real life. And the idea that a foul-mouthed bigot goes all "warm and cuddly" over immigrants he bullies and despises requires audiences to suspend disbelief. Is the underlying message of films like *Gran Torino* and *Crash* (below) that after a lifetime of bigotry, redemption is achievable in the final reel? Only in your Hollywood dreams.

Another screen racist undergoes a transformation in Paul Haggis's 2004 Oscar-winning film, *Crash*, a story about the collisions between people. The first scene sets up what will follow later in the film. Haggis opens with a rear-end crash involving an Asian woman and a white woman who proceed to blame each other during an escalating shouting match. These two characters do not reappear in the film. There are other scenes involving racial clashes, such as between a black detective and his white partner and between a white woman and her Latina housekeeper, but the significant ones concern a racist cop (Matt Dillon) living with his ailing father and his encounters with several black women.

Since Dillon's father is having difficulty receiving medical assistance from his black social worker, Dillon phones the worker, then goes to see her at her office, where they have a contentious meeting. Dillon thereupon stops a car containing two black passengers, a TV producer and his wife, on a pretext for harassment. He asks them to get out of the car, and with the husband watching Dillon searches ("feels up") the wife, much to the humiliation of the couple. This incident causes a dispute within the marriage because the wife is angry that her husband failed to intervene in her behalf. Later in the film, the TV producer's wife overturns her car and becomes trapped within it while gas leaks out from the tank. Coincidentally, Dillon's patrol car arrives on the scene, where he recognizes the woman as the one he previously searched, and proceeds to risk his life to free her before the car explodes and burns. Haggis provides no justification for Dillon's sudden turn of character, other than to have a white man save a black woman from certain death. Or is the film's message that even a racist has a good heart? If that is the intended message, it is certain to be offensive to African Americans.

Both *Crash* and *Gran Torino* share a flaw common to Hollywood-made movies, that is, a belief in the transformative nature of heroes in the final reel. In action movies audiences are more apt to accept such transformation because the film is inconsequential. But the films above deal with white bigots and racists who attain heroic stature in the final scene. What lesson does this impart to youngsters today? That a life of racial hatred is forgiven by one implausible act of kindness? Does that one act wash the slate clean of past transgressions? Maybe director Haggis should ask Martin Luther King Jr., Medgar Evers, Rodney King, and Trayvon Martin what they think. And should Haggis and Eastwood believe that their films express the view that decency exists in every human being, they misread the history of racism in America.

Yet another good example of "feel-good" racism is Stanley Kramer's 1967 film, *Guess Who's Coming to Dinner*, where the director tackles the issue of interracial marriage. While Kramer is to be commended for his willingness to undertake that subject in the 1960s when such a film was difficult to produce, good intentions alone are not enough. The story brings the team of Spencer Tracy and Katharine Hepburn once again to the screen as the Draytons, a couple whose liberal principles are challenged when their daughter (Katharine Houghton) brings home her fiancé (Sidney Poitier), a young doctor, to meet her parents. The Draytons are now faced with the moral dilemma of whether an interracial marriage is suitable for *their* daughter. To help the Draytons out of their predicament, Kramer has Poitier's parents express the view that in 1960s America such a union will face many difficulties and will even be illegal in some states. But in typical Hollywood fashion love wins out and the young couple receives the blessing of both sets of parents.

The film won two Oscars (for Hepburn and the screenplay) and some 20 nominations. But if Kramer had paid more than lip service to his liberal convictions, his film might have examined the issue in greater depth. Spike Lee tried to do just that in his film *Jungle Fever* (1991), in which a white woman of Italian background (Annabella Sciorra) has an affair with a married black office worker (Wesley Snipes). Although the film contains several love scenes (there were none in *Guess Who's Coming to Dinner*), Lee has the lovers returning to their respective families in the end. Admittedly, *Jungle Fever* could not have been made 30 years earlier, but still Kramer passed up an opportunity to examine the harder issue of anti-miscegenation laws that existed in the U.S. at the time. These interracial laws were struck down by the U.S. Supreme Court in the case of *Loving v. Virginia*,[19] but it was left to television to portray their story in a 1996 TV film, *Mr. & Mrs. Loving*. Richard Loving, a white man, married Mildred Jeter, a woman of African-American and American-Indian descent, in Washington, D.C., where interracial marriage was legal. But later, when they moved to Virginia, they were arrested for violating the Racial Integrity Act. With the aid of the ACLU, the Lovings prevailed in the courts. The Lovings were ordinary people who were deeply in love and simply wanted to live together like other married couples. This inspirational true story of a nonpolitical working-class couple who became civil rights heroes is the film Hollywood should have made.

As a measure of America's moral and social progress, it is interesting to note that when President Obama's parents married in 1960 their marriage would have been illegal—and he would have been considered illegitimate—in half of the states. Another equality yardstick lies in the increasing number of interracial marriages in the U.S. Consider that in 1970, three years after the *Loving* decision, fewer than 2 percent of married couples were interracial. By 2005, the proportion of interracial marriages had increased to 7.5 percent of all married couples.[20]

## How Good Intentions Lead to Bad Films

Sometimes Hollywood makes films with the best of intentions and some may become popular box office hits. But good intentions alone do not necessarily produce the right results. Both of the films in the following discussion, *The Blind Side* (2009) and *The Help* (2011) are cases in point. *The Blind Side* was a smash box office hit and won an Oscar for its star, Sandra Bullock. Unfortunately, this biopic of Michael Oher, who as an uneducated, homeless teen was befriended then adopted by a Southern white family who helped him to an education and a career as an National Football League (NFL) player, is a feel-good story that does a disservice to the kind deed that was done.

At its core, the film is the sort of rags-to-riches story that Hollywood loves to tell on the big screen, yet the author sees it as just another example of Hollywood peddling more of the same old feel-good racism. The Sandra Bullock character, Leigh Anne Tuohy, alternates throughout the movie between being Dirty Harry and Mother Teresa. In one scene she talks down and threatens a group of tough blacks from the Memphis projects and walks away triumphantly, a scenario that is highly implausible. Yet in other scenes, Leigh Anne appears saintly. During lunch with her wealthy female friends, she berates them for their racist attitudes. When they sheepishly congratulate her altruism by remarking that "you're changing that boy's life," she responds: "No, he's changing mine." After the Tuohys buy Michael a brand new car, he takes their son, S.J., for a ride and they begin to jive to the music when he takes his eyes off the road and rams into another vehicle. Michael is distraught and apologetic when Leigh Anne arrives on the scene and her response is to tell him: "It's not your fault." Of course it's his fault. His negligence could have killed both of them.

The above scenes reveal the real intention of this film: to broadcast the goodness of Leigh Anne and her over-privileged white family. The Tuohys, particularly Leigh Anne, dominate the film to such an extent that there is hardly any screen time for Michael Oher (Quinton Aaron). The script in fact gives him very few lines. This turns out to be Sandra

Bullock's Oscar story. What the Tuohys did was kind and generous, but does the film have to advertise their goodness like the Goodyear blimp?

When Michael is given screen time, he is lectured, comforted, and treated like a big puppy dog by Leigh Anne and her family, especially S.J., the young son. On the football field, his clueless football coach struggles to communicate with him. So who steps in? None other than pint-sized S.J., who has no trouble teaching Mike how to play left tackle. Then, to add insult to injury, his white momma provides on-the-field inspiration as she counsels Michael on how to play his position, which is to protect the QB: "This team is your family. You protect them," she says. In the next scene, there is Michael bowling over the defensive linemen.

In real life the Tuohys may well be an altruistic family, but as depicted in *The Blind Side*, they are just too good to be true. Except for Leigh Anne's lunch group, it is difficult to find any bigots in the film. All the white folks appear to love this big kid even though he would eat you out of house and home. The film is simply too self-righteous. When it's over, the audience has been exposed to the privileged life of white Southerners but learns very little about Michael Oher and the status of poor blacks in the Deep South.

As an antidote to all this Southern sugar, the reader should compare *The Blind Side* film version with Michael Oher's own story as recounted in his book, *I Beat the Odds: From Homelessness to The Blind Side and Beyond*.[21] While Michael expresses appreciation to the Tuohy family, he does not gush over them. On his dedication page, the Tuohys are listed second behind unidentified people who helped him. Then in the prologue, Michael corrects several errors in the movie version, such as his not knowing how to play football as a teenager and walking to the gym in November with cut-off shorts. He also challenges a newspaper article that reportedly quoted Leigh Anne as saying that he would have been dead or become a bodyguard to a gang leader if the Tuohys had not taken him into their family. His response to the article was : "I think that had to be a misquote because despite the sensationalist things that make for a more dramatic story, what my family knows and what I know is that I would have found my way out of the ghetto one way or another. Failure was not an option for me."[22] These words do not resonate with the lumbering, slow-witted Michael Oher portrayed in *The Blind Side*. The film version reduces its supposed central subject in every way possible, while portraying the Tuohys as candidates for sainthood. One film critic called this "the most insidious kind of racism."[23]

Why did Hollywood get race wrong in this film? Hardcore racism is not at issue. The studio heads, directors, and others who made the film are possibly misguided, but not bad people. Rather it is a question of the economics that governs most decisions within the film industry. Maybe the financial risk is too high for even well-intentioned directors and producers to make the kind of honest movie that one would like to come out of Hollywood. Instead, the film industry continues to make these feel-good movies that nurture white self-esteem, support white liberalism at no cost, and win an Oscar or two. In Hollywood, who could resist such a win-win situation?

Figure 12.1. *The Help*, 2011. Maid Octavia Spencer Delivering Her Special Pie to Her Ex-Employer. Reprinted with permission, Walt Disney Studios Motion Pictures/Photofest

## Case Study: *The Help*

Hollywood has a checkered history in its portrayal of race relations, off and on the screen. This is not because the studio heads are bigots but rather because the industry's bottom line is always about money and adherence to this principle requires that filmmakers not challenge the status quo or question the prevailing racial attitudes. The film industry accepted segregation and practiced discrimination, but later it readily embraced integration when it became the law of the land.

Like *The Blind Side*, the film *The Help* (2011) may have been produced with noble intentions, but its release caused much controversy, as it was applauded and condemned, praised and vilified by its supporter and detractors, and not always along racial lines. A national debate surrounded the film, disputing its merits and faults, and those who saw it either loved it or hated it.

*The Help* turned out to be the surprise box office hit of 2011. Based on the bestseller by Kathryn Stockett, which has sold over a million copies, the film was both praised and defended by film critics, white liberals, and several black organizations that openly spoke or wrote to support the film. A strong endorsement came from the widow of Medgar Evers, the civil rights activist, who was murdered in Mississippi in 1962. Mrs. Evers praised the film in a half-page ad in *The New York Times* two weeks before the annual Academy Awards in these words: "My hope is that this movie will continue to be taken into Schools so that this generation of children…will learn the true story of the struggle…[for civil rights]."[24]

The film was also endorsed by Roslyn Brock, the chairwoman of the NAACP, who "felt so proud" after seeing the film because her grandmother had been a domestic in Florida and when she died the family she took care of sent condolences. Brock urged NAACP members to "go see this movie."[25] Still another black organization, the Black Film Critics Circle, voted *The Help* the best film of the year. *The Help* garnered four Academy Award nominations, including best picture, eight NAACP Award nominations, four Screen Actors Guild Award nominations, and five award nominations in England from the British Academy of Film & Television Arts (BAFTA).

On the other hand, the African-American Film Critics Association (AAFCA) considered *The Tree of Life* as the best film of 2011, while ranking *The Help* at number 10.[26] But the harshest criticism came from the Association of Black Women Historians (ABWH), who issued an open statement to fans of the movie:

> Despite efforts to market the book and the film as a progressive story of triumph over racial injustice, *The Help* distorts, ignores, and trivializes the experiences of black domestic workers…. *The Help*'s representation of these women is a disappointing resurrection of Mammy—a mythical stereotype of black women who were compelled, either by slavery or segregation, to serve white families. Portrayed as asexual, loyal, and contented caretakers of whites, the caricature of Mammy allowed mainstream America to ignore the systemic racism that bound black women to backbreaking, low paying jobs where employers routinely exploited them. The popularity of this most recent iteration is troubling because it reveals a contemporary nostalgia for the days when a black woman could only hope to clean the White House rather than reside in it.[27]

Why did this film so divide its viewers? *The Help* may be viewed as a historical fable of black women who worked as maids and nannies for affluent white women in the Deep South so the latter could spend their days playing cards, enjoying gossipy lunches with their elite friends, and generally living a privileged lifestyle in 1960s Jackson, Mississippi. Essentially, these white women are portrayed as vacuous and closeted racists who leave the duties of home and children to their black maids, who prepare their meals, clean their homes, and raise their children. The latter responsibility is particularly poignant as it meant the maids did not have the time and energy for their own children. The two favorably cast white women in the film are Emma Stone (as Skeeter), a columnist for the local paper whose ambition is to be a serious writer, and Jessica Chastain (as Celia), who plays a well-meaning but somewhat naive wife considered to be "white trash" by the other women. By comparison, most all of the black women are wise, noble, and dedicated to their employers.

The story unfolds through the eyes of college graduate Skeeter, who has returned to her hometown during the early stages of the civil rights movement to discover that she has little in common with her former friends. Under the cover of ghostwriting a domestic column for the local paper, Skeeter interviews two black maids, Aibileen

(Viola Davis) and the feisty Minny (Octavia Spencer), to collect data for a book on black maids and their lives under the restrictions of the Jim Crow laws—which include requiring separate toilets for them and backdoor entrances so that they remain "invisible" to outsiders. Women dominate the film, whereas the white males are incidental characters and only two black men appear briefly.

Although the "separate but equal" doctrine of *Plessy v. Ferguson* (1896)[28] was declared unconstitutional in *Brown v. Board of Education*, the policy of integration was impeded by state and local governments and social codes aimed at keeping blacks in their subservient place. These social codes are presented in *The Help* as so ingrained in the culture that the black maids refuse to eat with their white employers, even when invited. The reader should understand that all social and entertainment facilities were divided into "white only" and "colored" sections, reminiscent of the Black Codes of the Reconstruction era. To be black in the South of the sixties was to dwell in the social underclass as emancipated servants to the white master.

As well as winning favor with film critics and white liberals, the film did very well at the domestic box office, grossing $170 million, an especially strong contemporary showing for a "social message" film. One argument in support of the film came from critics who admitted the film's flaws but maintained that, nevertheless, it provided an important civil rights lesson for a younger generation that might be ignorant of America's racist past. Furthermore, the argument continues, a more realistic, depressing film about blacks in the Deep South of the 1960s would be self-defeating since it probably would be a bust at the box office.[29] Other support came from critics and viewers who praised the film's acting, especially Davis, Spencer, and Chastain.

On the other side of the issue, the film's detractors raised several serious objections to it. One position saw the film as an apology for the South, with the overwhelming sweetness of the story and its light, sometimes humorous approach seen as an attempt to defuse the brutality and ugliness of segregation and its destructive effect on the black population. The film is shot in soft-color tones and concentrates largely on the lives of the affluent white class while implying that blacks did not have such a bad existence. But the author remembers his military time in the Jim Crow South of the 1950s where blacks would automatically step into the street as whites walked past them. In the movie theaters, whites had the center sections reserved for them while blacks were restricted to the side aisles. The theater bathrooms and water fountains were divided along racial lines. And in many southern cities there were on the law books so-called "vagrancy laws" that allowed the local police to stop and ask you to demonstrate that you had sufficient funds on your person. Needless to say, the vagueness of such laws allowed for arbitrary enforcement. The author remembers witnessing the application of this law, not only to blacks, but to Yankee soldiers who gave away their northern roots once they answered the question of "how much money you have on you, boy?" The wrong answer earned you a ticket straight to the local jail. These anecdotes represent the real South under Jim Crow rather than Hollywood's prettified version.

A related criticism is the film's underplaying of the violence and dangers blacks faced at that time. For example, Evers was assassinated in front of his house but the black maids and the theater audience hear about it on television, thereby softening the horror and the brutality of his murder. What is missing from *The Help* is any indication of the physical danger and smoldering violence that accompanied the civil rights movement in the South. There is only one scene where, while making an arrest, several black maids are manhandled by the police.

A third criticism focuses on the trying but fairly benign conditions under which these black women worked and lived. After all, one could argue that these women didn't have it so bad: they worked in a nice environment and ate good food that they had prepared. That may have been true, but the film contains at least one openly bigoted white woman, the sort who could, on a bad day, make the maid's day miserable simply because she woke up with a headache. One such is Hilly, played wonderfully by Bryce Dallas Howard as an insecure, unhappy wife with a white supremacy mean streak. Her maids are entirely at her mercy and she can (and does) fire them on the spot, in full knowledge there is no right of appeal to any outside agency. There is a scene in the film where a maid is accused of stealing three pieces of silverware (why take three? That's not even a complete table setting) and is immediately fired despite her denial. Another maid, Constantine, of long service to her employer and the one who raised Skeeter, is fired by Skeeter's mother because Constantine's daughter uses the front entrance instead of entering through the servant's quarters, thereby intruding into a luncheon meeting of the Daughters of the American Revolution.

These black maids must have lived in constant fear of their employers—afraid to speak a wrong word or make a mistake or fail at potty-training. The film minimizes the real anxiety and stressful conditions under which these maids labored every day of their working lives. To the best of the author's knowledge, there is little sociological data on how contemporary minority maids who work for white employers view them. But there are several sources that provide access to letters and stories where black maids/nannies (sometimes referred to as "nurses") bear witness to what it was like to work as a domestic. The consensus is that life for these black women was harsh, demanding, and often humiliating. One story of a black nurse published in a 1912 edition of *The Independent* revealed that she had to work 14 to 16 hours a day, was required to sleep in the house, usually with a small child, and was given one Sunday afternoon off every other week. She was not permitted to rest and was constantly on duty, ready to answer every "mammy do this" or "mammy do that" from her employer. When not tending to the children, she would be watering the garden, sweeping and mopping, darning and sewing, and helping the cook—all this work for $10 a month, excluding payment for her room and board. She was also at the mercy of the master, who tried to take sexual liberties with her.[30]

More recently, a 2005 documentary, *Maid in America*, follows three women maids working in Los Angeles.[31] Most of the more than 100,000 domestic workers in Los Angeles are women of color and the vast majority are immigrants, legal and illegal, from Central America, and are without rights and without union support. Like their fictional counterparts, domestics today are at the mercy of their employers. Only New York and California provide any protective laws for domestic workers.

How do the 2.5 million people who work in domestic services as maids, housekeepers, nannies, cooks, and more view their employers? Generally, they are viewed with resentment and anger as they labor for long hours without overtime pay, health insurance benefits, and paid vacations. In short, they continue to work under exploitative conditions in the 21st century.[32] This anecdotal documentary depicts a far different existence from that portrayed by the fictional black maids of *The Help*. Finally, *The Help*'s critics point out that the maids in the film accepted their status until Skeeter started to interview them and raise their racial consciousness. Blacks would question that assertion, although Hollywood has implied it in several films such as *Mississippi Burning*.

Skeeter is the heroine of the film even though the title implies that the movie's focus is on the black maids. It is Skeeter, after all, who initiates the interviews, which expand as the film progresses. This scenario reminds the author of a line in one of James Lee Burke's detective novels where New Orleans police Lieutenant Dave Robicheaux, after giving advice to a black man, wondered if by doing so he had been guilty of the Southern conceit that whites had to protect people of color from themselves.[33] Making Skeeter the centerpiece of *The Help* places her in the same position as Clint Eastwood's character in *Gran Torino*, namely, as the white savior of colored people.

I think the reader can understand why blacks would be offended by *The Help*'s unbalanced view of the civil rights movement—one led by whites (their masters) and supported by black followers (their servants). Admittedly, Spencer's character, Minny, exhibits some feistiness and expresses her displeasure at her employer. When she violates one of the social codes (using the house rather than the servant's bathroom), it results in her being fired by Hilly. Minny, however, exacts her revenge by baking one of her famous pies and presenting it to Hilly as a reminder of what Hilly will miss when Minny has left her employment. But once Hilly realizes the extra ingredient it contains, she makes a mad dash for the bathroom. The audience in the theater with me thought this scene hilarious. While some may consider Minny's payback funny, does it deserve this accolade from one film critic who described her as much of a civil rights activist as Rosa Parks, the seamstress who refused to move to the back of the bus in Montgomery, Alabama, thus initiating a city-wide bus boycott in 1955?[34] The comparison is not only ludicrous but insulting to the memory of Rosa Parks, a true civil rights heroine. Parks' act of defiance was not impulsive but planned. She had received training in nonviolent direct action similar to that received by the freedom riders and lunch-counter sit-in protesters. These people put their welfare and even their lives on the line. To even compare their actions to a maid who bakes a pie composed of human waste to give to a white woman in a piece of fiction is an affront of the first order.

Because *The Help* was a critical and financial success, it may seem petty to argue against the support it has received. A few of the film's supporters admitted its flaws and soft racial focus, but considered these minor blemishes in a film that otherwise de-

> scribed what life was like for black maids under Jim Crow. But there are some concerns about the validity of the film's representations. Good intentions alone do not trump the dubious racial messages the film delivered to audiences. Possibly it is too much to ask Hollywood to treat an important subject honestly and with integrity. But even more damaging is the fact that the film is being praised for the wrong reason. Living under segregation and Jim Crow was anything but pretty, noble, and funny for black people. That is *The Help*'s greatest omission.

It may prove useful to compare *The Help* with another film that expresses Hollywood's view of race a half-century ago. That would be director Douglas Sirk's film *Imitation of Life* (1959), a remake of the 1933 Fanny Hurst novel about two single mothers, one white, one black, trying to raise their daughters in post-WWII New York City. Sirk's career in Hollywood spanned more than 40 movies but his reputation blossomed after he retired, when critics remembered four of his 1950s films: *Magnificent Obsession* (1954), *All That Heaven Allows* (1955), *Written on the Wind* (1956), and *Imitation of Life*, which together accumulated six Oscar nominations and one win.

There are two narratives vying for attention in *Imitation of Life*. One narrative concerns the relationship between an ambitious white actress (played by Lana Turner) and her largely ignored daughter (Sandra Dee). The other involves the stormy relationship between a homeless black mother (Juanita Moore), whom Turner has taken in, and her light-skinned daughter (Susan Kohner), who is ashamed of her race and tries desperately to pass for white. Reportedly, Sirk promoted the first narrative because he feared that white audiences might not accept the dominance of a racial theme in 1959. The director was also apprehensive about casting a black actress to play the light-skinned daughter, and so he hired Kohner, of Mexican-Jewish descent, even though there were half dozen light-skinned and biracial actresses available.[35]

In viewing both films back-to-back, the author was struck by the similarities despite the half century that separates them. A close analysis of both films revealed the following qualities. First, the white characters in both films are dominant throughout, with the black characters accepting secondary roles despite having much more interesting and emotionally charged stories. While Moore and Kohner received Oscar nominations for their work, Turner and Dee did not.[36] This is similar to *The Help*, where Emma Stone (as Skeeter) failed to receive a best actress nomination even while the two black maids, Viola Davis and Octavia Spencer, were nominated for best supporting actress.

Second, Moore is treated as a maid/nanny almost immediately by Turner. It is true that Moore is beholden to Turner for taking her and her daughter off the streets, but would Moore so quickly assume the role of servant—running the daily routine of the household, doing all the domestic chores, and taking care of both daughters while Turner goes to auditions? Moore is very much like Davis and Spencer in *The Help*. She has been reduced to maid status and any pretense at equality is lost, since Moore addresses Turner as "Miss Lora" but is called "Annie" in return. The film establishes the class lines early when Turner, trying to get an acting part, tells her agent that Moore is her maid. That turns out to be the most honest line in the film.

Third, during a heart-to-heart talk about their daughters' problems, Turner makes it perfectly clear that having a daughter who falls in love with her mother's boyfriend is much more serious than having a daughter working in strip clubs and passing herself off as white. The comparison is insensitive and jarring. Turner's daughter has a crush on her mother's boyfriend and grows out of her romantic infatuation with an older man by the final reel. But Moore's daughter has deep-seated resentment over her race, is totally ashamed of her mother, and in trying to pass for white is beaten badly by her white boyfriend. Crushes come and go but problems associated with racial identity are not so easily resolved.

Fourth, when Moore is dying, she asks Turner to please follow her funeral plans, which include corresponding with a rather long list of friends. Turner is surprised and remarks that she never realized that Moore had so many friends and a life outside of her subservient role in Turner's home. The audience is just as amazed because Sirk fails to develop Moore's other life: she spends so much time in the house you would think she suffered from agoraphobia. What Turner expressed 50 years ago is characteristic of the white conceit that "the help" are not human beings but rather serve as functionaries allowing whites to live their chosen lifestyle. Does this attitude not remind you of the spoiled Southern white women in *The Help* who treated their maids as invisible except when their services were required? Isn't American history replete with examples where the white majority treated people of color as invisible entities? These similarities bind *The Help* and *Imitation of Life* together, demonstrating that Hollywood has learned little about developments in racial relations over the past half century.

More positively, Hollywood has recently produced a race-conscious film that is a more honest depiction of race in America than either *The Help* or *The Blind Side* since it examines racial issues from the perspective of the film's major African-American characters. *Lee Daniels' The Butler* (2013) is based on a true story of a black man, Cecil Gaines (played by Forest Whitaker), who served eight presidents as a butler on the White House staff. Gaines is the film's narrator as he relates his life story, beginning with his roots as the son of cotton pickers on a southern plantation and ending with him waiting to be honored by President Obama for his long service to the White House. The audience sees Gaines in two contexts: in his role as White House butler and as husband to a loving but unhappy wife (Oprah Winfrey) and father to two boys who follow different life paths. His younger son, Charlie, dies in the Vietnam War while his older son, Louis, joins the civil rights movement and becomes a U.S. congressman. The scenes between Gaines and Louis depict the intergenerational conflict and clash of values over civil rights and Vietnam that were present in many white families as well.

The strength of the movie is that, because it is Gaines' story, whites are secondary characters who move in and out of the plot, but never dominate it. Of most importance is the fact that these African Americans control their own fate, for better or worse. They make their own decisions and pay the price for them.

The author viewed the film with a mostly white audience that applauded as it ended, possibly as an expression of relief that Hollywood had made a film that depicted African

Americans as ordinary people who experience the joys and sorrows of life just as any other racial group. At last, Hollywood had made a film, quoting the Reverend Dr. Martin Luther King, where the characters "will not be judged by the color of their skin but by the content of their character."[37]

In summing up race in Hollywood, it can be stated that the film industry has taken several steps toward greater equality, off and on the screen, but much more remains to be achieved. In a recent study of popular films that included the topic of racial diversity within the industry, it was reported that minorities were underrepresented on screen and behind the camera.[38] Examining best picture-nominated films from 2007–10, the study found that of the 1,425 speaking characters, only 11.6 percent were black, 7 percent were Asian, and less than 2 percent were Hispanic. Looking at diversity behind the camera, the study revealed that less than 1 percent of the 180 directors were African American. These statistics demonstrate that racial diversity has yet to be achieved within the film industry. Also requiring greater attention is the occasional scene or piece of dialogue that, even if unintentional, contributes to racial and ethnic stereotyping in films. More people of color should be presented on screen other than in Tyler Perry movies. Many blacks continue to be invisible in the industry: even Perry, who has directed more than two dozen films, is omitted from a popular 1,600-page movie guide.[39] To provide opportunities for minorities and people of color to work behind the camera, an in-house mentoring system should be created to further their training as directors, screenwriters, cinematographers, and even studio executives. The major studios, at least, should establish internship opportunities for minority students who are studying for a career in the film industry. This list of suggestions is not meant to be exhaustive but to encourage incremental steps toward greater diversity within the industry.

A story recently broke in the media that actress Zoe Saldana would be cast as Nina Simone in a forthcoming biopic of the great jazz singer. While black critics questioned the casting because Saldana does not resemble Simone, their negative reaction focused more on Hollywood's tendency to cast light-skinned African Americans with white features as a more acceptable choice than, in this case, a darker but truer-to-life image of Simone.[40] So long as Hollywood continues to portray blacks on screen according to some studio's idea of what degree of color is acceptable to white America, there is little hope for change within the industry.

Chapter 13

# Hollywood and Women

## Cracks in the Celluloid Ceiling

"Women have made up half of the human race but you could never tell that by the books historians write."
—Arthur Schlesinger Jr., historian

"I spent my life searching for a man to look up to without lying down."
—Frances Marion, screenwriter and director

"Women are the only oppressed group in our society that lives in intimate association with their oppressors."
—Evelyn Cunningham, journalist

"It was we, the people; not we, the white male citizens; nor yet we, the male citizens; but we, the whole people, who formed the Union…women as well as men."
—Susan B. Anthony, feminist

"You know, when I first went into the movies Lionel Barrymore played my grandfather. Later he played my father and finally he played my husband. If he had lived I'm sure I would have played his mother. That's the way it is in Hollywood. The men get younger and the women get older."
—Lillian Gish, actress

The literature on women[1] in Hollywood movies is extensive and includes such notable scholars as Jeanine Basinger and Molly Haskell.[2] The objective in this chapter is to briefly review Hollywood's past history toward women, examine the present, and offer some suggestions that would advance their status in the film industry in the future. The chapter opens with a background description of Hollywood's treatment of women, from the early days of the film industry to the present, and then it describes how their status has changed over time. Following that discussion, the author examines specific films to illustrate how Hollywood gets women "right" and "wrong" in its movies. The chapter concludes with suggestions for furthering equality and extending opportunities to women within the film industry.

Unlike Hollywood's treatment of race relations, which moved slowly but progressively forward, its treatment of women followed an irregular path similar to the swings of the stock market. Women were the stars of early Hollywood until the advent of WWII. Thereafter, their fortunes declined for more than three decades until a renaissance of sorts began in the 1970s, marked by Sally Field's Oscar-winning performance as *Norma Rae* (1979). Whether this was due to the nascent feminist movement under way in the U.S. at the time or a reflection of the developing liberal trend within the industry, the status of women in Hollywood spiraled upward thereafter but continues to fall short of reaching equal treatment.

## Women in Early Hollywood

In the early years of the film industry, Hollywood treated women quite decently as compared to minorities. From its beginning, Hollywood was a non-unionized, male-dominated industry, where the actors, writers, directors, and technical staff, and even the glamour stars, were under the control of major studios through tight, restrictive contracts. But whereas minorities were badly treated by the studios, women played a prominent role in the early years of silent film. Possibly a few readers, especially older moviegoers, will recall the more prominent Hollywood female stars of the silent era like Mary Pickford and Lillian Gish, although writers and directors like Dorothy Arzner and Frances Marion remain largely unknown to most moviegoers today. To understand why this is the case is the purpose of this section.

Contrary to popular belief, women filled a variety of roles in the film industry's early years. They worked in front of and behind the camera as directors, film editors, producers, screenwriters, and technicians; a few even went into the distribution side of the business. Author and playwright Eleanor Gates, for instance, organized her own production company in 1914. By the next year, her company, the Liberty Feature Film Company, was producing two-reelers. Although the venture was ephemeral, it has the distinction of being the first production company managed completely by women.[3]

The early years of the film industry into the 1930s is often considered the "golden age" for women in Hollywood. Women like Alice Guy Blache, Lois Weber, Dorothy Arzner, and Frances Marion were film trailblazers as directors, writers, and producers. Guy Blache was a noted director and cinematographer in France before coming to the U.S., where she owned her own studio and was recognized as the first filmmaker to present a story or narrative on film. Weber was a successful director of the silent era; her films tackled social issues that affected women, like birth control. Arzner was a popular director in the 1930s, making 16 films in 15 years. Meanwhile, Marion wrote more than 300 scripts, directed and produced half a dozen films, and served as vice president and founder of the Screen Writers Guild (SWG). In 1917, she signed a contract as screenwriter with MGM that paid her $50,000 a year. Not only was Marion the highest-paid writer in the film industry from 1917 to 1930, but she was the first woman writer to ever win an Oscar and the first person to win two Academy Awards in any field.[4] Her friend Mary Pickford was the highest paid star in Hollywood at that time, and while she and Lillian Gish took screen roles that portrayed Victorian women who were virtuous, innocent, and in need of male protection, off screen they were independent and strong businesswomen.[5] For example, Pickford joined Charlie Chaplin, Douglas Fairbanks, and D.W. Griffith in creating United Artists—their own production and distribution company. By 1917 both Pickford and Frances Marion were surpassing the salaries of their male colleagues. At the height of her career, Pickford negotiated a huge contract for that era: a $40,000 signing bonus, $10,000 per week, and a percentage of the studio's profits.[6] She was the Julia Roberts of her day.

Director Dorothy Arzner left behind a significant body of work, done mostly in the twenties and thirties. In four of her films, *Honor Among Lovers* (1931), *Christopher Strong* (1933), *Craig's Wife* (1936), and *Dance Girl Dance* (1940), she portrayed strong women resisting the conventions of the patriarchal society and the social mores of the time. For example, in *Honor Among Lovers*, a secretary (Claudette Colbert) fills in for her boss (Frederic March) at an important board meeting and succeeds in persuading its members to accept March's proposals. March is delighted, but later, when March makes sexual advances, she rejects him and marries another man of lower status. Then in the film *Christopher Strong*, Katharine Hepburn plays an aviator who is also the mistress of the male lead. When Hepburn learns she is pregnant, she decides to return to flying. But rather than carry her pregnancy to term, she decides to end her life in a wild airplane ride.[7] The reader may want to compare the Hepburn decision with that made by the title characters in *Thelma and Louise* (1991), who decide to end their lives rather than face jail time. Hepburn's character realizes that she faces a bleak future as an unwed mother since abortion was illegal throughout the U.S. She and the child would also be stigmatized by the social mores of the 1930s. Hence, her suicide, while an act of desperation, is comprehensible. But Thelma and Louise driving off into the Grand Canyon abyss rather than face jail is less so. Feminists today may deride these choices as being weak portrayals of female independence, but it must be remembered that, in *Christopher Strong*'s time at least, movies were under the control of the Hays Office and later the Production Code, where no on-screen sins or crimes could go unpunished. To enjoy their sins, the code required screen characters to pay for them, one way or another.

Arzner may have made her strongest statement against what 1970s feminists called the "male gaze" in her film *Dance Girl Dance*. Arzner was critical of how Hollywood's male-centered movies tended to objectify the female body. In her film, two women in a dance company represent different attitudes toward their craft. Judy (Maureen O'Hara) is a dedicated student of ballet but male audiences are not interested in her dance movements. In contrast, Bubbles (Lucille Ball) is a sexy burlesque queen who bumps and grinds to the wild applause of the mostly male audience. No surprise that Bubbles becomes a "star" in her profession. At film's end, reserved Judy turns on the male audience that has been heckling her on stage with this rebuke:

> Go on, laugh, get your money's worth… I know you want me to tear my clothes off so you can look your 50 cents worth. Fifty cents for the privilege of staring at a girl the way your wives won't let you. What do you suppose we think of you up here with your silly smirks your mothers would be ashamed of?… We'd laugh right back at the lot of you, only we're paid to let you sit and roll your eyes and make your screamingly clever remarks. What's it for? So you can go home when the show's over, strut before your wives and sweethearts and play at being the stronger sex for a minute? I'm sure they see through you. I'm sure they see through you just like we do![8]

The golden era for women in film began its descent in the 1930s due to a combination of factors: the economic slump caused by the Great Depression, the advent of sound, the creation of Technicolor, the development of the star system, and the bitter competition for fewer jobs that led to adversarial relations among women in the industry.[9] But what may have affected women even more was the fact that the studios, desperate to stay in business, entered into economic partnerships with powerful lenders who favored a more traditional role for women as stay-at-home mothers in long-term marriages.[10]

Their descent hit bottom when the U.S. entered World War II, and with the encouragement of the government, Hollywood concentrated all of its resources in providing propaganda for the war effort by making films that supported our fighting Allies. Meanwhile, women served in the military and worked in war plants and defense factories. When the men returned home from the war, many women lost their jobs. True, there were women like Ida Lupino, who directed a number of movies in the forties and fifties, but she had little company in that regard. Others like Hepburn, Bette Davis, and Joan Crawford still could find acting work, but women were scarce in other sectors of the industry. Men had become the patriarchs of the industry, in charge of making, distributing, and financing movies. When women were superseded by men in the industry, Hollywood lost its female audience. The industry leaders preferred action-adventure movies that catered to boys and young men. Meanwhile, the pioneer women of early Hollywood were ignored and relegated to the dustbin of film history.

## Women in Post-WWII Hollywood

The years from the fifties to 1968, when MPAA President Jack Valenti replaced the Production Code with an age-based film-rating system, were a transition period for women within the industry. Female CEOs were rare and most actresses played secondary roles to male leads. The code placed restrictions on social and moral misbehavior on screen, rendering it extremely difficult for female characters to defy traditional values of home and family, let alone engage in unconventional behavior that rejected male dominance without being punished for it.

The demise of the code and the installation of the rating system improved the prospects for roles featuring strong and independent women. The caveat, however, was that men exercised almost total control over the writing, directing, and producing of films. With men in charge, attractive roles were written for male actors. Just at what point starring roles for women broke through these male-imposed obstacles is a matter of debate, but that they did is evident in films like *Norma Rae* (1979), where Sally Field leads the struggle to unionize a textile mill in the South, and *Alien* (1979), where Sigourney Weaver (Ripley) battles a slimy monster that has invaded her spacecraft. Strong, independent women who challenge male authority (*Norma Rae*) and serve as protectors for men (*Alien*) were now represented on screen.

Women in Hollywood movies in the eighties primarily fulfilled three screen roles: as feminine villains like Joan Crawford in *Mommie Dearest* (1981), as unstable and psychotic love interests like Glenn Close in *Fatal Attraction* (1987), and as victims for male slashers/

torturers in horror series such as *Friday the 13th* and *A Nightmare on Elm Street*. There were exceptions like *The Color Purple* (1985), but the decade belonged to the slashers and a whole series of macho men named Rocky, Rambo, and Conan.

Progress was developing on another front, however. Women like Polly Platt and Dawn Steel were breaking the "celluloid ceiling" and moving into executive positions. Platt worked as a producer, screenwriter, and production designer on a number of major films in the seventies and eighties, while Dawn Steel moved up the corporate ladder at Paramount Pictures until, in 1987, she reached the height of her career as head of Columbia Pictures.[11] The most celebrated female executive at that time, however, was Sherry Lansing, a former actress and scriptwriter at MGM, who became president of 20th Century Fox in 1980 at the age of 35. She later became CEO of Paramount Pictures in 1992, where, under her management, Paramount produced six of the 10 highest grossing films ever for the studio, including three best picture Academy Awards. Her track record as a studio head remains unmatched in Hollywood, as 80 percent of the films released under Lansing were box office hits. For her film achievements, Lansing was the first female studio head to receive a star on the Hollywood Walk of Fame, as well as the first woman executive to have her hands and feet enshrined on the sidewalk in front of Grauman's Chinese Theater. Before she retired in 2004, Lansing was named "the most powerful woman in Hollywood" by the trade publication *The Hollywood Reporter*.[12]

Women in Hollywood made their greatest advances as screen characters in the female-dominated scripts of the 1990s such as *Misery* (1990), *Blue Sky* (1991), *The Silence of the Lambs* (1991), *Thelma and Louise* (1991), *Dead Man Walking* (1995), and *Boys Don't Cry* (1999). These screen women challenged male supremacy in their featured roles as leads in well-received films. It is also important to note that during this decade, Julia Roberts became the first actress in modern times with the ability to "green light" a production, that is, determine if a film project would go forward.

Progress continued to be made at the administrative level as well. Lucy Fisher became vice chair of Columbia TriStar, Laura Ziskin became president of Fox 2000 Pictures, later joining Columbia to produce the financially successful first *Spiderman* (2002) film, while other women became CEOs in the television industry.[13] By the first decade of the 21st century, four of the six major Hollywood studios—Universal, Sony, Paramount, and Walt Disney's Buena Vista Motion Picture Group—had women in top decision-making positions.[14]

Despite these gains and the passage of federal equal opportunity legislation, complete equality remains to be achieved inside the industry. Women remain underrepresented on the big screen, considering they represent slightly more than half of the general population. In a study of Academy Award movies from 2007 to 2010, only 33 percent of speaking characters in Oscar-nominated films were female. But the most egregious underrepresentation is behind the camera. Only 14 percent of the films released during the study period were directed by females, although women did direct five of the films nominated for Best Picture.[15] Women are particularly absent from positions in screenwriting as well.[16] Nor have they fared well at Academy Award time. From 1930 through 2008, women have done best in costume design, art direction, and screenwriting. Of the 400 nominees for best director, only four women were nominated, but none had won until Kathryn Bigelow received an

Oscar for *The Hurt Locker*.[17] And of the 431 nominees for producers of the best picture, 32 were women but only five were awarded Oscars.

A study conducted by Professor Martha Lauzen, director of the Center for the Study of Women in Television and Film at San Diego State University, found that women directors had most success in independent films. Lauzen examined the offerings on the 2011–12 film festival circuit and discovered that women directors comprised 31 percent of filmmakers working on documentaries but only 23 percent of those involved in narrative films.[18] While research confirms the gains women directors are making in Hollywood, parity with men is still far off. For instance, women directed only 9 percent of the top 250 movies with the highest domestic box office in 2012. Although that percentage is quite small, still it represents the highest figure since 2000.[19]

But does it matter who directs movies? Take a similar situation in politics. Does it matter if women hold positions of power or influence in the political world? The policies of the 113th Congress might help answer that question since there are 101 women in both chambers, 20 in the U.S. Senate and 78 in the House (plus three non-voting members), including several in key leadership positions. While these figures confirm that women remain underrepresented, consider that 20 years ago in the 104th Congress, there were only 55 women members.[20] This gain does not necessarily forecast a shift in the policy agenda, but it could mean a slight change in attitudes toward women's issues. Recent research indicates that when women reach parity with men, their attitude toward welfare, poverty, and a safety net for those in need is more generous than when they are overwhelmed by the number of males, particularly in larger bodies like the U.S. Congress.[21] Similarly, in Hollywood directors have a voice in various aspects of the production: script, casting, interpretation. A 2011 University of Southern California (USC) study that examined the top 100 box office films released between 2007 and 2009 found that in 16 of the movies directed by men, 29 percent of the film characters were female, while in those directed by women, the number of female characters increased to 48 percent.[22]

Admittedly, so many variables are involved in the making of films and the winning of awards that it is impossible to determine whether discrimination plays any part in the selection process. In the case of women it is their absence from positions in the industry, such as directing, that may be the decisive factor. If that is the case, then the future appears brighter when we look at female directors like Kathryn Bigelow, who was behind action-adventure movies such as *Point Break* (1991), the Iraqi war film *The Hurt Locker*, and the critically acclaimed and controversial *Zero Dark Thirty* (2012), the story of the decade-long hunt for Osama bin Laden, for which she received an Oscar nomination. Bigelow has destroyed the Hollywood myth that women cannot make films that attract a wide audience, including men.

## Presenting Women on Screen

It would take more space than is available to present a comprehensive examination of how the film industry has treated women during its hundred-year history. Suffice it to state that the results have been mixed. It would be unfair, as well as inaccurate, to present a portrait of Hollywood as an intentionally sexist industry. But whether or not acts of discrimination in the form of a preference for male leads, for example, are intentional, the fact remains that women lag behind men in that department.

Below are samples of films where, in the author's view, Hollywood got women right and films where the industry got them terribly wrong. Hollywood does right by women when it treats them with intelligence and respect, featuring them in dramatic roles where their sexuality becomes irrelevant. On screen, as in life, there are women who commit crimes and act badly. But the stereotyping and the excessive objectifying, particularly the latter, should be rejected. In the college spring break movie *Spring Breakers*, the females in the film were largely reduced to being sex slaves for the male characters. But Professor Stacy Smith at USC's Annenberg School for Communication and Journalism found in one of her film studies that Hollywood has increased the sexualization of teens in the movies it makes for them.[23] What the research revealed is that female teenage characters are more likely to wear provocative clothing and appear partially naked than older women. Professor Smith commented that "the data speaks to an overemphasis on beauty, thinness and sexualization of women at younger and younger ages."[24]

Presenting women as sex objects is nothing more than male fantasy, but its depiction cheapens the industry. This is not a new complaint, as reported by Rita Moreno in her memoir, where she describes being typecast as a "Hispanic spitfire" or a "smoldering sexpot" in demeaning roles that were offered to her when she was well into her sixties.[25] Like race, gender should be neutralized on screen so audiences come to appreciate women for their human qualities—both good and bad.

## Getting Women Right

Hollywood put few impediments in the way of women during its early history. Actresses like Mary Pickford and Lillian Gish were the equals of their male leads and many of their scripts were written by women like Frances Marion and Dorothy Arzner. During this period, Hollywood made films for both sexes. This fact encouraged women to pursue a film career. One A-list actress, Katharine Hepburn, was a stage actress before she ventured into movies.[26] Her film career spanned 50 years, from the thirties to the eighties, and included 12 Oscar nominations and four best actress awards. Hepburn starred in over 40 movies, nine with her off-screen lover, Spencer Tracy. The Tracy-Hepburn films were popular with audiences, especially female, because the script treated the lead characters as equals, true partners in the relationship. In *Woman of the Year* (1942) Hepburn and Tracy are journalists; she covers the international scene, he covers sports. They meet, fall in love, marry, and spend the rest of the film arguing over whose career is more important. Does the reader need more than one guess who wins that argument? Then in the 1949 *Adam's Rib*, the two play lawyers, again as a married couple, on opposing sides of an "attempted murder" case. Tracy is the prosecutor, Hepburn the defense counsel. Tracy is sore that his wife should take such a case but he becomes downright belligerent after Hepburn shows him up in the courtroom and wins an acquittal for her client. It should be noted that Hepburn was independent off-camera as well as on and she was one of the few stars during the McCarthy era to speak out against the blacklist and not recant it later as screen tough guy Humphrey Bogart did. Like Frances Marion, Hepburn had too much self-respect to "lay down" for any man. Few actresses had her strength of character and determination. As one example, during the on-location shooting of *The African Queen* (1951), Bogart and director John Huston drank their way through the filming. Hepburn disapproved of their heavy drinking and made her point by declining the alcohol they offered her and drinking only water. For her pains, she came down with a severe case of dysentery, which Huston and Bogart were spared.

Given the right script, there were other actresses in Hollywood who also did their sex proud. One was Sally Field in her Oscar-winning performance as the title character in *Norma Rae* (1979). Without much support from her spouse and co-workers, Norma teams up with a Northern labor organizer to unionize the textile mill where she works. There is one powerful scene where Norma is fired for her union activities and told to vacate the premises. Instead, she shuts down her machine and climbs on a table, holding up a sign with one word on it: UNION. Slowly, one by one, her fellow workers turn off their machines until the entire plant is silent. It's a great moment of courage and defiance against callous and indifferent employers who exploit the working class.

Almost three decades later, Charlize Theron plays another gutsy woman who enters the male-dominated world of mining and is subjected to sexual harassment in the film *North Country* (2005). The movie is based on the real struggle of Lois Jenson, a single mother on welfare, to find work that will pay her enough to support her family.[27] Taking advantage of the 1974 mandate by the federal government that required steel companies to turn over 20 percent of their jobs to women and minorities, Jenson applies and is hired by Eveleth Mines in northern Minnesota. Once on the job, Jenson and the other female workers endure numerous acts of harassment, including being stalked after work. Tired of the abuse, they file a class action suit against the company. *North Country* is the fictionalized account of the first successful sexual harassment case in the U.S. In *Jenson v. Eveleth Mines*,[28] the court found enough evidence—graffiti, photos, and cartoons of a sexual nature, as well as incidents of verbal and physical abuse—to rule in favor of the women. After three trials and 14 years, the women were awarded $3.5 million in damages. Jenson served as an advisor on the film and attended its premiere. The movie took some liberties with the real facts, including compressing 20 years into two hours and making composites of several characters, but the essence of the dispute and the male behavior that gave rise to the litigation were accurate.

Two 1970s films examine the consequences of the rising American divorce rate. For comparison purposes, the divorce rate per 1000 population in the U.S. in 1950 was 2.6. By 1970 it had risen to 3.5 and it reached its peak in 1981 at 5.3, after which it leveled off and returned to its 1970 rate by 2009.[29] In Martin Scorsese's *Alice Doesn't Live Here Anymore* (1974), Ellen Burstyn, in her Oscar-winning role, finds herself a single mother when her husband leaves. Rather than feel sorry for herself, she takes her teenage son and moves to Phoenix, where she tries to become a singer. After several mishaps, including an unwise affair with an abusive married man, Burstyn finds romance and love the second time around. In the other film, Paul Mazursky's *An Unmarried Woman* (1978), New Yorker Jill Clayburgh has to adjust to being a single woman after her husband of 16 years leaves her for a younger woman. Like Burstyn, she refuses to collapse, and in one scene the audience sees her disposing of all of her husband's personal belongings as a symbol of her new independence. Also, like Burstyn, she has an unfortunate sexual fling before she finds the right man in artist Alan

Bates. What these woman share is their refusal to let the actions of men defeat them. The message of these films is that women can survive, and even blossom, without men.

*The Kids Are All Right*, released in summer 2010, was a small-budget film ($4 million) that turned a profit and received four Academy Award nominations. Although it failed to win an Oscar, the critics admired the original screenplay, direction, and acting. *The Kids Are All Right* is about a lesbian family where each of the women has given birth to a child from the same anonymous sperm donor. Nic (Annette Bening) and Jules (Julianne Moore) are a committed lesbian couple living in California. Nic is a doctor and the stricter parent; Jules is a carefree spirit whose attempts to start a business usually fail, and so by default, she fills the role of homemaker. When the film begins, Nic and Jules appear to be a happy couple, although like most married or committed couples, their daily lives are not without problems. Entering this domestic relationship is Paul (Mark Ruffalo), the sperm donor, who has been contacted by the children. Without their parents' knowledge, Joni and Laser meet with Paul, a co-op farmer and restaurant owner. The children like Paul and begin to spend more time with him until Jules and Nic discover their secret. The relationships become complicated when Nic starts to resent Paul's intrusion into family life and Jules, who is hired by Paul to redesign his backyard, embarks on an affair with him. The climax is reached when Nic uncovers the affair and has a showdown with Jules. Does Jules still love Nic? Is Jules going straight? The answers to these questions are "yes" and "no" as the film concludes with a happy ending.

Why is *The Kids Are All Right* also right about women? Although billed by Hollywood as a romantic comedy, the film is serious about its subject and neither patronizes the lesbian relationship nor elevates it to heroic heights. Quite possibly its objective portrayal is the result of the screenplay and direction by Lisa Cholodenko that relies heavily on her own lesbian relationship. Consequently, the nature of the relationship is not an issue but accepted for what it is. What *The Kids Are All Right* does is treat sex as a neutral factor and the same-sex relationship as similar to a straight relationship in having to cope with strains and infidelities. The Nic-Jules family, complete with teenagers, is not much different from heterosexual families, and thus the film implies that the children of such unions will grow up to become productive parents and citizens. And that message is delivered in reassuring tones and without warnings or hyperbole. In the author's opinion, a more appropriate title would have been: *The Kids Will Be All Right*.

Another low budget film, *Winter's Bone*, also opened during the summer of 2010 to positive reviews, but with small returns at the domestic box office. The star of the film, Jennifer Lawrence, plays Ree, a 17-year-old Ozark Mountain girl with a non-functioning mother and two young siblings who are on the verge of losing their home because their drug-dealing father has gone missing. Unless Ree locates him in time for his upcoming trial, the family will lose its home, since the father put it up as collateral for his bail. The family is dirt poor and its ramshackle house is everything to them. Ree then must locate her father within a week, and thus she embarks on a dangerous search among the family's kin who are involved in the local crystal meth drug trade. Everywhere she goes, she is warned to mind her own business and go home. Despite these threats to her life, Ree pushes on with the help of her uncle to unearth the truth and save the family home.

Director Debra Granik coached an Oscar-nominated performance out of 20-year-old Lawrence in this gritty film that focuses on rural poverty in an Ozark county unfamiliar to most of us. What Granik achieves in Lawrence's performance is a young woman of great strength and character who assumes the role of head-of-household in a dysfunctional family and manages to survive against all odds. Here is the teenager as a sensible, responsible, and persistent young woman rather than the fatuous airheads usually found in Hollywood's teen movies.

## Getting Women Wrong

Understandably, Hollywood gets women wrong when it fails to treat their screen characters with some modicum of logic, common sense, and respect, placing them in dramatic situations and then letting them respond in ways that reinforce sexual stereotypes. It would help if more women were writing the scripts and guiding the direction as they did in the industry's early years. It also would be beneficial if Hollywood refrained from catering to teenage boys and macho young men and if its film plots emphasized an interesting story rather than an exercise in special effects. Possibly then women might frequent the movie houses in the same numbers as in the past. Here are seven films that illustrate Hollywood's wrong-headed treatment of women.

A 1983 rape case[30] within the Portuguese community in New Bedford, Massachusetts, served as the basis for director Jonathan Kaplan's 1988 film, *The Accused*, which gave Jodie Foster her first Oscar. In the actual case, 23-year-old Cheryl Araujo was gang-raped on a pool table by four men in Big Dan's Tavern while other bar patrons watched but did not interfere. Consequently, six men were charged with rape. Araujo's cross-examination by the defense was so intense that it became a template for "blaming the victim" in future rape cases. According to the prosecution, Araujo left her house one night to buy cigarettes but the store where she usually bought them was closed. She then proceeded to walk into Big Dan's, the neighborhood bar, where two men approached her and asked her to leave with them. When she refused, she was grabbed from behind by a third man and slammed down onto a pool table, stripped to the waist and raped by several men. She managed to escape into the street where a passing motorist took her to a hospital. Defense counsel gave the jury a different version of that night's events. He claimed that Araujo went into the bar, but not to buy cigarettes. She drank enough to become legally drunk, played the jukebox, and watched some guys shoot pool, observations the defense hoped the jury would translate into consensual sex. The strategy failed as the jury found four of the men guilty of aggravated rape while it acquitted two others from aiding and abetting the crime. The case was a cause célèbre and it became the first trial to be televised by cable news.

But the film version did not adhere to the trial script. It differs in three respects from the actual events. First, in addition to the rape charges, the prosecutor in the film version unsuccessfully attempted to charge the 15 or so spectators who watched and cheered on the rapists with aiding and abetting. Second, the film eliminated the ethnicity of all the participants, an important point since Araujo and the bar patrons were of Portuguese descent rather than the WASPish-looking young men in the film. Changing their ethnicity may have spared hurt feelings but in a close-knit community that still respects the old traditions and customs, it diminishes the impact of the crime.[31] Crucial is the significance of how the film altered the reenactment of the rape scene. Although both sides presented different versions of events, the jury's decision indicated that it believed the prosecution. Yet Hollywood supported the defense's argument by having Foster play Araujo as a drunk, flirting with the men in the bar, dancing suggestively alone and together with one of the rapists while engaging in fondling and kissing, without objection, until she is slammed down on the pinball machine and gang-raped. This sequence runs almost 10 minutes and leaves the audience with the erroneous image that Araujo was a slut and a tramp. This fictionalized version of the actual rape promotes the "blame the victim" rape mentality.

An attempted rape drives the plot in Ridley Scott's 1991 film, *Thelma & Louise*. Thelma (Geena Davis), a young Arkansas housewife with an insufferable jerk for a husband, and Louise (Susan Sarandon), a middle-aged waitress in a relationship with a musician that doesn't seem to have a future, decide to spend a weekend together in the mountains. But no sooner are they on the road than they stop at a bar where Thelma has one too many margaritas while dancing nonstop with a cowboy. Feeling somewhat faint and sick, Thelma goes outsides to the parking lot where the cowboy aggressively tries to seduce her, pulling down her panties. But unlike Foster's character in *The Accused*, Thelma's reaction is to resist. When the cowboy persists, Thelma slaps him, which gets him angry and he attempts to rape her. Thelma is saved by Louise, who appears in the parking lot with a pistol that she places on the cowboy's head, yelling: "Let her go." As the women back away, the cowboy says that he was just having a little fun. To which, Louise replies: "In the future, when a woman is crying like that, she's not having any fun." The cowboy answers: "I should have gone ahead and fucked her," whereupon Louise shoots him dead. Thereafter, the film becomes a female buddy road movie: Thelma and Louise are chased by the police until they are surrounded. Their final act of defiance is to drive off into the Grand Canyon. Dramatic, yes, credible, no! The entire plot rests on the plausibility of the rape scene. Ninety-nine plus percent of women in a similar situation would have phoned the police, contacted the bar owner, screamed for help, or at least walked away. Instead Thelma and Louise decide to run and become fugitives who engage in robbery and other acts of violence. This film did not advance the feminist cause, but rather allowed Hollywood to substitute these women for macho men. *Thelma & Louise* is a step away from women's liberation.

The appearance of female strength and independence in Rod Lurie's 2000 political film *The Contender* is deceptive. The movie stars Joan Allen as a U.S. senator who is nominated by the president (Jeff Bridges) to take the place of the vice president, who has died in an accident. True to the real world of politics, her nomination is subject to confirmation by the Senate. The president's political rival (Gary Oldman), however, has his own agenda. During the confirmation hearings, Oldman attempts to smear the nominee's reputation by raising the issue of her sexual history, portraying Allen as a "party girl." Allen refuses to respond to the accusations, insisting that her personal life is her own business. Her nomination is in doubt when Oldman brings photos of Allen engaging in sexual activities during her college years. Still, Allen refuses to defend herself, much to the disappointment of her supporters. Hollywood however has a solution: Allen is *not* the woman in the photos! This surprise development requires the audience to believe all of the following: (1) an intelligent woman would jeopardize her historic promotion by remaining silent when all she has to say to the Senate is, "Hey boys, that isn't me;" (2) that Oldman and the other men on the Senate committee failed to confirm the identity of the woman in the photos before making the accusation; and (3) that in contemporary American politics when the personal life of a political candidate is under media scrutiny the wise course of action is to remain silent even when the accusation is false. Hollywood needs to depict a more realistic portrayal of independent women rather than rely on a phony free speech argument.

The premise behind *Set It Off* (1996) is that three African-American women (one a single mother with a young child), stuck in low-paying jobs and living in the Los Angeles projects, come to believe that their only option is to rob banks. This trio is joined by a fourth woman, played by Jada Pinkett Smith, who is unfairly dismissed from her bank teller's position because one of the robbers happens to be from her neighborhood. Of the group, Smith has a legitimate complaint because she cannot find work commensurate with her training. Frustrated, she joins these three desperate women in robbing banks, justifying her criminal activity on the grounds that the money they are stealing comes from "the system" and not the depositors. During their third bank job, three are shot dead and only Smith escapes to Mexico. In real life, many black women do menial work that keeps them under or at the poverty level, and many have the added burden of being single mothers.[32] These women could have availed themselves of social services and employment agencies. They could have looked to the protection offered by state and federal legislation. For three of the women, job training programs would have provided better jobs and improved pay. But as is usual in Hollywood films, the response to problem-solving is to rely on violence, whether it is by macho men or four desperate women. Such a fantastic plot as the one in *Set It Off* actually hampers progress toward informed gender and racial equality.

Barry Levinson's 1994 film, *Disclosure*, based on the Michael Crichton novel, is part computer technology special effects, part suspense thriller, and part male sex fantasy. The plot, filled with implausible situations and goofs (like having a hi-tech CEO not know how to use the electronic key card to enter his hotel room), has Michael Douglas playing a family man and computer expert for a Seattle high-tech corporation who discovers that he has been passed over for promotion to vice president. The position is given to an outsider, played by Demi Moore, Douglas's former lover, who now becomes his boss. The very first day on the job, Moore invites Douglas up to her office after hours for wine and…the reader can fill in the rest. Thinking Moore wants to discuss the problems he is having with his research project, Douglas reports as ordered. His boss asks him to pour the very expensive wine while she explains: "I like the boys under me to be happy," and proceeds to seduce him in a protracted sex scene. Within minutes, Moore removes her jacket, orders Douglas to rub her shoulders, kisses him, opens her blouse, sits on his lap, and undoes his pants zipper. This is not the typical business meeting. After his initial excitement, Douglas comes to his senses and struggles free. Moore is incensed at the rejection and accuses Douglas of sexual harassment. Despite the high-tech razzle-dazzle and the office intrigue, *Disclosure* is about the very serious subject of workplace harassment. How considerable is the problem? According to the Equal Employment Opportunity Commission (EEOC), 15,000 sex harassment complaints are filed each year.[33] However, the overwhelming number, approximately

# Hollywood and Women

90 percent, are brought by women against men for the logical reason that men control the boardrooms and executive positions in the corporate world. So why would Hollywood make a film that focuses on the 10 percent? Although it is true that the number of complaints filed by men is on the rise, *Disclosure* would like audiences to believe that sexual harassment is an equal opportunity offense. This is not only a distortion of the facts but a disservice to the majority of victims of workplace harassment—women.

Figure 13.1. Recreating the Judith Miller-Valerie Plame Affair in *Nothing But the Truth*, 2008. Reprinted with permission, Yari Film Group/Photofest

### Case Study: *Nothing But the Truth*

Rod Lurie's 2008 film *Nothing But the Truth* is a docudrama loosely based on the Judith Miller–Valerie Plame controversy that made headlines for several years.[34] The story began in February 2002 with allegations from the Bush administration that Iraq was seeking to buy uranium from Niger as a prelude to developing a nuclear bomb. To determine the credibility of the allegation, the CIA sent former Ambassador Joseph Wilson on a fact-finding mission to Niger. Wilson filed his report with the CIA in March 2002, asserting that there was no substance to the story. But in his 2003 State of the Union address, President George W. Bush nevertheless told Congress and the nation that the British government had learned that Saddam Hussein sought to buy large quantities of uranium from Africa.

This assertion was disputed by Wilson in an op-ed piece published in *The New York Times* on July 8, 2003, several months after the invasion of Iraq.[35] Eight days later, syndicated columnist Robert Novak reported in his article that Wilson's wife, Valerie Plame, worked for the CIA and had suggested sending him to Niger. Two days later, another article in *The Nation* identified Plame as a secret agent. Subsequently, Judith Miller, a reporter for *The New York Times*, was identified as one of the journalists who had been informed by a White House official that Plame was an undercover CIA operative. Miller was then subpoenaed by a Washington, D.C., grand jury investigating the leak, but refused to divulge her source. She was held in contempt and sentenced to 18 months' imprisonment. After spending 85 days in jail, Miller was released after her source, I. Lewis Libby, Vice President Dick Cheney's chief of staff, gave her permission to break her pledge of confidentiality. These are the facts of the actual Miller-Plame story but director Lurie twists these facts in *Nothing But the Truth* and in the end his film misrepresents both women and places them in a false light. As a consequence, he gets not one but two women wrong.

Lurie largely adheres to the Miller-Plame scenario during the film's first hour, but he abandons the actual facts as his film veers off in a completely fictional direction. In *Nothing But the Truth*, Kate Beckinsale plays the screen version of Judith Miller, a D.C. reporter for *The New York Times* who learns that the president has ignored the findings of a covert CIA operative (Vera Farmiga playing Valerie Plame) that the Venezuelan government was not involved in an assassination attempt against him. Despite this information, the president orders an air strike against Venezuela. Subsequently, Beckinsale names Farmiga as the covert agent, refuses to reveal her source, citing the protection of the First Amendment, and is subsequently jailed. The film correctly depicts the ensuing controversy, which pits the media and its support of First Amendment rights for journalists against the intelligence community and the government's insistence that secrecy is essential to national security.

Lurie, of course, has the right to make any film he likes if he can attract investors and a cast. But in *Nothing But the Truth* he misrepresents two women who suffered both personally and professionally for their principles: their images are needlessly distorted for Hollywood's benefit. First, Beckinsale suffers so much abuse in the film as to exaggerate her victimization and steer the audience in her favor. For instance, during her prison term Beckinsale's husband begins an affair that dooms their marriage and she eventually loses him to another woman. She also has to give up her son, as the boy decides to live with his father. While in prison, Beckinsale is placed into the general female population, which includes all criminal types. She is also sent to desegregation (isolation) for arguing with a guard and is later beaten by another inmate so badly that she requires hospitalization. After her release from prison, Beckinsale is arrested again by the government prosecutor (Matt Dillon) for impeding a federal investigation. When she persists in refusing to reveal her source, she is sentenced to two more years behind bars. The real Judith Miller spent 85 days in jail without any evidence that she was mistreated, beaten, or put into desegregation.[36]

Meanwhile Lurie's treatment of Farmiga as the screen version of Valerie Plame is less sympathetic. Farmiga's Plame is one cold, tough, foul-mouthed CIA operative who juggles home life with being a spy. Lurie attempts to balance her character by having Farmiga read stories to grade school children, but the scenes are underdeveloped. Although Farmiga has a husband and a daughter, the audience sees little of them. By film's end she also has lost her husband and child together with her privacy and her profession. Even the CIA turns against her, and in the final moment she is gunned down in front of her house by a right-wing shooter. (The real Valerie Plame's marriage is intact and she is very much alive). To add to the character falsification, it is revealed that the source of the information leaked to Beckinsale is none other than Farmiga's school-aged daughter, who inadvertently tells Beckinsale that her mom works for the CIA while both are on a school bus trip. Beckinsale later confirms this information from two other sources (one a drunk during a Washington party).

When a film takes its narrative from actual events, known as the docudrama, the filmmaker has a right to make minor alterations, but not to such an extent that the characters are distorted and the facts misrepresented. This is the slippery-slope problem of the docudrama format, where fiction is interwoven with fact. Filmmakers have a responsibility then to be sensitive to the potential harm caused by misrepresentation, particularly when, as in this situation, the actual persons depicted in the film can be readily recognized by most adults. No pre-film warning that it is fictional excuses the subsequent manipulation of the facts. Surely an experienced director like Lurie can recognize the danger signs.

In *The Contender* Lurie wants viewers to believe that an intelligent woman would prefer to remain silent and risk her confirmation as vice president rather than prove the falsity of the sexual charges against her. The film portrayal rings false and offends notable female senators like Hillary Clinton, Olympia Snowe, Elizabeth Warren, and others. Moreover, in *Nothing But the Truth* Lurie wants viewers to accept the premise that a prestigious Washington newspaper would hire a naive reporter like Beckinsale, who receives information from a kid and then doggedly pursues a First Amendment principle until it destroys her family. Even more bizarre is that the principle Beckinsale is defending to her detriment is one that the U.S. Supreme Court has repeatedly rejected since the case of *Branzburg v. Hayes*,[37] where the High Court ruled that journalists do not have a First Amendment privilege that protects them from testifying before a grand jury or from providing evidence to a grand jury. When Judith Miller challenged her subpoena before the U.S. Court of Appeals for the D.C. Circuit,[38] it held that Miller had no First Amendment privilege to refuse to disclose the identity of the source that leaked Valerie Plame's identity as a covert agent.[39] While the High Court has given free speech wide latitude, it has yet to hold First Amendment rights as absolute. Libel, obscene material, and national security are three exclusions to First Amendment protection. Then why did the film have Beckinsale pursue her free speech principle to the bitter end?

In contrast to the seriousness of *Nothing But the Truth*'s subject matter, another film, *Serious Moonlight* (2009), a romantic comedy, presents a more offensive depiction of women. In this silly film, Meg Ryan plays a high-powered lawyer who earns enough money to afford an idyllic vacation home in the country that she shares with her husband of 13 years. As the film begins, Ryan appears content with her marriage, her career, and her life. Then one day she unexpectedly returns early to her country house to find her husband in the process of writing a "Dear Jane" letter informing her that he is leaving for Paris with his young girlfriend. This is not an unfamiliar film narrative but in *Serious Moonlight*, Ryan responds to the upsetting news by knocking her husband (Tim Hutton) out with a flower pot and then proceeding to duct tape him to a chair while he is unconscious. Ryan's plan is to keep him captive until he agrees to abandon his girlfriend and remain with her because she knows, despite his denials, that he truly loves her. Her strategy is to woo and win her husband back with wedding pictures, his favorite chocolate chip cookies (which she quickly bakes for him), and her enduring love. Yet her husband is not persuaded. He yearns for his younger girlfriend and cannot wait to run away to the romantic Paris portrayed in American films. This is the plot for the first half of the film. Ryan wants to save her marriage because, as she explains to Hutton, she hates eating alone or going to the movies by herself. Ryan's treatment of her husband begins at simple assault and escalates to the felony charge of holding a person against his will. The irony here is that Hutton is a lousy husband: lazy, jealous and unhappy and there is no reason why any sane woman would want to keep him.

In the final scene, Ryan and Hutton are both tied up, with Hutton on the toilet and his pants down around his ankles, joined by the girlfriend, also trussed up, and with robbers downstairs ransacking the house. Ryan's character in *Serious Moonlight* insults women in many ways but particularly because it perpetuates the myth that women need men and cannot lead productive and happy lives without them. Surprisingly, both the screenwriter and the director were women. The release of this film insults the memory of the strong, independent women of Hollywood's past: Frances Marion, Mary Pickford, Dorothy Arzner, Ida Lupino, and Katharine Hepburn, among others.

More than a decade ago, a 2000 Mel Gibson movie asked *What Women Want*. In the film Gibson discovers the answer, but the author has come to believe that women are tired of all the old clichés about them and believes women wish to be considered for attributes beyond their sex. While the author would not presume to speak for women, he feels confident that they reject many of the screen images about them. Women would prefer not to be treated as sex objects or willing slaves simply to enhance the male ego. Women are more than their physical attributes and, I suspect, are tired of being portrayed as mindless bimbos, seductresses and husband stealers or as cold-hearted executives who emulate their male counterparts. The way to alter these images is to depict women in significant roles as scientists, engineers and administrators in plots that resonate with their peers. Finally, as many moviegoers would attest, the film industry has been unkind and unfair to women, especially as they mature. Screen star Lillian Gish recognized this sexist discrimination almost a century ago. Ask any actress over 50 today and she will tell you that roles for women are hard to come by in an industry where men age gracefully and women disappear from the screen. Women deserve more respect than that.

Is there a happy Hollywood ending for women? Possibly. Recent signs indicate that there are sections within the film industry where women rival men as major players. Women have made major inroads in the entertainment industry as publicity agents, agents for writers and actors, and as lawyers to Hollywood clients. While these women are not "household names," at least they now have a presence in areas that were formally reserved for men. In addition, more women are entering the executive ranks: Stacey Snider is co-chair and CEO of DreamWorks Studios, Donna Langley is co-chair of Universal Pictures, Amy Pascal is co-chair of Sony Pictures Entertainment, Elizabeth Gabler is president of Fox 2000 Pictures, and Sue Kroll is president of worldwide marketing for Warner Brothers.[40]

The author is encouraged, after discovering the Indiewire blog site "Women and Hollywood," to learn that women are speaking out about their second-class status and are actively taking steps to remedy the situation. The blog is committed to reporting exclusively about news and issues that concern women in film, both on the screen as actors and behind the scenes as writers, directors, cinematographers, and producers. But the blog is more than a reporting outlet, as it also serves as a good resource for information on organizations like the San Francisco Film Society that fund film projects and provide news about film awards and grants available to screenwriters and documentary filmmakers. In August 2012, the blog reported on a forum sponsored by *The New York Times* online opinion forum that asked seven women (and one man) in the film business to respond to the question "How Can Women Gain Influence in Hollywood?"[41] To summarize the discussion, the author divided their responses into two categories:

Table 13.1. Suggestions and Action Plans

| **Suggestions** | **Action Plans** |
| --- | --- |
| Studios should increase publicity of successful films made by women | Lobby for legislation that would require mandates in hiring women for behind-the-scenes positions |
| The industry needs to do more extensive research on female movie attendance to prove to the studios that films written, directed, and produced by women can attract an audience | Lobby for legislation for tax exceptions to women who want to own their own production companies |
| Established women in the industry should become role models for younger women | Lobby financial institutions to back successful female producers |
| Women need to support (financial, involvement) the Geena Davis Institute on Gender in Media and The Center for the Study of Women in Television & Film at San Diego State | |

The work being done by former actor Geena Davis is particularly noteworthy. Davis has established the Geena Davis Institute on Gender in Media, a research-based organization dedicated to the promotion of gender balancing, reduction in stereotyping, and the expansion of female characters on children's shows and programming. One institute study reported the following findings:

- Male roles predominate over the presence of women on the screen.
- There are fewer female speaking parts in family films, prime time programming, and children's shows.
- Females are more likely than men to be pictured in sexy clothes that expose more flesh.
- Females are more likely to receive comments on their physical appearance than men.
- Female screen characters are less likely to be represented as being at the peak of their profession. That role is usually reserved for men.
- Women are underrepresented on screen as engineers, scientists, mathematicians, and technology experts.[42]

In view of the negative indicators that confirm the unequal status of women relative to men in the film industry, women should remain united and committed to assist each other rather than act as competitors. Women in positions of power within the industry should strive to redefine the meaning of success. Money, of course, is always a consideration but it should not be the predominant reason for giving a green light to a film project. Success is an ambiguous term with several possible meanings. For example, *The New York Times* forum applied the term in reference to the 2011 comedy *Bridesmaids*, written by and starring women, because the film had a $170 million domestic gross. Women in executive positions within the industry have an opportunity to enlarge the meaning of success to include small, low-budget films similar to *Wendy and Lucy* and *Winter's Bone*, which received critical acclaim but did not overwhelm at the box office.

Furthermore, several of the proposed direct action plans seem impractical. Is it realistic to expect the state of California to enact regulatory legislation that might impact the economy of the southern part of the state? Rather than lobbying the government, a better approach might be to bring pressure to bear on those banks that loan money to the film studios to not reject funding for a film project because its director is a woman and its plot seemingly would appeal only to women. In that regard, women should organize into an effective pressure group that capitalizes on their growing numbers within the industry. Also, women should say NO to situations that demean and marginalize them, such as excessive sex and nudity in roles that diminish their self-respect and make them feel ashamed of their profession. And in the future when Seth MacFarlane or any other male host of the Oscars wants to sing a song and perform a dance number to "we saw your boobs," the author hopes all the women in the audience have the courage to walk out—and take their husbands and boyfriends with them! If women in Hollywood are serious about equality, they will need to fight to restore the "golden days" when their predecessors worked in all phases of the industry and had the guts to look men in the eye and not look up to them on their backs.

The road ahead may be long and arduous. But women need to remember that even the election of the first black president did not end inequality or eliminate acts of discrimination. It is only if they form a unified front that women will truly advance within the film industry.

Chapter 14

# Epilogue

## Is There a Future for Political Films in Hollywood?

"Independent film is really a way of thinking. I used to think it was where the money comes from, but now it's clearly about having a vision and a point of view when you want to tell a story."
—Director Nancy Savoca

"The independent film movement, as we knew it, just doesn't exist anymore, and maybe it can't exist anymore."
—Director Steven Soderbergh

"To create what it does, Hollywood has to draw young people, often of unstable temperament, from all over the world. It plunges them into exacting work—surrounds them with a sensuous life—and cuts them off from the normal sources of living."
—Max Lerner, *America as a Civilization*

The author ended his first edition (2000) with the same question: do political films have a future in Hollywood? At that time he considered three answers: yes, no, and maybe, much to the chagrin of readers. But the conditional nature of the response was warranted by the status of the film industry at the time. An optimistic "yes" would depend on whether certain conditions developed, a "no" if different factors depressed the film market, and a "maybe" if both positive and negative factors cancelled each other, signaling a return to the status quo. I am sorry if I disappoint the 4th edition reader but the inconclusive "maybe" remains firmly entrenched. Why?—because there are at least a half-dozen factors at play that could impact the film industry and lead to any one of three scenarios.

For the first two editions the author considered the "fledgling indies" market as the most promising outlet for inexpensive but edgier and riskier films, including those delivering political messages. The independent film market, commonly known as the "indies," is best defined in terms of the following characteristics:

- First, the films are usually produced outside the traditional studio system

- Second, the films are generally made on modest budgets and are financed by the filmmakers themselves, their family and friends, or by funds secured from non-traditional, outside sources
- Third, the films are distributed, if at all, outside the usual theater chains, and
- Lastly, the films are made by young directors at the beginning of their careers or by established "auteurs" who are in a position to freelance.

The author's initial assessment rested on the potential of the independent film movement to use the medium for political action and change or as a stage on which to raise political issues. Would the growth and popularity of modest, low-budget indie movies made by young filmmakers in the 1990s and early 2000s, those that played at Sundance, Tribeca, and other film festivals, continue to impress film studios? The prognosis at the time looked promising, as film festivals flourished, film schools multiplied, and film students flocked to screenwriting and directing workshops. By the time the 3rd edition was published in 2010, the economic recession was at work in the U.S. and affected many industries, including Hollywood. One notable example was the studio downsizing that occurred. For example, a few major studios closed subsidiaries that had produced lower-budget films. Warner Brothers shut down the New Line Cinema, Picturehouse, and Warner Independent Pictures divisions that made their riskier and less expensive pictures. Besides, the states that had once provided incentives to film studios were no longer in a generous mood. Michigan, which had converted an old GM factory into a state-of-the-art film studio in 2011 and poured millions of dollars into its renovation, had to scale back because the number of film projects committed to using the facility declined and the promised thousands of jobs never materialized. This forced the state to default on the interest due on the state-issued bonds that had financed the facility. In light of the persistence of the recession and unemployment, other states joined the recession bandwagon and ended their subsidies to the film industry. So, the economy was one troubling sign, but there were others, including a diminishing theater audience, especially the over 55 crowd, decreasing returns on DVD sales, and a growing and heavy reliance by the studios on foreign markets to turn box office losses into gains.[1]

Because Hollywood is in continuous transformation, constantly reinventing itself, absolute predictions are imprudent. The variables involved in film production are too numerous to enable an informed answer to what the future holds for political film. There are, however, enough warning signs to warrant uneasiness within the industry despite technological advances, the constant stream of new filmmakers coming out of New York University, the University of Southern California, and other film schools, and the creative talent and artistic energy of a select group of writers, directors, and producers. To the author, the most sensible recourse therefore is to examine the more important variables that could affect the film industry's future course.

## Warning Signs: Hollywood Filmmaking

The film industry is like no other. It is so unique that it is not considered at Harvard Business School as a model for other businesses. It is more akin to gambling than an exercise in venture capitalism. In laymen's terms, it is a crapshoot, where the risks are high, with the failures expensive disasters, but where the rewards equate to winning the national lottery. The industry shares certain essentials with other commercial enterprises, such as an organizational structure with a clear line of command and a product that is created and marketed to the public, but there the similarities end.

Six major studios dominate contemporary Hollywood, but each is a subsidiary to its parent unit, a conglomerate:

Table 14.1. Major Studio Market Share[2]

| Conglomerate | Major Studio | U.S./Canada Market Share |
|---|---|---|
| Sony | Columbia Pictures | 17% |
| Time Warner | Warner Bros Pictures | 15.4% |
| Walt Disney Co. | Walt Disney Pictures | 14.3% |
| Comcast | Universal Pictures | 13.6% |
| News Corporation | 20th Century Fox | 10.6% |
| Viacom | Paramount Pictures | 8.5% |

In addition, the major studios have production and distribution divisions that make and distribute movies under various brand names such as TriStar Pictures, New Line Cinema, Touchstone Pictures, Focus Features, Fox Searchlight Pictures, and Paramount Vantage. The six major film studios and their subsidiaries control almost 90 percent of the American and Canadian box office.[3]

There are also three smaller film production companies that are referred to as "mini-majors"—Reliance ADA Group (DreamWorks), Lions Gate Entertainment (The Weinstein Company, Summit Entertainment, and Lionsgate Films), and MGM Holdings (United Artists, Metro-Goldwyn-Mayer)—that account for the remainder of the North American market share.[4] The conglomerate organizational structure is led by executives who are not exclusively "movie people" but rather media CEOs who consider films as just another product line. These Harvard-trained MBAs staff their offices with accountants and lawyers who worry about the numbers and are committed to protecting the interests of the firm. Actors and directors are viewed as employees, well compensated but outside the decision-making process. In short, contemporary movies are controlled not by artists or creators but by number crunchers. In this context, films are not cooperative artistic projects but commodities to be marketed and sold to audiences.

American filmmaking is not for the fainthearted. One day you are "king of the hill" and the next you are leading tours past the homes of Hollywood stars. The story of the Weinstein Brothers is a good example.[5] New Yorkers by birth, they entered the entertainment business at an early age promoting rock concerts upstate. After several years the brothers took their savings and put it into a film company, Miramax, named for their parents. They spent most of the 1980s trying to gain recognition, finally hitting pay dirt with the distribution of the documentary *The Thin Blue Line* (1988), followed a year later with the Steven

Soderbergh film *sex, lies and videotape* (1989), which became a hit of the indie movement. The nineties belonged to the Weinsteins, as they enjoyed a series of critical and financial hits, including *Pulp Fiction* (1994), *The English Patient* (1996), *Good Will Hunting* (1997), and *Shakespeare in Love* (1998). Their string of successes paid off when the Disney Corporation bought Miramax for $80 million, but retained the brothers to lead the company. In 2005, the brothers left Miramax to form their own production outfit, The Weinstein Company. Their new venture began successfully but by 2008 the Weinsteins, like others in the industry, were in financial trouble. The company had to downsize staff, make other reductions, and put future film projects on hold. They even had to hire an advisor to restructure the company's finances. Few in Hollywood would have believed that the successful leaders of Miramax, a company that had received 249 Academy Award nominations, including 11 for best picture, while winning 60 Oscars, three for best film, would have trouble securing financing for their next picture. Within a decade the boy wonders of the nineties were on a downward slide. But just as quickly, their fortunes were revived when their film *Inglourious Basterds* (2009), directed by Quentin Tarantino, struck gold at the box office.[6] Three years later the Weinsteins had another hit on their hands, Tarantino's *Django Unchained* (2012), which was a box office success and won two Oscars.

This tale of the rise-fall-rise of the Weinsteins illustrates the precarious nature of the film business. It also uncovers three facts about the industry that make predicting its future an exercise in futility. Filmmaking begins with a project (a script outline, at least) for a film that requires investors, either banks or private individuals. Naturally, the larger the projected film budget, the higher the risk. While smaller projects require less funding, they are more vulnerable to the volatility of the economy. A few misses at the box office and financing is much harder to secure. And if you are a young filmmaker like Joshua Marston, financing can become a Kafkaesque nightmare. Marston began his career as a journalist and photographer before moving into film, where his accomplishments include a tongue-in-cheek yet accurate flowchart depicting the film production process in 29 steps: from finding a script to getting the green light. To maneuver through his 29 steps requires the patience of a Job, the persistence of a bulldog, and a little bit of luck. Progressing from step 1 (finding an intern to read through piles of scripts and uncover a brilliant story) to step 29 (after months and even years, the film project receives the green light to start production) is like feeling your way through a booby-trapped maze.[7] In between steps 1 and 29, Marston cons writers and directors to work for him, maxes out his credit card, goes to Vegas to make a score, and almost loses his sanity in the process.

Even if Marston's flow chart is an exaggeration, getting financing for a major studio production is no longer considered automatic regardless of the stellar reputation of the director, writer, and cast. Take two A-list film people, actor Brad Pitt and director Steven Soderbergh, who were collaborating on a baseball movie in 2009 called *Moneyball* when Sony shut it down, incurring a $10 million dollar loss.[8] Pitt did not want to abandon the project however, because he yearned to play the lead role of Oakland's GM Billy Beane. Together with Sony executive Amy Pascal, Pitt secured the services of several new writers, another director, and working with a lower budget eventually was able to make *Moneyball*. Released in 2011, the film failed to make money for Sony but it did receive six Oscar nominations.[9]

# Epilogue

An even stranger situation can occur in Hollywood land—namely, despite your reputation for turning out quality, Oscar-winning movies, you still may have trouble making the kind of movies for which you and your company are noted. Who would believe that DreamWorks, where director Steven Spielberg makes critically acclaimed films like *War Horse* and *Lincoln*, could find itself in a situation where it may not be able to secure the financing necessary to make such excellent films in the future, having instead to settle for more mundane but commercial fare?[10] In the film business, you cannot make movies without financial backing and that assistance often rests on the returns of your last film.

Securing funding is the starting point in a long process to determine whether a movie goes into production. The availably of bank financing is very much tied to the state of the economy and remains the key to future film production. When the recession hit Hollywood in 2007–08, it had an immediate effect on the attainability of bank loans. Banks became more cautious in approving loans, particularly for blockbuster projects with $100+ million budgets. Inside the industry the accepted formula for producing and marketing a film is this: you double the film's costs to cover the marketing expenses. This means a film that costs $100 million usually requires another $100 million for advertising and marketing. With costs like these, Hollywood has turned to multiple funding sources. For instance, the credits of seven production companies appeared on the screen before the opening scene of Spielberg's $65 million film, *Lincoln*. And this list did not include all of the investors.[11]

To continue producing films in a tight credit market, Hollywood has responded with cooperative or joint financing, joining several studios together to produce films, as DreamWorks did with *Lincoln*. These multi-studio projects have recently extended to foreign studios and overseas investors, giving some Hollywood films the appearance of a global cinematic venture. A perfect example was the very expensive film *Cloud Atlas* (2012). The directors, Andy and Lana Wachowski, transferred the bestseller to the screen, but that process involved three different directors utilizing two separate production crews. The film had a $100 million budget, with Germany contributing $18 million. One-third of the cost, however, was lent by backers in China, Korea, and Singapore.[12] A similar financing deal enabled a Bruce Willis film, *Looper* (2012), to get made. According to sources, the entire $30 million cost was financed by Chinese backers who received 50 percent of the profits and required that changes be made to the film in exchange for the financing.[13]

The trend towards multinational financing raises a host of important questions, primarily: how will foreign financing affect the content of Hollywood films? Since the foreign market accounts for almost 70 percent of box office receipts, will American audiences soon have to view films aimed to please the movie crowd in Beijing and New Delhi rather than Williamsport, PA, and Prescott, AZ? Is multinational financing the wave of the future or a temporary, pragmatic response to current economic conditions? It is too early to tell, but one aspect of Hollywood filmmaking—the blockbuster—is already affected. A useful illustration is to follow the path of the very successful film franchise *Pirates of the Caribbean*:

Table 14.2. Comparison Box Office for Pirates of the Caribbean Franchise[14]

| Film Title | Budget | Domestic Gross | Foreign Gross | %Foreign BO Receipts |
|---|---|---|---|---|
| #1. *Curse of the Black Pearl* | $140m | $305m | $348m | 53 |
| #2. *Dead Man's Chest* | $225m | $423m | $642m | 60 |
| #3. *At World's End* | $300m | $309m | $654m | 67 |
| #4. *On Stranger Tides* | $250m | $241m | $802m | 76 |
| #5. Scheduled for 2015 release | | | | |
| #6. Sixth film proposed | | | | |

The data tell the whole story and it would make no sense in any other business except Hollywood, where money trumps all other concerns. It is obvious from the above chart that the *Pirates of the Caribbean* series is running out of steam. By the fourth film, *On Stranger Tides*, the domestic box office failed to match the production costs. If we add at least another $100 million for advertising and ancillary costs, then the film lost money at home. That usually would signal the end for most film series. Then why is the studio planning a fifth and even a sixth film? Two words: foreign market. *On Stranger Tides* may have lost the interest of the North American market but foreign audiences made it a one billion dollar hit. In Hollywood, this fact alone ensures more sequels to come.

If Hollywood succumbs to the potentially rich non-European overseas market, which seems to enjoy fantasy, science fiction, action thrillers, and animation films, what chance do political films like *The Ides of March*, *Argo*, or even *Lincoln* have? All of these films draw on the type of political content that is central to America's cinematic history but irrelevant to foreign audiences. Not surprisingly, the foreign receipts for these films failed to match their domestic gross, a sure sign in Hollywood that similar films in the future must do well domestically in order for comparable political subjects to be considered again.

There is one more warning sign regarding the production end of the film business. Twenty years ago, state governments, fearing that Hollywood would take its business to Canada, and convinced that making films in-state would bring in money and help the local economy, joined the Hollywood incentive bandwagon by offering film companies tax incentives of various kinds, including credits against the state income tax, sales tax exemptions, fee-free use of state facilities and locations, cash rebates to cover production expenses, and, in some cases, even direct cash grants. In 2009, 45 states provided incentives to film companies amounting to $1.5 billion. *Lincoln*, for example, received $3.5 million from the state of Virginia. But the Michigan Studio fiasco mentioned previously, which cost the state millions, is making state governments rethink the whole idea of film incentives.[15] Should state film incentives decline or even be abolished, it will encourage Hollywood to do its filming elsewhere, even though the overseas location may not be a good fit for an American production. None of the above signs favor the growth of the political film genre.

## Obstacles and Concerns: Political Films

Should the film industry move exclusively toward multinational financing and co-production filming, political film will be adversely affected. But even assuming that scenario will not materialize, at least in the near future, the status of political films remains at risk. One detriment to its existence lies in the change that has taken place in the indie market over the past decade. Producers and distributors used to attend film festivals looking to buy modest, low-budget movies at bargain prices of under $1 million. Recent signs, however, indicate that the financial success of the indies has encouraged buyers to express more interest in $10 million dollar films that can be marketed to return five to 10 times the purchase price. It appears that the era of making quirky, politically risky movies that sold for under $1 million and made a profit is coming to a close. The buyers' expectations are much greater for a $10 million dollar film, and consequently that fact may affect the subject content. Should that happen, it is not hard to imagine what will become of the young film student with a digital camera, a $20,000 to $30,000 budget, and the dream of making a film about poverty, environmental pollution, sexual harassment, or cyber bullying.

In another sense, success places an obstacle in the path of the young filmmaker. American performers in the arts have chosen a career where only a few reach the highest plateau. They labor in an industry with a high failure rate and where only those popular at the box office reach stardom. So when a young filmmaker makes his first indie film, financed by family and friends, and receives encouragement on the festival circuit, who can blame him or her for dreaming of becoming the next Martin Scorsese or Kathryn Bigelow? When the film is bought at Sundance or Tribeca and plays in New York or Los Angeles to good reviews and shows decent box office returns, audiences will wish that filmmaker well and remember the name. But success can be a virus in the film business. If a filmmaker's work is critically received and makes money too, one of the major studios is likely to bankroll his or her next project and entrust the filmmaker with a larger budget. But success in Hollywood comes at a price. The studio will require that next project with its $50 million budget to be supervised and subjected to studio control over costs, casting, and content. Few in the industry have been able to make the upward climb while retaining their independence and creativity. The reality in Hollywood is that even A-list writers, directors, and actors are at the mercy of the conglomerates that now own and run the studios. There are a few exceptions, of course, but one or two financial failures, even for names like Spielberg, Eastwood and Scorsese, will make it difficult to secure backing for future projects. Even these respected filmmakers may have to make movies to please accountants, lawyers, foreign investors, and overseas audiences that have little interest in American history or politics. The global cinema that all the film critics write about in a positive way will be a bonanza to those in the industry who specialize in blockbusters or pure entertainment, but it will surely not advance a cinema dedicated to addressing the important social, economic, and political problems that face the world today.

There is one last factor working against political film that offers an even greater challenge because it lies within the values of corporate capitalism that the film industry has adopted. The Wall Street ideology of measuring success solely in terms of profits may serve those who make money without producing any tangible product or providing a necessary service, but it will not help a high-risk business like filmmaking. These corporate values, shared by Hollywood and mainstream American culture, present obstacles to any in the industry whose films offer alternatives to the status quo.

In his book *Cinema of Outsiders*, Emanuel Levy, professor of film and sociology, describes four such shared values that inhibit a proactive cinema from developing in Hollywood today.[16] One is the avoidance and even loathing of political movies, because the citizenry distrusts politicians and is wary about the exercise of power and authority. Consider President Obama's reform of the healthcare system. Merely the suggestion that a policy is "coming from Washington" is enough to raise cries of "socialism" among members on the right and their conservative media allies. Hollywood films support this popular distrust of government and are reluctant to confront the country's political institutions, preferring instead to blame misguided individuals and impersonal bureaucracies. Professor Levy also accuses Hollywood of exploiting the cult of individualism that permeates the American character by depicting film heroes and heroines as righteous individuals fighting alone, often successfully, against overwhelming odds.

Americans have become used to these glorified screen figures: boy ranger Jefferson Smith taking on the U.S. Senate filibuster, lawyer Frank Gavin winning a malpractice suit against the Catholic Church, plant manager Jack Godell shutting down a damaged nuclear power plant against the orders of its CEOs, and machine operator Norma Rae bringing unionization to a Southern textile mill at great cost to herself. Consequently, most of the action that occurs in standard Hollywood fare is by characters operating as individuals rather than in groups or as part of a larger community. Whether these fictional characters are exposing political corruption, protecting the environment, ensuring that the law produces just results, or advancing the rights of workers, they alone achieve the end result rather than a political party, interest group, or community organization. Collective action smacks too much of socialism for conservative Hollywood and probably mainstream America too.

Finally, Levy reminds us that the film industry avoids making films that identify any political ideology for fear of offending potential customers. The Hollywood studio heads are not conservative because they are Republicans, but rather because their goal is to make money in a high-risk business. That attitude translates too often into supporting the status quo: corporate capitalism, established institutions, the nuclear family, and the religious and cultural values of the majority.

If you tally up all these warning signs, obstacles, and concerns and add them to the preference of American moviegoers for pure entertainment, then the future for political film looks depressing indeed. Can it be that the author's grandchildren will never see films like *Mr. Smith Goes to Washington*, *On the Waterfront*, or *Casablanca*? These films did not require special effects, a booming stereo sound track, and gratuitous sex and violence to deliver their stories.

Still, there are indications that political film is not entirely dead in Hollywood. One encouraging sign is that young people are continuously drawn to work in the film industry as filmmakers, writers, and actors. Enrollment remains steady in top-graded films schools like USC, UCLA, and NYU—institutions that taught George Lucas, Francis Ford Coppola, and Martin Scorsese their craft. The number of first-time film directors who attend film school has doubled since 1980. Presently there are 120 colleges that offer degrees in film production or cinema studies. At UCLA film school, the number of students enrolled since the sixties has doubled. At USC, graduate enrollment in cinema arts has remained steady while undergraduate enrollment has risen 30 percent.[17] And in New York City, a different kind of film school has been created. Named the Ghetto Film School, it operates summers and weekends during the school year. Its ambition is to become a selective high school for the cinema arts.[18] These are all signs that young people continue to find careers in the film industry attractive. Many of them will likely begin their careers making short subjects, documentaries and films for the indie market.

The most telling evidence of this filmmaking phenomenon is the growth of film festivals and the number of films submitted to be juried. Film festivals have multiplied exponentially throughout the U.S., including a number that require no fee for submission. What is most impressive about these fee-free film festivals is the fact that a few of them, like the African Diaspora Film Festival and the Boston Jewish Film Festival, book racial and ethnic films. Such festivals are in response to the staggering number of films that seek exposure. Sundance, for instance, has grown from several hundred entries to an estimated 12,000 submissions, even though the festival accepts only 200 films to be screened.[19] Certainly, these numbers indicate that the independent film movement is still breathing.

What is glaring, however, is the lack of interest within the ranks of educators to recognize film as a medium to convey the kind of ideas that are worthy of First Amendment protection as articulated by the U.S. Supreme Court in *Burstyn v. Wilson*.[20] To promote such use of the medium, time should be set aside in the curriculum, as early as grade school, to introduce youngsters to films that teach about the human condition and that introduce them to the various peoples of the world. When the author spent a year at the University of Nottingham in England's East Midlands, he made friends with the director of the local downtown movie theatre where he witnessed classes of schoolchildren entering the theater to view and discuss films of special interest. The purpose behind these showings was to lay the foundation for a more informed and selective film audience as the children grew into adults. Additionally, the theater would occasionally offer special film lectures on a variety of subjects to a packed audience. The author, in fact, presented a film lecture program on Noam Chomsky, American linguist and political activist, to a crowd that enjoyed wine and hors d'oeuvres during intermission.

Another favorable sign is that there exists a small group of filmmakers in the industry that is dedicated to making the kind of challenging films that *they* want to make. Filmmakers like Kathryn Bigelow (*The Hurt Locker*, *Zero Dark Thirty*), Kimberley Peirce (*Stop-Loss*), George Clooney (*The Ides of March*, *Good Night, and Good Luck*), Ben Affleck (*Argo*), and Courtney Hunt, whose first feature, *Frozen River* (2008), received an Oscar nomination, show us that not all of Hollywood has joined the commercial assembly line. It remains to be seen whether they can keep from falling under the financial control of those who only make movies for money.

Still another positive indicator is the constant development of new technology that provides greater opportunities, especially to the indie filmmaker. Two developments deserve attention. Hollywood's latest strategy for low-budget films is to bypass theaters and release them directly to DVD. This strategy is not meant to pass off bad films to moviegoers, but rather to maximize profits for films that, for whatever reason, lack sufficient audience appeal. In these cases the studio develops a film project for under $10 million with the intention of releasing it to DVD, where the studio believes it will gross three times its cost. Apparently, the strategy is paying off, because 675 such films were released direct to DVD in 2007.[21] The number fell to 129 in 2010, but despite the decline, the strategy still will attract young filmmakers who want to make political films and distributors who are willing to market such films because of the minimal risk involved.[22] In a similar vein, a growing number of states are subsidizing these low-budget films destined for limited release as a means of stimulating the local economy and creating jobs. Some of these films go directly to DVD, others to film festivals in search of a buyer.[23]

Another potential source for filmmakers lies in making campaign videos and movies supporting political candidates and their parties. The past two presidential elections in 2008 and 2012 found both candidates and their respective parties utilizing media as a campaign tool to deliver campaign propaganda .The flow of political images and video streams began with Michael Moore's partisan campaign film, *Slacker Uprising*, which could be downloaded free from the Internet. The film's objective was to mobilize the vote, particularly among younger voters. Conservatives responded quickly to the liberal challenge. David Zucker's 2008 release, *An American Carol*, was a satirical comedy aimed squarely at Michael Moore and his liberal supporters. In the film, an old grandfather type actor is telling the folks at a July 4th barbecue a story about a documentary filmmaker and Michael Moore look-alike that hates America and is determined to abolish the national holiday. The Michael Moore clone refuses to celebrate, and that night he is visited by three ghosts, General George Patton, President George Washington and country western singer Trace Adkins, who give Moore a lesson in American patriotism.[24]

By the 2012 campaign, the Obama and Romney campaigns were using all of the new technologies—Internet, email, texting and social networks such as Facebook, Twitter, and MySpace—to woo voters, with the Obama team adding the option to make a contribution. This strategy to target small contributors paid off: Obama raised more money than Romney overall and received 57 percent of his contributions from those who gave under $200 compared to Romney's 24 percent.[25]

But the most intrusive media campaign against a presidential candidate was the partisan documentary *2016: Obama's America* by conservative thinker Dinesh D'Souza, which was discussed in chapter 3. The documentary, although critical of the president, did not affect the outcome of the 2012 election, but may have paved the way for future such offerings from other partisan voices. If they are prepared for the consequences, that is—D'Souza soon discovered that entering the political arena automatically makes you a media target.[26]

Who knows what new technology will develop in the future? Films already are streamed to computers, iPods, and iPhones. The ability to deliver low-budget films to individuals is another plus for young filmmakers who want to make experimental, off-beat, and even political films. But the overriding question remains: are these positive signs enough to offset the more negative indicators? Only time will provide the answer.

# Epilogue

The tragic events of September 11 remind us of the crucial role played by the media in an interconnected world. We see signs everywhere that filmic images are replacing the printed word. These mostly Western images are transmitted around the globe, and since the U.S. dominates the international market, Hollywood has a special responsibility to diversify such images and to avoid cultural expansionism. Here is where an independent film movement can make its greatest contribution. The best hope for global peace and understanding lies in a continuous stream of alternative films produced by politically conscious filmmakers who are willing to make the kind of films that mainstream Hollywood refuses to either consider or undertake because of their greater financial risk. This can only be achieved if American audiences become selective filmgoers, avoiding the banal, cheap, sexually vulgar, and excessively violent films that have become the staple of Hollywood. If American audiences truly want to see fewer films aimed at teenagers and action junkies, then they will have to prove it to Hollywood at the box office by staying away. Seniors have shown that they will return to theaters if Hollywood makes movies like *The Best Exotic Marigold Hotel* (2011), where seven elderly Britons are enticed to travel to India. Made for $10 million, it racked up four times its cost in the U.S. market alone and eventually went on to earn a total gross of $136 million.[27]

Winston Churchill was right: in a democracy people get what they deserve. That is what he meant when he described democracy as the best and the worst form of government. Hollywood is not a trendsetter; its inclination is to follow the box office returns. It is up to the public to indicate our film preferences by the choices we make. Buying tickets to a movie is one form of approval, staying home sends a different message. Between May and July 4th, 2013, the studios released 13 blockbuster films costing $100 million or more.[28] Many of these are intended for the global market and it may not matter what the public does, but at least Americans can express their discontent by not patronizing them.

Should we tell Hollywood that Americans appreciate quality films that move and inspire us? Should we tell the industry that adults are tired of films made for teenage libidos and macho men while the rest of the population is ignored? Or should we just continue to accept and support the cookie-cutter junk that fills the multiplexes? The choice is ours.

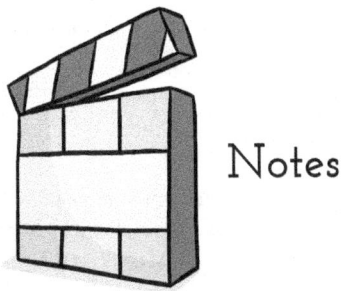

# Notes

## Prologue. President Obama Returns to the White House

1. Scott Rohter, "Snow White and the Seven Republican Dwarfs Sizing up the Field for 2012," October 2011, at http://www.lessgovisthebestgov.com/Snow-White-seven-Republican-dwarfs.html (accessed May 17, 2013). There were changes in the "dwarfs'" makeup, as Tim Pawlenty and Gary Johnson dropped out of the primary race.
2. "2012 Election Results Map," Politico, accessed December 27, 2012, http://www.politico.com/2012-election/map/#/President/2012/.
3. http://www.americanprogress.org/issues/progressive-movement/news/2012/11/08/44348/the-return-of-the-obama-coalition/ (accessed November 18, 2012).
4. Campbell Brown, "The President Gives Hollywood a Pass on Violence," *The Wall Street Journal*, April 4, 2013, A15. Brown, a former anchor for CNN and NBC, suggested the president was well placed to influence the entertainment industry given his influential friends and supporters in Hollywood and she was disappointed he hadn't taken the opportunity.

## Chapter 1. Film and Politics: The Hollywood-Washington Connection

1. Richard Maltby and Ian Craven, *Hollywood Cinema* (Cambridge: Blackwell, 1995), 363.
2. Steven J. Ross, *Hollywood Left and Right* (New York: Oxford University Press, 2011). The following discussion on debunking the entertainment myth comes from Ross's various sections of his examination of "political Hollywood."
3. Ibid., 304.
4. Ibid., 409–18.
5. Quoted in Paul Krugman's column, *The New York Times*, May 30, 2003, A29.
6. For a more complete list of entertainers turned politicians before Schwarzenegger, see *The New York Times*, August 8, 2003, A14.
7. http://www.cnn.com/election/2008. Data based on Federal Election Commission report, November 20, 2008. Together the candidates raised close to $1 billion.
8. Over $2 billion more will be spent on Congressional races and the remainder by Super PACs. The data come from the Center for Responsive Politics at http://www.opensecrets.org/news/2012/10/2012-election-spending-will-reach-6.html (accessed November 3, 2012).
9. *The New York Times*, Week in Review, February 25, 2004, sec. 4, 1. On the other hand, sportspeople tended to give more money to McCain.
10. *The New York Times*. Week in Review, March 4, 2007, sec. 4, 2.
11. See http://mediamythalert.wordpress.com/2010/11/06/follow-the-money-a-made-up-watergate-line/ (accessed October 23, 2012). The film's screenwriter, William Goldman, invented the line.
12. Neal Gabler, *Life: The Movie: How Entertainment Conquered Reality* (New York: Alfred A. Knopf, 1998).
13. James Traub, "The Celebrity Solution," *The New York Times*, March 9, 2008, 38–43.

14. Reported in *The New York Times*, February 16, 2009, C1.
15. http:///finance.yahoo.com/news/top-vip-donors-Obama-romney-070040339.html (accessed November 3, 2012).
16. See http:///finance.yahoo.com/news/clooney-aids-obama-campaign-geneva-fundraiser-095401777.html (accessed August 27, 2012) and CNN Wire Staff, "Obama fundraiser at George Clooney's home nets $15 million," at http:/cnn.com/2012/05/11/politics/california-obama-fundraiser, May 11, 2012.
17. Reported in *The New York Times*, December 1, 1998, A24.
18. Ronald Brownstein develops this theme in Part II of his book *The Power and the Glitter* (New York: Pantheon, 1990).
19. *The New York Times*, May 7, 2009, A26.
20. Neal Gabler in *An Empire of Their Own: How the Jews Invented Hollywood* (New York: Crown, 1988).
21. Ross, *Hollywood Left and Right*, 73.
22. See Roland Flamini, *Thalberg: The Last Tycoon and the World of MGM* (New York: Crown, 1994).
23. See Kevin Brownlow, *Behind the Mask of Innocence* (New York: Alfred A. Knopf, 1990), chapter 6.
24. Details of the campaign can be found in Greg Mitchell, *The Campaign of the Century* (New York: Random House, 1992); Immanuel Ness and James Ciment, *The Encyclopedia of Third Parties in America*, vol. 1 (New York: M.E. Sharpe, 2000), 249–50; *The New York Times Book Review*, July 2, 2006, sec. 7, 10–11; and in a recent posting by Andrew Glass, "Hollywood-Washington political ties rich in history," found at http://dyn.politico.com, April 29, 2007.
25. Paul Buhle and Dave Wagner, *Radical Hollywood* (New York: The New Press, 2002), Introduction. The film list would include such classics as *Casablanca*, *Lawrence of Arabia*, *Mr. Smith Goes to Washington*, and *The Wizard of Oz*. For the view that Hollywood is under the control of left-liberals today, see James Hirsen, *Tales from the Left Coast* (New York: Crown Forum, 2003).
26. See Frances Stoner Saunders, *The Cultural Cold War* (New York: The New Press, 1999).
27. John Daly, "The Right Stuff and the Wrong Stuff: The Curious History of an Epic Historical Film" (paper presented at the Far West Popular Culture meeting, Las Vegas, February 2004).
28. Simon Montlake, "Hollywood's Secret Weapon to Combat Piracy in China," at http://www.forbes.com/sites/simonmontlake/2012/11/02/hollywoods-secret-weapon-to-combat-piracy-in-china (accessed November 2, 2012).
29. Nicole Allan, "How to Make a Hollywood Hit," *The Atlantic* online, May 2012 (accessed November 5, 2012).
30. Sources disagree as to the percentage of revenue coming from foreign markets before the 1990s. Some cite 40 percent, others 30 percent. The discrepancy really does not affect the generalization that Hollywood today is relying more on foreign markets to turn a profit. See Christina Klein, "The Asia Factor in Global Hollywood," http://yaleglobal.yale.edu, March 23, 2003; Michael Edwards, "The Imbalance of trade," at http://www.jamaicaobserver.com, November 14, 2003, and Hy Hollinger and Cynthia Littleton, "Worldwide Opening," at http://www.hollywoodreporter.com, July 28, 2005.
31. Brent Lang, "Overseas Markets are Hollywood's Box Office Superheroes," August 16, 2012 at http://movies.yahoo.com/news/never-mind-avengers-overseas-markets-hollywoods-box-office-123850176.html.
32. John Schrems, *Understanding Principles of Politics and the State* (Lanham, MD: University Press of America, revised edition, 2011).
33. Mark Sachleben and Kevan M. Yenerall, *Seeing the Bigger Picture* (New York: Peter Lang, second edition, 2012).
34. The material on Guevara comes from novelist-playwright Ariel Dorfman's "Heroes and Icons," from "*Time* 100 Persons of the Century," online, June 14, 1999 as reprinted at http://content.time.com/time/magazine/

article/0,9171,991227,00.html (accessed March 11, 2013) and "Che Guevara" at http://en.wikipedia.org/wiki/Che_Guevara (accessed January 25, 2010).

35. *Che* was completed in 2008 but released in the U.S. in 2009. Although no budget estimate was available, the film's worldwide gross was a paltry $1.7 million, with almost 90 percent earned in the U.S.

36. Even with its A-list cast and romantic plot, Beatty's film, which cost between $32 and $35 million, had a domestic gross of only $40 million. In that same year, *Raiders of the Lost Ark* earned $209 million in the U.S.

37. Walter Benjamin, "The Work of Art in the Age of Mechanical Reproduction," in Hannah Arendt, ed., *Illuminations* (New York: Schocken Books, 1968).

38. The quote by Cassavetes is in Michael Genovese, *Politics and the Cinema* (Lexington, MA: Ginn Press, 1986), 67. Certainly, Neal Gabler agreed with that assessment in his book *An Empire of Their Own*, detailing how the Jewish immigrants who founded Hollywood portrayed an idealized version of the U.S. in their new films.

39. Dan Nimmo, "Political Propaganda in the Movies: A Typology," in James Combs, ed., *Movies and Politics: The Dynamic Relationship* (New York: Garland Publishing, 1993), 271–94.

40. Ibid., 283–84.

41. Mark C. Neely Jr., "The Young Lincoln," in Mark C. Carnes, ed., *Past Imperfect: History According to the Movies* (New York: Henry Holt & Company, 1995), 124–27.

42. Harry Keyishian, *Screening Politics: The Politician in American Movies, 1931–2001* (Lanham, MD: The Scarecrow Press, 2003), 184–87.

43. Neely Jr., "The Young Lincoln," 126.

44. Keyishian, *Screening Politics*, 180–83.

45. Joseph E. Persico, *Franklin and Lucy* (New York: Random House, 2008). FDR's ability to cover up the affair tells us how much the media's attitude towards our leaders has changed.

46. "Nixon Film as History," panel at the American History Association meeting, January 1997. See http://www.c-spanvideo.org/program/77654-1 (accessed October 30, 2012).

47. Keyishian, *Screening Politics*, 109–12.

48. William H. Chafe, "*Mississippi Burning*," in Carnes, ed., *Past Imperfect*, 274–77.

49. See Ernest R. May, "Thirteen Days in 145 Minutes," *National Forum* 81, no. 2 (Spring 2001): 34–37, and Michael Nelson, "Thirteen Days Doesn't Add Up," *The Chronicle of Higher Education*, February 2, 2001, sec. 2, B15–16.

50. These three films are cited by Ernest Giglio, "Using Film to Teach Political Concepts," *European Political Science* 1, no. 2 (Spring 2002): 53–58, as examples that require corrections and analysis before use in the classroom.

51. This is the viewpoint express by Richard B. Stinnett in *Day of Deceit: The Truth about FDR & Pearl Harbor* (New York: Free Press, 1999).

52. There are several critical critiques of *Argo* but I took most of it from a posting by NPR reporter David Haglund, "How Accurate is *Argo*?" posted on October 12, 2012 by Slate.com at http://www.slate.com/blogs/browbeat/2012/10/12/argo_true_story_the_facts_and_fiction_behind_the_ben_affleck_movie.html.

53. Stephen Vaughn, *Ronald Reagan in Hollywood* (New York: Cambridge University Press, 1994).

54. See Ernest Giglio, "The Decade of '*The Miracle*' 1952–1962: A Study in the Censorship of the American Motion Picture" (Ph.D. diss., Syracuse University, 1964) and I.C. Jarvie (editor) et al., *Children and the Movies: Media Influences and the Payne Fund Controversy* (New York: Cambridge University Press, 1996).

55. Jane Kellogg, "'*Dark Knight Rises*' Shooting: 10 New Developments in the Aurora, Colo., Massacre," *The Hollywood Reporter* online, July 22, 2012 at http://www.hollywoodreporter.com/news/dark-knight-rises-shooting-james-holmes-aurora-colorado-barak-obama-352839.

56. William R. Elliott and William J. Schenck-Hamlin, "Film, Politics and the Press: The Influence of '*All the President's Men*,'" *Journalism Quarterly* 56, no. 3 (1979): 546–53.

57. Thomas S. Bateman, Tomoaki Sakano, and Mokoto Fujita, "Roger, Me, and My Attitude: Film Propaganda and Cynicism toward Corporate Leadership," *Journal of Applied Psychology* 77, no. 5 (1992): 768–71.

## Chapter 2. In Search of the Political Film

1. The literature on *Casablanca* is too large to cite here but a few noteworthy sources include Aljean Harmetz, *Round Up the Usual Suspects* (New York: Hyperion, 1992); Howard Koch, "*Casablanca*": *Script and Legend* (New York: Overlook Express, 1992); and Randy Roberts and Robert E. May, "You Must Remember This: The Case of Hal Wallis's *Casablanca*" in Roberts and May, *Learning to Think Critically: Film, Myth, and American History* (New York: HarperCollins, 1993). If you are interested in what happened to Rick and Cpt. Renault, read Michael Walsh, *As Time Goes By* (Little, Brown & Co., 1998). For a new perspective on the film, see Eric D. Snider, "What's the Big Deal?: *Casablanca* (1942)," June 22, 2010, at http://www.film.com/movies/whats-the-big-deal-casablanca-1942 (accessed October 4, 2012).

2. http://www.loc.gov/rr/mopic/miggen.html#Political (accessed August 9, 2013).

3. The definition must be understood in the context of the largely collaborative work by the Internet's *Wikipedia* encyclopedia. Go to http://en.wikipedia.org/wiki/Political_cinema (accessed October 4, 2012).

4. Clifford Geertz, *The Interpretation of Cultures* (New York: Basic Books, 1973), 196.

5. See for example, Terry Christensen, *Reel Politics* (New York: Blackwell, 1987); Gary Crowdus, ed., *The Political Companion to American Film* (Chicago: Lake View Press, 1994); and Mark Litwak, *Reel Power* (London: Sedgwick & Jackson, 1987) as scholars, critics, and writers who fit into this group.

6. Terry Christensen, *Reel Politics: American Political Movies from "Birth of a Nation" to "Platoon"* (New York: Basil Blackwell, 1987), 228–38.

7. Genovese, *Politics and the Cinema*, 2–3.

8. The data come from http://www.boxofficemojo.com/movies/?id=wiigapatow.htm.

9. *Lincoln* grossed $180 million at home and was the 13th ranked film among the year's top grossing films. See http://boxofficemojo.com/movies/?id=lincoln.htm.

10. John Simon, *Movies into Film* (New York: Dell Publishing Co., 1970), 66.

11. Ibid.

12. Peter J. Haas, "A Typology of Political Film," Working Paper #11, Political Film Society series, March 2000.

13. Terry Christensen and Peter J. Haas, *Projecting Politics: Political Messages in American Films* (Armonk, NY: M.E. Sharpe, 2005).

14. Ibid., 4.

15. Kevin Brownlow, *Behind the Mask of Innocence* (New York: Alfred A. Knopf, 1990), chapter 2.

16. Christensen and Haas, *Projecting Politics*, 308–24.

17. Cass Sunstein, "Free Speech Now," *University of Chicago Law Review* 59 (1992): 304.

18. On this point, see Nimmo, "Political Propaganda in the Movies: A Typology," in *Movies and Politics*, 277. For the view that the film was about Hollywood, see Crowdus, *Political Companion*, 153–54, and Christensen, *Reel Power*, 93.

19. The story is related at http://www.current.org/doc/doc0210foreman.html. The documentary *Darkness at High Noon* was aired on PBS in September 2002.

20. Christine Noll Brinckmann, "The Politics of Force of Evil: An Analysis of Abraham Polonsky's Preblacklisted Film," *Prospects* 6 (1981): 369.
21. Peter Biskind, *Seeing Is Believing: How Hollywood Taught Us to Stop Worrying and Love the Fifties* (New York: Pantheon Books, 1983), 5.
22. Crowdus, *Political Companion*, 235–36, maintains that Kramer's social message pictures were commercial successes because he provided simple-minded solutions to complex problems. For example, in *Guess Who's Coming to Dinner*, the film suggests that racism can be resolved at the personal level of two families having a friendly discussion over a cup of coffee. Furthermore, Crowdus questions Kramer's political liberalism since off-screen he deserted friends during the time of McCarthyism and the blacklist.
23. See Charles Chaplin, *My Autobiography* (New York: Simon and Schuster, 1964) and David Robinson, *Chaplin: His Life and Art* (New York: McGraw-Hill, 1985).
24. Don B. Morlan, "A Pie in the Face: The Three Stooges Anti-Aristocracy Theme in Depression-Era American Film" (paper presented at the annual meeting of the Popular Culture Association, Chicago, April 1994), "Slapstick Contributions to World War II Propaganda: The Three Stooges and Abbott & Costello," *Studies in Popular Culture* 17 (Oct. 1994): 29–43, and "Pre-World War II Propaganda: Film as Controversy" (paper presented at the annual meeting of the American Political Science Association, Chicago, September 1995).
25. Leonard Maltin, *The Great Movie Shorts* (New York: Crown Publishers, 1972) identifies the Stooges as "low comedians" who recycled one basic plot formula in all their films. All their story lines developed from that one premise. Maltin admits that the Stooges made one political film, *Three Dark Horses*, a satire about a crooked presidential campaign. But the public embraced the shorts and ignored the film.
26. *Jacobellis v. Ohio*, 378 U.S. 184 at 197 (1964).

## Chapter 3. Nonfiction Film: Picturing Reality?

1. Bill Nichols, *Blurred Boundaries* (Bloomington: Indiana University Press, 1994), 47–48.
2. See Jill Godmilow, "How Real Is the Reality in Documentary Film?" *History and Theory* 36, no. 4 (December 1997): 80–81.
3. Richard M. Barsam, "From Nonfiction Film: A Critical History," in Gerald Mast and Marshall Cohen, eds., *Film Theory and Criticism*, 3rd ed. (New York: Oxford University Press, 1985), 583–85.
4. http://www.boxofficemojo.com/movies/?id=fahrenheit911.htm (accessed July 18, 2013).
5. Guido Convents, "Documentaries and Propaganda before 1914," *Framework* 35 (1988): 107–08.
6. Reported in Tom W. Hoffer and Richard Alan Nelson, "Docudrama on American Television," *Journal of the University Film Association* 30, no. 2 (Spring 1978): 22, ft.3.
7. The Library of Congress, "The Motion Picture Camera Goes to War," March 1998, http://www.loc.gov/loc/lcib/9803/film.html (accessed March 12, 2013).
8. See Steven J. Ross, "Struggles for the Screen: Workers, Radicals, and the Political Uses of Silent Film," *American Historical Review* 96, no. 2 (April 1991): 333–67.
9. Richard M. Barsam, *Nonfiction Film*, rev. ed. (Bloomington: Indiana University Press, 1992), 32–38.
10. Brian Winston, *Claiming the Real: The Documentary Film Revisited* (London: British Film Institute, 1995), 69–70.
11. Ross, "Struggles for the Screen," 349–61.
12. See Barsam, *Nonfiction Film*, chapter 10, for a discussion of American films made during World War II.
13. "What is "Documentary" Film?" at http://documentaryarchive.com/defining_documentary.html and "Documentary Film History" at http://documentaryarchive.com/documentary_history.html (accessed July 18, 2013).

14. See Barry Keith Grant, *Voyages of Discovery: The Cinema of Frederick Wiseman* (Urbana: University of Illinois Press, 1992), where the author describes Wiseman's films as "voyages of discovery" in which both the filmmaker and the viewer rediscover themselves, and Thomas W. Benson and Carolyn Anderson, *Reality Fictions: The Films of Frederick Wiseman*, 2nd ed. (Carbondale: Southern Illinois University Press, 2002).

15. For the complete story, see Benson and Anderson, *Reality Fictions*, chapter 2.

16. *Commonwealth v. Wiseman*, Superior Court, Civil Action No. 87538, 1 August 1991, Memorandum of Decision, Re: Motion for Reconsideration.

17. The information on *Primate* comes from an article by David Stewart, "Fred Wiseman's novelistic samplings of reality," February 27, 2004, http://www.current.org/wp-content/themes/current/archive-site/doc/doc802wiseman.shtml and a review on the film by Leo Goldsmith, "Primate," Not Coming to a Theater Near You, June 8, 2008, http://www.notcoming.com/reviews/primate.

18. Grant, *Voyages of Discovery*, 27–34.

19. Ibid., 9.

20. Benson and Anderson, *Reality Fictions*, 306.

21. Ibid., 2.

22. Interview reprinted in "Frederick Wiseman," *Wikipedia*, January 21, 2013, http://en.wikipedia.org/w/index.php?title=Frederick_Wiseman&oldid=525081127.

23. "What is 'Documentary' film?" http://docmentaryarchive.com/definig_documentary.html (accessed July 18, 2013).

24. See Raymond Fielding, *The March of Time, 1945–51* (New York: Oxford University Press, 1978), chapter 8, 187–201. Fielding claims that the newsreel took footage originally filmed in Germany and reshot most of it around Hoboken, New Jersey, using anti-Nazi German Americans.

25. According to Matthew Bernstein, "Documentaphobia and Mixed Modes," in Barry Keith Grant and Jeannette Sloniowski, eds., *Documenting the Documentary* (Detroit: Wayne State University Press, 1998), 397, Moore admitted to the fact in an interview.

26. See the reviews and commentary by Richard Corliss in *Time*, February 12, 1990, 58; Pauline Kael in *The New Yorker*, January 8, 1990, 90–92; and John Simon in *National Review*, June 11, 1990, 54. Michael Moore's second endeavor, *Canadian Bacon*, a feature film with Hollywood actors, did not fare well at the box office or with critics.

27. The story was reported in *The New York Times*, February 25, 2007, 23.

28. Richard Bernstein, "'Roger and Me': Documentary? Satire? Or Both?" *The New York Times*, February 1, 1990, C20.

29. See Miles Orwell, "Documentary and the Power of Interrogation: '*American Dream*' and '*Roger & Me*,'" *Film Quarterly* 48 (Winter 1994/95): 10–18.

30. Lincoln Steffens, *The Shame of the Cities* (New York: Hill & Wang, 1957).

31. The debate at the 2005 American Historical Association (AHA) is reported in John E. O'Connor, "Michael Moore: Cinematic Historian or Propagandist?" *Film & History* 35, no. 2 (2005), 7–16.

32. For arguments for and against the film see A.O. Scott, "Open Wide and Say 'Shame,'" *The New York Times*, June 22, 2004, B1; Atul Gawande, "Sick and Twisted," *The New Yorker*, July 23, 2007, 21–22; "What's Lacking in '*Sicko*,'" *The New York Times*, July 7, 2007, B5; and Philip M. Boffey, "Some Thoughts on Sickness After Seeing '*Sicko*,'" *The New York Times*, July 5, 2007, A14.

33. The article, "A Conservative Answer to Michael Moore," is at http://www.nysun.com/new-york/conservative-answer-to-michael-moore/8027, January 21, 2005.

34. The story is revealed in Christy Lemire, "Film Questions Michael Moore's Tactics," March 11, 2007, http://www.washingtonpost.com/wp-dyn/content/article/2007/03/11/AR2007031100874.html.

35. Alan Rosenthal, ed., *Why Docudrama?* (Carbondale: Southern Illinois University Press, 1999), xiv.
36. Good background material is found in Tom W. Hoffer and Richard Alan Nelson, "Docudrama on American Television," 21–27, as well as Rosenthal, *Why Docudrama? Part I*, 1–11.
37. See Rebecca Liss, "Oliver Stone's World Trade Center Fiction," August 9, 2006, http://www.slate.com/articles/news_and_politics/life_and_art/2006/08/oliver_stones_world_trade_center_fiction.html accessed March 12, 2013).
38. These criticisms were reported at "World Trade Center," *Wikipedia*, January 31, 2013. http://en.wikipedia.org/w/index.php?title=World_Trade_Center&oldid=534317074.
39. Review by Peter Bradshaw, *The Guardian*, September 29, 2006, http://www.guardian.co.uk/film/2006/sep/29/actionandadventure?INTCMP=SRCH. Another critical review is by Phillip French, *The Observer*, October 1, 2006, http://www.guardian.co.uk/film/2006/oct/01/drama?INTCMP=SRCH.
40. See http://en.wikipedia.org/wiki/United_93_(film).Three months previously, the A&E cable network aired a made-for-TV movie, *Flight 93*, on the same subject. However, it failed to receive the same acclaim as Greengrass's film. But both films illustrate that the communications system on the ground was inadequate to deal with a national emergency.
41. For a rare critique of *United 93*, see Frank Rich's op-ed column "Too Soon? It's Too Late for 'United 93,'" *The New York Times*, May 7, 2006, sec. 4, 12. Compare Rich's view with that of David Thomson, "Films of Infamy," *The New York Times*, April 30, 2006, sec. 4, 15. Both grapple with the question of when it is appropriate to film a national tragedy.
42. Quoted in David Culbert, "Our Awkward Ally: Mission to Moscow," in O'Connor and Jackson, eds., *American History/American Film*, 145, ft. 62.
43. See Welch, *Propaganda and the German Cinema, 1933–1945*, 123–25.
44. A 2013 documentary, "Defiant Requiem," recreates a performance of Verdi's *Requiem* by Jewish inmates at the Terezin concentration camp for their Nazi guards, fellow prisoners and the International Red Cross. Ralph Gardner Jr., "History's Requiem," *The Wall Street Journal*, April 4, 2013, A18.
45. See Winston, *Claiming the Real*, 74–78 and 108–9; David Hackett, film review of *The Wonderful, Horrible Life of Leni Riefenstahl*, *American Historical Review* 100, no. 4, (Oct. 1995), 1227–28; and Frank P. Tomasulo, "The Mass Psychology of Fascist Cinema," in Grant and Sloniowski, eds., *Documenting the Documentary*, 99–118. Tomasulo argues that Riefenstahl's film created a spectacle rather than documented one because of the presence of 16 cameramen, 135 technicians, and several high-ranking Nazi officers—all for the purpose of constructing a mythic representation of Hitler and the nation as one entity, with Hitler in the role of the strong father figure destined to lead a confused Germany in restoring its rightful place as a world power.
46. Reported in Anna Maria Sigmund, *Women of the Third Reich* (Ontario, Canada: NDE Publishing, 2000), 101.
47. Ibid., 108.
48. See Jurgen Trimborn, *Leni Riefenstahl: A Life* (Faber & Faber, 2007 ) and Steven Bach, *Leni: The Life & Work of Leni Riefenstahl* (Alfred A. Knopf, 2007).
49. Don B. Morlan, "Pre-WWII Propaganda: Film as Controversy" (paper presented at the annual meeting of the American Political Science Association, Chicago, Sept. 1995).
50. See Melvin Small, "Buffoons and Brave Hearts: Hollywood Portrays the Russians, 1939–1944," *California Historical Society* 52 (winter 1973): 326–37.
51. This is an edited version taken from the 1943 film as reprinted in *The New York Times*, January 10, 2010, Arts & Leisure, 4. Howard Koch, who wrote the screenplay, was blacklisted after the HUAC hearings.
52. See Culbert in O'Connor and Jackson, *American History/American Film*, 121–45. Culbert insists that Stalin, acting as the Soviet censor, only permitted some two dozen American films, including *Mission to Moscow*, to be shown in the Soviet Union between 1939 and 1945. The film remains a source of embarrassment to Warner Brothers, its distributor, since the studio denied the author permission to use a photo still from the movie.

53. Reported by Palash Ghosh, "How Many People Did Joseph Stalin Kill?" at http://www.ibtimes.com/how-many-people-did-joseph-stalin-kill-1111789, March 5, 2013 (accessed August 22, 2013).

54. For a subjective eyewitness account of the filming, consult blacklisted director Herbert Biberman's book, *Salt of the Earth* (Boston: Beacon Press, 1965). A more scholarly and objective account is found in James J. Lorence, *The Suppression of Salt of the Earth* (Albuquerque: University of New Mexico Press, 1999).

55. James Dao, "When the Bullets Flew, They Didn't Care That I Was a Woman," *The New York Times*, January 25, 2013, A1.

56. Max Fisher, "Map: Which Countries Allow Women in Front-line Combat Roles?" *WorldViews* (blog), *The Washington Post*, January 25, 2013, http://www.washingtonpost.com/blogs/worldviews/wp/2013/01/25/map-which-countries-allow-women-in-front-line-combat-roles/.

57. James Risen, "Military Has Not Solved Problem of Sexual Assault, Women Say," *The New York Times*, November 2, 2012, A15.

58. Ibid.

59. Department of Defense, "Annual Report on Sexual Assault in the Military: Fiscal Year 2011," on their Sexual Assault Prevention and Response Office website, April 10, 2012, http://www.sapr.mil/media/pdf/reports/Department_of_Defense_Fiscal_Year_2011_Annual_Report_on_Sexual_Assault_in_the_Military.pdf.

60. "Tailhook: Scandal Time," *Newsweek*, July 5, 1992, http://www.thedailybeast.com/newsweek/1992/07/05/tailhook-scandal-time.html (accessed February 26, 2013).

61. "Aberdeen Scandal," *Wikipedia*, last modified August 25, 2012, http://en.wikipedia.org/w/index.php?title=Aberdeen_scandal&oldid=509158597.

62. "2003 United States Air Force Academy Sexual Assault Scandal," *Wikipedia*, last modified February 7, 2013, http://en.wikipedia.org/w/index.php?title=2003_United_States_Air_Force_Academy_sexual_assault_scandal&oldid=537131707.

63. James Dao, "Instructor for Air Force is Convicted in Sex Assaults," July 20, 2012, http://www.nytimes.com/2012/07/21/us/lackland-air-force-base-instructor-guilty-of-sex-assaults.html?pagewanted=all&_r=0 (accessed February 26, 2013).

64. Colonel Ann Wright, "The Dark Side of the Prestigious Marine Barracks," May 8, 2012, http://www.truthdig.com/report/item/the_dark_side_of_the_the_prestigious_marine_barracks-20120508 (accessed February 26, 2013).

65. Dan Nimmo, "Political Propaganda in the Movies: A Typology," in Combs, ed., *Movies and Politics*, 271–94.

66. The material on Reverend Wright comes from Billy Hallowell, "This is How Obama 'Founding Father' Rev. Wright, His Church & Black Liberation Theology Shaped the President's Worldview," October 15, 2012, http://www.theblaze.com/stories/2012/10/15/this-is-how-obama-founding-father-rev-wright-trinity-united-black-liberation-theology-shaped-the-presidents-worldview/, and the source for the material on Ayers is from "Putting on Ayers," December 6, 2008, http://www.snopes.com/politics/obama/ayers.asp (accessed August 22, 2013).

67. "Weapons of Mass Instruction: Terrorism, Propaganda Film, Politics and Us: New Media, New Messages," *Studies in Popular Culture* 27, no. 3 (April 2005): 59–73.

## Chapter 4. Kiss, Kiss, Bang, Bang: Hollywood, Sex & Violence

1. For a discussion of early film censorship, see Ernest Giglio, "The Decade of '*The Miracle*' 1952–1962: A Study in the Censorship of the American Motion Picture" (Ph.D. diss., Syracuse University, 1964).

2. Terry Ramsaye, *A Million and One Nights* (New York: Simon and Schuster, 1926), vol. I, 256.

3. See Charles Lyons, *The New Censors: Movies and the Culture Wars* (Philadelphia: Temple University Press, 1997).

4. See Thomas Doherty, *Pre-Code Hollywood: Sex, Immorality, and Insurrection in American Cinema* (New York: Columbia University Press, 1999) and Mark Vieira, *Sin in Soft Focus: Pre-Code Hollywood* (New York: Harry N. Abrams, 1999).
5. Anthony Ferri and William M. Thompson, "An Assessment of Ethics in American Movies" (paper presented at the Far West Popular Culture meeting, Las Vegas, March 15, 2009).
6. Congressional Record, 67th Cong., 2d Sess., 1922, LXII, Part 9, 9657.
7. There has been renewed scholarly interest in the code, possibly due to its placement online at "The Motion Picture Production Code of 1930 (Hays Code)," *ArtsReformation.com*, http://www.artsreformation.com/a001/hays-code.html.
8. Lyons, *The New Censors*, 14.
9. Lyrics reproduced in Gregory D. Black, *Hollywood Censored* (Cambridge, UK: Cambridge University Press, 1994), 75.
10. See Marybeth Hamilton, *When I'm Bad, I'm Better: Mae West, Sex, and American Entertainment* (Berkeley: University of California Press, 1997), 191.
11. Black, *Hollywood Censored*, 75.
12. Ibid. see chapter 2, 21–49.
13. Ibid., see chapter 6, 149–97, for details on the activities of the legion during the 1930s.
14. Richard Brisbin Jr., "From State and Local Censorship to Ratings: Substantive Rationality, Political Entrepreneurship, and Sex in the Movies," *Political Film Society*, Working Paper Series #9, 5.
15. Vieira, in *Sin in Soft Focus*, refers to Breen as the "Hitler of Hollywood."
16. Jeanine Basinger, *I Do and I Don't* (New York: Alfred A. Knopf, 2013).
17. Michael Asimow, "Divorce in the Movies: From the Hays Code to *Kramer v. Kramer*," *Legal Studies Forum* 24, no. 2 (2000): 221–67.
18. For a detailed account of the battle between Selznick and the Breen Office, see Leonard J. Leff and Jerold L. Simmons, *The Dame in the Kimono: Hollywood, Censorship, and the Production Code from the 1920s to the 1960s* (New York: Grove Weidenfeld, 1990).
19. See Sam Staggs, *Born to Be Bad: The Untold Story of Imitation of Life* (New York: St. Martin's Press, 2009).
20. *U.S. v. Paramount Pictures*, 334 U.S. 131 (1947).
21. 343 U.S. 495 (1952).
22. Jon Lewis, *Hollywood v. Hard Core: How the Struggle over Censorship Saved the Modern Film Industry* (New York: New York University Press, 2000) advances the theory that the rating system was in response to two occurrences; the first being a box office slump that plagued the industry in 1968–1973 and secondly, the financial success of soft-porn independent films like *Last Tango in Paris* (1973) and hard-core porno films like *Behind the Green Door* (1972) and *Deep Throat* (1972). Hollywood was saved from financial ruin, Lewis contends, because the studios rallied behind the rating system in order to control the production and distribution of mainstream films. Taken together with Supreme Court decisions that restricted porno films, the industry was able to reposition sexually explicit fare to the film fringes.
23. For a profile on Valenti and his achievements as MPAA president, see Connie Bruck, "The Personal Touch," *The New Yorker*, August 13, 2001, 42–59.
24. For the story behind the establishment of the rating system, see Jack Valenti, *The Voluntary Movie Rating System* (Washington, DC: Motion Picture Association of America, 1996).
25. Ibid., 3.
26. See his statement before the Subcommittee on Telecommunications and Internet, House Committee on Energy and Commerce, June 22, 2007. Glickman's tenure was brief, as he retired in 2010 after six years as MPAA chief.
27. Edited version of the current ratings from the CARA website at http://www.filmratings.com.

28. Ibid.
29. Interview with *Los Angeles Times* critic Sonja Bolle, in *Stanford Magazine*, July/August 2008. Graves told Bolle that the reason for anonymity is to protect the reviewers from industry pressure.
30. "Bullying in School: How Bad Is It?" *KSL.com*, http://www.ksl.com/index.php?sid=19873354&nid=481.
31. Jim Dubreuil, and Eamon McNiff, "Bullied to Death in America's Schools," *ABC News*, October 15, 2010, http://abcnews.go.com/2020/TheLaw/school-bullying-epidemic-turning-deadly/story?id=11880841.
32. Colleen Curry, "Staten Island Teen Bullied Before Taking Her Life," *ABC News*, January 4, 2012, http://abcnews.go.com/US/staten-island-teen-bullied-suicide-family/story?id=15287910.
33. Katherine Bindley, "Bullying and Suicide: The Dangerous Mistake We Make," *Huffington Post*, February 8, 2012, http://www.huffingtonpost.com/2012/02/08/bullying-sucide-teens-depression_n_1247875.html.
34. Ibid.
35. Dubreuil and McNiff, "Bullied to Death in America's Schools."
36. "11 Facts about Bullying," *DoSomething.org*, http://www.dosomething.org/tipsandtools/11-facts-about-school-bullying.
37. The statement was reprinted in Jeremy Kinser, "Bully Doc Gets R Rating: Can't Be Shown in Schools," *SheWired*, February 24, 2012, http://www.shewired.com/2012/02/24/bully-doc-gets-r-rating-cant-be-shown-schools.
38. "PG-13 Granted to *Bully* by MPAA without Cutting Crucial Scene," *ComingSoon.net*, reprinting an announcement by The Weinstein Company, April 5, 2012, http://www.comingsoon.net/news/movienews.php?id=88950.
39. In the author's experience, *Spring Breakers* is the kind of film one would have seen in the adult theaters along 42nd in the Times Square section of Manhattan before it was cleaned up. The film is one long spring break party, containing stimulated sex acts, nudity, drug usage, unrestrained use of alcohol, and suggestive sex acts, particularly by women. It is one of the most vulgar films the author has seen in a decade.
40. http://www.imdb.com/title/tt1477855/parentalguide?ref_=tt_stry_pg (accessed December 28, 2012).
41. Article by Richard Corliss, "Censuring the Movie Censors," September 2, 2006, http://www.imdb.com/title/tt1477855/parentalguide?ref_=tt_stry_pg (accessed December 28, 2012).
42. Dick admitted using detectives and surveillance on the staff but things got messy when it was learned that CARA had made a copy of *This Film Is Not Yet Rated* without Dick's permission.
43. *The Sunday Times*, February 9, 1997, 4.
44. The appeal statistics were reported in *The New York Times*, December 19, 2004, sec. 2, 2 in a story about the appeal of the R-restrictive rating given to the film *Hotel Rwanda*. By a 10 to 3 vote, CARA gave the film a PG-13 rating. *The Times* noted that this was a rare instance of CARA making information public.
45. Stories of the film cuts were reported in *The New York Times*, January 30, 1992, C15 and March 15, 1992, H17 and the *Westchester Dispatch*, February 16, 1992, F1. The R-rated version contained scenes of sexual bondage, one rough sex scene that bordered on rape, and several brutal killings. Rumor had it that the cuts involved a shot of Michael Douglas's penis in a turgid state and an oral sex scene. Supposedly these scenes were included in the film version released in Europe. In the U.S., however, an NC-17 version appeared on laser disc, while an unrated director's cut was made available on video in addition to the edited R-rated version.
46. Manohla Dargis, "The Closing of the American Erotic," *The New York Times*, The Week in Review, February 13, 2011, 3. Dargis claims the change was made without making any cuts, which is unusual for CARA. However, anything is possible in Hollywood since most decisions occur behind closed doors.
47. The statistics from 2000–2008 were furnished to the author by CARA, June 24, 2009. The data from 2009–2011 was collected by assistant Loryn Isaacs, August 13, 2012, from http:www.filmratings.org/filmRatings_Cara/#/ratings.
48. Scott Bowles, "Is R the Scarlet Letter for Most Audiences?" *USA Today*, June 26, 2013, 2D.

49. Arthur DeVany and W. David Wells, "Does Hollywood Make Too Many R-rated Movies? Risk, Stochastic Dominance, and the Illusion of Expectation," *Journal of Business*, 75, no. 3 (July 2002): 425–52.
50. Data from *Box Office Mojo* at http://www.boxofficemojo.com/movies/?id=battleship.htm and http://www.boxofficemojo.com/movies/?id=johncarterofmars.htm (accessed July 24, 2013).
51. The author raised this issue with a filmmaker while in New York. He explained that the industry today, especially the big major studios, count heavily on *one* big hit to carry them through the entire year. There may be some merit in this explanation since Hollywood is not run like a traditional business.
52. Valenti, *The Voluntary Movie Rating System*, 11.
53. Federal Trade Commission 7th Report, "Marketing Violent Entertainment to Children," December 2009 at http://www.ftc.gov/os/2009/12/P994511violententertainment.pdf (accessed March 13, 2013).
54. "Study of Kids Trying to Get into R-Rated Movies Finds That Theaters Are Way Less Cool Now," at http://www.avclub.com/articles/study-of-kids-trying-to-get-into-r-rated-movies-fin, 95433/ (accessed July 23, 2013). But in 2011, that percentage had declined to 24 percent.
55. Trey Graham, "Despite ID Policy, R-rating Rarely Bars Teens from Screens," *USA Today*, June 16, 1999, 4D. Admittedly, this is an old report but recent FTC reports indicate that at least one-fifth to one-third of teenagers get in to see restricted films, one way or another.
56. See *The New York Times*, April 18, 2006, B2 and June 5, 2006, B2.
57. Before the 1952 *Burstyn* decision, consult: *Gitlow v. New York*, 268 U.S. 652 (1925); *Whitney v. California*, 274 U.S. 357 (1927); *Near v. Minnesota*, 283 U.S. 697 (1931); *Thornhill v. Alabama*, 310 U.S. 88 (1940); *West Virginia State Board v. Barnette*, 319 U.S. 624 (1943); After 1952, consult: *Roth v. U.S.*, 354 U.S. 476 (1957); *New York Times Co. v. Sullivan*, 376 U.S. 255 (1964); *Brandenburg v. Ohio*, 395 U.S. 444 (1969); *New York Times v. U.S.*, 403 U.S. 713.
58. Federal Trade Commission, *Report on Marketing Violent Entertainment to Children* (September 2000), especially 4-21. President Clinton requested the report after the Columbine High School shootings.
59. See L. Rowell Huesmann, Jessica Moise-Titus, Cheryl-Lynn Podolski, and Leonard D. Eron, "Longitudinal Relations Between Children's Exposure to TV Violence and Their Aggressive and Violent Behavior in Young Adulthood: 1977–1992," *Developmental Psychology* 39, no. 2 (2003): 201–21.
60. See especially two articles: Victor C. Strasburger, "Go Ahead Punk, Make My Day: It's Time for Pediatricians to Take Action against Media Violence," and Theresa Webb, Lucille Jenkins, Nickolas Browne, Abdelmonen A. Afifi, and Jess Kraus, "Violent Entertainment Pitched to Adolescents: An Analysis of PG-13 Films," both in *Pediatrics* 119, no. 6 (June 1, 2007), accessed online at http://pediatrics.aappublications.org/.
61. Because of the free speech provision of the First Amendment, courts have been reluctant to award plaintiffs damages for "harm done" by literary texts and the entertainment media. In a case involving Oliver Stone's film *Natural Born Killers*, the victim of a holdup shooting sued Stone and Time Warner after her assailant told police she and her boyfriend saw the film and wanted to be like "Mickey and Mallory," the killers in the movie. *Byers v. Edmondson*, La. Court of Appeal, First Circuit, No. 2001 CA 1184, June 5, 2002.
62. Their website is http://www.kids-in-mind.com and their reviews are updated weekly.

## Chapter 5. HUAC and the Blacklist: The Red Scare Comes To Hollywood

1. See the work of Dan Nimmo, "Political Propaganda in the Movies: A Typology," in James Combs, ed., *Movies and Politics* (New York: Garland Publishing, 1993); Gary Crowdus, ed., *The Political Companion to American Film* (Chicago: Lake View Press, 1994); and Terry Christensen, *Reel Politics* (New York: Blackwell Publishers, 1987).
2. See his interview in *The New York Times*, March 14, 1999, sec. 2, 7.
3. Victor Navasky, "Has *Guilty by Suspicion* Missed the Point?" *The New York Times*, March 31, 1991, H9.

4. See Greg Mitchell, *Tricky Dick and the Pink Lady: Richard Nixon vs. Helen Gahagan Douglas—Sexual Politics and the Red Scare* (New York: Random House, 1950).

5. Richard Fried, *Nightmare in Red* (New York: Oxford University Press, 1990), 42.

6. See, e.g., David M. Oshinsky, *A Conspiracy So Immense* (New York: Free Press, 1983); Richard Rovere, *Senator Joe McCarthy* (New York: Harcourt, Brace, 1959); Thomas C. Reeves, *The Life and Times of Senator Joe McCarthy* (New York: Stein and Day, 1982); and Albert Fried, *McCarthyism: The Great American Red Scare* (New York: Oxford University Press, 1997).

7. *American Heritage*, 3rd ed., s.v. "McCarthyism." But according to Richard Rovere, *Senator Joe McCarthy*, 7, cartoonist Herbert Block in *The Washington Post* first used the term.

8. S.Prt. 107-84, Executive Sessions of the Senate Permanent Subcommittee on Investigations of the Committee on Government Operations, vol. I–V, 83rd Congress, First Session, 1953–54.

9. James Edward Peters, *Arlington National Cemetery: Shrine to America's Heroes* (Arlington, VA: Woodbine House, 1986), 97. The FBI objected to Hammett being buried at Arlington.

10. Albert Fried, *McCarthyism: The Great American Red Scare*, 1–9.

11. See stories by Bernard Weinraub in *The New York Times*, October 1, 1997, B3 and October 5, 1997, sec. 4, 5.

12. A. O. Scott, "News in Black, White and Shades of Gray," Review of *Good Night, and Good Luck* in *The New York Times*, September 23, 2005, B1.

13. Fried, *Nightmare in Red*, 88.

14. Ted Morgan, *Reds: McCarthyism in Twentieth-Century America* (New York: Random House, 2003).

15. John Patrick Diggins, *The Proud Decades* (New York: Norton, 1989), 175–76.

16. M. Stanton Evans, *Blacklisted by History* (New York: Crown Forum, 2007).

17. David Oshinsky, *A Conspiracy So Immense* (New York: Free Press, 1983).

18. Mike Nielsen and Gene Mailes, *Hollywood's Other Blacklist* (London: British Film Institute, 1995).

19. Ibid. In their book, Nielsen and Mailes combine scholarship with oral history. Other valuable sources include Richard and Louis Perry, *A History of the Los Angeles Labor Movement* (Berkeley: University of California Press, 1963); Hugh Lovell and Tasile Carter, *Collective Bargaining in the Motion Picture Industry* (Berkeley: University of California Press, 1955); Murray Ross, *Stars and Strikes* (New York: Columbia University Press, 1941); and U.S. House of Representatives, Committee on Education and Labor, *Jurisdictional Disputes in the Motion Picture Industry* (Washington: Government Printing Office, 1948).

20. Quoted in Nielsen and Mailes, *Hollywood's Other Blacklist*, 130.

21. Ibid., 155.

22. Ibid., chapters 5 and 8.

23. See Robbie Lieberman, "Communism, Peace Activism, and Civil Liberties: From the Waldorf Conference to the Peekskill Riot," *Journal of Popular Culture* 18, no. 3 (Fall 1995): 59–65.

24. See U.S. Congress, House Committee on Un-American Activities, *Hearings Regarding the Communist Infiltration of the Motion Picture Industry*, 80th Congress, 1st. sess., 1947.

25. To Cooper's credit, however, he later supported blacklisted writer Carl Foreman during the filming of *High Noon* when Stanley Kramer wanted to fire him. Cooper told Kramer, "If he goes, I go."

26. Larry Ceplair and Steven Englund, *The Inquisition in Hollywood* (Garden City: Anchor Press/Doubleday, 1980), 371–73. Of the 58 informers, the authors identify 31 or slightly more than half, as important Hollywood artists. The "naming of names" varied from one informer to another. For example, writer Martin Berkeley gave up 155 names to the committee, while at the other extreme writer Gertrude Purcell identified only one colleague as a communist. See Appendix 7, in Ceplair and Englund, 447–48.

27. Reported in Walter Bernstein, *Inside Out: A Memoir of the Blacklist* (Cambridge, MA: Da Capo Press, 2000), 153–54.

28. The high estimate of 250 Hollywood workers who lost jobs and were placed on the blacklist comes from the American Movie Classics 1995 documentary *Blacklist: Hollywood on Trial*, while the lower figure of 200 is cited by Brian Neve in his *Film and Politics in America* (London: Routledge, 1992), 271. Ceplair and Englund, *The Inquisition in Hollywood*, 387, put the number blacklisted at 212. However, Dalton Trumbo, in a 1957 TV program, identified 235 writers alone who were blacklisted and could not work under their real names. If Trumbo was correct, the blacklist would have had to exceed 250 names. See Dalton Trumbo papers, State Historical Society of Wisconsin (hereafter cited as SHSW).

29. Dan Georgakas, "Hollywood Blacklist" in *Encyclopedia of the American Left* (New York: Garland, 1990), 327–28.

30. Some of the organizations included The Civil Rights Congress, National Federation for Constitutional Liberties, The Actors Laboratory, the Screen Writers Guild, and the Hollywood Writers Mobilization.

31. Herbert Biberman papers, SHSW. When called to testify, Ferrer swore under oath that he was not a communist.

32. Victor S. Navasky, *Naming Names* (New York: Penguin Books, 1981), 236. In his defense, Edward Dmytryk in his memoir, *Odd Man Out: A Memoir of the Hollywood Ten* (Carbondale: Southern Illinois University Press, 1996), reasons that he did not want to be punished further for a cause he no longer believed in; his flirtation with the CPUSA rested on anti-fascist grounds rather than ideological principle.

33. Dalton Trumbo papers, SHSW.

34. Richard Schickel, "The Hollywood Ten: Printing the Legend," in *Schickel on Film* (New York: Morrow, 1989), 95–120.

35. Neve, *Film and Politics in America*, 176–80.

36. Communist Party headquarters in New York refused to provide any membership data to the author, thereby continuing the speculation as to its actual strength as opposed to government figures and academic estimates. Edward Schapsmeier and Frederick Schapsmeier in their book *Political Parties and Civic Action Groups* (Westport, CT: Greenwood Press, 1981), 110–112, present the votes garnered by Communist Party candidates in the presidential elections as follows: in 1932, 102,785 votes out of 40 million cast; in 1936, the number totaled 80,159; and in 1940, votes dropped to 46,251. Of course, these votes do not imply actual party membership. Another scholar, L. Sandy Maisel, in his book *Political Parties and Elections in the United States* (New York: Garland Publishing, 1991), 177–78 puts Communist Party membership at 75,000 based upon registration at the party's 1938 convention. Since party membership was on the decline after peaking in 1932, it is conceivable that membership dropped to 40,000–50,000 by World War II.

37. Georgakas, *Encyclopedia of the American Left*, 328.

38. See Joyce Milton, *Tramp: The Life of Charlie Chaplin* (New York: HarperCollins, 1996), which focuses on Chaplin's political life. Also consult Charles Chaplin, *My Autobiography* (New York: Simon and Schuster, 1964).

39. Nixon, of course, would make his political mark later during the Hiss-Chambers spy hearings. Of the other eight HUAC members, J. Parnell Thomas, committee chair, would end up in prison for defrauding the government, Karl Mundt would be elected to the U.S. Senate, and the remaining members would fade from the political scene.

40. Richard A. Schwartz, "How the Hollywood Blacklist Worked" (paper presented at the annual meeting of the American Culture Association/Popular Culture Association, Orlando, April 1998), claims that the studios relied on a list of 300 names of alleged communists furnished by the American Legion. That list was converted into a de facto blacklist.

41. Pamphlet found in the Albert Bessie papers, SHSW. The pamphlet listed some of the biggest stars in Hollywood at the time, including Humphrey Bogart, Lauren Bacall, Charlie Chaplin, Melvyn Douglas, Gene Kelly, Frank Sinatra, Orson Welles, Danny Kaye, Katherine Hepburn, Gregory Peck, and Burt Lancaster, the majority of whom were never cited or named as communists or fellow travelers by any other source. True, nothing came of the mobilization efforts but the fact that this unsubstantiated pamphlet was taken seriously by HUAC says plenty about the committee and the Red Scare hysteria.

42. Larry Ceplair, "Hollywood Left," in *Encyclopedia of the American Left*, 330–32.

43. See Ceplair and Englund, *The Inquisition in Hollywood*, 66–79.

44. The number comes from Richard Schickel, *Schickel on Film* (New York: Morrow, 1989), 101.

45. Dorothy B. Jones, "Communism and the Movies: A Study of Film Content," in John Cogley, *Report on Blacklisting I: Movies* (New York: The Fund for the Republic, 1956), 197.

46. Dalton Trumbo papers, SHSW. The film scripts offered as evidence to the committee included *A Guy Named Joe*, *Thirty Seconds Over Tokyo*, *Our Vines Have Tender Grapes*, and *Kitty Foyle*. Trumbo also had letters of praise from the military and juvenile court judges for several of his films. As a general rule, HUAC would not permit the reading of statements or the introduction of evidence during the hearings.

47. See Paul Buhle and Dave Wagner, *Blacklisted: The Film Lover's Guide to the Hollywood Blacklist* (New York: Palgrave Macmillan, 2003).

48. See Dorothy B. Jones, "Communism and the Movies: A Study in Film Content," Table 8, 272. The list includes only 150 films because nine were described as unclassified.

49. Quoted in Ring Lardner Jr., papers, SHSW. Friendly HUAC witness writer Ayn Rand testified that the film was communist because it showed the Russian people in a better socioeconomic position than was actually true. Similarly, Lela Rogers testified that the film *None But the Lonely Heart* was communist propaganda because it was critical of the free enterprise system. See the Biberman-Sondegaard papers, SHSW. She also complained about *Tender Comrade* on grounds that five women sharing a house during wartime was socialism.

50. T. Bennett, "Culture, Power, and Mission to Moscow: Film and Soviet-American relations during WWII," *The Journal of American History* 88, no. 2 (September 2001): 489–519. I am indebted to Herman Schloss for this source.

51. Quoted in the Ned Young papers, SHSW (cf. earlier note).

52. Larry Parks papers, SHSW. Parks made one film in England after the hearings, but Columbia Pictures refused to pick up his option after his HUAC testimony, an action that basically ended his film career.

53. Abraham Polonsky papers, SHSW. Polonsky also wrote screenplays; however, he went 17 years before he received screen credit for his work.

54. Albert Maltz papers, SHSW. Maltz surmised that the Army pressured the government to deny assistance in the film's production. Maltz attributes other rejections directly to the HUAC hearings and the blacklist. 20th Century Fox purchased his novel *The Journey of Simon McKeever*, but the screenplay was shelved due to pressure from the Motion Picture Alliance.

55. *The New York Times*, March 19, 2009, A21.

56. Ceplair and Englund, *The Inquisition in Hollywood*, 425.

57. Information from the Turner Classic Movie documentary *The John Garfield Story*, telecast on November 21, 2008.

58. Andy Mersler, "How Blacklisting Hurt Hollywood Children," *The New York Times*, August 31, 1995, C13.

59. See Michael Wilson and Deborah Silverton Rosenfelt, *Salt of the Earth* (New York: Feminist Press, 1978) and James J. Lorence, *The Suppression of "Salt of the Earth"* (Albuquerque: University of New Mexico Press, 1999). Lorence's book is an exceptional piece of scholarship and the best source for information on the strike and the making of the film.

60. Lorence, *The Suppression of "Salt of the Earth,"* 195.

61. See Emma Horcombe, "Attitudes to Informing and the Informer" (master's dissertation, University of Nottingham, UK 1994).

62. Arthur Miller, "Are You Now or Were You Ever?" from *The Guardian/The Observer* online, June 17, 2000, http://www.writing.upenn.edu.

63. According to Fried, *McCarthyism: The Great American Red Scare*, 135–37, Kazan took out a one-page ad in *The New York Times* in the form of an open letter to the American people to explain his decision to cooperate with HUAC. His reasoning for informing on friends and colleagues came down to his disenchantment with the Communist Party because it had become authoritarian and manipulative. Of course, this is specious reasoning since Kazan could have preserved his honor, if not his career, by accepting the Miller-Hellman position of restricting his testimony to himself.

64. Letter to *The New York Times*, September 14, 1994, A18.

65. Was it coincidental that 40 years had to pass before Miller's play reached the screen? When the film version of *The Crucible* opened in 1996, the critics found its story of witchcraft in 17th- century Salem powerful drama. But historians disputed its accuracy.

66. Kazan became a victim of contemporary Hollywood's unofficial blacklist since the film industry refused to honor him for his lifetime achievement until the Motion Picture Academy had a change of heart and awarded Kazan an honorary Oscar at the 1999 Academy Awards. For more on this issue, see Editorial, *The New York Times*, January 19, 1997, 14 and *The New York Times*, January 13, 1999, B3.

67. Neve, *Film and Politics in America*, 171–210. As a rule, these films were financial flops as well as artistic disasters. Not one appeared on the top 10 box office hits for the decade. Instead the list was populated by children's' films, historical epics, and musicals.

68. See Lynne Arany, Tom Dyja and Gary Goldsmith, *The Reel List* (New York: Dell Publishing, 1995), 283.

69. See Tom C. Williams, "*The Day the Earth Stood Still*: Cold War Parable or Messianic Metaphor?" (paper presented at the annual meeting of the American Culture Association/Popular Culture Association, Las Vegas, March 1996).

70. See Stuart Samuels, "The Age of Conspiracy and Conformity: *Invasion of the Body Snatchers* (1956)," in John O'Connor and Martin A. Jackson, *American History/American Film* (New York: Frederick Unger, 1979), 203–17.

71. See Arany, Dyja and Goldsmith, *The Reel List*, 284.

72. Ceplair and Englund, *The Inquisition in Hollywood*, 335–36.

73. Vivian Gornick, "The Left in the Fifties," *Lincoln Center Theatre Review*, no. 35 (Spring/Summer 2003): 12.

74. Peter Biskind, *Easy Riders, Raging Bulls: How the Sex-Drugs-and-Rock 'n' Roll Generation Saved Hollywood* (New York: Simon & Schuster, 1998), advances the thesis that the success of *Easy Rider* (1964) heralded a decade of rebellious young filmmakers whose screen work challenged (and saved the industry) from the old studio system.

## Chapter 6. Real to Reel Politicians: Idealists, Saviors, and Scoundrels

1. For the perspective on Nixon, see Irv Letofsky, "All the Presidents' Movies (And Not All PG)," *The New York Times*, April 13, 1997, sec. 2, 29; for the view on Reagan, see Elizabeth Traube, *Dreaming Identities: Class, Gender and Generation in 1980s Hollywood Movies* (Boulder: Westview Press, 1992), 48.

2. Besides feature films, this figure includes shorts, newsreels, cartoons, travelogues, etc.

3. See Sidney Wise, "Politicians: A Film Perspective," *News for Teachers of Political Science*, no. 32 (winter 1982): 1–3; and Robert Thompson, "American Politics on Film," *Journal of Popular Culture* 20 (Summer 1986): 27–47.

4. See Richard Maltby and Jan Craven, *Hollywood Cinema* (Oxford: Blackwell Publishers, 1995), 361–411.

5. Steven J. Ross, "The Visual Politics of Class: Silent Film and the Public Sphere, *Film International*, April 28, 2011, http://filmint.nu/?p=1735 (accessed June 30, 2012). Also see Kevin Brownlow, *Behind the Mask of Innocence* (New York: Alfred A. Knopf, 1990), chapter 6.

6. See Philip John Davies, "Hollywood in elections and elections in Hollywood," in Philip John Davies and Paul Wells, eds., *American Film and Politics from Reagan to Bush Jr.* (Manchester, UK: Manchester University Press, 2002).
7. 531 U.S. 98, 121 S.Ct. 525, 148 L.Ed. 2d 388 (2000).
8. *The New York Times*, September 7, 2012, C16.
9. See William L. Riordon, *Plunkitt of Tammany Hall* (New York: E.P. Dutton & Co., 1963).
10. *All the King's Men* was a critical success, as it was nominated for eight Academy Awards, winning three Oscars for Best Picture, Actor, and Supporting Actress. Despite an all-star cast, a 2006 remake opened and disappeared quickly from theaters. When, 40 years later, Hollywood decided to make a film about Huey's brother, Earl, three-time governor of Louisiana, the results were also less gratifying. The film *Blaze* (1989) proved a disappointment despite the casting of Paul Newman in the title role. Quite possibly the film's problem lay in the script, since it was based on the memoirs of Earl's lover, stripper Blaze Starr. In this case, the combination of politics and sex failed to mesh.
11. In real life, Meade Esposito, Kings County political boss, was convicted of influence peddling and bribery. Donald Manes, his Queens counterpart, committed suicide just as Aiello does in the film. But not all deals end in prison or death. While the film crew was permitted to shoot inside most of City Hall, Mayor Giuliani put the Mayor's Office and the ceremonial Blue Room off limits. All was not lost, however. The studio struck a deal with the City Council Speaker. In return for the use of his large office to reconstruct a set to resemble the Mayor's Office and Blue Room, the Speaker had his office painted, carpeted and redecorated for free. No taxpayers objected to the deal, although rumor had it that some Council colleagues were envious.
12. Recall a similarity with the real-life situation in the Democratic Party when Governor Mario Cuomo was picked to make the presidential nominating speech at the 1984 convention. Cuomo's stirring speech placed him high among Democratic presidential contenders for 1988, although he declined to be a candidate. Also, Franklin Roosevelt's nomination of Al Smith at the 1924 convention failed to win the nomination for Smith, but it did raise Roosevelt's stock among Democratic Party delegates and voters.
13. Newsletter #173 of the Political Film Society, July 15, 2003.
14. Oldman made the charge in *Premier* 14, no. 3 (November 2000): 93–98. The charge was repeated on the Mr. Showbiz website and later reported in *The New York Times*, October 16, 2000, C16.
15. See Michael G. Krukones, "Motion Picture Presidents of the 1930s," in Peter C. Rollins and John E. O'Connor, eds, *Hollywood's White House: The American Presidency in Film and History* (Lexington: The University Press of Kentucky, 2003).
16. The information on the vote of the 13th Amendment comes from the movie and http://en.wiki/Thirteenth_Amendment_to_the_United_States_Constitution (accessed November 29, 2012). The information on Eddie came from http://histclo.com/pres/Ind19/lincoln/lincolne.html.
17. Z. Byron Wolf, "Screenwriter Admits Lincoln Inaccuracy, But Points Out It Is a Movie," *ABC News Blogs*, February 8, 2013, http://abcnews.go.com/blogs/politics/2013/02/screenwriter-admits-lincoln-inaccuracy-but-points-out-it-is-a-movie/.
18. Abraham Lincoln, "Letter to Horace Greeley," August 22, 1862, cited at http://www.nytimes.com/1862/08/24/news/letter-president-lincoln-reply-horace-greeley-slavery-union-restoration-union.html (accessed March 14, 2013).
19. For 110 years, the number of deaths stood at 618,222, with 360,222 from the North. But new research has raised that number to 750,000. See Guy Gugliotta, "New Estimate Raises Civil War Death Toll," *The New York Times*, April 2, 2012, http://www.nytimes.com/2012/04/03/science/civil-war-toll-up-by-20-percent-in-new-estimate.html?pagewanted=all.
20. David Brooks, "Why We Love Politics," *The New York Times*, November 23, 2012, A27.
21. Historian Ron Briley notes in "Hollywood and the American Presidency: A Nation Seeks to Define Itself" (paper presented at the annual meeting of the American Political Science Association, Washington, Aug.

1977) that the film was criticized because President Hammond used authoritarian methods to achieve his goals. It was no coincidence that William Randolph Hearst produced the film in conjunction with MGM, and that it opened in the early days of Roosevelt's New Deal administration.

22. For development of this view, see Deborah Carmichael, "Gabriel Over the White House," in Rollins and O'Connor, eds., *Hollywood's White House*, 159–79.

23. Kevan M. Yenerall and Christopher S. Kelley, "Shysters, Sycophants, and Sexual Deviants: The Hollywood Presidency in the 1990s," in Robert Watson, ed. *White House Studies Compendium*, vol. 3 (Hauppauge, NY: Nova Publishers, 2007), 213–30.

24. Historically, presidents did not have "doubles," but in crowded situations, the Secret Service is likely to use two limousines and one president to confuse would-be assassins. Reportedly, however, Presidents Bush (the elder) and Clinton had Secret Service agents who closely resembled them in appearance. See Maureen Dowd, "Film View: Of Hems and Haws: The Insider's Guide to *Dave*," *New York Times*, May 16, 1993, sec. 2, 17.

25. Yenerall and Kelley, "Shysters, Sycophants, and Sexual Deviants."

26. Ralph R. Donald, "Fictional Presidents as Antagonists in American Motion Pictures: The New Antihero for the Post-Watergate Era," published in *American Studies Today Online*, http://www.americansc.org.uk/Online/Fictional_Presidents.htm.

27. George McGovern, "Nixon and Historical Memory: Two Reviews," *Perspectives, AHA Newsletter* 34, no. 3 (March 1996): 3. A view of the Watergate scandal, rather than of Nixon himself, is presented in *All the President's Men* (1976), based on the book by Carl Bernstein and Bob Woodward, the two young *Washington Post* reporters whose investigations exposed the political corruption. *All the President's Men* became the top grossing film in 1976.

28. See Peter Rollins, "Hollywood's President 1944–1996: The Primacy of Character," in Rollins and O'Connor, ed., *Hollywood's White House*, 251–61.

29. See the results at http://legacy.c-span.org/PresidentialSurvey/Overall-Ranking.aspx, February 16, 2009 (accessed August 26, 2013).

30. Ibid.

31. Ibid.

32. The sources for this information are many, including *The New York Times*, April 17, 2009, 1 and April 22, 2009, 1, and *Newsweek*, April 27, 2009, 28–9 and May 4, 2009, 11.

33. Similarly, *The Manchurian Candidate* was withdrawn from theatrical circulation for 25 years after the Kennedy assassination.

34. Why is Barbara Jean, rather than Walker, assassinated? Political scientist G. Alan Tarr's review in *Notes for Teachers of Political Science*, no. 22 (Summer 1979), 21, asserts that Altman's choice reflects his view that Americans are indifferent to politics, preferring instead the private lives of celebrities such as a country-western singer. Symbolically her death is much more significant than the assassination of any political candidate.

35. Robert S. Robins and Jerrold M. Post, *Political Paranoia: The Psychopolitics of Hatred* (New Haven, CT: Yale University Press, 1997).

36. Actually Robbins and Post, 240, counted eight different conspiracy loci in the film, e.g., the CIA, military, Dallas police, weapons manufacturers, establishment press, renegade anti-Castro Cubans, the White House, and the Mafia. Take your pick!

37. See Gerald Posner, "Garrison Guilty: Another Case Closed," *New York Times Magazine*, sec. 6, August 6, 1995, 40–41. Historian Stanley Karnow agrees with Posner and other Stone critics on the unsubstantiated notion that Kennedy intended to withdraw from Vietnam, one reason for his death. See his "JFK," in Mark C. Carnes, *Past Imperfect: History According to the Movies* (New York: Henry Holt & Co., 1995), 270–73.

38. See the advertisement for the *JFK* opening in *The New York Times*, December 15, 1991, sec. 2, 10, with a large photo of Kevin Costner portraying D.A. Garrison in the film, with the blurb:

He's a District Attorney,
He will risk his life, the lives of his family,
everything he holds dear
for the one thing he holds sacred...the truth.

Also see the ad for *JFK* in The New York Times, April 2, 1992, C17, where the text includes this dedication: "The truth is the most important value we have."

39. See Ray Pratt, *Projecting Paranoia* (Lawrence: University Press of Kansas, 2001).
40. The Internet Movie Database (IMDB) information is also confusing. It shows the film either being completed or released in 2003 and later states the release date as 2007. The only certainty here is that the film was made, was shown at festivals, and was never reviewed by film critics.
41. The film's domestic gross was under $1 million, http://www.boxofficemojo.com/movies/?id=assassination ofrichardnixon.htm.
42. Reported in *The New York Times*, June 5, 2006, A19.
43. Michael Barkun, "Conspiracy Thinking in Contemporary America," *Maxwell Perspective* (Syracuse University) 8, no. 1 (Fall 1997): 23.
44. Robert Alan Goldberg, *Enemies Within: The Culture of Conspiracy in Modern America* (New Haven, CT: Yale University Press, 2001).
45. In his article "Mr. Carter Goes to Washington," *Journal of Popular Film & Television* 25, no. 2 (Summer 1997): 57–67, Allen Rostron contends that Jimmy Carter came to Washington much like Jefferson Smith—an innocent outsider from a small town who wanted to restore decency and morality to government. Carter failed in Washington, whereas the fictional Smith succeeded, Rostron argues, because in real politics, Carter had to contend with external factors like the backlash from Vietnam and Watergate.
46. Michael Canning, "The Hill on Film: Hollywood's Take on the U.S. Congress and Its Members" (paper presented at the annual meeting of the American Political Science Association, Washington August 1997).
47. William M. Jones, "Monumental Disasters: From *Mr. Smith Goes to Washington* to *Independence Day*" (paper presented at the annual meeting of the American Political Science Association, Washington, August 1997), concludes that the present trend in Hollywood to find national symbolic monuments and revered public buildings expendable and, therefore, subject to destruction reflects the current cynicism on the part of American filmmakers. This attitude deviates considerably from Frank Capra's *Mr. Smith Goes to Washington*, where the physical structures are treated as national shrines.

## Chapter 7. Picturing Justice: The Law and Lawyers in Hollywood Films

1. Stewart Macaulay, "Images of Law in Everyday Life: The Lesson of School, Entertainment, and Spectator Sports," *Law & Society Review* 21, no. 2 (1987): 185–218.
2. Hearst Corporation, *The American Public, the Media and the Judicial System* (New York: Hearst Corporation, 1983).
3. Macaulay, 192–97.
4. Michael Asimow and Shannon Mader, *Law and Popular Culture* (New York: Peter Lang Publishing, 2004). See chapter 1, "Introduction to Law and Popular Culture," 3–15.
5. 384 U.S. 436 (1966).
6. 467 U.S. 649, 104 S. Ct. 2626, 81 L. Ed. 2d 550 (1984).
7. Adam Banner, "Miranda, McVeigh, and the Boston Marathon Bombing: Where's the Distinction?" at http://www.huffingtonpost.com/adam-banner/miranda,-McVeigh-and-the-b_b_3245308.html (accessed July 26, 2013).
8. John Denvir, ed., *Legal Reelism: Movies as Legal Texts* (Urbana: University of Illinois Press, 1996), introduction.

9. Timothy Lenz, *Changing Images of Law in Film & Television* (New York: Peter Lang, 2003), 8–14.
10. Ibid., 15–16.
11. David Ray Papke, "Law, Cinema and Ideology: Hollywood Legal Films of the 1950s," *UCLA Law Review* 40, no. 6 (2001): 1473.
12. The films include *Anatomy of a Murder, Compulsion, I Want to Live, Inherit the Wind, Judgment at Nuremberg, To Kill a Mockingbird, Twelve Angry Men, Witness for the Prosecution*, and *The Young Philadelphians*.
13. William G. Hyland Jr., "Creative Malpractice: The Cinematic Lawyer," *Texas Review of Entertainment & Sports Law* 9 (Spring 2008): 231.
14. Stefan Machura, "An Analysis Scheme for Law Films," *University of Baltimore Law Review* 36 (Spring 2007): 329.
15. "The Significance of the Frontier in American History," first presented to the American Historical Association in 1893 and later republished in Turner's essays, *The Frontier in American History* (New York: Henry Holt & Co., 1920).
16. For a detailed discussion of 1930s westerns, see Francis M. Nevins, "Through the Great Depression on Horseback," in John Denvir, ed., *Legal Reelism*, 44–69.
17. For a discussion of film vigilantism, see Frankie Y. Bailey, "Getting Justice: Real Life Vigilantism and Vigilantism in Popular Films" (paper presented at the annual meeting of the Criminal Justice Sciences Association, Pittsburgh, March 1992).
18. Bruce Watson, "Hang 'Em First, Try 'Em ater," *Smithsonian* 29, no. 8 (June 1998): 96–107. Watson claims that the real Judge Bean was a paunchy fellow with a gray beard, hardly resembling actor Paul Newman. It is also dubious whether Bean actually hanged anybody. Nor did Bean die in a climactic shootout; rather his death took place in a bar after a drinking binge.
19. For data on Southern lynching, see W. Fitzhugh Brundage, *Lynching in the New South* (Urbana: University of Illinois Press, 1993); and Stewart E. Tolenay and E. M. Beck, *A Festival of Violence: An Analysis of Southern Lynching, 1882–1930* (Urbana: University of Illinois Press, 1995). For shocking photos of lynchings, see Leon F. Litwack, *Without Sanctuary: Lynching Photographs in America* (San Francisco: Twin Palms, 2000).
20. Quoted in Paul Bergmann and Michael Asimow, *Reel Justice: The Courtroom Goes to the Movies* (Kansas City: Andrews and McMeel, 1996), 226. The authors note that there were 66 lynchings in the early years of the Depression, 1933–35. Moreover, it was rare for lynch mob participants to be apprehended and punished.
21. For a case study, see Leonard Dinnerstein, *The Leo Frank Case* (New York: Columbia University Press, 1968). Dinnerstein came to the conclusion that Frank was innocent but convicted of the murder of Mary Phagan, the 13-year-old girl who worked in his Atlanta, Georgia, factory, on the basis of circumstantial evidence, the damaging testimony of the black janitor, which tarnished Frank's reputation, and the pervasive climate of anti-Semitism in the South. When Governor Slaton commuted Frank's sentence, Jewish businesses were told by vigilantes to close or suffer the consequences. Meanwhile, Christians were warned to avoid patronizing Jewish merchants.
22. Herbert Packer, *The Limits of the Criminal Sanction* (Stanford: Stanford University Press, 1968).
23. The Warren Court decisions included *Mapp v. Ohio*, 367 U.S. 643 (1961), which extended the federal exclusionary rule as to illegally obtained evidence to the states; *Escobedo v. Illinois*, 378 U.S. 478 (1964), which expanded constitutional protections for the accused during police interrogation; and *Miranda v. Arizona*, 384 U.S. 436 (1966), which set down rules that the police had to follow before making an arrest, including the right to remain silent and to have an attorney present during questioning.
24. See Lenz, *Changing Images of Law*, chapter 2, for a thorough discussion of this point and an analysis of the *Dirty Harry* and *Death Wish* movies.
25. *Goldman v. Weinberger*, 475 U.S. 503 (1985). The Congress reversed the military regulation two years later.
26. Bergmann and Asimow, *Reel Justice*, 76.

27. Alan M. Dershowitz, *The Best Defense* (New York: Vintage Books, 1983), xvi.
28. See Bergmann and Asimow, *Reel Justice*, 232–38.
29. Ibid., 14–20.
30. Hyland, "Creative Malpractice," at 262, reports that a similar case occurred in New York City where a lawyer, who was an associate in one of the city's largest firms, sued when he was fired when the firm learned he had AIDS. Several years after his death, his family won a $500,000 award from the firm. The family also sued the producers of *Philadelphia* for its failure to compensate them for serving as technical advisers on the film. That suit was settled during the trial.
31. Ibid., at 266.
32. Ibid., at 267.
33. *Blood Work* had a $50 million budget but grossed only $26 million at home. See http://www.boxofficemojo.com/movies/?id=bloodwork.htm (accessed March 16, 2013).
34. Terence Rattigan, *The Winslow Boy* (New York: Dramatist Play Service, 1946, renewed 1973).
35. Leonard Maltin, *1997 Movie & Video Guide* (New York: Penguin Books, 1996).
36. According to Gerald Leonard Cohen, *Origin of the Term "Shyster"* (Frankfurt: Peter Lang, 1982), 1, lexicographers agree that the term originated in the 1840s in New York City newspapers to describe unscrupulous lawyers of that era. The word later was applied to other professions. There is some support, however, for the view that the term comes from the Shylock character in Shakespeare's *The Merchant of Venice*.
37. See Andrew Bergman, *We're in the Money* (New York: New York University Press, 1971), 18–29.
38. For a discussion of gangster films in the 1930s, see Roger Dooley, *From Scarface to Scarlett: American Films in the 1930s* (New York: Harcourt Brace Jovanovich, 1981), 289–300.
39. See http://pre-code.com/pre-code-lawyer-man-1932/ (accessed March 16, 2013).
40. Quoted in David Ray Papke, "Myth and Meaning: Francis Ford Coppola and Popular Response to the Godfather Trilogy," in John Denvir, ed., *Legal Reelism*, 3.
41. For the development of this argument, see Christine Noll Brinckmann, "The Politics of Force of Evil: An Analysis of Abraham Polonsky's Preblacklisted Film," *Prospects* 6 (1981): 357–86.
42. Bergmann and Asimow, *Reel Justice*, 306. The legal errors and unethical conduct depicted in the film include the following: (1) Gavin breaks into a mailbox to intercept a letter—a federal offense, (2) Gavin turns down a settlement without consulting his clients (either act would get him disbarred), and (3) the trial judge conspires with the defense to protect the Boston Archdiocese.
43. See Mary Kay O'Malley, "Through a Different Lens: Using Film to Teach Family Law," *Family Court Review* 49, no. 4 (October 2011): 715–22; and David Ray Papke, "Skepticism Bordering on Distrust: Family Law in the Hollywood Cinema," *Family Court Review* 50, no. 1 (January 2012): 13–22.
44. The following discussion is taken from Papke, ibid.
45. The data come from http://www.divorcestatistics.info (accessed September 24, 2012).
46. See David Papke, "Skepticism Bordering on Distrust: Family Law in the Hollywood Cinema," 20.
47. Mary Kay O'Malley, "Through a Different Lens: Using Film to Teach Family Law," 716.
48. Papke, "Skepticism Bordering on Distrust: Family Law in the Hollywood Cinema," 20.
49. For a discussion of these films, see Dooley, *From Scarface to Scarlett*, 317–18; and Ric Sheffield, "On Film: A Social History of Women Lawyers in Popular Culture 1930 to 1990," *Loyola of Los Angeles Entertainment Law Journal* 14 (1993): 73–114.
50. Sheffield, "On Film: A Social History of Women Lawyers in Popular Culture 1930 to 1990," 79.
51. For a contrary view that these early female lawyer films ultimately allowed the patriarchal power structure to win and dominate the action, see Cynthia Lucia, "Women on Trial: The Female Lawyer in the Hollywood Courtroom, *Cineaste* 19 (1993): 32–37.

# Notes

52. ABA Commission on women in the Profession, "A current glance at Women in the Law 2009, http://www.americanbar.org/conte/dam/aba/migrated/women/reports/CurrentGlanceStatistics2009.authcheckdam.pdf (accessed March 22, 2013).

53. See Lucia, "Women on Trial," 35.

54. See Bergman and Asimow, *Reel Justice*, 90–93.

55. On Law, Culture & Society Forum, "Erin Brockovich Biography," http://www.forumonlawcultureandsociety.org/biography/erin-brockovich (accessed March 22, 2013).

56. Kathleen Sharp, "Erin Brockovich: The Real Story," April 14, 2000, http://www.salon.com/2000/04/14/sharp/(accessed March 22, 2013)

57. Frank Sanello, *Reel v. Real: How Hollywood Turns Fact into Fiction* (Lanham, MD: Taylor Trade Publishing, 2003), 266–69.

58. Six months after his release, Kenny fell from a wall to his death. His sister Betty, however, continues to work for wrongfully convicted prisoners. http://rogerebert.suntimes.com/apps/pbcs.dll/article?AID=/20101013/REVIEWS/101019992/1023 (accessed March 22, 2013).

59. *The New York Times*, January 25, 2008, E1.

60. Examples may be found on the ABA website, http://www.americanbar.org/groups/women.html

61. Data from ibid. (accessed September 21, 2012).

62. Catherine Ho, "Law school applications continue to slide," at http://www.washingtonpost.com/business/capitalbusiness/law-school-applications-continue-to-slide/2013/06/02/db4929b0-c93f-11e2-9245-773c0123c027_story.html (accessed July 26, 2013).

63. The reason why the figure is an estimate is that only the MPAA would have those statistics and the organization refused to respond to the author's request for the data. The exact figure is complicated by the terminology that is used with the data. For example, Hollywood produces many more films than it releases to theaters. And of the films intended for release, some will be withdrawn due to the rating received. Hence, the smallest number that remains is the actual number of films that reach local theaters. For example, in 1988 the film industry produced 601 features. But only 294 had theatrical releases. Hence, roughly half of the films produced in 1988 reached the big screen. In addition, when writers use a larger figure, say 150,000 or 180,000 films made by Hollywood in the last century, the reader has to understand that these figures include features, shorts, newsreels, cartoons, etc. Information furnished by the Library of Congress.

64. See Richard K. Sherwin, *When the Law Goes Pop: The Vanishing Line Between Law & Popular Culture* (Chicago: University of Chicago Press, 2002).

65. See Asimow, "Bad Lawyers in the Movies," 561.

66. Leo J. Shapiro Associates, "Public Perceptions of Lawyers Consumer Research Findings, A Report Prepared for the ABA, April 2002, http://www.cliffordlaw.com/abaillinoisstatedelegate/publicperceptions1.pdf (accessed March 22, 2012).

67. Humphrey Taylor, "Trust in Priests and Clergy Falls 26 Points in Twelve Months," *Harris Interactive*, Harris Poll # 63, November 27, 2002, http://www.harrisinteractive.com/vault/Harris-Interactive-Poll-Research-Trust-in-Priests-and-Clergy-Falls-26-Points-in-Twelve-Months-2002-11.pdf (accessed March 22, 2013).

68. See Mark Tushnet, "Class Action: One View of Gender and Law in Popular Culture," in Denvir, ed., *Legal Reelism*, 244–60.

69. Laura Grosshans, "Representations of Women Lawyers in Popular Culture," *Cardozo Public Law, Policy & Ethics Journal* 4 (April 2006): 457.

70. Sheffield, "On Film: A Social History of Women Lawyers in Popular Culture 1930 to 1990," 109–111.

71. See Lucia, "Women on Trial," 37.

## Chapter 8. Hollywood Goes To War: From the Great War to the Good War to the Forgotten War

1. Corel All-Movie Guide 2, 1996.
2. "Top Domestic War Movies" at http://top5ofanything.com/index.php?h=407f1ef1 (accessed March 23, 2013).
3. The statistics are from Peter Hart, *The Darkest Hour on the Western Front* (New York: Pegasus Books, 2009).
4. The quote and discussion comes from William Boyd, "Why World War I Resonates," *The New York Times Sunday Review*, Op-Ed, January 22, 2012, 8. The military data were compiled by Susan Everett from her book, *The Two World Wars, Vol. I—World War I* (Lincoln, NE: Bison Books, 1980), found at "Timeline: 1914–1918—Casualty Figures," *World War I: Trenches on the Web*, accessed March 20, 2012, http://www.worldwar1.com/tlcrates.htm. The figures do not include civilian casualties or those who died from diseases due to the war. After checking several resources, it is not surprising that the author found no two sources were the same.
5. According to Peter Rollins and John O'Connor, eds., *Hollywood's WWI: Motion Picture Images* (Bowling Green, OH: Popular Press, 1997), there is little footage of World War I that is real. Much of the material was either censored or staged. The warring nations, for example, would not permit filming on the front lines or in the trenches.
6. Thomas Doherty, *Projections of War: Hollywood, American Culture and World War II* (New York: Columbia University Press, 1993), 88–91.
7. Ibid., 97.
8. Bernard F. Dick, *The Star-Spangled Screen: The American World War II Film*, rev. ed. (Lexington: University of Kentucky Press, 1996), 93–94.
9. See Sally E. Parry, "Confessions of an Interventionist: Did Hollywood Encourage the U.S. to Enter World War II?" (paper presented at the Popular Culture Association meeting, San Diego, March 1999).
10. Estimates of losses vary and depend on sources and the timeframe utilized. Taking only the period from 1939 to 1945—from the invasion of Poland to the Japanese surrender—the total number of deaths due to the war has been estimated to range from 30 million to 60 million. American casualties, dead and wounded, are placed at around one million, with at least 400,000 dead.
11. See Israel Gutman, editor in chief, *Encyclopedia of the Holocaust*, vol. 4 (New York: Macmillan Publishing Co., 1990); Richard C. Lukas, *The Forgotten Holocaust: The Poles under German Occupation* (Lexington: University of Kentucky Press, 1986); and Betty Alt and Silvia Folts, *Weeping Violins: The Gypsy Tragedy in Europe* (Kirksville, MO: Thomas Jefferson University Press, 1996).
12. See James E. Wise Jr. and Anne Collier Rehill, *Stars in Blue: Movie Actors in America's Sea Services* (Annapolis: Naval Institute Press, 1997).
13. By 1942 Lew Ayres was an established Hollywood star, best remembered as Dr. Kildare. When the war came, Ayres refused combat duty on religious grounds and served instead as a medic and chaplain's aide. The film studios shunned him until 1948. The plight of conscientious objectors has yet to be fully detailed, although their numbers are considerable. In World War I, 60,000 were classified as objectors but only 4,000 served in that capacity. In World War II, 12,000 objectors served in the Civilian Service Program (CSP), with another 6,000 imprisoned. About 5,000 men served as objectors during the Korean conflict. The war in Vietnam saw over 171,000 eligible men declare themselves objectors and war resistors and flee to Canada to avoid the draft. Philip Borkholder (Executive Director, National Interreligious Service Board for Conscientious Objectors), email to author, July 9, 1997. For the story of the CSP, see Albert N. Keim, *The CPS Story: An Illustrated History of Civilian Public Service* (Intercourse, PA: Good Books, 1990). For mistreatment of COs during the Vietnam period, see Stephen M. Kohn, *Jailed for Peace* (Westport, CT: Greenwood Press, 1986).
14. See William M. Tuttle Jr., *Daddy's Gone to War* (New York: Oxford University Press, 1993), 148–54.

15. Clayton R. Koppes and Gregory D. Black, *Hollywood Goes to War* (Berkeley: University of California Press, 1987), 325. Recent research by Thomas Schatz, "World War II and the Hollywood War Film," in Nick Browne, ed., *Refiguring Genres* (Berkeley: University of California Press, 1998), 103–04, places the figure of World War II-related Hollywood features closer to 20 percent of the 1,636 films made between Pearl Harbor and the end of the war. Of these 340 war-related films, Schatz found that the most popular type were the combat films, followed by espionage and home front movies.

16. Jeanine Basinger, *The World War II Combat Film* (New York: Columbia University Press, 1986).

17. Bradbury Science Museum, Los Alamos, New Mexico. The figures are from the National Archives, viewed July 13, 2012. For readers interested in WWII and the atomic bomb, this is a must visit.

18. *Encyclopaedia Britannica*, "Haakon VII," http://www.britannica.com/EBchecked/topic/250650/Haakon-VII (accessed July 30, 2013).

19. See Ann Dorr, "The Women Who Flew—but Kept Silent," *New York Times Magazine*, May 7, 1995, sec. 6, 70–71; and Melissa Fay Greene, "The Flygirl," *Life*, June 1999, 80–86. These women were buried without military honors and those who survived received no benefits.

20. I am indebted to Dawn Letson, former librarian at the Texas Woman's University, for this information.

21. Sally E. Parry, "How Proudly Did We Serve?: Popular Culture Images of Army Nurses in World War II" (paper presented at the Popular Culture Association meeting, Philadelphia, April 1995).

22. For the real life story of 72 nurses trapped on Bataan and imprisoned for three years on Corregidor, read Elizabeth M. Norman, *We Band of Angels* (New York: Random House, 1999).

23. The $21 million Women's Memorial was dedicated in October 1997.

24. Although WWII was fought on a segregated basis, Hollywood has yet to tell the real story of African-American soldiers during the war. Most black soldiers were prohibited from combat and were assigned to do menial tasks like building roads, digging latrines, and loading ships. See Brent Staples, "Reliving WWII with a Captain America of a Different Color," *New York Times Magazine*, December 1, 2002, sec.4, 8. For the story of black soldiers in combat, see David P. Colley, *Blood for Dignity: The Story of the First Integrated Combat Unit in the U.S. Army* (New York: St. Martin's Press, 2003).

25. See Basinger, *The World War II Combat Film*, 28; and Koppes and Black, *Hollywood Goes to War*, 248–77. In his unpublished paper, Ralph R. Donald, "Savages, Swine and Buffoons: Hollywood's Selected Stereotypical Characterizations of the Japanese, Germans and Italians in Films Produced During World War II" (paper presented at the Popular Culture Association meeting, Orlando, April 1998), advances the thesis that a descending order of brutality existed in Hollywood World War II movies. He maintains that the Italians received the most neutral characterization, usually portrayed as buffoons and hapless soldiers. The Nazis were despised and often depicted as military gangsters, but Hollywood distanced them from the German people. Donald argues that the most vicious attacks were saved for the Japanese, resulting in negative images "unmatched in American film propaganda," 7.

26. The entire episode is described in Koppes and Black, *Hollywood Goes to War*, 72–77.

27. Recent research by Iris Chang, *The Rape of Nanking: The Forgotten Holocaust of WWII* (New York: Basic Books, 1997), describes Japanese atrocities in the Chinese city of Nanking in 1937 where 200,000 to 350,000 civilians were slaughtered, nearly half of the population. Yet American feeling toward the Japanese probably was influenced more by the attack on Pearl Harbor.

28. Hollywood tried to redeem itself after the war when MGM released *Go for Broke* (1951), a film about the exploits of the 442nd Regimental Combat Team composed mainly of Japanese-American (Nisei) volunteers. The Nisei fought in seven major European campaigns and suffered 9,486 casualties. Their bravery and courage under fire earned them over 18,000 individual decorations and seven presidential citations. Two facts are interesting about the film version. First, Hollywood wisely focused on the Nisei rather than Van Johnson, the white male star. Second, the film became a blatant piece of postwar propaganda. After the credits, the film displays President Roosevelt's message of support for the establishment of Nisei units, commenting that being American is a matter of heart and not race or ancestry. But it was Roosevelt

who issued Executive Order 9066, which began the evacuation and internment of over 115,000 Japanese-Americans (three-quarters of whom were U.S. citizens) from the West Coast.

29. Kathryn Kane, "The World War II Combat Film, 1942–45," in Wes D. Gehring, ed., *Handbook of American Film Genres* (Westport, CT: Greenwood Press, 1988), 85–86.

30. On the other hand, not every World War II film is a commercial success. Terrence Malick's version of the James Jones novel, *The Thin Red Line* (1998), flopped at the box office.

31. James Bradley, *Flags of our Fathers* (New York: Bantam Books, 2000).

32. See their stories in "Buffalo Soldier," *Wikipedia*, March 19, 2013, http://en.wikipedia.org/w/index.php?title=Buffalo_Soldier&oldid=545379167; *People* 70, no. 15 (October 2008): 104; and *The New York Times*, June 6, 2009, A10.

33. The story is available from http://www.cafebabel.co.uk/article/27029/spike-lee-miracleatstanna-francesco-bruni.html, October 20, 2008 and from http://www.jewishvirtuallibrary.org/jsource/Holocaust/Stazzema.html, "The Sant'Anna di Stazzema Massacre," August 1944 (accessed March 23, 2013).

34. The Internet Movie Database, http://www.imdb.com/title/tt1046997/?ref_=fn_al_tt_1, reports the film budget was roughly $45 million but its domestic gross only reached $8 million (accessed March 23, 2013).

35. The first film about the Tuskegee Airmen was made by HBO for cable in 1995 and featured Laurence Fishburne and Cuba Gooding Jr. *The Tuskegee Airmen* is a different film than *Red Tails* because the emphasis is on the training of these men to become pilots despite doubts by the Washington brass and the racist attitudes by white officers. Its aerial scenes cannot compare to what Lucas did in *Red Tails* but the story on the ground rings truer.

36. See the review in *The New York Times*, January 20, 2012, C13.

37. Visit the Tuskegee Airmen website at http://www.tuskegeeairmen.org. In 1998, President Clinton approved the establishment of a National Historic Site at Moton Field in Tuskegee, Alabama, to commemorate their contribution to WWII.

38. For an analysis of the film, see Sally E. Parry, "So Proudly They Serve: American Women in World War II Films" (paper presented at the annual meeting of the American Political Science Association, San Francisco, August–Sept. 1996).

39. Richard Schickel, "The Hollywood Ten: Printing the Legend," in *Schickel on Film* (New York: Morrow, 1989), 106.

40. The Harold Russell character (Homer) represented the more than 670,000 Americans who suffered war wounds, with 83,000 receiving treatment at VA hospitals. See Tuttle, *Daddy's Gone to War*, 216.

41. Tom Brokaw, *The Greatest Generation* (New York: Random House, 1998).

42. See http://www.wwiimemorial.com/ (accessed March 23, 2013).

43. There were rumors that the project was in financial trouble. But an examination of the 2011 Auditor's Report at http://www.nationalww2museum.org/about-the-museum/annual-report.html indicates a stable financial situation. However, the museum carries heavy entrance fees: museum + all exhibits for adults $32, for seniors $29 and for students and active military $23. Only WWII vets get free entry. http://www.nationalww2museum.org/visit/index.html

44. See Doherty, *Projections of War*, Appendix, 304–08.

45. Ibid., 229.

46. Bruce Shapiro, "Lugging the Guts into the Next Room," http://www.salon.com/1998/07/30/30media/ (accessed March 23, 2013). The warrior myth perpetuated by the military is that combat soldiers fight and die heroically for God and country. Any combat soldier will tell you otherwise.

47. Basinger, *The World War II Combat Film*, 125–31. Ford's film, *December 7th*, has an interesting history. This government-funded film of the Japanese attack on Pearl Harbor alienated the U.S. Navy because it implied naval complacency before the assault. As a consequence, the government confiscated the film's negative and

instead released an edited version, which, nonetheless, won an Academy Award. The complete uncensored version was withheld from public view until the 1990s.

48. See Doherty, *Projections of War*, 237.
49. For a contrary view of the film by a military historian, see Roger J. Spiller, "War in the Dark," *American Heritage* 50, no. 1 (February–March 1999): 41–51.
50. Peter Bart and Peter Guber, *Shoot Out* (New York: The Berkley Publishing Group, 2002), 82.
51. Material from the Bradbury Science Museum, Los Alamos, NM, and "Why the Bomb?" brochure by the Los Alamos Education Group NM (undated).
52. Other estimates place the total casualties for Hiroshima at between 135,000 and 150,000 and between 64,000 and 75,000 for Nagasaki three days later. The figures cited are from "The Atomic Bombings of Hiroshima and Nagasaki: Chapter 10—Total Casualties," Lillian Goldman Law Library, accessed March 20, 2013, http://avalon.law.yale.edu/20th_century/mp10.asp.
53. Gar Alperovitz, *The Decision to Use the Atomic Bomb* (New York: Alfred A. Knopf, 1995).
54. Paul Boyer, *By the Bomb's Early Light* (Chapel Hill: University of North Carolina Press, 1994), 183. The poll participants were given four choices: (a) should not have used the bomb, (b) approved dropping both bombs, (c) should have dropped more bombs, and (d) should have dropped one somewhere (presumably over water) to impress the Japanese and then use one over land if the Japanese failed to surrender.
55. Tsuyoshi Hasegawa, *Racing the Enemy: Stalin, Truman, and the Surrender of Japan* (Cambridge, MA: Harvard University Press, 2006).
56. The films are *Pork Chop Hill* and *The Bridges at Toko-Ri*. See "*Military History* Magazine's 100 Greatest War Movies (2007)," *The One-Line Review* (blog), accessed March 20, 2013, http://1linereview.blogspot.com/2010/10/military-history-magazines-100-greatest.html.
57. Just as the Korean War interrupted the life of William Holden's character in the film, it also interrupted the baseball career of the Boston Red Sox Hall of Famer Ted Williams. Similar to Holden's character, Williams had served in WWII and was recalled into the marines for two years, flying the jets seen in the film. See User Reviews at http://www.imdb.com/title/tt0046806/?ref_=sr_1 (accessed July 30, 2013).
58. Basinger, *The World War II Combat Film*, 176–79.
59. Reported in Lewis H. Carlson, "*The Manchurian Candidate* and Other Korean War POW films" (paper presented at the Popular Culture Association meeting, New Orleans, April 2000).
60. For details on the torture memos, see stories in *Newsweek*, May 11/May 18, 2009, 6 & 37; and *The New York Times*, Week in Review, columns by Frank Rich and Nicholas Kristof, April 26, 2009, 14. On American interrogation techniques used at Guantanamo, see *The New York Times*, Week in Review, July 6, 2008, 1.
61. President Roosevelt interned more than 115,000 Japanese-Americans during World War II on the basis of an executive order despite the fact that three-quarters were American citizens. In *Korematsu v. U.S.*, 323 U.S. 214 (1944) and other cases, the Supreme Court upheld the internment order on national security grounds. Less known to the public is the treatment accorded to Italian-Americans, mostly aliens, who were interned during the war in military camps in Montana, Minnesota, and Ellis Island and were forced to leave their homes on the West Coast, and were branded "enemy aliens" by the U.S. government. The introduction of the Wartime Violation of Italian American Civil Liberties Act in 1997 was an attempt by Congress to force the Justice Department to document government mistreatment of Italian-Americans during the war.
62. 374 U.S. 483 (1954).
63. "The Rediscovery of World War II," *AARP Newsletter*, May 1999, 22.
64. Michael Walzer, *Just and Unjust Wars*, 2nd ed. (New York: Basic Books, 1992), 117–24.
65. See the reports in *The New York Times*, April 21, 2000, A6 and January 12, 2001, 1.
66. Bruce Cumings, *The Korean War* (New York: Modern Library, 2010). Cuming's also noted that President Truman "considered" using the atomic bomb on North Korea.

67. Ubuntaworks, "The Barbaric War", http://www.uwpep.org/Index/KOREAN_WAR.html, no date (accessed March 23, 2013).
68. David Halberstam, *The Coldest Winter: America and the Korean War* (New York: Hyperion, 2007). Another excellent source on the Korean War is T.R. Fehrenbach, *This Kind of War* (Washington, D.C.: Brassey's, Inc., 1963).

## Chapter 9. Remembering Vietnam on Film: Lessons Learned and Forgotten

1. Charles Molir, "History and Hindsight: Lessons from Vietnam," *The New York Times*, April 30, 1985, 6.
2. Transcript of lecture delivered at the Naval War College, December 10, 1964.
3. Lawrence Wright, *In the New World* (New York: Alfred Knopf, 1987), 119–22.
4. Quoted in Andrew Martin, *Receptions of War: Vietnam in American Culture* (Norman: University of Oklahoma Press, 1993), 107.
5. Michael Coyne, *The Crowded Prairie* (London: I. B. Tauris Publishers, 1997), 145, characterizes *The Green Berets* as "a John Wayne western set in Vietnam."
6. See Thomas Doherty, *Projections of War: Hollywood, American Culture, and World War II* (New York: Columbia University Press, 1993), 282–98; and Richard T. Jamesson, ed., *They Went Thataway: Redefining Film Genres* (San Francisco: Mercury House, 1994), 263–79.
7. Joseph Conrad, *Heart of Darkness*, ed. Robert Kimbrough, 2nd ed. (New York: W.W. Norton & Company, 1971). According to Kimbrough, *Heart of Darkness* appeared in three different versions: a magazine version in 1899, a book edition in 1902, and a revised edition in 1921 considered by scholars to be Conrad's final text.
8. See Mark C. Carnes, *Past Imperfect: History According to the Movies* (New York: Henry Holt & Co., 1995).
9. According to Arnold R. Isaacs, *The War, Its Ghosts, and Its Legacy* (Baltimore: John Hopkins University Press, 1998), the idea that politicians, along with a hostile media and subversive demonstrators, prevented victory in Vietnam is a myth. Instead, Isaacs' thesis is that the country turned against the war when the military failed to win in the field.
10. Michael Rogin, *Ronald Reagan, the Movie* (Berkeley: University of California Press, 1988), 7, reports that after the American hostages in Lebanon, taken as part of the 1985 TWA skyjacking, were released, the president watched *First Blood, Part 2* and supposedly told aides, "Boy, I saw *Rambo* last night. Now I know what to do the next time this happens."
11. Marita Sturken, "Reenactment, Fantasy, and the Paranoia of History: Oliver Stone's Docudramas," *History and Theory* 36, no. 4 (December 1997): 66.
12. William J. Palmer, *The Films of the Eighties* (Carbondale: Southern Illinois University Press, 1993), 16–60.
13. Ibid., 18.
14. Ibid., 21.
15. See Frank P. Tomosulo, "The Politics of Ambivalence: *Apocalypse Now* as Prowar and Antiwar Film," in Linda Dittmar and Gene Michaud, eds., *From Hanoi to Hollywood* (New Brunswick, NJ: Rutgers University Press, 1990), 145–58.
16. See Palmer, *The Films of the Eighties*, 61–113.
17. See Leonard Quart, "*The Deer Hunter*: The Superman in Vietnam," in Dittmar and Michaud, *From Hanoi to Hollywood*, 159–68.
18. See "Cost of the Vietnam War," *Vietnam Agent Orange Relief and Responsibility Campaign*, accessed March 25, 2013, http://www.vn-agentorange.org/edmaterials/cost_of_vn_war.html.
19. James Kurth, "The U.S. Victory in Vietnam: Lost and Found," *The Intercollegiate Review* 41, no. 2 (Fall 2006): 14–22.
20. George F. Will, "Is It 1966 in Washington?" *Time*, October 5, 2009, 25.

21. The interventionist analysis comes from Peter Huchthausen, *America's Splendid Little Wars* (New York: Viking, 2003). The author is a retired naval captain.
22. For an analysis that suggests more significance than normally accorded the film, see Pat Aufderheide, "Vietnam: Good Soldiers" in Mark Crispin Miller, ed., *Seeing Through Movies* (New York: Pantheon Books, 1990), 81–111.
23. Quoted in Maureen Dowd, "A Different Bush Conforms to a Nation's Mood," *The New York Times*, March 2, 1991, A7.
24. Michael Norman, "Carnage and Glory, Legends and Lies," *The New York Times*, sec. 2, July 7, 1996, 19.
25. There were multiple reasons for Swofford's bitterness besides the lack of action: his girlfriend had jilted him, his buddy committed suicide after being drummed out of the Marine Corps, and another writer suggested that the film had taken dialogue from his published book on the Gulf War. See "*Jarhead*," IMDb, accessed March 26, 2013, http://www.imdb.com/title/tt0418763/; and *The New York Times*, November 9, 2005, B1.
26. See David Rieff, "Were Sanctions Right?" *The New York Times Magazine*, sec.6, July 27, 2003, 40–46. Also see *Paying the Price: Killing the Children of Iraq*, Bullfrog Films, 2000. In effect, the sanctions killed more people than the two atomic bombs dropped on Japan during WWII.
27. The idea comes from Bosah Ebo, "War as Popular Culture: the Gulf Conflict and the Technology of Illusionary Entertainment," *Journal of American Culture* 18, no. 3 (Fall 1995): 19–25.
28. The discussion and analysis comes from the following sources: Robert Freeman, "Is Iraq Another Vietnam? It Is Already Lost," *Common Dreams*, October 22, 2006, http://www.commondreams.org/views06/1022-26.htm; Danny Schechter, "Those Vietnam Parallels," *Common Dreams*, October 24, 2006, http://www.commondreams.org/views06/1024-34.htm; Tim Kane and David Gentilli, "Is Iraq Another Vietnam? Not for U.S. Troop Levels," *The Heritage Foundation*, July 21, 2006, http://www.heritage.org/research/reports/2006/07/is-iraq-another-vietnam-not-for-us-troop-levels; Nathaniel Fick, "Is Iraq Another Vietnam?" *The Washington Post*, November 19, 2006, sec. Arts & Living, http://www.washingtonpost.com/wp-dyn/content/article/2006/11/16/AR2006111601135.html.
29. See Neta C. Crawford, "Just War Theory and the U.S. Counterterror War," *Perspectives on Politics* 1, no. 1 (March 2003): 5–25.
30. In Michael Walzer's *Just and Unjust Wars*, 2nd ed. (New York: Basic Books, 1992), 97–101, Professor Walzer concludes that the Vietnam War was unjust because the U.S. could not justify its intervention for two reasons. First, the South Vietnamese government could not survive without external support. Therefore it lacked public support despite American aid. Second, when the U.S. intervened militarily, it did so to pursue its own policies. The war, then, became an American war fought in another country. In contrast, Korea was a just war because the North Korean aggression was undisputed and because the goal of counter-intervention was to restore the status quo rather than win a military victory. Michael Ryan and Douglas Kellner, *Camera Politica* (Bloomington: Indiana University Press, 1990), 194–216, agree with Walzer that Vietnam was an unjust war but for a different reason. For Ryan and Kellner, the U.S. involvement was unjust because it lent support to a corrupt and undemocratic regime.
31. See Michael Anderegg, ed., *Inventing Vietnam: The War in Film and Television* (Philadelphia: Temple University Press, 1991), where he argues that, even though Vietnam was given life through film, the visual images remain subjective creations of the filmmakers.
32. Anthony Swofford, *Jarhead* (New York: Scribner & Sons, 2003), 114.
33. Reported in Norman, "Carnage and Glory, Legends and Lies," 19.

## Chapter 10. Mission Accomplished? Hollywood and the Afghanistan-Iraq War Films

1. The quotes are taken from a transcript of the president's speech at http://www.cnn.com/2003/US/05/01/bush.transcript, May 1, 2003.

2. William Dalrymple, "The Ghosts of Afghanistan's Past," *The New York Times*, Sunday Review, April 14, 2013, 5.

3. Statistics from "Operation Iraqi Freedom (OIF) Casualty Status," U.S Department of Defense, accessed February 17, 2013, http://www.defense.gov/news/casualty.pdf.

4. Michael R. Gordon, "Failed Efforts and Lost Chances of America's Last Months in Iraq," *The New York Times*, September 23, 2012, 1.

5. "Iraq after the U.S. Withdrawal," *The New York Times*, December 19, 2011, A12.

6. Jason Lyall, "Afghanistan's Lost Decade," *Foreign Affairs*, December 15, 2011, http://www.foreignaffairs.com/articles/136787/jason-lyall/afghanistans-lost-decade.

7. *The New York Times*, Editorial, "Beginning of the End," February 19, 2012, 10.

8. Tom Vanden Brook, "Taliban Targets Afghan Troops," *USA Today*, August 20, 2012, 1.

9. *The New York Times*, Editorial, "Time to Pack Up," October 14, 2012, 10.

10. ABC News made the pronouncement: http://abcnews.go.com/Politics/afghan-war-now-longest-war-us-history/story?id=10849303, June 7, 2010 (accessed April 23, 2013).

11. http://icasualties.org/ (accessed April 23, 2013).

12. http://www.redding.com/news/2013/mar/16/more-than-50000-us-troops-injured-in-iraq-and/ (accessed April 23, 2013).

13. http://www.militaryspot.com/news/troops-and-vets-urged-to-tap-va-services-and-benefits/, April 22, 2013.

14. https://research.hks.harvard.edu/publications/workingpapers/citation.aspx?PubId=8956, March 28, 2013.

15. http://costsofwar.org/article/civilians-killed-and-wounded (accessed April 23, 2013).

16. Luke Mogelson, "A Beast in the Heart," *The New York Times Magazine*, May 1, 2011, 34–41ff; James Dao, "U.S. Identifies Army Sergeant in Killing of 16," *The New York Times*, March 17, 2012, 1; and Nicholas D. Kristoff, "When War Comes Home," *The New York Times*, Sunday Review, November 11, 2012, 1.

17. Nicholas D. Kristof, "War Wounds," *The New York Times*, Sunday Review, August 12, 2012, 1.

18. James Dao, "For a Soldier Disfigured in War, a Way to Return to the World," *The New York Times*, January 31, 2012, 1.

19. This information comes from a series on returning veterans run in *The New York Times* during 2012. On suicide and sexual abuse see Elisabeth Bumiller, "Active-Duty Suicides Reach Record High; Sex Crimes Also on the Rise," January 20, 2012, A11; and Nicholas D. Kristof, "A Veteran's Death, the Nation's Shame," April 15, 2012, 1. On alcohol and drug abuse see James Dao, "Report Urges Update of Military Substance Abuse Strategies," September 18, 2012, A13; and Richard A. Friedman, "Why Are We Drugging Our Soldiers," April 22, 2012, 9.

20. An argument could be made against including *Charlie Wilson's War* because the storyline involves the fight by the mujahedeen against the Soviet invaders. However, it relates to the current situation in Afghanistan and Iraq because of the clandestine operation by an American congressman to aid the Afghans and because it preaches the simplistic notion that American involvement can achieve positive results. Furthermore, if you consider that the most commercial of these films, *Charlie Wilson's War*, earned 60 percent of the $110 million domestic gross, the financial failure of the other five is even more pronounced. Box office figures are from http://www.boxofficemojo.com/movies/?id=charliewilsonswar.htm (accessed April 24, 2013).

21. Box office figures from http://www.boxofficemojo.com/movies/?id=darkknight.htm (accessed April 24, 2013).

22. http://www.imdb.com/title/tt0995832/reviews?ref_=tt_urv, summer 2008 (accessed April 24, 2013).

23. See *The New York Times*, June 23, 2008, C4.

24. Reported at "Extraordinary Rendition," *Wikipedia*, last updated March 27, 2013, http://en.wikipedia.org/w/index.php?title=Extraordinary_rendition&oldid=547227130. However, the Clinton accusation, originally reported in a *Wall Street Journal* editorial, March 11, 2005 was disputed at http://mediamatters.

org/research/2005/03/11/wsj-editorial-claimed-clinton-pioneered-bush-re/132875 (accessed January 10, 2010). The clandestine CIA rendition program, in which terrorist suspects are transported to third countries for interrogation, was ruled in violation of human rights by the European Court of Human Rights in Strasbourg, France, recently in a case involving a German man seized by Macedonia and handed over to the CIA for rendition to Afghanistan, where he was imprisoned and tortured. The case was reported by Nicholas Kulish, "Court Finds Rights Violation in CIA Rendition Case," *The New York Times*, December 13, 2012, A13.

25. See "Charlie Wilson (Texas Politician)," *Wikipedia*, last modified April 3, 2013, http://en.wikipedia.org/wiki/Charlie_Wilson_(Texas_politician) (accessed August 7, 2013).

26. Gregory Feifer, *The Great Gamble* (New York: HarperCollins Publishers, 2009).

27. 425 F. 3rd 549 (9th Cir. 2005).

28. Louis Jacobson, "'Stop-loss' stopped in early 2011," Politifact.com, November 4, 2011, http://www.politifact.com/truth-o-meter/promises/obameter/promise/144/end-the-stop-loss.

29. *The New York Times*, Arts & Leisure, March 23, 2008, 1–15.

30. The story was reported in *The New York Times*, Ari Karpel, "Whitewash in Wartime," August 15, 2010, 11. The documentary *The Tillman Story* was also reviewed in the *Times*, August 20, 2010, C1.

31. See Julian E. Barnes, "Calling the shots on war movies," *Los Angeles Times*, July 7, 2008, http://articles.latimes.com/2008/jul/07/nation/na-armyfilms7?pg=3.

32. The estimated budget for *The Lucky Ones* was $15 million. It opened on only 425 screens in selected cities, grossing $183,000 for the weekend. In wider release several weeks later, the film did not do much better, earning $266,967. Afterward, the film disappeared from theaters altogether. See http://www.boxofficemojo.com/movies/?id=luckyones.htm (accessed April 24, 2013).

33. *The New York Times*, April 22, 2008, 18. In 2006, 249 enlistment waivers were given to army recruits who had been convicted of felonies. That number doubled in 2007.

34. The story was reported in *The New York Times*, January 13, 2008, 1.

35. The story ran in the print and TV media for days. See *The New York Times*, November 9, 2009, 1 and the following week's newspaper for a recap of the story and an update on developments.

36. See Jim Sheeler, *Final Salute* (New York: Penguin Press, 2008).

37. See John Barry, "A Matter of Honor," *Newsweek* 153, no. 8 (February 23, 2009): 32.

38. *The New York Times*, February 27, 2009, A13.

39. "*The Hurt Locker*," Box Office Mojo, accessed April 10, 2013, http://boxofficemojo.com/movies/?id=hurtlocker.htm. With worldwide distribution, the film grossed $49 million, a disappointing amount for an Academy Award winner.

40. See Scott Shane, "Portrayal of C.A.A. torture in Bin Laden Film Reopens a Debate," *The New York Times*, December 13, 2012, 1. In his review, David Denby, "Dead Reckoning," *The New Yorker*, December 24 & 31, 2012, 130–32, writes that the Maya character was based on a real agent. Also see Logan Hall, "Secrets of *Zero Dark Thirty*," *Rolling Stone*, January 17, 2013, 20.

41. Scott Shane, "Acting C.I.A. Chief Critical of Film '*Zero Dark Thirty*,'" *The New York Times*, December 23, 2012, 33.

42. Story at http://news.yahoo.com/analysis---zero-dark-thirty--opens-wide-----to-controversy-185306375.html (accessed January 12, 2013).

43. Michael Cieply, "Hollywood Makes Case for '*Zero Dark Thirty*,'" *The New York Times*, January 20, 2012, 22.

44. "The Senate Censors," *The Wall Street Journal*, February 28, 2013, A14. The *Journal*'s viewpoint was seconded by Ali H. Soufan in an op-ed, "Torture, Lies and Hollywood," *The New York Times*, February 24, 2013, 4, where the former FBI special agent argued that torture led the agency away from bin Laden.

45. Karen Greenberg, "How '*Zero Dark Thirty*' Reminds Americans How Much They Love Torture," Common Dreams, http://www.commondreams.org/view/2013/01/10-6, January 10, 2013.

46. In a series of cases beginning in the 19th century [*Hopt v. Utah*, 110 U.S. 574 (1884)] and into the 20th, culminating in *Miranda v. Arizona*, 384 U.S. 436 (1966), the court has sought to protect those suspected and accused of crimes by validating that the confession was voluntary by invoking the 14th, 5th, and 6th Amendments. The court has continued the right against coerced confessions into the 21st century.

47. This is the domestic gross as of March 24, 2013. See "*Zero Dark Thirty*," Box Office Mojo. Because of its content the film's producers would not expect a substantial box office gross from overseas.

48. Film scholars like Terry Christensen, Peter Haas, and Michael Coyne take a broader view of what constitutes a "political film" than the author. And contrary to the author, Coyne believes that the idea of political films as box office poison is part of Hollywood mythology. See chapter 2 for further discussion on this point. Also of interest is Gary Crowdus's book *A Political Companion to American Film* (Chicago: Lake View Press, 1994), which contains segments on war films, political films, etc.

49. There is a very good synopsis of U.S. interventions at Zoltán Grossman, "From Wounded Knee to Libya: A Century of U.S. Military Interventions," Evergreen State College, (accessed April 10, 2013), http://academic.evergreen.edu/g/grossmaz/interventions.html. Details about U.S. and NATO policy in Libya are from Ivo H. Daalder and James G. Stavridis, "NATO's Victory in Libya," *Foreign Affairs*, March/April 2012, http://www.foreignaffairs.com/articles/137073/ivo-h-daalder-and-james-g-stavridis/natos-victory-in-libya. For a leftist view of the Libyan intervention, see Lance Selfa, "Libya's revolution, U.S. intervention, and the Left," in *International Socialist Review* 77 (May–June 2011), at http://isreview.org/issues/77/feat-libya&left.shtml.

50. Michael Scheuer, "No Matter Who Wins, the Next President Will—without Question—Be an Interventionist War President," Non-Intervention.com (blog), November 5, 2012, http://non-intervention.com/1075/no-matter-who-wins-the-next-president-will-without-question-be-an-interventionist-war-president/.

51. Ibid.

52. In North Africa, the U.S. provided intelligence to the French to identify the military forces of al Qaeda. See Adam Entous et al., "U.S. Boosts War Role in Africa," *The Wall Street Journal*, March 4, 2013, 1. To the Syrian Coalition, the U.S. provided non-military aid in the form of food and military supplies, but disappointed the rebels who wanted weapons, see "New Syrian Aid Slammed by Rebels," *The Wall Street Journal*, March 1, 2013, A2. See Mark Landler et al., "Obama Says U.S. Will Recognize Rebels in Syria," *The New York Times*, December 12, 2012, 1, for the story of a civil war that has claimed at least 40,000 lives.

53. The following analysis comes from two works by Max Boot: *Invisible Armies* (New York: Liveright, 2013) and the article "The Guerrilla Myth," *The Wall Street Journal*, Review, January 19–20, C1.

54. See Fred Kaplan, *The Insurgents: David Petraeus and the Plot to Change the American Way of War* (New York: Simon & Schuster, 2013).

55. For what it is worth, the Library of Congress acknowledges "war films" as a separate genre in its classification system but divides it into fiction (commercial) and nonfiction (documentary). The difference between the AFI figure and that of the IMDB is that the latter's definition is more inclusive and when it includes war as a secondary subject, it expands further to 2,403. One fact is certain: the Hollywood war film of any kind has been on the decline since the end of WWII. Zoran Sinobad, Reference Librarian, Library of Congress emails to the author, August 6 and August 8, 2013.

56. "Frequently Asked Questions," The National WWII Museum, accessed April 11, 2013, http://www.nationalww2museum.org/about-the-museum/frequently-asked-questions.html.

57. 57.The data come from "Hall of Heroes: Medal of Honor," Iraq and Afghanistan Veterans of America, http://iava.org/hall-heroes-medal-honor; and "Hall of Heroes: Meet Dakota Meyer," http://iava.org/blog/hall-heroes-honor-dakota-meyer#meyer (accessed April 11, 2013).

## Chapter 11. Hollywood Confronts Nuclear War and Global Terrorism

1. *The New York Times*, October 30, 2007, D1. Other facilities that produced nuclear materials were at Oak Ridge, Tennessee, and Hanford, Washington.
2. *The New York Times Book Review*, May 15, 2005, sec. 7, 7–8.
3. Bradbury Science Museum, Los Alamos National Laboratory, visited on July 13, 2012.
4. William J. Broad, "New Books Revive Old Talk of Spies," *The New York Times*, May 11, 1999, D1.
5. Michael Walsh, "Iowa-Born, Soviet Trained," *Smithsonian* 40, no. 2 (May 2009): 40–47.
6. Paul Boyer, *By the Bomb's Early Light* (Chapel Hill: University of North Carolina Press, 1994).
7. "ShockWave," *Time*, July 31, 1995, 50. These are conservative figures because countless other deaths were likely caused by radioactivity. *The Catholic Light*, August 3, 1995, 2, put the Hiroshima deaths attributed to the atomic blast at 200,000, with another 39,000 dead in the Nagasaki blast. By any count, the numbers are considerable. However, estimates of the damage from the March 1945 air raids on Tokyo range from 100,000 to 200,000 deaths, while the total number of Japanese dead from conventional bombs and fire bombs was put at 500,000. On the other hand, estimates of the number of American casualties, had President Truman opted for an invasion of the Japanese islands, vary from 100,000 to 200,000. Revisionist historian Gar Alperovitz disputes these figures in his book *The Decision to Use the Atomic Bomb* (New York: Alfred A. Knopf, 1995). Moreover, Alperovitz maintains that the number of American casualties was not the deciding factor in Truman's decision. Instead, he argues that Truman used the atom bomb as part of his post-war diplomacy to send a message to the Soviets to stay out of Asia.
8. Winston Churchill said that 1.5 million American and British lives would be saved. The president of the Japanese Medical Association believed that use of the atom bomb saved millions of Japanese lives because it broke the government's will to resist and prevented an invasion of the islands. See Harvard Nuclear Study Group, *Living with Nuclear Weapons* (New York: Bantam Books, 1983), 72–73; and John P. Roche, *The History and Impact of Marxist-Leninist Organizational Theory* (Cambridge, MA: Institute of Foreign Policy Analysis, 1984), 66–67.
9. For a case study on the film, consult Nathan Reingold, "A Footnote to History: MGM Meets the Atomic Bomb," in Philip S. Cook, Douglas Goney, and Lawrence W. Lichty, *American Media* (Washington, DC: The Wilson Center Press, 1989). According to Jack Shaheen, ed., *Nuclear War Films* (Carbondale: Southern Illinois University Press, 1978), 8, the film was cut and reedited several times. One scene between an officer and a crew member that was mercifully left on the cutting room floor involved this verbal exchange: Crew Member: "Is it true that if you fool around with this stuff [atomic equipment] long enough, you don't like girls anymore?" To which the officer replied: "I hadn't noticed it."
10. History repeated itself when the Smithsonian Museum in Washington, DC, ran into controversy when it planned to mark the 50th anniversary of the dropping of the A-bombs to end World War II. Originally, the museum intended a big exhibition to include material on the decision to use the bomb, the horror caused by the bomb, and the subsequent arms race that followed the Cold War—all centered on the fuselage of the *Enola Gay*. But criticism from veterans groups and members of Congress that the planned exhibition exaggerated Japanese suffering and minimized Japanese aggression forced the museum to cut back. When the exhibition officially opened what remained were the plane, a video, and a plaque. For the story, see *The New York Times*, February 5, 1995, E5.
11. See Michael Walzer, *Just and Unjust Wars*, 2nd ed. (New York: Basic Books, 1992).
12. See "How Hollywood Learned to Start Worrying and Hate the Bomb," *American Film* 8, no. 1 (October 1982): 57–63. Other film stars who were active in the anti-nuke campaign besides Newman included Ellen Burstyn, Jill Clayburgh, Sally Field, Meryl Streep, and Joanne Woodward.
13. See Mick Broderick, *Nuclear Movies* (Jefferson, NC: McFarland & Co., 1991), Filmography, 55–191.
14. The original *Godzilla* (1954) movie was a low-budget Japanese film that reflected the horrors of Hiroshima and Nagasaki. The film was edited and released in the U.S. in 1956 as *Godzilla, King of the Monsters*. Raymond Burr starred in a film that identified Godzilla as a radioactive monster terrorizing Japan.

15. See Nora Sayre, *Running Time: Films of the Cold War* (New York: The Dial Press, 1982), chapter VII, for a Cold War analysis of science fiction films of the fifties.

16. Jane Caputi has tried to establish a relationship between certain horror films such as *Night of the Living Dead* and the nuclear age. Her thesis is that although such films make no explicit references to nuclear technology, the ghouls are byproducts of nuclear contamination. See her "Films of the Nuclear Age," *Journal of Popular Film and Television* 16, no. 3 (Fall 1988): 100–07.

17. See Cyndy Hendershot, "The Atomic Scientist, Science Fiction Films, and Paranoia," *Journal of American Culture* 20, no. 1 (spring 1997): 31–41. The 2008 remake of *The Day the Earth Stood Still*, starring Keanu Reeves, was a financial success with a worldwide gross of $230 million, but the film critics thought the original was much better.

18. Reported in Lawrence Suid, "The Pentagon and Hollywood: *Dr. Strangelove*," in John O'Connor and Martin Jackson, eds, *American History/American Film*, 224. The same lack of cooperation was accorded the Stanley Kubrick film *Dr. Strangelove*.

19. Richard Ostrom, "Re-Viewing *Dr. Strangelove*: The Funniest Things Were the Most Realistic" (paper presented at the annual meeting of the Far West Popular Culture Association, Las Vegas, January/February 2003). Political scientist Dan Lindley agrees that the Russian Doomsday device was an unlikely weapon, yet mass destruction was possible as a consequence of nuclear war, especially since there were 34,000 nuclear weapons in existence at the time.

20. See Bonnie Szumski, ed., *Nuclear War: Opposing Viewpoints* (St. Paul: Greenhaven Press, 1985), 15–42.

21. Ted Guy, "The Doomsday Blueprints," *Time*, August 10, 1992, 32–34.

22. A number of incidents and mishaps have occurred in the UK involving American nuclear planes, dating as far back as the 1950s. But since the UK has an Official Secrets Act that allows the government of the day to operate in secret, information about such matters must be secured through utilization of the Freedom of Information Act in the U.S. Finally, in 1996, the Ministry of Defense, after prodding by the Campaign for Freedom of Information in the UK, admitted to 20 nuclear incidents since 1960 but assured the public that none involved the release of radioactive material. Whether one should trust the credibility of a government that often hides behind closed doors or believe journalist I.F. Stone's maxim that "all governments are run by liars" is the reader's choice.

23. "April 26, 1986. Chernobyl. The World's Worst Nuclear Disaster," at http://www.chernobyl.com.ua. Also see Holly Stratts, "Chernobyl: Aftermath of a Catastrophe," *Villanova Magazine* 11, no. 4 (Fall 1996): 26. Also see the book by Grigori Medvedev, the chief engineer at Chernobyl at the time of the explosion, *The Truth About Chernobyl* (New York: Basic Books, 1991) where Medvedev not only provides an insider's description and analysis of what happened, but also claims that there had been 11 accidents in the Soviet Union and 12 in the U.S. involving nuclear reactors that provided data that could have predicted the disaster at Chernobyl.

24. The material on the Fukushima Daiichi disaster come from the following sources: "Fukushima Daiichi Nuclear Accident," Nuclear Energy Agency, March 8, 2013, http://www.oecd-nea.org/fukushima/; "Fukushima Daini Nuclear Power Plant," http://en.wikipedia.org/wiki/Fukushima_Daini_Nuclear_Power_Plant; and "Fukushima Daiichi Site: Cesium-137 Is 200 Times Greater Than at Chernobyl Accident," Salem-News.com, May 7, 2012, http://salem-news.com/articles/may072012/fukushima-reality.php.

25. Martin Fackler, "Leaks Into Pacific Persist at Japan Nuclear Plant," *The New York Times*, August 7, 2013, A6.

26. The phrase "survival of the fittest" came from 19th-century philosopher Herbert Spencer's work *Principles of Biology* (1864) after reading Charles Darwin. Spencer's theory of social evolution was raised in the U.S. Supreme Court case, *Lochner v. New York*, 198 U.S. 45 (1905), which involved a law limiting the number of hours a baker could work during the week. The court majority struck down the law but in his dissent, Justice Oliver Wendell Holmes wrote: "The Fourteenth Amendment does not enact Mr. Herbert Spencer's Social Statics."

27. See Gregory A. Waller, "Re-placing *The Day After*," *Cinema Journal* 26, no. 3 (Spring 1987): 3–20.

Notes 353

28. The film had a considerable budget in the $110–115 million range but worldwide took in over $378 million. It seems like the author is the only one who didn't like it.
29. James Hoge's review of Graham Allison' book, *Nuclear Terrorism* (New York: Henry Holt & Co., 2004) in *The New York Times Book Review*, September 5, 2004, sec. 7, 8.
30. See "Warheads Taken from Romanian Train," BBC, July 18, 2011, sec. Europe, http://www.bbc.co.uk/news/world-europe-14189205; and Alina Wolfe-Murray, "64 Missile Warheads Stolen from Romanian Train," DeseretNews.com, July 18, 2011, http://www.deseretnews.com/article/700152554/64-missile-warheads-stolen-from-Romanian-train.html.
31. See Carl Boogs and Tom Pollard, "Hollywood and the Spectacle of Terrorism," http://www.tandfonline.com/doi/full/10.1080/07393140600856151 (accessed April 17, 2013).
32. See David Gritten, "Spooks Stuck in a Time Warp," *The Telegraph*, August 3, 2002 http://www.telegraph.co.uk/culture/film/3580908/Spooks-stuck-in-a-time-warp.html. The film did well, grossing over $100 million in the U.S.
33. Jack G. Shaheen, *Reel Bad Arabs: How Hollywood Vilifies a People* (New York: Interlink Publishing Group, 2001). An answer to Shaheen is in Mark Whittington's article, "Does Hollywood Vilify Arab Terrorists?" May 1, 2008, http://voices.yahoo.com/does-hollywood-vilify-arab-terrorists-1429363.html?cat=40.
34. Quoted in Broderick, *Nuclear Movies*, 1.
35. Paul Boyer, *By the Bomb's Early Light*, 183. The poll participants were given four choices: (a) should not have used the bomb, (b) approved dropping both bombs, (c) should have dropped more bombs, and (d) should have dropped one somewhere (presumably over water) to impress Japanese and then use over land if the Japanese failed to surrender.
36. Quoted in Strada, "Kaleidoscopic Nuclear Images of the Fifties," 182.
37. Cited in Philip Taubman, *The Partnership: Five Cold Warriors and Their Quest to Ban the Bomb* (New York: HarperCollins Publishers, 2012).
38. See *The New York Times*, September 11, 1996, A5; and "Nuclear Testing," CTBTO Preparatory Commission, http://www.ctbto.org/nuclear-testing/ (accessed April 15, 2013). The U.S. and China signed the treaty but have yet to ratify it, while India, Pakistan, and North Korea refused to sign it.
39. http://www.un.org/en/members/growth.shtml (accessed August 8, 2013).
40. Both countries have stockpiles of operational and non-operational nuclear weapons. According to the Arms Control Association, "Nuclear Weapons: Who Has What at a Glance," November 2012, http://www.armscontrol.org/print/2566, the Russians have approximately 1,499 deployed strategic warheads and another 1,022 nondeployed strategic warheads, plus some 2,000 tactical nuclear warheads. The U.S., meanwhile, has approximately 5,113 nuclear warheads, including tactical, strategic and nondeployed, with an estimated 500 tactical nuclear warheads (accessed April 17, 2013).
41. Reported in *The New York Times*, July 7, 2009, 1.
42. *The New York Times*, Sunday Review Editorial, October 30, 2011, 10; and news story in *The New York Times*, May 16, 2012, A4.
43. See Bill Keller, "The Thinkable" *The New York Times Magazine*, May 4, 2003, sec. 6, 48–53ff; and William Broad, "Facing a Second Nuclear Age," *The New York Times*, August 3, 2003, sec. 4, 1, 12.
44. The analysis is from Lawrence Wright, "The Double Game," *The New Yorker*, May 16, 2011, http://www.newyorker.com/reporting/2011/05/16/110516_fact__wright (accessed April 17, 2013).
45. David Williams, "Pakistan to Overtake Britain as World's Fifth Largest Nuclear Power," *Mail Online*, February 21, 2011, http://www.dailymail.co.uk/news/article-1359231/Pakistan-overtake-Britain-worlds-fifth-largest-nuclear-power.html.
46. See "North Korea's Nuclear Tests," BBC, February 12, 2013, http://www.bbc.co.uk/news/world-asia-17823706; "North Korea Nuclear Programme," BBC, April 2, 2013, http://www.bbc.co.uk/news/

world-asia-pacific-11813699; and Sung-Yoon Lee, "Why North Korea's Rocket Mattered," *The New York Times* Op-Ed, April 14, 2012, A17.

47. The material on Iran comes from Seymour M. Hersh, "Iran and the Bomb," *The New Yorker*, June 6, 2011, 30–35; and Rick Gladstone and Alan Cowell, "Iran's President Unfazed in Parliamentary Grilling," *The New York Times*, March 14, 2012, http://www.nytimes.com/2012/03/15/world/middleeast/iran-ahmadinejad-questioned-before-parliament-majlis.html?pagewanted=all.

48. See Avner Cohen, *Israel and the Bomb* (New York: Columbia University Press, 1998).

49. Fredrik Dahl, "Iran Has Enough Uranium for 5 Bombs: expert," May 26, 2012, http://www.infowars.com/iran-has-enough-uranium-for-5-bombs-expert/ (accessed April 17, 2013).

50. Ron Rosenbaum, *How the End Begins: The Road to a Nuclear World War III* (New York: Simon & Schuster, 2011).

51. Henry A. Kissinger, "Our Nuclear Nightmare," *Newsweek* 153, no. 7 (February 16, 2009): 40–42.

52. See Taubman, *The Partnership: Five Cold Warriors and Their Quest to Ban the Bomb*. Besides Kissinger, the other Cold War warriors included Sidney Drell, Sam Nunn, Bill Perry, and George Schultz.

## Chapter 12. Hollywood, Race, and Obama: Feel-Good Racism

1. Roger Fristoe, "Asian Images in Film Introduction," http://www.tcm.com/this-month/article/196827%7C0/Race-Hollywood-Asian-Images-in-Film-Tuesdays-Thursdays-in-June-.html (accessed April 19, 2013).

2. http://en.wikipedia.org/wiki/Sessue_Hayakawa (accessed August 9, 2013).

3. The material on Oscar Micheaux and his films come from Patrick McGilligan, *Oscar Micheaux: The Great and Only* (New York: Harper Collins, 2007), and Carrie Golus, "Doc Films Screening pre-1950s 'Race Films' that Students will be Discussing in Seminar," *Chicago Chronicle* 21, no 7 (2002), http://chronicle.uchicago.edu/020110/racefilms.shtml. Micheaux did get his star on the Hollywood Walk of Fame in 1987.

4. The material on Robeson comes largely from "Paul Robeson, Jr.," *Wikipedia*, last modified June 13, 2012, http://en.wikipedia.org/wiki/Paul_Robeson_Jr; "Paul Robeson, a Brief Biography," Computer Professionals for Social Responsibility—Chicago Chapter, http://.www.cpsr.cs.uchicago.edu/robeson/bio.html (accessed July 15, 2009); and from a documentary on Robeson, televised over WPSX-3, Penn State University.

5. "Buffalo Soldier," *Wikipedia*, last modified March 19, 2013, http://en.wikipedia.org/w/index.php?title=Buffalo_Soldier&oldid=545379167.

6. 347 U.S. 483 (1954). In the follow-up case, *Brown v. Board of Education II*, 349 U.S. 294 (1955), the Court dictated that its desegregation order was to be implemented "with all deliberate speed."

7. The material on Poitier comes mainly from his memoir, *The Measure of a Man* (New York: HarperCollins, 2000); an article by Marilyn Milloy, "Sidney Poitier," in *AARP*, Sept/Oct. 2008, 38–42ff; and information on him at "Sidney Poitier," *Wikipedia*, last modified April 13, 2013, http://en.wikipedia.org/wiki/Sidney_Poitier.

8. The material on Lee comes from "Spike Lee Filmography," *Wikipedia*, last modified April 17, 2013, http://en.wikipedia.org/wiki/Spike_Lee_filmography.

9. The story played in the press and media for weeks. Here are several sources: *The New York Times*, July 24, 2009, 1, July 31, A10; *The New York Times Magazine*, August 2, 2009, 11; and *The New York Post*, July 27, 2009, 15.

10. The material on the Trayvon Martin-George Zimmerman incident has been extensive. A good summary covering the first year of the case can be found at http://www.cnn.com/2013/02/25/justice/florida-zimmerman-5-things, February 26, 2013.

11. In 2012, Florida was among two dozen states that had enacted such a law, which permits citizens to act, even with deadly force, if they believe their lives are threatened. Florida's "stand your ground" law is

explained at http://www.ehow.com/about_4577787_florida-selfdefense-laws.html. The term is "stand and defend" in some states, "stand your ground" in others. Regardless of the language used, these laws provide grounds for killing someone in self-defense.

12. *The New York Times* followed the story for days; see reports on November 29, 2012, A14; December 1, 2012, A16; and December 15, 2012, A11. It should be noted that the "stand and defend" law is not an absolute defense. In another case where a married woman fired a shot at the ceiling in her home for fear of her husband who had threatened her, the trial judge refused to accept it. See http://www.cbsnews.com/8301-504083_162-57434757-504083/fla-woman-marissa-alexander-gets-20-years-for-warning-shot-did-she-stand-her-ground, May 15, 2012.

13. http://www.hlntv.com/article/2013/07/15/jordan-davis-michael-dunn-zimmerman-trayvon-martin (accessed August 10, 2013).

14. Thomas Powell, *The Persistence of Racism in America* (Lanham, MD: University Press of America, 1992). Professor Powell's book deserves a wider audience.

15. Reported in *The New York Times*, December 13, 2012, A17.

16. See "54th Regiment Massachusetts Volunteer Infantry," *Wikipedia*, last modified 17 April 2013, http://en.wikipedia.org/wiki/54th_Massachusetts_Volunteer_Infantry

17. Thomas Powell, "Feel-Good Racism," *The New York Times*, May 24, 1992, E11.

18. William H. Chafe, "*Mississippi Burning*," in Mark C. Carnes, ed., *Past Imperfect* (New York: Henry Holt & Co., 1995).

19. 388 U.S. 1 (1967). The Lovings lived in Virginia in 1959 in violation of the state's anti-miscegenation law. They pleaded guilty and received a one-year sentence that they could avoid if they left Virginia and did not return for 25 years. They did leave the state but returned in 1963 to challenge the law.

20. See Michael J. Rosenfeld, "The Steady Rise of Non-traditional Romantic Unions," Council on Contemporary Families, March 8, 2007, http://www.contemporaryfamilies.org/marriage-partnership-divorce/unions.html.

21. Michael Oher, *I Beat the Odds: From Homelessness to "The Blind Side" and Beyond* (New York: Gotham Books, 2011).

22. Ibid., xv.

23. Melissa Anderson, "Saintly White People Do the Saving in *The Blind Side*," November 17, 2009, http://www.villagevoice.com/2009-11-17/film/saintly-white-people-do-the-saving-in-the-blind-side/(accessed September 26, 2012).

24. *The New York Times*, Arts & Leisure, February 12, 2012, 13.

25. Nicole Sperling, "Black leaders Give '*The Help*' a Hand in Marketing," *Los Angeles Times*, August 9, 2011, http://articles.latimes.com/2011/aug/09/business/la-fi-ct-help-marketing-20110809.

26. http://latimesblogs.latimes.com/movies/2011/12/african-american-critics-tree-of-life-best-film-2011.html, December 12, 2011.

27. "An Open Statement to the Fans of *The Help*," Association of Black Women Historians, http://www.abwh.org/index.php?option=com_content&view=article&id=2:open-statement-the-help (accessed February 15, 2012).

28. 163 U.S.537 (1896).

29. John McWhorter, "*The Help* Isn't Racist, Its Critics Are," *The New Republic* online, August 17, 2011, http://www.newrepublic.com/article/film/93779/the-help-black-racism#.

30. Negro Nurse, "More Slavery at the South," *The Independent*, January 25, 1912, reprinted at http://docsouth.unc.edu/fpn/negnurse/negnurse.html.

31. The film was written and directed by Anayansi Prado and distributed in 2005.

32. Maggie Galehouse, "Maids Step Out of the Shadows," *The Houston Chronicle*, August 23, 2011, http://www.chron.com/life/article/Maids-step-out-of-the-shadows-1798874.php, and originally found at "A Critical Review of the Novel *The Help*" (blog), http://acriticalreviewofthehelp.wordpress.com/2011/10/23/who-make-up-todays-help-in-america/.

33. *A Stained White Radiance* (New York: Pocket Books, 1992).

34. Owen Gleiberman, "Is '*The Help*' a Condescending Movie for White Liberals? Actually, the Real Condescension Is Calling It That," Inside Movies, *Entertainment Weekly*, August 14, 2011, http://insidemovies.ew.com/2011/08/14/is-the-help-a-movie-for-white-liberals/.

35. Kirk auditioned other white actresses, including Natalie Wood, for the Kohner role but not one black or biracial actress. See Sam Staggs, *Born to Be Hurt: The Untold Story of "Imitation of Life"* (New York: St. Martin's Press, 2009).

36. Ibid., 22. This may seem like a minute point but Moore, who stole the movie, was paid $5,550 for her role, while Turner's wardrobe alone cost $23,645. Does that fact tell you anything?

37. "I Have a Dream" speech by Martin Luther King, Jr. at the Lincoln Memorial, August 28, 1963, http://www.chicagonow.com/tween-us/2013/08/sharing-martin-luther-king-jr-s-i-have-a-dream-speech-with-tweens-and-teens/ (accessed August 28, 2013).

38. Stacy L. Smith, Marc Choueiti, and Stephanie Gall, "Asymmetrical Academy Awards® 2: Another Look at Gender in Best Picture Nominated films from 1977 to 2010," (Annenberg School for Communication & Journalism, USC, White Paper, 2011).

39. Leonard Maltin, *Leonard Maltin's Movie Guide* (New York: Penguin Books, 2009).

40. The story appeared in *The New York Times*, September 13, 2012, C1. Not long after, a controversy developed over the casting; see http://www.huffingtonpost.com/2012/11/20/zoe-saldana-nina-simone-biopic-casting-controversy_n_2165356.html.

## Chapter 13. Hollywood and Women: Cracks in the Celluloid Ceiling

1. In the 3rd edition, the author used the word "gender" rather than women." But since gender refers to the social and cultural roles associated with their sex, the term has been changed to "women" in this 4th edition. Thanks to Harry M. Benshoff and Sean Griffin, whose book *America on Film*, 2nd ed. (West Sussex, UK: Blackwell Publishing Ltd, 2009) made the word usage clearer.

2. See Jeanine Basinger, *A Woman's View: How Hollywood Spoke to Women 1930–1960* (Hanover, NH: University Press of New England, 1993); and Molly Haskell, *From Reverence to Rape: The Treatment of Women in the Movies*, 2nd ed. (Chicago: The University of Chicago Press, 1987).

3. See Karen Ward Maher, *Women Filmmakers in Early Hollywood* (Baltimore: The Johns Hopkins University Press, 2006).

4. See Cari Beauchamp, *Without Lying Down: Frances Marion and the Powerful Women of Early Hollywood* (Berkeley: University of California Press, 1997); and Benshoff and Griffin, *America on Film*, chapter 10.

5. See Benshoff and Griffin, *America on Film*, chapter 10.

6. Cari Beauchamp, *Without Lying Down*.

7. See Beverle Houston, "Missing in Action: Notes on Dorothy Arzner," *Wide Angle* 6, no 3 (1934): 24–31.

8. Judy's speech is reported at "*Dance, Girl, Dance* (1940): Quotes," IMDb, accessed July 30, 2012, http://www.imdb.com/title/tt0032376/quotes.

9. See Alice Tynan, "The Silenced Majority—Women in Early Hollywood," November 20, 2005, http://www.myspace.com/kalikala0122/blog/62847229 (accessed April 25, 2013).

10. Benshoff and Griffin, *America on Film*, chapter 10.

11. The material on Platt came from "Polly Platt," *Fandango*, accessed April 22, 2013, http://www.fandango.com/pollyplatt/biographies/p106651; while the material on Steel came from her obituary at http://www.

independent.co.uk/news/obituaries/obituary-dawn-steel-1290471.html, December 24, 1997 (accessed April 24, 2013).

12. The information on Lansing comes from "Sherry Lansing," *Wikipedia*, last modified March 17, 2013, http://www.en.wikipedia.org/wiki/Sherry_Lansing; and Guylaine Cadorette, "Trade Lists 100 Most Powerful Women," December 3, 2002, http://www.hollywood.com/news/brief/1701360/trade-lists-100-most-powerful-women?page=all (accessed April 25, 2013).

13. The material on Ziskin comes from "Laura Ziskin," *Wikipedia*, last modified February 26, 2013, http://en.wikipedia.org/wiki/Laura_Ziskin; and on Lucy Fisher from http://articles.latimes.com/1995-10-19/business/fi-58845_1_sony-pictures (accessed April 26, 2013). Four years later Fisher went on to join her husband's Sony-based production company. Also see "The 10 Most Powerful Women in Television," May 16, 2011, http://www.adweek.com/news/television/10-most-powerful-women-television-131635 (accessed April 26, 2013).

14. See Nancy Hass, "Hollywood's New Old Girls' Network," April 24, 2005, http://www.nytimes.com/2005/04/24/movies/24hass.html?_r=0. Also see Mollie Gregory's book *Women Who Run the Show* (New York: St. Martin's Press, 2002) for an account of the rise of women in the Hollywood workplace since the 1970s.

15. "Academy Award-Nominated Movies Lack Females, Racial Diversity," *USC Annenberg News*, February 22, 2012, http://annenberg.usc.edu/News%20and%20events/News/120222SmithGender.aspx.

16. In an article by Denise and William Bielby, "Women and Men in Film: Gender Inequality among Writers in a Culture Industry," *Gender & Society* 10, no.3 (June 1996): 248–70, the authors make the case that in contemporary Hollywood the screenwriters are 80 percent male.

17. Alexander Huls, "12 Female Directors Who Should Have Been Nominated for Oscars," January 14, 2013, http://flavorwire.com/363078/12-female-directors-who-should-have-been-nominated-for-oscars (accessed August 27, 2013).

18. Reported by Melissa Silverstein, "Women Directors Are More Successful in the Indie World," September 5, 2012, http://blogs.indiewire.com/womenandhollywood/women-directors-are-way-more-successful-in-the-indie-world.

19. Carrie Rickey, "Female Directors Gain Ground, Slowly," *The New York Times*, Arts & Leisure, January 13, 2013, 17.

20. Jennifer E. Manning and Ida A. Brudnick, Congressional Research Service, "Women in the United States Congress, 1917–2013," September 26, 2013, 102-03.

21. Tali Mendelberg and Christopher F. Karpowitz, "More Women, but Not Nearly Enough," *The New York Times*, Op-Ed, November 9, 2012, A27. But one area where women may influence policy concerns sexual abuse in the military. In 2013, seven women sat on the Senate Armed Services Committee that will almost certainly make changes in present Pentagon policy regarding sexual abuse. See Jennifer Steinhauer, "Women in the Senate Gain Strength in Rising Numbers," *The New York Times*, June 3, 2013, A1 and also http://www.senate.gov/general/committee_membership/committee_memberships_SSAS.htm (accessed August 12, 2013).

22. Rickey, "Female Directors Gain Ground, Slowly," 17.

23. Stacy L. Smith and Crystal Allene Cook, "Gender Stereotypes: An Analysis of Popular Films and TV," Annenberg School for Communication, USC, White Paper, 2011, http://www.thegeenadavisinstitute.org/research (accessed March 8, 2012).

24. The quote is at *USA Today*, Weekend, April 22–24, 2009, p. 1. But see Dr. Smith's research in Stacy L. Smith and Marc Choueiti, "Gender Inequality in Cinematic Content? A Look at Females on Screen & Behind-the-Camera in Top-Grossing 2008 Films," Annenberg School for Communication & Journalism, USC, White Paper, 2008. For more on hypersexualization of women in film, see Robin H. Pugh Yi and Craig T. Dearfield, "The Status of Women in the U.S. Media 2012," Women's Media Center, White Paper, 2012, http://www.womensmediacenter.com (accessed March 5, 2012).

25. Rita Moreno, *Rita Moreno: A Memoir* (New York: Penguin Group, 2013). In addition to the stereotyping and often humiliating roles, Moreno describes acts of sexual abuse during filming where her male costars would run their hands over her body.

26. See "Katherine Hepburn," *Wikipedia*, last modified April 17, 2013, http://en.wikipedia.org/wiki/Katherine_Hepburn.

27. The background material on Jenson, the legal case, and the film come from http://www.callsam.com/the-bernstein-advantage/legal-resource-center/important-legal-news/movie-qnorth-courtryq-how-a-lawsuit-made-a-difference (accessed April 26, 2013) and from the book by Clara Bingham and Laura Leedy Gansler, *Class Action: The Story of Lois Jensen and the Landmark Case that Changed Sexual Harassment Law* (New York: Doubleday, 2002). The case is at *Jensen v. Eveleth Taconite Co., 61 FEP Cases 1252 (D. Minn.)*.

28. 130 F.3d 1287 (8th Circuit Court of Appeals, 1997). What this court did was to overturn an initial award of $10,000 to each plaintiff and order a new trial. Before that trial began, however, Eveleth Mines settled for $3.5 million to the 15 plaintiffs.

29. The statistics on both marriage and divorce are at "U.S. Divorce Statistics," *Divorce Magazine.com*, http://www.divorcemag.com/statistics/statsUS.shtml (accessed August 22, 2009).

30. The facts of the case come from various sources: "Cheryl Araujo," *Wikipedia*, last modified March 12, 2013, http://en.wikipedia.org/wiki/Cheryl_Araujo; Lynn S. Chancer, "New Bedford, Massachusetts, March 6, 1983–March 22, 1984: The 'Before and After' of a Group Rape," *Gender and Society* 1, no. 3 (Sept. 1987): 239–260, http://www.d.umn.edu/cla/faculty/jhamlin/3925/Readings/newBedford.pdf (accessed April 26, 2013); and Janet Maslin, "Sex Scenes: Handle with Utmost Care," *The New York Times*, October 16, 1988, http://www.nytimes.com/1988/10/16/movies/film-view-sex-scenes-handle-with-utmost-care.html (accessed April 26, 2013).

31. Ernest F. Norden, "Portuguese Americans," http://www.everyculture.com/multi/Pa-Sp/Portuguese-Americans.html (accessed August 12, 2013).

32. According to Rose Kreider at the Census Bureau, government family statistics may show the race of the child but not the race of the parent. That reduces statistics to a guessing game. Current estimates from the 2008 Population Survey indicate that there are roughly 11 million black children in the U.S. With 5,791,000 living with their mothers only, and since most children live with same-race mothers, it looks like somewhere around 50 percent of black children live with their mothers and not their fathers. Email from Dr. Kreider to author, September 1, 2009. Other data on this subject estimate 45 to 55% live with their mothers only. But this is a guesstimate.

33. The statistics come from "Sexual Harassment in the Workplace," Sexualharassmentlawfirms.com, http://www.sexualharassmentlawfirms.com/SexualHarassmentWorkplace.cfm (accessed August 24, 2009).

34. The Miller-Plame affair dominated the media for several years. Several books and another film, *Fair Game*, based on Plame's memoir, presented both sides of the story. The author's synopsis was culled from several sources, including *The New York Times* and websites like SourceWatch and *Wikipedia*. See "Judith Miller," SourceWatch, The Center for Media and Democracy, last modified June 3, 2012, http://www.sourcewatch.org/index.php?title=Judith_Miller; and "Biography," JudithMiller.com, http://www.judithmiller.com/about (accessed March 3, 2012); "Plame Affair," *Wikipedia*, last modified February 25, 2013, http://en.wikipedia.org/wiki/Plame_affair; and "Judith Miller," *Wikipedia*, last modified April 10, 2013, http://en.wikipedia.org/wiki/Judith_Miller_(journalist).

35. Joseph Wilson, "What I Didn't Find in Africa," July 6, 2003, http://www.nytimes.com/2003/07/06/opinion/what-i-didn-t-find-in-africa.html?pagewanted=all&src=pm (accessed April 26, 2013).

36. "Judith Miller," SourceWatch.

37. 408 U.S. 665 (1972).

38. U.S. Court of Appeals for the District of Columbia Circuit, In re Grand Jury Subpoena, Judith Miller No. 04-3138 (2005).

## Notes

39. Miller was eventually allowed to name I. Lewis Libby, Vice President Cheney's chief of staff, as her source. A year later, Richard Armitage, former deputy secretary of state, admitted that he had been the original source of the leak to Washington Post reporter Bob Woodward and columnist Robert Novak. *The New York Times*, September 8, 2006, A22.
40. See http://www.elle.com/pop-culture/reviews/reel-world-women-power-in-hollywood-514517, November 8, 2010 (accessed April 26, 2013). Recently the Academy elected director Lisa Cholodenko and producer Kathleen Kennedy to its board of governors. Reported at http://blogs.indiewire.com/womenand hollywood (accessed July 22, 2012).
41. See Melissa Silverstein, "How Can Women Gain More Influence in Hollywood? A NY Times Forum Debate," *Women and Hollywood* (blog), Indiewire, August 15, 2012, http://blogs.indiewire.com/women andhollywood/how-can-women-gain-more-influence-in-hollywood-a-ny-times-forum-debate.
42. Ximera Ramirez, "13 Ways Females are Underrepresented, Stereotyped and Sexualized on Screen," care2.com, November 24, 2012, http://www.care2.com/causes/13-ways-females-are-underrepresented-stereotyped-and-sexualized-on-screen.html.

## Chapter 14. Epilogue: Is There a Future for Political Films in Hollywood?

1. This analysis comes from several sources: John Lippman, "Studios Summer Schooling," *The Wall Street Journal*, September 3, 2004, w8; Joe Bieerman, "A Couple of Thoughts on the NY Times (Magazine) Articles on the State of Global Cinema," http://people.umass.edu/~comm342/mb.html, November 15, 2004 (accessed April 6, 2013); Aabha Rathee, "Should Hollywood Studios Focus on the Foreign Audiences?" Wall St. Cheat Sheet, April 5, 2012, http://www.wallstcheatsheet.com/stocks/should-hollywood-studios-focus-on-the-foreign-audience.html/; and Louise Story, "Michigan Town Woos Hollywood but Ends Up with a Bit Part," *The New York Times*, December 3, 2012, http://www.nytimes.com/2012/12/04/us/when-hollywood-comes-to-town.html
2. The data came from "Major Film Studio," *Wikipedia*, last modified April 13, 2013, http://en.wikipedia.org/wiki/Major_film_studio. The market share percentages are from 2012.
3. Ibid.
4. Ibid.
5. The material on the Weinsteins, Miramax, and the Weinstein Company came from "Harvey Weinstein," *Wikipedia*, last modified April 25, 2012, http://en.wikipedia.org/wiki/Harvey_Weinstein.
6. Box Office Mojo reported that the film cost an estimated $70 million but earned a worldwide gross of $139 million during its first two weeks. Eventually the film grossed $321 million worldwide. See http://boxofficemojo.com/movies/?id=inglouriousbasterds.htm (accessed April 27, 2013).
7. Joshua Marston, "Get a Hollywood Studio to Green Light Your Picture, In 29 Easy Steps," *Planet Money* (blog), National Public Radio, November 12, 2012, http://www.npr.org/blogs/money/2012/11/08/164690843/get-a-hollywood-studio-to-green-light-your-picture-in-29-easy-steps.
8. Reported in *The New York Times*, July 2, 2009, B1.
9. http://www.imdb.com/title/tt1210166/?ref_=sr_1 (accessed April 29, 2013).
10. Michael Cieply and Brooks Barnes, "DreamWorks: A Studio's Real-Life Drama," *The New York Times*, January 30, 2012, B1.
11. "*Lincoln*," IMDb, http://www.imdb.com/title/tt0443272/companycredits?ref_=tt_dt_co (accessed April 10, 2013). The financing was complicated because it came at the beginning of the recession. DreamWorks received a $325 million loan from JP Morgan Chase & Co and an equal amount from the Mumbai-based Reliance Big Entertainment. Then DreamWorks split the film's expenses with partners Participant Media and 20th Century Fox. The Disney Company lent $200 million toward distribution. And there might have been one or two other investors. See Michael White, "Spielberg's '*Lincoln*' Risks Losses for DreamWorks

12. Story by Nicholas Kulish and Michael Cieply, "Around the World in One Movie: Film Financing's Global future," *The New York Times*, December 6, 2011, 1.

13. See Helen Pidd, "Sci-fi blockbuster *Looper* achieves Chinese box office first," *The Guardian*, October 1, 2012, http://www.guardian.co.uk/film/2012/oct/01/looper-sci-fi-blockbuster-china (accessed April 29, 2013).

14. Lauren A.E. Schuker, "Plot Change: Foreign Forces Transform Hollywood Films," *The Wall Street Journal*, August 2, 2010, http://online.wsj.com/article/SB10001424052748704913304575371394036766312.html.

15. Glenn Harlan Reynolds, "The Hollywood Tax Story They Won't Tell at the Oscars," *The Wall Street Journal*, February 23–24, 2013, A11. While Michigan scaled back its incentive program, Iowa ended its and several other states are having second thoughts.

16. Emanuel Levy, *Cinema of Outsiders: The Rise of American Independent Film* (New York: New York University Press, 1999).

17. The admission data comes from http://cinema.usc.edu, courtesy of Alicia Woods, Communications & Public Relations Department at USC.

18. See Ben Sisario, "In the Bronx, a Film School with a Ghetto Name," *The New York Times*, September 13, 2007, http://www.nytimes.com/2007/09/13/movies/13ghet.html, and Larry Rohter, "A Bronx Film School Tale," *The New York Times*, September 5, 2010, http://www.nytimes.com/2010/09/06/movies/06ghetto.html (both accessed April 29, 2013).

19. See "Festival Program," Sundance Film Festival, http://www.sundance.org/festival/festival-program (accessed April 12, 2013).

20. *Burstyn v. Wilson*, 343 U.S. 495 (1952).

21. Brooks Barnes, "Direct-to-DVD Releases Shed Their Loser Label," *The New York Times*, January 28, 2008, C1.

22. Lurker, "Movies Released straight to DVD," *Linked in Hollywood* (blog), March 14, 2011, http://linkedinhollywood.com/2011/03/14/movies-released-straight-to-dvd/.

23. Michael Cieply, "States Underwrite Films, Some in Narrowest Release," *The New York Times*, March 19, 2009, 1.

24. Jericho Parms, "From Box Office to Ballot Box" *The Independent*, November 1, 2008, http://www.independent-magazine.org/08/10/box-office-ballot-box (accessed May 1, 2013).

25. http://elections.nytimes.com/2012/campaign-finance (accessed May 1, 2013). At the end, the Obama campaign had raised $80 million more than the Romney campaign.

26. See Ariel Kaminer, "Star Commentator Is Out as Christian College President After Scandal," *The New York Times*, October 19, 2012, A24. D'Souza was president of King's College, a conservative Christian institution, when he was spotted at a South Carolina motel with a woman not his wife. The media reports led D'Souza to resign.

27. http://www.boxofficemojo.com/movies/?id=bestexoticmarigoldhotel.htm (accessed May 1, 2013).

28. Brooks Barnes, "Save My Blockbuster!" *The New York Times*, Arts & Leisure, June 30, 2013, 1. The economic pull of global markets is so strong that even failures cannot halt the overseas trend. Even though 3-D movies have not fared well at home, the studios are committed to making some five dozen more. See Michael Cieply, "Appeal of 3-D Wanes, but New Releases Are Still Planned," *The New York Times*, August 12, 2013, B1.

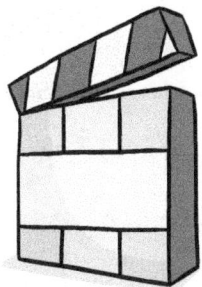

# Selected Bibliography

## Books

Allison, Graham. *Nuclear Terrorism*. New York: Henry Holt & Co., 2004.

Alperovitz, Gar. *The Decision to Use the Atomic Bomb*. New York: Alfred A. Knopf, 1995.

Alt, Betty, and Silvia Folts. *Weeping Violins: The Gypsy Tragedy in Europe*. Kirksville, MO: Thomas Jefferson University Press, 1996.

Anderegg, Michael, ed. *Inventing Vietnam: The War in Film and Television*. Philadelphia: Temple University Press, 1991.

Arany, Lynne, Tom Dyja, and Gary Goldsmith. *The Reel List*. New York: Dell Publishing, 1995.

Asimow, Michael, and Shannon Mader. *Law and Popular Culture*. New York: Peter Lang Publishing, 2004.

Aufderheide, Pat. "Vietnam: Good Soldiers." In *Seeing Through Movies*, edited by Mark Crispin Miller, 81–111. New York: Pantheon Books, 1990.

Bach, Steven. *Leni: The Life & Work of Leni Riefenstahl*. New York: Alfred A. Knopf, 2007.

Barsam, Richard M. "From Nonfiction Film: A Critical History." In *Film Theory and Criticism*, 3rd edition, edited by Gerald Mast and Marshall Cohen, 583–85. New York: Oxford University Press, 1985.

Barsam, Richard M. *Non-Fiction Film*. Revised edition. Bloomington: Indiana University Press, 1992.

Bart, Peter, and Peter Guber. *Shoot Out*. New York: The Berkley Publishing Group, 2002.

Basinger, Jeanine. *A Woman's View: How Hollywood Spoke to Women 1930–1960*. Hanover, NH: University Press of New England, 1993.

Basinger, Jeanine. *I Do and I Don't*. New York: Alfred A. Knopf, 2013.

Basinger, Jeanine. *The World War II Combat Film*. New York: Columbia University Press, 1986.

Beauchamp, Cari. *Without Lying Down: Frances Marion and the Powerful Women of Early Hollywood*. Berkeley: University of California Press, 1997.

Benjamin, Walter. "The Work of Art in the Age of Mechanical Reproduction." In *Illuminations: Essays and Reflections*, edited by Hannah Arendt. New York: Schocken Books, 1968.

Benshoff, Harry M., and Sean Griffin. *America on Film*. 2nd edition. West Sussex, UK: Blackwell Publishing Ltd, 2009.

Benson, Thomas W., and Carolyn Anderson. *Reality Fictions: The Films of Frederick Wiseman*. 2nd edition. Carbondale: Southern Illinois University Press, 2002.

Bergman, Andrew. *We're in the Money*. New York: New York University Press, 1971.

Bergmann, Paul, and Michael Asimow. *Reel Justice: The Courtroom Goes to the Movies*. Kansas City: Andrews and McMeel, 1996.

Bernstein, Matthew. "Documentaphobia and Mixed Modes." In *Documenting the Documentary*, edited by Barry Keith Grant and Jeannette Sloniowski. Detroit: Wayne State University Press, 1998.

Bernstein, Walter. *Inside Out: A Memoir of the Blacklist*. Cambridge, MA: Da Capo Press, 2000.

Biberman, Herbert. *Salt of the Earth*. Boston: Beacon Press, 1965.

Bingham, Clara, and Laura Leedy Gansler. *Class Action: The Story of Lois Jensen and the Landmark Case That Changed Sexual Harassment Law*. New York: Doubleday, 2002.

Biskind, Peter. *Easy Riders, Raging Bulls: How the Sex-Drugs-and-Rock 'n' Roll Generation Saved Hollywood.* New York: Simon & Schuster, 1998.

Biskind, Peter. *Seeing Is Believing: How Hollywood Taught Us to Stop Worrying and Love the Fifties.* New York: Pantheon Books, 1983.

Black, Gregory D. *Hollywood Censored.* Cambridge, UK: Cambridge University Press, 1994.

Boot, Max. *Invisible Armies.* New York: Liveright, 2013.

Boyer, Paul. *By the Bomb's Early Light.* Chapel Hill: University of North Carolina Press, 1994.

Bradley, James. *Flags of our Fathers.* New York: Bantam Books, 2000.

Broderick, Mick. *Nuclear Movies.* Jefferson, NC: McFarland & Co., 1991.

Brokaw, Tom. *The Greatest Generation.* New York: Random House, 1998.

Brownlow, Kevin. *Behind the Mask of Innocence.* New York: Alfred A. Knopf, 1990.

Brownstein, Ronald. *The Power and the Glitter.* New York: Pantheon, 1990.

Brundage, W. Fitzhugh. *Lynching in the New South.* Urbana: University of Illinois Press, 1993.

Buhle, Paul, and Dave Wagner. *Blacklisted: The Film Lover's Guide to the Hollywood Blacklist.* New York: Palgrave Macmillan, 2003.

Buhle, Paul, and Dave Wagner. *Radical Hollywood.* New York: The New Press, 2002.

Canemaker, John. "World War II Animated Propaganda Cartoons." In Crowdus, *A Political Companion to American Film*, 496–500.

Carmichael, Deborah. "*Gabriel Over the White House.*" In *Hollywood's White House: The American Presidency in Film and History*, edited by Peter C. Rollins and John E. O'Connor, 159–79. Lexington: The University Press of Kentucky, 2003.

Carnes, Mark C. *Past Imperfect: History According to the Movies.* New York: Henry Holt & Co., 1995.

Ceplair, Larry, and Steven Englund. *The Inquisition in Hollywood.* Garden City, NY: Anchor Press/Doubleday, 1980.

Chafe, William H. "*Mississippi Burning.*" In *Past Imperfect: History According to the Movies*, edited by Mark C. Carnes, 274–77. New York: Henry Holt & Co., 1995.

Chang, Iris. *The Rape of Nanking: The Forgotten Holocaust of WWII.* New York: Basic Books, 1997.

Chaplin, Charles. *My Autobiography.* New York: Simon and Schuster, 1964.

Christensen, Terry, and Peter J. Haas. *Projecting Politics: Political Messages in American Films.* Armonk, NY: M.E. Sharpe, 2005.

Christensen, Terry. *Reel Politics.* New York: Blackwell, 1987.

Cohen, Avner. *Israel and the Bomb.* New York: Columbia University Press, 1998.

Cohen, Gerald Leonard. *Origin of the Term "Shyster."* Frankfurt: Peter Lang Publishing, 1982.

Colley, David P. *Blood for Dignity: The Story of the First Integrated Combat Unit in the U.S. Army.* New York: St. Martin's Press, 2003.

Coyne, Michael. *Hollywood Goes to Washington.* London: Reaktion Books, 2008.

Coyne, Michael. *The Crowded Prairie.* London: I.B. Tauris Publishers, 1997.

Crowdus, Gary, ed. *The Political Companion to American Film.* Chicago: Lake View Press, 1994.

Culbert, David. "Our Awkward Ally: Mission to Moscow." In *American History/American Film*, edited by John E. O'Connor and Martin A. Jackson. New York: Frederick Ungar, 1988.

Cumings, Bruce. *The Korean War.* New York: Modern Library, 2010.

Davies, Philip John. "Hollywood in Elections and Elections in Hollywood." In *American Film and Politics from Reagan to Bush Jr.*, edited by Philip John Davies and Paul Wells. Manchester, UK: Manchester University Press, 2002.

Denvir, John, ed. *Legal Reelism: Movies as Legal Texts.* Urbana: University of Illinois Press, 1996.

Dershowitz, Alan M. *The Best Defense.* New York: Vintage Books, 1983.

Dick, Bernard F. *The Star-Spangled Screen: The American World War II Film.* Revised edition. Lexington: University of Kentucky Press, 1996.

# Selected Bibliography

Diggins, John Patrick. *The Proud Decades*. New York: Norton, 1989.

Dinnerstein, Leonard. *The Leo Frank Case*. New York: Columbia University Press, 1968.

Dmytryk, Edward. *Odd Man Out: A Memoir of the Hollywood Ten*. Carbondale: Southern Illinois University Press, 1996.

Doherty, Thomas. *Pre-Code Hollywood: Sex, Immorality, and Insurrection in American Cinema*. New York: Columbia University Press, 1999.

Doherty, Thomas. *Projections of War: Hollywood, American Culture and World War II*. New York: Columbia University Press, 1993.

Dooley, Roger. *From Scarface to Scarlett: American Films in the 1930s*. New York: Harcourt Brace Jovanovich, 1981.

Evans, M. Stanton. *Blacklisted by History*. New York: Crown Forum, 2007.

Everett, Susan. *The Two World Wars, Vol. I: World War I*. Lincoln, NE: Bison Books, 1980.

Fehrenbach, T.R. *This Kind of War*. Washington, D.C.: Brassey's, Inc., 1963.

Feifer, Gregory. *The Great Gamble*. New York: Harper Collins Publishers, 2009.

Fielding, Raymond. *The March of Time, 1945–51*. New York: Oxford University Press, 1978.

Flamini, Roland. *Thalberg: The Last Tycoon and the World of MGM*. New York: Crown Publishers, 1994.

Fried, Albert. *McCarthyism: The Great American Red Scare*. New York: Oxford University Press, 1997.

Fried, Richard. *Nightmare in Red*. New York: Oxford University Press, 1990.

Gabler, Neal. *An Empire of Their Own: How the Jews Invented Hollywood*. New York: Crown Publishers, 1988.

Gabler, Neal. *Life: The Movie: How Entertainment Conquered Reality*. New York: Alfred A. Knopf, 1998.

Geertz, Clifford. *The Interpretation of Cultures*. New York: Basic Books, 1973.

Genovese, Michael. *Politics and the Cinema*. Lexington, MA: Ginn Press, 1986.

Georgakas, Dan. "Hollywood Blacklist." In *Encyclopedia of the American Left*. New York: Garland, 1990.

Georgakas, Dan, and Lenny Rubenstein, eds. *The Cineaste Interviews*. Chicago: Lake View Press, 1983.

Giglio, Ernest. *Rights, Liberties and Public Policy*. Aldershot, UK: Ashgate Publishing, 1995.

Goldberg, Robert Alan. *Enemies Within: The Culture of Conspiracy in Modern America*. New Haven, CT: Yale University Press, 2001.

Grant, Barry Keith. *Voyages of Discovery: The Cinema of Frederick Wiseman*. Urbana: University of Illinois Press, 1992.

Gregory, Mollie. *Women Who Run the Show*. New York: St. Martin's Press, 2002.

Gutman, Israel, editor in chief. *Encyclopedia of the Holocaust, vol. 4*. New York: Macmillan Publishing Co., 1990.

Halberstam, David. *The Coldest Winter: America and the Korean War*. New York: Hyperion, 2007.

Hamilton, Marybeth. *When I'm Bad, I'm Better: Mae West, Sex, and American Entertainment*. Berkeley: University of California Press, 1997.

Harmetz, Aljean. *Round Up the Usual Suspects*. New York: Hyperion, 1992.

Hart, Peter. *The Darkest Hour on the Western Front*. New York: Pegasus Books, 2009.

Harvard Nuclear Study Group. *Living with Nuclear Weapons*. New York: Bantam Books, 1983.

Hasegawa, Tsuyoshi. *Racing the Enemy: Stalin, Truman, and the Surrender of Japan*. Cambridge, MA: Harvard University Press, 2006.

Haskell, Molly. *From Reverence to Rape: The Treatment of Women in the Movies*. 2nd edition. Chicago: The University of Chicago Press, 1987.

Hearst Corporation. *The American Public, the Media and the Judicial System*. New York: Hearst Corporation, 1983.

Hirsen, James. *Tales from the Left Coast*. New York: Crown Forum, 2003.

Huchthausen, Peter. *America's Splendid Little Wars*. New York: Viking, 2003.

Isaacs, Arnold R. *The War, Its Ghosts, and Its Legacy*. Baltimore: John Hopkins University Press, 1998.

Jamesson, Richard T., ed. *They Went Thataway: Redefining Film Genres*. San Francisco: Mercury House, 1994.

Jarvie, I.C., ed., et al., *Children and the Movies: Media Influences and the Payne Fund Controversy*. New York: Cambridge University Press, 1996.

Jones, Dorothy B. "Communism and the Movies: A Study of Film Content." In *Report on Blacklisting I: Movies*, by John Cogley. New York: The Fund for the Republic, 1956.

Kane, Kathryn. "The World War II Combat Film, 1942–45." In *Handbook of American Film Genres*, edited by Wes D. Gehring, 85–6. Westport, CT: Greenwood Press, 1988.

Kaplan, Fred. *The Insurgents: David Petraeus and the Plot to Change the American Way of War*. New York: Simon & Schuster, 2013.

Keim, Albert N. *The CPS Story: An Illustrated History of Civilian Public Service*. Intercourse, PA: Good Books, 1990.

Keyishian, Harry. *Screening Politics: The Politician in American Movies, 1931–2001*. Lanham, MD: The Scarecrow Press, 2003.

Koch, Howard. *Casablanca: Script and Legend*. New York: Overlook Express, 1992.

Kohn, Stephen M. *Jailed for Peace*. Westport, CT: Greenwood Press, 1986.

Koppes, Clayton R., and Gregory D. Black. *Hollywood Goes to War*. Berkeley: University of California Press, 1987.

Krukones, Michael G. "Motion Picture Presidents of the 1930s." In *Hollywood's White House: The American Presidency in Film and History*, edited by Peter C. Rollins and John E. O'Connor. Lexington: The University Press of Kentucky, 2003.

Leff, Leonard J., and Jerold L. Simmons. *The Dame in the Kimono: Hollywood, Censorship, and the Production Code from the 1920s to the 1960s*. New York: Grove Weidenfeld, 1990.

Lenz, Timothy. *Changing Images of Law in Film & Television*. New York: Peter Lang Publishing, 2003.

Levy, Emanuel. *Cinema of Outsiders: The Rise of American Independent Film*. New York: New York University Press, 1999.

Lewis, Jon. *Hollywood v. Hard Core: How the Struggle over Censorship Saved the Modern Film Industry*. New York: New York University Press, 2000.

Ling, Bettina. *Aung San Suu Kyi: Standing Up for Democracy in Burma*. New York: The Feminist Press, 1999.

Litwack, Leon F. *Without Sanctuary: Lynching Photographs in America*. San Francisco: Twin Palms, 2000.

Litwak, Mark. *Reel Power*. London: Sedgwick & Jackson, 1987.

Lorence, James J. *The Suppression of Salt of the Earth*. Albuquerque: University of New Mexico Press, 1999.

Lovell, Hugh, and Tasile Carter. *Collective Bargaining in the Motion Picture Industry*. Berkeley: University of California Press, 1955.

Lukas, Richard C. *The Forgotten Holocaust: The Poles Under German Occupation*. Lexington: University of Kentucky Press, 1986.

Lyons, Charles. *The New Censors: Movies and the Culture Wars*. Philadelphia: Temple University Press, 1997.

Maher, Karen Ward. *Women Filmmakers in Early Hollywood*. Baltimore: The Johns Hopkins University Press, 2006.

Maisel, L. Sandy. *Political Parties and Elections in the United States*. New York: Garland Publishing, 1991.

Maltby, Richard, and Ian Craven. *Hollywood Cinema*. Cambridge: Blackwell, 1995.

Maltin, Leonard. *1997 Movie & Video Guide*. New York: Penguin Books, 1996.

Maltin, Leonard. *Leonard Maltin's Movie Guide*. New York: Penguin Books, 2009.

Maltin, Leonard. *The Great Movie Shorts*. New York: Crown Publishers, 1972.

Martin, Andrew. *Receptions of War: Vietnam in American Culture*. Norman: University of Oklahoma Press, 1993.

McGilligan, Patrick. *Oscar Micheaux: The Great and Only*. New York: Harper Collins, 2007.

Medved, Michael. *Hollywood v. America*. New York: HarperCollins, 1992.

Medvedev, Grigori. *The Truth about Chernobyl*. New York: Basic Books, 1991.

Milton, Joyce. *Tramp: The Life of Charlie Chaplin*. New York: HarperCollins, 1996.

Mitchell, Greg. *The Campaign of the Century*. New York: Random House, 1992.

## Selected Bibliography

Mitchell, Greg. *Tricky Dick and the Pink Lady: Richard Nixon vs. Helen Gahagan Douglas—Sexual Politics and the Red Scare*. New York: Random House, 1950.

Morgan, Ted. *Reds: McCarthyism in Twentieth-Century America*. New York: Random House, 2003.

Navasky, Victor S. *Naming Names*. New York: Penguin Books, 1981.

Neely, Mark C., Jr., "The Young Lincoln." In *Past Imperfect: History According to the Movies*, edited by Mark C. Carnes, 124–27. New York: Henry Holt & Company, 1995.

Ness, Immanuel, and James Ciment. *The Encyclopedia of Third Parties in America*, vol. 1. New York: M.E. Sharpe, 2000, 249–50.

Neve, Brian. *Film and Politics in America*. London: Routledge, 1992.

Nevins, Francis M. "Through the Great Depression on Horseback." In Denvir, *Legal Reelism*, 44–69.

Nichols, Bill. *Blurred Boundaries*. Bloomington: Indiana University Press, 1994.

Nielsen, Mike, and Gene Mailes. *Hollywood's Other Blacklist*. London: British Film Institute, 1995.

Nimmo, Dan. "Political Propaganda in the Movies: A Typology." In *Movies and Politics: The Dynamic Relationship*, edited by James Combs, 271–94. New York: Garland Publishing, 1993.

Norman, Elizabeth M. *We Band of Angels*. New York: Random House, 1999.

Oher, Michael. *I Beat the Odds: From Homelessness to "The Blind Side" and Beyond*. New York: The Penguin Group, 2011.

Oshinsky, David M. *A Conspiracy So Immense*. New York: Free Press, 1983.

Packer, Herbert. *The Limits of the Criminal Sanction*. Stanford: Stanford University Press, 1968.

Palmer, William J. *The Films of the Eighties*. Carbondale: Southern Illinois University Press, 1993.

Papke, David Ray. "Myth and Meaning: Francis Ford Coppola and Popular Response to the Godfather Trilogy." In Denvir, *Legal Reelism*, 3.

Perry, Richard, and Louis Perry. *A History of the Los Angeles Labor Movement*. Berkeley: University of California Press, 1963.

Persico, Joseph E. *Franklin and Lucy*. New York: Random House, 2008.

Peters, James Edward. *Arlington National Cemetery: Shrine to America's Heroes*. Arlington, VA: Woodbine House, 1986.

Poitier, Sidney. *The Measure of a Man*. New York: HarperCollins, 2000.

Powell, Thomas. *The Persistence of Racism in America*. Lanham, MD: University Press of America, 1992.

Pratt, Ray. *Projecting Paranoia*. Lawrence: University Press of Kansas, 2001.

Puttnam, David. *Movies and Money*. With Neil Watson. New York: Knopf, 1997.

Quart, Leonard. "*The Deer Hunter*: The Superman in Vietnam." In *From Hanoi to Hollywood*, edited by Linda Dittmar and Gene Michaud, 159–168. New Brunswick, NJ: Rutgers University Press, 1990.

Ramsaye, Terry *A Million and One Nights*. New York: Simon and Schuster, 1926.

Reeves, Thomas C. *The Life and Times of Senator Joe McCarthy*. New York: Stein and Day, 1982.

Reingold, Nathan. "A Footnote to History: MGM Meets the Atomic Bomb." In *American Media*, by Philip S. Cook, Douglas Goney, and Lawrence W. Lichty. Washington, DC: The Wilson Center Press, 1989.

Riordon, L. *Plunkitt of Tammany Hall*. New York: E.P. Dutton & Co., 1963.

Roberts, Randy, and Robert E. May. "You Must Remember This: The Case of Hal Wallis's *Casablanca*." In *Learning to Think Critically: Film, Myth, and American History*. New York: HarperCollins, 1993.

Robins, Robert S., and Jerrold M. Post. *Political Paranoia: The Psychopolitics of Hatred*. New Haven, CT: Yale University Press, 1997.

Robinson, David. *Chaplin: His Life and Art*. New York: McGraw-Hill, 1985.

Roche, John P. *The History and Impact of Marxist-Leninist Organizational Theory*. Cambridge, MA: Institute of Foreign Policy Analysis, 1984.

Rogin, Michael. *Ronald Reagan, the Movie*. Berkeley: University of California Press, 1988.

Rollins, Peter, and John O'Connor, eds. *Hollywood's WWI: Motion Picture Images*. Bowling Green, OH: Popular Press, 1997.

Rollins, Peter. "Hollywood's Presidents 1944–1996: The Primacy of Character." In *Hollywood's White House: The American Presidency in Film and History*, edited by Peter C. Rollins and John E. O'Connor, 251–61. Lexington: The University Press of Kentucky, 2003.

Rosenbaum, Ron. *How the End Begins: The Road to a Nuclear World War III*. New York: Simon & Schuster, 2011.

Rosenthal, Alan, ed. *Why Docudrama?* Carbondale: Southern Illinois University Press, 1999.

Ross, Murray. *Stars and Strikes*. New York: Columbia University Press, 1941.

Ross, Steven J. *Hollywood Left and Right*. New York: Oxford University Press, 2011.

Rovere, Richard. *Senator Joe McCarthy*. New York: Harcourt, Brace, 1959.

Ryan, Michael, and Douglas Kellner. *Camera Politica*. Bloomington: Indiana University Press, 1990.

Sachleben, Mark, and Kevan M. Yenerall. *Seeing the Bigger Picture*. 2nd edition. New York: Peter Lang Publishing, 2012.

Samuels, Stuart. "The Age of Conspiracy and Conformity: Invasion of the Body Snatchers (1956)." In *American History/American Film*, edited by John E. O'Connor and Martin A. Jackson, 203–17. New York: Frederick Unger, 1979.

Sanello, Frank. *Reel v. Real: How Hollywood Turns Fact into Fiction*. Lanham, New York: Taylor Trade Publishing, 2003.

Saunders, Frances Stoner. *The Cultural Cold War*. New York: The New Press, 1999.

Sayre, Nora. *Running Time: Films of the Cold War*. New York: The Dial Press, 1982.

Schapsmeier, Edward, and Frederick Schapsmeier. *Political Parties and Civic Action Groups*. Westport, CT: Greenwood Press, 1981.

Schatz, Thomas. "World War II and the Hollywood War Film." In *Refiguring Genres*, edited by Nick Browne, 103–4. Berkeley: University of California Press, 1998.

Schickel, Richard. *Schickel on Film*. New York: Morrow, 1989.

Schrems, John. *Understanding Principles of Politics and the State*. Revised edition. Lanham, MD: University Press of America, 2011.

Shaheen, Jack, ed. *Nuclear War Films*. Carbondale: Southern Illinois University Press, 1978.

Sheeler, Jim. *Final Salute*. New York: Penguin Press, 2008.

Sherwin, Richard K. *When the Law Goes Pop: The Vanishing Line Between Law and Popular Culture*. Chicago: University of Chicago Press, 2002.

Sigmund, Anna Maria. *Women of the Third Reich*. Richmond Hill, ON: NDE Publishing, 2000.

Simon, John. *Movies into Film*. New York: Dell Publishing Co., 1970.

Staggs, Sam. *Born to be Hurt: The Untold Story of "Imitation of Life."* New York: St. Martin's Press, 2009.

Steffens, Lincoln. *The Shame of the Cities*. New York: Hill & Wang, 1957.

Stinnett, Richard B. *Day of Deceit: The Truth about FDR & Pearl Harbor*. New York: Free Press, 1999.

Suid, Lawrence. "The Pentagon and Hollywood: *Dr. Strangelove*." In *American History/American Film*, edited by John E. O'Connor and Martin A. Jackson. New York: Frederick Ungar, 1988.

Swofford, Anthony. *Jarhead*. New York: Scribner & Sons, 2003.

Szumski, Bonnie, ed. *Nuclear War: Opposing Viewpoints*. St. Paul, MN: Greenhaven Press, 1985.

Taubman, Philip. *The Partnership: Five Cold Warriors and Their Quest to Ban the Bomb*. New York: HarperCollins, 2012.

Tolenay, Stewart E., and E. M. Beck. *A Festival of Violence: An Analysis of Southern Lynching, 1882–1930*. Urbana: University of Illinois Press, 1995.

Tomasulo, Frank P. "The Mass Psychology of Fascist Cinema." In *Documenting the Documentary*, edited by Barry Keith Grant and Jeannette Sloniowski. Detroit: Wayne State University Press, 1998.

Tomosulo, Frank P. "The Politics of Ambivalence: *Apocalypse Now* as Prowar and Antiwar Film." In *From Hanoi to Hollywood*, edited by Linda Dittmar and Gene Michaud, 145–158. New Brunswick, NJ: Rutgers University Press, 1990.

# Selected Bibliography

Traube, Elizabeth. *Dreaming Identities: Class, Gender and Generation in 1980s Hollywood Movies*. Boulder, CO: Westview Press, 1992.

Trimborn, Jurgen. *Leni Riefenstahl: A Life*. New York: Faber & Faber, 2007.

Turner, Frederick Jackson. *The Frontier in American History*. New York: Henry Holt & Co., 1920.

Tushnet, Mark. "Class Action: One View of Gender and Law in Popular Culture." In Denvir, *Legal Reelism*, 244–60.

Tuttle, William M., Jr. *Daddy's Gone to War*. New York: Oxford University Press, 1993.

U.S. House of Representatives, Committee on Education and Labor. *Jurisdictional Disputes in the Motion Picture Industry*. Washington, DC: Government Printing Office, 1948.

Valenti, Jack. *The Voluntary Movie Rating System*. Washington, DC: Motion Picture Association of America, 1996.

Vaughn, Stephen. *Ronald Reagan in Hollywood*. New York: Cambridge University Press, 1994.

Vieira, Mark. *Sin in Soft Focus: Pre-Code Hollywood*. New York: Harry N. Abrams, 1999.

Walzer, Michael. *Just and Unjust Wars*. 2nd edition. New York: Basic Books, 1992.

Welch, David. *Propaganda and the German Cinema, 1933–1945*. New York: Oxford University Press, 1983.

Wilson, Michael, and Deborah Silverton Rosenfelt. *Salt of the Earth*. New York: Feminist Press, 1978.

Winston, Brian. *Claiming the Real: The Documentary Film Revisited*. London: British Film Institute, 1995.

Wise, James E., Jr., and Anne Collier Rehill. *Stars in Blue: Movie Actors in America's Sea Services*. Annapolis, MD: Naval Institute Press, 1997.

Wright, Lawrence. *In the New World*. New York: Knopf, 1987.

Yenerall, Kevan M., and Christopher S. Kelley. "Shysters, Sycophants, and Sexual Deviants: The Hollywood Presidency in the 1990s." In *White House Studies Compendium*, vol. 3, edited by Robert Watson, 213–30. Hauppauge, NY: Nova Publishers, 2007.

## Articles

Asimow, Michael. "Divorce in the Movies: From the Hays Code to *Kramer v. Kramer*." *Legal Studies Forum* 24, no. 2 (2000): 221–67.

Barkun, Michael. "Conspiracy Thinking in Contemporary America." *Maxwell Perspective* (Syracuse University) 8, no. 1 (Fall 1997): 23.

Bateman, Thomas S., Tomoaki Sakano, and Mokoto Fujita. "Roger, Me, and My Attitude: Film Propaganda and Cynicism toward Corporate Leadership." *Journal of Applied Psychology* 77, no. 5 (1992): 768–71.

Bennet, T. "Culture, Power, and *Mission to Moscow*: Film and Soviet-American relations during WWII." *The Journal of American History* 88, no. 2(2001): 489–519.

Bielby, Denise, and William Bielby. "Women and Men in Film: Gender Inequality among Writers in a Culture Industry." *Gender & Society* 10, no. 3 (June 1996): 248–70.

Brinckmann, Christine Noll. "The Politics of *Force of Evil*: An Analysis of Abraham Polonsky's Preblacklisted Film." *Prospects* 6 (1981): 369.

Brisbin, Richard, Jr. "From State and Local Censorship to Ratings: Substantive Rationality, Political Entrepreneurship, and Sex in the Movies." *Political Film Society*, Working Paper Series #9, 5.

Bruck, Connie. "The Personal Touch." *The New Yorker*, August 13, 2001, 42–59.

Caputi, Jane. "Films of the Nuclear Age." *Journal of Popular Film and Television* 16, no. 3 (Fall 1988): 100–07.

Chancer, Lynn S. "New Bedford, Massachusetts, March 6, 1983–March 22, 1984: The 'Before and After' of a Group Rape." *Gender and Society* 1, no. 3 (Sept. 1987): 239–260.

Convents, Guido. "Documentaries and Propaganda before 1914." *Framework*, no. 35 (1988): 107–08.

Crawford, Neta C. "Just War Theory and the U.S. Counterterror War." *Perspectives on Politics* 1, no. 1 (March 2003): 5–25.

DeVany, Arthur, and W. David Wells. "Does Hollywood Make Too Many R-rated Movies? Risk, Stochastic Dominance, and the Illusion of Expectation." *Journal of Business* 75, no. 3 (July 2002): 425–52.

Donald, Ralph R. "Fictional Presidents as Antagonists in American Motion Pictures: The New Antihero for the Post-Watergate Era." *American Studies Today Online*. http://www.americansc.org.uk/Online/Fictional_Presidents.htm.

Ebo, Bosah. "War as Popular Culture: The Gulf Conflict and the Technology of Illusionary Entertainment." *Journal of American Culture* 18, no. 3 (Fall 1995): 19–25.

Elliott, William R., and William J. Schenck-Hamlin. "Film, Politics and the Press: The Influence of *All the President's Men*." *Journalism Quarterly* 56, no. 3 (1979): 546–53.

Gans, Herbert J. "Hollywood Entertainment: Commerce or Ideology?" *Social Science Quarterly* 74, no. 1 (1993): 150–53.

Giglio, Ernest. "Using Film to Teach Political Concepts." *European Political Science* 1, no. 2 (Spring 2002): 53–58

Godmilow, Jill. "How Real Is the Reality in Documentary Film?" *History and Theory* 36, no. 4 (December 1997): 80–81.

Gornick, Vivian. "The Left in the Fifties." *Lincoln Center Theatre Review*, no. 35 (Spring/Summer 2003): 12.

Grosshans, Laura. "Representations of Women Lawyers in Popular Culture." *Cardozo Public Law, Policy & Ethics Journal* 4, no. 2 (April 2006): 457.

Haas, Peter J. "A Typology of Political Film." Working Paper #11, Political Film Society series, March 2000.

Hammer, Joshua. "A Free Woman." *The New Yorker*, January 24, 2011, 24–30.

Hendershot, Cyndy. "The Atomic Scientist, Science Fiction Films, and Paranoia." *Journal of American Culture* 20, no. 1 (Spring 1997): 31–41.

Heuston, Sean. "Weapons of Mass Instruction: Terrorism, Propaganda Film, Politics and Us: New Media, New Messages." *Studies in Popular Culture* 27, no. 3 (April 2005): 59–73.

Hoffer, Tom W., and Richard Alan Nelson. "Docudrama on American Television." *Journal of the University Film Association* 30, no. 2 (Spring 1978): 22, ft.3.

Houston, Beverle. "Missing in Action: Notes on Dorothy Arzner." *Wide Angle* 6, no. 3 (1934): 24–31.

"How Hollywood Learned to Start Worrying and Hate the Bomb." Special issue, *American Film* 8, no. 1 (October 1982): 57–63.

Huesmann, L. Rowell, Jessica Moise-Titus, Cheryl-Lynn Podolski, and Leonard D. Eron. "Longitudinal Relations Between Children's Exposure to TV Violence and Their Aggressive and Violent Behavior in Young Adulthood: 1977–1992." *Developmental Psychology* 39, no. 2 (2003): 201–21.

Hyland, William G., Jr. "Creative Malpractice: The Cinematic Lawyer." *Texas Review of Entertainment & Sports Law* 9 (Spring 2008): 231.

Jowett, Garth S. "Hollywood, Propaganda and the Bomb: Nuclear Images in Post World War II Film." *Film and History* 18, no. 2 (May 1988): 27.

Jowett, Garth S. "Propaganda and Communication: The Re-emergence of a Research Tradition." *Journal of Communication* 37, no. 1 (Winter 1987): 113–14.

Keller, Laura. "Freedom of the Screen: Joseph Burstyn and *The Miracle*." *New York Archives* 1, no. 4 (Spring 2002): 23–25.

Kurth, James. "The U.S. Victory in Vietnam: Lost and Found." *The Intercollegiate Review* 41, no. 2 (Fall 2006): 14–22.

Lieberman, Robbie. "Communism, Peace Activism, and Civil Liberties: From the Waldorf Conference to the Peekskill Riot." *Journal of Popular Culture* 18, no. 3 (Fall 1995): 59–65.

Lucia, Cynthia. "Women on Trial: The Female Lawyer in the Hollywood Courtroom." *Cineaste* 19 (1993): 32–37.

Macaulay, Stewart. "Images of Law in Everyday Life: The Lesson of School, Entertainment, and Spectator Sports." *Law & Society Review* 21, no. 2 (1987): 185–218.

Machura, Stefan. "An Analysis Scheme for Law Films." *University of Baltimore Law Review* 36 (Spring 2007): 329.

# Selected Bibliography

Manning, Jennifer E. and Ida A. Burdnick, "Women in the United States Congress, 1917-2013. *Congressional Research Service* (Sept 26, 2013): 102-03.

McGovern, George. "Nixon and Historical Memory: Two Reviews." *Perspectives, AHA Newsletter* 34, no. 3 (March 1996): 3.

Morlan, Don P. "Slapstick Contributions to World War II Propaganda: The Three Stooges and Abbott & Costello." *Studies in Popular Culture* 17 (Oct. 1994): 29–43.

O'Connor, John E. "Michael Moore: Cinematic Historian or Propagandist?" *Film & History* 35, no. 2 (2005): 7–16.

O'Malley, Mary Kay. "Through a Different Lens: Using Film to Teach Family Law." *Family Court Review* 49, no. 4 (Oct 2011): 715–22

Orwell, Miles. "Documentary Film and the Power of Interrogation: '*American Dream*' and '*Roger & Me*'." *Film Quarterly* 48 (Winter 1994/95): 10–18.

Papke, David Ray. "Law, Cinema and Ideology: Hollywood Legal Films of the 1950s." *UCLA Law Review* 40, no. 6 (2001): 1473.

Papke, David Ray. "Skepticism Bordering on Distrust: Family Law in the Hollywood Cinema." *Family Court Review* 50, no. 1 (January 2012): 13–22.

Ribstein, Larry E. "Wall Street and Vine: Hollywood's View of Business." U Illinois Law & Economics Research Paper No. LE05-010, March 8, 2009. http://ssrn.com/abstract=563181 or http://dx.doi.org/10.2139/ssrn.563181.

Ross, Steven J. "Struggles for the Screen: Workers, Radicals, and the Political Uses of Silent Film." *American Historical Review* 96, no. 2 (April 1991): 333–67.

Ross, Steven J. "The Visual Politics of Class: Silent Film and the Public Sphere." *Film International*, April 28, 2011. http://filmint.nu/?p=1735.

Rostron, Allen. "Mr. Carter Goes to Washington." *Journal of Popular Film & Television* 25, no. 2 (Summer 1997): 57–67.

Sheffield, Ric. "On Film: A Social History of Women Lawyers in Popular Culture 1930 to 1990." *Loyola of Los Angeles Entertainment Law Journal* 14 (1993): 73–114.

Small, Melvin. "Buffoons and Brave Hearts: Hollywood Portrays the Russians, 1939–1944." *California Historical Society* 52 (Winter 1973): 326–37.

Spiller, Roger J. "War in the Dark." *American Heritage* 50, no. 1 (February–March 1999): 41–51.

Strada, Michael J. "Kaleidoscopic Nuclear Images of the Fifties." *Journal of Popular Culture* 20, no. 3 (1986): 191.

Strasburger, Victor C. "Go Ahead Punk, Make My Day: It's Time for Pediatricians to Take Action against Media Violence." *Pediatrics* 119, no. 6 (June 1, 2007). http://pediatrics.aappublications.org/.

Stratts, Holly. "Chernobyl: Aftermath of a Catastrophe." *Villanova Magazine* 11, no. 4 (Fall 1996): 26.

Sturken, Marita. "Reenactment, Fantasy, and the Paranoia of History: Oliver Stone's Docudramas." *History and Theory* 36, no. 4 (December 1997): 66.

Sunstein, Cass. "Free Speech Now." *University of Chicago Law Review* 59 (1992): 304.

Thompson, Robert. "American Politics on Film." *Journal of Popular Culture* 20 (Summer 1986): 27–47.

Waller, Gregory A. "Re-placing *The Day After*." *Cinema Journal* 26, no. 3 (Spring 1987): 3–20.

Walsh, Michael. "Iowa-Born, Soviet Trained." *Smithsonian* 40, no. 2 (May 2009): 40–47.

Watkins, Peter. "The Fear of Commitment." *Literature/Film Quarterly* 11, no. 4 (1983): 221–33.

Watson, Bruce. "Hang 'Em First, Try 'Em Later." *Smithsonian* 29, no. 8 (June 1998): 96–107.

Webb, Theresa, Lucille Jenkins, Nickolas Browne, Abdelmonen A. Afifi, and Jess Kraus. "Violent Entertainment Pitched to Adolescents: An Analysis of PG-13 Films." *Pediatrics* 119, no. 6 (June 1, 2007). http://pediatrics.aappublications.org/.

Welsh, James. "Banned in Britain." *American Film* 8, no. 1 (October 1982): 64, 69–71.

Wise, Sidney. "Politicians: A Film Perspective." *News for Teachers of Political Science* 32 (Winter 1982): 1.

Zweigenhaft, Richard L. "Students Surveyed about Nuclear War." *Bulletin of the Atomic Scientists* (February 1985): 26–27.

## Cases

*Abrams v. U.S.*, 250 U.S. 616 (1919)
*Brandenburg v. Ohio*, 395 U.S. 444 (1969)
*Brown v. Board of Education*, 347 U.S. 483 (1954)
*Burstyn v. Wilson*, 343 U.S. 495 (1952)
*Bush v. Gore*, 531 U.S. 98 (2000)
*Byers v. Edmondson*, L.A. Court of Appeals (First Circuit, No. 2001, CA 1184, 2002)
*Commonwealth v. Wiseman*, Superior Court (Civil Action No. 87538, 1991)
*Escobedo v. Illinois*, 378 U.S. 478 (1964)
*Gitlow v. New York*, 268 U.S. 652 (1925)
*Goldman v. Weinberger*, 475 U.S. 503 (1985)
*Home Building and Loan Association v. Blaisdell*, 290 U.S. 398 (1934)
*Hopt v. Utah*, 110 U.S. 574 (1884)
*Jacobellis v. Ohio*, 378 U.S. 184 (1964)
*Jensen v. Eveleth Taconite Co.*, 61 FEP Cases 1252 (D. Minn., 1993)
*Jenson v. Eveleth Mines*, 130 F. 3d 1287 (Eighth Circuit Court of Appeals, 1997)
*Korematsu v. U.S.*, 323 U.S. 214 (1944)
*Lochner v. New York*, 198 U.S. 45 (1905)
*Loving v. Virginia*, 388 U.S. 1 (1967)
*Mapp v. Ohio*, 367 U.S. 643 (1961)
*Miranda v. Arizona*, 384 U.S. 436 (1966)
*Near v. Minnesota*, 283 U.S. 697 (1931)
*New York v. Quarles*, 467 U.S. 649 (1984)
*New York Times v. U.S.*, 403 U.S. 713 (1971)
*New York Times Co. v. Sullivan*, 376 U.S. 255 (1964)
*Roe v. Wade*, 410 U.S. 113 (1973)
*Roth v. U.S.*, 354 U.S. 476 (1957)
*Santiago v. Rumsfeld*, 425 F. 3rd 549 (Ninth Circuit 2005)
*Thornhill v. Alabama*, 310 U.S. 88 (1940)
U.S. Court of Appeals for the District of Columbia Circuit, In re Grand Jury Subpoena, Judith Miller, 438 F 3rd 1138 (2006)
*U.S. v. Paramount Pictures*, 334 U.S. 131 (1947)
*West Virginia State Board v. Barnette*, 319 U.S. 624 (1943)
*Whitney v. California*, 274 U.S. 357 (1927)

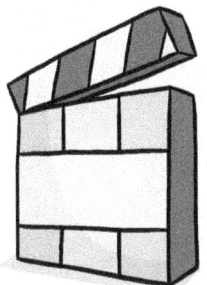

# Selected Filmography

(*) denotes film is available on video

## Features

*Abe Lincoln in Illinois* (USA: 1940) Director: John Cromwell. Screenplay: Robert Sherwood. Cast: Raymond Massey, Gene Lockhart, Ruth Gordon. 110 mins. (*)

*Above and Beyond* (USA: 1952) Directors: Melvin Frank, Norman Panama. Screenplay: Norman Panama, Beirne Lay Jr., Frank Panama. Cast: Robert Taylor, Eleanor Parker, James Whitmore. 122 mins. (*)

*Absolute Power* (USA: 1996) Director: Clint Eastwood. Screenplay: William Goldman. Cast: Clint Eastwood, Gene Hackman, Ed Harris. 121 mins. (*)

*The Accused* (USA: 1988) Director: Jonathan Kaplan. Screenplay: Tom Topor. Cast: Jodie Foster, Kelly McGillis. 101 mins. (*)

*Action in the North Atlantic* (USA: 1944) Director: Lloyd Bacon. Screenplay: John Howard Lawson. Cast: Humphrey Bogart, Raymond Massey, Alan Hale, Julie Bishop. 126 mins. (*)

*Adam's Rib* (USA: 1950) Director: George Cukor. Screenplay: Garson Kanin. Cast: Spencer Tracy, Katharine Hepburn, Judy Holliday, Tom Ewell. 101 mins. (*)

*Advise and Consent* (USA: 1962) Director: Otto Preminger. Screenplay: Wendell Mayes. Cast: Don Murray, Charles Laughton, Henry Fonda, Walter Pidgeon, Lew Ayres. 139 mins. (*)

*The African Queen* (USA: 1951) Director: John Huston. Screenplay: James Agee, John Huston. Cast: Humphrey Bogart, Katharine Hepburn. 105 mins. (*)

*Air Force One* (USA: 1997) Director: Wolfgang Peterson. Screenplay: Andrew W. Marlowe. Cast: Harrison Ford, Glenn Close, Gary Oldman. 124 mins. (*)

*The Alamo* (USA: 2004) Director: John Lee Hancock. Screenplay: Leslie Bohem, Stephen Gaghan. Cast: Dennis Quaid, Billy Bob Thornton, Jason Patric. 137 mins. (*)

*Alamo Bay* (USA: 1985) Director: Louis Malle. Screenplay: Alice Arlan. Cast: Ed Harris, Ho Nguyen, Amy Madigan. 99 mins. (*)

*Alice Doesn't Live Here Anymore* (USA: 1974) Director: Martin Scorsese. Screenplay: Robert Getchell. Cast: Ellen Burstyn, Kris Kristofferson. 105 mins. (*)

*Alien* (USA: 1979) Director: Ridley Scott. Screenplay: Dan O'Bannon. Cast: Tom Skerritt, Sigourney Weaver. 117 mins. (*)

*All Quiet on the Western Front* (USA: 1930) Director: Lewis Milestone. Screenplay: Lewis Milestone, Maxwell Anderson, Del Andrews, George Abbott. Cast: Louis Wolheim, Lew Ayres. 140 mins. (*)

*All the King's Men* (USA: 1949) Director: Robert Rossen. Screenplay: Robert Rossen. Cast: Broderick Crawford, John Ireland, Mercedes McCambridge, Joanne Dru. 109 mins. (*)

*All the President's Men* (USA: 1976) Director: Alan J. Pakula. Screenplay: William Goldman. Cast: Robert Redford, Dustin Hoffman, Jason Robards Jr. 135 mins. (*)

*An American Carol* (USA: 2008) Director: David Zucker. Screenplay: David Zucker et al. Cast: Kevin Farley, Kelsey Grammer. 83 mins. (*)

*American Pie* (USA: 1999) Director: Paul Weitz. Screenplay: Adam Herz. Cast: Jason Biggs, Chris Klein. 95 mins. (*)

*American Pie 2* (USA: 2001) Director: J.B. Rogers. Screenplay: David H. Steinberg, Adam Herz. Cast: Jason Biggs, Shannon Elizabeth. 91 mins. (*)

*The American President* (USA: 1995) Director: Rob Reiner. Screenplay: Aaron Sorkin. Cast: Michael Douglas, Annette Bening, Martin Sheen, Michael J. Fox. 115 mins. (*)

*American Psycho* (USA: 2000) Director: Mary Harron. Screenplay: Mary Harron. Cast: Christian Bale, Reese Witherspoon. 101 mins. (*)

*Anatomy of a Murder (USA: 1959)* Director: Otto Preminger. Screenplay: Wendell Mayes. Cast: James Stewart, George C. Scott, Lee Remick, Arthur O'Connell. 161 mins. (*)

*And Justice for All* (USA: 1979) Director: Norman Jewison. Screenplay: Barry Levinson, Valerie Curtin. Cast: Al Pacino, Jack Warden, Christine Lahti. 120 mins. (*)

*Angels from Hell* (USA: 1968) Director: Bruce Kessler. Screenplay: Jerome Wish. Cast: Tom Stern, Arlene Martel, Ted Markland, Stephen Oliver. 86 mins. (*)

*Ann Carver's Profession* (USA: 1933) Director: Edward Buzzell. Screenplay: Robert Riskin. Cast: Fay Wray, Gene Raymond. 68 mins.

*Apocalypse Now* (USA: 1979) Director: Francis Ford Coppola. Screenplay: Francis Ford Coppola, John Milius. Cast: Marlon Brando, Martin Sheen, Robert Duvall. 153 mins. (*)

*Apollo 13* (USA: 1995) Director: Director: Ron Howard. Screenplay: William Broyles Jr., Al Reinert. Cast: Tom Hanks, Ed Harris, Bill Paxton, Gary Sinise. 140 mins. (*)

*Argo* (USA: 2012) Director: Ben Affleck. Screenplay: Chris Terrio et al. Cast: Ben Affleck, Alan Arkin, John Goodman. 120 mins. (*)

*Armageddon* (USA: 1998) Director: Michael Bay. Screenplay: Tony Gilroy, Shane Salerno, Jonathan Hensleigh, Jeffrey Abrams. Cast: Bruce Willis, Billy Bob Thornton, Ben Affleck. 144 mins. (*)

*The Assassination of Richard Nixon* (USA/Mexico: 2004) Director: Niels Mueller. Screenplay: Kevin Kennedy, Niels Mueller. Cast: Sean Penn, Jack Thompson. 95 mins. (*)

*Baby Doll* (USA: 1956) Director: Elia Kazan. Screenplay: Tennessee Williams. Cast: Eli Wallach, Carroll Baker, Karl Malden. 115 mins. (*)

Baby Face (USA: 1933) Director: Alfred E. Green. Screenplay: George Markey et al. Cast: Barbara Stanwyck, George Brent. 71 mins.

*Back to Bataan* (USA: 1985) Director: Edward Dmytryk. Screenplay: Ben Barzman, Richard Landau. Cast: John Wayne, Anthony Quinn. 95 mins. (*)

*Bad Company* (USA: 2002) Director: Joel Schumacher. Screenplay: Gary Goodman, David Himmelstein. Cast: Anthony Hopkins, Chris Rock. 116 mins. (*)

*Basic Instinct* (USA: 1992) Director: Paul Verhoeven. Screenplay: Joe Eszterhas. Cast: Michael Douglas, Sharon Stone, George Dzundza, Jeanne Tripplehorn. 123 mins. (*)

*Bataan* (USA: 1943) Director: Tay Garnett. Screenplay: Robert D. Andrews. Cast: Robert Taylor, George Murphy, Thomas Mitchell. 115 mins. (*)

*Battle Cry of Peace* (USA: 1915) Directors: J. Stuart Blackton, Wilfred North. Screenplay: J. Stuart Blackton. Cast: Charles Richman, L. Rogers Lytton, Charles Kent. Nine reels.

*Battle of the Bulge* (USA: 1965) Director: Ken Annakin. Screenplay: Philip Yordan, Milton Sperling, John Melson. Cast: Henry Fonda, Robert Shaw, Robert Ryan, Dana Andrews. 167 mins. (*)

*The Beast from 20,000 Fathoms* (USA: 1953) Director: Eugene Lourie. Cast: Paul Christian, Paula Raymond, Cecil Kellaway, Kenneth Tobey. 80 mins. (*)

*The Beginning or the End?* (USA: 1947) Director: Norman Taurog. Screenplay: Robert Considine. Cast: Brian Donlevy, Robert Walker, Tom Drake, Beverly Tyler. 112 mins.

*Behind Enemy Lines* (USA: 2001) Director: John Moore. Screenplay: John Thomas. Cast: Owen Wilson, Gene Hackman. 106 mins. (*)

*Behind the Rising Sun* (USA: 1943) Director: Edward Dmytryk. Screenplay: Emmet Lavery. Cast: Tom Neal, J. Carrol Naish. 88 mins. (*)

*The Best Man* (USA: 1964) Director: Franklin J. Schaffner. Screenplay: Gore Vidal. Cast: Henry Fonda, Cliff Robertson, Lee Tracy, Margaret Leighton. 104 mins. (*)

*The Best Years of Our Lives* (USA: 1946) Director: William Wyler. Screenplay: Robert Sherwood. Cast: Fredric March, Myrna Loy, Dana Andrews, Harold Russell, Teresa Wright. 170 mins. (*)

*A Better Life* (USA: 2011) Director: Chris Weitz. Screenplay: Eric Eason. Cast: Demian Bichir, Eddie Sotelo. 98 mins. (*)

*Beyond a Reasonable Doubt* (USA: 2009) Director: Peter Hyams. Screenplay: Peter Hyams, Douglas Morrow. Cast: Michael Douglas, Jesse Metcalfe, Amber Tamblyn. 106 mins.(*)

*Beyond Rangoon* (UK/USA: 1995) Director: John Boorman. Screenplay: Alex Lasker, Bill Rubenstein. Cast: Patricia Arquette, U Aung Ko. 100 mins. (*)

*Big Jim McLain* (USA: 1952) Director: Edward Ludwig. Screenplay: James Edward Grant, Richard English, Eric Taylor. Cast: John Wayne, Nancy Olson, James Arness. 90 mins. (*)

*The Big Parade* (USA: 1925) Director: King Vidor. Screenplay: Lawrence Stallings, Harry Behn. Cast: John Gilbert, Renee Adoree, Hobart Bosworth. 141 mins. (*)

*The Big Red One* (USA: 1980) Director: Samuel Fuller. Screenplay: Samuel Fuller. Cast: Lee Marvin, Robert Carradine, Mark Hamill. 113 mins. (*)

*The Birth of a Nation* (USA: 1915) Director: D.W. Griffith. Screenplay: D.W. Griffith, Frank Woods. Cast: Henry B. Walthall, Mae Marsh, Miriam Cooper, Lillian Gish. 100 mins. (*)

*Black Hawk Down* (USA: 2001) Director: Ridley Scott. Screenplay: Ken Nolan. Cast: Josh Hartnett, Ewan McGregor. 144 mins. (*)

*The Blind Side* (USA: 2009) Director: John Lee Hancock. Screenplay: John Lee Hancock. Cast: Sandra Bullock, Quinton Aaron. 129 mins. (*)

*Blockade* (USA: 1938) Director: William Dierterle. Screenplay: John Howard Wilson. Cast: Madeleine Carroll, Henry Fonda, Leo Carrillo, John Halliday. 85 mins. (*)

*Blood Work* (USA: 2002) Director: Clint Eastwood. Screenplay: Brian Helgeland. Cast: Clint Eastwood, Jeff Daniels. 110 mins. (*)

*Blow-Up* (UK/Italy: 1966) Director: Michelangelo Antonioni. Screenplay: Tonino Guerra, Michelangelo Antonioni. Cast: David Hemmings, Vanessa Redgrave, Sarah Miles. 111 mins. (*)

*Blue Valentine* (USA: 2010) Director: Derek Cianfrance. Screenplay: Derek Cianfrance. Cast: Ryan Gosling, Michelle Williams. 112 mins (*)

*Bob Roberts* (USA: 1992) Director: Tim Robbins. Screenplay: Tim Robbins. Cast: Tim Robbins, Giancarlo Esposito, Alan Rickman. 105 mins. (*)

*Body and Soul* (USA: 1925) Director: Oscar Micheaux. Screenplay: Oscar Micheaux. Cast: Paul Robeson, Mercedes Gilbert. 102 mins. (*)

*Bolshevism on Trial* (USA: 1919) Director: Harley Knoles. Screenplay: Thomas Dixon, Harry Chandler. Cast: Robert Frazer, Leslie Stowe. 85 mins.

*Boom Town* (USA: 1940) Director: Jack Conway. Screenplay: John Lee Mahin. Cast: Clark Gable, Spencer Tracy. 119 min. (*)

*Born on the Fourth of July* (USA: 1989) Director: Oliver Stone. Screenplay: Oliver Stone, Ron Kovic. Cast: Tom Cruise, Willem Dafoe, Tom Berenger. 144 mins. (*)

*Bound* (USA: 1996) Directors: Andy and Larry Wachowski. Screenplay: Andy and Larry Wachowski. Cast: Jennifer Tilly, Gina Gershon. 107 mins. (*)

*A Boy and His Dog* (USA: 1975) Director: L.Q. Jones. Screenplay: Harlan Ellison, L.Q. Jones. Cast: Don Johnson, Suzanne Benton, Jason Robards Jr., Charles McGraw. 87 mins. (*)

*Boys Don't Cry* (USA: 1999) Director: Kimberly Peirce. Screenplay: Kimberly Peirce, Andy Bienen. Cast: Hilary Swank, Chloe Sevigny. 119 mins. (*)

*The Boys in Company C* (USA: 1977) Director: Sidney J. Furie. Screenplay: Sidney J. Furie. Cast: Stan Shaw, Andrew Stevens, James Canning. 127 mins. (*)

*Boyz n the Hood* (USA: 1991) Director: John Singleton. Screenplay: John Singleton. Cast: Larry Fishburne, Ice Cube. 107 mins. (*)

*Braddock: Missing in Action III* (USA: 1988) Director: Aaron Norris. Screenplay: James Bruner, Chuck Norris. Cast: Chuck Norris. 101 mins. (*)

*The Brave One* (USA: 1957) Director: Irving Rapper. Screenplay: Dalton Trumbo, Harry S. Franklin. Cast: Michel Ray. 100 min. (*)

*The Brave One* (USA: 2007) Director: Neil Jordan. Screenplay: Roderick Taylor, Bruce A. Taylor. Cast: Jodie Foster, Terrence Howard. 122 mins. (*)

*Braveheart* (USA: 1995) Director: Mel Gibson. Screenplay: Randall Wallace. Cast: Mel Gibson, Sophie Marceau. 177 mins. (*)

*Brian's Song* (USA: 1971) Director: Buzz Kulik. TV Script: William Blinn. Cast: James Caan, Billy Dee Williams. 73 mins. (*)

*Bridesmaids* (USA: 2011) Director: Paul Feig. Screenplay: Kristen Wiig, Annie Mumolo. Cast: Kristen Wiig, Maya Rudolph. 125 mins. (*)

*The Bridge on the River Kwai* (UK: 1957) Director: David Lean. Screenplay: Michael Wilson, Carl Foreman. Cast: William Holden, Alec Guinness, Jack Hawkins, Sessue Hayakawa. 161 mins. (*)

*Brokeback Mountain* (USA: 2005) Director: Ang Lee. Screenplay: Larry McMurtry. Cast: Heath Ledger, Jake Gyllenhaal. 134 mins. (*)

*Broken Blossoms* (USA: 1919) Director: D.W. Griffith. Screenplay: D.W. Griffith. Cast: Lillian Gish, Richard Barthelmess. 95 mins. (*)

*Brothers* (USA: 2009) Director: Jim Sheridan. Screenplay: David Benioff. Cast: Tobey Maguire, Jake Gyllenhaal, Natalie Portman. 104 min.*

*Buffalo Soldiers* (UK/Germany: 2001) Director: Gregor Jordan. Screenplay: Eric Weiss. Cast: Joaquin Phoenix, Ed Harris, Scott Glenn. 98 mins. (*)

*Bulworth* (USA: 1998) Director: Warren Beatty. Screenplay: Warren Beatty, Jeremy Pikser. Cast: Warren Beatty, Halle Berry. 108 mins. (*)

*Cabin in the Sky* (USA: 1943) Director: Vincente Minnelli. Screenplay: Joseph Schrank. Cast: Lena Horne, Ethel Waters. 100 mins. (*)

*The Caine Mutiny* (USA: 1954) Director: Edward Dmytryk. Screenplay: Stanley Roberts. Cast: Humphrey Bogart, Jose Ferrer, Van Johnson, Fred MacMurray. 125 mins. (*)

*The Campaign* (USA: 2012) Director: Jay Roach. Screenplay: Chris Henchy, Shawn Harwell. Cast: Will Ferrell, Zach Galifianckis. 85 mins. (*)

*Canadian Bacon* (USA: 1994) Director: Michael Moore. Screenplay: Michael Moore. Cast: Alan Alda, Kevin Pollak, John Candy, Rhea Perlman. 91 mins. (*)

*The Candidate* (USA: 1972) Director: Michael Ritchie. Screenplay: Jeremy Larner. Cast: Robert Redford, Peter Boyle, Don Porter, Allan Garfield. 105 mins. (*)

*Cape Fear* (USA: 1962) Director: J. Lee Thompson. Screenplay: James Webb. Cast: Gregory Peck, Robert Mitchum. 105 mins. (*)

*Cape Fear* (USA: 1991) Director: Martin Scorsese. Screenplay: Wesley Strick. Cast: Robert De Niro, Nick Nolte, Jessica Lange. 128 mins. (*)

*Career Woman* (USA: 1936) Director: Lewis Seiler. Screenplay: Lamar Trotti. Cast: Erville Alderson, Edward S. Brophy. 75 mins.

*Casablanca* (USA: 1942) Director: Michael Curtiz. Screenplay: Julius J. Epstein, Philip C. Epstein, Howard Koch. Cast: Humphrey Bogart, Ingrid Bergman, Paul Henreid, Claude Rains. 102 mins. (*)

*Casualties of War* (USA: 1989) Director: Brian DePalma. Screenplay: David Rabe. Cast: Sean Penn, Michael J. Fox, Thuy Thu Le. 120 mins. (*)

*Changling* (USA: 2008) Director: Clint Eastwood. Screenplay: J. Michael Straczynski. Cast: Angelina Jolie, John Malkovich. 141min. (*)

*Charlie Wilson's War* (USA: 2007) Director: Mike Nichols. Screenplay: Aaron Sorkin. Cast: Tom Hanks, Julia Roberts. 102 mins. (*)

*Che* (USA/Spain/France: 2008) Director: Steven Soderbergh. Screenplay: Peter Buchanan, Benjamin A. van der Veen. Cast: Benicio del Toro, Franka Potente. 269 min. (*)

## Selected Filmography

*The China Syndrome* (USA: 1979) Director: James Bridges. Screenplay: Mike Gray, T.S. Cook, James Bridges. Cast: Jane Fonda, Jack Lemmon, Michael Douglas. 123 mins. (*)

*Christopher Strong* (USA: 1933) Director: Dorothy Arzner. Screenplay: Zoe Akins. Cast: Katharine Hepburn, Colin Clive. 77 mins. (*)

*Chrome and Hot Leather* (USA: 1971) Director: Lee Frost. Screenplay: Michael Haynes, David Neibel, Don Tait. Cast: William Smith, Tony Young, Michael Haynes, Peter Brown. 91 mins. (*)

*Citizen Kane* (USA: 1941) Director: Orson Welles. Screenplay: Herman Mankiewicz, Orson Welles. Cast: Orson Welles, Joseph Cotton. 119 mins. (*)

*City Hall* (USA: 1996) Director: Harold Becker. Screenplay: Bo Goldman, Paul Schrader, Nicholas Pileggi. Cast: Al Pacino, John Cusack, Bridget Fonda, Danny Aiello. 111 mins. (*)

*A Civil Action* (USA: 1998) Director: Steven Zaillian. Screenplay: Steven Zaillian. Cast: John Travolta, Robert Duvall. 113 mins. (*)

*Civilization* (USA: 1916) Director: Thomas Ince. Screenplay: C. Gardner Sullivan. Cast: Howard Hickman, Enid Markey, Lola May. 80 mins. (*)

*Class Action* (USA: 1991) Director: Michael Apted. Screenplay: Samantha Shad. Cast: Mary Elizabeth Mastrantonio, Gene Hackman, Larry Fishburne, Donald Moffat. 110 mins. (*)

*The Client* (USA: 1994) Director: Joel Schumacher. Screenplay: Akiva Goldsman. Cast: Susan Sarandon, Tommy Lee Jones. 119 mins. (*)

*A Clockwork Orange* (Great Britain: 1971) Director: Stanley Kubrick. Screenplay: Stanley Kubrick. Cast: Malcolm McDowell, Patrick MaGee. 137 mins. (*)

*Cloud Atlas* (USA/Germany/Hong Kong/Singapore: 2012) Directors: Tom Tykwer, Andy Wachowski et al. Screenplay: Lana Wachowski et al. Cast: Tom Hanks, Halle Berry. 172 mins. (*)

*Collateral Damage* (USA: 2002) Director: Andrew Davis. Screenplay: Ronald Roose, David Griffiths. Cast: Arnold Schwarzenegger. 108 mins. (*)

*The Color Purple* (USA: 1985) Director: Steven Spielberg. Screenplay: Menno Meyjes. Cast: Whoopi Goldberg, Danny Glover, Oprah Winfrey. 152 mins. (*)

*Coming Home* (USA: 1978) Director: Hal Ashby. Screenplay: Robert C. Jones. Cast: Jane Fonda, Jon Voight, Bruce Dern. 130 mins. (*)

*Commandos Strike at Dawn* (USA: 1943) Director: John Farrow. Screenplay: Irwin Shaw. Cast: Paul Muni, Anna Lee. 98 mins. (*)

*The Commission* (USA: 2003) Director: Mark Sobel. Screenplay: Mark Sobel. Cast: Martin Landau, Sam Waterston, Martin Sheen. 102 mins.

*Compulsion* (USA: 1959) Director: Richard Fleischer. Screenplay: Richard Murphy. Cast: Orson Welles, Diane Varsi, Dean Stockwell, Bradford Dillman. 103 mins. (*)

*Comrade X* (USA: 1940) Director: King Vidor. Screenplay: Ben Hecht. Cast: Clark Gable, Hedy Lamarr, Oscar Homolka. 87 mins. (*)

*Confessions of a Nazi Spy* (USA: 1939) Director: Anatole Litvak. Screenplay: Milton Krims, John Wexley. Cast: Edward G. Robinson, Paul Lucas, George Sanders. 110 mins.

*Conspiracy Theory* (USA: 1996) Director: Richard Donner. Screenplay: Brian Hegeland. Cast: Mel Gibson, Julia Roberts. 135 mins. (*)

*The Conspirator* (USA: 2010) Director: Robert Redford. Screenplay: James D. Soloman. Cast: Robin Wright, James McAvoy. 122 mins. (*)

*The Contender* (USA/Germany/UK: 2000) Director: Rod Lurie. Screenplay: Rod Lurie. Cast: Jeff Bridges, Joan Allen, Gary Oldman. 126 mins. (*)

*Conviction* (USA: 2010) Director: Tony Goldwyn. Screenplay: Pamela Gray. Cast: Hilary Swank, Sam Rockwell. 107 mins. (*)

*The Cooler* (USA: 2003) Director: Wayne Kramer. Screenplay: Frank Hannah, Wayne Framer. Cast: William H. Macy, Maria Bello. 102 mins. (*)

*Counsellor at Law* (USA: 1933) Director: William Wyler. Screenplay: Elmer Rice. Cast: John Barrymore, Beebe Daniels, Melvyn Douglas, Doris Kenton. 78 mins. (*)

*Country* (USA: 1984) Director: Richard Pearce. Screenplay: Bill Wittliff. Cast: Jessica Lange, Sam Shepard, Wilford Brimley. 109 mins. (*)

*Courage of the Commonplace* (USA: 1917) Director: Ben Turbett. Five reels.

*Courage under Fire* (USA: 1996) Director: Edward Zwick. Screenplay: Patrick Sheane Duncan. Cast: Denzel Washington, Meg Ryan. 115 mins. (*)

*The Court Martial of Billy Mitchell* (USA: 1955) Director: Otto Preminger. Screenplay: Emmet Lavery, Milton Sperling (uncredited: Ben Hecht, Dalton Trumbo, Michael Wilson). Cast: Gary Cooper, Charles Bickford, Ralph Bellamy, Rod Steiger. 100 mins. (*)

*Craig's Wife* (USA: 1936) Director: Dorothy Arzner. Screenplay: Mary C. McCall Jr. Cast: Rosalind Russell, John Boles. 75 mins. (*)

*Crash* (USA/Germany: 2005) Director: Paul Haggis. Screenplay: Paul Haggis, Bobby Moresco. Cast: Matt Dillon, Don Cheadle. 112 min. (*)

*Crash* (USA: 1996) Director: David Cronenberg. Screenplay: David Cronenberg. Cast: James Spader, Holly Hunter. 100 mins. (*)

*Crash Dive* (USA: 1943) Director: Archie Mayo. Screenplay: Jo Swerling. Cast: Tyrone Power, Ann Baxter, Dana Andrews. 105 mins. (*)

*Crossfire* (USA: 1947) Director: Edward Dmytryk. Screenplay: John Paxton. Cast: Robert Young, Robert Mitchum, Robert Ryan. 86 mins. (*)

*The Crucible* (USA: 1996) Director: Nicholas Hytner. Screenplay: Arthur Miller. Cast: Daniel Day-Lewis, Winona Ryder, Paul Scofield. 123 mins. (*)

*Cry Havoc* (USA: 1944) Director: Richard Thorpe. Screenplay: Paul Osborn. Cast: Margaret Sullivan, Ann Sothern, Joan Blondell. 97 mins. (*)

*D.C. Sniper: 23 Days of Fear* (USA: 2003) Director: Tom McLoughlin. TV Script: Dave Erickson. Cast: Charles Dutton, Jay O. Sanders. 120 mins. (*)

*The Da Vinci Code* (USA: 2006) Director: Ron Howard. Screenplay: Akiva Goldsman. Cast: Tom Hanks, Audrey Tautou. 148 mins. (*)

*Dance, Girl, Dance* (USA: 1940) Director: Dorothy Arzner. Screenplay: Frank Davis, Tess Slesinger. Cast: Maureen O'Hara, Lucille Ball. 88 mins.

*Dangerous Hours* (USA: 1919) Director: Fred Niblo. Cast: Lloyd Hughes. 88 mins. (*)

*The Dark Horse* (USA: 1946) Director: Will Jason. Cast: Jane Darwell, Dick Elliott, Donald MacBride, Phillip Terry. 59 min. (*)

*The Dark Knight* (USA: 2008) Director: Christopher Nolan. Screenplay: Jonathan and Christopher Nolan. Cast: Christian Bale, Heath Ledger, Maggie Gyllenhaal. 152 min. (*)

*The Dark Knight Rises* (USA: 2012) Director: Christopher Nolan. Screenplay: Jonathan Nolan et al. Cast: Christian Bale, Gary Oldman. 165 mins. (*)

*Dave* (USA: 1993) Director: Ivan Reitman. Screenplay: Gary Ross. Cast: Kevin Kline, Sigourney Weaver, Frank Langella. 110 mins. (*)

*The Day After* (USA: 1983) Director: Nicholas Meyer. Screenplay: Edward Hume. Cast: Jason Robards Jr., JoBeth Williams, John Lithgow, Steve Guttenberg. 126 mins. (*)

*The Day the Earth Stood Still* (USA: 1951) Director: Robert Wise. Screenplay: Edmund H. North. Cast: Michael Rennie, Patricia Neal, Hugh Marlowe, Sam Jaffe. 92 mins. (*)

*Days of Glory* (USA: 1943) Director: Jacques Tourneur. Screenplay: Casey Robinson, Melchior Lengyel. Cast: Tamara Tourmanova, Gregory Peck, Alan Reed, Maria Palmer. 86 mins. (*)

*Death Wish* (USA: 1974) Director: Michael Winner. Screenplay: Wendell Mayes. Cast: Charles Bronson, Vincent Gardenia, William Redfield, Hope Lange. 93 mins. (*)

*Death Wish II* (USA: 1982) Director: Michael Winner. Screenplay: David Engelbach, Brian Garfield. Cast: Charles Bronson, Jill Ireland. 89 mins. (*)

## Selected Filmography

*Deep Impact* (USA: 1998) Director: Mimi Leder. Screenplay: Bruce Joel Rubin, Michael Tolkin. Cast: Robert Duvall, Morgan Freeman. 120 mins. (*)

*The Deer Hunter* (USA: 1978) Director: Michael Cimino. Screenplay: Deric Washburn, Michael Cimino. Cast: Robert De Niro, Christopher Walken, Meryl Streep, John Savage. 183 mins. (*)

*The Defense Rests* (USA: 1934) Director: Lambert Hillyer. Screenplay: Jo Swerling. Cast: Jack Holt, Jean Arthur. 70 mins. (*)

*Defenseless* (USA: 1991) Director: Martin Campbell. Screenplay: James Hicks, Jeff Burkhart. Cast: Barbara Hershey, Sam Shepard, Mary Beth Hurt, J.T. Walsh. 106 mins. (*)

*The Departed* (USA: 2006) Director: Martin Scorsese. Screenplay: William Monahan. Cast: Jack Nicholson, Matt Damon, Leonardo DiCaprio. 151 mins. (*)

*Desperate Journey* (USA: 1942) Director: Raoul Walsh. Screenplay: Arthur T. Horman. Cast: Errol Flynn, Ronald Reagan, Raymond Massey, Nancy Coleman. 108 mins. (*)

*Deterrence* (USA: 1999) Director: Rod Lurie. Screenplay: Rod Lurie. Cast: Kevin Pollak, Timothy Hutton. 101 mins. (*)

*The Devil's Advocate* (USA: 1997) Director: Taylor Hackford. Screenplay: Jonathan Lemkin, Tony Gilroy. Cast: Al Pacino, Keanu Reeves. 144 mins. (*)

*Dick* (USA: 1999) Director: Andrew Fleming. Screenplay: Andrew Fleming, Sheryl Longin. Cast: Dan Hedaya, Kirsten Dunst, Michelle Williams. 94 mins. (*)

*Dirty Harry* (USA: 1971) Director: Don Siegel. Screenplay: Harry Julian and Rita Fink. Cast: Clint Eastwood, Harry Guardino. 102 mins. (*)

*Disclosure* (USA: 1994) Director: Barry Levinson. Screenplay: Paul Attanasio. Cast: Michael Douglas, Demi Moore. 127 mins. (*)

*Dive Bomber* (USA: 1941) Director: Michael Curtiz. Screenplay: Frank Wead, Robert Buckner. Cast: Errol Flynn, Fred MacMurray, Ralph Bellamy, Alexis Smith. 130 mins. (*)

*Django Unchained* (USA: 2012) Director: Quentin Tarantino. Screenplay: Quentin Tarantino. Cast: Jamie Foxx, Christopher Waltz, Leonardo DiCaprio. 165 mins. (*)

*Do the Right Thing* (USA: 1989) Director: Spike Lee. Screenplay: Spike Lee. Cast: Danny Aiello, Spike Lee, John Turturro. 120 mins. (*)

*Dr. Strangelove or: How I Learned to Stop Worrying and Love the Bomb* (UK: 1964) Director: Stanley Kubrick. Screenplay: Terry Southern, Peter George, Stanley Kubrick. Cast: Peter Sellers, George C. Scott, Sterling Hayden, Keenan Wynn. 93 mins. (*)

*The Eagle and the Hawk* (USA: 1933) Director: Stuart Walker. Screenplay: Seton I. Miller, Bogart Rogers, John Monk Saunders. Cast: Fredric March, Cary Grant, Dennis O'Keefe. 68 mins. (*)

*Easy Rider* (USA: 1964) Director: Dennis Hopper. Screenplay: Dennis Hopper, Peter Fonda, Terry Southern. Cast: Peter Fonda, Dennis Hopper, Jack Nicholson. 94 mins. (*)

*Edge of Darkness* (USA: 1943) Director: Lewis Milestone. Screenplay: Robert Rossen. Cast: Errol Flynn, Ann Sheridan, Walter Huston, Nancy Coleman. 120 mins. (*)

*The Emperor Jones* (USA: 1933) Director: Dudley Murphy. Screenplay: DuBose Heyward. Cast: Paul Robeson. 72 mins. (*)

*The English Patient* (USA: 1996) Director: Anthony Minghella. Screenplay: Anthony Minghella. Cast: Ralph Fiennes, Juliette Binoche, Kristin Scott Thomas. 160 mins. (*)

*Erin Brockovich* (USA: 2000) Director: Steven Soderbergh. Screenplay: Susannah Grant. Cast: Julia Roberts, Albert Finney. 130 mins. (*)

*The Execution of Eddie Slovak* (USA: 1974) Director: Lamont Johnson. Screenplay: Richard Levinson, William Link. Cast: Martin Sheen, Ned Beatty, Gary Busey. 122 mins. (*)

*Executive Action* (USA: 1973) Director: David Miller. Screenplay: Dalton Trumbo. Cast: Burt Lancaster, Robert Ryan, Will Geer. 91 mins. (*)

*Executive Power* (USA: 1997) Director: David Corley. Screenplay: David Corley. Cast: Craig Sheffer, Andrea Roth. 105 mins. (*)

*Extremely Loud and Incredibly Close* (USA: 2011) Director: Stephen Daldry. Screenplay: Eric Roth. Cast: Tom Hanks, Thomas Horn. 129 mins. (*)

*Eyes Wide Shut* (USA/UK: 1999) Director: Stanley Kubrick. Screenplay: Stanley Kubrick. Cast: Tom Cruise, Nicole Kidman. 159 mins. (*)

*Fail Safe* (USA: 1964) Director: Sidney Lumet. Screenplay: Walter Bernstein. Cast: Henry Fonda, Dan O'Herlihy, Walter Matthau, Larry Hagman. 111 mins. (*)

*Fair Game* (USA: 2010) Director: Doug Liman. Screenplay: Jez Butterworth et al. Cast: Naomi Watts, Sean Penn. 108 mins. (*)

*Far from Heaven* (France/USA: 2002) Director: Todd Haynes. Screenplay: Todd Haynes. Cast: Julianne Moore, Dennis Quaid. 107 mins. (*)

*The Farmer's Daughter* (USA: 1947) Director: H.C. Potter. Screenplay: Hella Wvolijoki (Juhni Tervataa), Larry Rivkin, Laura Kerr. Cast: Loretta Young, Joseph Cotten, Ethel Barrymore. 97 mins. (*)

*Fat Man and Little Boy* (USA: 1989) Director: Roland Joffe. Screenplay: Bruce Robinson, Tony Garnett, Roland Joffe. Cast: Paul Newman, Dwight Schultz, Bonnie Bedelia, John Cusack. 127 mins. (*)

*Fatal Attraction* (USA: 1987) Director: Adrian Lyne. Screenplay: James Dearden. Cast: Michael Douglas, Glenn Close. 119 mins. (*)

*The Fearmakers* (USA: 1958) Director: Jacques Tourneur. Screenplay: Chris Appley. Cast: Dana Andrews, Dick Foran. 83 mins. (*)

*A Few Good Men* (USA: 1992) Director: Rob Reiner. Screenplay: Aaron Sorkin. Cast: Tom Cruise, Jack Nicholson, Demi Moore, Kevin Bacon. 138 mins. (*)

*The Fighting 69th* (USA: 1940) Director: William Keighley. Screenplay: Fred Niblo, Norman Reilly Raine, Dean Franklin. Cast: James Cagney, Pat O'Brien. 90 mins. (*)

*The Finest Hour* (USA: 1991) Director: Shimon Dotan. Screenplay: Shimon Dotan. Cast: Rob Lowe, Gale Hansen, Tracy Griffith. 105 mins. (*)

*Fired Up!* (USA: 2009) Director: Will Gluck. Screenplay: Freedom Jones. Cast: Eric Christian Olsen, Nicholas D'Agosto. 91 mins. (*)

*The Firm* (USA: 1993) Director: Sydney Pollack. Screenplay: David Rabe. Cast: Tom Cruise, Jeanne Tripplehorn, Gene Hackman. 154 mins. (*)

*First Blood* (USA: 1982) Director: Ted Kotcheff. Screenplay: Sylvester Stallone. Cast: Sylvester Stallone, Richard Crenna, Brian Dennehy. 96 mins. (*)

*Five* (USA: 1951) Director: Arch Oboler. Screenplay: Arch Oboler. Cast: Susan Douglas, William Phipps. 93 mins. (*)

*The Five Heartbeats* (USA: 1991) Director: Robert Townsend. Screenplay: Robert Townsend, Keenen Ivory Wayans. Cast: Robert Townsend, Diahann Carroll. 120 mins. (*)

*Fixed Bayonets* (USA: 1951) Director: Samuel Fuller. Screenplay: Samuel Fuller. Cast: Richard Basehart, Gene Evans. 92 mins. (*)

*Flags of Our Fathers* (USA: 2006) Director: Clint Eastwood. Screenplay: William Broyles Jr., Paul Haggis. Cast: Ryan Phillippe, Jesse Bradford, Adam Beach. 131 mins. (*)

*Flight Command* (USA: 1940) Director: Frank Borzage. Screenplay: Wells Root. Cast: Robert Taylor, Ruth Hussey, Walter Pidgeon. 110 mins. (*)

*For Whom the Bell Tolls* (USA: 1943) Director: Sam Wood. Screenplay: Dudley Nichols. Cast: Gary Cooper, Ingrid Bergman, Akim Tamiroff. 168 mins. (*)

*Force of Evil* (USA: 1948) Director: Abraham Polonsky. Screenplay: Abraham Polonsky. Cast: John Garfield, Thomas Gomez, Marie Windsor, Sheldon Leonard. 78 mins. (*)

*Foreign Correspondent* (USA: 1940) Director: Alfred Hitchcock. Screenplay: Robert Benchley, Charles Bennett, Joan Harrison, James Hilton. Cast: Joel McCrea, Laraine Day, Herbert Marshall, George Sanders. 120 mins. (*)

*Forrest Gump* (USA: 1994) Director: Robert Zemeckis. Screenplay: Eric Roth. Cast: Tom Hanks, Robin Wright, Sally Field, Gary Sinise. 142 mins. (*)

# Selected Filmography

*The Fortune Cookie* (USA: 1966) Director: Billy Wilder. Screenplay: Billy Wilder, I.A.L. Diamond. Cast: Jack Lemmon, Walter Matthau, Ron Rich, Cliff Osmond. 125 mins. (*)

*The Fourth Protocol* (USA: 1987) Director: John MacKenzie. Screenplay: Frederick Forsythe, Richard Burridge, George Axelrod. Cast: Michael Caine, Pierce Brosnan, Ned Beatty, Joanna Cassidy. 119 mins. (*)

*Friday the 13th* (USA: 1980) Director: Sean S. Cunningham. Screenplay: Victor Miller. Cast: Betsy Palmer. 95 mins. (*)

*From Dusk to Dawn* (USA: 1913) Director: Frank E. Wolfe. Screenplay: Frank E. Wolfe. Cast: Clarence Darrow. Five reels.

*From Here to Eternity* (USA: 1953) Director: Fred Zinnemann. Screenplay: Daniel Taradash. Cast: Burt Lancaster, Montgomery Clift, Frank Sinatra, Deborah Kerr. 118 mins. (*)

*The Front* (USA: 1976) Director: Martin Ritt. Screenplay: Walter Bernstein. Cast: Woody Allen, Zero Mostel, Herschel Bernardi, Michael Murphy. 95 mins. (*)

*Frost/Nixon* (USA: 2008) Director: Ron Howard. Screenplay: Peter Morgan. Cast: Frank Langella, Michael Sheen. 122 min. (*)

*Frozen River* (USA: 2008) Director: Courtney Hunt. Screenplay: Courtney Hunt. Cast: Melissa Leo, Misty Upham. 96 mins. (*)

*Full Metal Jacket* (USA: 1987) Director: Stanley Kubrick. Screenplay: Michael Herr, Gustav Hasford, Stanley Kubrick. Cast: Matthew Modine, R. Lee Ermey, Vincent D'Onofrio, Adam Baldwin. 116 mins. (*)

*Fury* (USA: 1936) Director: Fritz Lang. Screenplay: Fritz Lang, Bartlett Cormack. Cast: Spencer Tracy, Sylvia Sidney, Walter Abel. 96 mins. (*)

*Gabriel Over the White House* (USA: 1933) Director: Gregory LaVaca. Screenplay: Carey Wilson, Bertram Bloch. Cast: Walter Huston, Karen Morley, Franchot Tone. 87 mins. (*)

*Gandhi* (UK: 1982) Director: Richard Attenborough. Screenplay: John Briley. Cast: Ben Kingsley, Candice Bergen, Edward Fox. 188 mins. (*)

*Gangs of New York* (USA: 2002) Director: Martin Scorsese. Screenplay: Steven Zailian. Cast: Leonardo DiCaprio, Daniel Day-Lewis. 166 mins. (*)

*Gentleman's Agreement* (USA: 1947) Director: Elia Kazan. Screenplay: Moss Hart. Cast: Gregory Peck, Dorothy McGuire, John Garfield. 118 mins. (*)

*The Ghost Breakers* (USA: 1940) Director: George Marshall. Screenplay: Walter DeLeon. Cast: Bob Hope, Paulette Goddard. 85 mins. (*)

*Giant* (USA: 1956) Director: George Stevens. Screenplay: Fred Guiol, Ivan Moffat. Cast: Rock Hudson, Elizabeth Taylor, James Dean. 201 mins. (*)

*Gladiator* (UK/USA: 2000) Director: Ridley Scott. Screenplay: David Franzoni. Cast: Russell Crowe, Joaquin Phoenix. 155 mins. (*)

*The Glass Key* (USA: 1942) Director: Stuart Heisler. Screenplay: Jonathan Latimer. Cast: Alan Ladd, Veronica Lake, Brian Donlevy, William Bendix. 85 mins. (*)

*Glory* (USA: 1989) Director: Edward Zwick. Screenplay: Kevin Jarre. Cast: Matthew Broderick, Denzel Washington, Morgan Freeman. 122 mins. (*)

*Go for Broke* (USA: 1951) Director: Robert Pirosh. Screenplay: Robert Pirosh. Cast: Van Johnson. 92 mins. (*)

*Go Tell the Spartans* (USA: 1978) Director: Ted Post. Screenplay: Wendell Mayes. Cast: Burt Lancaster, Craig Wasson. 114 mins. (*)

*The Godfather* (USA: 1972) Director: Francis Ford Coppola. Screenplay: Mario Puzo, Francis Ford Coppola. Cast: Marlon Brando, Al Pacino, Robert Duvall, James Caan. 171 mins. (*)

*The Godfather: Part 2* (USA: 1974) Director: Francis Ford Coppola. Screenplay: Mario Puzo, Francis Ford Coppola. Cast: Al Pacino, Robert De Niro, Diane Keaton, Robert Duvall. 200 mins. (*)

*The Godfather: Part 3* (USA: 1990) Director: Francis Ford Coppola. Screenplay: Francis Ford Coppola. Cast: Al Pacino, Diane Keaton, Andy Garcia, Joe Mantegna. 170 mins. (*)

*Godzilla* (USA: 1998) Director: Roland Emmerich. Screenplay: Dean Devlin, Roland Emmerich. Cast: Matthew Broderick, Jean Reno. 140 mins. (*)

*Gone with the Wind* (USA: 1939) Director: Victor Fleming. Screenplay: Sidney Howard. Cast: Clark Gable, Vivien Leigh, Olivia de Havilland, Leslie Howard. 231 mins. (*)

*The Good Earth* (USA: 1937) Director: Sidney Franklin. Screenplay: Talbot Jennings and Tess Slesinger. Cast: Luise Rainer, Paul Muni. 138 mins. (*)

*Good Morning, Vietnam* (USA: 1987) Director: Barry Levinson. Screenplay: Mitch Markowitz. Cast: Robin Williams, Forest Whitaker, Bruno Kirby, Richard Edson. 121 mins. (*)

*The Good Mother* (USA: 1998) Director: Leonard Nimoy. Screenplay: Michael Bortman. Cast: Diane Keaton, Liam Neeson. 103 mins. (*)

*Good Night, and Good Luck* (USA: 2005) Director: George Clooney. Screenplay: Grant Heslov, George Clooney. Cast: David Strathairn, George Clooney, Frank Langella. 93 mins. (*)

*Good Will Hunting* (USA: 1997) Director: Gus Van Sant. Screenplay: Matt Damon, Ben Affleck. Cast: Robin Williams, Matt Damon, Ben Affleck. 126 mins. (*)

*Goodfellas* (USA: 1990) Director: Martin Scorsese. Screenplay: Nicholas Pileggi. Cast: Robert De Niro, Ray Liotta, Joe Pesci. 145 mins. (*)

*Gran Torino* (USA: 2008) Director: Clint Eastwood. Screenplay: Nick Schenk. Cast: Clint Eastwood, Bee Vang, Ahney Her. 117 mins. (*)

*The Grapes of Wrath* (USA: 1940) Director: John Ford. Screenplay: Nunnally Johnson. Cast: Henry Fonda, Jane Darwell, John Carradine, Charley Grapewin. 129 mins. (*)

*The Great Dictator* (USA: 1940) Director: Charles Chaplin. Screenplay: Charles Chaplin. Cast: Charles Chaplin, Paulette Goddard, Jack Oakie. 127 mins. (*)

*The Great Escape* (USA: 1963) Director: John Sturges. Screenplay: James Clavell, W.R. Burnett. Cast: Steve McQueen, James Garner, Richard Attenborough. 168 mins. (*)

*The Great McGinty* (USA: 1940) Director: Preston Sturges. Screenplay: Preston Sturges. Cast: Brian Donlevy, Akim Tamiroff. 82 mins. (*)

*The Great Train Robbery* (USA: 1903) Director: Edwin S. Porter. Screenplay: Edwin S. Porter. Cast: Marie Murray, Broncho Billy Anderson, George Barnes. 10 mins. (*)

*The Green Berets* (USA: 1968) Directors: John Wayne, Ray Kellogg. Screenplay: James Lee Barrett. Cast: John Wayne, David Janssen, Jim Hutton. 141 mins. (*)

*Green Zone* (USA: 2010) Director: Paul Greengrass. Screenplay: Brian Helgeland. Cast: Matt Damon, Greg Kinnear. 115 mins. (*)

*Guadalcanal Diary* (USA: 1943) Director: Lewis Seiler. Screenplay: Jerome Cady, Richard Tregaskis, Lamar Trotti. Cast: Preston Foster, Lloyd Nolan, William Bendix, Richard Conte. 93 mins. (*)

*Guess Who's Coming to Dinner* (USA: 1967) Director: Stanley Kramer. Screenplay: William Rose. Cast: Katharine Hepburn, Spencer Tracy, Sidney Poitier, Katherine Houghton. 108 mins. (*)

*Guilty as Sin* (USA: 1993) Director: Sidney Lumet. Screenplay: Larry Cohen. Cast: Don Johnson, Rebecca DeMornay, Jack Warden, Stephen Lang. 120 mins. (*)

*Guilty by Suspicion* (USA: 1991) Director: Irwin Winkler. Screenplay: Irwin Winkler. Cast: Robert De Niro, Annette Bening. 105 mins. (*)

*Gung Ho!* (USA: 1943) Director: Ray Enright. Screenplay: Joseph Hoffman, Lucien Hubbard, W.S. LeFrancois. Cast: Robert Mitchum, Randolph Scott, Noah Beery Jr., Alan Curtis. 88 mins. (*)

*Hamburger Hill* (USA: 1987) Director: John Irvin. Screenplay: Jim Carabatsos. Cast: Michael Dolan, Daniel O'Shea, Dylan McDermott, Tommy Swerdlow. 104 mins. (*)

*Heartbreak Ridge* (USA: 1986) Director: Clint Eastwood. Screenplay: Jim Carabatsos. Cast: Clint Eastwood, Marsha Mason. 130 mins. (*)

*The Help* (USA: 2011) Director: Tate Taylor. Screenplay: Tate Taylor. Cast: Viola Davis, Emma Stone, Octavia Spencer. 146 mins. (*)

*The Heroes of Desert Storm* (USA: 1991) Director: Don Ohlmeyer. Screenplay: Lionel Chetwynd. Cast: Daniel Baldwin, Angela Bassett. 93 mins. (*)

## Selected Filmography

*High Noon* (USA: 1952) Director: Fred Zinnemann. Screenplay: Carl Foreman. Cast: Gary Cooper, Grace Kelly, Lloyd Bridges, Lon Chaney Jr. 85 mins. (*)

*Home of the Brave* (USA: 1949) Director: Mark Robson. Screenplay: Carl Foreman. Cast: Lloyd Bridges, James Edwards, Frank Lovejoy. 86 mins. (*)

*The Homesteader* (USA: 1919) Director: Oscar Micheaux. Screenplay: Oscar Micheaux. Cast: Charles D. Lucas. (Film is lost)

*Honor Among Lovers* (USA: 1931) Director: Dorothy Arzner. Screenplay: Austin Parker. Cast: Claudette Colbert, Fredric March. 75 mins.

*The Hurt Locker* (USA: 2008) Director: Kathryn Bigelow. Screenplay: Mark Boal. Cast: Jeremy Renner, Anthony Mackie. 131 mins. (*)

*Hyde Park on Hudson* (USA: 2012) Director: Roger Mitchell. Screenplay: Roger Mitchell. Cast: Bill Murray, Laura Linney. 94 mins. (*)

*I Am a Fugitive from a Chain Gang* (USA: 1932) Director: Mervyn LeRoy. Screenplay: Howard J. Green. Cast: Paul Muni, Glenda Farrell, Preston Foster. 93 mins. (*)

*I Married a Communist* (USA: 1950) Director: Robert Stevenson. Screenplay: Charles Grayson, Robert Hardy Andrews. Cast: Laraine Day, Robert Ryan, John Agar. 73 mins.

*I Want You* (USA: 1951) Director: Mark Robson. Screenplay: Irwin Shaw. Cast: Dana Andrews, Dorothy McQuire, Farley Granger. 101 mins. (*)

*I Was a Communist for the FBI* (USA: 1951) Director: Gordon Douglas. Screenplay: Crane Wilbur, Matt Cvetic. Cast: Frank Lovejoy, Dorothy Hart, Phil Carey. 83 mins.

*The Ides of March* (USA: 2011) Director: George Clooney. Screenplay: George Clooney et al. Cast: Ryan Gosling, George Clooney. 101 mins. (*)

*I'm No Angel* (USA: 1933) Director: Wesley Ruggles. Screenplay: Mae West. Cast: Mae West, Cary Grant, Edward Arnold. 88 mins. (*)

*Imitation of Life* (USA: 1959) Director: Douglas Sirk. Screenplay: Eleanor Griffin et al. Cast: Lana Turner, John Gavin, Sandra Dee. 125 mins. (*)

*In the Heat of the Night* (USA: 1967) Director: Norman Jewison. Screenplay: Stirling Silliphant. Cast: Sidney Poitier, Rod Steiger. 109 mins. (*)

*In the Land of Blood and Honey* (USA: 2011) Director: Angelina Jolie. Screenplay: Angelina Jolie. Cast: Zana Marjanovic, Goran Kostic. 127 mins. (*)

*In the Valley of Elah* (USA: 2007) Director: Paul Haggis. Screenplay: Paul Haggis. Cast: Tommy Lee Jones, Charlize Theron. 121 mins. (*)

*Independence Day* (USA: 1996) Director: Roland Emmerich. Screenplay: Dean Devlin, Roland Emmerich. Cast: Will Smith, Bill Pullman, Jeff Goldblum. 145 mins. (*)

*Indiana Jones and the Kingdom of the Crystal Skull* (USA: 2008) Director: Steven Spielberg. Screenplay: David Koepp. Cast: Harrison Ford, Cate Blanchett. 122 min. (*)

*Inglourious Basterds* (USA/Germany: 2009) Director: Quentin Tarantino. Screenplay: Quentin Tarantino. Cast: Brad Pitt, Eli Roth. 153 mins. (*)

*Inherit the Wind* (USA: 1960) Director: Stanley Kramer. Screenplay: Nathan E. Douglas (aka Ned Young), Harold Jacob Smith. Cast: Spencer Tracy, Fredric March, Gene Kelly. 128 mins. (*)

*Intruder in the Dust* (USA: 1949) Director: Clarence Brown. Screenplay: Ben Maddow. Cast: David Brian, Claude Jarmen Jr., Juano Hernandez. 87 mins. (*)

*Invasion of the Body Snatchers* (USA: 1956) Director: Don Siegel. Screenplay: Daniel Mainwaring. Cast: Kevin McCarthy, Dana Wynter, Larry Gates, King Donovan. 80 mins. (*)

*It Came from Beneath the Sea* (USA: 1955) Director: Robert Gordon. Screenplay: Hal Smith, George Worthing Yates. Cast: Kenneth Tobey, Faith Domergue, Ian Keith, Donald Curtis. 80 mins. (*)

*It Came from Outer Space* (USA: 1953) Director: Jack Arnold. Screenplay: Ray Bradbury. Cast: Richard Carlson, Barbara Rush, Charles Drake, Russell Johnson. 81 mins. (*)

*It Can't Happen Here* (MGM, unproduced)

*J. Edgar* (USA: 2011) Director: Clint Eastwood. Screenplay: Dustin Lance Black. Cast: Leonardo DiCaprio, Armie Hammer. 137 mins. (*)

*Jagged Edge* (USA: 1985) Director: Richard Marquand. Screenplay: Joe Eszterhas. Cast: Jeff Bridges, Glenn Close, Robert Loggia. 108 mins. (*)

*Jarhead* (Germany/USA: 2005) Director: Sam Mendes. Screenplay: William Broyles Jr. Cast: Jake Gyllenhaal, Jamie Foxx. 125 mins. (*)

*The Jazz Singer* (USA: 1927) Director: Alan Crosland. Screenplay: Alfred A. Cohn. Cast: Al Jolson. 89 mins. (*)

*JFK* (USA: 1991) Director: Oliver Stone. Screenplay: Oliver Stone, Zachary Skiar. Cast: Kevin Costner, Sissy Spacek, Kevin Bacon, Tommy Lee Jones. 189 mins. (*)

*Johnny Guitar* (USA: 1953) Director: Nicholas Ray. Screenplay: Philip Yordan. Cast: Joan Crawford, Ernest Borgnine, Sterling Hayden, Mercedes McCambridge. 110 mins. (*)

*Judge Priest* (USA: 1934) Director: John Ford. Screenplay: Dudley Nichols, Lamar Trotti. Cast: Will Rogers, Stepin Fetchit, Anita Louise, Henry B. Walthall. 80 mins. (*)

*Jungle Fever* (USA: 1991) Director: Spike Lee. Screenplay: Spike Lee. Cast: Anabella Sciorra, Wesley Snipes. 131 mins. (*)

*The Kids Are All Right* (USA: 2010) Director: Lisa Cholodenko. Screenplay: Lisa Cholodenko, Stuart Blumberg. Cast: Julianne Moore, Annette Bening, Mark Ruffalo. 106 mins. (*)

*A King in New York* (USA: 1957) Director: Charlie Chaplin. Screenplay: Charles Chaplin. Cast: Charlie Chaplin, Dawn Addams, Michael Chaplin. 105 mins. (*)

*King of the Pecos* (USA: 1936) Director: Joseph Kane. Screenplay: Bernard McConville, Dorrell McGowan, Stuart E. McGowan. Cast: John Wayne, Muriel Evans, Cy Kendall, Jack Clifford. 54 mins. (*)

*The Kingdom* (USA, German: 2007) Director: Peter Berg. Screenplay: Matthew Michael Carnahan. Cast: Jamie Foxx, Chris Cooper, Jennifer Cooper. 110 mins. (*)

*The King's Speech* (UK/USA/Australia: 2010) Director: Tom Hooper. Screenplay: David Seidler. Cast: Colin Firth, Geoffrey Rush. 118 mins. (*)

*Knock on Any Door* (USA: 1949) Director: Nicholas Ray. Screenplay: Daniel Taradash, John Monks Jr. Cast: Humphrey Bogart, John Derek, George MacCready. 100 mins. (*)

*Kramer vs. Kramer* (USA: 1979) Director: Robert Benton. Screenplay: Robert Benton. Cast: Dustin Hoffman, Meryl Streep. 105 mins. (*)

*Kundun* (USA: 1997) Director: Martin Scorsese. Screenplay: Melissa Mathison. Cast: Tenzin Thuthob Tsarong, Gyurme Tethog, Robert Lin (II). 135 mins. (*)

*Ladies Courageous* (USA: 1944) Director: John Rawlins. Screenplay: Doris Gilbert. Cast: Loretta Young, Geraldine Fitzgerald. 88 mins. (*)

*The Last Hurrah* (USA: 1958) Director: John Ford. Screenplay: Frank Nugent. Cast: Spencer Tracy, Jeffrey Hunter, Diane Foster, Pat O'Brien. 121 mins. (*)

*The Last Woman on Earth* (USA: 1961) Director: Roger Corman. Screenplay: Robert Towne. Cast: Antony Carbone, Edward Waine, Betsy Jones-Moreland. 71 mins. (*)

*Lawyer Man* (USA: 1932) Director: William Dieterle. Screenplay: Riam James, James Seymour. Cast: William Powell, Joan Blondell. 70 mins. (*)

*Lee Daniels' The Butler* (USA: 2013) Director: Lee Daniels. Screenplay: Danny Strong. Cast: Forest Whitaker, Oprah Winfrey. 132 mins. (*)

*Legal Eagles* (USA: 1986) Director: Ivan Reitman. Screenplay: Jim Cash, Jack Epps Jr. Cast: Robert Redford, Debra Winger, Daryl Hannah, Brian Dennehy. 116 mins. (*)

*Legally Blonde* (USA: 2001) Director: Robert Luketic. Screenplay: Karen McCullah. Cast: Reese Witherspoon, Luke Wilson. 96 mins. (*)

*Legally Blonde 2: Red, White and Blonde* (USA: 2003) Director: Charles Herman-Wurmfeld. Screenplay: Amanda Brown, Eve Ahlert. Cast: Reese Witherspoon, Sally Field. 95 mins. (*)

*Letters from Iwo Jima* (USA: 2006) Director: Clint Eastwood. Screenplay: Iris Yamashita. Cast: Ken Watanabe. 141 mins. (*)

# Selected Filmography

*The Life and Times of Judge Roy Bean* (USA: 1972) Director: John Huston. Screenplay: John Milius. Cast: Paul Newman, Stacy Keach, Ava Gardner, Jacqueline Bisset. 124 mins. (*)

*Lilies of the Field* (USA: 1963) Director: Ralph Nelson. Screenplay: James Poe. Cast: Sidney Poitier, Lilia Skala. 93 mins. (*)

*Lincoln* (USA: 2012) Director: Steven Spielberg. Screenplay: Tony Kushner. Cast: Daniel Day-Lewis, Sally Field, David Strathairn. 150 mins. (*)

*Abe Lincoln in Illinois* (USA: 1940) Director: John Cromwell. Screenplay: Robert E. Sherwood. Cast: Raymond Massey, Ruth Gordon. 110 mins. (*)

*The Lincoln Lawyer* (USA: 2011) Director: Brad Furman. Screenplay: John Romano. Cast: Matthew McConaughey, Marisa Tomei. 118 mins. (*)

*Lions for Lambs* (USA: 2007) Director: Robert Redford. Screenplay: Matthew Michael Carnahan. Cast: Robert Redford, Meryl Streep, Tom Cruise. 92 mins. (*)

*Little Caesar* (USA: 1930) Director: Mervyn LeRoy. Screenplay: Francis Faragoh, Robert E. Lee. Cast: Edward G. Robinson, Glenda Farrell, Sidney Blackmer, Douglas Fairbanks Jr. 80 mins. (*)

*Little Tokyo, U.S.A.* (USA: 1942) Director: Otto Brower. Screenplay: George Bricker. Cast: Preston Foster, Brenda Joyce. 64 mins.

*The Longest Day* (USA: 1962) Director: Ken Annakin. Screenplay: Bernhard Wicki. Cast: John Wayne, Richard Burton, Red Buttons, Robert Mitchum. 179 mins. (*)

*Losing Isaiah* (USA: 1995) Director: Stephen Gyllenhaal. Screenplay: Naomi Foner. Cast: Jessica Lange, Halle Berry. 111 mins. (*)

*The Lucky Ones* (USA: 2008) Director: Neil Burger. Screenplay: Neil Burger, Dirk Wittenborn. Cast: Tim Robbins, Rachel McAdams, Michael Pena. 115 mins. (*)

*M*A*S*H* (USA: 1970) Director: Robert Altman. Screenplay: Ring Lardner Jr. Cast: Donald Sutherland, Elliott Gould, Robert Duvall. 116 mins. (*)

*Mad Max* (USA: 1980) Director: George Miller. Screenplay: George Miller. Cast: Mel Gibson, Joanne Samuel. 93 mins. (*)

*The Majestic* (USA: 2001) Director: Frank Darabont. Screenplay: Michael Sloane. Cast: Jim Carrey. 152 mins. (*)

*Malcolm X* (USA: 1992) Director: Spike Lee. Screenplay: Spike Lee, Arnold Perl, James Baldwin. Cast: Denzel Washington, Angela Bassett, Albert Hall, Al Freeman Jr. 201 mins. (*)

*Man Hunt* (USA: 1941) Director: Fritz Lang. Screenplay: Dudley Nichols. Cast: Walter Pidgeon, Joan Bennett, George Sanders. 105 mins. (*)

*The Man Who Shot Liberty Valance* (USA: 1962) Director: John Ford. Screenplay: Willis Goldbeck, James Warner Bellah. Cast: James Stewart, John Wayne, Vera Miles, Lee Marvin. 123 mins. (*)

*The Man with the Golden Arm* (USA: 1955) Director: Otto Preminger. Screenplay: Walter Newman. Cast: Frank Sinatra, Eleanor Parker, Kim Novak. 119 mins. (*)

*The Manchurian Candidate* (USA: 2004) Director: Jonathan Demme. Screenplay: Daniel Pyne, Dean Georgaris. Cast: Denzel Washington, Meryl Streep, Liev Schreiber. 130 mins. (*)

*The Manchurian Candidate* (USA: 1962) Director: John Frankenheimer. Screenplay: George Axelrod, John Frankenheimer. Cast: Frank Sinatra, Laurence Harvey, Janet Leigh, James Gregory, Angela Lansbury. 126 mins. (*)

*Manhattan Project* (USA: 1986) Director: Marshall Brickman. Screenplay: Marshall Brickman. Cast: John Lithgow, Christopher Collet, Cynthia Nixon, Jill Eikenberry. 112 mins. (*)

*Mars Attacks!* (USA: 1996) Director: Tim Burton. Screenplay: Len Brown et al. Cast: Jack Nicholson, Glenn Close. 106 mins. (*)

*A Martyr to His Cause* (USA: 1911) Produced by the AFL's McNamara Legal Defense Committee. Two reels.

*The Mask of Fu Manchu* (USA: 1932) Director: Charles Brabin. Screenplay: Irene Kuhn, Edgar Allan Woolf. Cast: Boris Karloff, Lewis Stone. 68 mins. (*)

*Meet John Doe* (USA: 1941) Director: Frank Capra. Screenplay: Robert Riskin, Richard Connell, Robert Presnell. Cast: Gary Cooper, Barbara Stanwyck, Edward Arnold. 135 mins. (*)

*Men in War* (USA: 1957) Director: Anthony Mann. Screenplay: Philip Yordan. Cast: Robert Ryan, Aldo Ray. 102 mins. (*)

*The Messenger* (USA: 2009) Director: Oren Moverman. Screenplay: Alessandro Camon, Oren Moverman. Cast: Woody Harrelson, Ben Wilson. 105 min. (*)

*Michael Clayton* (USA: 2007) Director: Tony Gilroy. Screenplay: Tony Gilroy. Cast: George Clooney, Tom Wilkinson, Tilda Swinton. 120 mins. (*)

*Milk* (USA: 2008) Director: Gus Van Sant. Screenplay: Dustin Lance Black. Cast: Sean Penn, Josh Brolin, Emile Hirsch. 127 min. (*)

*Miracle at St. Anna* (USA/Italy: 2008) Director: Spike Lee. Screenplay: James McBride. Cast: Derek Luke, Michael Ealy. 160 mins. (*)

*Missing* (USA: 1982) Director: Costa-Gavras. Screenplay: Costa-Gavras, Donald Stewart. Cast: Jack Lemmon, Sissy Spacek, John Shea. 122 mins. (*)

*Missing in Action* (USA: 1984) Director: Joseph Zito. Screenplay: James Bruner. Cast: Chuck Norris, M. Emmet Walsh. 101 mins. (*)

*Missing in Action 2: The Beginning* (USA: 1985) Director: Lance Hool. Screenplay: Steve Bing. Cast: Chuck Norris, Soon-Teck Oh. 96 mins. (*)

*Mission to Moscow* (USA: 1943) Director: Michael Curtiz. Screenplay: Howard Koch. Cast: Walter Huston, Ann Harding, Oscar Homolka. 123 mins.

*Mississippi Burning* (USA: 1988) Director: Alan Parker. Screenplay: Chris Gerolmo. Cast: Gene Hackman, Willem Dafoe, Frances McDormand, Brad Dourif. 127 mins. (*)

*Mo' Better Blues* (USA: 1990) Director: Spike Lee. Screenplay: Spike Lee. Cast: Denzel Washington, Wesley Snipes, Spike Lee. 127 mins. (*)

*Modern Times* (USA: 1936) Director: Charles Chaplin. Screenplay: Charles Chaplin. Cast: Charles Chaplin, Paulette Goddard. 85 mins. (*)

*Mommie Dearest* (USA: 1981) Director: Frank Perry. Screenplay: Robert Getchell. Cast: Faye Dunaway, Diana Scarwid. 129 mins. (*)

*Moneyball* (USA: 2011) Director: Bennett Miller. Screenplay: Steven Zaillian, Aaron Sorkin et al. Cast: Brad Pitt, Jonah Hill. 133 mins. (*)

*Monster's Ball* (USA: 2001) Director: Marc Forster. Screenplay: Milo Addica, Will Rokos. Cast: Billy Bob Thornton, Halle Berry. 111 mins. (*)

*The Moon Is Blue* (USA: 1953) Director: Otto Preminger. Screenplay: F. Hugh Herbert. Cast: William Holden, David Niven, Maggie McNamara. 99 mins. (*)

*The Moon Is Down* (USA: 1943) Director: Irving Pichel. Screenplay: Nunnally Johnson. Cast: Cedric Hardwicke, Henry Travers, Lee J. Cobb. 90 mins.

*The Mortal Storm* (USA: 1940) Director: Frank Borzage. Screenplay: Claudine West, George Froeschel, Anderson Ellis. Cast: Margaret Sullavan, James Stewart, Robert Young. 100 mins. (*)

*The Mouthpiece* (USA: 1932) Directors: Elliott Nugent, James Flood. Screenplay: Joseph Jackson, Earl Baldwin. Cast: Warren William, Sidney Fox, Mae Madison, Aline MacMahon. 90 mins.

*Mr. and Mrs. Loving* (USA: Director: Richard Friedenberg Screenplay: Richard Friedenberg. Cast: Timothy Hutton, Lela Rochon. 105 mins. (*)

*Mr. Smith Goes to Washington* (USA: 1939) Director: Frank Capra. Screenplay: Sidney Buchman. Cast: James Stewart, Jean Arthur, Edward Arnold, Claude Rains. 130 mins. (*)

*Music Box* (USA: 1989) Director: Constantin Costa-Gavras. Screenplay: Joe Eszterhas. Cast: Jessica Lange, Frederic Forrest, Lukas Haas, Armin Mueller-Stahl. 126 mins. (*)

*Mutiny on the Bounty* (USA: 1935) Director: Frank Lloyd. Screenplay: Talbot Jennings, Jules Furthman, Carey Wilson. Cast: Charles Laughton, Clark Gable, Franchot Tone. 132 mins. (*)

## Selected Filmography

*My Cousin Vinny* (USA: 1992) Director: Jonathan Lynn. Screenplay: Dale Launer. Cast: Joe Pesci, Ralph Macchio, Marisa Tomei. 120 mins. (*)

*My Fellow Americans* (USA: 1996) Director: Peter Segal. Screenplay: Jack Kaplan. Cast: Jack Lemmon, James Garner, Dan Akroyd. 101 mins. (*)

*My Son John* (USA: 1952) Director: Leo McCarey. Screenplay: Myles Connolly, Leo McCarey, John Mahin. Cast: Helen Hayes, Robert Walker, Dean Jagger, Van Heflin. 122 mins.

*Nashville* (USA: 1975) Director: Robert Altman. Screenplay: Joan Tewkesbury. Cast: Keith Carradine, Lily Tomlin, Henry Gibson, Ronee Blakely, Barbara Harris. 159 mins. (*)

*Natural Born Killers* (USA: 1994) Director: Oliver Stone. Screenplay: Quentin Tarantino, Oliver Stone. Cast: Woody Harrelson, Juliette Lewis, Robert Downey Jr., Tommy Lee Jones. 119 mins. (*)

*Network* (USA: 1976) Director: Sidney Lumet. Screenplay: Paddy Chayefsky. Cast: Faye Dunaway, William Holden, Peter Finch. 120 mins. (*)

*A Nightmare on Elm Street* (USA: 1984) Director: Wes Craven. Screenplay: Wes Craven. Cast: John Saxon, Ronee Blakley. 92 mins. (*)

*Ninotchka* (USA: 1939) Director: Ernst Lubitsch. Screenplay: Billy Wilder. Cast: Greta Garbo, Melvyn Douglas. 110 mins. (*)

*Nixon* (USA: 1995) Director: Oliver Stone. Screenplay: Oliver Stone. Cast: Anthony Hopkins, Joan Allen, Powers Boothe, Ed Harris. 190 mins. (*)

*No Way Out* (USA: 1987) Director: Roger Donaldson. Screenplay: Robert Garland. Cast: Kevin Costner, Sean Young, Gene Hackman, Will Patton. 114 mins. (*)

*Norma Rae* (USA: 1979) Director: Martin Ritt. Screenplay: Harriet Frank Jr., Irving Ravetch. Cast: Sally Field, Ron Leibman, Beau Bridges, Pat Hingle. 114 mins. (*)

*North Country* (USA: 2005) Director: Niki Caro. Screenplay: Michael Seitzman. Cast: Charlize Theron, Frances McDormand. 126 mins. (*)

*The North Star* (USA: 1943) Director: Lewis Milestone. Screenplay: Lillian Hellman. Cast: Anne Baxter, Dana Andrews, Walter Huston, Farley Granger. 105 mins. (*)

*Nothing But a Man* (USA: 1964) Director: Michael Roemer. Screenplay: Robert Getchell, Robert M. Young. Cast: Ivan Dixon, Abbey Lincoln. 92 mins. (*)

*Nothing But the Truth* (USA: 2008) Director: Rod Lurie. Screenplay: Rod Lurie. Cast: Kate Beckinsale, Matt Dillon. 108 mins. (*)

*Objective, Burma!* (USA: 1945) Director: Raoul Walsh. Screenplay: Ranald MacDougall, Lester Cole. Cast: Errol Flynn, James Brown, William Prince, George Tobias. 142 mins. (*)

*On the Beach* (USA: 1959) Director: Stanley Kramer. Screenplay: John Paxon, James Lee Barrett. Cast: Gregory Peck, Ava Gardner, Fred Astaire, Anthony Perkins. 133 mins. (*)

*On the Waterfront* (USA: 1954) Director: Elia Kazan. Screenplay: Budd Schulberg. Cast: Marlon Brando, Rod Steiger, Eva Marie Saint, Lee J. Cobb. 108 mins. (*)

*The Ox-Bow Incident* (USA: 1943) Director: William A. Wellman. Screenplay: Lamar Trotti. Cast: Henry Fonda, Harry Morgan, Dana Andrews, Anthony Quinn. 75 mins. (*)

*The Package* (USA: 1989) Director: Andrew Davis. Screenplay: John Bishop. Cast: Gene Hackman, Tommy Lee Jones, Joanna Cassidy, Dennis Franz. 108 mins. (*)

*Panic in Year Zero!* (USA: 1962) Director: Ray Milland. Screenplay: John Morton (II), Jay Simms. Cast: Ray Milland, Jean Hagen, Frankie Avalon, Mary Mitchell. 92 mins. (*)

*The Parallax View* (USA: 1974) Director: Alan J. Pakula. Screenplay: David Giler, Lorenzo Semple Jr., Loren Singer. Cast: Warren Beatty, Hume Cronyn, William Daniels, Paula Prentiss. 102 mins. (*)

*The Path to 9/11* (USA: 2006) Director: David L. Cunningham. Screenplay: John Miller, Michael Stone. Cast: Harvey Keitel, Wendy Crewson. 240 mins. (*)

*Patton* (USA: 1970) Director: Franklin J. Schaffner. Screenplay: Francis Ford Coppola, Edmund H. North. Cast: George C. Scott, Karl Malden. 171 mins. (*)

*The Peacemaker* (USA: 1997) Director: Mimi Leder. Screenplay: Andrew and Leslie Cockburn. Cast: George Clooney, Nicole Kidman. 124 mins. (*)

*Pearl Harbor* (USA: 2001) Director: Michael Bay. Screenplay: Randall Wallace. Cast: Ben Affleck, Josh Hartnett. 183 mins. (*)

*The Pelican Brief* (USA: 1993) Director: Alan J. Pakula. Screenplay: Alan J. Pakula. Cast: Julia Roberts, Denzel Washington. 141 mins. (*)

*The People Against O'Hara* (USA: 1951) Director: John Sturges. Screenplay: John Monk Jr. Cast: Spencer Tracy, Diana Lynn, Pat O'Brien. 102 mins.

*The Perfect Husband: The Laci Peterson Story* (USA: 2004) Director: Roger Young. TV Script: Dave Erickson. Cast: Dean Cain. 120 mins.

*Philadelphia* (USA: 1993) Director: Jonathan Demme. Screenplay: Ron Nyswaner. Cast: Tom Hanks, Denzel Washington. 125 mins. (*)

*Pinky* (USA: 1949) Director: Elia Kazan. Screenplay: Philip Dunne, Dudley Nichols. Cast: Jeanne Crain, Ethel Waters, Ethel Barrymore. 102 mins. (*)

*Pirates of the Caribbean: At World's End* (USA: 2007) Director: Gore Verbinski. Screenplay: Ted Elliott et al. Cast: Johnny Depp, Orlando Bloom. 167 mins. (*)

*Pirates of the Caribbean: Curse of the Black Pearl* (USA: 2003) Director: Gore Verbinski. Screenplay: Ted Elliott et al. Cast: Johnny Depp, Orlando Bloom. 143 mins. (*)

*Pirates of the Caribbean: Dead Man's Chest* (USA: 2006). Director: Gore Verbinski. Screenplay: Ted Elliott et al. Cast: Johnny Depp, Keira Knightley. 151 mins. (*)

*Pirates of the Caribbean: On Stranger Tides* (USA: 2011) Director: Rob Marshall. Screenplay: Ted Elliott et al. Cast: Johnny Depp, Penelope Cruz. 136 mins. (*)

*Platoon* (USA: 1986) Director: Oliver Stone. Screenplay: Oliver Stone. Cast: Charlie Sheen, Willem Dafoe, Tom Berenger. 113 mins. (*)

*Point Break* (USA: 1991) Director: Kathryn Bigelow. Screenplay: W. Peter Lliff. Cast: Patrick Swayze, Keanu Reeves. 122 mins. (*)

*Pork Chop Hill* (USA: 1959) Director: Lewis Milestone. Screenplay: James R. Webb. Cast: Gregory Peck, Harry Guardino, Rip Torn, George Peppard. 97 mins. (*)

*Presumed Innocent* (USA: 1990) Director: Alan J. Pakula. Screenplay: Frank Pierson. Cast: Harrison Ford, Brian Dennehy, Bonnie Bedelia, Greta Scacchi. 127 mins. (*)

*Primary Colors* (USA: 1998) Director: Mike Nichols. Screenplay: Elaine May. Cast: John Travolta, Emma Thompson. 140 mins. (*)

*Prisoner of War* (USA: 1954) Director: Andrew Marton. Screenplay: Allen Rivkin. Cast: Ronald Reagan, Steve Forrest. 80 mins.

*The Public Enemy* (USA: 1931) Director: William Wellman. Screenplay: Kubec Glasmon, John Bright. Cast: James Cagney, Edward Woods, Jean Harlow, Jean Blondell. 83 mins. (*)

*Pulp Fiction* (USA: 1994) Director: Quentin Tarantino. Screenplay: Quentin Tarantino, Roger Avary. Cast: John Travolta, Samuel L. Jackson. 154 mins. (*)

*The Rack* (USA: 1974) Director: Arnold Laven. Screenplay: Stewart Stern. Cast: Paul Newman, Wendell Corey. 100 mins. (*)

*The Rainmaker* (USA: 1997) Director: Francis Ford Coppola. Screenplay: Francis Ford Coppola. Cast: Matt Damon, Danny DeVito. 135 mins. (*)

*A Raisin in the Sun* (USA: 1961) Director: Daniel Petrie. Screenplay: Lorraine Hansberry. Cast: Sidney Poitier, Ruby Dee, Claudia McNeil. 128 mins. (*)

*Rambo: First Blood Part II* (USA: 1985) Director: George Pan Cosmatos. Screenplay: James Cameron, Kevin Jarre, Michael Kozoll, Phil Alden Robinson, Sylvester Stallone. Cast: Sylvester Stallone, Richard Crenna. 93 mins. (*)

*The Reagans* (USA: 2003) Director: Robert Allan Ackerman. TV Script: Jane Marchwood. Cast: Judy Davis, James Brolin. 120 mins.

# Selected Filmography

*Recount* (USA: 2008) Director: Jay Roach. Screenplay: Danny Strong. Cast: Kevin Spacey, Laura Dern. 116 mins. (*)

*Red Corner* (USA: 1997) Director: Jon Avnet. Screenplay: Robert King. Cast: Richard Gere, Bai Ling. 119 mins. (*)

*Red Dawn* (USA: 1984) Director: John Milius. Screenplay: Kevin Reynolds. Cast: Powers Boothe, Ron O'Neal, Patrick Swayze. 114 mins. (*)

*The Red Kimona* (USA: 1925) Director: Walter Lang. Screenplay: Dorothy Arzner. Cast: Priscilla Bonner, Tyrone Power Sr. 77 min. (*)

*The Red Menace* (USA: 1944) Director: R. G. Springsteen. Screenplay: Albert Demond, Gerald Geraghty. Cast: Robert Rockwell, Hanna Axman. 81 mins. (*)

*Red Nightmare* (USA: 1962) Director: George Waggner. Produced for the Department of Defense. Cast: Peter Brown, Jeanne Cooper, Jack Kelly. 30 mins.

*Red River* (USA: 1948) Director: Howard Hawkes. Screenplay: Borden Chase, Charles Schnee. Cast: John Wayne, Montgomery Clift, Walter Brennen, Joanna Dru. 133 mins. (*)

*Red Tails* (USA: 2012) Director: Anthony Hemingway. Screenplay: John Ridley et al. Cast: Cuba Gooding Jr, Terrence Howard. 125 mins. (*)

*Redacted* (USA: 2007) Director: Brian De Palma. Screenplay: Brian De Palma. Cast: Happy Anderson, Patrick Carroll. 90 mins. (*)

*Red-Headed Woman* (USA: 1932) Director: Jack Conway. Screenplay: Anita Loos et al. Cast: Jean Harlow, Chester Morris. 79 mins. (*)

*Reds* (USA: 1981) Director: Warren Beatty. Screenplay: Trevor Griffiths, Warren Beatty. Cast: Warren Beatty, Diane Keaton, Jack Nicholson. 194 min. (*)

*Rendition* (USA: 2007) Director: Gavin Hood. Screenplay: Kelley Sane. Cast: Reese Witherspoon, Jake Gyllenhaal. 122 mins. (*)

*Rescue Dawn* (USA: 2007) Director: Werner Herzog. Screenplay: Werner Herzog. Cast: Christian Bale, Steve Zahn, Jeremy Davies. 126 mins. (*)

*Reservoir Dogs* (USA: 1992) Director: Quentin Tarantino. Screenplay: Quentin Tarantino. Cast: Harvey Keitel, Tim Roth, Michael Madsen, Steve Buscemi. 100 mins. (*)

*Reversal of Fortune* (USA: 1990) Director: Barbet Schroeder. Screenplay: Nicholas Kazan. Cast: Jeremy Irons, Glenn Close, Ron Silver, Annabella Sciorra. 112 mins. (*)

*The Right Stuff* (USA: 1993) Director: Philip Kaufman. Screenplay: Philip Kaufman. Cast: Sam Shepard, Scott Glenn, Ed Harris. 193 mins. (*)

*Rolling Thunder* (USA: 1977) Director: John Flynn. Screenplay: Paul Schrader. Cast: William Devane, Tommy Lee Jones. 99 mins. (*)

*Roots* (USA: 1977) Director: Marvin Chomsky, John Erman. TV Script: William Blinn, M. Charles Cohen. Cast: Le Var Burton, Edward Asner. 573 mins. (*)

*Rules of Engagement* (USA: 2000) Director: William Friedkin. Screenplay: Stephen Gaghan. Cast: Tommy Lee Jones, Samuel L. Jackson. 127 mins. (*)

*Runaway Jury* (USA: 2003) Director: Gary Fleder. Screenplay: Brian Koppelman. Cast: John Cusack, Gene Hackman, Dustin Hoffman. 127 mins. (*)

*The Russians Are Coming, the Russians Are Coming* (USA: 1966) Director: Norman Jewison. Screenplay: William Rose. Cast: Carl Reiner, Eva Marie Saint, Alan Arkin. 126 min. (*)

*Salt of the Earth* (USA: 1954) Director: Herbert Biberman. Screenplay: Michael Wilson. Cast: Rosaura Revueltas, Juan Chacon, Will Geer. 94 mins. (*)

*Salvador* (USA: 1986) Director: Oliver Stone. Screenplay: Oliver Stone. Cast: James Woods, James Belushi, John Savage, Michael Murphy. 123 mins. (*)

*Sands of Iwo Jima* (USA: 1949) Director: Allan Dwan. Screenplay: Harry Brown, James Edward Grant. Cast: John Wayne, Forrest Tucker, John Agar, Richard Jaeckel. 109 mins. (*)

*Saving Jessica Lynch* (USA: 2003) Director: Peter Markle. TV Script: John Fasano. Cast: Laura Regan, Nicholas Guilak. 120 mins.

*Saving Private Ryan* (USA: 1998) Director: Steven Spielberg. Screenplay: Robert Rodat. Cast: Tom Hanks, Edward Burns, Matt Damon, Tom Sizemore. 170 mins. (*)

*Savior* (USA: 1998) Director: Predrag Antonijevic. Screenplay: Robert Orr. Cast: Dennis Quaid. 103 mins. (*)

*Scarface* (USA: 1931) Director: Howard Hawkes. Screenplay: Ben Hecht, W.R. Burnett. Cast: Paul Muni, Ann Dvorak, Karen Morley. 93 mins. (*)

*Scarlet Pages* (USA: 1930) Director: Ray Enright. Cast: Elsie Ferguson, John Halliday. 65 mins.

*Scary Movie* (USA: 2000) Director: Keenen Ivory Wayans. Screenplay: Wayans et al. Cast: Jon Abrahams, Carmen Electra. 88 mins. (*)

*Schindler's List* (USA: 1993) Director: Steven Spielberg. Screenplay: Steven Zallian. Cast: Liam Neeson, Ben Kingsley, Ralph Fiennes. 195 mins. (*)

*Seabiscuit* (USA: 2003) Director: Gary Ross. Screenplay: Gary Ross. Cast: Jeff Bridges, Chris Cooper, Tobey Maguire. 141 mins. (*)

*Secret Honor* (USA: 1985) Director: Robert Altman. Screenplay: Donald Freen, Arnold Stone. Cast: Philip Baker Hall. 90 mins. (*)

*The Seduction of Joe Tynan* (USA: 1979) Director: Jerry Schatzberg. Screenplay: Alan Alda. Cast: Alan Alda, Barbara Harris, Meryl Streep, Melvyn Douglas. 107 mins. (*)

*Sergeant York* (USA: 1941) Director: Howard Hawks. Screenplay: Abe Finkel, Harry Chandler, Howard Koch, John Huston. Cast: Gary Cooper, Joan Leslie, Walter Brennan. 134 mins. (*)

*Serious Moonlight* (USA: 2009) Director: Cheryl Hines. Screenplay: Adrienne Shelly. Cast: Meg Ryan, Timothy Hutton. 93 mins. (*)

*Set It Off* (USA: 1996) Director: F. Gary Gray. Screenplay: Takashi Bufford. Cast: Jada Pinkett Smith, Queen Latifah. 121 mins. (*)

*Seven Years in Tibet* (USA: 1997) Director: Jean-Jacques Annaud. Screenplay: Becky Johnston. Cast: Brad Pitt, David Thewlis, B.D. Wong. 139 mins. (*)

*sex, lies, and videotape* (USA: 1989) Director: Steven Soderberg. Screenplay: Steven Soderberg. Cast: James Spader, Andie MacDowell, Peter Gallagher. 101 mins. (*)

*Shakespeare in Love* (UK/USA: 1998) Director: John Madden. Screenplay: Marc Norman, Tom Stoppard. Cast: Joseph Fiennes, Gwyneth Paltrow. 122 mins. (*)

*She Done Him Wrong* (USA: 193) Director: Lowell Sherman. Screenplay: Harvey Theu, John Bright. Cast: Mae West, Cary Grant. 65 mins. (*)

*Showboat* (USA: 1936) Director: James Whale. Screenplay: Oscar Hammerstein II. Cast: Irene Dunne, Allan Jones, Paul Robeson. 113 mins, (*)

*Showgirls* (USA: 1995) Director: Paul Verhoeven. Screenplay: Joe Eszterhas. Cast: Elizabeth Berkley, Kyle MacLachlan, Gina Gershon. 131 mins. (*)

*The Siege* (USA: 1998) Director: Edward Zwick. Screenplay: Lawrence Wright. Cast: Denzel Washington, Bruce Willis, Annette Bening. 116 mins. (*)

*Silkwood* (USA: 1983) Director: Mike Nichols. Screenplay: Nora Ephron, Alice Arlen. Cast: Meryl Streep, Kurt Russell, Cher. 131 mins. (*)

*Since You Went Away* (USA: 1944) Director: John Cromwell. Screenplay: David O. Selznick. Cast: Claudette Colbert, Jennifer Jones, Shirley Temple, Joseph Cotton. 172 mins. (*)

*So Proudly We Hail* (USA: 1943) Director: Mark Sandrich. Screenplay: Alan Scott. Cast: Claudette Colbert, Paulette Goddard, Veronica Lake. 126 min. (*)

*Song of Russia* (USA: 1943) Director: Gregory Ratoff. Screenplay: Paul Jarrico, Richard Collins. Cast: Robert Taylor, Susan Peters. 107 mins.

*Speechless* (USA: 1994) Director: Ron Underwood. Screenplay: Robert King. Cast: Michael Keaton, Geena Davis, Christopher Reeve. 98 mins. (*)

Selected Filmography

*Spiderman* (USA: 2002) Director: Sam Raimi. Screenplay: David Koepp. Cast: Tobey Maguire, William Dafoe, Kirsten Dunst. 121 mins. (*)

*Spring Breakers* (USA: 2012) Director: Harmony Korine. Screenplay: Harmony Korine. Cast: James Franco. 93 mins.(*)

*Stalag 17* (USA: 1953) Director: Billy Wilder. Screenplay: Billy Wilder, Edwin Blum. Cast: William Holden, Don Taylor, Otto Preminger. 120 mins. (*)

*Star Wars* (USA: 1977) Director: George Lucas. Screenplay: George Lucas. Cast: Mark Hamill, Carrie Fisher, Harrison Ford, Alec Guinness. 121 mins. (*)

*State of Play* (USA: 2009) Director: Kevin Macdonald. Screenplay: Matthew Michael Carnahan, Tony Gilroy. Cast: Russell Crowe, Ben Affleck, Rachel McAdams. 127 min. (*)

*State of the Union* (USA: 1948) Director: Frank Capra. Screenplay: Myles Connolly, Anthony Veiller, Russell Crouse, Howard Lindsay. Cast: Spencer Tracy, Katharine Hepburn, Angela Lansbury, Van Johnson. 124 mins. (*)

*The Steel Helmet* (USA: 1951) Director: Samuel Fuller. Screenplay: Samuel Fuller. Cast: Gene Evans, Robert Hutton, Richard Loo. 84 mins. (*)

*Stop-Loss* (USA: 2008) Director: Kimberly Peirce. Screenplay: Mark Richard, Kimberly Peirce. Cast: Ryan Phillippe, Abbie Cornish. 113 mins. (*)

*Storm Warning* (USA: 1951) Director: Stuart Heisler. Screenplay: Daniel Fuchs, Richard Brooks. Cast: Ronald Reagan, Ginger Rogers. 93 min. (*)

*Stormy Weather* (USA: 1943) Director: Andrew L. Stone. Screenplay: Frederick J. Jackson. Cast: Lena Horne, Bill Robinson. 77 mins. (*)

*The Story of GI Joe* (USA: 1945) Director: William A. Wellman. Screenplay: Leopold Atlas, Guy Endore, Philip Stevenson. Cast: Burgess Meredith, Robert Mitchum, Freddie Steele. 108 mins.

*A Streetcar Named Desire* (USA: 1951) Director: Elia Kazan. Screenplay: Tennessee Williams. Cast: Vivien Leigh, Marlon Brando, Kim Hunter. 122 mins. (*)

*Sudden Death* (USA: 1995) Director: Peter Hyams. Screenplay: Gene Quintano, Karen Baldwin. Cast: Jean-Claude Van Damme, Powers Boothe. 110 mins. (*)

*Suddenly* (USA: 1954) Director: Lewis Allen. Screenplay: Richard Sale. Cast: Frank Sinatra, Sterling Hayden, James Gleason, Nancy Gates. 75 mins. (*)

*The Sum of All Fears* (USA/Germany: 2002) Director: Phil Alden Robinson. Screenplay: Paul Attanasio. Cast: Ben Affleck, Morgan Freeman. 124 mins. (*)

*Summertree* (USA: 1971) Director: Anthony Newley. Screenplay: Edward Hume, Stephen Yafa. Cast: Michael Douglas, Brenda Vaccaro, Jack Warden. 89 mins. (*)

*Sunrise at Campobello* (USA: 1960) Director: Vincent J. Donehue. Screenplay: Dore Schary. Cast: Ralph Bellamy, Greer Garson, Hume Cronyn, Jean Hagen. 143 mins. (*)

*Suspect* (USA: 1987) Director: Peter Yates. Screenplay: Eric Roth. Cast: Dennis Quaid, Cher, Liam Neeson. 101 mins. (*)

*Swing Vote* (USA: 2008) Director: Joshua Michael Stern. Screenplay: Jason Richman, Joshua Michael Stern. Cast: Kevin Costner, Kelsey Grammer. 119 mins. (*)

*Syriana* (USA: 2005) Director: Stephen Gaghan. Screenplay: Stephen Gaghan. Cast: George Clooney, Matt Damon. 126 min. (*)

*Taking Chance* (USA: 2009) Director: Ross Katz. Screenplay: Ross Katz, Michael Strobl. Cast: Kevin Bacon, Tom Aldredge. 77 mins. (*)

*Tanner '88* (USA: 1988) Director: Robert Altman. Screenplay: Gary Trudeau. Cast: Michael Murphy, Pamela Reed, Cynthia Nixon. 120 mins. (*)

*Tarantula* (USA: 1955) Director: Jack Arnold. Screenplay: Robert M. Fresco, Martin Berkeley. Cast: Leo G. Carroll, John Agar, Mara Corday. 81 mins. (*)

*Taxi Driver* (USA: 1976) Director: Martin Scorsese. Screenplay: Paul Schrader. Cast: Robert DeNiro, Jodie Foster, Harvey Keitel. 112 mins. (*)

*The Teahouse of the August Moon* (USA: 1956) Director: Daniel Mann. Screenplay: John Patrick. Cast: Marlon Brando, Glenn Ford. 123 mins. (*)

*Tender Comrade* (USA: 1943) Director: Edward Dmytryk. Screenplay: Dalton Trumbo. Cast: Ginger Rogers, Robert Ryan, Ruth Hussey, Patricia Collinge. 101 mins. (*)

*Testament* (USA: 1983) Director: Lynne Littman. Screenplay: John Sacret Young, Carol Amen. Cast: Jane Alexander, William Devane, Ross Harris, Roxana Zal. 90 mins. (*)

*Thelma and Louise* (USA: 1991) Director: Ridley Scott. Screenplay: Callie Khouri. Cast: Susan Sarandon, Geena Davis. 128 mins. (*)

*Them!* (USA: 1954) Director: Gordon Douglas. Screenplay: Ted Sherdeman, Russell Hughes. Cast: James Whitmore. Edmund Gwenn, Joan Weldon, James Arness. 93 mins. (*)

*They Were Expendable* (USA: 1945) Directors: John Ford, Robert Montgomery (uncredited). Screenplay: Frank W. Weed. Cast: John Wayne, Robert Montgomery, Donna Reed. 135 mins. (*)

*They Won't Forget* (USA: 1937) Director: Mervyn LeRoy. Screenplay: Robert Rossen, Aben Kandel. Cast: Claude Rains, Otto Kruger, Lana Turner, Alan Joslyn, Edward Norris. 95 mins. (*)

*The Thin Red Line* (USA: 1998) Director: Terrence Malick. Screenplay: Terrence Malick. Cast: Sean Penn, Nick Nolte, John Cusack, Woody Harrelson, George Clooney. 166 mins. (*)

*The Thing* (USA: 1951) Director: Christian Nyby. Screenplay: Charles Lederer. Cast: Kenneth Tobay, James Arness, Margaret Sheridan. 87 mins. (*)

*Thirteen Days* (USA: 2000) Director: Roger Donaldson. Screenplay: David Self. Cast: Kevin Costner, Bruce Greenwood, Steven Culp. 147 mins. (*)

*Three Kings* (USA: 1999) Director: David O. Russell. Screenplay: David O. Russell. Cast: George Clooney, Mark Wahlberg. 114 mins. (*)

*Thurgood* (USA: 2011) Director: Michael Stevens. Screenplay: George Stevens Jr. Cast: Laurence Fishburne. 105 mins. (*)

*A Time to Kill* (USA: 1996) Director: Joel Schumacher. Screenplay: Akiva Goldsman. Cast: Matthew McConaughey, Sandra Bullock, Samuel L. Jackson. 149 mins. (*)

*To Kill a Mockingbird* (USA: 1962) Director: Robert Mulligan. Screenplay: Horton Foote. Cast: Gregory Peck, Brock Peters, Robert Duvall, Philip Alford, Mary Badham. 129 mins. (*)

*To the Shores of Hell* (USA: 1965) Director: Will Zens. Screenplay: Will Zens, Robert McFadden. Cast: Marshall Thompson, Kiva Lawrence. 82 mins. (*)

*Traffic* (Germany/USA: 2000) Director: Steven Soderbergh. Screenplay: Stephen Gaghan. Cast: Michael Douglas, Benicio del Toro, Don Cheadle. 147 mins. (*)

*Trial* (USA: 1955) Director: Mark Robson. Screenplay: Don Mankiewicz. Cast: Glenn Ford, Dorothy McGuire, Arthur Kennedy. 105 mins.

*True Believer* (USA: 1989) Director: Joseph Ruben. Screenplay: Wesley Strick. Cast: James Woods, Robert Downey Jr. 103 mins. (*)

*True Colors* (USA: 1991) Director: Herbert Ross. Screenplay: Kevin Wade. Cast: John Cusack, James Spader, Imogen Stubbs, Mandy Patinkin. 111 mins. (*)

*True Lies* (USA: 1994) Director: James Cameron. Screenplay: James Cameron. Cast: Arnold Schwarzenegger, Jamie Lee Curtis. 141 mins. (*)

*Truman* (USA: 1995) Director: Frank Pierson. Screenplay: Tom Rickman. Cast: Gary Sinise, Diana Scarwid, Richard Dysart. 135 mins. (*)

*U-571* (France/USA: 2000) Director: Jonathan Mostow. Screenplay: Jonathan Mostow. Cast: Matthew McConaughey, Bill Paxton, Harvey Keitel. 116 mins. (*)

*Uncommon Valor* (USA: 1983) Director: Ted Kotcheff. Screenplay: Joe Gayton. Cast: Gene Hackman, Fred Ward, Patrick Swayze, Randall Cobb. 105 mins. (*)

*Unfaithful* (USA/Germany: 2002) Director: Adrian Lyne. Screenplay: Alvin Sargent. Cast: Diane Lane, Richard Gere. 124 mins. (*)

# Selected Filmography

*United 93* (USA/France/UK: 2006) Director: Paul Greengrass. Screenplay: Paul Greengrass. Cast: David Alan Basche. 111 mins. (*)

*An Unmarried Woman* (USA: 1978) Director: Paul Mazursky. Screenplay: Paul Mazursky. Cast: Jill Clayburgh, Alan Bates. 124 mins. (*)

*Unthinkable* (USA: 2010) Director: Gregory Jordan. Screenplay: Peter Woodward. Cast: Samuel L. Jackson, Michael Sheen. 97 mins. (*)

*The Verdict* (USA: 1982) Director: Sidney Lumet. Screenplay: David Mamet. Cast: Paul Newman, James Mason, Charlotte Rampling, Jack Warden. 122 mins. (*)

*A View from the Bridge* (France: 1961) Director: Sidney Lumet. Screenplay: Norman Rosten. Cast: Raf Vallone, Maureen Stapleton, Jean Sorel, Carol Lawrence. 110 mins.

*W* (USA: 2008) Director: Oliver Stone. Screenplay: Stanley Weiser. Cast: Josh Brolin, James Cromwell, Richard Dreyfuss. 129 min. (*)

*Wag the Dog* (USA: 1997) Director: Barry Levinson. Screenplay: David Mamet, Hilary Henkin. Cast: Dustin Hoffman, Robert DeNiro. 120 mins. (*)

*Wake Island* (USA: 1942) Director: John Farrow. Screenplay: W.R. Burnett, Frank Butler. Cast: Robert Preston, Brian Donlevy, William Bendix, MacDonald Carey. 88 mins. (*)

*A Walk in the Sun* (USA: 1946) Director: Lewis Milestone. Screenplay: Robert Rossen. Cast: Dana Andrews, Richard Conte, John Ireland, Lloyd Bridges. 117 mins. (*)

*War Games* (USA: 1983) Director: John Badham. Screenplay: Lawrence Lasker, Walter Parkes. Cast: Matthew Broderick, Dabney Coleman, John Wood, Ally Sheedy. 113 mins. (*)

*War Horse* (USA: 2011) Director: Steven Spielberg. Screenplay: Lee Hall et al. Cast: Jeremy Irvine, Emily Watson. 146 mins. (*)

*The War of the Roses* (USA: 1989) Director: Danny DeVito. Screenplay: Michael Leeson. Cast: Michael Douglas, Kathleen Turner. 118 mins. (*)

*The Way We Were* (USA: 1973) Director: Sydney Pollack. Screenplay: Arthur Laurents. Cast: Barbra Streisand, Robert Redford. 118 mins. (*)

*We Were Soldiers* (USA/Germany: 2002) Director: Randall Wallace. Screenplay: Randall Wallace. Cast: Mel Gibson, Madeleine Stowe. 138 mins. (*)

*Welcome to Sarajevo* (UK /USA: 1997) Director: Michael Winterbottom. Screenplay: Frank Cottrell Boyce. Cast: Woody Harrelson, Marisa Tomei, Stephen Dillane. 102 mins. (*)

*Wendy and Lucy* (USA: 2008) Director: Kelly Reichardt. Screenplay: Jon Raymond. Cast: Michelle Williams. 80 mins. (*)

*What Price Glory?* (USA: 1926) Director: Raoul Walsh. Screenplay: James T. O'Donohoe. Cast: Edmund Lowe, Victor McLaglen. 120 mins. (*)

*Where Are My Children?* (USA: 1916). Director: Lois Weber, Phillips Smalley (uncredited). Screenplay: Lois Weber, Phillips Smalley (uncredited). Cast: Tyrone Power Sr. 62 min.

*Who's Afraid of Virginia Woolf* (USA: 1966) Director: Mike Nicholas. Screenplay: Ernest Lehman. Cast: Richard Burton, Elizabeth Taylor, George Segal, Sandy Dennis. 127 mins. (*)

*The Wild One* (USA: 1953) Director: Laszlo Benedek. Screenplay: John Paxton. Cast: Marlon Brando, Mary Murphy. 79 mins. (*)

*Wilson* (USA: 1944) Director: Henry King. Screenplay: Lamar Trotti. Cast: Alexander Knox, Charles Coburn, Geraldine Fitzgerald, Thomas Mitchell. 154 mins. (*)

*Wings* (USA: 1927) Director: William Wellman. Screenplay: Hope Loring, Louis D. Lighton. Cast: Charles (Buddy) Rogers, Clara Bow, Richard Arlen. 139 mins. (*)

*Winter Kills* (USA: 1979) Director: William Richert. Screenplay: William Richert. Cast: Jeff Bridges, John Huston, Anthony Perkins, Richard Boone. 97 mins. (*)

*Winter's Bone* (USA: 2010) Director: Debra Granik. Screenplay: Debra Granik et al. Cast: Jennifer Lawrence, John Hawkes. 100 mins. (*)

*Within Our Gates* (USA: 1919) Director: Oscar Micheaux. Screenplay: Oscar Micheaux. Cast: Evelyn Preer. 77 mins.
*Woman of the Year* (USA: 1942) Director: George Stevens. Screenplay: Ring Lardner Jr., Michael Kanin. Cast: Katharine Hepburn, Spencer Tracy. 112 mins. (*)
*World Trade Center* (USA: 2006) Director: Oliver Stone. Screenplay: Andrea Berloff. Cast: Nicholas Cage, Michael Pena. 129 mins. (*)
*The World, the Flesh, and the Devil* (USA: 1959) Director: Ranald MacDougall. Screenplay: Ferdinand Reyher, Ranald MacDougall. Cast: Harry Belafonte, Inger Stevens, Mel Ferrer. 95 mins. (*)
*A Yank in the R.A.F.* (USA: 1941) Director: Henry King. Screenplay: Karl Tunberg, Darrell Ware, Darryl F. Zanuck. Cast: Tyrone Power, Betty Grable, John Sutton. 98 mins. (*)
*You Nazty Spy* (USA: 1940) Director: Jules White. 18 min.
*Young Mr. Lincoln* (USA: 1939) Director: John Ford. Screenplay: Lamar Trotti. Cast: Henry Fonda, Alice Brady, Marjorie Weaver, Arleen Whelan. 100 mins. (*)
*Zero Dark Thirty* (USA: 2012) Director: Kathryn Bigelow. Screenplay: Mark Boal. Cast: Jessica Chastian, Mark Strong. 157 mins. (*)

## Documentaries

*2016: Obama's America* (USA: 2012) Directors: Dinesh D'Souza, John Sullivan. 87 mins. (*)
*American Dream* (USA: 1989) Director: Barbara Kopple. 100 mins. (*)
*America's Answer* (USA: 1918) Produced by the U.S. Signal Corps and the Committee on Public Information.
*Baptism of Fire* (Germany: 1940) Director: Fritz Hippler. 50 mins.
*The Battle of Midway* (USA: 1942) Director: John Ford. 28 mins.
*The Battle of San Pietro* (USA: 1944) Director: John Huston. 43 mins. (*)
*Belfast, Maine* (USA: 2000) Director: Frederick Wiseman. 245 mins.
*The Big One* (USA: 1998) Director: Michael Moore. 96 mins. (*)
*Boxing Gym* (USA: 2010) Director: Frederick Wiseman. 91 min. (*)
*Bowling for Columbine* (USA: 2002) Director: Michael Moore. 120 mins. (*)
*Britain Prepared* (Great Britain: 1915) Produced by the British War Propaganda Bureau.
*Bully* (USA: 2012) Director: Lee Hirsch. 98 mins. (*)
*Capitalism: A Love Story* (USA: 2009) Director: Michael Moore. 127 mins.
*Can Mr. Smith Get to Washington, Anymore?* (USA: 2006) Director: Frank Popper. 82 mins. (*)
*Dear America: Letters Home from Vietnam* (USA: 1988) Director: Bill Couturie. 85 mins. (*)
*December 7th: The Movie* (USA:1943 ) Directors: John Ford, Gregg Toland. Narrators: Walter Huston, Harry Davenport, Dana Andrews, Paul Hurst. 82 mins. (*)
*The External Jew* (Germany: 1940). Director: Fritz Hippler.
*Fahrenheit 9/11* (USA: 2004) Director: Michael Moore. 122 mins. (*)
*Fahrenhype 9/11* (USA: 2004) Director: Alan Peterson. 80 mins. (*)
*Generation Kill* (USA: 2008) Directors: Suzanne White, Simon Cellan Jones. 360 mins. (*)
*The Ground Truth* (USA: 2006) Director: Patricia Foulkrod. 72 mins. (*)
*Gunner Palace* (USA: 2004) Directors: Petra Epperlein, Michael Tucker. 85 mins. (*)
*Harlan County, U.S.A.* (USA: 1976) Director: Barbara Kopple. 103 mins. (*)
*High School* (USA: 1968) Director: Frederick Wiseman. 75 mins.
*Hospital* (USA: 1970) Director: Frederick Wiseman. 84 mins.
*An Inconvenient Truth* (USA: 2006) Director: David Guggenheim. 96 mins. (*)
*Indoctrinate U* (USA: 2007) Director: Evan Coyne Maloney.
*The Invisible War* (USA: 2012) Director: Kirby Dick. 93 mins. (*)

## Selected Filmography

*Juvenile Court* (USA: 1973) Director: Frederick Wiseman. 144 mins. (*)

*Maid in America* (USA: 2005) Director: Anayansi Prado. 58 mins.

*Manufacturing Dissent* (Canada: 2007) Directors: Rick Caine, Debbie Melnyk. 97 mins. (*)

*Massacre in Mazar* (Ireland: 2002) Director: Jamie Doran.

*The Memphis Belle* (USA: 1943) Director: William Wyler. 45 mins. (*)

*Michael and Me* (USA: 2005) Director: Larry Elder. 90 mins. (*)

*Michael Moore Hates America* (USA: 2004) Director: Michael Wilson. 125 mins. (*)

*Nanook of the North* (USA: 1922) Director: Robert Flaherty. 55 mins.

*No End in Sight* (USA: 2007) Director: Charles Ferguson. 102 mins. (*)

*A Perfect Candidate* (USA: 1996) Directors: R.J. Cutler, David Van Taylor. 105 mins. (*)

*Pershing's Crusaders* (USA: 1918) Produced by the Committee on Public Information.

*The Plow That Broke the Plains* (USA: 1934) Director: Pare Lorentz. 49 mins. (*)

*Primate* (USA: 1974) Director: Frederick Wiseman. 105 mins. (*)

*Public Housing* (USA: 1997) Director: Frederick Wiseman. 200 mins. (*)

*The Ramparts We Watch* (USA: 1940) Director: Louis de Rochemont. Screenplay: Robert L. Richards, Cedric R. Worth. Cast: Non-professional actors. 90 mins.

*Report from the Aleutians* (USA: 1943) Director: John Huston. U.S. Signal Corps. 47 mins.

*Restrepo* (USA: 2010) Directors: Tim Hetherington, Sebastian Junger. 93 mins. (*)

*Rethink Afghanistan* (USA: 2009) Director: Robert Greenwald. 75 mins.

*The River* (USA: 1937) Director: Pare Lorentz. Produced by the Farm Security Administration. 31 min. (*)

*Roger and Me* (USA: 1989) Director: Michael Moore. 91 mins. (*)

*Sicko* (USA: 2007) Director: Michael Moore. 123 mins. (*)

*Slacker Uprising* (USA: 2008) Director: Michael Moore. 102 mins. (*)

*State Legislature* (USA: 2007) Director: Frederick Wiseman. 217 mins.

*Taxi to the Dark Side* (USA: 2007) Director: Alex Gibney. 106 mins. (*)

*The Thin Blue Line* (USA: 1988) Director: Errol Morris. 103 mins. (*)

*This Film Is Not Yet Rated* (USA: 2006) Director: Kirby Dick. 98 mins. (*)

*Titicut Follies* (USA: 1967) Director: Frederick Wiseman. 89 mins. (*)

*Triumph of the Will* (Germany: 1934) Director: Leni Riefenstahl. 115 mins. (*)

*Uncovered: The War on Iraq* (USA: 2004) Director: Robert Greenwald. 87 mins. (*)

*Under Four Flags* (USA: 1918) Director: S.L. Rothafel. Produced by the U.S. Army Signal Corp.

*The War Room* (USA: 1993) Director: Chris Hegedus, D.A. Pennebaker. 93 mins. (*)

*The War Tapes* (USA: 2006) Director: Deborah Scranton. 97 mins. (*)

*Why We Fight* series (USA: 1943–45) Director: Frank Capra. U.S. War Department Productions.

# Index

20th Century Fox, 12, 110, 295
20th Century-Fox's Movietone News, 192
*2016: Obama's America*, 16, 29, 65, 318
40 Acres and a Mule, 272
9/11 Commission, 137
9/11 terrorist attacks, 221–22, 241

## A

Aaron, Quinton, 167
ABC, 255
*Abe Lincoln in Illinois*, 17, 31
*Above and Beyond*, 247
*Absolute Power*, 130, 139
*The Accused*, 169–70, 300–1
Acheson, Dean, 18
*Action in the North Atlantic*, 184
*Adam's Rib*, 168, 297
*Advise and Consent*, 29, 122–23
Affleck, Ben, 9, 19–20, 257, 317
Afghanistan, 264
Afghanistan/Iraq Wars, 59–61, 179, 215, 221, 225–28
    statistics about, 227–28
    Hollywood productions relating to, 228–41
African Diaspora Film Festival, 317
*The African Queen*, 298
Aidid, Mohamed, 217
Aiello, Danny, 121
*Air Force One*, 27, 112, 128
al Qaeda, 226, 265
al-Sadr, Moktada, 226
*Alamo Bay*, 26
Albee, Edward, 73
Albert, Eddie, 182
Alda, Alan, 16, 138
Alexander, Jane, 255
*Alice Doesn't Live Here Anymore*, 298
*Alien*, 294
*All God's Chillun' Got Wings*, 269
*All Quiet on the Western Front*, 180, 199
*All That Heaven Allows*, 287
*All the King's Men*, 121
*All the President's Men*. 7, 21, 142

Allen, Joan, 124
Allen, Woody, 90
Alperovitz, Gar, 193
Altman, Robert, 117, 132, 135, 199
Ambrose, Stephen, 191
AMC, 75
*America's Answer*, 180
American Association for Suicide Prevention, 77
*An American Carol*, 318
American Civil Liberties Union, 156
American Civil War, 28
*American Dream*, 43, 47
American Federation of Labor, 41
American Film Institute, 271
American Film Renaissance, 51
American Legion, 102
*American Pie 2*, 87
American Political Science Association, 24
*The American President*, 36
Amet, Edward, 41
*An Inconvenient Truth*, 43
*And Justice for All*, 144–45, 155, 170
*Anatomy of a Murder*, 142, 156
Anderson, Stanley, 128
Andrews, Dana, 185, 191, 199
*Angels from Hell*, 212
*Ann Carver's Profession*, 168
Antonioni, Michelangelo, 73
*Apocalypse Now*, 31, 207–8, 210–11
*Apollo 13*, 11
Arab Spring, xxi
Araujo, Cheryl, 300
Arbuckle, Fatty, 69
*Argo*, 19–20, 314
Aristotle, 175
*Armageddon*, 128
Arness, James, 249
Arnold, Edward, 122
Arthur, Jean, 168
Arzner, Dorothy, 292–93, 297, 306
Ashby, Hal, 209
Asimow, Michael, 142, 174
Asner, Ed, 136
*The Assassination of Richard Nixon*, 137

Association of Black Women Historians, 283
*Atom Man versus Superman*, 248
*Attack of the Fifty-Foot Woman*, 29
Ayers, Lew, 180, 182
Ayers, William, 65

## B

Babbitt, Bruce, 117
*Baby Doll*, 73
*Baby Face*, 68
Bachman, Michele, xviii
*Back to Bataan*, 184, 198, 206
Bacon, Kevin, 236
*Bad Company*, 11
Bale, Christian, 214
Bales, Robert, 227
Ball, Lucille, 293
Barkun, Michael, 137
Barrymore, John, 161
Barsam, Richard, 40
Barthelmess, Richard, 268
*Basic Instinct*, 29, 82
Basinger, Jeanine, 72, 183, 189, 291
Bates, Alan, 298–299
*Battle Cry of Peace*, 179
*The Battle of Midway*, 192
*The Battle of San Pitro*, 192
*Battle of the Bulge*, 188
*Battleship*, 83
*The Beast from 20,000 Fathoms*, 249
Beatty, Warren, 3–4, 8, 14–15, 26, 116, 135, 139
Beckinsale, Kate, 304–5
*The Beginning of the End*, 247
*Behind Enemy Lines*, 218
*Behind the Rising Sun*, 187
Belafonte, Harry, 3, 271
Bellamy, Ralph, 124
Bello, Maria, 79
Bening, Annette, 36, 299
Bennett, T., 103
Berg, Peter, 257
Bergman, Ingrid, 32
Bernstein, Carl, 7, 142
Berry, Halle, 272
Bessie, Alvah, 100
Best, Willie, 268
*The Best Defense*, 156
*The Best Exotic Marigold Hotel*, 319
*The Best Man*, 114–15
*The Best Years of Our Lives*, 191, 199, 212
*A Better Life*, 26
*Beyond a Reasonable Doubt*, 164
Biberman, Herbert, 100, 104, 106

*Big Jim McLain*, 13
*The Big One*, 40, 48
*The Big Red One*, 223
*The Big Parade*, 178, 180
Bigelow, Kathryn, 233, 237, 239, 295–96, 317
bin Laden, Osama, 222, 226, 239, 242, 262
*The Birth of a Nation*, 6, 20, 28, 64, 178, 243, 267, 269
Biskind, Peter, 30
Black, Gregory, 71
*Blackhawk Down*, 217
blacklist. *See* House Un-American Activities Committee
Blacklist Company, 105–9
Blackton, J. Stuart, 179
Blair, Betsy, 105
*The Blind Side*, 167, 280–81
*Blood Work*, 158
Bloody Friday, 96
*Blow-Up*, 73
*Blue Sky*, 295
*Blue Valentine*, 82
Boal, Mark, 239
*Bob Roberts*, 115–16, 138
*Body and Soul*, 270
Bogart, Humphrey, 23, 32, 152, 154, 181, 297–98
*Bolshevism on Trial*, 42
Bond, Ward, 98
Bono, Sonny, 6
Boot, Max, 242–43
*Born on the Fourth of July*, 209
Bosnia War, 31, 217–18
Boston Jewish Film Festival, 317
Boston Marathon, xxi, 143
*Bowling for Columbine*, 40, 48, 51
*A Boy and His Dog*, 256
Boyer, Paul, 246
*Boys Don't Cry*, 232, 295
*The Boys in Company C*, 207–8
*Boyz in the Hood*, 272
Bradbury, Ray, 250
*Braddock: Missing in Action III*, 210
Bradley, James, 188–89, 192
Brando, Marlon, 73, 107, 208, 268
*Branzburg v. Hayes*, 305
*The Brass Verdict*, 158
*The Brave One*, 150–51
breakpoint.com, 87
Breasseale, J. Todd, 233–34
Brecht, Bertolt, 97, 100
Breen, Joseph, 69, 71–73
Brewer, Roy, 106
*Bridesmaids*, 26, 308
*Bridge Over the River Kwai*, 188, 196
*The Bridges at Toko-Ri*, 196

# Index

Bridges, Jeff, 124, 135
*Britain Prepared*, 41
British Academy of Film and Television Arts, 283
British Board of Film Classification, 81, 85, 150
Brock, Roslyn, 283
Broderick, Matthew, 252
Brokovich, Erin, 170–71
Brokaw, Tom, 191
*Brokeback Mountain*, 31, 85
*Broken Blossoms*, 268
Bromberg, J. Edward, 105
Bronson, Charles, 149
*Brothers*, 233–35
Brown, Clarence, 274
*Brown v. Board of Education*, 198, 270, 276, 284
Brownlow, Kevin, 28
Bruckheimer, Jerry, 217
Bryan, William Jennings, 156
Buena Vista Motion Picture Group, 295
*Buffalo Soldiers*, 11
Buhle, Paul, 10
*Bulletin of Atomic Scientists*, 261
Bullock, Sandra, 166–67, 280–81
*Bully*, 76–79, 88
bullying, 76–79
*Bulworth*, 4, 26, 116–17
Bundy, George, 18
Bureau of Motion Pictures, 182
Burger, Neil, 233
Burstyn, Ellen, 298
*Burstyn v. Wilson*, 73, 317
Burton, Tim, 129
Buscemi, Steve, 237
Bush, George H.W., 133, 217–18
Bush, George W., 5, 16, 118, 217–19, 236, 303
    film portrayal of, 48–49, 59, 117, 131
    Iraq/Afghanistan War and, 221, 225–26, 231, 243
    Michael Moore and, 29, 48–49
    *W.*, 132–33
Bush, Jeb, 132–33
*Bush v. Gore*, 118
*The Butler*, 288
*By the Bomb's Early Light*, 246

## C

*Cabin in the Sky*, 270
Cage, Nicholas, 53
Cagney, James, 68, 181
Cain, Herman, xviii
*The Caine Mutiny*, 152
Caine, Rick, 51
Cameron, James, 256

*The Campaign*, 117, 119
Campaign for Economic Democracy, 3
Camus, Albert, 245
*Can Mr. Smith Get to Washington, Anymore?*, 122
*Canadian Bacon*, 43
*The Candidate*, 111, 115
*Cape Fear*, 143–44
*Capitalism: A Love Story*, 50
Capra, Frank, 15, 35, 42, 46, 114, 120, 122, 138, 192
Carabatsos, Jim, 213, 216
Carmike, 75
Carnahan, Russ, 122
*Career Woman*, 168
Carrey, Jim, 90
Carter, Jimmy, 19, 216
Cartwright, James E., 262
*Casablanca*, 23, 32, 181
Cassavetes, John, 15
*Casualties of War*, 209, 213, 230
CBS News, 229
censorship. *See* film, censorship
Chacón, Juan, 106
Chafe, William, 277
Chan, Charlie, 268
Chaplin, Charlie, 10, 32–33, 101–2, 181, 293
Charles, Ray, 275
*Charlie Wilson's War*, 228, 231
Chastain, Jessica, 239, 283
*Che*, 14, 30
Cheney, Dick, 304
Cher, 169, 170
Chernobyl, 253
*China Beach*, 213
*The China Syndrome*, 3, 25, 52, 252–53
Cholodenko, Lisa, 299
Christensen, Terry, 25, 27–29, 37
*Christopher Strong*, 293
*Chrome and Hot Leather*, 212
Churchill, Winston, 185, 319
Cimino, Michael, 209
*Cinema of Outsiders*, 315
Cinemark, 75
*Citizen Kane*, 23
*City Hall*, 36, 121–22
*A Civil Action*, 163–64, 173
Civil War, 28, 64, 126, 147, 178, 200–1, 206, 275
*Civilization*, 179
Clancy, Tom, 257
Clarke, Mae, 68
*Class Action*, 169-70, 174
Clayburgh, Jill, 298
Clementi, Tyler, 77
*The Client*, 158
Clinton, Bill, xviii, 5, 8, 65, 131, 138, 217–18, 231

Clinton, Hillary, 229, 305
Clooney, George, 7, 8, 14, 26, 93, 119–20, 164, 170, 175, 219, 256, 317
Close, Glenn, 169, 294
*Cloud Atlas*, 313
CNN, 229, 240
Cobb, Lee J., 107
Code and Rating Administration (CARA), 74–75, 78–82, 87–88
Code Red, 152–53
Cohn, Roy, 94
Colbert, Claudette, 191, 293
Cold War, 91, 109, 131
Cole, Lester, 100
*Collateral Damage*, 11
Collins, Lily, 167
Collins, Richard, 100
Colson, Chuck, 87
Columbia Pictures, 248, 295
combat films, 18, 178–91, 196–99, 206–13, 216, 219–27, 231–38, 270
*Coming Home*, 3, 207, 209–10, 212
*Commandos Strike at Dawn*, 185–86
*The Commission*, 136
Committee for the First Amendment, 98
Committee on Public Information (CPI), 41
*Common Dreams*, 239
communism, 13, 30, 91–94, 98, 101, 122–23, 145. *See also* Joseph McCarthy; House Un-American Activities Committee
Communist Party of the United States of America (CPUSA), 93, 96, 98, 101
Comprehensive Nuclear Test Ban Treaty, 261
*Compulsion*, 156
Condon, Richard, 135
*Confessions of a Nazi Spy*, 180
Connelly, Michael, 158
Connors, Chuck, 268
Conrad, Joseph, 208
*The Conspirator*, 26
*Conspiracy Theory*, 137
*The Contender*, 124
*Conviction*, 171-72
*The Cool World*, 44
*The Cooler*, 79–80
Coolidge, Calvin, 180
Cooper, Gary, 16, 97, 104, 151, 181
Copland, Aaron, 93, 185
Coppola, Francis Ford, 28, 160, 208
Corman, Roger, 254
Costner, Kevin, 18, 36, 118, 136
Cotton, Joseph, 113
Coughlin, Charles, 181
*Counsellor at Law*, 161–62

*Country*, 25
*Courage of the Commonplace*, 42
*Courage Under Fire*, 219
*The Court Martial of Billy Mitchell*, 151–52
*Craig's Wife*, 293
Crain, Jeanne, 270
Crane, Stephen, 210
*Crash* (1996), 81
*Crash* (2005), 230, 278–79
*Crash Dive*, 183, 185
Crawford, Broderick, 121
Crawford, Joan, 109, 294
*Crazy Horse*, 44
Creel Committee, 181
Creel, George, 180
Crichton, Michael, 302
Cronenberg, David, 81
*Crossfire*, 31
Crowley, James, 272–73
*The Crucible*, 108
Cruise, Tom, 153, 157, 230, 241
*The Crusades*, 52
*Cry Havoc*, 186–87
Cuban missile crisis, 134, 139, 197, 252
Culbert, David, 55
Cummings, Amanda, 77
Curie, Marie, 275
Cusack, John, 121, 123, 138

D

Dafoe, Willem, 18, 277
Damon, Matt, 158, 237–38
*Dance Girl Dance*, 293
Dandridge, Dorothy, 275
*Dangerous Hours*, 42
Daniels, Lee, 288
*The Dark Horse*, 113
*The Dark Knight*, 228
*The Dark Knight Rises*, xx, 21
Darrow, Clarence, 156
Dassin, Jules, 105
*Dave*, 129–30
Davies, Jeremy, 214
Davies, Joseph, 57, 103
*The Da Vinci Code*, 85
Davis, Bette, 294
Davis, Geena, 36, 301, 308
Davis, Viola, 284, 287
Davis, Jordan, 273
*The Day After*, 254–55
*The Day the Earth Stood Still*, 109, 249–50
*Days of Glory*, 57, 185
*D.C. Sniper: 23 Days of Fear*, 52

# Index

De Mille, Cecil B., 52
De Mornay, Rebecca, 170
De Niro, Robert, 5, 89–91, 98, 209, 212
De Palma, Brian, 79, 82, 209, 230, 235
de Rochemont, Louis, 42
DeVito, Danny, 165
*Dead in a Blue Dress*, 272
*Dead Man Walking*, 295
*Dear America: Letters Home from Vietnam*, 222
*Death Wish*, 149–50
*Death Wish II*, 149
*December 7th: The Movie*, 192
Dee, Sandra, 287
*Deep Impact*, 128
*The Deer Hunter*, 31, 207, 209–11
*The Defense Rests*, 168
*Defenseless*, 169–70
Demme, Jonathan, 157
Denvir, John, 143
Department of Defense, 183
Derek, John, 154
Dern, Laura, 118
Dershowitz, Alan, 156
Desert Storm, 219–20. *See also* Afghanistan/Iraq Wars; Persian Gulf War
*Desert Storm: Cockpit Videos of Bomb Runs*, 219
*Desert Storm: Eagles over the Gulf*, 219
*Desert Triumph*, 219
*Desperate Journey*, 187
*Deterrence*, 129, 139
*The Devil's Advocate*, 163
DiCaprio, Leonardo, 37
*Dick*, 129, 130
Dick, Kirby, 62, 75, 80–81
Dillon, Matt, 278–79, 304
*Dirty Harry*, 4, 143, 149
*Disclosure*, 302–3
Disney Corporation, 12, 48, 312
Disney, Walt, 97
Division of International Information, 42
Dixon, Ivan, 276
*Django Unchained*, 67, 79, 312
Dmytryk, Edward, 97–100, 190
*Do the Right Thing*, 272
docudrama. *See* film, docudrama
Dodd, Christopher, xxi, 2, 73, 79, 239
Dole, Bob, 117
*Dolorita's Passion Dance*, 68
Donald, Ralph, 131
Donaldson, Roger, 35
Douglas, Kirk, 104
Douglas, Melvyn, 111, 123
Douglas, Michael, 36, 164–65, 203–4, 302
*Downsize This!*, 48

*Downton Abbey*, 179
*Dr. Strangelove*, 251
*Dragon Seed*, 268
*Dreams From My Father*, 65
DreamWorks, 12, 124, 307, 311, 313
*Dressed to Kill*, 82
Drury, Allen, 122
D'Souza, Dinesh, 16, 29, 65, 318
Dukakis, Michael, 117
Dunn, Michael, 273
Duvall, Robert, 211

# E

*The Eagle and the Hawk*, 180
Eagleton, Tom, 115
Eastwood, Clint, xviii, 4, 26, 30, 37, 130–31, 143, 149, 158, 188, 216, 277–78, 286
*Edge of Darkness*, 185
Einstein, Albert, 261
Eisenhower, Dwight D., 145, 236, 261
Elder, Larry, 50–51
Eliot, T. S., 255
Empire Zinc Corporation, 106
*The Emperor Jones*, 269–70
Enfield, Cy, 101
*The English Patient*, 312
Enola Gay, 247
Enterprise Productions, 162
Equal Employment Opportunity Commission, 172, 302
*ER*, 219
*Erin Brockovich*, 170
Evans, Stanton, 94–95
Evers, Medgar, 133, 279, 282
*Eyes Wide Shut*, 82
*The Execution of Eddie Slovak*, 105
*Executive Action*, 135
*Executive Power*, 130, 139
*Exodus*, 104
*Extremely Loud and Incredibly Close*, 26

# F

*Fail Safe*, 250–51
*Fair Game*, 37
Fairbanks, Douglas, 10, 182, 293
*Fahrenheit 9/11*, 16, 29, 40, 48–49, 65, 240
*Fahrenhype 9/11*, 51
Fall, Bernard, 204
*The Farmer's Daughter*, 113
Farmiga, Vera, 304–5
*Fat Man and Little Boy*, 247–48

*Fatal Attraction*, 294
Faulkner, William, 72, 274
*The Fearmakers*, 108
Federal Bureau of Investigation (FBI), 21, 26, 30, 37, 42, 93–94. *See also* House Un-American Activities Committee
Federal Trade Commission, 74, 84, 86
Federated Film Corporation, 42
Feiffer, Gregory, 231
Feinstein, Dianne, 239
*Fellow Travelers in Hollywood*, 102
Ferguson, Charles, 60
Ferguson, Elsie, 168
Fermi, Enrico, 246
Ferrell, Will, 119
Ferrer, José, 98, 152
*A Few Good Men*, 152–53
Field, Sally, 292, 294, 298
*The Fifth Witness*, 158
*The Fighting 69th*, 181
film
    awards and nominations, 47–48, 60, 62, 79, 83, 93, 110, 178, 191, 233, 239, 271, 278–79, 283
    biopics, 275
    censorship of, 48, 68–69, 71–73, 85, 234
    classification, 85
    conspiracy theories in, 137–38
    content, 12, 81–83, 109–10
    docudrama, 52–54
    documentary, 43–51, 192–93
    earnings/revenues, 11–12, 19, 26, 31, 40, 43, 70, 81, 84–85, 112, 175–76, 178, 229, 233, 240, 244, 247, 311–12, 314
    festivals, 8, 48, 51, 136, 255, 296, 310, 315, 317–18
    financing, 116, 229, 274, 294, 312–15
    frontier violence in, 146–48
    as history, 16–20
    as ideology, 13–15
    independent film movement, 317
    internal integrity of, 83–84
    Internet and, 87, 229, 318
    movie rating system of, 73–88
    nonfiction, 39–43
    nuclear accidents, 252–54
    nuclear age, 247–50
    nuclear survival, 254–56
    nuclear terrorism, 256–60
    nuclear war, 245–47, 260–62. *See also* film, portraying nuclear war
    as politicizing agent, 20–21
    politics and, 1–2, 6–7
    political. *See* political films
    portrayal of law and lawyers, 141–46, 153–72
    portrayal of military justice in, 151–57
    portrayal of presidents in, 112, 115–20, 124–33
    portrayal of race in, 267–89
    Production Code and, 69–73
    as propaganda, 15–16, 55–66
    science fiction, 249–50
    second nuclear age and, 260–62
    sex and violence in, 67–88
    types of, 27
    urban vigilantism in, 148–51
    wave theory, 207–8
*filmvalues.com*, 87
*Final Salute*, 236
*Fired Up!*, 87
*The Firm*, 157
*First Blood*, 210
Fishburne, Lawrence, 275
Fisher, Lucy, 295
*Five*, 254
*The Five Heartbeats*, 272
*Fixed Bayonets*, 198
*Flags of Our Fathers*, 188
Flaherty, Robert, 40, 43, 46
Flynn, Errol, 25, 184, 186–87
Focus Features, 311
Fonda, Henry, 115, 122, 124, 146–47, 182, 250
Fonda, Jane, 3, 212
*Force of Evil*, 30, 162, 175
Ford, Gerald, 133, 136, 215
Ford, Glenn, 154–55
Ford, Harrison, 28, 112, 128, 170
Ford, John, 17, 31, 113–14, 120, 171, 184, 192
Foreman, Carl, 16, 30, 105
*Forrest Gump*, 31–32
*For Whom the Bell Tolls*, 104
*Force of Evil*, 161
Forsythe, John, 155
*The Fortune Cookie*, 160
Foster, Jodie, 150, 170, 300–1
Foulkrod, Patricia, 61
*The Fourth Protocol*, 248
Fox 2000 Pictures, 295, 307
Fox Searchlight Pictures, 311
Francis, Robert, 152
Frank, Leo, 148
Frankenheimer, John, 134
Franklin, Carl, 272
Freeman, Morgan, 8, 128
*Friday the 13th*, 295
Fried, Albert, 93
*From Dusk to Dawn*, 41
*From Here to Eternity*, 73, 196
*The Front*, 90
Frontier Films, 42

# Index

Frost, David, 132
*Frost/Nixon*, 132
*Frozen River*, 80, 317
Fuchs, Klaus, 246–47
Fukushima Daiichi Nuclear Power Plant, 253
*Full Metal Jacket*, 209–10, 213
Fuller, Sam, 198, 216, 223
*Fury*, 31, 147–48

## G

Gable, Clark, 182
Gabler, Elizabeth, 307
*Gabriel Over the White House*, 127, 138
Gagnon, Rene, 188
Galifianakis, Zach, 119
Gardner, Ava, 250
Garfield, John, 105, 133, 161–62
Garfield, Julie, 105
Garner, James, 129
Garrett, Betty, 105
Gates, Eleanor, 292
Gates, Henry Louis Jr., 272–73
Gazzara, Ben, 156
Geena Davis Institute on Gender in Media, 308
Geer, Will, 106
Geertz, Clifford, 24
*Generation Kill*, 228-29, 232–33
Genovese, Michael, 25–27, 29
*Gentleman's Agreement*, 31
*Gentlemen Prefer Blonds*, 29
George, Peter, 251
Gephardt, Dick, 122
Geraghty, Brian, 237
Gershwin, Ira, 185
Ghetto Film School, 317
*The Ghost Breakers*, 268
Giamatti, Paul, 119
*Giant*, 11
Gibbs, Calvin, 227
Gibney, Alex, 60
Gibson, Mel, 137, 213, 256, 306
Gilbert, John, 180
Gingrich, Newt, xviii
Gish, Lillian, 292, 297, 306
*The Glass Key*, 120
Glickman, Dan, xxi, 73
*Glory*, 275
*Go Tell the Spartans*, 207, 222
*The Godfather*, 28, 143, 160–61
*Godzilla*, 248
Goebbels, Joseph, 55–56
Goetz, Bernard, 150
Goldberg, Robert Alan, 137

Goldwyn, Samuel, 5, 9
*Gone with the Wind*, 28, 72, 182
*The Good Earth*, 268
*Good Morning Vietnam*, 222
*The Good Mother*, 165–66
*Good Night, and Good Luck*, 93
*Good Will Hunting*, 312
Gore, Al, 43, 117–18, 132
Gomez, Thomas, 161
Gornick, Vivian, 110
Gosling, Ryan, 119, 120
*Gran Torino*, 277–79, 286
Granik, Debra, 300
Grant, Lee, 104
*The Grapes of Wrath*, 26, 31
Graves, Joan,
*The Great Dictator*, 33, 181
*The Great Escape*, 188
*The Great Gamble*, 231
*The Great McGinty*, 120
*The Great Train Robbery*, 146
Greenberg, Karen, 239
*The Green Berets*, 11, 184, 206, 244
*Green Zone*, 237
Greenglass, David, 246–47
Greengrass, Paul, 54, 237
Greenwald, Robert, 59
Grenada, invasion of, 178, 210, 215–16
Grierson, John, 40
Griffith, D.W., 6, 28, 64, 178, 267–69, 293
Grisham, John, 144, 157
*The Ground Truth*, 61
Groves, Leslie, 246
*Guadalcanal Diary*, 184, 188
*Guess Who's Coming to Dinner*, 32, 279
Guevara, Ernesto, "Che," 14
*Guilty as Sin*, 170
*Guilty by Suspicion*, 89–90, 98
Gulf War. *See* Persian Gulf War
*Gung Ho!*, 185
*Gunner Palace*, 60
Guy Blache, Alice, 292
Gyllenhaal, Jake, 220, 234

## H

Haakon VII, 186
Haas, Peter, 27–29, 37
Hackman, Gene, 18, 36, 130–31, 174, 212, 277
Haggis, Paul, 230, 234, 278–79
Halberstam, David, 201
Hall, Philip Baker, 132
*Hamburger Hill*, 209–11, 213
Hammer, Armie, 37

Hammett, Dashiell, 93, 120
Hanks, Tom, 7, 8, 18, 157, 191, 229, 231
Hansberry, Lorraine, 275
Harding, Warren G., 180
*Harlan County, USA*, 43
Harlow, Jean, 68
Harrelson, Woody, 237
Hart, Gary, 4, 8, 117, 131
Harvey, Laurence, 134
Hasan, Nidal, 235
Hasegawa, Tsuyoshi, 193
Haskell, Molly, 291
Hayakawa, Sessue, 268
Hayden, Tom, 3, 204
Hayes, Ira, 188
Hays, Will, 2, 69
Hays Office, 70, 293
HBO, 275
HBO Films, 236, 276
Head, Jae, 167
Hearst Corporation, 142
Hearst, William Randolph, 9
*Heart of Darkness*, 208
*Heartbreak Ridge*, 216
Hellman, Lillian, 104, 107, 185
*The Help*, 280, 282–88
Hentschel, Irv, 96
Hepburn, Katharine, 32, 114, 168, 268, 279, 293–94, 297, 306
Hernández, Juano, 274, 276
Hershey, Barbara, 169–70
Herzog, Werner, 214
Heston, Charlton, 3, 271
Hetherington, Tim, 238
Heuston, Sean, 66
Hitchcock, Alfred, 181
*High Noon*, 16, 29, 30, 90
*High School I*, 45
*High School II*, 45
Hirsch, Lee, 78
*History by Hollywood*, 16
Hitler, Adolf, 33, 39, 55–56, 58
Hoffman, Dustin, 5, 165
Hoffman, Philip Seymour, 119–20
Holden, William, 196
Holiday, Billie, 275
Holliday, Judy, 168
Hollywood
　against unions, 95–97
　blacklist, 89–91, 95–98
　communist threat in, 101–4
　future of political films in, 309–10
　*Miranda v. Arizona* reaction in film, 143
　movie rating system, 73–88
　political influence in, 8–12
　possible end of war films, 243–44
　social responsibility of, 86–88
　stars funding politicians, 7–8
　women and, 291–308
*Hollywood Left and Right*, 2
Hollywood Ten, 90, 96–99, 190, 243
*Home of the Brave*, 270
*The Homesteader*, 268
*Honor Among Lovers*, 293
Hood, Gavin, 230–31
Hoover, Herbert, 9
Hoover, J. Edgar, 26, 30, 91, 101
*Hospital*, 45
Houghton, Katharine, 279
House Un-American Activities Committee (HUAC), 6, 30, 32, 97–98, 107–9, 162, 185, 191, 269
　Communist threat in, 101–4
　Hollywood blacklist, 89–91, 95–98
　Hollywood Ten, 90, 98–99
　Joseph McCarthy and, 91–95
Houston, Walter, 127
Howard, Bryce Dallas, 285
Howard, Leslie, 182
Howard, Ron, 132
HUAC. *See* House Un-American Activities Committee
Hubbard, Jim, 50–51
Hughes, Howard, 106
Hughes, Langston, 276
Hunt, Courtney, 317
Huntsman, Jon, xviii
*The Hurt Locker*, 233, 237, 241, 296
Hussein, Saddam, 54, 59, 219–20, 226, 241, 303
Huston, John, 298
Huston, Walter, 138
Hutton, Tim, 306
*Hyde Park on Hudson*, 18, 34–36, 79–80, 88
Hyland, William G., Jr., 145, 157

# I

*I Am a Fugitive from a Chain Gang*, 31
IA Progressives, 96
*The Ides of March*, 26, 37, 117, 119–20, 314
IFC Films, 48
*I Beat the Odds*, 281
*I Married a Communist*, 13, 108
*I Want You*, 199
*I Was a Communist for the FBI*, 13, 108
*I'm No Angel*, 70
*Imitation of Life*, 72, 287
Ince, Thomas, 179

*In the Heat of the Night*, 271, 275
*In the Land of Blood and Honey*, 218
*In the New World*, 204
*In the Valley of Elah*, 228, 230, 235, 241
*Indiana Jones and the Kingdom of the Crystal Skull*, 228
*Independence Day*, 27, 112, 128
Independent Productions Corporation, 106
Independent Progressive Party, 105
Indochina Peace Campaign, 3
*Indoctrinate U*, 50
*Inglourious Basterds*, 312
*Inherit the Wind*, 156
Institute for Science and International Security, 264
International Alliance of Theatrical & Stage Employees (IA), 96
*Intruder in the Dust*, 31, 274
*Invasion of the Body Snatchers*, 109
*The Invisible War*, 61–64
Iran, 262–64
Iranian hostage crisis, 216
Iraq War, 132, 220
*The Iron Curtain*, 13
*Iron Man 3*, 12
*Invasion of the Body Snatchers*, 249
Irvin, John, 209
*It Came from Beneath the Sea*, 249
*It Came from Outer Space*, 249–50
*It Can't Happen Here*, 72
*It's a Wonderful Life*, 103

## J

*J. Edgar*, 26, 37
Jackson, Andrew, 133
Jackson, Jesse, 117
Jackson, Samuel L., 166, 257, 259
*Jagged Edge*, 169
Janssen, David, 206
*Jarhead*, 220
Jarrico, Paul, 106
*The Jazz Singer*, 268
Jenson, Lois, 298
*Jenson v. Eveleth Mines*, 298
Jeter, Mildred, 279
Jewison, Norman, 256
*JFK*, 29–30, 134, 136–37
Jimeno, Will, 53
John Birch Society, 251
*John Carter*, 83
*Johnny Guitar*, 90, 109
Johnson, Lyndon B., 73, 93, 131, 221, 264, 276
Johnson, Van, 152
Jolie, Angelina, 166, 218
Jolson, Al, 268

Jones, Dorothy B., 102
Jones, James, 73
Jones, Paula, 5
Jones, Tommy Lee, 136, 230, 235, 257
Jordan, Barbara, 117
Jordan, Michael, 48
Juárez, Benito, 52, 275
*Judge Priest*, 113
Junger, Sebastian, 238
*Jungle Fever*, 272, 279
*Just and Unjust Wars*, 200
just war theory, 221–22
*Juvenile Court*, 45

## K

Kael, Pauline, 58, 107
Kahn, Gordon, 101
Kahn, Herman, 252
Kai-shek, Chiang, 95
Kaplan, Jonathan, 300
Karloff, Boris, 268
Karnes, Dave, 53–54
Kazan, Elia, 42, 107–8
Keaton, Diane, 15, 166
Keaton, Michael, 36
Kelley, Christopher, 131
Kelly, Gene, 105
Kennedy, Arthur, 155
Kennedy, Bobby, 133
Kennedy, John F., 52, 93, 131, 133, 135–36, 139
Kennen, George F., 215
Kidman, Nicole, 256
*The Kids Are All Right*, 31, 299
*kids-in-mind.com*, 87
Kim, Jong-il, 263
Kim, Jong-un, 263
*King of the Pecos*, 146
*A King in New York*, 29, 32
King, Martin Luther Jr., 133, 279, 289
King, Rodney, 279
*The Kingdom*, 257–58
Kissinger, Henry, 264–65
Kline, Kevin, 129
Knight, Phil, 48
*Knock on Any Door*, 154
Knox, Alexander, 124
Koch, Ed, 121
Koch, Howard, 101
Kohner, Susan, 72, 287
Kopple, Barbara, 43, 47
Korean War, 128, 194–200, 236
*The Korean War*, 201
Kosovo, 217

Koval, Abram, 246
Kovic, Ron, 209
Kramer, Stanley, 32, 250, 279
*Kramer vs. Kramer*, 165–66
Kroll, Sue, 307
Kubrick, Stanley, 82, 209, 251–52
Kuwait, 218, 232, 241
Kurth, James, 214–15

## L

Labor Film Services, 42
*La Danse: The Paris Opera Ballet*, 44
*Ladies Courageous*, 186
Lafollette, Robert, 92
Lahti, Christine, 170
Lancaster, Burt, 207
Landau, Martin, 136
Lane, Mark, 135
Lang, Fritz, 147, 164
Lange, Jessica, 169
Langella, Frank, 132
Langley, Donna, 307
Lansing, Sherry, 295
Lardner, Ring, Jr., 100, 110
*Lassie Come Home*, 103
*The Last Hurrah*, 120
*The Last Woman on Earth*, 254
Laurents, Arthur, 90
Lauzen, Martha, 296
law and lawyer films. *See* film, portraying lawyers
Lawrence, Jennifer, 299–300
Lawson, John Howard, 42, 98–100, 105
*Lawyer Man*, 160
League of Women Voters, 97
Lebanon, US military involvement in, 216
Leder, Mimi, 256
Lee, Bill, 272
Lee, Canada, 105, 271
Lee, Harper, 154
Lee, Spike, 189, 270, 272, 279
*Legal Eagles*, 169
*Legally Blonde 2*, 28–29, 123
Legion of Decency, 69, 71, 87
Lemmon, Jack, 129, 160, 252–53
Lenz, Timothy, 143, 149
*Letters from Iwo Jima*, 189
Levin, Carl, 239
Levinson, Barry, 302
Levy, Emanuel, 315
Lewinski, Monica, 5
Lewis, Sinclair, 72
Libby, I. Lewis, 304
Liberty Feature Film Company, 292

Liberty Film Festival, 51
Liddy, G. Gordon, 130
*The Life and Times of Judge Roy Bean*, 147
*Lilies of the Field*, 271
*Lincoln*, 26, 313–14
Lincoln, Abraham, 200
  assassination of, 133
  case study of film portrayal, 125–27
  portrayal in films, 124, 154
*The Lincoln Lawyer*, 158–59
*Lions into Lambs*, 230, 241
Lions Gate Entertainment, 311
Lionsgate Films, 48, 234, 311
Lipper, Ken, 121
*Little Caesar*, 68, 70
*Little Tokyo, USA*, 187
Logan, Lara, 229
Lombard, Carole, 182
Long, Huey, 121
Long, Tyler, 77
*The Longest Day*, 178, 188
*Looper*, 313
Lorence, James, 106
Lorentz, Pare, 41, 56
Losey, Joseph, 105
*Losing Isaiah*, 166–67
*Lost City in the Jungle*, 248
Loving, Richard, 279
*Loving v. Virginia*, 279–80
Lucas, George, 190
*The Lucky Ones*, 233
Lumet, Sidney, 250
Lupino, Ida, 294, 306
Lurie, Rod, 124, 303–5

## M

Macauley, Stewart, 142
MacFarlane, Seth, 308
Machura, Stefan, 145
Mackie, Anthony, 237
Macy, William, 79
*Mad Max*, 256
Mader, Shannon, 142
Madonna, 166
*Magnificent Seven*, 287
Maguire, Tobey, 234
*Maid in America*, 285
Mailes, Gene, 95
*The Majestic*, 90
Malcolm X, 133
*Malcolm X*, 272
Malden, Karl, 107
Malick, Terrence, 184

# Index

Malik, Art, 256
Maloney, Evan Coyne, 50–51
Maltz, Albert, 42, 99–100, 105
*The Man Who Shot Liberty Valance*, 114, 146, 171
*The Man With the Golden Arm*, 73
Mann, Anthony, 198
March, Fredric, 156, 191
*The Manchurian Candidate*, 29, 134, 197
Manhattan Project, 245–46, 248
*The Manhattan Project*, 247
*Manufacturing Dissent*, 51
March, Fredric, 180, 196, 293
*March of Time*, 46
Marion, Frances, 292–93, 297, 306
*Marketing Violent Entertainment to Children*, 84
*Mars Attacks!*, 129
Marshall, George, 193
Marshall, Thurgood, 275–76
Marston, Joshua, 312
Martin, Trayvon, 273, 279
*A Martyr to His Cause*, 41
Marvin, Lee, 114
*M\*A\*S\*H*, 11, 199
*The Mask of Fu Manchu*, 268
Massey, Raymond, 124
Mastrantonio, Mary Elizabeth, 169, 174
Matthau, Walter, 160, 175
Matusow, Harvey, 97
Mayer, Louis B., 2, 3, 9, 103
Mazursky, Paul, 298
McAdams, Rachel, 234
McBride, James, 189
McCain, John, 7, 239
McCambridge, Mercedes, 109
McCarthy, Eugene, 115, 145
McCarthy, Joseph, 91–95, 101–2, 249
McCarthyism, 32, 91–95, 109
McConaughey, Matthew, 157, 159
McGillis, Kelly, 169–70
McGovern, George, 4, 18, 131
McGraw, Tim, 167
McKinley, William, 133
McNamara, Robert, 18
Medvedev, Roy Aleksandrovich, 58
*Meet John Doe*, 120
Melnyk, Debbie, 51
*The Memphis Belle*, 192
*Men in War*, 198–99
Mendes, Sam, 220
Menjou, Adolphe, 97
*The Messenger*, 233, 236–37
Metro-Goldwyn-Mayer, 311
MGM, 57, 73, 103, 110, 181, 186–87, 247, 292, 295
MGM Holdings, 311

MGM's News of the Day, 192
*Michael & Me*, 51
*Michael Clayton*, 145, 164, 170, 173, 175
*Michael Moore Hates America*, 51
Micheaux, Oscar, 268–70
Milestone, Lewis, 101, 185, 199
*Milk*, 31
Miller, Arthur, 107–8
Miller, Judith, 304–5
Milosevic, Slobodan, 217
*Miracle at St. Anna*, 189, 270
Miramax, 48, 311–12
*Misery*, 295
*Missing in Action*, 210
*Missing in Action II: The Beginning*, 210
*Mission to Moscow*, 57–58, 64, 99, 103
*Mississippi Burning*, 18, 277, 286
Mitchell, Roger, 34
*Mo' Better Blues*, 272
*Mommie Dearest*, 294
*Moneyball*, 312
Monroe, Marilyn, 107
Montgomery, Robert, 182
*The Moon Is Blue*, 25, 73
*The Moon Is Down*, 187
Moore, Demi, 153, 302
Moore, Juanita, 287–88
Moore, Julianne, 299
Moore, Michael, 16, 21, 29, 40, 43, 46–51, 65, 318
    conservative backlash against, 50–51
    as documentary director, 46–50
Moreno, Rita, 297
Morgan, Harry, 146
Morgan, Ted, 94
Morlan, Don, 33, 57
Morris, Dick, 51
*The Mortal Storm*, 181
Moss, Carrie-Anne, 259
Mostel, Joshua, 105
Mostel, Zero, 105
Motion Picture Academy, 47, 98
Motion Picture Alliance for the Preservation of American Ideals, 97
Motion Picture Association of America, 1, 2, 69, 73, 81, 84
Motion Picture Producers and Distributors of America, 69
*The Mouthpiece*, 160
movieguide.com, 87
*Mr. & Mrs. Loving*, 279
*Mr. Smith Goes to Washington*, xvii, 15–16, 29, 35, 122, 163
Muni, Paul, 68
Murphy, George, 2–3, 6

Murray, Bill, 35
Murray, Don, 122
Murrow, Edward R., 93, 181
*Music Box*, 169
Mussolini, Benito, 33
*My Cousin Vinny*, 160
*My Fellow Americans*, 129
*My Son John*, 108
Myers, Henry, 69

# N

Nader, Ralph, 117
*Nanook of the North*, 40, 46
*Nashville*, 135
National Amusements, 75
National Association for Colored People, 105
National Association of Theatre Owners (NATO), 83
Nazi Party, 39, 55–57
NBC, 53
Neely, Mark E., 17
Neeson, Liam, 166
New Line Cinema, 310–11
*Network*, 50
Newman, Paul, 147, 162, 170, 175, 197, 247
Nichols, Mike, 116, 231, 253
Nicholson, Jack, 15, 129, 153
Nielsen, Mike, 95
*A Nightmare on Elm Street*, 295
Nimmo, Dan, 16, 64
Nitti, Frank, 96
*Nixon*, 18, 131–32
Nixon, Richard, 3, 52, 102, 112, 130–31, 142, 214–15, 264
*No Easy Day*, 239
*No End in Sight*, 60
*No Way Out*, 31, 35
Noriega, Manuel, 216–17
*Norma Rae*, 26, 292, 294, 298
Norris, Chuck, 210
Norris, Frank, 45, 48
*North Country*, 298
North Korea, 262–64
North, Oliver, 65
*The North Star*, 57, 104, 185
*Nothing But a Man*, 274
*Nothing But the Truth*, 303–5
Novak, Robert, 304
nuclear
    accidents, 252–54
    age, 247–49, 249–50
    survival, 254–56
    terrorism, 256–60
    war, 245–47, 260–62. *See also* film, portraying nuclear war

# O

Obama, Barack, 4, 7–8, 17, 49, 65, 133, 138, 221, 229, 272, 280, 288, 315, 318
    Afghanistan/Iraq Wars and, 59–60, 225–26, 232, 236, 239–40
    avoidance of war, 241–43
    presidential campaign of 2012, xvii–xxi
Obama, Michelle, xviii
*Objective Burma*, 184
O'Connor, Edwin, 120
Odets, Clifford, 101
Oher, Michael, 167, 280
Oland, Warner, 268
Oldman, Gary, 124
Office of War Information (OWI), 57, 104, 181, 183, 185, 187
O'Hara, Maureen, 293
*On Stranger Tides*, 314
*On the Beach*, 250, 265
*On the Waterfront*, 107
O'Neill, Eugene, 269–70
Operation Desert Storm, 219
Oppenheimer, J. Robert, 246–47, 261
Ornitz, Samuel, 100, 105
Oshinsky, David, 95
Ostrom, Richard, 251
*The Ox-Bow Incident*, 146–47

# P

Pacino, Al, 36, 79, 121, 144, 155, 163, 170
*The Package*, 248
Packer, Herbert, 148
Pakistan, 263
Palmer, William, 210
Panama, 215, 217
*Panic in Year Zero!*, 254–55
Papke, David Ray, 145, 165, 167
*The Parallax View*, 4, 135
Paramount, 186, 255, 295
Paramount Vantage, 311
Paramount News, 192
Parker, Alan, 18, 277
Parker, Charlie, 275
Parks, Larry, 97, 101, 105
Parks, Rosa, 286
Partial Test Ban Treaty, 261
Pascal, Amy, 307, 312
*Past Imperfect*, 16

# Index

Pasteur, Louis, 275
Patrick, Deval, xviii
*Patton*, 112, 188
Paul, Ron, xviii
Paulk, Joey, 228
*Payne Fund Studies*, 20
*The Peacemaker*, 256–57
Pearl Harbor, 19, 32, 57, 152, 181, 183, 186–87, 193–94, 257
*Pearl Harbor*, 18
Peck, Gregory, 154, 185, 199, 250
Peirce, Kimberley, 232, 317
*The Pelican Brief*, 157–58
Pelosi, Nancy, 8
Pena, Michael, 53, 234
Penn, Sean, 137
*The People Against O'Hara*, 162
*A Perfect Candidate*, 65, 117
*The Perfect Husband*, 52–53
Perry, Rick, xviii, 289
*Pershing's Crusaders*, 180
*Persian Gulf: The Images of a Conflict*, 219
Persian Gulf War, 215, 219–21, 241
Persico, Joseph, 18
Pesci, Joe, 159
Peters, Susan, 57
Peterson, Alan, 51
Peterson, Laci, 53
Petraeus, David, 243
*Philadelphia*, 157
Phillippe, Ryan, 159
Pichel, Irving, 101
Pickford, Mary, 10, 292–93, 297, 306
Picturehouse, 310
*Pinky*, 270
*Pirates of the Caribbean*, 313–14
Pitt, Brad, 312
Plame, Valerie, 304–5
*Platoon*, 209–11, 213
Platt, Polly, 295
*Plessy v. Ferguson*, 276, 284
*The Plow That Broke the Plains*, 41
Plunkitt, George Washington, 120
*Point Break*, 295
Poitier, Sidney, 3, 32, 270–72, 275–76, 279
Polonsky, Abraham, 30, 90, 98, 105, 162
political films, 23–24, 111–13
    content of, 12
    definition of, 23–24
    effect of, 31–35
    future of, 309–10, 315–19
    Hollywood and, 2–3
    intent of, 29–31
    location and, 35–36
    major characters in, 36–37
    narrative in, 37–38
    obstacles and concerns, 315–19
    portrayal of political assassinations, 133–38
    portrayal of capital crimes and misdemeanors in, 122–24
    portrayal of political campaigns and conventions in, 113–20
    portrayal of political machines in, 120–22
    portrayal of presidents in, 124–33
    practical politics and, 4–6
    schools of thought about, 24–29
Pollak, Kevin, 129
Popular Front, 98, 101
*Pork Chop Hill*, 198–99, 211
Portman, Natalie, 8
Post, Jerrold, 135
Powell, Colin, 219
Powell, Thomas, 273, 277
Powell, William, 160
Power, Tyrone, 182, 185
Pratt, Ray, 136
Preminger, Otto, 104
*Presumed Innocent*, 170
*Primary Colors*, 5–6, 116, 139
*Primate*, 45
Prince, Phoebe, 77
*Prisoner of War*, 197
Production Code, 21, 67–73, 124, 174, 186, 293–94
Production Code Administration (PCA), 69, 71–72
*Projecting Politics*, 28–29
propaganda film. *See* film, propaganda
*The Public Enemy*, 68, 70
*Public Housing*, 45
Pullman, Bill, 28, 112, 128
*Pulp Fiction*, 312
Putin, Vladimir, 246
Puzo, Mario, 160
Pyle, Ernie, 184–185

## Q

Qaddafi, Muammar, 242
Quaid, Dennis, 217–218

## R

race, 267–89
Racial Integrity Act, 280
Rabe, David, 213
Rabinowitch, Eugene, 261
*The Rack*, 197–98
*Radar Men from the Moon*, 248

*Radical Hollywood*, 10
Rainer, Luise, 268
Raines, Claude, 23
*The Rainmaker*, 158
*A Raisin in the Sun*, 275
*Rambo: First Blood, Part II*, 112, 210
*The Ramparts We Watch*, 42
Rampling, Charlotte, 163, 170
Randolph, Martha, 105
Rather, Dan, 219
Rattigan, Terence, 159
*Recount*, 117–18
Reagan, Ronald, 2–3, 6, 47, 97, 104, 112, 133, 197, 212, 216
reality fictions. *See* films, documentary
*Red Alert*, 251
*Red Badge of Courage*, 210
*Red Channels*, 105
*Red-Headed Woman*, 68
*The Red Kimona*, 28
*The Red Menace*, 13, 58, 108
*Red Nightmare*, 58
Red Scare, 102, 104–6
*Red Stars*, 102
*Red Tails*, 37, 190
*Redacted*, 228, 230, 235, 240
Redford, Robert, 8, 26, 90, 111, 115, 117, 138, 229, 230
*Reds*, 4, 14–15
Reed, John, 4
*Reel Bad Arabs: How Hollywood Vilifies a People*, 260
*Reel Politics*, 25
Reeves, Keanu, 163
Regal Entertainment Group, 75
Reichardt, Kelly, 80
Reliance ADA Group, 311
*Rendition*, 228, 230, 240
Rennie, Michael, 249
Renner, Jeremy, 237
*Report from the Aleutians*, 192
*Rescue Dawn*, 213
*Restrepo*, 238
*Rethink Afghanistan*, 59
*The Reversal*, 158
*Reversal of Fortune*, 156
Revueltas, Rosaura, 106–7
Rice, Elmer, 161
Rich, Robert, 104
Richards, Ben, 227
Richards, Mark, 232
Riefenstahl, Leni, 15, 29, 39, 55, 57–58
*The Right Stuff*, 11
*The River*, 41
RKO, 187

RKO-Pathe News, 192
Roberts, Julia, 157, 170, 231, 293, 295
Robertson, Cliff, 115
Robertson, Pat, 117
Robeson, Paul, 97, 268–69, 271
Robins, Robert, 135
Robbins, Tim, 115, 138, 234
Robinson, Edward G., 68
Rockwell, Sam, 171
*Roe v. Wade*, 52
*Roger and Me*, 21, 40, 43, 46–47
Rogers, Ginger, 190
Rogers, Will, 113
*Rolling Thunder*, 212
Romney, Ann, xviii
Romney, Mitt, xviii–xix, 7, 65, 242, 318
Rooney, Mickey, 196
Roosevelt, Eleanor, 17, 34
Roosevelt, Franklin D., 17, 19, 34, 79, 95, 103, 127–28, 181, 245
Roosevelt, Theodore, 133
*Roots*, 52
Rosenberg, Ethel, 247
Rosenberg, Julius, 247
Ross, Steven, 2, 4
Rossen, Robert, 101
Rove, Karl, 132
Ruffalo, Mark, 299
*Rules of Engagement*, 257
Rumsfeld, Donald, 60
*Runaway Jury*, 144
*Rush to Judgment*, 135
Russell, David O., 219
Russell, Harold, 191
*The Russians Are Coming, The Russians Are Coming*, 256
Rutherford, Lucy Mercer, 18
Ryan, Meg, 219, 306
Ryan, Paul, xviii

# S

Sachleben, Mark, 13
Saint, Eva Marie, 107
Saldana, Zoe, 289
*Salt of the Earth*, 26, 58, 64, 105–7, 136
Salt, Waldo, 101
San Francisco Film Society, 307
*Sands of Iwo Jima*, 183, 188, 210
*Sandstorm in the Gulf: Digging out*, 219
Santiago, Emiliano, 231
*Santiago v. Rumsfeld*, 231
Santorum, Rick, xviii
Sarandon, Susan, 158, 301

# Index

Saunders, Frances, 11
Savage, John, 209
*Saving Jessica Lynch*, 53
*Saving Private Ryan*, 18, 178, 188, 193, 222, 244
*Savior*, 217
Sawyer, Diane, 219
*Scarface*, 68, 70, 79
*Scarlet Pages*, 168
Scheuer, Michael, 242
Schickel, Richard, 99
*Schindler's List*, 187–88
Schlesinger, Arthur Jr., 18, 200
Schlichtmann, Jan, 163
Schreiber, Liev, 134
Schulberg, Budd, 107
Schwartz, Liz, 105
Schwarzenegger, Arnold, 2, 4, 6, 115, 256
Schwarzkopf, Norman, 219
Sciorra, Annabella, 279
Scopes, John T., 156
Scopes Monkey Trial, 156
Scorsese, Martin, 144, 298
Scott, Adrian, 99–100, 105
Scott, Randolph, 185
Scott, Ridley, 217, 301
Scranton, Deborah, 60
Screen Actor's Guild, 104
Screen Writers Guild, 292
*screenit.com*, 87
*Seabiscuit*, 32
*The Seduction of Joe Tynan*, 16, 123, 138
*The Sea Hawk*, 25
*Secret Honor*, 132
*See It Now*, 93
Selznick, David O., 72
Sereika, Chuck, 53
*Sergeant York*, 181, 210
*Serious Moonlight*, 306
*Set It Off*, 302
*sex, lies and videotape*, 312
Shaheen, Jack, 260
*Shakespeare in Love*, 312
*Shame of the Cities*, 48
*She Done Him Wrong*, 70
Shaw, Robert Gould, 275
Sheeler, Jim, 236
Sheen, Charlie, 211
Sheen, Martin, 136, 208
Sheen, Michael, 259
Sheridan, Jim, 234
Sherman, William Tecumseh, 178
Sherwood, Robert, 17
Shigeta, James, 268
Shute, Neville, 250
*Sicko*, 40, 49
*The Siege*, 257
Siegel, Don, 249
*Sign of the Cross*, 52
*The Silence of the Lambs*, 295
*Silkwood*, 52, 252–54
Silver, Ron, 156
Simon, John, 27
Sinatra, Frank, 105, 134
*Since You Went Away*, 190–91
Sinclair, Upton, 9–10, 45, 48
Singleton, John, 272
Sinise, Gary, 124, 128
Sirk, Douglas, 287
*Slacker Uprising*, 46, 318
Slaton, John, 148
Smith, Dwight L., 227
Smith, Jeff, 122
Smith, Jefferson, 138
Smith, Jennifer, 61
Smith, Kate, 10
Smith, Jada Pinkett, 302
Smith, Roger, 21, 46
Smith, Stacy, 297
*Smith v. Allwright*, 276
Smith, Will, 271
Snider, Stacey, 307
Snipes, Wesley, 279
Snowe, Olympia, 305
*So Proudly We Hail*, 186–87
Sobel, Mark, 136
Soderbergh, Steven, 14, 30, 170, 312
Sondergaard, Gale, 104
*Song of Russia*, 57, 99, 103
Sony Pictures, 239, 295, 307
Sorkin, Aaron, 231
Spader, James, 123
Spanish-American War, 52, 104
Spanish Civil War, 42, 104
*Spartacus*, 104
*Speechless*, 36
Spencer, Herbert, 255
Spencer, Octavia, 284, 287
Spielberg, Steven, 124, 179, 188, 193, 313
*Spiderman*, 295
*Spring Breakers*, 67, 80, 297
*Stalag 17*, 188, 196
Stalin, Joseph, 58, 103
Stallone, Sylvester, 210
Stanwyck, Barbara, 68
*State Legislature*, 45
*State of Play*, 9
*State of the Union*, 113–14
Steel, Dawn, 295

*The Steel Helmet*, 198, 223
Steffens, Lincoln, 48
Steinem, Gloria, 117
Stevens, George, 192
Stewart, Jimmy, xviii, 29, 114, 122, 146, 156, 182
Stockett, Kathryn, 282
Stone, Emma, 283, 287
Stone, Oliver, 5, 14, 18, 53–54, 131–32, 134, 136–37, 209, 211, 213, 217
*Stop-Loss*, 228, 232, 241
*Stormy Weather*, 270
*The Story of GI Joe*, 184–85
Stowe, Harriet Beecher, 271
Streep, Meryl, 123, 134, 165, 230
*A Streetcar Named Desire*, 73
Streisand, Barbra, 7, 90
Students for a Democratic Society, 204
Sturges, Preston, 120
Suckley, Daisy, 18
*Suddenly*, 134–35
*The Sum of All Fears*, 257
*Summertree*, 203, 205
Summit Entertainment, 311
Sundance Film Festival, 8, 117, 310, 315
*Sunrise at Campobello*, 17–18, 127–28
Sunstein, Cass, 29
*Superman*, 248
*Suspect*, 142, 169–70
Swank, Hilary, 171
*Swing Vote*, 117–19
Swinton, Tilda, 170, 175
Swofford, Anthony, 223
*Syriana*, 85
Szilard, Leo, 251

## T

*Taking Chance*, 229, 233, 236
Talabani, Jalal, 226
Taliban, 262–63
*Tanner '88*, 117, 135
Tarantino, Quentin, 79, 312
*Tarantula*, 249
*Taxi Driver*, 212
*Taxi to the Dark Side*, 60
Taylor, Ken, 19–20
Taylor, Robert, 97, 182
*The Teahouse of the August Moon*, 268
Teller, Edward, 246, 252, 261
Temple, Shirley, 6
*Tender Comrade*, 190–91
*Terminator*, 4
*Testament*, 254–56

Thatcher, Margaret, 216
*Them!*, 249
Theron, Charlize, 298
*They Were Expendable*, 184
*They Won't Forget*, 31, 147–48
*The Thin Red Line*, 184
*The Thing*, 109, 249
*Thelma and Louise*, 293, 295, 301
*The Thin Blue Line*, 311
*This Film Is Not Yet Rated*, 75, 80
Thomas, Jason, 54
Thompson, Fred, 6
*Three Kings*, 219
Three Stooges, 33
*Thurgood*, 275–76
Tibbits, Paul, 247
Tillman, Pat, 233
*A Time to Kill*, 157
*Titicut Follies*, 44–45
*To Kill a Mockingbird*, 154, 173
*To the Shores of Hell*, 206
Toler, Sidney, 268
Tolstoy, Leo, 73
Touchstone Pictures, 311
Townsend, Leo, 99
Townsend, Robert, 272
Tracy, Spencer, 32, 114, 120, 147–48, 156, 162, 168, 175, 279, 297
Tradeau, Gary, 117
Travolta, John, 5, 116
*The Tree of Life*, 283
Trevor, Claire, 168
*Trial*, 154–55
TriStar Pictures, 82, 311
*Triumph of the Will*, 15, 29, 39, 55–56, 58, 64
*True Believers*, 163, 173
*True Colors*, 123–24, 138
*True Lies*, 256
*Truman*, 127–28
Truman, Harry, 95, 127–28, 133, 139, 193–94, 261
Trumbo, Dalton, 96, 98, 100, 103–5, 110, 135, 190, 243
Tucker, Michael, 60
Turow, Scott, 170
Turner, Frederick Jackson, 146
Turner, Kathleen, 165
Turner, Lana, 287–88
Turner, Tina, 275
Tuskegee Airmen, 190
Tsarnaev, Dzhokhar, 143
Tsarnaev, Tamerlan, 143

# Index

## U

*U-571*, 19
*Uncle Tom's Cabin*, 271
*Uncommon Valor*, 212
*Uncovered: The War on Iraq*, 59
*Under Four Flags*, 180
*Unfaithful*, 70
Uniform Code of Military Justice, 151–52
Union of Russian Workers, 92
*United 93*, 54
United Artists, 311
United Service Organization (USO), 183
Universal-International, 248
Universal Pictures, 231, 295, 307
Universal Newsreel, 192
*An Unmarried Woman*, 298–99
*Unthinkable*, 259–60
U.S. Court of Military Appeals, 151
U.S. Information Agency, 42

## V

Valenti, Jack, 2, 73, 294
Vaughn, Stephen, 20
Ventura, Jessie, 115
*The Verdict*, 145, 162–63, 170, 173
Verhoeven, Paul, 82
Vidal, Gore, 114
*Vietnam: A Television History*, 213
Vietnam War, 31, 131, 203–7
    political expediency in film production, 211–14
    wave theory of movies about, 207–10
*A View from the Bridge*, 108
Voight, Jon, 212
Von Braun, Werner, 252
von Bulow, Claus, 156

## W

*W*, 5, 6, 132
Wachowski, Andy, 313
Wachowski, Lana, 313
*Wag the Dog*, 5, 6, 139
Wagner, Dave, 10
*Wake Island*, 183–84, 187–88, 198
*A Walk in the Sun*, 184
Walken, Christopher, 209
Walker, Luis, 63
Walters, Barbara, 219
Walters, Francis, 107
Walzer, Michael, 200–1, 222

war films. *See* Afghanistan/Iraq Wars; Civil War; combat films; Desert Storm; Kuwait; Pearl Harbor; Spanish Civil War; World War I; World War II
*War Games*, 252
*War Horse*, 179, 313
*The War of the Roses*, 165
War Relocation Authority, 187
*The War Room*, 65, 117
*The War Tapes*, 60
Warner Brothers, 52, 58, 96, 103, 147, 181, 186, 307, 310
Warner, Harry, 9
Warner Independent Pictures, 310
Warner, Jack, 9, 103
Warren Commission, 135–37
Warren, Elizabeth, 305
Warren, Robert Penn, 121
Washington, Denzel, 7, 134, 157–58, 219, 257, 271
Watanabe, Ken, 189
Watergate, 131, 145, 174, 215
Waterston, Sam, 136
wave theory, 207–8
*The Way We Were*, 90
Wayne, John, 11, 98, 108, 146, 184, 206, 221
*We Were Soldiers*, 213–14
Weaver, Sigourney, 294
Weber, Lois, 292
Weiner, Anthony D., 9
Weinstein Company, 75, 78, 311–12
Welch, Joseph, 89, 94
Welch, Laura, 132
*Welcome to Sarajevo*, 31, 217
Welles, Orson, 156
*Wendy and Lucy*, 80, 308
West, Mae, 70–71
*West Wing*, 231
*What Price Glory?*, 180
*What Women Want*, 306
Whitaker, Forest, 288
*Who's Afraid of Virginia Woolf?*, 73
*Why We Fight*, 15, 29, 42, 46, 64
*The Wild One*, 73
Wilder, Billy, 160
Wilkinson, Tom, 164, 170
Will, George, 215
Williams, Robin, 222
Williams, Tennessee, 73
Willis, Bruce, 257, 313
Wilson, Charlie, 231
Wilson, Joseph, 303–4
Wilson, Michael, 50–51, 104
Wilson, Woodrow, 17, 41, 127–28, 180–81
*Wilson*, 17, 31, 127–28

Winfrey, Oprah, 288
Winger, Debra, 169
*Wings*, 180
Winkler, Irwin, 89, 91
*Winter Kills*, 135–36
*Winter's Bone*, 299–300, 308
Wiseman, Frederick, 43, 44–46
Witherspoon, Reese, 28–29, 123, 230
*Within Our Gates*, 268–69
*The Wizard of Oz*, 103
*Woman of the Year*, 297
Women Air Force Service Pilots (WASP), 186
women in Hollywood, 291–92
    early days, 292–94
    getting women right in films, 297–300
    getting women wrong in films, 300–8
    on screen, 296–97
Wong, Anna May, 268
Wood, Sam, 104
Woods, James, 163, 175
Woodward, Bob, 7, 142
*The World, the Flesh, and the Devil*, 254
*World Trade Center*, 53, 54
World War I, 41, 52, 179–82
World War II, 42–43, 182–94
Wouk, Herman, 152
Wray, Fay, 168
Wright, Evan, 228
Wright, Jeremiah, 65
Wright, Lawrence, 205
*Written on the Wind*, 287–88
*www.moviemom.com*, 87
Wyler, William, 192

Ziering, Amy, 62
Zimmerman, George, 273
Ziskin, Laura, 295
Zola, Emile, 52, 275
*Zombies of the Stratosphere*, 248
Zucker, David, 318
Zwick, Edward, 275

# X

*The X-Files*, 137

# Y

Yenerall, Kevan, 13, 131
Yerkes Regional Primate Research Center, 45
*You Nazty Spy*, 33
Young, Loretta, 113, 138, 186
*Young Mr. Lincoln*, 17, 154, 173
Young, Ned, 105

# Z

Zahn, Steve, 214
Zanuck, Darryl F., 17
*Zero Dark Thirty*, 37, 88, 239–40, 243, 296